The Hosta Handbook

The Hosta Handbook

Mark R. Zilis

Q & Z Nursery, Inc.
Rochelle, Illinois

The Hosta Handbook

Published by
Q & Z Nursery, Inc.
11409 E. Flagg Rd.
Rochelle, IL 61068

ISBN: 0-9679440-0-7

CONTENTS

CONTENTS

HOSTA DESCRIPTIONS

CONTENTS *(Continued)*

CONTENTS *(Continued)*

CONTENTS *(Continued)*

CONTENTS *(Continued)*

CONTENTS *(Continued)*

CONTENTS *(Continued)*

To Peter Ruh
a good friend and living hosta legend
who never lost faith that I would actually
finish this project

ACKNOWLEDGMENTS

Many people have been instrumental to the success of *The Hosta Handbook*. Not only were they gracious in their hospitality, but continued to encourage me to complete this book, despite its seemingly endless nature. I am particularly grateful to Pete and Jean Ruh of Chesterland, Ohio who permitted me to thoroughly dissect their massive collection and hosted me so many times at their home that I am embarrassed to reveal the number. The numerous conversations with Pete have supplied me with an incredible wealth of historical information of which I have only been able to describe in limited detail in this work. I am also indebted to Van Wade, who allowed me to measure, photograph, and study his incredible collection during numerous visits. His opinions also helped solidify my thinking about many plants. Other people who allowed me to study their collections include Jim Schwarz of Dubuque, Iowa, Bernie and Jane Diesen of Plattsmouth, Nebraska, Clarence and Marge Soules of Indianapolis, Indiana, Herb and Dorothy Benedict of Hillsdale, Michigan, the late Larry Englerth of Hopkins, Michigan, and numerous other hosta collectors and nurserymen who witnessed me standing in the middle of their collections, photographing and measuring their plants. I am also grateful to Hideko Gowen of Excelsior, Minnesota, Yoshimichi Hirose of Iwakuni City, Japan, Hajime Sugita of Okazaki, Japan, and the Watanabe family of Gotemba City, Japan for their help in my travels in Japan. I owe a debt of gratitude to Bob Olson and Bob Solberg who continually encouraged me to stick with the project. So many times, Bob Olson would say something like 'You've got to get that book done!'. Both Bobs not only offered encouragement, but their editorial skills as well. Also lending her considerable proofreading skills was Ann Strang, a great person to have as a friend. I am greatly indebted to my brother-in-law, Rick Vanous, and my sisters, Mary Beth Vanous and Cathy Sawner, for their efforts and encouragement. Also vital was my wife Katie, who maintained the fort at home while I was off gallivanting around the country studying plants and has been an integral part of finishing this project. My son, Andy, also lent his assistance by using his computer graphics skills to develop the diagram of leaf blade shapes. A special mention goes to Mary Pratt of Peoria, who proposed an idea to me back in 1983, i.e., 'Why don't you write a book about hostas?'. She also offered me encouragement numerous times and helped me with my initial studies of hostas in Japan. Perhaps the final bit of motivation came from my four children who have frequently asked 'Hey Dad, weren't you writing a book about hostas?'

Mark R. Zilis

May 7, 2000

Photos in *The Hosta Handbook*

The photographs that appear in this book were taken over a period of twenty years in various gardens and nurseries throughout the United States and Japan. I am very grateful to the many gardeners and collectors who carefully maintained their plants which allowed me to photograph them at their best. I would also like to thank Bob Solberg for allowing me to use his photo of *H. plantaginea* 'Aphrodite'.

INTRODUCTION

When I first began seriously gathering data for a book on hostas in 1983, I never would have guessed that it would take this long to complete the project. *The Hosta Handbook* represents my observations, measurements, and interpretations about many of the hostas that I have viewed. I realize that my descriptions may differ from what others have seen, and my opinions may just be that, mine alone. As best as possible, I wrote everything from an objective viewpoint and tried to not give any personal or business considerations much weight. I utilized and noted the works of other writers whenever it was essential to the understanding of various topics. This book was written with the intention of it being carried around in the garden, a kind of field guide for hostas. It does not completely describe all hostas in existence. Instead I have focused on hostas that have had the most impact in shade gardening. Among these are the traditional landscaping plants (e.g., *Hosta lancifolia*, 'Fortunei Hyacinthina', and 'Undulata Albomarginata'), important commercial cultivars, and species that have some horticultural importance. The latter group includes all that I saw growing in the wild in Japan plus any that have been widely grown in Japanese or American collections. Of course, since thousands of hostas now exist, I was left with the prospect of ignoring the vast majority of them. I have partially solved that dilemma by briefly describing or naming many other hostas under the categories of "seedlings, sports, and other related types" and "other similar types" that follow each of the 278 major listings. This adds at least a mention of over 1300 more hostas. Unfortunately I have not been able to describe or mention many fine plants, but that will have to wait for a future date.

The Hosta Handbook has been written from a horticultural perspective. My main concern has been how each hosta will perform in a garden environment. The only deviations from this center around the few species that I observed growing in the wild, but even my descriptions of them are horticulturally oriented. Over the course of the last 20 years, I have witnessed the numbers of hostas grow from a few hundred significant types to a few thousand. Not only are more people growing hostas, but more are being hybridized than ever and more sports are being discovered in gardens, nurseries, and tissue culture labs. Data needed to be taken from more sources at more times of the year. The numbers of photographs that I felt were necessary not only to publish, but to study each variety, mushroomed significantly. That, however, was my task, and the result is a relatively small summary of all of the data and photography that went into the project.

A BRIEF HISTORY OF HOSTAS

Hostas are native to Japan, Korea, and China. They can be found in a wide variety of habitats in these countries, including woodlands, marshes, grasslands, and alongside streams and rivers. Hostas were first brought over to Europe during the 1800's and, by the end of the century, *Hosta lancifolia*, *H. plantaginea*, *H. ventricosa*, and numerous Fortunei-types had become established parts of American shade gardens as well. Hostas had become ordinary, almost forgotten plants by the time an upsurge in interest in herbaceous perennials began during the 1970's in the U.S. At about the same time, the fledgling American Hosta Society (founded in 1968) encouraged the hybridization and development of new hostas. By the early 1980's, a few nurseries were using the relatively new propagation technique of plant tissue culture to fill the increased demand for hostas. Instead of this creating a glut of new plants, the demand for hostas intensified. Varieties that had been owned by only a few collectors could now be purchased by even the average gardener. Hosta collections also grew by leaps and bounds. The largest numbered less than 500 in 1980, but by 1990, anyone could order twice that many from the many mail-order nurseries that had sprung up. The membership of the American Hosta Society, too, grew at a fast pace. What was once a very small group grew into the thousands during the 1980's. By the mid-1990's hostas had become the top-selling herbaceous perennials in the nursery industry, passing up daylilies which would have been unthinkable only a few years ago.

Today interest in hostas continues to increase, though not quite at the same overheated, 1980's pace. Almost every nursery offering herbaceous perennials sells a wide selection of hostas. Landscapers and landscape architects, who had long ignored hostas and other perennials, now routinely include them in plans. The numbers of new hostas being introduced continues to increase at a faster and faster pace. The emphasis seems to be on unusual forms, different patterns of variegation, and slug-resistance. No longer can an average, thin-leaved variety be introduced and gain wide acceptance for very long. Interest in hostas not only has increased in the United States, but in Europe, Canada, New Zealand, and Australia as well. Renewed appreciation for one of their national treasures has also occurred in Japan where exciting new forms continue to be identified in the wild and developed in collections.

With all of the increased interest and focus on hostas, awareness of problems concerning hostas has also increased. Virus, nematode, fungal and bacterial problems have been identified. Hosta collectors and growers have become more aware of the more "traditional" pests that plague hostas including slugs, black vine weevils, cutworms, and deer.

TAXONOMY OF THE GENUS *HOSTA*

In the plant world hierarchy, hostas are monocotyledonous, flowering (angiosperms) herbaceous perennials that belong to the genus *Hosta* which traditionally has been a member of the Lily family (*Liliaceae*). Recently it has been proposed to consider a separation of the genus into its own family, the *Hostaceae* (Schmid, 1991). The genus has been known under a variety of names besides *Hosta*, the most notable being *Funkia*, a name which persists to some extent as a common name. Gardening literature and nursery catalogs from the early part of the twentieth century reveal that *Funkia* was preferred by many authors. It took until the 1970's for *Hosta* to finally become the exclusive name for the genus. In botanical writings, however, the name *Hosta* became accepted much earlier. Liberty Hyde Bailey's *Cyclopedia of American Horticulture* from 1919 listed the genus as *Hosta* with *Funkia* being described as an outdated, alternate name.

A few publications concerning *Hosta* taxonomy are worth noting. Fumio Maekawa's 1940 monograph entitled "The Genus *Hosta*" which appeared in the Japanese *Journal of the Faculty of Science* (from the Imperial University, Tokyo) is considered the benchmark description of the genus. (It was reprinted with all Latin portions translated in two issues of *The American Hosta Society Bulletin*, (No. 4, March 1972, pp. 12-64, and No. 5, March 1973, pp. 12-59).

Maekawa (1972) listed the following 39 *Hosta* species:

> *H. atropurpurea*
> *H. capitata*
> *H. cathayana*
> *H. clausa*
> *H. clavata*
> *H. crispula*
> *H. decorata*
> *H. densa*
> *H. ensata*
> *H. fluctuans*
> *H. gracillima*
> *H. helonioides*
> *H. hippeastrum*
> *H. kikutii*
> *H. kiyosumiensis*

H. lancifolia
H. longipes
H. longissima
H. minor
H. montana
H. nakaiana
H. nigrescens
H. okamii
H. opipara
H. pachyscapa
H. plantaginea
H. rectifolia
H. rhodeifolia
H. rupifraga
H. sacra
H. sieboldiana
H. sparsa
H. tardiva
H. tokudama
H. tortifrons
H. tosana
H. undulata
H. ventricosa
H. venusta

Maekawa also described several botanical varieties and forms of his species.

Over the years various additions and modifications were made to Maekawa's monograph. In 1954 Nils Hylander of Sweden published "The Genus *Hosta* in Swedish Gardens" in *Acta Horti Bergiani* (16, 11: 331-420). His work, while not a complete review of the genus, added *H. albomarginata* (later to become *H. sieboldii*), *H. elata*, *H. fortunei*, and *H. tardiflora* to the list of species. Curiously only varieties of *H. fortunei* were described, not the species itself. *H. tardiflora* was derived from *H. sparsa* as listed by Maekawa. *H. albomarginata* came out of Maekawa's *H. lancifolia thunbergiana albo-marginata*. Also significant was the addition of *H. sieboldiana* var. *elegans* (previously known as *H. fortunei robusta*) and changing the plant that Maekawa described as *H. cathayana* to *H. lancifolia*.

Dr. Noboru Fujita (1978) presented a much different view of hostas in "The Genus Hosta in Japan", printed in *The American Hosta Society Bulletin*. Of significance was the elimination of *Hosta montana* (lumping it with *H. sieboldiana*); making *H. gracillima* a variety of *H. longipes*; and listing the species *H. alismifolia*, *H. shikokiana*, *H. pulchella*, and *H. tsushimensis*. Though some of Fujita's work was accepted, the changes to *H. montana* (and *H.*

sieboldiana), *H. gracillima*, and other species have been dismissed as a being too radical.

Despite the work of Maekawa, Hylander, Fujita, and others, the status of *Hosta* taxonomy was generally viewed as confused into the 1980's. Complicating the issue were misidentifications of imported plants and the seemingly artificial assignments of variegated plants as species, e.g., *Hosta undulata, H. albomarginata, H. crispula,* and *H. decorata.*

In 1991 W. George Schmid published his book, *The Genus Hosta*, which stands as the watershed event of hosta taxonomy. He aggressively reviewed all of the problems surrounding the taxonomy of the genus and made numerous revisions. In his work most variegated "species" became cultivars. It also set straight the identification of most *Hosta* species, varieties, and forms, and solved numerous other nagging problems. In Appendix A-Part 5 (Schmid, 1991), the following 43 species are listed:

> *H. aequinoctiiantha*
> *H. alismifolia*
> *H. atropurpurea*
> *H. calliantha*
> *H. capitata*
> *H. cathayana*
> *H. clausa*
> *H. clavata*
> *H. crassifolia*
> *H. densa*
> *H. fluctuans*
> *H. gracillima*
> *H. hypoleuca*
> *H. ibukiensis*
> *H. jonesii*
> *H. kikutii*
> *H. kiyosumiensis*
> *H. laevigata*
> *H. longipes*
> *H. longissima*
> *H. minor*
> *H. montana*
> *H. nakaiana*
> *H. nigrescens*
> *H. okamotoi*
> *H. pachyscapa*
> *H. plantaginea*
> *H. pulchella*
> *H. pycnophylla*
> *H. rectifolia*

> *H. rohdeifolia* f. *viridis*
> *H. rupifraga*
> *H. shikokiana*
> *H. sieboldiana*
> *H. sieboldii*
> *H. takahashii*
> *H. takiensis*
> *H. tardiva*
> *H. tibae*
> *H. tsushimensis*
> *H. ventricosa*
> *H. venusta*
> *H. yingeri*

Significant botanical varieties and forms listed by Schmid (1991) include:

> *H. clausa* var. *normalis*
> *H. kikutii* var. *caput-avis*
> *H. kikutii* var. *kikutii* f. *leuconata*
> *H. kikutii* var. *polyneuron*
> *H. longipes* var. *caduca*
> *H. longipes* f. *hypoglauca*
> *H. longipes* var. *latifolia*
> *H. longipes* f. *sparsa*
> *H. longipes* f. *viridipes*
> *H. longipes* var. *vulgata*
> *H. longissima* var. *longifolia*
> *H. montana* f. *macrophylla*
> *H. plantaginea* var. *japonica*
> *H. sieboldii* f. *angustifolia*
> *H. sieboldii* f. *okamii*
> *H. sieboldii* f. *spathulata*

The following were formerly designated as species or botanical varieties by others but were reduced to cultivar level by Schmid (1991):

> 'Crispula'
> 'Decorata'
> 'Decorata Normalis'
> 'Elata'
> 'Fortunei'
> 'Fortunei Albomarginata'
> 'Fortunei Albopicta'
> 'Fortunei Aurea'
> 'Fortunei Aureomarginata'
> 'Fortunei Hyacinthina'
> 'Fortunei Stenantha'
> 'Helonioides'
> 'Helonioides Albopicta'
> 'Lancifolia'

H. montana 'Aureomarginata'
'Opipara'
H. plantaginea 'Aphrodite'
H. rohdeifolia 'Rohdeifolia'
H. sieboldiana 'Elegans'
H. sieboldii 'Alba'
H. sieboldii 'Kabitan'
H. sieboldii 'Subcrocea'
'Tardiflora'
'Tokudama'
'Tokudama Aureonebulosa'
'Tokudama Flavocircinalis'
'Undulata'
'Undulata Albomarginata'
'Undulata Erromena'
'Undulata Univittata'
H. ventricosa 'Aureomaculata'
H. ventricosa 'Aureomarginata'

Throughout *The Hosta Handbook* I have utilized the taxonomy of George Schmid with only a few exceptions. I have retained *Hosta lancifolia* as a species and not utilized 'Lancifolia' (or *H. cathayana* of Maekawa). Secondly, I have retained the Japanese *H. longipes lancea* and not reverted to *H. longipes sparsa*. My reasons for these diversions are explained in the main text.

HOSTA NOMENCLATURE

A few basic rules of nomenclature have been followed throughout *The Hosta Handbook*. As an example, the name *Hosta plantaginea* signifies a plant in the *Hosta* genus, with the specific epithet of *plantaginea*. Together these two words comprise a species name. Species names should be written in *italics* or underlined, e.g., *Hosta plantaginea* or <u>Hosta plantaginea</u>. It is always acceptable to abbreviate the name *Hosta* to *H.* when it has been completely spelled out in the previous text. In general gardening literature such a practice is common. If the most recent "*H*" genus referred to *Hosta*, then an abbreviated *H.* would automatically mean "*Hosta*". At the same time, if *Hemerocallis* or *Heuchera* were being discussed, the next "*H.*" would refer to them instead. For example, "The genus *Hosta* represents plants that are mainly native to Japan. *H. plantaginea*, however, is native to China. The genus *Hemerocallis* can also be found in eastern Asia. *H. minor* is often found in marshy grasslands." The first "*H.*" represented *Hosta*, for *Hosta plantaginea*, the second "*H.*" stood for *Hemerocallis*. Since *The Hosta Handbook* talks almost exclusively about the genus *Hosta*, "*H.*" generally refers to *Hosta*. In the same manner, the specific epithet can also be abbreviated when it has been recently discussed. For example, *Hosta sieboldiana* 'Frances Williams' can be listed simply as *H. s.* 'Frances Williams'.

Also important is a general understanding of the botanical varieties and forms. The word "variety" in botanical jargon signifies a distinct grouping in nature that, while still being part of the same species, varies slightly, often exclusive to a certain geographical area. For example, *Hosta longipes* var. *latifolia* refers to a distinct branch of *Hosta longipes* found in Japan. In general literature, it can be written as simply *Hosta longipes latifolia* without the variety designation. Often, too, the "type" for a species is given a varietal name the same as the specific epithet, e.g., *Hosta longipes* var. *longipes*, *H. kikutii* var. *kikutii* or *H. sieboldiana* var. *sieboldiana*. Such plants represent the typical plant of the species, but their varietal designations are generally omitted, i.e., *H. longipes*, *H. kikutii*, and *H. sieboldiana*. A *forma*, abbreviated "f.", refers to a distinct form. For example *Hosta longipes* f. *hypoglauca* differs from the species by having red petioles and is normally written *Hosta longipes hypoglauca*.

Another optional style involves the inclusion of the species name when referring to cultivars. When a cultivar can be referred back to a species, I sometimes include it to give the reader a reference point. In the case of *Hosta sieboldiana* 'Frances Williams', I know that the cultivar 'Frances Williams' is a cultivated form of the species *Hosta sieboldiana*. If I am familiar with *H. sieboldiana*, I automatically understand a lot about the flowering habits (color, size, time, scapes), mound size, leaf size, foliar substance, etc. of 'Frances Williams' itself. Referring to this plant as *H.* 'Frances Williams' is acceptable, but omits helpful information. When *Hosta fortunei* was considered a species, I always added it to any *H. fortunei* form. This meant that such plants as 'Gold Standard' or 'Francee' would be written as *H. fortunei* 'Gold Standard' and *H. fortunei* 'Francee'. With the loss of its species designation, it is no longer easy to associate Fortunei-type plants by their common characteristics. I do not advocate, however, calling these plants 'Fortunei Gold Standard' and 'Fortunei Francee'. 'Fortunei Albopicta', 'Fortunei Aureomarginata', 'Fortunei Hyacinthina' and others are acceptable combinations because these so-called "Latinized" cultivar names were formerly designated as botanical varieties of a species. The same is also true for any other species now considered a cultivar such as 'Decorata', 'Crispula', 'Tokudama', 'Opipara', and 'Undulata'.

The term "cultivar", too, has come into some question recently. I have always understood it to mean a "cultivated variety", i.e., a plant that was developed in cultivation, not the wild. (Individual plants found in the wild, varying from the species, e.g., streaked mutations, can be given a "forma" designation if they represent significant, distinct differences.) Additionally "cultivar" has been used synonymously with "clone" in current usage. Henry Ross of the Gardenview Horticultural Park in Strongsville, Ohio first alerted me to this problem a few years ago. The actual meaning of the term "cultivar" is much broader and can signify a related group of plants, not necessarily a clone. In *A Dictionary of Botany* (Little and Jones, 1980, p. 101), a "cultivar" is defined as follows:

> "A contraction of "cultivated variety". It refers to a plant type within a particular cultivated species that is distinguished by one or more characteristics; horticulturally, such plants are of considerable economic importance."

The same book (ibid, p. 85) defines a "clone" as

> "A group of genetically identical individuals resulting from asexual, vegetative multiplication, i.e. by mitosis; any plant propagated vegetatively and therefore considered a genetic duplicate of its parent."

Though the two definitions are similar, they are not the same. A clone can be a cultivar, but not all cultivars are clones. 'Gold Standard' is a clone and a cultivar. *H. sieboldiana* 'Elegans', however, is a cultivar, but not a clone, due to its widespread propagation by seed. Just about every other hosta "cultivar" is also a clone.

Plants propagated by tissue culture should be clonal material, no different from plants propagated through other vegetative means, e.g., division. Whenever a sport occurs, whether in tissue culture or the ground, it should be considered a new cultivar (and clone) because of the change in chloroplast genes.

The name Plantainlily (sometimes written as Plantain-lily) is the so-called "common name" for plants of the genus *Hosta*, presumably because the foliage resembles Plantain leaves and the flowers are lily-like. "Plantainlily", though, has fallen out of favor in deference to simply using "hosta". Some writers have also employed "hosta" as the plural (instead of "hostas"), though this is linguistically incorrect. In Japan hostas are known under the name "Giboshi" (pronounced "ge-boash"). Additional Japanese words are added before "Giboshi" to describe specific types, e.g., "Oba Giboshi" represents *H. montana* and "Iwa Giboshi" identifies *H. longipes*. Additional terms are added to describe forms or seedlings. For example, "Ogon Oba Giboshi" stands for a gold (ogon) form of *H. montana.* Forms of Japanese words commonly used in hosta names include "hime" (dwarf), "nishiki" (streaked), "shiro" (white), "hana" or "bana" (flower), "fukurin" (margined, usually denoting a white margin), "kifukurin" (gold-margined), and "murasaki" (purple).

Japanese cultivar names in Romaji (the Japanese language in Roman letters) must be used, not an English translation. Thus, the name 'Nishiki Iwa' should not be listed as 'Streaked Rock'. (Likewise cultivars introduced in German should not be translated into English.) This is in keeping with Article 28.1 of the "International Code of Nomenclature for Cultivated Plants - 1995" (1995 ICNCP) (Trehane, 1995). This rule basically states that translated names are not allowed. Also, according to Article 28.6, whenever the particle "no" is used in a Japanese name, it should be hyphenated before and after "no", e.g., 'Uzu-no-Mai'. Some difficulty occurs when attempting to list Japanese cultivars or forms of species. For example, "Ogon Oba Giboshi" would mean a gold-leaved type of *Hosta montana*. Writing this name as *Hosta montana* 'Ogon', however, is not acceptable since 'Ogon' is commonly used for gold-leaved forms of many species. Current thinking is that such a plant should be labelled *Hosta montana* 'Ogon Oba' or simply, *Hosta* 'Ogon Oba'. Although this seems awkward, it is probably the only way that such plants can include their proper Japanese names.

The same 1995 ICNCP also lists several rules pertaining to naming new hostas. Article 17.10 states that each cultivar name can consist of no more than 30 letters and 10 syllables. Interestingly hyphens, apostrophes, commas, exclamation points, and periods are acceptable in cultivar names according to Article 17.19. Such words as "group", "strain", "seedling", "sport", "selection", and "hybrid" cannot be included in cultivar names according to Article 17.16. Article 17.17 states that the words "improved" or "transformed" cannot be incorporated into a cultivar name. Article 17.6 states that each word of a cultivar must be capitalized with a few exceptions, one being the Japanese particle "no" (hence, 'Uzu-no-Mai').

One unusual usage of terminology that I incorporate throughout *The Hosta Handbook* occurs when generally referring to groups of plants related by a common species. I sometimes utilize the terms "Sieboldianas" and "Montanas" to refer to the plants related to *Hosta sieboldiana* and *Hosta montana*. The same happens for a few former species groups such as the "Fortuneis", the "Undulatas", and the "Tokudamas". I also freely use "Tardianas" to refer to the group of *H.* 'Tardiflora' X *H. sieboldiana* 'Elegans' hybrids developed by Eric Smith. While this usage of specific epithets may make botanical purists cringe, it has become very common in horticultural jargon.

THE AMERICAN HOSTA SOCIETY AND HOSTA REGISTRATION

From a small band of enthusiasts who gathered on July 7th, 1968 at Swarthmore College in Pennsylvania for the first national convention, the American Hosta Society (AHS) has grown by leaps and bounds. Today its membership numbers over 4000. Each year the AHS publishes two issues of *The Hosta Journal* as well as the *Hosta Yearbook*. Annual conventions have been held in such cities as Iowa City, Iowa, Peoria, IL, Atlanta, GA, Columbus, OH, Minneapolis, MN, Portland, OR, Raleigh, NC, Wilmington, DE, Indianapolis, IN, and Ann Arbor, MI just to name a few. Convention events include a leaf show (with judging), garden tours, speakers, an auction, and more. The AHS also sponsors scientific forums, gives grants for scientific research, and serves as the registration body of the genus *Hosta*. The national display garden for the American Hosta Society is located at the Minnesota Landscape Arboretum where the registrar also is based.

The arboretum's Andersen Horticultural Library houses the records of Frances R. Williams which includes her extensive correspondence with other hosta collectors. From the 1930's until her death in 1969, Frances communicated with Eunice Fisher of Wisconsin, Alex Cumming (developer of 'Honeybells') of Connecticut, Elizabeth Nesmith of Fairmount Gardens in Massachusetts (Frances' close friend and introducer of her hostas), botanist Nils Hylander of Sweden, Gus Krossa of Michigan, George Robinson of Oxford, England, H. A. Zager of Iowa, and others. From her Winchester, Massachusetts garden Frances Williams developed some of the first hosta cultivars including the plant named for her, *H. sieboldiana* 'Frances Williams'. Other Frances Williams hostas include 'Louisa', 'Lavender Lady', 'Snow Flakes', 'Purple Profusion', 'Sweet Susan', 'Betsy King', 'Tinker Bell', 'Dorothy', 'Sunlight', and 'Golden Circles'. Articles by Frances Williams extolling the virtues of hostas appeared in such journals as *The New York Botanic Garden Journal*, *Horticulture*, and *Popular Gardening*. Frances lived to see the formation of the American Hosta Society which certainly owes her a great debt.

One of Frances Williams's correspondents, Eunice Fisher, was the first Secretary-Treasurer of the American Hosta Society. Eunice had collected and grown hostas for many years from her Oshkosh, Wisconsin farm. During the 1970's, she authored and self-published three editions of the first book on hostas entitled *Hosta: The Aristocratic Plant for Shady Gardens*. Eunice also introduced over 40 hosta cultivars including 'Blue Rock', 'Candy Hearts', 'Fond

Hope', 'Happy Hearts', 'Heartleaf', 'Silver Award', 'Silver Bowl', and 'Unique'. She had a fairly extensive list of hostas for sale as well. Some of my first intensive studies of hostas were of a large group that she sold to Cantigny Museum and Gardens in Wheaton, Illinois, located only a mile from my old nursery site.

Another great influence in the early history of the American Hosta Society was Alex Summers, the first president and editor of *The Bulletin of the American Hosta Society* (later to become *The Hosta Journal*). Others prominent in the early AHS include Paul Aden, hosta collector and introducer of an outstanding group of hostas ('Sum and Substance', 'Blue Angel', 'Fragrant Bouquet', 'Just So', 'Gold Edger', 'Gold Regal', and 'Blue Mammoth', just to name a few); Pauline Banyai, developer of 'Gold Standard'; Bob Savory of Minnesota (nurseryman and developer of 'Golden Tiara', 'Lemon Lime', 'Tiny Tears' and 'Baby Bunting'); and Eldren Minks, second president of the AHS and hosta hybridizer ('Alvatine Taylor', 'Banana Sundae' and 'Regal Ruffles'). Throughout the years many other individuals have provided leadership and enthusiasm in various capacities with the AHS. Presidents such as Jim Cooper, Olive Bailey Langdon, Vic Santa Lucia, and Bob Olson have led the society through a phenomenal period of change and growth. Warren Pollock also stands out for changing the official publication of the AHS from a single yearly, black and white bulletin to a twice-yearly journal laden with numerous high quality color photos. Throughout all the years, various hybridizers and nurserymen have contributed mightily to the AHS by being dedicated to the development and introduction of new hostas. Standouts include Mildred Seaver, Kevin Vaughn, Bill and Eleanor Lachman, Peter Ruh, Van Wade, Bob Kuk, Mary Chastain, Herb and Dorothy Benedict, Jim Wilkins, Russ O'Harra, Ken Anderson, Clarence and Marge Soules, and Roy Klehm.

An important function of the American Hosta Society is its role as the International Registration Authority (IRA) for the genus *Hosta*. Any person wishing to authenticate the origin and description of a new hosta should register it with the AHS. Registration of a hosta secures its name and gives credit to the originator, registrant, nominant (namer), and introducer of each plant. If accurate data is supplied, the registration can serve as a useful source of information for those interested in learning about new hostas. A hosta can be registered by filling out a relatively simple form and supplying facts concerning the origin of the plant, who developed it, if it is a seedling or sport, etc. Plant size, leaf color and size, and flowering data are also required along with a single print or slide of the plant. More detailed, but optional information, can also be supplied on the two page form.

A plant should be registered if it is a new seedling or sport that has merit. The registrar, however, will not make judgements as to the value of a plant. The registrar's job is to check that the name has not been previously registered or is an established name in the nursery trade.

Registration forms can be obtained from the following address:

Hosta Registrar
Minnesota Landscape Arboretum
P.O. Box 39
3675 Arboretum Drive
Chanhassen, MN 55317

Despite there being over 4000 named hostas in the world, less than half that number have been registered. Unlike the genus *Hemerocallis* where registration is almost a prerequisite to marketing a new introduction, hostas are often named and introduced with registration occurring long afterward.

The American Hosta Society also offers numerous other services and publications. To find out more about all of these or to join the AHS, contact Cindy Nance, Membership Secretary, 338 E. Forestwood, Morton, IL 61550 for more information.

To foster more local interest in hostas, the AHS has created 8 regions covering the U.S. and Canada. Some of these groups hold annual conventions, much like the national AHS event. The Midwest Regional Hosta Society has been active for many years, long before the regional divisions were established. Recent Midwest conventions have been held in Chicago, Omaha, Dubuque, Iowa, Minneapolis, Peoria, and Madison, WI.

With the increased interest in hostas, over 70 local societies have also been formed. These groups cover many parts of the country and offer gardeners the opportunity for year-round hosta activities. Local hosta societies include The Carolina Hosta Society, the Central Illinois Society, the Delaware Valley Hosta Society, the Dubuque Regional Hosta Society, the Harshbarger Hosta Society (Iowa), The Indianapolis Hosta Society, the Metro Detroit Hosta Society, The Michigan Hosta Society, the Minnesota Hosta Society, the Northern Illinois Hosta Society, the Mississippi Valley Hosta Society, the Shady Choice Hosta Society, the Tri-State Hosta Society, and the Wisconsin Hosta Society.

There is also an ever-increasing number of websites devoted to hostas. The American Hosta Society maintains its own website, www.hosta.org.

GROWING HOSTAS

Across the world, hostas can be found in just about any temperate climate. Notable hosta areas include Japan, Korea, and China, where they are native, and the United States, Canada, and Europe. They also can be grown in any other area of the world that receives frost. Hostas have been grown in Argentina, Chile, Russia, Australia, New Zealand, and South Africa. Across the broad range of climates in the U.S., they can be found in almost any state. Though not common in California, Florida, Arizona, New Mexico, Louisiana, and Nevada, hostas will survive at high elevations in these states or in isolated areas that receive frost. Hostas require about 700 hours of temperatures below 40°F to satisfy the dormancy which naturally occurs when light levels are reduced in the fall. In northern Illinois, the first hostas begin to go dormant in late September, but many will continue to grow into October or November unless cut down by frost. In a greenhouse environment not receiving artificial light, most hostas go dormant in late November.

LIGHT. The amount of light that hostas should receive is dependent upon the climate. Generally in the U.S., hostas grown in cooler northern regions will tolerate more direct sunlight than those grown in the southern U.S. The ideal light level for hostas in northern Illinois is bright, dappled sunlight which creates a condition that I call "open shade". Such a setting may receive about one or two hours of direct sunlight each day. Hostas can also be grown in "partial shade", generally defined as 2-4 hours of direct, but less intense, morning sunlight. A good example of this would be on the east side of a building. In contrast "partial sun" can be defined as an area that receives at least 3 or 4 hours of direct, afternoon sunlight. This would be enough for most sun-loving herbaceous perennials, but only a few hostas will tolerate such conditions. At the other extreme, deep shade, as found in a dense woods, limits the potential for growth. Hostas will survive with deep shade, but the leaves tend to be thinner, wider, and fewer than in very bright conditions. Ironically, many hostas grow under dense shade in their native habitats.

SOIL. Hostas do best in rich, organic soil which is humusy and well-aerated. Clay-loam soils provide a good environment, but generally need to be lightened with such amendments as Canadian sphagnum peat moss, mushroom compost, pine bark, or decomposing leaves. Sandier soils provide better conditions for hosta root development. A sandy-clay-loam generally offers the ideal combination of fertility and good aeration.

Also important is soil pH. Hostas will tolerate a pH range

31

of 5.5 to 7.5, but the ideal seems to be 6.0 to 6.5. At pH extremes, some soil nutrients are not available for uptake. Often iron is tied up, leading to chlorosis (yellowing) of the foliage. For soils that are only slightly acid (pH 6.5-7.0) or alkaline (above pH 7.0), acidity can be increased by adding elemental sulfur or incorporating Canadian Sphagnum peat moss into the soil. A general recommendation would be to add 8-12 cubic feet of peat moss to the soil per 100 square feet of planting space dug down to a depth of 8-12". The pH of very acid soils can be increased by adding dolomitic lime.

FERTILIZATION. When planting a new growing area, incorporating dried fertilizers can be beneficial. A 5-10-5 or 10-10-10 will supply the soil with the additional fertility that hostas crave. High nitrogen fertilizers (as would be used for a lawn, e.g., 30-5-5) can produce tremendous growth, but may make the plants more susceptible to various fungal or bacterial rots. Slow-release fertilizers can also be used, but with some caution. Fertilizer is released into the soil for root uptake over a period of time that varies from 30 to 180 days. With high temperatures and excessive moisture, however, nutrient discharge increases, sometimes leading to problems. A small amount of slow-release fertilizer placed at the base of newly planted hostas would probably be the most conservative approach. A 2-3" layer of decomposed manure added to a new planting bed will also improve soil fertility. Though the N-P-K rating is usually low, the overall quantity used makes a difference. The main caution is to make sure that the manure has been aged for at least one or two years. Horse and sheep manures are best, but cow manure can also be acceptable. Chicken or turkey manure must be well-aged, five years or more, to be usable for garden purposes.

Established plantings also benefit from supplemental fertilization. Dried or slow-release fertilizers or manure can be worked into the surface of the soil in the spring at the time of emergence. Throughout the growing season, liquid fertilization can also be beneficial. Such fertilizers give a brief, but not long-lasting, shot of nutrition. Newly planted hostas may not be able to take full advantage of liquid fertilizers until they regrow fine root hairs often damaged at the time of planting. Fertilization should stop about six weeks before the first fall frost.

MOISTURE. Careful attention should be given to soil moisture level during the first few years after planting. This becomes especially crucial during the hottest parts of the summer, July and August in northern areas. New plantings of slow-growing hostas are most vulnerable to fluctuations in moisture levels. Many Sieboldianas and Tokudamas grow so slowly that if the root system dries out at an early stage, the plants seem to shrink in size over time. A trick to establishing such varieties as 'Great Expectations', 'Tokudama Aureonebulosa', and 'Blue Ice', is to place the plant with pot directly into the garden. This has the effect of keeping more water near the soil surface. After a year or two, the container can be removed.

MULCHES. Mulches can be helpful in retaining soil moisture and can reduce competition from weeds. Recommended mulches around new plantings include mushroom compost, decomposed leaves, pine needles, pine bark, shredded oak bark, cocoa bean mulch, and dried grass clippings. Mulches can also reduce the incidence of winter-kill in late-season plantings caused by heaving. This occurs when extreme temperature fluctuations from day to night during mid to late winter gradually push the plants out of the soil. The exposed crown and roots of heaved plants tend to dry out and eventually die. In northern areas of the U.S., it is advisable to place a 3-4" layer of mulch around any hostas planted after September 1.

PESTS: Slugs, etc. The negative side of using mulch is that it may harbor slugs that chew holes in hosta foliage. Slugs thrive in the cool, moist environments that mulches create. If mulches are to be used, liberal amounts of slug-bait must be applied early in the growing season. Begin applying bait when the hostas have just started to emerge, but before any damage becomes evident. Since they feed at night, slugs are not usually noticed until they've done a lot of damage. Generally they begin feeding just after dusk, and will continue to feed throughout the night. Occasionally on very humid, cloudy days, they can be found feeding during the daytime, but that is fairly rare. Once hostas have become established in the garden, mulches can be eliminated altogether to reduce the slug problem.

Other damaging pests include cutworms, black vine weevils, sowbugs, inchworms, and striped blister beetles. The latter is a fairly rare but particularly ravenous beast that can consume hosta foliage like no other insect. I have only seen them in July in northern Illinois. Fortunately, they can be controlled by a number of chemical sprays. Oil sprays have not been effective, however. Most other pests can be controlled by one pesticide or another. Occasionally woolly leaf hoppers create a white, fuzzy appearance on *Hosta ventricosa* scapes in July, but do no apparent damage. Aphids will feed on new growth, but this is generally confined to greenhouses. The same can be said for spider mites which feed on hostas under very dry, greenhouse conditions. Mites can be found on the leaf underside, often in great numbers, and cause the top surface to appear lightly speckled. *Hosta plantaginea* and related hybrids are good indicator plants for spider mite damage. Oil sprays and other chemicals are very effective in controlling mites. In the garden, such infestations occur only under drought conditions.

PESTS: Nematodes. Foliar nematodes are the newest pests to be of concern in the hosta garden. The main symptom is interveinal browning that becomes very evident in late summer. Nematodes overwinter in the crown of the plant. In spring they make their way into the leaf blade and begin feeding and multiplying in the areas between the veins. In Illinois they can be first spotted about the middle of July, but are not very noticeable until early August. Foliar nematodes are generally spread by splashing water meaning that they are more of a problem in rainy environments or with overhead watering systems. The problem cannot be solved by just removing infected foliage, though this certainly will help. If the plant is heavily infested, it should be discarded. Valuable plants can be saved by soaking infected individual divisions in a water bath held at 120°F for 15-20 minutes. This will usually kill any adult nematodes and their eggs. Such plants should then be potted and isolated for at least six months before moving back into the garden. For gardens with heavier infestations, a few sprays have been effective. Most need to be applied several times by a licensed applicator. Because of the increasing difficulties with foliar nematodes, significant research is underway that may offer safer chemical controls.

Foliar nematodes were virtually unknown to U.S. collectors until about 1991. Imports of a few rare hostas carried the nematodes that gradually spread to other gardens on divisions of these plants. At first some collectors chose to ignore the problem and, as a result, the problem spread further than it ever should have. Still, most landscapes are not affected by foliar nematodes. Many nurseries and collectors are now aware of the problem and are actively working to eradicate it.

PESTS: Four-legged types. Much bigger pests that consume hosta foliage by the bushel-load are deer. They have become an increasing problem in some communities and are not easy to control. In the spring, they feed on new hosta foliage, occasionally chewing the plant back to the ground. During the growing season, deer will feed on almost any type of hosta, but are especially attracted to fragrant-flowered types. I am not sure if they are attracted to the succulence of the new, active growth or their sugary sweetness, but hostas related to *H. plantaginea* are tops on the deer menu. If given the choice of tough, chewy *H. sieboldiana* 'Elegans' or sweet, succulent 'Honeybells' foliage, the latter is always preferred. Though music (classic, rap, country, or rock), hair, human urine, hot pepper sprays, dogs, cats, scarecrows, pie pans, and soap, plus a wide variety of applied chemicals, can successfully control deer, the best controls are mechanical. Peter Ruh of Chesterland, Ohio invented an ingenious series of barriers that has kept his vast collection generally safe from the many deer in his area.

Mice, rats, moles, ground squirrels, rabbits, and voles can also invade gardens and destroy plants. Damage to hostas varies with the pest, but it can range from mild to severe. Rabbits will sometimes chew new foliage, but usually are not a major problem. At the other extreme are voles, which voraciously consume hosta roots, though often leaving the crowns intact. (These can be replanted in fresh soil.) When left unchecked, voles have been known to wreak havoc in many a hosta collection. Most of these rodents can be controlled with various traps and poisons. Adding pea gravel or crushed granite to the garden sometimes deters burrowing types. Probably the best rodent control, however, is a cat with a good instinct for hunting (not all have it).

FUNGI, BACTERIA, AND VIRUSES. A few fungal and bacterial problems occasionally cause crown rot in hostas. The so-called "Southern Blight" is, perhaps, the best known rot problem. It usually shows up in gardens in July or August and can rapidly spread if left unchecked. The first symptoms are a lightening of the leaf blade, though in no distinct pattern. At some point tugging on a leaf will easily pull it away and reveal a mass of white, fiber-like growths at the ground, crown level. If the infection has not gone too far, the plant can be saved by digging it out of the ground and removing any remaining foliage. The roots should be thoroughly cleansed of soil with a garden hose (making sure any excess water does not spread to the rest of the garden). The clump can then be soaked in a dilute (10-20%) bleach solution. The amount of time is debatable, but 1-2 hours should suffice. After drying for a day or two, the treated plant should be potted and isolated for at least three months. Periodic observations will reveal if the plant is free of blight. Back in the garden, as much of the soil surrounding the old infected plant should be removed and new bleach solution can be poured into the hole which should be later filled with new soil. One unfortunate result is that hostas should not be planted back into the same spot. Various fungicides can also be used to control rot problems, but they need to be applied repeatedly to be effective. Factors that encourage rot in hostas include high nitrogen fertilization and hot, humid conditions. Crown rot may also develop in the spring, usually as a secondary effect of winter-kill. The crown may have been killed back due to low temperatures or heaving, and then a rot begins to deteriorate the remaining tissue. Too often gardeners will assume that the rot is the cause of the problem rather than a byproduct. Such plants can sometimes be saved through the same methods as used for Southern Blight.

A few viruses have also been known to infect hostas. They exhibit a variety of symptoms that are pictured in the "Hosta Problem Solving Guide" at the back of this book. Unlike foliar nematode, rot, and other pest problems, there are no cures for viral infections. Good sanitation is the best defense. Pruning shears or knives used in dividing or maintaining hostas should be cleaned with a 50% bleach solution and air-dried. By passing an infected knife from plant to plant, it is possible to infect clean tissue. Sometimes confusing is the fact that not all leaves of virus-infected material will show symptoms. If one part of the plant is diseased, the whole plant is diseased. Also misleading are various, tiny spots that may develop on hosta leaves due to wind, mechanical damage, or dryness. Light spring frosts, too, can cause a light flecking of the foliage that can mimic a virus. All of these are non-infectious phenomena that probably account for most spots on leaves.

OTHER PROBLEMS. A variety of other problems can afflict hostas including spring frost damage, winter damage, spring desiccation burn on golden Sieboldiana-types, meltout, the drawstring effect, fairy ring (center-clump dieback), and chemical damage. The latter problem occurs when herbicides are absorbed by actively growing plants. The result is a thickening of foliage or scapes. Sometimes collectors are fooled into thinking that they are seeing a sport, but that is not the case. I have observed some very bizarre, flattened scapes with flower buds popping out all over from exposure to 2,4-D or 2,4,5-T. Chemicals that leach from some railroad ties used in landscaping can also cause grotesque growth patterns. Similar-looking damage can be the result of cold winter temperatures. If the temperatures are severe in early winter, the outer layers of dormant hosta buds are sometimes damaged. When growth begins in the spring, the damaged tissue appears contorted. Eventually newer, normal foliage will emerge unless the buds are heavily affected.

Spring frost damage can be problematic in certain parts of the country. In the southern U.S. *Hosta montana* 'Aureomarginata' and *H. plantaginea* are often subject to this problem. In about one out of ten years in northern Illinois, *H. plantaginea*, *H. lancifolia*, and a few others are damaged by late spring frosts. Affected plants usually recover, though the clump size will be reduced. If the main bud has been killed, secondary side buds will emerge and produce new, but smaller, shoots.

Spring is also the time for the so-called "spring desiccation burn" or "spring burn" that afflicts many Sieboldianas with gold in the foliage. This occurs when the leaves are rapidly expanding in spring and the nighttime temperatures dip into the low 40's. If the foliage is then subjected to wind and direct sunlight in the morning, the gold areas can desiccate and develop a light brown appearance within a few days. Eventually these areas turn orangy brown, creating the so-called "rust". *H. sieboldiana* 'Frances Williams', 'Golden Sunburst', and 'Borwick Beauty' are examples of Sieboldianas that burn heavily in spring. Interestingly blue-green parts of the foliage never burn. Similarly the white margins of such Sieboldianas as 'Northern Halo' or 'Northern Exposure' do not burn. There has been a major effort among collectors to identify non-burning, gold-margined Sieboldiana forms. 'Olive Bailey Langdon', so far, seems to be the best. Though it develops an occasional spot, the problem is minimal. Other cultivars that show promise are described in this book. If susceptible plants are kept out of direct light, the amount of burning is reduced. Also, in cooler, more humid climates, spring burn is not as severe.

The "drawstring effect" develops in a few white-margined varieties when the margin stops expanding during the growing season, while the center (green, blue-green or gold) continues to expand. The difference in growth patterns leads to distortion and pressure on the relatively thin margin which can begin tearing. Eventually the torn areas start to turn brown and can become quite unsightly. Many of these drawstring plants originated as tissue culture mutations, but not all. Unfortunately I introduced a few of these plants, the first being 'Lunar Eclipse'. As a mutation of 'August Moon', 'Lunar Eclipse' showed promise as a young plant but developed the drawstring effect after reaching maturity. The distortion is enhanced in gardens that are heavily fertilized. In such settings, other cultivars that are not normally associated with this problem may also develop it. I have seen 'Francee', 'Gloriosa', and others become distorted due to intense fertilization. While I do not recommend growing plants that develop the "drawstring effect", cutting off the first flush of growth will result in a normal-looking set of foliage being produced. A similar problem occurs when the margins of some hostas seem to just fall away. This occurs in such varieties as 'Brim Cup' and 'Knockout'. At a young stage of development, the foliage appears attractive, but with maturity, the margins partially drop out and produce a jagged, sawtooth effect. Again, this problem is aggravated by heavy fertilization.

When a hosta has not been divided for a number of years, the center of the clump often dies out and produces a "fairy ring". This condition is called center-clump dieback. It is most evident in early spring when the foliage begins to emerge from the ground. Once growth has commenced, the mound develops to normal proportions. Occasionally a plant with this condition will begin to rot in the center portions, which will lead to the eventual destruction of the whole clump. The best strategy for clumps with a fairy ring formation is to dig them up, divide them, replant healthy sections, and discard the center area. The soil from the old clump should be either replaced or amended with fresh organic matter and fertilizer. If no rot has occurred, a hosta can be planted back into the same place.

"Meltout" occurs when the white center of a leaf desiccates, turns brown, and drops out. Such leaves generally take on the appearance of a holey, brown and white mess. Meltout can be reduced by growing susceptible cultivars in bright, moist locations.

Sunburn is another problem that can be avoided by moving a plant to a different part of the garden. It usually occurs when leaves receive too much light before surrounding shade trees have fully developed in spring. Large sections of leaves will first turn light yellow, then crispy brown. Occasionally a fungus will infect the affected areas and continue disintegration of the foliage.

Refer to the "Hosta Problem Solving Guide" at the back of the book for further discussion of many of these problems.

HOSTA COMPANIONS

In most gardens, hostas require some overhead planting to create a shaded environment. A variety of trees and shrubs can serve this purpose, some better than others. The best trees include a number of oaks (white, black, red, burr, pin, and swamp white), some maples, lindens, hickories, elms, pines, spruces, ash, larch, and dogwoods. Interestingly hostas will also grow under Black Walnut trees whose roots emit toxic substances that prevent many other plants from growing. I've seen many beautiful hosta collections planted under Sugar and Norway Maples, but their fibrous root systems must be kept at bay. I once developed a new garden bed near a Norway Maple and found it filled with tree roots within three weeks. Crabapples offer a quick solution to create shade, but the low-lying branches of some varieties present a pruning challenge. *Malus hupehensis*, the Tea Crabapple, with its decidedly vase-shaped habit, would be a good selection. Slightly more exotic shade trees include Katsuratree (*Cercidiphyllum japonicum*), Carolina Silverbell (*Halesia carolina*), Black Tupelo (*Nyssa sylvatica*), Japanese Pagodatree (*Sophora japonica*), Japanese Maple (*Acer palmatum*) and Redbud (*Cercis canadensis*). Similarly combinations of large shrubs can provide adequate shade for hostas. Good choices include Witchhazels (*Hamamelis vernalis, H. japonica, H. x intermedia*), Viburnums (*V. dentatum, V. lantana, V. lentago,* and *V. dilatatum*), Sweetshrub (*Calycanthus floridus*), Cotoneasters (*C. multiflorus, C. lucidus*), Rhododendrons (*R. mucronulatum, R. catawbiense,* and the P.J.M. hybrids) and Mockorange (*Philadelphus coronarius*). In the wild I've seen hostas shaded by *Miscanthus sinensis*, the Maiden Grass. Other tall grasses and perennials can be used in the same manner.

A large number of perennials combine well with hostas in shaded landscapes. Ferns offer a contrast in texture and have nearly the same growing requirements. Some of the best are Woodferns (*Dryopteris marginalis, D. spinulosa*), Lady Fern (*Athyrium filix-femina*), Hay-scented Fern (*Dennstaedtia punctilobula*), Sensitive Fern (*Onoclea sensibilis*), Japanese Painted Fern (*A. goeringianum* 'Pictum'), Christmas Fern (*Polystichum acrostichoides*), and Cinnamon Fern (*Osmunda cinnamomea*). I don't recommend interplanting Ostrich Fern (*Matteuccia pensylanica*) with hostas or any other perennial. They are much too aggressive and will eventually suffocate anything within reach. Good flowering perennials to use include the Hellebores (*Helleborus orientalis* and *H. niger*), which offer interesting foliage as well as early season flowers. The Japanese Toadlilies (*Tricyrtis*) also provide attractive foliage, but their orchid-like flowers are produced late in the season. Other good shade-loving perennials include Heart-leaf Brunnera (*Brunnera macrophylla*), Snakeroot (*Cimicifuga*), Barrenwort (*Epimedium*), Primrose (*Primula*), and Violas (*Viola*). Woodland wildflowers can also be effectively combined in a shade garden with hostas. Virginia Bluebells (*Mertensia virginica*) bloom in April in northern Illinois and begin to die back at the same time as hosta foliage emerges and develops in May. Other good woodland wildflowers include Trilliums, Jack-in-the-Pulpit (*Arisaema triphyllum*), Blue Cohosh (*Caulophyllum thalictroides*), Cranesbill (*Geranium maculatum*), Hepatica (*Hepatica acutiloba* and *H. americana*), Mayapple (*Podophyllum peltatum*), Bloodroot (*Sanguinaria canadensis*), Solomon's Seal (*Polygonatum biflorum*), Solomon's Plume (*Smilacina racemosa*), and Foamflower (*Tiarella cordifolia, T. wherryi*, and various new hybrid forms). Spring-flowering bulbs can be used in the same way in the shade garden. Snowdrops, Crocus, Scilla, Puschkinia, Daffodils, Hyacinths, Tulips, and Alliums are but a few of the many choices available. An unusual bulb to plant is the Magic Lily (*Lycoris squamigera*) which produces a large mound of foliage in the spring that dies back to the ground by early summer, only to flower (without foliage) in August, just about at the time when you've forgotten about it.

Hostas can be effectively used as specimens in a sea of ground cover. Good ground covers to combine with hostas include Japanese Spurge (*Pachysandra terminalis*), Sweet Woodruff (*Galium odoratum*), European Wild Ginger (*Asarum europeum*), Creeping Lilyturf (*Liriope spicata*), *Lamium maculatum* cultivars ('White Nancy', 'Beacon Silver'), and some forms of English Ivy (*Hedera helix*). Not recommended are Goutweed (*Aegopodium podograria*) and Crownvetch (*Coronilla varia*) which can so dominate an area that survival of any hostas growing near them becomes secondary to the fight to rid the garden of these weedy plants. Wintercreeper Euonymus (*Euonymus fortunei coloratus*) and Periwinkle (*Vinca minor*), though not as aggressive, also do not mix well with hostas.

PROPAGATION, HYBRIDIZATION, AND MUTATION SELECTION

DIVISION. Even in this day of plant tissue culture, the most common form of hosta propagation continues to be division. This is a relatively easy process that any gardener or nurseryman can successfully employ to multiply hostas. Individual shoots or divisions are separated from a clump (with attached crown and roots) and allowed to grow as new, separate plants. Hostas can be divided at almost any time of the year that the ground can be worked, but the best time is in spring, just after the plants have begun to grow. Spring-divided hostas develop roots early in the growing season and then have a full growing season to become established. Summer is also a good time to divide hostas, and tends to be the most convenient time for most nurserymen and gardeners. Fall division can be successful, but only if precautions are taken to reduce the possibility of winter damage (thick mulches).

The actual process of dividing a hosta is simple. In the garden, the clump to be divided is dug by loosening the soil around the perimeter of the plant with a shovel and lifted out of the ground. A clean, sharp knife or shovel is then inserted into the clump between shoots. By making vertical cuts, individual shoots are cut apart and separated. The amount of cutting is determined by age of the clump and the number of divisions desired. Clumps older than five or six years (from an original single division) may yield many divisions when divided. A rapidly-growing cultivar such as 'Royal Standard' can be separated into twenty or more divisions after about five years growth in good soil. On the other hand, slower growers, such as 'Tokudama Aureonebulosa' or *H. sieboldiana* 'Elegans', might yield only three or four divisions over the same period of time.

The formation of divisions does not happen overnight. Shoots emerge in the spring from dormant buds which were formed one to three years prior. Generally buds can be found in the crown tissue at the base of actively growing shoots. Some of these buds will become the following year's shoots, while others will become active in succeeding years. Expansion of these buds occurs throughout the growing season. The number of buds formed at the base of each shoot varies with variety and age of the plant. Small plants of most hostas do not generally form more than one or two buds for the following year's growth. In fact a single bud is typical for small hosta divisions or plantlets after the first season of growth.

Recently there have been attempts to speed up the process of division through the application of growth regulators to actively growing plants. The basic concept is to stimulate dormant buds to prematurely begin active growth. Once a cluster of new shoots has formed, these can then be divided. The cytokinin Benzyladenine or "BAP" has been the most popular growth regulator employed, though there are many others that could be utilized. Growth regulators offer exciting possibilities to anyone wishing to increase their stock of new varieties, but they should be used with caution.

PLANT TISSUE CULTURE. During the last twenty or so years, plant tissue culture (or micropropagation) has become the principle means of increase for the newest hostas. Tissue culture is basically a type of division done under sterile conditions on a miniature scale. The ultimate goal is to rapidly increase large numbers of varieties in demand. Usage of plant tissue culture has made a significant impact upon the availability of hostas throughout the United States and abroad. Varieties that were once extremely rare and could only be found in a few collector's gardens are now available to any home gardener. In the tissue culture process, very small shoots are multiplied in sterile, nutrient media (in test tubes or flasks) which optimizes their growth. Through the stimulation of growth regulators in the media, shoot multiplication or root formation occurs. Instead of waiting a whole growing season for new buds to develop, cultured hostas develop new shoots within five or six weeks of the start. By repeated dissection or "subculturing" every six weeks, a single shoot can potentially yield the same number of divisions in one year that would take ten or more years outside. The new plantlets that result are generally grown for at least two months in a greenhouse environment before they can be transplanted into larger containers or the ground.

Tissue-cultured plants are no different genetically from those propagated by division. Over the years the term "originator's stock" has cropped up to identify plants propagated by division. This term has become somewhat blurred in the sense that many "originator's stock" plants were developed in tissue culture. Some would argue that plants propagated by division are larger than those out of tissue culture. Certainly a single division cut out of a five-year-old clump of *H. sieboldiana* 'Elegans' will be larger than a single tissue culture plantlet. Such plants, though, should never be considered a retail, saleable size. Given the proper growing environment, plants from tissue culture will become just as large as divisions.

SEED GERMINATION. Propagation by seed can yield large numbers of plants in a fairly short period of time. It is easy to understand why many nurserymen resorted to seed propagation of the slow-multiplying *H. sieboldiana* 'Elegans' (see page 400). Unfortunately most hosta cultivars do not come true-to-type from seed. Seed germination, of course, is a very important part of hybridizing programs. In the past, too, seeds have been the original source for new types of hostas collected in the wild. The only hosta that can be reliably multiplied by seed is *Hosta ventricosa*. This species from China develops most of its embryos through "apomixis", which is also known as asexual embryo formation. Such embryos are genetic carbon-copies of the mother plant. In the mix of seedlings, however, are a few sexual embryos that are slightly different from the mother plant.

Hosta seeds are formed in pods, one pod per flower. Pod size and shape range considerably. The pods of *H. sieboldiana* 'Elegans' (15/32" long by 1/8" wide), *H. ventricosa* (1 1/4" by 3/8"), and *H. plantaginea* (2 3/4" by 3/8") cover the range of sizes found in most hostas. The number of seeds per pod averages around thirty, but this can vary considerably. The percentage of viable seeds will also differ. Though a seed may form, it may not contain a living embryo and will not germinate. White seeds are not viable, but some brown seeds that are completely flat are also non-viable. Viable seeds are usually very dark brown in color and are thickened at one end. In comparing these same three hostas, 'Elegans' averages about 34 viable seeds per pod, while *H. plantaginea* forms as many as eighty seeds, but only about 30 are usually viable. *H. ventricosa* pods yield about 25 seeds, with nearly all viable.

The percentage of flowers forming seed pods varies with the type of hosta and weather conditions. Generally pod set will be poor under very rainy or extremely hot conditions. Every flower of some hostas, e.g., *H. ventricosa* and *H. sieboldiana* 'Elegans', seems to form a seed pod, meaning that several hundred seeds can be produced by one plant. On the other hand, hostas such as 'Krossa Regal' or 'Undulata' rarely form seed pods. 'Royal Standard' can be put into the class of "sparse pod formers". One year I found only fifty seed pods in a large planting of 'Royal Standard' which produced over 100,000 flowers during its three-week blooming period. These seed pods, too, averaged only one viable seed per pod. Assuming the formation of about 25 seeds per pod (24 non-viable, 1 viable), this calculates to a .002% fertility level or a 99.998% level of sterility.

Hosta seeds are usually collected in the fall as the seed pods turn yellow, just before they naturally dehisce and disperse the seed. Collected seed pods should be placed into clean, dry paper bags and stored in a cool, dry environment. Under such conditions hosta seeds remain viable for about nine months. Freezing hosta seeds or, better yet, storing them at 33-40°F, allows them to remain viable for several years.

Seeds can be germinated in flats of soil, either in a greenhouse or outdoors in spring or early summer. A good germination mix consists of peat and perlite, one part each. Seeds can be covered with a thin (about 1/4") layer of vermiculite which retains moisture but also provides excellent aeration. The seed flats should be watered well with clear (not fertilized) water after sowing, using a mist nozzle to reduce washing-out. Germination generally takes about 2-3 weeks. Seedlings can be transplanted into larger pots once they have developed 2-3 leaves, usually about 4-6 weeks following germination.

HYBRIDIZATION. Hybridization and mutation selection are the chief means of developing new types of hostas. A hybrid is created when the flowers of two distinct hostas are crossed. The actual process of hybridizing involves taking the pollen from the anthers of one plant and placing it upon the stigmatic surface of another. In a protected greenhouse environment, successful pollination can occur any time during the day. Outdoors this must be done early in the day to prevent bee pollination. Bumblebees are great natural pollinators that can begin work as early as 5 a.m. Any unprotected flower is likely to be bee-pollinated, eventually resulting in so-called "open-pollinated" seedlings. Open-pollinated seedlings are usually "selfed", i.e. the pollen and eggs are from the same plant. Such plants are not hybrids, but can exhibit some genetic diversity nonetheless.

Once pollination occurs, successful pod formation can be determined in about four days for most crosses. Pods that are developing at that time will continue to maturation. Occasionally a pod will drop off after 1-2 weeks, but that is fairly rare. Fully mature, dark brown seeds are ready to be harvested 30 days after pollination, even though the pods are still green. Seed pods do not ripen and turn brown until fall, even for early blooming types.

Perhaps the greatest challenge to hybridization is not in the process itself, but in the selection of superior seedlings. Leaf color is the easiest trait to distinguish. Often foliage colors will be evident right after germination, and certainly within the first year after germination. Many other characteristics, however, do not manifest themselves for several years. Also seedlings often bear traits that change as the plant matures. What may be a cute, wavy-leaved plant as a two-year-old seedling, may flatten out and be less attractive with age.

MUTATIONS. Mutation (or sport) selection is another way to develop new hostas. As a group, hostas exhibit a high mutation rate. By far the most common type of mutation occurs when the chlorophyll changes or mutates into another form. The net result is a "sport" (the resulting, mutated plant) with foliage colors different from the original or "mother" plant. In the wild in Japan, hosta mutations frequently occur. Wild collected sports have come out of *H. montana*, *H. longipes*, *H. sieboldii*, *H. kikutii*, *H. kiyosumiensis*, and others. In gardens and tissue culture labs, the number of mutations that have occurred is equally as exciting. Sometimes, it seems that a single hosta cultivar will yield an endless stream of new forms. Cultivars such as 'Golden Tiara', 'Gold Standard', 'Francee', and 'August Moon' have yielded a large number of sports. For every valuable sport, though, there are many more unusable or poor sports. Like seedling selection it is important to be able to distinguish which sports have potential.

HOSTA DESCRIPTIONS

GUIDE TO READING DESCRIPTIONS

The format for each hosta description is fairly obvious, but, for clarity's sake, a few words are in order. First, unless noted, all descriptive information and listed data originated from my own extensive note-taking and measurements in a variety of gardens, nurseries, greenhouses, and native sites. All leaf, mound, flower, scape, etc. measurements were taken with a measuring tape (actually a few dozen) and are listed in inches in *The Hosta Handbook*. I attempted to view each hosta in as many sites and as many times as possible. This gave me the broadest view of how each plant responded to differences in environment, geography, and time of year.

Every listing begins with a boxed-in area that can be thought of as a quick guide to each plant. One could probably get a good feel for all the listed plants by just reading these areas and studying the accompanying photo. Besides the name and any common names that I have encountered (including any Japanese names), I describe the "**key features**" for which each plant is known. Next comes the **mound size**, height by width of each clump. The height is stated first since this is the determining factor for categorizing a hosta size (dwarf, small, medium, etc.). Normally I list a size that could be found in many collections, but occasionally note a much larger size that I observed only in a limited number of settings. Keep in mind that the listed dimensions represent well-grown, mature clumps and can vary considerably from garden to garden. For a slow-growing cultivar such as 'Blue Ice', it may take eight or ten years under ideal conditions to achieve the listed 8" by 18" mound dimensions. At the same time, with a less than optimum environment, 8" by 18" might never be achieved. Faster-growing cultivars can also range considerably. While I've seen several clumps of 'Francee' reach 21" high by 50" wide, some will certainly become no larger than 16" high by 36" wide. I can recall a clump of 'Sum and Substance' in a very dry environment with intense tree root competition only achieve about half of its potential size after several years.

Right below the box is a "**spacing**" designation. This was suggested to me by a nursery friend of mine who thought it would be helpful for planning landscapes. Next comes the heart of my 16 years of data-taking: descriptions of the **leaves** and the **flowers**. The "**comments**" section ends the main listing for each variety. Lastly are the "**Seedlings, Sports, and Other Related Types**" and "**Other Similar**

Types" sections. In these groupings I attempt to list and/or briefly describe hostas that are either genetically related to the main plant or have a similar appearance.

A more detailed look at each section of the descriptions:

spacing

This represents the average distance to space each variety in the landscape. Although this is somewhat based upon the mature width of the plant, growth rate is also a consideration. Some hostas grow so slowly that recommending a spacing of 72" would mean 5-10 years of a very bare-looking garden.

leaves

Technically a hosta leaf consists of a blade and a petiole. In common vernacular, however, the terms "leaf" and "blade" are used almost interchangeably and that is how they are treated throughout *The Hosta Handbook*. Leaves originate from the growing point or meristem of each shoot. Each shoot connects to a "crown", which joins the foliage and the root system. When a shoot is separated with connecting crown and roots, this is termed a "division".

(1) **Leaf Size**. (length by width of the blade, in inches)

For each leaf, the longest length and the widest width is listed. Like mound size, leaf size can vary considerably with the environment, age of the plant, and rate of growth.

(2) **Leaf Color**. (light green; medium green; dark green; bluish green; blue-green; chartreuse; medium gold; bright gold; white-margined & green-centered; white-margined & blue-green-centered; white-margined & gold-centered; gold-margined & green-centered; gold-margined & blue-green-centered; green-margined & white-centered; blue-green-margined & white-centered; green-margined & gold-centered; blue-green-margined & gold-centered; streaked; mottled)

The actual description of leaf color is truly in the eye of the beholder. Most observers can agree on the general color categories, e.g., gold, green, blue, white-margined & green-centered, etc., but getting more specific becomes a debate. What is white to some, may be creamy white to others. How about differentiating between the various shades of gold? "Gold" ranges from chartreuse to light yellow. It should be noted that in many AHS registrations the term "yellow-gold" is used to describe gold. This really does not give the reader much specific information. In the same light, some registrations depict chartreuse as yellowish green or greenish yellow.

Time of the year can also influence foliage color. Most

hosta collectors are familiar with the dramatic color changes that occur in such cultivars as 'Fortunei Albopicta' (gold-centered in spring, then green), 'Gold Standard' (green in spring, then gold-centered), and *H. ventricosa* 'Aureomaculata' (gold-centered in spring, then shiny, dark green). Many seasonal changes, however, are more subtle. Yellow margins often slowly turn creamy white, depending not only on the season, but also on the amount of direct sunlight received. Most blue-green types turn green, again being influenced by environmental factors such as light and moisture. A few hostas also develop notable fall color displays. I attempt to note as many of these seasonal changes as possible.

In variegated hostas, margin width varies from as narrow as 1/64" to as wide as 3-4". Whenever possible, width of the margin is listed.

Also influencing the color effect of hosta foliage is the appearance of the top leaf surface. Most hostas have a "dull" or non-shiny top, but many are shiny. These are described as shiny, slightly shiny, or very shiny.

(3) **Leaf Underside**. (shiny (glabrous), very shiny, whitish shiny, thick bloom, moderate bloom, thin bloom)

The condition of the leaf underside is an important identification characteristic. While any bloom (a whitish wax) on the top surface of the leaf will wear away, an underside bloom usually remains intact the whole growing season. The term "whitish shiny" depicts an underside which appears shiny and white at the same time but is not covered with a bloom. *Hosta minor* and *H. yingeri* are good examples of "whitish shiny" undersides.

(4) **Blade Shape**. (linear, very narrowly elliptic, narrowly elliptic, elliptic, broadly elliptic, rotund, lanceolate, narrowly ovate, ovate, broadly ovate, very broadly ovate, heart-shaped, elliptic-ovate, broadly oblong-ovate, triangular) **See Diagram 1.**

I use the chart of leaf blade shapes described on page 320 of the *Royal Horticultural Society Supplement to the Dictionary of Gardening* (Synge, 1956) as a guide. I deviate from this chart only to create new shapes that better describe hosta leaves, e.g., elliptic-ovate and broadly oblong-ovate. When important I describe the blade base, which can vary from wedge-shaped (usually with an elliptic blade) to round to slightly lobed (subcordate) to deeply lobed or heart-shaped (cordate). The combination of a deeply lobed base and a broadly ovate blade usually results in the leaf being described as "heart-shaped". Additionally I note the leaf tip when it is curved or very long, occasionally when it is very short or blunt.

Diagram 1. Blade Shapes

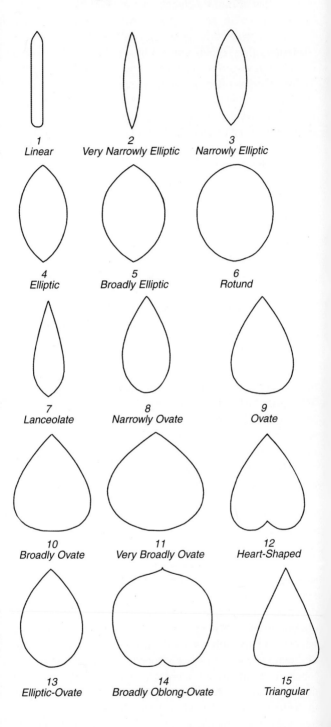

1
Linear

2
Very Narrowly Elliptic

3
Narrowly Elliptic

4
Elliptic

5
Broadly Elliptic

6
Rotund

7
Lanceolate

8
Narrowly Ovate

9
Ovate

10
Broadly Ovate

11
Very Broadly Ovate

12
Heart-Shaped

13
Elliptic-Ovate

14
Broadly Oblong-Ovate

15
Triangular

Andrew 2

An important factor in blade shape is the maturity of the plant. As a hosta ages, the blade generally widens. Sometimes it seems hard to believe that a juvenile plant with very narrow foliage is the same cultivar as a mature plant with very wide, broadly ovate foliage.

(5) **Margin**. (slightly rippled, heavily rippled, wavy, very wavy, not wavy)

Any rippling or waviness of the leaf margin is noted. Ripples (or ruffles) are very small and generally confined to the edge of the leaf. A "piecrust" margin has a large number of small ripples along the whole length of the margin. Waves are much broader and less defined, often extending throughout the whole blade. I sometimes counted ripples or waves, starting at the base and ending at the tip. Thus, the number listed is the amount that can be found on one-half of the blade.

Most hostas have a slightly wavy margin or blade. It is very rare for living tissue such as a hosta leaf to be perfectly flat. Rather than describing such hostas such as *H. lancifolia* and *H. venusta* as "flat", I have used the term "not wavy".

(6) **Texture**. (smooth; slightly, moderately or heavily (intensely) corrugated; unruly)

The surface of most hosta leaves is either smooth or corrugated (rugose). The term "corrugation" describes the appearance of a leaf with small, concave depressions in the leaf blade. Each depression can be thought of as a pucker or a dimple. I recently heard the term "warts" used for small, convex dimples. An older term for corrugation is "seersucker".

Corrugation usually develops with maturity. Even the most heavily corrugated cultivars have a smooth texture when young.

Unruliness describes a very "unsettled" appearance as found in 'Bold Ruffles' or 'Fantastic'. It usually is a combination of extreme waviness and heavy corrugation.

(7) **Cupping**. (deeply, moderately, or slightly)

Cupping is produced when the leaf blade has a concave character. This is a genetic trait that is often passed on to seedlings. Depth of cupping varies considerably over the range of cupped-leaved hostas, with the deepest measuring about 3". Some leaves are inversely or downwardly cupped, as in 'Blue Umbrellas'.

(8) **Substance** (thick, good, better than average, average, thin)

Substance refers to the thickness of the leaf blade. Thicker leaves are more pest resistant and better able to withstand drought and resist mechanical damage. Thin leaves are susceptible to slug damage.

(9) **Vein Pairs**. (3-21)

The portion of the petiole that extends into the leaf blade and divides the blade lengthwise into two equal halves is termed the "midrib". The midrib tends to be wider and thicker toward the base of the leaf, becoming veinlike near the tip. On each side of the midrib are matching pairs of veins. Each hosta bears a characteristic number of vein pairs at maturity. Hostas related to *H. sieboldiana* normally have 16-18 vein pairs, though the range is 14-21. Other typical vein pair numbers are 3-5 for *H. venusta* and *H. sieboldii*, 6-7 vein pairs for *H. nakaiana*, 7-8 for 'Golden Tiara' and its derivatives, 8-9 for *H. ventricosa*, 7-10 for the Undulatas, 9-11 for *H. plantaginea*, 9-11 for the Fortunei types, 11-12 for the Tardiana Series, and 14-16 for *H. montana*. Less than mature plants bear fewer vein pairs.

Counting vein pairs is a relatively simple process. Start at the tip and count the veins on one side of the blade, all the way to the base. For larger hostas often there is a very short pair of veins near the base. These should also be counted.

Veins can also be very prominent or hardly noticeable. Though a secondary ornamental feature, deeply impressed veins add to the appearance of such types as *H. kikutii yakusimensis*, *H. montana macrophylla*, and 'Yellow River'. Often deeply impressed vein pairs make prominent ridges that can be felt on the leaf underside. Very rarely, the veins are almost indistinguishable as for *H. longissima longifolia*. Occasionally, too, the arrangement of vein pairs will be irregular or will merge in mid-leaf, usually resulting from an unruly leaf surface, e.g., 'Bold Ruffles' and 'Koryu'.

(10) **Other Leaf Characteristics**.

Other descriptive leaf elements include the color of the petiole (green, purplish red, reddish purple, covered with purple-red dots, etc.), shape of the petiole (curved or flattened), and fall color of the mound. Colored petioles have been the focus of a number of breeders, with the long-term goal of extending the color into the blade. Unless the plant is large with a distinctly upright habit, such petioles are barely noticeable in the garden. Normally petioles have a curved shape, but occasionally they will appear almost "flat". A number of hostas produce attractive fall colors including 'Fortunei Hyacinthina', 'Crispula', 'Krossa Regal', 'Fortunei Gigantea', and *H. sieboldiana* 'Elegans'. The best colors are produced in cool (without frost), dry falls. Timing for fall color varies by variety, with the Fortuneis coming earliest (late September in northern Illinois) and the Sieboldianas last (late October).

flowers

Hosta flowers are complete, i.e., they contain all of the basic flower parts. The showy, ornamental parts are the six tepals (the three petals and three sepals as a combined unit), generally referred to as the "petals". The male parts of hosta flowers are the six anthers, which bear the pollen and are held on long, threadlike filaments. On the single day of flowering, the anthers "dehisce" or break open exposing the pollen which can be carried via insects (not wind) from flower to flower. The pollen is received by the stigma which is the surface at the end of the long, tubular style. At the base of the style is the ovary which becomes the seed pod once fertilization is completed. The pedicel is the short stalk which connects the flower to the scape.

(1) **season of bloom**.

Depending upon the variety, hostas bloom from mid-June into October. Most of my flowering data was derived from observations taken in northern Illinois, Iowa, north and central Ohio, Minnesota, and Michigan. A few times I note the state where I observed a hosta in bloom. Usually a general blooming season is described (e.g., late June into mid-July), but a few specific dates are listed when I have been able to determine them.

(2) **flower color**.

Hosta flower colors vary from pure white to bright purple. Only a few hostas have a pure white color, *Hosta plantaginea* being the most notable example. Almost all *H. sieboldiana* and 'Tokudama' types have near-white flowers. These appear white from a distance but have a pale lavender, mid-petal stripe. A majority of hostas bear flowers with some shade of lavender (very pale, pale, medium). *H. montana* typifies the very pale lavender group, while 'Undulata Erromena' exemplifies the pale lavender group. The medium lavender color represents a rich color, almost verging on pink. 'Antioch', 'Crusader', and 'Tall Boy' are good examples of this group. Many of the Tardianas produce flowers in an unusual shade of lavender that I call "pale bluish lavender". There seems to be a great deal of blue pigment in these flowers. Purple flowers generally have more red pigment than lavender flowers. Purple flowers can vary from pale to medium to very deep or bright. There are a number of hostas with attractive purple flowers including *H. sieboldii*, *H. ventricosa*, 'Peedee Elfin Bells', 'Temple Bells', *H. capitata*, and *H. venusta*. Over the years I have heard of red-flowered and pink-flowered hostas, but none have ever turned out to be so.

Other than pure white, hosta flowers are rarely a single,

solid color. Many hosta flowers are striped, streaked or mottled. Some have translucent margins (which appear white), while others have a white center. Due to their relatively small size and narrow shape, such patterns are usually noticeable only from a close distance. They are, however, good diagnostic features.

(3) **flower length by width**.

Flower length is the distance from the scape to the end of the petals. This includes the length of the pedicel. Width is measured as the greatest distance that the petal tips reach at the peak of bloom. It was often difficult to determine these measurements and they are sometimes omitted from the descriptions.

(4) **flower shape**.

The "average" hosta flower is shaped like a funnel, as for 'Undulata', but this does vary from a narrow funnel (sharp petal angle, e.g., 'Fortunei Hyacinthina') to an open funnel (wide angle, e.g., 'August Moon'). Less common are the trumpet shape of *H. plantaginea* flowers and the bell shape of *H. ventricosa*. A bell shape is produced by an inflated area halfway between the base and the tip of the flower. Some bell-shaped flowers have only a slightly inflated area and are categorized as being "semi-bell-shaped", as in *H. rohdeifolia*. The petals of *H. plantaginea* flowers flare out near the tips, creating a trumpet shape. A few hostas have petals that are "reflexed", i.e. turned back at the tip.

There are an increasing number of cultivars with double flowers. *H. plantaginea* 'Aphrodite' is the most prominent of this group. The doubleness is created by extra sets of petals or petaloid stamens. The latter basically are filaments that are petal-like and they usually bear the anthers. Such anthers often do not develop normally.

With the discovery of *H. yingeri* and *H. laevigata*, the term "spider flowers" entered hosta jargon (Schmid, 1991). These species bear flowers with relatively narrow petals.

(5) **scapes.**

The flower stalk of a hosta is termed a "scape". Scapes originate in the crown and generally reach or rise above the foliage mound. The complete process of scape lengthening takes about two to three weeks, after which flowering begins.

Scape heights are usually not uniform in any single clump and vary by year and age of the plant. Older plants produce taller scapes, except in dry years when they can be considerably shorter. A wide range of heights can be expected from a clump in full bloom. When a single height is listed in *The Hosta Handbook*, it reflects the tallest scape that was measured. When possible, a range of scape heights is noted.

When relevant scape colors, leaves, bracts, and number are also noted.

(6) **seed pod formation**.

As often as possible, the development of seed pods is noted. Most hostas will produce seed pods, but there are quite a number that are nearly sterile. Other plants only occasionally form a seed pod, as in most Fortuneis, *H. nigrescens*, and the Undulatas.

(7) **other flowering information**.

When important other flowering habits have been described such as the location of the flowers on the scape (e.g., in dense clusters or in the upper 6" of the scape), any unusual scape habits (e.g., recumbent, crooked), and reblooming possibilities. Of course flower fragrance is also indicated.

"Scape bud" is a specialized term used occasionally in *The Hosta Handbook*. It denotes the large bud-like appearance of the flower bud cluster just before the buds begin to separate and open. The appearance of the scape bud is a diagnostic feature for a number of hostas including *H. montana*, *H. capitata*, and *H. ventricosa*.

comments

My personal opinions, the history of a cultivar, and other facts relevant to the hosta being described are covered in this section. For many hostas, landscape value, mound habit, sun tolerance, related sports, and breeding potential are also discussed.

Any AHS registration information is also listed. This information was obtained from my 1983 visit to the registrar's office, the checklists of registered cultivars published by the AHS (*The Genus Hosta List of Registered Cultivars*, 1993 and *The Genus Hosta List of Registered Cultivars: Supplement I,* 2000), and listings of registrations in *The Hosta Journal* and *The Bulletin of the American Hosta Society*.

seedlings, sports, and other related types

Plants that are known seedlings or sports of the listed hosta are described in this section. Information obtained from American Hosta Society registrations is contained within special brackets { }, just after the name. This bracketed information contains the year of registration (followed by a lower case "r", e.g., 1986r), anyone (including plant societies and nurseries) known to be involved in originating, naming, introducing or registering the hosta and the parentage of the plant. Some descriptive information from the registration may also be included within the special brackets. One deviation from published lists of registered cultivars is not using the term "hybrid" for open-pollinated seedlings. As previously stated, open-pollinated seedlings are most often selfed seedlings and, hence, not hybrids. Instead of calling something an *H. sieboldiana* 'Elegans' hybrid, it is referred to as an *H. sieboldiana* 'Elegans' seedling. After the AHS registration data, any notes, measurements, or comments about the plant are listed. This can range from nothing to a complete plant description. When the words "sport" or "seedling" are used by themselves within the brackets, this indicates that the sublisted plant is a sport or seedling of the major listing. For example, under 'Fortunei Hyacinthina', 'Alaskan Halo' is listed as follows:

'Alaskan Halo': {1997r, P. Ruh; sport}

This means that 'Alaskan Halo' was registered in 1997 by Peter Ruh and is a sport of 'Fortunei Hyacinthina'. At the same time, under 'Fortunei Hyacinthina', 'Imperial Potentate' is described as:

'Imperial Potentate': {1999r, R. & D. Benedict; sport of 'Crowned Imperial'}

This means that 'Imperial Potentate' is a 1999 registration of Ralph (Herb) and Dorothy Benedict and is a sport of 'Crowned Imperial', which is a sport of 'Fortunei Hyacinthina'.

Descriptions of the pod parent (for hybrids), the "mother plant" (from which something sported), and other sports that were derived from the same mother plant are sometimes included in this section. Unfortunately I have not been able to describe every related hosta, especially if I have not seen them in a garden. There are quite a few hostas that were registered ten to twenty years ago, but were never introduced for sale or shared among collectors. These plants are included to show the possibilities for hybridizing or sport selection. For such hostas I have added such comments as "have never seen", "rare" or "rarely grown".

When possible, I have included a date of introduction for sale. This is especially important when the date of registration differs significantly from the time of introduction.

other similar types

This section denotes hostas that appear similar to the main listing, but are not necessarily genetically related. These listings can vary from simply a name to a complete description with any AHS registration information in the same special brackets, {   }.

Abbreviations.
For both **"seedlings, sports, and other related types"** and **"other similar types"** sections, I have employed the following abbreviations:

AHS = American Hosta Society
Aug = August
avg = average
BHHS = British Hosta and Hemerocallis Society
betw = between
bl = blue
bl-gr = blue-green
br = bright
chartr = chartreuse
cntr = center; cntrd = centered
corrug = corrugation
cv = cultivar
dk = dark
dvlpd = developed
e = early
esp = especially
fl = flower; fls = flowers
fr = from
fragr = fragrant
go = gold
go-cntrd = gold-centered
go-mgd = gold-margined
gr = green
imm = immature
intro = introduction
IRA = International Registration Authority
lav = lavender
lf = leaf; lvs = leaves
lg = large
lt = light
md =mound
med = medium
med-lg = medium-large
mgd = margined; mgn = margin
N = Nursery (Nurseries)
Oct = October
pl = plant
prob = probably
r = registration
sc = scape or scapes
sdlg = seedling
Sept = September
sl = slight or slightly
strkd = streaked

subst, substd = substance, substanced
t.c. = tissue culture
und = underside
upr = upright
v = very
vp = vein pairs
wh = white
wh-mgd = white-margined
wh-cntrd = white-centered
wi = with
ylw = yellow

'Abba Dabba Do'

key features: large mound of green-centered, gold-margined foliage; sport of 'Sun Power'
mound size: 28" high by 60" wide (up to 35" by 75")

spacing: 48"
leaves: 12 1/4" long by 8 1/2" wide; slightly wavy, 1/4" wide gold margin; medium to dark green center; thin underside bloom; ovate shape with a deeply lobed base and a curved tip; slight corrugation; good substance; 15-17 vein pairs
flowers: early to late July; pale lavender; 2 1/4" long by 1 5/8" wide; 40" scapes, up to 47" high
comments: This sport of 'Sun Power' was introduced by Tony Avent in 1993 and registered in 1998. It becomes a huge mound of wavy, variegated foliage and makes an excellent background plant in the shaded garden. It is almost indistinguishable from Russ O'Harra's 'Sun Banner', another 'Sun Power' sport.

seedlings, sports, and other related types:

'Abba Aloft': {1990r, P. Aden; 'Sun Power' sport wi gr-centered, chartreuse-mgd lvs} have never seen

'Abba Dew': {1999r; K. Brill; 'Sun Power' sport} lvs have a muted, light green center & gold mgns; originator's 5-year-old plant 20" by 57" wi 11" by 7" lvs; center lighter green than 'Abba Dabba Do'

'Flint Hill': {1999r, S. Matthews; 'Sun Power' sport; lvs med green wi gold mgns}

'Sun Banner': {1999r by the Russ O'Harra Hosta Society for R. O'Harra; sport of 'Sun Power'} medium to dark green-centered, gold-mgd lvs

other similar types:

'Yellow River'

'Abiqua Drinking Gourd'

key features: deeply cupped, thick-substanced, blue-green foliage
mound size: 24" high by 46" wide

spacing: 36"
leaves: 11" long by 11" wide; deep blue-green color; blade very broadly ovate to rotund; cupped 3" deep; moderate underside bloom; heavily corrugated; thick substance; 15-16 vein pairs
flowers: late June into mid-July; near-white color; near the top of the foliage mound on 24-30" scapes
comments: 'Abiqua Drinking Gourd' may have the most deeply cupped foliage of any hosta cultivar. The combination of cupping, excellent blue-green color, and corrugation makes it a cultivar worth growing as a specimen, hybridizing plant, or conversation piece.

'Abiqua Drinking Gourd' was registered by Walden West in 1989 as a hybrid of 'Tokudama' X *H. sieboldiana*.
seedlings, sports, and other related types:
none listed
other similar types:
'Alabama Bowl', 'Love Pat', 'Quilted Cup', 'Sea Lotus Leaf', 'Silver Bowl'

'Abiqua Moonbeam'
key features: gold-margined, green-centered sport of 'August Moon'
mound size: 20" high by 55" wide (up to 27" by 68")

spacing: 36"
leaves: 9 1/4" long by 8" wide; 1" to 2" wide gold margin, medium to dark green center; thin underside bloom; broadly oblong-ovate shape; moderate corrugation; good substance; 11-12 vein pairs
flowers: mid-July into early August; pale lavender; 1 3/4" long by 1 1/2" wide; open funnel shape; scapes 20-30" high; many seed pods develop
comments: 'Abiqua Moonbeam' was the first registered (Walden West, 1987) green-centered sport of the hosta classic, 'August Moon', though 'Mayan Moon' was introduced into the trade earlier. I have not been able to distinguish between the two. Several other green-centered 'August Moon' sports have also been introduced. Most are similar to 'Abiqua Moonbeam' with a few exceptions.

'Abiqua Moonbeam' represents the first significant hosta in Walden West's "Abiqua" (**ah**-be-kwa, not ah-**bee**-kwa) series.
seedlings, sports, and other related types:
'Gemini Moon': sport of 'Abiqua Moonbeam' recently found at Wade & Gatton N; much wider gold margin and a narrower green center
other similar types:
'August Beauty', 'Carolina Moon', 'Dark Moon', 'Indiana Knight', 'Jupiter', 'Kiwi Sunlover', 'Mayan Moon', 'Muted Moon', 'Saturn'

'Abiqua Recluse'

key features: medium-large mound of bright gold, slug-resistant foliage

mound size: 23" high by 48" wide

spacing: 24-36"

leaves: 11" long by 8 3/4" wide; bright gold color; very thin underside bloom; blade ovate and sometimes cupped; slight to moderate corrugation; good substance; 13-15 vein pairs

flowers: late June into mid-July; near-white with a pale lavender mid-petal stripe; 2 1/2" by 1 5/8"; wide-open funnel shape; in dense clusters near the top of 30-35" scapes; fertile

comments: Registered in 1989 by Walden West as a hybrid of 'White Vision' X 'Sum and Substance', 'Abiqua Recluse' makes a medium-large mound of gold foliage that can be useful in brightening deeply shaded areas.

seedlings, sports, and other related types:

'Academy Blushing Recluse': {1999r, S. Chamberlain; sport wi gold-mgd, green-centered lvs}

'Electrum Stater': {1997r, A. Malloy; sport wi wh-mgd, go-cntrd lvs} mgns creamy yellow early; thick substance

'Paradigm': {1999r, Walden West & C. Purtyman; sport} green-margined, gold-centered foliage; impressive

'Wooden Nickel': {1999r, Walden West & J. Hyslop; sport; lvs dk green wi a greenish ylw mgn}

other similar types:

'Abiqua Gold Shield', 'August Moon', 'City Lights', 'White Vision'

Hosta aequinoctiiantha (Ohigan Giboshi)
key features: medium-sized mound of green foliage; late season flowers subtended by white bracts
mound size: 18" high by 36" wide

spacing: 18-24"
leaves: 9" long by 5" wide; medium to dark green; slightly shiny top; whitish shiny underside; ovate shape; margin irregularly rippled; long, thin tip; petiole purple dotted; average substance; 9-11 vein pairs
flowers: early to late September; pale lavender color; 2 1/8" long by 1 5/8" wide; subtended by large white bracts; scapes 18-20" high, tending to droop as flowering proceeds

comments: As a species native to Japan, *Hosta aequinoctiiantha* is mainly known to collectors and taxonomists. Its chief ornamental value lies in its late flowering season and the impressive white bracts that are very attractive just before flowering. Garden-grown specimens of this species grow much larger than plants in the wild.

Some taxonomists consider this a variety of *Hosta longipes* (*Hosta longipes* var. *aequinoctiiantha*).
seedlings, sports, and other related types:
At a nursery in Okazaki, Japan I observed a patch of bright gold *H. aequinoctiiantha* seedlings.
other similar types:
Hosta longipes

61

Hosta alismifolia (Baran Giboshi)
key features: medium-sized mound of shiny, dark green foliage; native to Honshu Island in Japan
mound size: 20" high by 44" wide

spacing: 18-24"
leaves: 11" long by 3 1/2" wide; shiny, dark green color; blade narrowly ovate to elliptic-ovate; moderate marginal waviness; smooth texture; good substance; 11 vein pairs
flowers: late July; medium purple (with a whitish petal margin, halfway from the throat to the tip); 1 15/16" long by 13/16" wide; scapes 37" high; forms seed pods

comments: Although the Baran Giboshi is a fairly obscure Japanese species found in only a few American collections, it deserves more attention. The shiny, dark green foliage and upright mound habit make it an ornamentally superior plant. In Japan I saw a few plants of *Hosta alismifolia* in a mountainous area of Aichi Prefecture (Honshu Island) among grasses near *H. longissima longifolia* (but not in standing water as the latter species prefers). At a lower elevation I observed *H. alismifolia* growing near *Hosta sieboldii spathulata* in a deciduous forest. A white-backed form can also be found in the same areas as the species. There are two other forms of *Hosta alismifolia* in Japan: one with scapes that reached 60" high and a bright gold-leaved form (Ogon Baran Giboshi).

seedlings, sports, and other related types:
'Gosan Gold Sword': {1989r, W. Schmid; *H. alismifolia* X *H. rectifolia* 'Ogon'; lvs emerge yellow green, turning yellow}

other similar types:
Hosta sieboldii spathulata

'Allan P. McConnell'
key features: dense, rounded mound of foliage with thin, white margins
mound size: 13" high by 39" wide

spacing: 24-30"

leaves: 4 1/4" long by 3" wide; green center with a thin (1/32" to 1/16"), white margin; occasional grayish green streaks into the center of the leaf from the margin; dull top surface, slightly shiny underside; ovate blade shape with a rounded base; slightly wavy; smooth texture; average substance; 5 vein pairs

flowers: mid-July into early August; lavender; medium purple in bud, 1 1/2" long by 1 1/8" wide; 19" scapes; many seed pods develop

comments: 'Allan P. McConnell' makes an ideal edger or rock garden plant and has proven to be a good grower in both garden and nursery situations. Its combination of a very rounded, dense mound habit and small, thin white-margined foliage creates a distinctive appearance that cannot be mistaken for any other hosta. Mildred Seaver registered 'Allan P. McConnell' with the AHS in 1980 with unknown parentage. It is often misspelled "Alan P. McConnell" or "Allen P. McConnell".

seedlings, sports, and other related types:

'Ivory Pixie': {1982 r, M. Seaver; sport} white-cntrd, gr-mgd lvs; very weak; haven't seen since 1986

'Shades Of Mercy': {1998r, R. Snyder; sport; center of lf streaked; white mgns}

other similar types:

'Little White Lines', 'Pilgrim'

'Alvatine Taylor'

key features: large mound of gold-margined, blue-centered foliage

mound size: 24" high by 48" wide (up to 30" by 58")

spacing: 48"

leaves: 10" long by 7 1/4" wide; 1" to 2" wide margin which changes from chartreuse to medium gold by mid-summer; center blue-green changing to dark green; thick underside bloom; blade ovate, broadening with maturity; not wavy; little or no corrugation; good substance; 14 vein pairs

flowers: mid-June to early July; near-white color with a pale lavender mid-petal stripe; 2 1/8" long by 1 1/4" wide; many scapes up to 42" high; forms many seed pods

comments: I first viewed 'Alvatine Taylor' in the Minks garden in 1990 and, since that time, have been impressed with its attractive variegation. The rich blue center contrasts nicely with the gold margin. It makes an excellent specimen or background plant that can serve as a "non-burning" substitute for 'Frances Williams' in the landscape.

'Alvatine Taylor' forms a large number of seed pods and, with all of its good characteristics, can be a useful addition to any breeding program. The all-gold form, 'Doubloons,' often develops when propagated by tissue culture.

'Alvatine Taylor' was registered in 1990 by Fairway Enterprises (Eldren and Nancy Minks' nursery) as a sport of 'Lady in Waiting'. It was pictured on the cover of the fall 1998 issue of *The Hosta Journal*.

seedlings, sports, and other related types:

'Doubloons': all-gold sport fr Q & Z N introduced in 1995; impressive, lg md of bright gold foliage

'Lady In Waiting': {1980r by A. Arett; hybrid of 'Tokudama' X 'Elegans'} 24" by 52" md; bl-gr lvs, 14" by 11" (17-18 vp); near-wh fls, June-July, on sc up to 42"; "mother plant" of 'Alvatine Taylor'

other similar types:
'Abiqua Moonbeam', 'June Dove', 'Tokudama Flavocircinalis'

'Ani Machi' (Ani Machi Giboshi) ('Geisha')
key features: dense, medium-sized mound of gold-centered foliage
mound size: 18" high by 36" wide

---

spacing: 24"
leaves: 7 1/4" long by 3 3/4" wide; 1 1/2" wide green margin, 2" wide center that changes from medium gold in early spring to pale green by the end of summer; blade shape elliptic to narrowly ovate with a rounded base and a few broad, distinct waves; leaf tip curved 90 degrees on most leaves; average substance; 7 vein pairs

flowers: mid-August to mid-September; medium purple color, 2" long by 15/16" wide; scapes 26-28" high with purple-red dots

comments: Ani Machi Giboshi can be found in many Japanese collections and is the same plant that has been sold as 'Geisha'. It is not, however, the plant that Kevin Vaughn registered under this name in 1983. Whatever the history, it grows into an impressive, medium-sized mound of center-variegated foliage that has ornamental interest even as the center color changes to green. Its late flowering season also adds to its value in the shaded garden. It certainly can be used as a replacement for 'Undulata Unvitatta' in landscapes.

seedlings, sports, and other related types:
'Apple Court': {1998r, P. Scolnik; sport} wh-cntrd, gr-mgd lvs

Two other sports are known including an all-green form and one that is gold in spring, changing to green (the center color of 'Ani Machi Giboshi').

other similar types:
'Undulata'

'Antioch'

key features: large-sized, flowing mound of white-margined foliage
mound size: 24" high by 56" wide

spacing: 36"
leaves: 10 3/4" long by 7 1/2" wide; medium green center; margins chartreuse when leaves first emerge changing to greenish yellow, then yellow by mid-May and creamy white by early June; margins 1/4" to 1 1/4" wide in upper 2/3 of the blade (toward the tip), nearly disappearing in the lower third; blade ovate with a slightly lobed base and long tip; two to three long waves down each margin; blade generally curves downward, contributing to the flowing mound effect; slightly shiny top and a thin bloom on the underside; no corrugation; better than average substance; 9-10, deeply impressed vein pairs, especially noticeable on the green portion of the leaf
flowers: July 10 to 31; medium lavender; 1 7/8" long by 7/8" wide; narrow funnel shape; 16-34" scapes; one mature clump had over 30 scapes; limited seed pod formation
comments: 'Antioch' has become one of the premier white-margined hostas for shade gardens. It stands out in any collection and, because of its vigorous growth habit, quickly makes an impact in landscape plantings. Though registered with the AHS in 1979 (by Peter Ruh for Paul Hofer), it actually has a much longer history in the United States and Europe. Originally developed by Cynthia Tompkins in the 1920's, it has been sold under a variety of names including *Hosta fortunei aureo-marmorata*, 'Moorheimii' and 'Spinners'. Additionally 'Fortunei Albomarginata' ('Silver Crown') is often confused with 'Antioch'.

'Aspen Gold'
key features: slug-resistant, medium-large mound of golden, 'Tokudama'-like foliage
mound size: 20" high by 43" wide (up to 26" by 60")

spacing: 24-30"
leaves: 9 1/4" long by 8 1/2" wide; medium to bright gold; thin bloom on top surface, thick underside bloom; blade oblong-ovate shape with a heart-shaped base; heavily corrugated; no purple dots on petioles; thick substance; 16-17 vein pairs
flowers: late June into early July; near-white color with a pale lavender petal midrib; 1 3/4" long by 1" wide; scapes range from 16" to 24" high, generally just topping the foliage mound; fertile

comments: Its bright gold foliage makes 'Aspen Gold' useful as a specimen or accent in the middle or at the front of the flower border. It can also be effective in small groups and looks especially good in combination with 'Tokudama Flavocircinalis' and 'Tokudama Aureonebulosa'. The intense corrugation and thick substance of the foliage are also outstanding.

'Aspen Gold' is an open-pollinated seedling of 'Tokudama' introduced by Vivian Grapes of Nebraska in the 1970's. It was registered by the AHS in 1986.

seedlings, sports, and other related types:

'Abiqua Ariel': {1999r, Walden West & J. Hyslop; 'Aspen Gold' X 'Golden Chimes' sdlg} 18" by 39" md of bright gold lvs, 8" by 6 3/4" (13 vp); also thick subst & moderate corrug

'Aardvark': {1991r, D. Savory; 'Aspen Gold' sdlg} med-sized md of chartreuse to gold-centered, green-margined foliage that is also thick-substanced & heavily corrugated; dense clusters of near-white fls from early to late July (Ohio)

'Golden Chimes': {1979r, V. Grapes; 'Tokudama' sdlg} med-sized md of thick, bright gold foliage; near-white fls, late June into July; a sibling of 'Aspen Gold'

'Golden Teacup': {1989r, J. & J. Wilkins; 'Aspen Gold' X 'Gold Regal'} deeply cupped, gold leaves; near-white flowers in July; beautiful plant

'Green Aspen': {1986r, C. Owens; selfed sdlg of 'Aspen Gold'; green foliage}

'Millie's Memoirs': {1999r, H. Hansen & Shady Oaks N; sport wi green-centered, gold-mgd lvs}

'Hoosier Homecoming': sport wi very thin, wh mgns (gold center); 1997 AHS "convention plant" in Indianapolis

'Sun Glow': {1974r, P. Aden; 'Aspen Gold' sdlg} 20" by 55" md of med to bright gold lvs, 9" by 7 3/4"; pale lav fls, late June into July on 30" sc

'Tranquility': {1995r, J. & J. Wilkins; sport of an 'Aspen Gold' sdlg} 16" by 34" md of thick, bl-green-centered, gold-mgd lvs, 8" by 6 1/2" (14 vp); margin 1/2" wide

other similar types:

'Gold Cup', 'Golden Bullion', 'Golden Medallion', 'Golden Nugget', 'Golden Rajah', 'King Tut'

'August Moon'

key features: medium-large mound of broad, golden foliage; a hosta "classic"

mound size: 20" high by 42" wide

spacing: 24-30"

leaves: 9 1/2" long by 8" wide; medium to bright gold color, brighter with some direct sunlight; slight bloom on underside; broadly oblong-ovate shape; moderate corrugation; good substance; 10-11 vein pairs

flowers: July 17 to August 7; pale lavender color; 1 3/4" long by 1 1/2" wide; open funnel shape; about 24 per scape; held at a right angle to the scapes which measure 19-27" in height; many, short, thick (3/4" by 1/4") seed pods develop

comments: Despite being one of the oldest hosta cultivars, 'August Moon' remains highly rated. It is notable for its bright gold color, corrugation, and good substance. Though the foliage appears Sieboldiana-like at a glance, the flowers differ significantly. They appear about three weeks later than most Sieboldianas and are lavender and more widely flared. The leaves also carry fewer vein pairs and the growth rate is more rapid. It has been used in hybridizing and recently has been the source of a bewildering number of sports, the most significant being 'Abiqua Moonbeam' and 'September Sun'. Just when you think that you've seen all of the sport possibilities, another shows up with a name in a garden.

A complete description was published in the first *Bulletin of the American Hosta Society* (Summers, 1969), but it was not considered registered by the AHS until 1996. Peter Ruh registered 'August Moon' for R. Langfelder, the originator, and Alex Summers, the introducer and namer. Its parentage is unknown.

I registered (unfortunately) the first sport of 'August Moon', 'Lunar Eclipse', in 1985. This plant develops the dreaded "drawstring" effect with maturity which can cause the leaf margins to tear and become unsightly (see discussion of "Drawstring Effect" on page 594).

seedlings, sports, and other related types:

Sports related to 'August Moon' include the following:

'Abiqua Moonbeam': {1987r, Walden West} green center, gold mgn **(see page 59)**

'August Beauty': green center, gold mgn

'Carolina Moon': {1997r, A. Breiwick; lvs med gr with a lt gr mgn}

'Crescent Moon': {1988r, Walters Gardens} 'Lunar Eclipse' sport wi gr-cntrd, wh-mgd lvs

'Dark Moon': green center, gold mgn; fr Alex Summers

'Dianne': {1985r, C. Owens} streaked lvs

'Hub City': green foliage; 'September Sun' sport fr Q & Z N (1997)

'Indiana Knight': {1990r, G. Goodwin} gr center, chartreuse mgn

'Indiana Moonshine': {1996r; C. Harstad; lvs med gold wi a lt gr mgn}

'Jupiter': green cntr, gold mgn fr Q & Z N (1997)

'Kiwi Kaniere Gold': {1999r, B. Sligh; fast-growing md of gold foliage}

'Kiwi Sunlover': {1999r, B. Sligh; green-centered, gold-mgd lvs}

'Lunar Eclipse': {1985r, M. Zilis & T & Z N} gold cntr wi a narrow white, drawstring mgn

'Lunar Magic': {1994r, R. Lydell; 'Lunar Orbit' sport} gold cntr, wide gr mgn

'Lunar Night': {1998r; R. Lydell; sport of 'Lunar Magic'; dk gr lvs}

'Lunar Orbit': {1991r, R. Lydell} gold-cntrd; wide, green mgn

'Mayan Moon': green cntr, gold mgn from Bill Mitchell (1986)

'Muted Moon': {1995r, P. Ruh} dk gr cntr, chartr mgn

'Saturn': chartreuse cntr, gold mgn; fr Pauline Banyai (1991 or earlier)

'September Sun': {1985r, R. Solberg} gold cntr, gr mgn **(see page 387)**

'September Surprise': {1997r, Walters Gardens} chartr cntr, gr mgn

Seedlings related to 'August Moon' include:

'Alpine Aire': {1980r, E. Minks, 'August Moon' X 'Wogon Gold'} 18" by 44" md of chartreuse to br gold lvs, 9" by

6 3/4" (10 vp); pal lav fls in early Aug on 43" sc; shows hybrid character; rare

'Glory': {1985r, R. Savory; 'August Moon' sdlg} 16" by 42" md of bright gold lvs, 9" by 8" (12 vp); sported to 'Old Glory' {1999r, H. Hansen & Shady Oaks N; lvs gold wi a dk green mgn}

'Honey Moon': {1982r, K. Anderson} (*H. venusta* X 'August Moon'); 21" by 49" md; chartreuse, heart-shaped lvs, 5 1/4" by 5" (9 vp)

'Maui Buttercups': {1991r, W. Vaughn; 'Frances Williams' X 'August Moon'} v bright gold, cupped lvs

'Michigan Gold': {1984r, R. Benedict; 'August Moon' X 'Aspen Gold'} 16" by 42" md of bright gold lvs, 10" by 7" (12 vp); bright gold even in deep shade

'Moon Waves': {1994, M. Plater-Zyberk & R. Solberg} listed as a mutation of 'August Moon' but no doubt a seedling; 20" by 44" md of heavily rippled, med gold lvs, 11" by 6" (13 vp)

'Radiance': {1980r, K. Anderson; parentage unknown} 24" by 50" md of brilliant, shimmering gold lvs, 9 5/8" by 7 1/2" (12 vp); near-white fls, early to late July on 24" sc

'Squash Casserole': {1995r, T. Avent; 'Hirao Elite' X 'August Moon'} ruffled, medium gold foliage

other similar types:
'Abiqua Recluse', 'Banana Muffins', 'Butter Yellow', 'Golden Friendship', 'Harvest Moon', 'Prairie Glow'

'Azure Snow'

key features: blue-leaved *Hosta hypoleuca* seedling; forms a medium-large mound
mound size: 20" high by 45" wide

spacing: 24-30"
leaves: 14" long by 10" wide; intense blue-green color; thick bloom on top and underside surfaces; oblong-ovate blade shape; lightly rippled margin; no corrugation; good substance; 11-13 vein pairs
flowers: August 10 to September 1; medium lavender color; scapes 18" high
comments: 'Azure Snow' has the distinction of being the only *Hosta hypoleuca* seedling with blue foliage. The effect is created by the thick bluish bloom that not only covers the leaf underside, but the top as well. Though the mound habit is somewhat open, it makes an interesting specimen in the garden. Peter Ruh grew this plant from seeds that he obtained in 1982 and registered it in 1991.

seedlings, sports, and other related types:
'Lemon Meringue': {1991r, P. Ruh; *H. hypoleuca* sdlg} 26" by 50" md of bright gold lvs, 16" by 12" (13-15 vp); sl corrug & lightly rippled; pale lav fls fr mid-July into August; 'Azure Snow' sibling
'Thor': {1994r, P. Ruh} green-leaved *H. hypoleuca* sdlg; 17" by 28" md; lvs 14" by 8" (12 vp); pale lav fls in Aug; sibling of 'Azure Snow'
other similar types:
'Maekawa'

'Baby Bunting'

key features: small, dense mound of bluish green leaves
mound size: 11" high by 26" wide

spacing: 24"

leaves: 2 3/4" long by 2 1/2" wide; grayish blue early, turning dark green; thin underside bloom; blade nearly round in shape; 6 vein pairs

flowers: late June into mid-July; bright purple; 19" scapes; many seed pods develop

comments: 'Baby Bunting' becomes a very dense mound of bluish green foliage that is useful as a low ground cover or edging plant. Bob Savory registered it in 1982 as a hybrid of 'Rough Waters' X a seedling.

The specimens that I have seen varied considerably due to differences in soil fertility and site. Plants growing in soil of average fertility may not reach the listed 11" by 26" mound dimensions.

seedlings, sports, and other related types:

'Hope': {1999r, H. Hansen & Shady Oaks N; sport with greenish ylw-mgd, green-centered lvs; purple fls}

'Pandora's Box': {1996r, H. Hansen & Shady Oaks N; sport} very attractive, white-centered foliage; 4" by 10" md; lvs 2 1/4" by 1 5/8" wi a pure white center & 1/2" gr mgn; purple fls on white scapes, 12" high

other similar types:

'Popo'

'Beatrice'

key features: small mound of narrow, highly variable foliage; purple flowers; breeding plant
mound size: 11" high by 25" wide (up to 15" by 30")

spacing: 18"
leaves: 5" long by 1 1/2" wide; color varies considerably but in true form green with irregular white streaks that range from subtle to predominant throughout the leaf; slightly shiny top, moderately shiny underside; narrowly elliptic blade shape; slightly wavy margin; smooth texture; thin substance; 6 vein pairs
flowers: very late July into mid-August; bright purple; 2 3/8" long by 1 3/4" wide; 22-31" scapes; forms seed pods (variegated seedlings often result)
comments: 'Beatrice' is no longer widely grown in gardens, yet it stands as one of the most significant hostas ever introduced for its role in breeding programs in the 1970's and 1980's. Its ability to produce variegated seedlings led many hybridizers to use 'Beatrice' as the pod parent, and today hundreds of hosta cultivars can be traced back to it.

As a garden plant, 'Beatrice' is highly variable with leaf colors ranging from streaked to margined to solid-colored forms. A good sampling of the variation in 'Beatrice' is on display at Wade and Gatton Nurseries where the following foliage types can be found:

    (1) white-centered leaves with a green margin;
    (2) green-centered leaves with a gold margin;
    (3) streaked foliage with a gold edge;
    (4) streaked foliage with a predominance of green.

I have also seen a green-centered form with pure white

margins and numerous other streaked forms in other collections.

'Beatrice' is a Frances Williams origination that she selected in 1958 from a lot of 350 *H. sieboldii* seedlings (Williams, 1959a) and named for the daughter of a friend (Williams, 1966). Though the original plant had variegated foliage, three green-leaved siblings (two had white flowers, one purple-flowered) were also propagated over the years as 'Beatrice', confusing the identity of the plant. (My first purchase of 'Beatrice' turned out to be a green-leaved plant with white flowers.)

Some of the sports and siblings of 'Beatrice' have been named, though none of them have become very significant in either the nursery or collector's trade.

seedlings, sports, and other related types:

'Bold Edger': {1983r, K. Vaughn; hybrid of 'Beatrice' X 'Frances Williams'} medium-sized md of wh-mgd lvs **(see page 98)**

'Breeder's Choice' {1987r, K. Vaughn; "Vaughn 73-2" (= 'Beatrice' X 'Beatrice') X 'Frances Williams'} 12" by 31" md of heavily streaked & mottled lvs, often wi a creamy white mgn, 6 1/8" by 4 3/4" (8-10 vp); lav fls on 22" sc, late June into July; outstanding breeding plant **(see page 101)**

'Carnival': {1986r, W. & E. Lachman; a hybrid of a 'Beatrice' sdlg X a sdlg} med-sized md of gold-mgd lvs **(see page 110)**

'Celebrity': {1995r, W. & E. Lachman; hybrid of a 'Beatrice' F6 sdlg X 'Frances Williams'} impressive 26" by 56" md; lvs green-cntrd, gold-mgd, 10 1/2" by 7 1/2" (13 vp)

'Cherry Berry': {1991r, W. & E. Lachman; hybrid of two sdlgs} introduced for sale in 1992 by Hatfield Gardens which listed 'Beatrice' in its background; sm md of wh-cntrd lvs; br red sc bear purple fls in Aug **(see page 113)**

'Christmas Tree': {1982r, M. Seaver; 'Frances Williams' X 'Beatrice'} lg md of wh-mgd lvs **(see p. 116)**

'Galaxy': {1987r, W. & E. Lachman; 'Beatrice' sdlg X 'Frances Williams' sdlg} lg md of strkd lvs **(see p. 176)**

'Golden Fountain': {1993r, J. Dishon; 'Beatrice' X 'Green Fountain'} 23" by 45", fountain-like md of shiny, golden foliage; lvs 14 1/2" by 5 1/2" (8 vp)

'Green Beatrice': {1987r by P. Ruh for F. Williams as an *H. sieboldii* sdlg} one of the green-leaved, purple-flowered 'Beatrice' siblings that Frances Williams originally selected in 1958; lvs 6" by 2 1/2" (6 vp); bigger md than 'Beatrice'; not widely grown

'Metallica': {1991r, W. & E. Lachman; 'Beatrice' seedling X 'Blue Moon'} 13" by 33" md of bluish foliage that becomes a shiny, dk gr by July; lvs 7" by 5 1/2" (10 vp); lav fls on 36" sc in Aug

'Mildred Seaver': {1981r, K. Vaughn; "Vaughn 73-2" (= 'Beatrice' X 'Beatrice') X 'Frances Williams'} lg md of white-margined foliage **(see page 294)**

'Mistress Mabel': {1995r, W. & E. Lachman; ('Beatrice' F6 sdlg X 'Blue Moon') X *H. plantaginea*} lvs creamy white-mgd wi a shiny, dk gr cntr

'Noel': {1983r, R. Benedict; 'Beatrice' sport} sm md of white-centered lvs, 4 1/2" by 2"; br purple fls July-Aug

'Royal Bells': {1999r, J. Dishon; ('Beatrice' X *H. kikutii*) X ('August Moon' X *H. kikutii*) lg, purple fls in August} 16" by 41" md of heavily rippled, creamy yellow-mgd lvs, 10" by 4" (10 vp); outstanding!

'Rusty Bee': {1998r, A. Malloy; 'Beatrice' sdlg; light green lvs & red petioles}

'Starburst': {1973r, M. Eisel; 'Beatrice' sdlg} sm md of lvs wi mgns that change from ylw to creamy white; lf cntr varies fr green to strkd fr mound to mound; close to 'Beatrice'; rare

'Summer Fragrance': {1983r, K. Vaughn; "Vaughn 73-2" (= 'Beatrice' X 'Beatrice') X *H. plantaginea*} 26" by 57" md of white-margined lvs, 12" by 8 3/4" (10 vp); fragrant, v pale lav fls, mid-Aug into Sept on 36" sc; first cultivar with white-mgd foliage & fragr fls

'Temple Bells': {1992r, P. Banyai; sdlg of a gr-lvd 'Beatrice' sdlg} dense md, 14" by 32"; dk gr lvs; impressive show of bell-shaped purple fls in Aug; one of the best for flower effect

'Top Banana': {1983r, K. Vaughn; 'Beatrice' X 'Frances Williams'; wh-cntrd, gr-mgd lvs} med-sized md of creamy white-centered lvs with thin green margins; rare

'Valencia': {1995r, W. Zumbar; 'Beatrice' X 'Iron Gate Delight'; wh-mgd, streaky-cntrd lvs}

'White Dove': {1995r, R. & D. Benedict; selfed 'Beatrice' sdlg} sm md which nicely combines white-margined foliage and white fls

'White Swan': {1995r, R. & D. Benedict; selfed 'Beatrice' sdlg} sm md of wh-cntrd lvs; white fls

'William Lachman': {1981r, K. Vaughn; "Vaughn 73-2" (= 'Beatrice' X 'Beatrice') X 'Frances Williams'} med-lg md of heavily streaked foliage; 20" by 48" md; 8 3/4" by 6 3/4" lvs (11 vp); important breeding plant

other similar types:

'Neat Splash', 'Yellow Splash'

'Big Daddy'
key features: large mound of slug-resistant, blue-green foliage
mound size: 25" high by 66" wide

spacing: 30-36"
leaves: 15" long by 10 1/2" wide; rich, blue-green color changing to deep green by late summer; thick top and underside bloom; blade broadly ovate with deeply lobed bases; often cupped; intense corrugation; thick substance; 16-17 vein pairs
flowers: mid-June into early July; near-white color; in dense clusters; 24-32" scapes; heavy seed pod formation; typical *Hosta sieboldiana* flowering habits
comments: 'Big Daddy' becomes an impressive, large mound of slug-resistant, blue-green foliage. The leaves tend to cup more than other Sieboldianas, especially in contrast to 'Big Mama' to which it is often compared. It was registered by Paul Aden in 1978 as a sport of a variegated 'Robusta' seedling.
seedlings, sports, and other related types:
'Big Mama': {1978r, P. Aden; 'Blue Tiers' X 'Blue Angel'}
    28" by 60" md of bl-green lvs, 13" by 10" (16 vp), v
    heavily corrugtd & thick-substd; near-wh fls, mid-June
    into July; typical 'Elegans'-type
'Geneva Remembrance': {1996r, G. & D. Stark & D. Dean;
    sdlg of 'Big Daddy'; dk gr to bl-gr lvs}
'Lakeside Masterpiece': {1998r, M. Chastain; sdlg X 'Big
    Daddy'; bl-gr lvs mgd in creamy white}
'Tucker Pucker': {1993r, R. Stephens; *H. montana* sdlg X
    'Big Daddy'; bl-gr lvs}
other similar types:
'Aqua Velva': {1983r, K. Vaughn; ('Polly Bishop' X 'Blue

Lace') X 'Summer Fragrance'} 26" by 60" md of 11" by 8" (13 vp) lvs that are blue-green early, turning a very attractive, shiny, dark green by mid-summer; lav fls on 32" scapes in mid-July

'Blue Beauty': {1986r, AHS for F. Shaw; unknown parentage} 23" by 50" md of heavily corrugated, bl-green lvs, 11 1/2" by 10 1/4" (14-15 vp); near-white fls from late June into mid-July on 27" sc; fertile; formerly 'Birchwood Blue Beauty'

'Sea Lotus Leaf' **(see page 384)**

'Big John'

key features: huge mound of dark green leaves; largest individual leaves of any hosta
mound size: 32" high by 72" wide

spacing: 48-60"
leaves: 17" long by 13" wide (up to 21" by 16 3/8"); bluish green color early, changing to medium to dark green by early summer; thin underside bloom; blade broadly oblong-ovate, generally wavy and downwardly puckered; margin rippled; moderate corrugation; good substance; 17-20 vein pairs
flowers: late June into mid-July; near-white with a pale lavender mid-petal stripe; 3" by 1 1/2"; in dense clusters on scapes, 31-35" high

comments: 'Big John' is synonymous with "huge" in hostas. Not only does the mound of foliage become massive, but the individual leaves are the largest of any hosta, narrowly beating out 'Sum and Substance' for that honor. The record-breaking, 21" by 16 3/8" leaf was measured in 1988 in Clarence Owens' original clump during the AHS national convention. Since then no leaf that I have measured (probably more than 5,000) has exceeded those dimensions.

'Big John' becomes the focal point of any shaded garden where it is grown, making an outstanding choice for the center of an island bed or as a background plant.

Clarence Owens registered 'Big John' in 1986 as a seedling of *H. sieboldiana* 'Mira'.

seedlings, sports, and other related types:
'Emerald City': {1996r, D. & J. Ward; 'Big John' X *H. montana macrophylla*} huge gr lvs, 17" by 12" (19 vp)
'Godzilla': {1996r, D. & J. Ward; 'Big John' X *H. montana macrophylla*; med green foliage}

other similar types:
'Bethel Big Leaf', 'Big Sam', 'Birchwood Elegance', 'Green Acres', 'King James', 'King Michael', *H. sieboldiana* 'Mira'

'Birchwood Elegance'
key features: huge mound of large, dark green foliage
mound size: 33" high by 77" wide

spacing: 48"
leaves: 18 1/2" long by 12 1/4" wide; dark green color; moderate underside bloom; broadly oblong-ovate blade that is also wavy; slight to moderate corrugation; good substance; 18-20 vein pairs
flowers: late June into July; near-white color with a pale lavender petal midrib; 2 1/4" long by 1 1/2" wide; scapes just under or near the top of the foliage, reaching 28-34" high
comments: 'Birchwood Elegance' makes an impressive, massive mound of dark green foliage that can be effective as a specimen or space-eating ground cover. It was developed in the 1960's by Florence Shaw and registered for her by the AHS in 1986. It exhibits many typical *H. sieboldiana* characteristics.

seedlings, sports, and other related types:

'Birchwood Green': {1986r by the AHS for F. Shaw} large mound of heavily corrugated, green foliage; 24" by 52" md, 12 1/2" by 10" lvs; near-wh fls, late June into July on 28" sc; same *H. sieboldiana* origin as 'Birchwood Elegance', probably a sibling

other similar types:

'Big John', 'Green Formal', 'Lake Erie'

'Birchwood Parky's Gold'
key features: dense mound of gold leaves; fast growth rate
mound size: 17" high by 43" wide

spacing: 24-30"
leaves: 6 1/8" long by 5" wide; color changes from pale chartreuse in mid-May to a medium gold by late June; pale yellow fall color; top surface has a dull finish; thin underside bloom; blade broadly ovate with a cordate base creating a heart shape; average substance; 9-10 vein pairs
flowers: July 2 to 21 (peak July 9 to 16); medium lavender color; 1 7/8" long by 15/16" wide; narrow funnel shape; about 22 per scape with 1-2 opening each day; scapes typically around 29" high (up to 36"); many scapes per clump; sparse pod formation

comments: A long-standing cultivar noted for its attractive golden foliage, fast growth rate, and attractive show of lavender flowers, 'Birchwood Parky's Gold' makes a valuable addition to any shaded landscape. Its gold color stands out on overcast days, in early morning, and at dusk.

'Birchwood Parky's Gold' was developed in the 1960's by Florence Shaw, the originator of the "Birchwood" hostas. The AHS registered it in 1986 as a 'Sunlight' hybrid, though this parentage is incorrect. It exhibits many characteristics of *Hosta nakaiana* and is certainly a hybrid

80

of it. It was once known as "Parkman Shaw 391" or 'Parkman Shaw' and has also been listed as 'Golden Glimmer' and "Golden Nakaiana".

seedlings, sports, and other related types:

'Birchwood Gold': {1986r by the AHS for F. Shaw} probably a sibling to 'Birchwood Parky's Gold'; 15" by 47" md of gold lvs, 6 5/8" by 5 3/4" (10 vp); lav fls in July; slightly larger than 'Birchwood Parky's Gold'

'Parky's Prize': {1999r, J. Hawes & A. Summers; sport; lvs green-centered, greenish ylw-mgd}

'Sweet Home Chicago': t.c. sport found at my nursery (Q & Z Nursery, Inc.); green-margined, gold-centered foliage; "convention plant" of the 1999 MRHS meeting held near Chicago; an attractive variation on a classic cultivar

'Teaspoon': {1998r, F. Nyikos; 'Birchwood Parky's Gold' X 'Golden Tiara'; lvs green-cntrd wi a mgn}

'Zuzu's Petals': {1999r, D. Savory; sport; lvs green-centered, yellow-mgd}

other similar types:

'Gold Cadet', 'Gold Drop', 'Gold Edger'

'Black Hills'

key features: dark green leaves in a medium-large mound

mound size: 22" high by 48" wide

---

spacing: 30"

leaves: 8 1/4" long by 7" wide; shiny, deep green; thick underside bloom; blade nearly rotund, heavily corrugated, unruly, and slightly cupped; good substance; 11 vein pairs.

flowers: late June into mid-July; pale lavender color, darker near the tips of petals and in bud; scapes just top the foliage, 20-30" high; in top 6-8" of scape; many seed pods develop

comments: Impressive for its shiny, dark green foliage and good growth rate, 'Black Hills' can be used in a variety of ways in the landscape. It is especially effective as a ground cover and offers an attractive contrast to white-margined Fortuneis. Bob Savory registered 'Black Hills' in 1983 as a 'Green Gold' seedling but it shows evidence (number of vein pairs, blooming season, and fertility) of also having *H. sieboldiana* in its background.

seedlings, sports, and other related types:

'Indian Hills': {1989r, D. Savory; 'Black Hills' X sdlg} dk green, heavily corrug lvs, 8" by 6" (14 vp)

'Neat and Tidy': {1980r, L. Simpers; 'Golden Circles' sdlg} 19" by 49" md of very unruly dark green foliage that is everything but what the name suggests; lvs 9 1/4" by 8" (11-13 vp); pale lav fls on 36" sc from early to late July; traits indicate a similar hybrid background as 'Black Hills'

'Puckered Giant': {1983r, L. Powell; *H. sieboldiana* 'Elegans' sdlg} 24" by 60" md of heavily corrugated, 12" by 9" (16 vp) lvs that are bluish early, shiny, dark green most of the season; near-white fls, early to late July on 36" sc; exhibits hybrid traits; acts like a bigger version of 'Black Hills'

'Sea Ebony': {1991r, R. Solberg & M. Seaver; parentage unknown} 21" by 42" md of heavily corrugated, slightly cupped, dark green lvs, 8 1/2" by 7 1/2" (15 vp); near-wh fls, late June into mid-July on 12-24" sc; Sieboldiana or Tokudama heritage; not well-known

other similar types:

'Black Beauty', 'Java', 'Joseph', 'Lakeside Accolade', 'Lakeside Black Satin', 'Lakeside Lollipop', 'Rosedale Spoons', 'Second Wind', 'Spinach Patch', 'Twisted Sister'

'Blue Angel'

key features: very large mound of deep blue-green foliage

mound size: 32" high by 70" wide (up to 36" by 85")

spacing: 48"

leaves: 16" long by 12 1/4" wide; deep blue-green color lasts until mid-summer, dark green thereafter; thick bloom on top and underside surfaces; blade broadly oblong-ovate shape with a deeply lobed base and long, distinct tip; margins moderately wavy; slight to moderate corrugation; thick substance; 16 vein pairs

flowers: June 25 to July 20 (peak July 8);

near-white color with a pale lavender midrib; 2 1/2" long by 2" wide; open funnel shape; as many as 4-5 open each day per scape; in very dense clusters well above the foliage on scapes that reach 36-44" high; sparse seed pod formation

comments: 'Blue Angel' has proven to be one of the finest cultivars in the large blue-leaved category of hostas. The giant-sized clump of striking, deep blue foliage and attractive clusters of flowers make this plant worth leaving space for in the garden. It has been a good performer in almost any area of the U.S. where hostas can be grown. Bob Solberg of Green Hill Farm reports that 'Blue Angel' ranks as the best big blue hosta for North Carolina gardens.

'Blue Angel' is a Paul Aden introduction from the 1970's that was registered with the American Hosta Society in 1986 as a hybrid of two seedlings. Although it exhibits many traits typical of *H. sieboldiana* 'Elegans', the narrower foliage and larger, wider flowers on taller scapes points to *H. montana* also being in its background.

seedlings, sports, and other related types:

'Angel Eyes': sport of 'Blue Angel' with foliage characteristics similar to 'Guardian Angel'

'Green Angel': {1990r, Klehm Nursery} green-leaved t.c. sport of 'Blue Angel' found in the mid-1980's; md 31" high by 83" wide; impressive & underrated

83

'Guardian Angel': {1995r, C. & R. Thompson; sport} misted white and green leaf center surrounded by a blue-green mgn; turns green by mid-summer; eye-catching specimen; introduced for sale by Green Hill Farm in 1998

'Grey Ghost': sport of 'Guardian Angel' from Bob Solberg; emerges emerges creamy white in spring (no blue-green border), changing to dark green by mid-summer

other similar types:

'Snowden': {1988r, BHHS for E. Smith; 'Fortunei Aurea' X *H. sieboldiana*} 27" by 50" md of wavy, long, blue-green lvs, 14" by 9 3/4" (14 vp); near-wh fls (open funnel shape), mid-June into July on 41" sc; outstanding large md of blue-green foliage

---

'Blue Arrow'

key features: rich blue foliage in a medium-sized mound; slug-resistant; semi-upright habit

mound size: 16" high by 36" wide (up to 20" by 48")

spacing: 24"

leaves: 8" long by 4 1/2" wide; deep blue-green color lasts into late summer; blade roughly tri-angular often with a squarish base; moderately wavy along the margin; good substance; 12 vein pairs

flowers: late July into mid-August; pale bluish lavender; 2 1/8" long by 3/4" wide; 25-30" scapes (occasionally to 35" or so); many seed pods develop

comments: 'Blue Arrow' is impressive for its slug-resistant, wavy, blue-green leaves and good growth rate. The leaves are carried in a semi-upright manner creating an interesting effect. Though not "officially" a Tardiana, it displays all of the characteristics of that group and certainly ranks highly among blue-leaved hostas. Ken Anderson registered 'Blue Arrow' in 1982 with parentage unknown.

seedlings, sports, and other related types:
none listed
other similar types:
'Blue Dimples', 'Blue Wedgwood', 'Winfield Blue'

'Blue Betty Lou'
key features: semi-upright mound of thick, cupped blue-green foliage
mound size: 24" high by 55" wide

---

spacing: 36"
leaves: 11 1/2" long by 9" wide; blue-green color; broadly oblong-ovate shape; deeply cupped; moderately corrugated; blade generally wavy, slightly unruly; good substance; distinctive tip; 17-19 vein pairs
flowers: early to late July; medium lavender; 2 1/4" long by 1" wide; scapes up to 46" high; many seed pods develop
comments: 'Blue Betty Lou' has a distinctive appear-

ance that cannot be confused with any other hosta. The combination of deep blue foliage color, cupping, and semi-upright mound habit creates its unique character. Clarence Owens registered 'Blue Betty Lou' in 1987 as a hybrid of 'True Blue' X 'Gold Regal' and it is safe to say that he combined the best characteristics of both parents in this plant.
seedlings, sports, and other related types:
none
other similar types:
'Blue Bayou': {1987r, K. Vaughn; sixth generation sdlg from 'Frances Williams'} large, semi-upr md of blue-green foliage; similar to 'Blue Betty Lou' in md habit, leaf traits, and flowering; impressive pl

'Blue Blazes'

key features: large mound of deep blue-green foliage; good growth rate

mound size: 27" high by 60" wide

spacing: 36-48"

leaves: 13 1/2" long by 10" wide; blue-green color, dark green by mid-July; very broadly ovate to oblong-ovate blade; moderate corrugation; somewhat unruly; good substance; 16-18 vein pairs

flowers: late June into mid-July; near-white color (with a pale lavender midrib); 2 1/2" long by 1 1/8" wide; 33" scapes; many seed pods develop

comments: Kevin Vaughn registered 'Blue Blazes' in 1988 as a hybrid between 'Blue Boy' X 'Polly Bishop'. The result is an impressive mound of large, blue-green foliage that has the look of a Sieboldiana with a slightly better growth rate. It is certainly worth considering as a background plant or very large ground cover.

seedlings, sports, and other related types:

'Something Blue': {1991r, P. Ruh for L. Simpers; 'Blue Beauty' X 'Blue Boy'} 22" by 50" md of deep blue-green lvs, 9" by 8" (15 vp); pale lav fls on 26" sc from late June into mid-July

'Moongate Flying Saucer': {1996r, C. Isaacs & R. Solberg; 'Serendipity' X 'Blue Blazes'} bluish green foliage early, becoming dark green; 13" by 37" md; 6 1/2" by 5" (11 vp) lvs that are slightly cupped and corrugated; avg substance; pale lav fls in mid-June in North Carolina (early July, northern Illinois), about a week later than 'Moongate Little Dipper'

'Moongate Little Dipper': {1996r, C. Isaacs & R. Solberg; 'Serendipity' X 'Blue Blazes'} shiny, dark green foliage; 13" by 36" md; 6" by 5" lvs which are cupped, moderately corrgtd, and thick-substd; pale purple fls, in whorls around 21" sc in e July; outstanding for shiny, cupped, dk gr lvs & attractive fls; underrated

other similar types:
'Big Daddy', 'Sea Grotto'

'Blue Cadet'
key features: dense mound of bluish green foliage; fast growth rate
mound size: 15" high by 38" wide

spacing: 24"
leaves: 5 1/4" long by 4" wide; bluish green color in May and June, fading to a dark green by July 1, turning gold toward the end of October; moderate underside bloom; blade nearly a perfect heart shape with a cupped base; average substance; slight corrugation; 8-9 vein pairs
flowers: July 8 to 25; purplish lavender color; 1 3/4" long by 1 1/4" wide; funnel shape; clustered near the top of the scape, typical of *H. nakaiana*-types; scapes 14-21" high; many scapes per plant; heavy seed pod formation
comments: 'Blue Cadet' has attained great popularity amongst gardeners and nurserymen alike. It does not possess the bluest color or the greatest substance, but the dense, symmetrical mound habit, fast growth rate, and good flowering habits contribute to its continuing status as a hosta favorite. 'Blue Cadet' has been widely used as a ground cover and an edging plant. It also works well in combination with 'Gold Drop', 'Gold Edger', and 'Birchwood Parky's Gold'.

Paul Aden registered 'Blue Cadet' in 1974 as a seedling of 'Tokudama', but it tends to be much more like *H. nakaiana* in both foliage and flowering characteristics. In the same year, Paul also registered 'Gold Cadet' which was once considered to be a gold-leaved version of 'Blue Cadet'. It does not differ much from 'Gold Drop' or 'Gold Edger'.

seedlings, sports, and other related types:

'Blue Heaven': {1976r, P. Aden, 'Blue Cadet' X a sdlg} thick-substanced, blue foliage; thicker subst and bluer than 'Blue Cadet'; Tardiana-like

'Booka': {1986r, H. Weissenberger; 'Blue Cadet' sdlg; blue-green lvs}

'Daniel': {1986r, H. Weissenberger; 'Blue Cadet' sdlg; blue-green lvs}

'Lakeside Neat Petite': {1991r, M. Chastain; *H. venusta* X 'Blue Cadet'} sm, dense md of gr foliage **(see page 267)**

'Lynne': {1986r, H. Weissenberger; 'Blue Cadet' sdlg; lvs blue-green, turning a glossy green}

'Margie Weissenberger': {1986r, H. Weissenberger; 'Blue Cadet' sdlg; blue-green lvs}

'Pauline Brac': {1986r, H. Weissenberger; 'Blue Cadet' sdlg} med-sized md of bluish leaves (5 1/2" by 4 1/2"); lav fls on 20" sc in July

'Stephen': {1986r, H. Weissenberger; 'Blue Cadet' sdlg; bl-green lvs}

'Tot Tot': {1978r, P. Aden; 'Blue Cadet' X *H. venusta*} sm mound (7" by 21") of green lvs, 2 1/2" by 2", with 6 vp and a thin underside bloom; pale purple fls with whitish petal margins, early to mid-July on 13-19" sc; useful rock garden pl; effective in flower, one clump having 45 scapes

other similar types:

'Banyai's Dancing Girl': {1987r, P. Banyai; 'Blue Boy' sdlg} 17" by 40", dense md of heart-shaped, bl-green lvs, 5 1/2" by 4 1/2" (11 vp); pale purple fls, early to late July, in dense clusters near the top of 20-24" sc; v similar to 'Blue Cadet' in foliage & flower

'My Blue Heaven': {1997r, P. Banyai & E. Elslager; unknown parentage} 15" by 42", dense md of heart-shaped, bl-green lvs, 5 1/2" by 4 1/4" (11 vp); fls produced in early to late July; similar to 'Blue Cadet'

'Pacific Blue Edger': a Dan Heims introduction from 1988 or earlier that is very similar to 'Blue Cadet'; med-sized md of heart-shaped, bl-green foliage; lav fls in July on 24-30" sc; sported to 'Flash Dance' {1999r, M. Laviana & A. Malloy; lvs streaked with yellow}

Several other hostas have the "'Blue Cadet' look" (dense, rounded mound of heart-shaped, bluish green foliage topped by dense clusters of lavender flowers in July). These include:

'Abiqua Blue Edger', 'Abiqua Trumpet', 'Barbara', 'Carl', 'Dear Heart', 'Drummer Boy', 'Heart of Chan', 'Heart Throb', 'Oakview', 'Pelham Blue Thump', 'Peter Pan', 'Serendipity'

'Blue Danube'
key features: deep blue, slug-resistant foliage; a Tardiana
mound size: 18" high by 48" wide

spacing: 30-36"
leaves: 8" long by 6" wide; intense blue-green color; thick underside bloom; broadly ovate blade shape; slight to moderate corrugation; slightly wavy; thick substance; 12 vein pairs
flowers: late July into August; pale lavender; 20" scapes
comments: 'Blue Danube' is a second generation Tardiana (TF 2 x 24) seedling from the 1960's breeding program of Eric Smith. It rates highly for its intensity of blue foliage color, even among the Tardianas. It has a slow growth rate, but eventually becomes a fairly dense mound of slug-resistant blue leaves.

The British Hosta and Hemerocallis Society registered 'Blue Danube' for Eric Smith in 1988.
seedlings, sports, and other related types:
none listed
other similar types:
'Brother Ronald', 'Hadspen Blue', 'Nordatlantik' ('North Atlantic')

'Blue Dimples'

key features: deep blue, slug-resistant foliage; dense mound habit; a Tardiana
mound size: 18" high by 45" wide

spacing: 30-36"
leaves: 8 3/4" long by 5 1/2" wide; thick bloom creates a very deep blue color that lasts late into the season; thick underside bloom; oblong-ovate shape with a flattened base; margins slightly wavy; thick substance; 11-12 vein pairs
flowers: July 18 to August 14; very pale lavender with light petal margins; 1 7/8" long by 1 1/8" wide; scapes 20-24" high; many seed pods form
comments: 'Blue Dimples' continues to be admired by many as one of the bluest cultivars ever developed. Another of the Tardianas (TF 2 x 8), it has been widely grown over the last 15 years and can now be found in many gardens. There is some confusion, however, as to the real identity of 'Blue Dimples'. In the early 1980's, many hosta enthusiasts felt that 'Blue Wedgwood' and 'Blue Dimples' were mixed up. Most nurseries and collectors switched labels, i.e. 'Blue Wedgwood' plants became 'Blue Dimples' and vice-versa. Though well-intentioned, this was probably a mistake. I do not, however, advocate switching back. Since most of these plants now follow this new designation, another change would forever confuse the two. In any case, both are wonderful, slug-resistant blue-leaved hostas with similar flowers and foliage. The main difference between them are that the leaves of 'Blue Dimples' are slightly longer while 'Blue Wedgwood' leaves are more triangular in outline.

The British Hosta and Hemerocallis Society registered 'Blue Dimples' for Eric Smith in 1988.

seedlings, sports, and other related types:
none listed
other similar types:
'Blue Diamond', 'Blue Wedgwood', 'Winfield Blue'

'Blue Ice'
key features: dwarf-sized mound of thick blue foliage
mound size: 8" high by 18" wide

spacing: 15"
leaves: 4" long by 3 1/2" wide; deep blue-green color that can last into late summer; thick underside bloom; very broadly ovate, almost heart-shaped blade; slightly corrugated; cupped; thick substance; 9 vein pairs
flowers: mid-August; near-white to very pale lavender; in dense clusters on 8-10" scapes
comments: 'Blue Ice' ranks as one of Herb (Ralph) Benedict's best introductions. In the small-sized mound category, it is one of the best for slug-resistance and blue foliage color. Herb registered 'Blue Ice' in 1987 as a hybrid of 'Dorset Blue' X 'Blue Moon', making it at least the equivalent of a third generation Tardiana. Like its parents, it has a very slow growth rate, but is well worth the wait to reach mature size.
seedlings, sports, and other related types:
'Blue Chip': {1997r, R. Benedict & R. Olson; selfed 'Dorset Blue' sdlg} thick, deep blue foliage; 9" by 18" md; 4" by 3 1/4" lvs (9 vp)
'Blue Clown': {1996r; R. & D. Benedict & J. & E. Stratton; selfed 'Dorset Blue' sdlg} 12" by 22" md of thick-substanced, blue-green lvs, 6" by 4 1/2" (10 vp); med lav fls, mid-July into Aug on 18" scapes
other similar types:
'Blue Beard', 'Blue Moon', 'Winsome Blue'

'Blue Mammoth'

key features: huge mound of slug-resistant, blue foliage
mound size: 34" high by 65" wide

spacing: 48"

leaves: 16" long by 12" wide; deep blue-green color into mid-summer; thick bloom on top and underside; broadly ovate shape with a deeply lobed base; moderately to heavily corrugated; broadly wavy and generally unruly; thick substance; 18-20 vein pairs

flowers: mid-June into mid-July; near-white color with a pale lavender petal midrib, more lavender in bud; 2 3/4" long by 1 1/4" wide; narrow funnel shape; scapes at the top of the mound, 30-36" high; many seed pods form

comments: As a gigantic mound of heavily corrugated, deep blue foliage, 'Blue Mammoth' becomes the focal point of almost any shaded garden. It has a somewhat open mound habit and can be very effectively used as a specimen or background plant. Though it is a typical blue Sieboldiana in many ways, it is larger than most in overall size and individual leaf dimensions.

'Blue Mammoth' is another fine introduction from Paul Aden first offered for sale in the mid-1980's.

seedlings, sports, and other related types:

'Blue Delight': {1993r, E. Moore; 'Blue Mammoth' sport; med bl-green foliage}

other similar types:

'Eleanor J. Reath', 'Gray Cole', 'Ryan's Big One', 'Silver Anniversary', 'Trail's End', 'Woodland Blue'

'Blue Moon'

key features: dense mound of intensely blue, deeply cupped foliage; slug-resistant; a Tardiana
mound size: 10" high by 23" wide

spacing: 18-24"
leaves: 5" long by 4 1/4" wide; deep blue-green color lasting well into July; thick underside bloom; blade very broadly ovate, deeply cupped, and heavily corrugated; thick substance; 10-11 vein pairs

flowers: late July into early August; whitish; on short scapes

comments: Though developed in the 1960's (with all of the other Tardianas),

'Blue Moon' (TF 2 x 2) continues to be highly desirable because of its excellent blue color, slug resistance, and small size. The leaves are also neatly cupped and attractively corrugated.

In the late 1980's, it was discovered that a plant similar to 'Love Pat' was being mistakenly sold as 'Blue Moon'. This plant has since been named 'Blue Splendor'. It becomes a much larger mound of foliage (19" high by 40" wide or more) with larger leaves (10" long by 9" wide) and it blooms much earlier (from late June into early July in northern Illinois) than 'Blue Moon'.

The true 'Blue Moon' was registered in 1976 by Paul Aden for Eric Smith, the originator of the Tardianas.

seedlings, sports, and other related types:

'Blue Ice': {1987r, R. Benedict, 'Dorset Blue' X 'Blue Moon'} sm md of deep blue lvs **(see page 91)**

'Cherub': {1989r, W. & E. Lachman; 'Crepe Suzette' X 'Blue Moon'} sm, dense md of heart-shaped, creamy white-mgd foliage **(see page 115)**

'Deep Blue Sea': {1994r, C. Seaver; 'Blue Moon' sdlg} rich blue foliage; excellent substance

'Full Moon': {1991r, W. & E. Lachman; selfed 'Blue Moon' sdlg} sm md of deeply cupped and corrugated, blue-green foliage; outstanding

'Minimoon': {1992r, W. & E. Lachman; selfed 'Blue Moon' sdlg} attractive, thick-substanced small blue

'Summer Joy': {1998r, R. Klehm, 'Blue Moon' sport} white-centered, blue-green-margined foliage; listed in the 2000 Robyn's Nest catalog (p. 32) as growing taller & faster than 'Blue Moon'

other similar types:
'Blue Chip', 'Dorset Blue'

'Blue Umbrellas'
key features: huge mound of dark green leaves that cup downward
mound size: 33" high by 72" wide

spacing: 48"

leaves: 15 1/2" long by 12" wide; bluish green color early, shiny, dark green from early June on; thick underside bloom; broadly ovate shape with a cordate base; blade generally inversely cupped (downward); slight to moderate corrugation; good substance; 16-18 vein pairs

flowers: late June to late July; very pale lavender color (petal margins paler than center); 2 1/8" long by 1 1/2" wide; scapes at or near the top of the foliage mound; fertile

comments: Its foliage is not very blue and there are many larger hostas, but 'Blue Umbrellas' is always a standout in any garden. The very large, shiny, dark green leaves that normally cup downward plus the open mound habit give 'Blue Umbrellas' a distinctive, attractive appearance. It has been offered for many years in the nursery trade and should continue to be widely grown. It was registered with the

AHS by Paul Aden 1978 as a hybrid of 'Tokudama' X *H. sieboldiana* 'Elegans'.

seedlings, sports, and other related types:
'Potomac Pride': {1995r, T. Avent; *H. yingeri* X 'Blue Umbrellas'} 24" by 50" md of shiny, dark green lvs, 12" by 8 1/2", good substance; bluish purple fls on 36" sc in July; 1995 AHS "convention" plant; fast growth rate

other similar types:
'Blackjack': {1990r, C. Owens; *H. sieboldiana* 'Mira' X *H. sieboldiana*} 29" by 72" md of heavily corrugated, thick-substd foliage that is bluish green early, becoming dark green by early summer; lvs 15" by 14" (19 vp); lf blade downwardly cupped & somewhat unruly

'Millennium': {1995r, J. & J. Wilkins; 'Herb Benedict' X 'Sagae'} 28" by 54", semi-upright md of thick-substanced, blue-green lvs, 16" by 12" (18 vp); lvs dark green by mid-summer; pale lav fl, late June into July on 40" sc; fertile; majestic, upright mound

'Placemat': {1990r, C. Soules; *H. sieboldiana* X 'Tokudama'} 24" by 60" md of rounded, shiny, dark green lvs, 12 1/2" by 11" (17 vp); whitish fls from late June into mid-July on 34" sc

'Blue Vision'
key features: large mound of thick, blue foliage
mound size: 25" high by 46" wide

spacing: 36"
leaves: 13" long by 9 1/2" wide; rich blue-green color created by a thick bloom on the top; becomes dark green by mid-summer; thick underside bloom; broadly ovate to elliptic shape with a slightly cordate base; moderate

cupping; intense corrugation; thick substance; 17-19 deeply impressed vein pairs

flowers: late June into early July; near-white color; 2 1/4" long by 1" wide; scapes 25-36" high; many seed pods develop

comments: The deep blue-green color, thick substance, and good corrugation make 'Blue Vision' an outstanding cultivar. With heavy fertilization and a lot of water, a mature clump will probably exceed the listed dimensions. It was registered in 1976 by Paul Aden as a hybrid of two seedlings.

seedlings, sports, and other related types:
'Blue Whirls': {1978r, P. Aden; sdlg X 'Blue Vision'} med-lg md of blue-green leaves that radiate from the center of the mound; md 23" by 52"; lvs 9 1/2" by 5 1/2" (12-13 vp), wavy and thick-substanced; pale lav fls, mid-July into Aug on 33" sc; a Tardiana-type

other similar types:
'Perry's True Blue', 'Sea Sapphire'

'Blue Wedgwood'
key features: medium-sized mound of deep blue foliage; slug-resistant; a Tardiana
mound size: 19" high by 44" wide

spacing: 30-36"
leaves: 7 1/2" long by 5 1/2" wide (up to 8" by 6 3/4"); very bright blue color produced by a thick bloom on the top surface, lasting into mid-summer; thick underside bloom; ovate shape with a slightly cupped, flattish base, being almost triangular in overall outline; 3-6 waves along the margin; slight corrugation; thick substance; 11-13 vein pairs

flowers: July 25 to August 20; very pale bluish lavender color with a contrasting, darker midrib; 1 3/4" long by

1 1/8" wide; scapes 20-27" high; seed pods develop

comments: When hosta collectors are asked to name the bluest cultivar, 'Blue Wedgwood' often comes to mind. In fact when 'Blue Wedgwood' is seen at its peak, the definition of blue in a hosta leaf is immediately understood. Besides foliage color, the excellent substance, good growth rate, and attractive flowers add to the beauty and value of this plant.

As discussed under 'Blue Dimples', the two cultivars were switched in the 1980's resulting in 'Blue Wedgwood' plants having shorter, more wedge-shaped leaves. 'Blue Wedgwood' was originally known as the Tardiana "TF 2 x 9" and is often misspelled 'Blue Wedgewood'. It was registered by the British Hosta and Hemerocallis Society for Eric Smith in 1988.

seedlings, sports, and other related types:
'Ace of Spades': {1993r, E. Lunsford; 'Blue Wedgwood' sdlg; dark green foliage}
'Punky': {1999r, R. Kuk; sport; yellow-centered, bl-green-mgd lvs}
'Winfield Blue': {1999r, M. Zilis} a plant of Tardiana origin; 18" by 45" md of intensely blue-green lvs, 7" by 5" (12-13 vp); pale lav fls, mid-July into early Aug, on 20-28" sc

other similar types:
'Blue Arrow', 'Blue Dimples'

'Bold Edger'
key features: medium-sized mound of green leaves neatly edged in white
mound size: 19" high by 45" wide

spacing: 30-36"
leaves: 8" long by 5 1/2" wide; medium to dark green center with a 3/4" to 1" wide margin that changes from yellow to creamy white as the season progresses; moderate underside bloom; blade broadly wavy and oblong-ovate in shape with a puckered base; little or no corrugation; better than average substance; 11-12 vein pairs
flowers: mid-July into mid-August; medium lavender color with darker, mid-petal striping; 2 7/8" long by 2" wide; wide-open funnel shape; scapes 20-28" high
comments: 'Bold Edger' becomes a fairly dense mound of distinctly margined foliage at maturity. It is an excellent choice for mass plantings because of its size, fast growth rate and attractive foliage. Kevin Vaughn bred this superb plant and registered it as a hybrid of 'Beatrice' X 'Frances Williams' in 1983.
seedlings, sports, and other related types:
none
other similar types:
'Emily Dickinson', 'Queen Josephine', 'Tambourine'

'Bold Ruffles'

key features: large mound of heavily corrugated, unruly blue-green foliage
mound size: 26" high by 50" wide

spacing: 36-40"
leaves: 13 1/2" long by 12 1/2" wide with an occasional leaf wider than long (e.g., 12 1/2" by 13 1/4"); blue-green in May-June, dark green from July into October when an orangy tan fall color develops; thick bloom on top and underside; very broadly ovate blade shape with a deeply lobed base and long, distinct tip; intensely corrugated; unruliness throughout the blade usually

creates concave or convex cupping; very thick substance; 17-18 vein pairs with some merging at mid-blade
flowers: very late June into mid-July; very pale lavender color with lighter petal margins; 2 1/4" long by 1 1/8" wide; scapes 29-37" high; blooms later and more lavender than other *H. sieboldiana* types; some seed pods develop
comments: When other cultivars with heavily corrugated, unruly foliage are compared to 'Bold Ruffles', they usually take second place. Even as a young plant, the foliage displays a distinct, ruffled and wavy character. Additionally, the blue-green color and thick, cardboard-like substance add to its appeal. It does have a slow growth rate, so heavy fertilization and watering are necessary for 'Bold Ruffles' to achieve its potential. Anne Arett of Minnesota registered 'Bold Ruffles' in 1975 as a sport of *H. sieboldiana* 'Elegans'.

seedlings, sports, and other related types:
'Locomotion': {1993r, Belle Gardens; 'Crested Surf' X 'Bold Ruffles'; intensely blue-green foliage}
'Peedee Dew Catcher': {1992r, U. Syre-Herz; 'City Lights' X 'Bold Ruffles'} 18" by 57" md of heavily corrugated, thick-substanced, gold lvs, 11" by 8 1/2" (17 vp); changes from chartreuse to gold; has sported to 'Dippity

Dew', which has green-centered, gold-mgd leaves {1999r, J. Schwarz}

'Peedee Granny Smith': {1992r, U. Syre-Herz; 'Shade Fanfare' X 'Bold Ruffles'; lvs lt blue, turn green}

other similar types:
'Fantastic', 'Lochness'

'Brave Amherst'

key features: rounded mound of blue leaves neatly edged in gold; thick substance
mound size: 20" high by 50" wide or more

spacing: 36"
leaves: 11 1/2" long by 9 1/2" wide; medium blue-green color with a 1/4" to 1" wide, gold margin; thick underside bloom; broadly ovate to rotund shape; slightly to moderately corrugated blade; blade tends to cup downward; good substance; 17 vein pairs
flowers: very late June into late July; registered as being near-white on 25" scapes

comments: I first saw 'Brave Amherst' growing at Soules Garden in Indianapolis in 1997 and was really taken with it. The round blade shape, sharp contrast between the blue center and thin, gold margins, and large mound size created an effect that I had not seen before. The above listed dimensions of 20" by 50" can probably be far surpassed by heavy fertilization. 'Brave Amherst' was registered by Bill and Eleanor Lachman (of Amherst, Massachusetts) in 1993 as a hybrid of 'Christmas Tree' X 'Reversed'.

seedlings, sports, and other related types:
none

other similar types:
'Christmas Tree', 'Grand Master'

'Breeder's Choice'

key features: medium-sized mound of heavily streaked foliage; premier breeding plant

mound size: 12" high by 31" wide

spacing: 24"

leaves: 6 1/8" long by 4 3/4" wide; heavily streaked and mottled center; creamy white margin; broadly ovate blade that is slightly wavy; slight corrugation; better than average substance; 8-10 vein pairs

flowers: late June into mid-July; lavender; 22" scapes; fertile

c o m m e n t s : 'Breeder's Choice' has rightly gained the reputation as a premier hybridizing plant. Kevin Vaughn registered 'Breeder's Choice' as a seedling of "Vaughn 73-2" (= 'Beatrice' X 'Beatrice') X 'Frances Williams' in 1987 and used it extensively in his breeding program. Some of its progeny include 'Heart's Content', 'Formal Attire', and 'Little Doll', all outstanding white-margined cultivars. Two heavily streaked 'Breeder's Choice' seedlings are 'Pin Stripe' and 'Pin Stripe Sister', which have become prominent breeding plants in their own right.

In the garden, 'Breeder's Choice' makes an attractive, splashy specimen plant, but the variegation can be unstable. I have seen one sport, 'Breeder's Choice Margined', which has green-centered, white-margined foliage. It becomes a larger mound (18" by 48") with larger-sized leaves (8 1/2" by 7").

seedlings, sports, and other related types:

'Cotillion': {1995r, W. Zumbar; 'Breeder's Choice' F1 X (*H. nakaiana* x 'Kii Hime' sdlg)} 10" by 23" md of 3 3/8" by 1 1/2" (4 vp) lvs with a 1/32" wide mgn

'Dress Blues': {1995r, W. Zumbar; 'Breeder's Choice' F1 X 'Halcyon'} semi-upright, 22" by 54" md of yellow-edged, blue-green foliage

'Formal Attire': {1988r, K. Vaughn; 'Breeder's Choice' X

'Frances Williams'} lg md of creamy white-mgd foliage **(see page 151)**

'Heart's Content': introduced in the 1992 Hatfield Gardens catalog as a Kevin Vaughn hybrid of 'Breeder's Choice' X 'Polly Bishop'; 22" by 46" md of heart-shaped, white-mgd foliage **(see page 222)**

'Little Doll': 'Breeder's Choice' X 'Blue Shadows' hybrid from Kevin Vaughn; 15" by 34" md of 5 1/2" by 5" lvs which are yellow margined early, changing to creamy white; moderately corrugated, rounded blade; good subst; lav fls in July; 1994 Hatfield Gardens introduction; outstanding

'Mildred Seaver': {1981r, K. Vaughn} from the same cross as 'Breeder's Choice', i.e. "Vaughn 73-2" X 'Frances Williams'; lg md of white-margined foliage **(see page 294)**

'Pin Stripe': {1983r, K. Vaughn} introduced in 1992 by Hatfield Gardens as a hybrid of 'Breeder's Choice' X 'Frances Williams'; streaked foliage; used as a breeding plant (registered, white-mgd sdlgs include 'Amazing Grace' {1999r}, 'Firefly' {1996r}, 'Grace McClure' {1998r}, and 'Pixie Vamp' {1996r} from Dick & Jane Ward)

'Pin Stripe Sister': sibling of 'Pin Stripe' developed by Kevin Vaughn; heavily variegated lvs that are mottled cream and green through center with a dark green margin; used as a breeding plant (registered open-pollinated, white-mgd sdlgs include 'Kaitlyn'{1998r}, 'Thumbelina'{1996r}, and 'Winsome' {1996r} from Dick & Jane Ward)

'William Lachman': {1981r, K. Vaughn; "Vaughn 73-2" X 'Frances Williams'} med-lg md of heavily streaked foliage; 20" by 48" md; 8 3/4" by 6 3/4" lvs (11 vp); from the same cross as 'Breeder's Choice' and equally as important as a breeding plant

other similar types:

'Beatrice'

'Brim Cup'

key features: cupped foliage with distinct, white margins that sometimes tear
mound size: 14" high by 40" wide

spacing: 24-30"
leaves: 7 1/2" long by 6 1/2" wide; medium to dark green center; white margin, about 1/2" wide, sometimes tearing; thin underside bloom; moderately cupped and corrugated; broadly ovate shape; good substance; 13 vein pairs

flowers: late June into mid-July; pale lavender; 1 3/4" long by 1" wide; open funnel shape; 21-25" scapes

comments: A plant with so much promise but, in the end, a disappointment best describes 'Brim Cup'. As a young plant, 'Brim Cup' looks great and is admired by hosta collectors and gardeners alike. With age, however, it develops a nasty habit of tearing along the margin (not to be confused with the "drawstring" effect). 'Brim Cup' is probably not worth promoting for landscape usage any longer, but does make a beautiful container plant. In Japan, where hosta collections are often completely containerized, I saw several 'Brim Cup' specimens used this way.

Paul Aden registered 'Brim Cup' in 1986 as a hybrid of "Aden 392" X 'Wide Brim'.

seedlings, sports, and other related types:

'Java': green-leaved sport of 'Brim Cup'; 16" by 45" md of cupped, corrugated foliage; good substance; attractive; 1994 Q & Z N introduction

other similar types:

'Snow Cap': {1980r, P. Aden; 'Wide Brim' X 'Royal Rainbow'}19" by 42" md; 7 1/2" by 6 1/4" lvs (13 vp) wi wide, white margins; near-wh fls in June-July; difficult to grow; margins often tear (not drawstring); not recommended

'Knockout': {1986r, P. Aden; hybrid of two sdlgs} similarly

103

afflicted with marginal tearing, perhaps even worse than 'Brim Cup'; 18" by 33" md of creamy white-mgd, bl-green-cntrd foliage; lvs 7 1/2" by 6 3/4" (12-13 vp); not recommended

---

'Brother Ronald'
key features: deep blue-green, slug-resistant foliage; dense clusters of white flowers; a Tardiana
mound size: 16" high by 35" wide

spacing: 30"
leaves: 7" long by 5" wide; deep blue-green color that is long-lasting; thick bloom on top and underside; ovate blade shape; slight cupping; moderate corrugation; thick substance; 12 vein pairs
flowers: mid-July into early August with peak of bloom on July 27 (northern Ohio); pure white color; 1 1/2" long by 7/8" wide; arranged around the scapes in dense clusters; scapes up to 18-20" high; will form seed pods

comments: 'Brother Ronald' ranks near the top of blue-leaved hostas, but its combination of blue foliage and white flowers makes it truly outstanding. Inexplicably it has seen only limited popularity, but hopefully that will change. 'Brother Ronald' was formerly known as "TF 2 x 30" (its Tardiana designation) and later, 'Hadspen White'. It was registered by the BHHS for Eric Smith in 1988.

seedlings, sports, and other related types:
'Osprey': another great Tardiana with blue foliage and white flowers
'September White': good blue foliage with white flowers that begin to bloom just when 'Brother Ronald' is finishing; a Tardiana-type from Herb Benedict; md 16" by 37"; lvs 6 1/2" by 4 3/4" (11 vp)

other similar types:
'Buckshaw Blue', 'Tokudama'

104

'Buckshaw Blue'

key features: intensely corrugated, deep blue foliage in a medium-sized mound; slug-resistant

mound size: 19" high by 54" wide

spacing: 36"

leaves: 8 1/4" long by 7" wide; deep blue-green color into mid-summer, dark green thereafter; thick bloom on top and underside; broadly ovate shape with a cordate base and slight tip; blade cupped and slightly wavy; intensely corrugated; thick substance; 16-18 vein pairs

flowers: mid-June into early July; near-white color with a pale lavender petal

midrib; 1 3/4" long by 1" wide; narrow funnel shape; 16-20" scapes

comments: The outstanding, deep blue color, thick substance, and deeply corrugated leaves make 'Buckshaw Blue' a worthwhile plant. It comes very close to 'Tokudama' in both foliage and flower. The AHS registered 'Buckshaw Blue' for Eric Smith in 1986 as a hybrid of *H. sieboldiana* X 'Tokudama', though it more likely is a selfed 'Tokudama' seedling.

seedlings, sports, and other related types:
none

other similar types:
'Blue Horizon', 'Blue Velvet', 'Moscow Blue', 'Tokudama'

'Camelot'

key features: bright blue, slug-resistant blue foliage in a medium-sized mound; a Tardiana

mound size: 17" high by 42" wide (up to 21" by 58")

spacing: 30-36"

leaves: 7 3/4" long by 6 1/4" wide; intense blue-green color into mid-summer; thick bloom on top and underside surfaces; blade broadly ovate, almost heart-like, with a slightly cupped, subcordate base; slight corrugation and waviness; thick substance; 12-13 vein pairs

flowers: late July into mid-August; very pale lavender color with a slightly darker petal midrib; 2 1/8" long by 1 3/8" wide; 16-22" scapes

comments: 'Camelot' is another second generation Tardiana (TF 2 x 27) from the late Eric Smith of England. The foliage color can best be described as a "frosty", bright blue. It also has rounder leaves than other Tardianas. Though virtually unknown ten years ago, it has become widely available within the last few years. The BHHS registered 'Camelot' for Eric Smith in 1988.

seedlings, sports, and other related types:
none

other similar types:
'Brother Ronald', 'Grey Goose', 'Hadspen Blue', 'Sherborne Songbird'

'Candy Hearts'

key features: rounded dense mound of heart-shaped, green foliage; fast growth rate
mound size: 17" high by 43" wide

spacing: 24-30"

leaves: 6" long by 4 7/8" wide; slightly bluish cast early, medium green color most of the season; gold fall color in late October; thin bloom on underside; blade heart-shaped (broadly ovate with a cordate base); slightly corrugated; moderately cupped; average substance; no purple dots on petiole; 9-10 vein pairs

flowers: July 3 to July 21 (northern Illinois); pale lavender color with a lighter throat; 1 7/8" long by 15/16" wide; narrow funnel shape; in tight clusters in the top 3-4" of the scapes; the 15-20" high scapes are just above the foliage mound; many seed pods develop

comments: 'Candy Hearts' has long been admired for its dense mound of attractive, heart-shaped foliage. It can be used as an edger or ground cover in the landscape. Despite the fact that it can form prolific numbers of seed pods, it has not been widely used in breeding work.

Peter Ruh registered 'Candy Hearts' in 1998 for Eunice Fisher who introduced it in the early 1970's. It is a seedling of *Hosta nakaiana* to which it shows many similarities, except for its ultimate size.

seedlings, sports, and other related types:

'Amber Maiden': {1988r, Walters Gardens; 'Candy Hearts' sport} 1/2" wide, muted pale green to chartreuse margin flows into a medium green center; a collector's plant

'Bountiful': {1971r, E. Fisher; *H. nakaiana* sdlg} 15" by 40" md; green lvs, 6 3/8" by 3 3/4" (8 vp); similar to 'Candy Hearts' in mound size and flowering but foliage narrower

'Cupid's Arrow': {1988r, Walters Gardens; 'Candy Hearts' sport} white-cntrd, green-mgd foliage; margins tend to be very ruffled; collector's plant

'Cupid's Dart': {1997r, Walters Gardens; sport of 'Heartsong'} sm, dense md of v narrow, elliptic-shaped lvs wi thin, white margins; acts like a juvenile form of 'Heartsong'; collector's plant

'Fair Maiden': {1993r, Walters Gardens & C. Falstad; sport of 'Amber Maiden'} white-mgd, dark green-centered lvs; lav fls; attractive contrast betw margin & center

'Happy Hearts': {1973r, E. Fisher; *H. nakaiana* sdlg} 16" by 38" md; 6 1/2" by 5 3/4" green lvs; very similar in foliage and flower to 'Candy Hearts'

'Heartleaf': {1971r, E. Fisher; *H. nakaiana* sdlg} 19" by 48" md; 7 3/4" by 6 3/4" green lvs; lav fls, on 16-25" sc, mid to late July; larger than 'Candy Hearts'

'Heartsong': {1984r, Walters Gardens; 'Candy Hearts' sport} same as 'Candy Hearts' except for thin, 1/8" wide, creamy white to white margin that does not "drawstring"

'Pinky': {1990r, P. Banyai; 'Blue Boy' sdlg} 22" by 47" md of cupped, bluish gr lvs, 6 1/2" by 6 1/2" (13 vp); lav fls, July 10 to Aug 1, on 34" sc; like a large version of 'Candy Hearts'

'Special Gift': {1973r, E. Fisher; *H. nakaiana* sdlg} 16" by 42" md; 6 5/8" by 5 1/2" gr lvs that are slightly more elongated than 'Candy Hearts'

other similar types:

'Gum Drop', 'Jade Scepter', 'Minnie Klopping', 'Pearl Lake', 'Purple Bouquet'

Hosta capitata
(Iya Giboshi; Kanzashi Giboshi)

key features: medium-sized mound of rippled, green foliage; clusters of large purple flowers
mound size: 16" high by 38" wide

spacing: 24-30"

leaves: 7" long by 4 1/4" wide; medium green color; dull top; whitish shiny underside; ovate to elliptic-ovate blade with ten or more, distinct, marginal ripples; blade droops downward at the tip; no purple dots evident on the petiole; no corrugation; average substance; 9-11 vein pairs

flowers: late June into early July; deep purple color with a white throat; 2 5/8" long by 1 1/4" wide; narrow funnel shape; in tight clusters at the top of 15-22" scapes; ball-like scape bud; many blunt-tipped seed pods form

comments: As a garden plant, *Hosta capitata* will never be at the top of popularity polls, but it makes an attractive specimen and can be valuable in breeding programs. The rippled leaf margins and large purple flowers which cluster at the top of the scapes are useful genetic traits. In Japan I observed two forms of *Hosta capitata* that were collected in the wild on Shikoku Island. The leaves of both were heavily rippled and medium green but one was significantly narrower than the other. The wider form (collected near Tokushima, a city on the eastern end of Shikoku Island) closely matches what we have grown under this name.

seedlings, sports, and other related types:

'Show Piece': {1998r, P. Ruh for E. Fisher & G. Krossa} 12" by 33" md; med green lvs, 6 1/8" by 4 1/2" (7 vp) wi a slightly rippled margin; pale purple fls produced in clusters at the ends of 22" sc from mid to late July; lf color yellow in spring (Fisher, 1979); probably a hybrid of *H. capitata* X *H. nakaiana*, circa 1970

'Tatted Lace': {1990r, Fairway Enterprises; *H. capitata* X 'Ruffles'} very close to *H. capitata* in both foliage and flower, i.e., heavily rippled, med green lvs and long, bright purple fls in July at the top of the scapes

other similar types:

H. minor, H. nakaiana, H. venusta

'Carnival'
key features: open mound of broad leaves with wide, creamy yellow margins
mound size: 18" high by 44" wide

spacing: 30"

leaves: 9" long by 7 1/2" wide; 1" to 1 1/2" wide yellow to creamy yellow margins that often streak into the medium to dark green center; many gray-green streaks also into center of leaf; broadly ovate blade that is slightly wavy; average substance; 12-13 vein pairs

flowers: mid-July into early August; medium lavender color; 1 3/4" long by 1 1/2" wide; scapes well above foliage, up to 30" high

comments: 'Carnival' is an ornamentally stunning cultivar that can be very effective as a specimen plant. The wide yellow margins lighten considerably in bright light, all the way to creamy white. Bill and Eleanor Lachman registered 'Carnival' in 1986 as a hybrid of a 'Beatrice' seedling X a seedling.

seedlings, sports, and other related types:

'Festival': {1998r, A. Malloy; 'Carnival' sport; heavily strkd green, yellow, & white lvs}

'Sherwood Forest': {1993r, W. & E. Lachman; 'Carnival' sdlg} moderately dense md of roundish, med green, unruly lvs; md 22" by 48"; lvs 9" by 8 1/2" (10 vp); lav fls begin opening in mid-July

110

other similar types:
'Celebrity', 'El Capitan', 'Carousel'

'Chantilly Lace'
key features: semi-upright mound of wavy-edged, white-margined foliage
mound size: 16" high by 40" wide

spacing: 30"

leaves: 6 3/8" long by 3" wide; 1/8" wide, white margin; medium to dark green center; moderate underside bloom; narrowly ovate to elliptic-ovate shape; smooth texture; blade distinctly wavy; better than average substance; 8 vein pairs

flowers: mid to late August; pale lavender; 2" long by 1 1/2" wide; scapes 19" high

comments: The horizontal manner in which the leaves are held combined with the white-margined color and waviness give 'Chantilly Lace' a distinctive appearance. The mound habit is fairly dense and the growth rate appears to be good. In the landscape, it can be used effectively as a specimen or ground cover.

'Chantilly Lace' is another great Lachman plant. Bill and Eleanor registered it in 1988 as a cross between 'Calypso' X 'Halcyon'.

seedlings, sports, and other related types:
none

other similar types:
'Gay Blade', 'Torchlight'

'Chartreuse Wiggles'

key features: low mound of narrow, very wavy, bright gold foliage
mound size: 10" high by 25" wide

'Chartreuse Wiggles' bordering 'Moonlight'

spacing: 15-18"
leaves: 5 1/2" long by 1" wide; chartreuse (in deep shade) to bright yellow color; slightly shiny top and underside; narrowly elliptic shape with a wedge-shaped base and curved tip; margin distinctly rippled, five or more per side; smooth texture; thin substance; 4-5 vein pairs
flowers: August; pale purple; 20" scapes
comments: Always a favorite of hosta aficionados, 'Chartreuse Wiggles' adds an interesting element to the shaded garden. The waviness of the narrow, golden foliage is ornamentally attractive and can be noticed from a distance. Its low, dense mound habit and good growth rate make 'Chartreuse Wiggles' an excellent edging plant.

It is of *Hosta sieboldii* origin, probably being a descendant of 'Kabitan' or 'Subcrocea'. Paul Aden registered this plant in 1976 as a seedling of 'Wogon Gold'.
seedlings, sports, and other related types:
'Lights Up': {1986, P. Aden; sdlg X 'Chartreuse Wiggles'} low md of small, narrow, wavy gold foliage
'Spring Lace': {1998r, C. Helsley; 'Chartreuse Wiggles' X 'Starburst'; lvs lt green wi a med gr mgn}
'Yellow Waves': {1978r, P. Aden, 'Wogon Gold' X 'Chartreuse Wiggles'} low, dense md of wavy, golden foliage; md 9" by 39"; similar to 'Chartreuse Wiggles' but lvs (7 1/2" by 2 1/2") wider & not as distinctly rippled
other similar types:
'Chartreuse Waves': low, dense md of wavy golden lvs (6 1/4" by 2 1/2") that are wider than 'Chartreuse Wig-

gles'; close to 'Yellow Waves'; haven't seen since 1986

'Golden Wiggler': v dense md of narrow, wavy, golden foliage; 8-yr old clump measured 7" by 18"; impressive for consistent waviness and dense mound habit; from Herb Benedict; have only seen in originator's garden

'Lauren': {1991r, D. Heinz; 'Saishu Jima' sdlg} dense md (14" by 30") of long, very wavy, bright gold lvs (5 1/4" by 1 1/4"); resembles 'Chartreuse Wiggles'

'Sea Wiggles': (1981r, M. Seaver; 'Sea Sprite' sdlg} low md of very wavy, narrow gold foliage

'Subcrocea': very similar low md of narrow, gold foliage but without the rippling **(see page 426)**

'Cherry Berry'

key features: small mound of white-centered foliage; bright red flower scapes in July-August

mound size: 12" high by 28" wide

spacing: 18"

leaves: 6 1/2" long by 2 5/8" wide; center yellow in spring, turning creamy white; 1/2" wide green margin; slightly shiny top and underside; elliptic blade shape; smooth texture; average substance; 6-7 vein pairs

flowers: late July to late August; light purple color with white petal margins; 2 1/2" long by 1 1/4" wide; bright red scapes, especially below the flowers; some seed pods develop, turning bright red; bracts on scape white-centered (like leaves)

comments: As if a dense mound of beautiful, white-centered foliage wasn't enough, 'Cherry Berry' becomes even more spectacular in flower! The bright red scapes that emerge from the foliage immediately draw the attention of even the most casual observer. The light purple flowers, too,

offer a nice color contrast to both scapes and foliage. Red seed pods develop after flowering and are attractive until fall. It has a good growth rate in containers, slower in the garden. It should be planted where it can receive some direct sunlight.

There has been a concerted effort amongst hybridizers to increase the amount of red on hosta petioles, but in a garden setting this has only limited ornamental value. Red scapes (and seed pods), on the other hand, make a better statement for "red" in a hosta.

'Cherry Berry' was registered in 1991 by Bill and Eleanor Lachman as a hybrid of two seedlings (#82-18-1 X #81-9-2). Hatfield Gardens introduced it for sale in 1992 and listed 'Flamboyant', 'Beatrice', and 'Frances Williams' in the background of those two seedlings.

seedlings, sports, and other related types:

'Maraschino Cherry': {1999r, M. Zilis & R. Solberg} green-lvd sport of 'Cherry Berry' introduced for sale in 1997 by Q & Z N; md 17" by 47"; med green lvs, 7 1/2" by 4" (10 vp); scapes greenish purple-red; impressive for v fast growth rate, making it a good ground cover; scapes ornamental but not as striking as 'Cherry Berry'

other similar types:

'Banana Boat': {1991r, W. & E. Lachman; sdlg #81-9 X 'Reversed'} med-sized md of creamy-centered foliage; largest lvs I've seen measured 6 1/4" by 3 1/2" (8 vp); lf center yellow, turning to creamy white; wide, dark green margins; introduced for sale by Hatfield Gardens in 1993

'Hot Lips': {1993r, H. Gowen, F. Riehl, & R. Benedict; parentage unknown} 16" by 38" md; 7 1/2" by 3 1/4" lvs wi a 3/4" wide, green mgn and wh center; purplish red petioles; similar to 'Cherry Berry' but forming a larger mound of foliage and blooming in late summer

'Island Charm': {1997r, G. Rasmussen & A. Malloy; 'Flamboyant' sdlg} 10" by 22" md of white-centered, gr-mgd lvs, 4 1/4" by 3 1/8", wi purple red petioles; pale purple fls in July on 18" sc; a striking, v attractive, low md of center-variegated foliage; sported to 'Pink Panther' {1998r, A. Malloy; lvs green-mgd wi a white & green-streaked center}

'Joyce Trott': {1988r, K. Vaughn; 'Flamboyant' X 'Sum and Substance'} similar foliage to 'Cherry Berry' with creamy white-cntrd lvs but margins tend to be wider and blade is wavier; md 10" by 23"; lvs 5 1/2" by 3 1/2"

'Sitting Pretty': {1987r, P. Aden; 'Reiko' X 'Amy Aden'} 6" by 18" md; lvs yellow to creamy white-centered, green-mgd, 5 1/2" by 3" (7 vp); bright purple fls in late July; has sported 'Junior Miss' {1999r, R. Klehm} low md of dk green-centered, creamy yellow-mgd lvs

---

'Cherub'
key features: low, dense mound of heart-shaped, creamy white-margined foliage
mound size: 11" high by 30" wide

spacing: 24"
leaves: 5" long by 4 1/2" wide; 1/2" wide margins that are creamy yellow early, creamy white by mid-summer; center medium green with some gray-green streaking from margin; thin underside bloom; heart-shaped blade that is not cupped; slight corrugation; better than average substance; 8-9 vein pairs
flowers: early to late July; lavender; 14-18" scapes; forms seed pods
comments: The wide, creamy white margins on a heart-shaped leaf combined with the dense mound habit make 'Cherub' one of the best small-sized white-margined hostas. It can be used as an edging plant or as a specimen for the

front of the shaded border. 'Cherub' is another fine Bill and Eleanor Lachman hosta which they registered in 1989 as a hybrid of 'Crepe Suzette' X 'Blue Moon'.

seedlings, sports, and other related types:

'Crepe Suzette': {1986r, W. & E. Lachman; 'Flamboyant' sdlg} sm md of creamy white-mgd foliage; 6" by 18" md; 4 1/2" by 2 1/2" lvs (5 vp) wi a 1/2" mgn; v pale purple fls, mid-late July; parent of 'Cherub' and similar to it in many ways

'Karen': {1999r, R. Olson; sport of ('Crepe Suzette' X 'Blue Moon'); white-mgd, bl-green-centered lvs}

'Nordic Racer': {1999r, R. Olson; 'Crepe Suzette' X 'Blue Moon'; lvs white-mgd wi a streaked bl-green & white center}

'Tea and Crumpets': Bill & Eleanor Lachman plant introduced for sale in the 1996 Hatfield Gardens catalog as a hybrid of "81-9-2" X 'Crepe Suzette'; small mound of cupped, white-margined foliage; margins change from yellow to creamy white; sported to 'Champagne and Caviar' {1999r, C. Helsley; center of lf streaked gr & white; creamy wh mgn}

other similar types:

'Heartsong'

'Moon River'

'Pilgrim': {1997r, G. Rasmussen & A. Malloy; 'Flamboyant' hybrid} low, dense md of green-centered foliage with wide margins that change from yellow to creamy white during the season

---

'Christmas Tree'

key features: medium-large mound of rounded, white-margined leaves; purple seed pods

mound size: 23" high by 56" wide

spacing: 36-48"

leaves: 9 3/4" long by 8 3/4" wide; dark green center with a 1/8-3/8" margin that changes from yellow in spring to creamy white by early summer; margins occasionally streak into the center of the leaf; thin underside bloom; blade broadly oblong-ovate with a deeply lobed base; moderately corrugated; good substance; 11-12 vein pairs

flowers: late June to late July; medium lavender color; 2 3/16" long by 1 1/2" wide; scapes 30-36" high; many seed pods develop, turning reddish purple by mid-August

comments: For almost fifteen years, 'Christmas Tree' has been widely grown and highly respected by nurserymen and hosta collectors. It offers durable, white-margined foliage that becomes a dense mound in a fairly short period of time. An often overlooked ornamental feature is the red color that the numerous seed pods develop by late summer.

'Christmas Tree' is a product of Kevin Vaughn's hybridizing program ('Frances Williams' X 'Beatrice') that Mildred Seaver raised and registered in 1982. There has been some speculation that the original 'Christmas Tree' was a streaked plant (like 'Christmas Tree Gala'). I had a chance to examine the registration for 'Christmas Tree' at the registrar's office in 1983. It stated that its leaves were "Green with very narrow yellow hit or miss edge. Young divisions have faint yellowish streaks". Draw your own conclusion.

seedlings, sports, and other related types:

'Christmas Gold': med-sized md of round, gold foliage; sport of 'Christmas Tree'; from Mildred Seaver

'Christmas Tree Gala': sport of 'Christmas Tree' with streaks throughout the leaf; no white margin; somewhat variable ranging from completely streaked & mottled to streaked wi a gr mgn; have seen in several gardens and is offered by some nurseries; good breeding plant

'Kevin Vaughn': sport of 'Christmas Tree' with the reverse leaf color pattern, i.e. white center, green margin; margin tends to streak into the center of the lf; named and introduced by Bill and Eleanor Lachman; attractive but have only seen in a leaf show (a form of 'Christmas Tree Gala' exists that appears to be the same)

'Sea Mist': sdlg of 'Christmas Tree' from Mildred Seaver; 16" by 38" md of moderately corrug lvs, 9" by 7 1/2" (16 vp), pale green-mgd wi a sl streaked, chartreuse center; fls on 30" scapes in late June-July

'Showboat': {1993r, W. & E. Lachman; 'Christmas Tree' X "81-9"} med-lg md of 9" by 6 1/2" lvs (13 vp) wi a wavy, 1" wide margin that changes from yellow to creamy white; lf center dk green; lav fls on 23" sc in July; outstanding

117

'Southern Pride': {1986r, N. Suggs; 'Fascination' X 'Christmas Tree'; light green lvs} rarely grown

other similar types:

'Grand Master': {1986r, P. Aden; hybrid of two sdlgs} broadly oblong-ovate, white-margined leaves; md 24" by 58"; lvs 10" by 7 1/2"; lav fls in July; red seed pods; very close to 'Christmas Tree'

'Citation'
key features: medium-sized mound of apple green-centered, creamy-margined leaves
mound size: 17" high by 38" wide

spacing: 24-30"
leaves: 7 1/2" long by 5 3/4" wide; 1/4" to 1" margin that changes from creamy yellow to white; chartreuse center turns pale green; thin underside bloom; ovate to elliptic-ovate blade shape that is slightly wavy at maturity; when young blade narrowly elliptic and noticeably twisted and wavy; smooth texture; average substance; 11-13, deeply impressed vein pairs

flowers: mid-July into August; pale lavender color; 2" long by 1" wide; 22" scapes

comments: 'Citation' belongs to the class of hostas that change dramatically as they mature. As a juvenile plant, the intense waviness dominates the relatively narrow leaves, and that seems to accentuate its multi-colored character. With maturity, the waviness almost totally disappears and the leaves broaden considerably. Still, 'Citation' is worth growing based upon its interesting seasonal color changes and dense mound appearance.

Paul Aden registered 'Citation' in 1980 as a hybrid of 'Vicki Aden' X a sibling. It achieved a fair amount of popularity in the mid-1980's but is becoming harder to find.

seedlings, sports, and other related types:
'Excitation': {1988r, P. Aden; 'Citation' sport}18" by 48"
    md; 9" by 6" lvs that change from chartreuse to med
    green & are slightly wavy at maturity; average-looking
other similar types:
'Crested Surf', 'Saint Elmo's Fire'

'City Lights'
key features: large mound of luminescent, golden
foliage; slug-resistant
mound size: 27" high by 55" wide

spacing: 36-48"
leaves: 12 1/4" long by 9" wide; very bright gold color that
almost glistens; moderate bloom covers the top (early in the
season) and underside surfaces; broadly ovate shape with a
heart-shaped base; can be cupped; heavily corrugated; thick
substance; 15-16 vein pairs
flowers: late June into mid-July; near-white (with a pale
lavender midrib); 2 1/2" long by 1 1/2" wide; in moderately
dense clusters on 31" scapes; funnel shape that is more open
than most Sieboldianas; sets seed well
comments: The aptly named 'City Lights' offers satiny
golden foliage that can brighten almost any shaded landscape. The good substance and attractive flowers also add to
its garden value. Simply put, it is one of the best gold-
leaved Sieboldiana-type hostas.

It was registered by Paul Aden in 1978 as a hybrid
between 'White Vision' X 'Golden Prayers'.
seedlings, sports, and other related types:
'Peedee Dew Catcher': {1992r, U. Syre-Herz; 'City Lights'
    X 'Bold Ruffles'} 18" by 57" md of heavily corrugated,
    thick-substanced, gold lvs 11" by 8 1/2" (17 vp);

changes from chartreuse to gold; has sported to 'Dippity Dew', which has green-centered, gold-mgd leaves {1999r, J. Schwarz}

other similar types:
'Aspen Gold', 'Gold Cup', 'Golden Rajah', 'Golden Waffles', 'King Tut', 'White Vision', 'Zounds'

Hosta clausa (Tsubomi Giboshi)
key features: spreading mound of green foliage; closed, purple flowers
mound size: 19" high by 45" wide (to 103" wide or more)

spacing: 48"
leaves: 7 1/2" long by 3 1/8" wide; dark green; shiny top and underside surfaces; narrowly ovate to elliptic blade; slightly wavy margins; no corrugation; intense red-purple dots on the petioles; average substance; 6-7 vein pairs
flowers: August 1 to 31; dark purple buds that remain closed until they drop; 1 7/8" long; scapes 30-44" high with purple-red dots; 22 scapes on one 18" by 46" clump; as many as 52 buds per scape; does not form seed pods
comments: At the peak of "bloom" in August, a mature planting of *Hosta clausa* can be quite striking. The effect is produced by the large numbers of scapes bearing many, bright purple buds over the spreading mound of dark green foliage. Each flower develops normally until the time of opening, then gradually droops and falls off after a few days. Even if the flowers are artificially opened and pollinated, they do not form pods. Bob Savory, however, used *H. clausa* as the pollen parent for 'Purple Lady Finger' which also has closed, purple flowers.

Though *Hosta clausa* is unusual and intriguing because of its flowering habits, its rhizomatous nature makes it a premier ground cover. One planting that I observed reached 103" wide and was in no danger of stopping! New shoots typically stretch 6-12" from the previous year's growth, but I've seen them as far away as 18" from the main clump.

Hosta clausa can be found growing wild in Korea, and is known as the Tsubomi Giboshi in Japan.

seedlings, sports, and other related types:

'Golden Arrow': {1996r, R. Herman; *H. clausa* sdlg; golden foliage}

'Livonia': {1997r by P. Ruh for G. Krossa, the originator} 14" high, rhizomatous md of shiny, dk green lvs, 6 1/4" by 2 1/2" (8 vp) wi red petioles; fls open normally, but close to *H. clausa* in foliage and rhizomatous nature

H. clausa 'Normalis': same as the species, except that the flowers open normally; known as Sakuhana Giboshi in Japan; md 20" by 54"; lvs 10" by 4 1/2"; bell-shaped, purple fls on 20-34" sc; readily forms seeds; not common

'Purple Lady Finger': {1982r, R. Savory} 16" by 45" md of narrowly elliptic green lvs, 7" by 1 1/2"; closed purple flowers in August-September on 24" scapes; overall appearance closely resembles *H. longissima* (In 1983 Bob told me that this was a hybrid of *H. longissima* X *H. clausa* and that the flowers reminded him of lady finger firecrackers.)

other similar types:

'Saishu Jima Closed': seedling of 'Saishu Jima' from Herb Benedict; dense md of wavy, narrow green foliage; 16" by 34" md; 4 1/2" by 1 3/4" lvs (3-4 vp); 2" long, med to dk purple fls in Aug that incompletely open; many scapes ranging from 28" to 41"; an intriguing plant worth growing

Hosta clavata (Ko Giboshi)
key features: small mound of narrow green foliage; flowers in September
mound size: 11" high by 24" wide

spacing: 18"
leaves: 5" long by 1 1/8" wide; dark green color; slightly shiny top; whitish shiny underside; narrowly elliptic blade shape; smooth texture; average substance; 4 deeply impressed vein pairs
flowers: August 31-September 15; purple with stripes; open funnel shape; 2" long by 1 3/4" wide; 14" scapes
comments: For a long time in the United States, a golden-leaved 'Subcrocea'-type plant was incorrectly grown under the name *Hosta clavata*. The true, green-leaved species was finally imported from reliable sources in Japan in the early 1990's. It roughly resembles *Hosta longissima* in leaf, mound appearance, and blooming season, though I have not compared flowers of the two side-by-side. Ornamentally it is average at best and its greatest use in the garden probably would be to feature its late season, purple flowers.

seedlings, sports, and other related types:
none

other similar types:
'Alma': {1995r by P. Ruh for G. Krossa, the originator} the golden-leaved plant long grown as *H. clavata* but not at all similar to it; still listed as such in some gardens; 8" by 20" md of br gold lvs, 5" by 1 7/8"; blade elliptic to narrowly ovate and thin-substanced wi occasional streaks of corrug; red-purple dots on petioles; fls in Aug on 28" sc; many seed pods develop

'Columbus Circle'

key features: medium-sized mound of creamy margined foliage
mound size: 17" high by 42" wide

spacing: 30-36"

leaves: 8 1/2" long by 5 3/4" wide; 1/4" to 1/2" wide margin that changes from yellow to creamy white during the season; center medium to dark green; thin underside bloom; blade ovate and slightly wavy; slight to moderate corrugation at maturity (smooth when young); slightly better than average substance; 11-12 vein pairs

flowers: mid-July into August; very pale lavender; 2 1/4" long by 1 1/2" wide; funnel shape; sturdy scapes, 32" high

comments: 'Columbus Circle' forms a moderately dense mound of foliage. The leaf margins change from yellow to creamy white by mid-summer, especially in bright light. The very pale lavender, almost white, flowers have a "Fortunei" look to them and are not especially decorative.

'Columbus Circle' is an introduction of Iron Gate Gardens.

seedlings, sports, and other related types:
none

other similar types:
'Bold Edger', 'Crusader', 'Leola Fraim'

'Coquette'

key features: medium-sized mound of white-margined foliage

mound size: 17" high by 42" wide

spacing: 36"

leaves: 7 1/4" long by 4 1/4" wide; 1/4" wide, creamy white margin; medium green center; very shiny underside; elliptic to ovate blade shape; moderately corrugated; average substance; 8 vein pairs

flowers: early to late August; medium purple color; dark purple buds; 3 1/8" long by 1" wide; long, narrow funnel shape; scapes 31-33" high

comments: 'Coquette' gives the appearance of being a 'Decorata' look-alike, but was registered by Herb Benedict in 1987 as a selfed seedling of 'Neat Splash'. The long, funnel-shaped, purple flowers make a nice show in late summer.

seedlings, sports, and other related types:

'Scooter': {1990r, R. & D. Benedict; 'Yellow Splash' sdlg} med-sized md; 6 1/2" by 4" (7 vp) lvs with very wide (3/8" to 5/8"), creamy white mgns & a green center; br purple fls, late July into August

other similar types:

'Abiqua Delight', 'Bold Edger', 'Bold Ribbons', 'Cordelia', 'Crested Surf', 'Decorata', 'Don Stevens', 'Ground Master', 'Neat Splash Rim'

'Cordelia'

key features: medium-sized mound of white-margined foliage; deep purple flowers

mound size: 14" high by 36" wide

spacing: 24"

leaves: 6 1/2" long by 3" wide; shiny, dark green center; creamy white (creamy yellow early) margin that is irregularly wavy; narrowly ovate shape; little or no corrugation; average substance; 7 vein pairs

flowers: mid-July into mid-August; very deep purple; 2 3/4" long; funnel-shaped; scapes 27" high

comments:

The fairly dense mound of white-margined foliage is reason enough to grow this variety, but the vivid purple flowers are really what makes 'Cordelia' stand out. It was registered in 1991 by Bob (Robert) Kuk as an open-pollinated seedling of 'Neat Splash'.

seedlings, sports, and other related types:

none listed

other similar types:

'Bold Ribbons', 'Coquette', 'Don Stevens', 'Ground Master', 'Little Bo Peep', 'Queen Josephine', 'Scooter'

'Crested Surf'

key features: dense mound of rippled, white-margined foliage; seasonal color changes

mound size: 16" high by 40" wide

spacing: 24-30"

leaves: 6" long by 2 1/2" wide; 1/8" wide, rippled margin that changes from gold to creamy white; center changes from gold to medium green by mid-summer; elliptic to elliptic-ovate blade shape; smooth texture; petiole neatly rippled along whole length, especially when juvenile, less at maturity; average substance; 7-8 vein pairs

flowers: early to late August; medium purple color; dark purple buds; 3" long by 1 1/4" wide; many reddish purple pods form

comments: Originally touted for its rippled petioles, the best ornamental feature of 'Crested Surf' lies in the foliage color which undergoes significant seasonal changes. When in an active phase of growth, it is possible to have gold-centered and green-centered (both with white margins) leaves at the same time. 'Crested Surf' has a fast growth rate which lends itself to usage as ground cover.

The rippled petioles of 'Crested Surf' were the sensation of the 1990 AHS convention leaf show. Leaves entered in that show took two major awards including the President's Exhibitor Trophy, the top honor. Herb and Dorothy Benedict registered 'Crested Surf' in 1990 as a selfed seedling of 'Neat Splash'.

seedlings, sports, and other related types:

'Fire Island': {1998r, W. Brincka; *H. longipes hypoglauca* X 'Crested Surf'; greenish yellow foliage}

'Locomotion': {1993r, Belle Gardens; 'Crested Surf' X 'Bold Ruffles'; intensely blue-green foliage}

other similar types:
'Citation', 'Mentor Gold', 'Saint Elmo's Fire', 'Stiletto'

'Crispula'
(Whiterim Plantainlily; Sazanami Giboshi)
key features: large mound of white-margined foliage; tall scapes of whitish flowers
mound size: 25" high by 54" wide

---

spacing: 36"
leaves: 11 1/2" long by 6 1/2" wide; 1/4" to 5/8" wide, white margins surround and, occasionally, streak into the medium green center; deep gold fall color in early October; slightly shiny underside; narrowly ovate shape with a rounded base and long, narrow tip that twists 90 degrees; irregular, but noticeable, marginal rippling; slight corrugation; slightly

better than average substance; 9-11 vein pairs; buds emerge early in the spring, showing white margins as soon as the leaves break out of the bud scales

flowers: July 1 to 26; very pale lavender with a whitish throat; 2 1/4" long by 1 5/8" wide; funnel-shaped; one to four open per scape each day; scapes 28-45" high; eight scapes with 29 to 38 buds per scape on one mature clump; scapes droop due to extensive seed pod development; seed pods measure 1" by 1/4" at maturity

comments: 'Crispula' makes an imposing, large mound of white-margined foliage that can be effectively used as a ground cover or a specimen. The distinct, white margins look good from April (when the buds emerge from the soil) into October when the attractive gold fall color develops. The almost white flowers emanate from the same "flower-like" scape bud typical of *Hosta montana*. I have always been able to distinguish it from other white-margined hostas through a combination of characteristics. First, the leaf tip twists about 90 degrees and the leaf margins have many, slight, irregular ripples. The shiny leaf underside and the *H. montana*-like flowers on 3-4' scapes also help in identification. I've seen this plant being grown under a variety of names including *Hosta montana albo-marginata* in Japan and as 'Dr. Jamison Harrison', *H. fortunei* 'Marginato-alba', and *Hosta marginato-alba* in the U.S. Some plants being sold as 'Fortunei Albomarginata', as well, are actually 'Crispula'.

Long considered a species (*Hosta crispula*) and still labelled as such in many gardens, it has been relegated to cultivar status, i.e. 'Crispula' (Schmid, 1991).

Several green-leaved plants that are either seedlings of 'Crispula' or look very similar to 'Crispula Viridis' have been introduced. All become a large mound of green foliage and most exhibit the same curved leaf tip and marginal rippling typical of 'Crispula'. This group includes five registered cultivars from Eunice Fisher, 'Daily Joy' {1973r}, 'Eunice Fisher' {1985r}, 'Great Desire' {1973r}, 'Greenwood' {1997r}, and 'Unique' {1997r}, plus 'Maui Hana' {1991r, W. Vaughn} and 'Woodland Green' {1990r, Simpers-Ruh}.

seedlings, sports, and other related types:

'Crispula Lutescens': yellow splotched lvs in spring; not especially attractive; spots may be viral in origin, though there is still some debate about this

'Crispula Viridis': the same as 'Crispula' except for all-green lvs; formerly *H. crispula viridis*

'Dewline': Chet Tompkins plant that is very similar to 'Crispula' in foliage and flower

'Lucy's Crinkles': {1991r, P. Banyai; 'Crispula' sdlg; dull, dark green foliage}

'Minuet': {1990r, R. Kuk; 'Crispula' sport} slightly smaller form but not dwarf; lvs 10" by 6 1/4" (10 vp) wi a 1/4", white margin

other similar types:

'Snow Crust', *H. montana* 'Mountain Snow'

'Crusader'

key features: dense, medium-sized mound of white-margined foliage; good flower effect

mound size: 18" high by 42" wide

spacing: 36"

leaves: 6 1/2" long by 5 1/2" wide; 1/8" to 1/4" wide margin, creamy yellow, changing to white; dark green center; thin underside bloom; broadly ovate blade; slightly wavy margins; slightly corrugated at maturity; good substance; 9-11 vein pairs

flowers: early to late August; medium lavender; 2" long; 24-32" scapes

comments:

'Crusader' ranks as one of the top white-margined cultivars for its foliage, excellent show of flowers, and good growth rate. Bill and Eleanor Lachman registered this hybrid of ('Resonance' X a seedling) X 'Halcyon' in 1989. It was introduced for sale by Hatfield Gardens in 1990 and has been widely propagated since.

seedlings, sports, and other related types:

An unnamed, all-green sport is known.

other similar types:

'Gay Blade', 'Tambourine'

'Cynthia'

key features: unusual gold blotches cover the leaves in spring, green later; large mound
mound size: 28" high by 67" wide

spacing: 48"

leaves: 12" long by 8 5/8" wide; green with large, chartreuse-blotched sections in spring, becoming all-green by mid-June; ovate shape with a rounded base and a long, distinct, curved tip; 10-12 distinct marginal ripples; slight to moderate corrugation; slightly better than average substance; 15 vein pairs

flowers: June 15 to July 7; pale lavender color with petal margins partially colored white; 2 5/8" long by 1 5/8" wide; funnel-shaped; 37" scapes tend to droop near the end of flowering due to weight of many developing seed pods

comments: As a green-leaved plant in mid-summer, 'Cynthia' is an attractive mound of large, piecrust-edged foliage that can be a useful background plant in the shaded garden. Step back about six weeks and 'Cynthia' stands as the center of attention. The unusually splotched foliage makes it either one of the most beautiful hostas ever developed or something that induces itching. This characteristic is not caused by a virus, but is a genetic trait that can be passed on to seedlings. Whatever your view of 'Cynthia', it does add interest to the spring garden.

Chet Tompkins of Canby, Oregon registered 'Cynthia' in 1984 as a cross of two seedlings. He wrote extensively about the interesting origins of 'Cynthia' and other Tompkins (from Chet and his mother, Cynthia) plants in *The American Hosta Society Bulletin* (Tompkins, 1984).

seedlings, sports, and other related types:

'Laella': a sibling to 'Cynthia' with similar splotchy colored foliage; rippled margins; from Chet Tompkins; have only seen in Chet's garden

'Toltec Idol': sdlg of 'Cynthia' wi attractive center variegation in spring; from Chet Tompkins

other similar types:

'Freckles': long-standing cultivar which has yellow splotches in spring, green thereafter; Sieboldiana-type; 26" by 63" md, 13" by 10" lvs; whitish fls in June

'Green Spot': {1998r by P. Ruh for E. Fisher} sport of 'Aureafolia' (now 'Starker Yellow Leaf'); v similar in seasonal foliage colors, mound habit, and flowers to 'Cynthia'; md 33" by 63" wi 12 1/8" by 8 1/8" lvs that are splotched and speckled in spring, green by mid-summer; pale lav fls on 37" sc in July

'Little Cyn': {1998r, R. Duback; unknown parentage} unusual splotchy green and yellow foliage that shows similarities to 'Cynthia'

'Starker Yellow Leaf':{1989r by P. Ruh for C. Starker} developed in the 1940's; formerly 'Starker Aureafolia' and 'Aureafolia'; 27" by 53" md of foliage that changes from gold-centered, green-margined in spring to deep green by mid-summer; lvs 13 1/2" by 9 3/4" (15-16 vp); lav fls in July on 42" sc; fertile; one of the first American cultivars, but now rarely grown

'Wolcott' (formerly 'Stone's Fantasy'): {1982r, Piedmont Gardens; *H. sieboldiana* sdlg} 30" by 61" md of foliage that is blotchy yellow when it first emerges; lvs 14 1/4" by 10 1/4"; pale lav fls on 44" sc, late June into mid-July; developed by David Stone

'Daybreak'

key features: wide mound of bright gold foliage; unusual, sprawling mound habit

mound size: 24" high by 60" wide

spacing: 48"

leaves: 14" long by 10 1/2" wide; brilliant, shiny gold color, even late in the season; thin underside bloom; ovate blade that is slightly wavy; smooth when young, slightly corrugated at maturity; good substance; 15-17 vein pairs

flowers: late July into August; lavender color (with lighter petal margins); 2" long by 1 1/4" wide; clustered at the end of 34" long scapes that tend to droop and lie in the foliage; many seed pods develop

comments: The brilliant gold foliage and wide-spreading, ground-hugging growth habit make 'Daybreak' invaluable as a ground cover, specimen, or background plant. I have not seen this plant "burn" as golden Sieboldianas often do, and it certainly competes with 'Sum and Substance' and 'Solar Flare' for the honor of "best big gold".

'Daybreak' is another outstanding introduction from Paul Aden who registered it in 1986 as a sport of a Japanese seedling of unknown origin.

seedlings, sports, and other related types:

'Day's End': {1999r, M. Zilis} sport of 'Daybreak'; lvs, 15" by 11", green-centered wi a 3/8" gold mgn; introduced for sale in 2000 by Q & Z N

'Night Shift': {1991r, D. Savory; 'Daybreak' sport; gold-centered, green-mgd lvs}

other similar types:

'Solar Flare', 'Sum and Substance'

'Decorata' (Otafuku Giboshi)

key features: medium-sized mound of white-margined foliage; rhizomatous; purple flowers

mound size: 15" high by 42" wide

spacing: 36"

leaves: 6 1/2" long by 4 1/2" wide; medium green center color with distinct, 1/4" wide, pure white margin; dull top surface, very shiny underside; oblong-ovate to broadly elliptic shape with a very slight tip and rounded base; no purple dots on petioles; slight corrugation; average substance; 6-7 vein pairs

flowers: July 31 to August 31; deep purple with a white

throat; semi-bell shape; 2 1/4" long by 1" wide; one to three open per scape per day; 33 scapes on one mature clump ranged from 12-31" high with most 22-28"; many, short, thick pods produce a nice winter effect

comments: As a landscape subject, 'Decorata' makes a good ground cover due to its rhizomatous nature. The white-margined foliage is attractive most of the growing season though slugs and/or direct sunlight can make it unsightly by late summer. The purple flowers are produced in great abundance in August and offer an attractive contrast to the variegated foliage. Seed pod formation is extensive.

The rhizomatous behavior of 'Decorata' is shared by only a few other hostas, the most notable being *Hosta clausa*. I once dug up an 11-year old clump of 'Decorata' (13 1/2" high by 44" wide) and found 56 divisions connected by a network of underground rhizomes. Two or three shoots were clustered at the end of each rhizome that ranged from 1/4" to 3/8" in diameter and were as much as 6" long. New rhizomes extended as branches, starting about 1/2" below the older ones. The roots grew as clusters along the rhizome in association with shoots or buds. For propagation purposes, clusters of shoots can easily be separated from the clump and replanted.

133

For many years 'Decorata' was known as 'Thomas Hogg' and, in fact, my first purchase of this plant was under this name. Evidently Thomas Hogg, the person, sent this plant to the U.S. from Japan and somehow his name was affixed to the plant. He also sent hostas to England where the name 'Thomas Hogg' was used for 'Undulata Albomarginata' until recently.

Maekawa (1973) listed 'Decorata' as a species, *Hosta decorata*, found in a garden on Honshu Island. Being only found in cultivation led Schmid (1991) to relegate this plant to cultivar status, hence the name 'Decorata'.

seedlings, sports, and other related types:

'Betsy King': {1986r by the AHS for F. Williams} 'Decorata' sdlg; named for Frances Williams' great-great-grandmother (Williams, 1959b); introduced for sale in 1960 by Fairmount Gardens; 15" by 40" md of med to dk gr lvs, 5 1/2" by 3 1/8" (5-6 vp); bell-shaped, deep purple fls on 18-25" sc, August; rhizomatous growth habit; similar to 'Decorata Normalis'; not widely grown

'Decorata Normalis': green-leaved version of 'Decorata' listed as *Hosta decorata* f. *normalis* (Maekawa, 1973)

'Goddess of Athena': {1987r, Kuk's Forest; selfed sdlg of 'Decorata'} med-sized md of lvs with wider, creamier, and more distinct, white margins than 'Decorata' **(see page 184)**

'Golden Plum': {1997r by P. Ruh for Lewis & A. Summers} 'Decorata'-type lvs that are gold early, green by mid-summer; bell-shaped med purple fls in Aug on 25" sc; probably a 'Decorata' sdlg

'Jingle Bells': {1986r by the AHS for V. Grapes} probably a hybrid of 'Decorata' X *H. sieboldii*; 17" by 39" md of dk green lvs, 7" by 3"; semi-bell-shaped, deep purple fls on 38" sc fr mid-Aug into Sept; developed before 1969; rarely grown anymore; like 'Decorata' in fl, *H. sieboldii spathulata* in foliage

'Kathleen': {1986r, C. Williams for F. Williams; possibly a hybrid of 'Fortunei' X 'Decorata'} 17" by 30", spreading md of green lvs, 6 1/2" by 4" (8 vp); lav fls in August; of historical interest

'Patrician': {1999r, E. Skrocki & T. Avent; parentage unknown} 15" by 44" md of green-centered, yellow-mgd lvs, 6" by 2 1/2" (5-6 vp); semi-bell-shaped purple fls on 26" sc in August that are very close to 'Decorata'; acts like a yellow-mgd version of 'Decorata'

other similar types:

'Coquette', 'First Impressions'

'Diamond Tiara'

key features: dense, medium-sized mound of white-margined foliage; 'Golden Tiara' sport

mound size: 18" high by 42" wide

spacing: 36"

leaves: 5 1/4" long by 4" wide; 1/16" to 7/16" wide, white margin, medium green center; dull top surface, shiny underside; ovate blade shape; slightly corrugated; slightly wavy margins; average substance; 6-7 vein pairs

flowers: mid-July into early August; pale purple in deep shade, bright purple with more light; 2 1/8" long by 1 1/4" wide; many 30"

scapes; sparse pod formation; will rebloom in August-September if scapes cut down right after flowering

comments: In viewing 'Diamond Tiara' in numerous gardens over the years, I have come to appreciate its value more and more. In fact it may be the most underrated plant of the whole "Tiara" series. It rapidly grows into a neat, dense mound of attractively variegated foliage. The contrast between the white margin and green center is especially striking. It has the typically good flowering habits of 'Golden Tiara' (many purple flowers neatly spaced over the foliage mound; can rebloom) and can be used in a variety of ways in the landscape.

I registered 'Diamond Tiara' as a sport of 'Golden Tiara' in 1985.

seedlings, sports, and other related types:

'Platinum Tiara': white-margined, gold-centered sport of 'Golden Scepter' **(see page 350)**

'Grand Prize': {1998r, Walters Gardens; 'Grand Tiara' sport; lvs med gr wi a pale ylw mgn that turns creamy white}

other similar types:

'Heartsong', 'Little White Lines', 'Moon River', 'Pilgrim'

'Donahue Piecrust'

key features: large mound of distinctly rippled, green foliage; best piecrust breeding plant

mound size: 28" high by 60" wide

spacing: 48"

leaves: 11 1/2" long by 7 1/2" wide; medium to dark green; slightly shiny top; ovate blade shape; 20 or more regular ripples along margin; long, thin tip that can be twisted 180 degrees; a few streaks of corrugation at maturity; good substance; 13-14 vein pairs

flowers: very late June into late July; pale lavender color; whitish bracts; scapes 40" high; many seed pods develop

comments: 'Donahue Piecrust' has the reputation of being the best parent for "piecrust" hostas. A very high percentage of its seedlings inherit the genetic trait for rippled margins. The regular marginal ripples are very prominent along the large, dark green leaves, making it an interesting specimen plant in the shaded garden.

'Donahue Piecrust' is a long-standing cultivar developed by the late Thomas Donahue of Massachusetts. It was registered in 1999 by Peter Ruh. Though its origins are not clear, it is probably a descendant of 'Fortunei Gigantea'.

seedlings, sports, and other related types:

'Lunatic Fringe': sdlg of 'Donahue Piecrust' from Mildred Seaver; unusual marginal tears; a leaf displayed at the 1991 AHS leaf show in NC created a lot of discussion; characteristic holds according to some reports

'Sea Frolic': 'Donahue Piecrust' sdlg from Mildred Seaver; 24" by 53" md of intensely rippled, wavy, green lvs, 13" by 9"; widely admired in the landscape & as a breeding plant

'Swirling Hearts': M. Zilis hybrid of 'Donahue Piecrust' X 'Heartleaf' from 1986; 27" by 81" md of dark green lvs.

136

11" by 7 5/8" (15-16 vp); slight marginal rippling; twisted tip much like 'Donahue Piecrust'; introduced for sale in 1997

'Trill': introduced in the 1993 Hatfield Gardens catalog as a hybrid of 'Donahue Piecrust' X 'Green Piecrust' from Kevin Vaughn; heavily rippled green lvs, 11 1/2" by 6 1/8" (12 vp); pale lav fls in July; fast growth rate

other similar types:
'Fortunei Gigantea', 'Green Piecrust', 'Green Ripples', 'Mesa Fringe', 'Ruffles', 'Sea Drift'

'Dorset Blue'
key features: small, dense mound of slug-resistant, blue foliage; a Tardiana
mound size: 10" high by 24" wide (up to 12" by 32")

spacing: 18"
leaves: 5 1/4" long by 4" wide; intense blue-green color; thick underside bloom; broadly ovate blade shape; moderately cupped; moderate to heavy corrugation with maturity; thick substance; 11-12 vein pairs
flowers: very pale lavender; mid to late August; in dense clusters on 16" scapes; seed pods develop
comments: Besides being an outstanding small, blue-leaved hosta, 'Dorset Blue' has also proven to be an excellent parent. Herb Benedict utilized it in developing such hostas as 'Blue Ice' and 'Blue Chip'. The only negative perhaps is its very slow growth rate, so fertilizer and water are necessary to give this plant a jump start.

'Dorset Blue' is a second generation Tardiana (TF 2 x 4). Paul Aden registered it for Eric Smith, the originator, in 1977.

seedlings, sports, and other related types:
'Blue Chip': {1997r, R. Benedict & R. Olson; selfed 'Dorset Blue' sdlg} thick, deep blue foliage; 9" by 18" md; 4" by 3 1/4" lvs (9 vp)

137

'Blue Clown': {1996r; R. & D. Benedict & J. & E. Stratton; selfed 'Dorset Blue' sdlg} 12" by 22" md of thick-substanced, blue-green lvs, 6" by 4 1/2" (10 vp); med lav fls, mid-July into Aug on 18" scapes

'Blue Ice': {1987r, R. Benedict, 'Dorset Blue' X 'Blue Moon'} sm md of deep blue lvs **(see page 91)**

'Blue Jay': {1987r, R. Benedict; selfed 'Dorset Blue' sdlg} deep blue foliage; 16" by 35" md; 6" by 4" lvs (11 vp)

'Salute': {1995r, R. & D. Benedict as a selfed 'Dorset Blue' F4 sdlg} semi-upright mound of narrow, wavy, blue foliage; 15" high md; 8" by 4 1/4" lvs (10 vp); pale lav fls, mid-August into Sept on 22" long, drooping scapes; acts more like a hybrid of *H. kikutii leuconata* X 'Tardiflora'

'Winsome Blue': Tardiana-type from Herb Benedict; very compact mound of deep blue, slug-resistant foliage; 6" by 10" md; 4" by 3 1/2" lvs (11 vp)

'Wolverine': {1995r, J & J Wilkins; sport of (sdlg X 'Dorset Blue')} 18" by 34" md; 7" by 3" lvs (8 vp) are gold-mgd (1/4" wide) wi a bl-green center; outstanding growth rate; v attractive contrast betw mgn & center of leaf; sported to all-blue 'Curtain Call' {1998r, J. Wilkins}

other similar types:

'Blue Hearts', 'Blue Moon'

'El Capitan'

key features: large mound of yellow-margined foliage
mound size: 26" high by 50" wide

spacing: 36"

leaves: 9" long by 7 1/2" wide; 1/2" to 3/4" wide, yellowish gold margin, deep green center; thick underside bloom; blade ovate with slightly wavy margins; moderately corrugated; good substance; 12 vein pairs

flowers: late July into mid-August; medium lavender; 2 1/4" long by 1 1/4" wide; scapes up to 40" high

comments: At maturity 'El Capitan' makes an impressive mound of yellow-edged foliage that can be used as a background plant, specimen or ground cover. It comes out of the breeding program of Bill and Eleanor Lachman who registered it in 1987 as a hybrid of a 'Beatrice' seedling X a seedling. Even with 'Beatrice' in its background, 'El Capitan' has excellent substance and attractive flowering, and becomes a fairly large mound.

seedlings, sports, and other related types:
none listed

other similar types:
'Carnival', 'Celebrity', 'Standing Ovation'

139

'Elvis Lives'

key features: semi-upright, medium-sized mound of wavy, blue-green foliage

mound size: 18" high by 40" wide (up to 25" by 72")

spacing: 30"

leaves: 9" long by 4 3/4" wide; bluish green into mid-summer, then dark green; moderate underside bloom; narrowly ovate blade; moderately rippled along the margin; smooth texture; average substance; 9-11 vein pairs

flowers: mid-July into early August; pale purple; slightly inflated funnel shape; 29" scapes that are covered with a thin bloom

comments: Upon introduction 'Elvis Lives' received a great deal of interest from many based upon its unusual name. Over time, however, it has earned respect for its attractive vase-shaped mound habit, rippled blue foliage, and excellent growth rate.

Tony Avent registered 'Elvis Lives' in 1995 as a hybrid of 'Peter Pan' X 'Green Fountain'.

seedlings, sports, and other related types:
none listed

other similar types:
'Twilight Time': a blue-leaved 'Spritzer'-type from Greg Johnson of Iowa; rippled blue lvs, 7" by 2 1/2"

'Embroidery'

key features: low, wide mound of green foliage; corrugated medium green margin, smoother in the lighter green center creating an "embroidered" effect

mound size: 15" high by 30" wide

spacing: 30"

leaves: 10 1/2" long by 8 1/2" wide; in spring margins slightly darker than the center into which it often streaks; center turns medium green by mid-June; very unruly with the leaf margins twisted and corrugated in streaks while the leaf center (usually) remains smooth except for an occasional streak of corrugation; purple dots on petioles; slightly shiny top, thin underside bloom; better than average substance; 12 vein pairs

flowers: late July into mid-August; near-white (a faint purple line down each petal midrib); 2 3/8" long by 1 3/8" wide; 24" high scapes have a tendency to droop as flowering proceeds; no seed pod formation

comments: 'Embroidery' may be the quintessential collector's plant. Not only is it unique amongst hostas with its corrugated margin contrasting a relatively smooth, lighter green center, but it has proven difficult to accurately reproduce via tissue culture. The result is low supply and high demand which equals high prices. At one point a single plant commanded $400 or more. Propagation by division will probably remain the best means to increase the supply of 'Embroidery' for some time to come.

I first viewed this plant in Paul Aden's garden in 1983 and naively thought that something had crushed his specimen. Only later did I learn that that was the way it was supposed to look! It truly is unique among hosta cultivars and certainly can be "the" conversation piece of any shaded garden.

Paul Aden named and introduced this plant in the early 1980's.

seedlings, sports, and other related types:

'Green Velveteen': {1999r, R. Klehm; sport} "smooth-leaved" sport of 'Embroidery' that often results when it is propagated by tissue culture; md 27" by 68"; lvs 17" by 9 3/8" (12 vp); beautiful, large mound of smooth, green foliage, more useful than 'Embroidery' in the landscape; also sterile

other similar types:

'Emerald Necklace': {1994r, R. Kuk; mutation of a 'Tardi-flora' sdlg} much different from 'Embroidery' but possessing a similar pattern of dark green, marginal puckering and a creamy white center in spring that changes to green during the summer; 16" by 33" md; lvs 5 1/2" by 4" (7-9 vp); lf center 1 1/2" wide; 2" long, med purple fls on scapes up to 47", late July into mid-Aug; many seed pods; interesting and unusual plant

---

'Emerald Tiara'

key features: dense, medium-sized mound of gold-centered, green-margined foliage
mound size: 17" high by 35" wide

spacing: 30"
leaves: 4 3/8" long by 3 3/8" wide; 3/4" green margin, medium gold center; shiny underside; ovate blade that is slightly wavy; little or no corrugation; average substance; 7 vein pairs
flowers: mid-July into early August; pale to bright purple depending on light level; 2" long by 1" wide; scapes 20-30" high; some pod formation

comments: 'Emerald Tiara' was registered in 1988 by Walters Gardens as a sport of 'Golden Scepter' (which sported from 'Golden Tiara'). It ranks as one of the best in the "Tiara" series. It becomes a very dense mound of gold-centered, green-margined foliage that can really stand out if given one to two hours of direct sunlight per day. 'Emerald Tiara' has a good growth rate, perhaps only slightly slower than that of 'Golden Tiara' and faster than 'Golden Scepter'. I have seen it used effectively in gardens in combination with some of the other "Tiaras", but it can also be used as a specimen or as a ground cover.

seedlings, sports, and other related types:

'Emerald Scepter': t.c. sport of 'Golden Tiara' from my nursery (Q & Z N); named in 1991; 8" by 20" md of lvs wi a light green mgn & a gold center that can turn creamy white in bright light; differs from 'Emerald Tiara' in foliage colors, smaller size, and being less vigorous

'Green with Envy': dense, small (9 1/2" by 27") md of gold-centered, green-mgd lvs, 4" by 3" (6 vp); purple fls in July on 24" sc; a sport of 'Dawn' from England

'Topaz Tiara': {1998r, Walters Gardens; 'Grand Tiara' sport; yellow to greenish ylw-cntrd, green-mgd lvs} the equivalent of 'Emerald Tiara' in the 'Grand Tiara' series of sports

other similar types:

'Amy Elizabeth', 'Crown Prince', 'Enchantress', 'June Bug', 'Just So', 'Little Sunspot', 'Pooh Bear', 'Sweet Home Chicago', 'Wylde Green Cream'

'Emily Dickinson'

key features: dense, medium-sized mound of white-margined foliage; fragrant, purple flowers in August

mound size: 17" high by 40" wide

spacing: 30"

leaves: 7" long by 4 1/2" wide; 1/2" to 1" wide margin that changes from yellow to creamy white, medium green center; shiny underside; blade ovate and slightly wavy; smooth texture; average substance; 7-9 vein pairs

flowers: early to late August; medium purple; 2 1/2" long; fragrant; scapes to 30" high

comments: 'Emily Dickinson' offers a pleasing combination of white-margined foliage and fragrant, purple flowers that bloom in August. The Lachmans (Bill and Eleanor) registered it in 1987 as a hybrid of a 'Neat Splash' seedling X *Hosta plantaginea* and, like its parents, has a good growth rate. Hatfield Gardens introduced it for sale in 1990.

seedlings, sports, and other related types:

'Austin Dickinson': {1992r, W. & E. Lachman; 'Resonance' X *H. plantaginea*} med-sized md of white-margined (creamy yellow early), green-centered foliage; fragrant fls in late summer; similar to 'Emily Dickinson' in foliage and flower but 'Austin Dickinson' lvs tend to be rounder, less wavy and have a wider margin

other similar types:

'Lacy Belle'

'Fan Dance'
key features: medium-sized mound of gold-centered, green-margined foliage
mound size: 18" high by 36" wide

spacing: 30"
leaves: 7 3/4" long by 5 1/4" wide; thin (1/4" wide), dark green margin; center changes from light gold to creamy yellow; very shiny underside; blade ovate at maturity, more elliptic when juvenile; not wavy; slightly corrugated; average substance; 7-8 vein pairs
flowers: late July into mid-August; light purple with darker streaking on petals; 1 15/16" long by 1" wide; narrow funnel shape; bunched in the top 6" of 20-29" scapes
comments: I first viewed 'Fan Dance' in 1988 in the Benedict garden where it had sported from 'Dorothy'. At that time, Herb was debating its merits and actually considered "throwing it onto the mulch pile". I'm glad he didn't! 'Fan Dance' is impressive for its bright gold center that nicely contrasts with the thin, but dark green margin and makes an excellent specimen plant.

Herb Benedict registered this plant in 1987.
seedlings, sports, and other related types:
'Dorothy': {1986r by the AHS for F. Williams; 'Decorata' X 'Fortunei'} "mother plant" of 'Fan Dance'; rhizomatous, 20" by 44" md of dk green lvs, 7 3/4" by 5 1/2" (8-9 vp); flowering the same as 'Fan Dance'; a Frances Williams hybrid named in 1960 (Williams, 1960a) and introduced for sale by Fairmount Gardens in 1961 (Williams, 1961)
other similar types:
'Janet', 'Okay Dokey'

'Fantastic'
key features: large mound of heavily corrugated, unruly blue foliage; slug-resistant
mound size: 23" high by 50" wide (up to 27" by 56")

spacing: 48"

leaves: 12 1/2" long by 10 1/2" wide; bluish cast in spring, then dark green; thin underside bloom; broadly ovate to nearly rotund blade shape; blade irregularly puckered and creased, cupped upward or downward; intense corrugation magnifies unruly appearance; thick substance; 16-18 vein pairs

flowers: mid-June into early July; near-white color with a pale lavender midrib; 2" long by 1 1/8" wide; narrow funnel shape; 22-30" scapes, some under or just reaching the top of the foliage; seed pods develop

comments: 'Fantastic' ranks as the one of the most unruly, twisted-leaved hosta cultivars. The intense corrugation, creasing, and cupping combine to create the "unsettled" look that many find very attractive. 'Fantastic' shows *Hosta sieboldiana* characteristics in both foliage and flower. It was registered by Marge Soules in 1988 as an *H. sieboldiana* seedling.

seedlings, sports, and other related types:
none listed

other similar types:
'Bold Ruffles' **(see page 99)**

'Evelyn McCafferty': {1975r, A. Arett} lg md of unruly blue-green foliage; 28" by 47" md; 13 1/2" by 12" lvs that are also heavily corrugated; near-wh fls on 27" sc, late June into mid-July; the plant closest to 'Fantastic' in all respects; possibly a 'Tokudama' sdlg

'Lochness': {1988r, W. & E. Lachman; 'Sea Monster' X a sdlg} lg md of blue-green foliage; leaves also heavily corrugated and unruly; near-white fls, late June into July, in dense clusters; slug-resistant

---

'Fascination'
key features: medium-large mound of highly variable, streaked foliage; breeding plant
mound size: 18" high by 50" wide

spacing: 30"
leaves: 8" long by 6 3/4" wide; color variable from plant to plant, leaf to leaf; most streaked, showing a combination of chartreuse with large streaks of white, gold, and a yellow-green mosaic; some pale green-margined with a gold center that also may be streaked; moderate bloom on underside; ovate shape with a rounded base; slightly wavy margins; slight to moderate corrugation; average substance; 9-11 vein pairs
flowers: mid-July into early August; pale lavender color; 1 7/8" long by 1 3/8" wide; narrow funnel shape; 22" scapes; not especially ornamental; fertile
comments: At one time 'Fascination' could be found in many hosta collections, providing a splash of color. The true, streaked form, however, can only be maintained by constantly culling the off-color divisions that typically develop. Nowadays it has fallen out of favor with collectors in deference to newer, easier-to-maintain plants.

Its role as a pod parent in hybridizing, however, has been very important, owing to the high percentage of variegated seedlings that often result. Paul Aden introduced a number of variegated 'Fascination' seedlings during the 1980's including 'Amy Aden', 'Bravo', 'Fragrant Bouquet', 'Splish Splash', 'Sunshine Kid', and 'Whoopee'. More recently others have utilized 'Fascination' to produce such cultivars as 'Lakeside April Snow', 'Merry Sunshine', and 'Sally and Bob'. Additionally, some 'Fascination' sports have been named and probably supersede it in popularity.

'Fascination' was registered by Paul Aden in 1978 as a hybrid of 'Flamboyant' X 'High Fat Cream'.

seedlings, sports, and other related types:

'Amy Aden': {1980r, P. Aden; 'Fascination' X 'High Fat Cream'} low md; lvs strkd wi thin, ylw mgns; variable; lav fls in July on 17" sc

'Bravo': {1980r, P. Aden; 'Reversed' X 'Fascination'} 17" by 44" md of wh-mgd lvs (8" by 3"); leaf center varies from streaked and mottled to solid green

'Candle Glow': {1990r, Fairway Enterprises; 'Fascination' sdlg} 16" by 32" md of heavily streaked foliage; 6 1/2" by 4 1/4" lvs; lav fls on 30" sc, early to late July

'Color Accord': {1982r, P. Aden; 'Fascination' X a sibling} haven't seen

'Color Glory': {1980r, P. Aden; 'Fascination' X 'Intrigue'} registered plant does not match the description of the gold-centered Sieboldiana-type sold under this name

'Comeuppance': {1982r, P. Aden; 'Vicki Aden' X 'Fascination'} haven't seen

'Double Edge': {1982r, P. Aden; 'Flamboyant' X 'Fascination'} saw a slide of it in 1983

'Fascinator': {1989r, J. Wilkins & C. Owens; sport of 'Golden Fascination'} gold-cntrd, green-mgd lvs

'Fragrant Bouquet': {1982r, P. Aden; 'Fascination' X 'Fragrant Summer'} outstanding combination of variegated foliage and fragrant flowers **(see page 169)**

'Golden Fascination': {1986r, AHS} gold-leaved sport of 'Fascination'; 24" by 63" md, 9 3/4" by 7 1/4" lvs (12 vp); more vigorous and more widely grown than 'Fascination'

'High Fat Cream': {1976r, P. Aden; hybrid of two sdlgs} one of the parents of 'Fascination' with unstable foliage **(see page 225)**

'Intrigue': {1978r, P. Aden; 'Flamboyant' X 'High Fat Cream'} 20" by 40" md of highly variable foliage; some lvs green-mgd wi a creamy white center; rarely grown

'Lakeside April Snow': {1994r, M. Chastain; 'Fascination' X 'Lakeside Symphony'} lvs chartreuse wi creamy white margins

'Lakeside Cha Cha': {1994r, M. Chastain; 'Fascination' X *H. montana*; lvs lt gr wi a creamy wh mgn}

'Loleta Powell': {1980r, P. Aden; 'Fascination' X 'Intrigue'} med-sized md of highly variable, variegated foliage; not grown much anymore

'Love Joy': {1980r, P. Aden; 'Fascination' X a sibling}

med-sized md of white-mgd, gold-centered foliage; very rare

'Merry Sunshine': {1998r, E. Elslager; 'Fascination' X *H. hypoleuca*} green-cntrd, creamy yellow-mgd foliage; very attractive

'Sally and Bob': {1994r, C. Owens; 'William Lachman' X 'Fascination'} predominantly green foliage streaked throughout the center with white, yellow and mottled sections

'Southern Pride': {1986r, N. Suggs; 'Fascination' X 'Christmas Tree'} rarely grown

'Splish Splash': {1980r, P. Aden; 'Fascination' X 'Intrigue'} med-sized md of streaked foliage that varies from plant to plant; many lvs center-streaked and yellow-mgd; pale lav fls in July; has sported to 'Richland Surprise', a 17" by 36" md of gold-mgd, green-centered foliage (6 1/2" by 4 3/8") {1999r, V. Wade} & the green-lvd 'Richland Green Splish' {1999r, V. Wade}

'Sunshine Kid': {1980r, P. Aden; 'Fascination' X 'High Fat Cream'} neat sm md of gold-mgd, green-centered lvs; attractive, but rarely grown

'Whoopee': {1980r, P. Aden; 'Flamboyant' X 'Fascination'} med-sized md of heavily streaked foliage; highly variable from plant to plant; not grown much anymore

other similar types:

'Hoopla': medium-sized md of heavily streaked foliage; a Paul Aden introduction had some popularity in the early 1980's but now rarely grown; sports include:

> 'Good as Gold': med-sized md of gold foliage; widely grown
>
> 'Gaiety': {1986r, Paul Aden} gold-centered, white-mgd lvs, 9" by 5 1/2" (11 vp); 12" by 40" md; pale lav fls in July on 22" sc; widely grown

'Shenanigans': Paul Aden introduction from the early-1980's; 20" by 49" md of heavily streaked, highly variable foliage; lvs 9 3/8" by 7 1/2" (10-11 vp); pale lav fls in mid-July; tends to sport to numerous stable forms, esp wi white-margined, green-centered lvs; another rarity these days

Hosta fluctuans **(Kuronami Giboshi)**
key features: large mound of green foliage; lavender flowers on tall scapes; native to Japan
mound size: probably 31" high by 70" wide in cultivation, smaller in the wild

comments: For this plant the "Comments" section must come first.

I have never seen a verified specimen of this species in Japan and there is debate as to whether it can be found in the wild. Schmid (1991) indicated that it may be possible to find it in northern Japan. He questioned, however, whether 'Sagae' (long known as *Hosta fluctuans* 'Variegated' in the West) has any relation to *H. fluctuans*. He states "Its Western name is technically incorrect because its connection to *H. fluctuans* has not been definitely established" (Schmid, 1991, p. 49).

For several reasons, I do believe that 'Sagae' is a sport of *H. fluctuans*. First, Fumio Maekawa (1972) clearly describes *Hosta fluctuans* and shows two photos, both in and out of bloom. The flowering habits (tall scapes, flowers clustered in the upper portion of the scape, flower shape, drooping scape habit) and the foliage (shape, waviness, tip, underside, and mound habit) closely match what would be an all-green 'Sagae'. A major discrepancy seems to be the 9-10 vein pairs that Maekawa listed for *H. fluctuans*. Schmid (1991) also lists *H. fluctuans* as having 9-10 vein pairs, but also ascribes the same number to *H. fluctuans* 'Variegated' (= 'Sagae'). Over the years of extensive measurements I have found that mature leaves of 'Sagae' generally have 13 vein pairs. I discount any differences as simply being the result of Maekawa and Schmid using data from immature foliage. The size of leaves that Maekawa described for *H. fluctuans* (roughly 8-10" long by 4-7" wide) approximates the size of numerous leaves on large, but not fully grown plants that I have measured. For example in 1983 I measured a leaf of 'Sagae' in Mildred Seaver's garden at 9 1/4" long by 8 1/8" wide. This leaf had 9 vein pairs. Similarly an 8 3/4" by 7 1/2" leaf of 'Sagae' in a West Chicago, IL garden had 10 vein pairs. Other measurements of immature leaves at other sites reveal similar vein pair numbers. The leaf sizes that Schmid (1991) lists for both *H. fluctuans* (8-12" by 5-7") and 'Sagae' (8-12" by 5-8") fall into what I consider less than mature foliage. Mature 'Sagae' leaves actually range from 13" to 14" long by 10 1/4" to 11 1/4" wide in size and have 13 vein pairs.

seedlings, sports, and other related types:
'Sagae': the gold-margined "classic" that can also be listed
    as *Hosta fluctuans* 'Sagae' **(see page 376)**

other similar types:
'Green Sheen', 'Green Wedge', *H. nigrescens* 'Elatior'

'Formal Attire'

key features: large mound of foliage with very wide, creamy white margins
mound size: 26" high by 60" wide

spacing: 48-60"
leaves: 10 1/4" long by 8 1/2" wide; yellow to creamy white margin, up to 1" wide, medium to dark green center; broadly ovate blade with a deeply lobed base; moderately corrugated; somewhat wavy; better than average substance; 12 vein pairs
flowers: late July into mid-August; pale lavender; 2 1/2" long by 1 1/2" wide; slightly inflated funnel shape; scapes 36" high

comments: I have always thought 'Formal Attire' to be one of the most appropriately named hostas. The very thick creamy margins sharply contrast the green center and give it a distinctive appearance. Though the substance is not quite as thick as many Sieboldianas, that is secondary to the greatness of this plant. It becomes a large mound of foliage and can be effectively used in a variety of ways in the landscape including as a background plant, a specimen, or even as a large ground cover. Grow this plant!!!

'Formal Attire' was registered as a seedling of 'Breeder's Choice' X 'Frances Williams' in 1988 by Kevin Vaughn.

seedlings, sports, and other related types:
none listed

other similar types:
H. sieboldiana 'Northern Exposure', 'Robert Frost'

'Fortunei' (Fortune's Plantainlily)
key features: a "cultivated species" possessing characteristics shared by many introduced cultivars

---

comments: Despite being the common factor in a great number of cultivars, there is no single plant that can be labeled *Hosta* 'Fortunei'. In his 1954 monograph, Nils Hylander (1954) described *Hosta fortunei* as being a common plant in Sweden with five significant varieties (*H. fortunei* var. *stenantha, H. fortunei* var. *albopicta, H. fortunei* var. *rugosa, H. fortunei* var. *obscura, H. fortunei* var. *hyacinthina*), but nowhere does he delineate a separate *Hosta fortunei* plant. Its species designation was changed by Schmid (1991), who relegated *Hosta fortunei* and its varieties to cultivar status. Thus, *Hosta fortunei* became *Hosta* 'Fortunei', *H fortunei* var. *hyacinthina* became *H.* 'Fortunei Hyacinthina', etc. In any case, all of these plants possess certain similar characteristics that make the careful observer of hostas know a "Fortunei" when he or she sees one. It should be noted that 'Fortunei Gigantea', which Hylander (1954) described as *Hosta elata*, is not closely related to this group and is actually a type of *H. montana*.

Typical Fortunei traits are included in the following list.

Mound
(1) medium-large size (18-24" high by 40-50" wide)
(2) dense habit

Leaves
(3) 9-10" long by 6-7" wide
(4) ovate (to broadly ovate) blade shape
(5) thin underside bloom (often on top surface as well)
(6) limited or no corrugation
(7) average to better than average substance
(8) 9-10 vein pairs
(9) better than average sun-tolerance

Flowers
(10) open mid-July into August (northern Illinois)
(11) pale lavender color
(12) narrow funnel shape
(13) scapes well above the leaf mound

Other
(14) fast growth rate
(15) limited seed pod formation
(16) few viable seeds in the pods that do form
(17) readily mutate in gardens and tissue culture labs
(18) good landscaping plant

Many introduced cultivars also belong to the Fortunei group. Before the species name was ruled illegitimate, I always attached the name *Hosta fortunei* to the cultivar, e.g., *Hosta fortunei* 'Francee', *Hosta fortunei* 'Gold Standard', etc. Separate cultivars, other than the "Latinized" group (formerly Latin names converted to cultivars), should no longer have the name 'Fortunei' attached to it. For example, 'Aoki' and 'Francee' would be proper listings, not 'Fortunei Aoki' and 'Fortunei Francee'.

The so-called "Latinized" cultivars include:
'Fortunei Albomarginata': white-margined foliage
'Fortunei Albopicta': gold-centered leaves in spring; green thereafter; fertile form
'Fortunei Aurea': gold leaves in spring; green thereafter
'Fortunei Aureomarginata': gold-margined leaves
'Fortunei Hyacinthina': bluish green in spring; the source of many sports
'Fortunei Obscura': green leaves
'Fortunei Rugosa': green foliage that is heavily corrugated

'Fortunei Stenantha': green foliage
'Fortunei Viridis': green foliage; sport of 'Fortunei Albopicta'

Some of the cultivars belonging to the 'Fortunei' group include:
'Alaskan Halo', 'Antioch', 'Aoki', 'Aoki Variegated', 'Arctic Rim', 'Brenda's Beauty', 'Broad Band', 'Captain Kirk'. 'Carol', 'Chelsea Babe', 'Counter Point', 'Crowned Imperial', 'Emerald Crust', 'Fisher's Cream Edge', 'Francee', 'Gloriosa', 'Gold Standard', 'Granary Gold', 'Green Gold', 'Helen Field Fischer', 'Heliarc', 'Jade Beauty', 'Janet', 'Janet Day', 'Jester', 'Julia', 'Klopping Variegated', 'Krossa Variegated', 'La Vista', 'Lady Lou', 'Mary Marie Ann', 'Maya', 'Minuteman', 'Moonlight', 'North Hills', 'Patriot', 'Patriot's Fire', 'Raven', 'Revelations', 'Richland Gold', 'Rossing's Pride', 'Sarah Jane', 'Sharmon', 'Shogun', 'Simper's Blue Leaf', 'Snow Crust', 'Snowdrift', 'Something Different', 'Striptease', 'Sundance', 'Thea', 'Viette's Yellow Edge', 'Vivian', 'White Christmas', 'White Lightning', 'Windsor Gold', 'Zager Blue', 'Zager Green', 'Zager Green Rim', 'Zager's White Edge'

'Fortunei Albomarginata'
key features: medium-large mound of white-margined foliage; also known as 'Silver Crown'
mound size: 23" high by 54" wide

spacing: 40"
leaves: 10 5/8" long by 6 1/4" wide; white margin up to 3/4" wide, narrowing significantly in the lower third of the leaf; center medium green; slightly shiny top; thin underside bloom; ovate blade with a long, curved tip and rounded, folded base; distinctly wavy margins; no corrugation; better than average substance; 9-10 vein pairs

154

flowers: mid-July into early August; pale lavender; 2" long by 1" wide; narrow funnel shape; dense cluster of 24-40" scapes; 27 scapes on one mature clump

comments: Plants sold under this name can vary as it has been considered a convenient name to use for any white-edged Fortunei. When listed as 'Silver Crown', however, they are usually fairly consistent. Like most other Fortuneis, it has an excellent growth rate and becomes a fairly dense, flowing mound at maturity that can be used in a variety of ways in the landscape. The scapes also tend to bunch toward the center of the clump creating an attractive flower habit.

The AHS registered this plant as *H. fortunei* 'Albo-marginata' in 1987. In 1991 the name was changed to 'Fortunei Albomarginata' (Schmid, 1991).

seedlings, sports, and other related types:

'Antioch' **(see page 66)**

'Dragon Wings': {1996r, W. Lefever} *H. montana* X 'Fortunei Albomarginata'; large md of green lvs

'North Hills': {1986r, AHS for A. Summers; sport} 21" by 44" md wi lvs 10" by 6 1/4" with a 1/8" to 1/4" wide creamy wh mgn; typical Fortunei fls; sets seed; slightly narrower margin and smaller mound than 'Fortunei Albomarginata'; developed in the early 1970's

'Vivian': {1993r by P. Ruh for V. Grapes; 'Fortunei Stenantha Variegated' sport} lg md; lvs dk gr-cntrd wi a pure wh mgn; formerly *H. fortunei* 'Stenantha Albo-marginata' and *H. fortunei* 'Stenantha Variegated'; similar to 'Fortunei Albomarginata' and sometimes sold as such

other similar types:

'Chameleon': {1986r, Caprice Farm N; unknown parentage} 28" by 70" md; lvs 12" by 8" (10-12 vp) wi a green center & a margin that changes from white to greenish white by late June (Iowa); similar to variegated 'Fortunei Stenantha'-types

(note: The name 'Chameleon' was also used for a hybrid of 'Fortunei Aurea' X 'Fortunei Albomarginata' from England. That plant has mottled cream-yellow-green foliage.)

'Jade Lancer': 24" by 68" (up to 30" by 88") md of white-mgd lvs, 9 1/2" by 5" (up to 13" by 7") wi 11 vp; lav fls from mid to late July on sc up to 48" high; could easily be mistaken for 'Fortunei Albomarginata' or 'Antioch'; from Chet Tompkins

'Shogun': 24" by 68" md of creamy white-mgd lvs, 9 5/8" by 6 3/4" (up to 11" by 7 1/4") wi 9-11 vp; 1/2" mgn narrows to 1/32" near the base; lav fls on 39" sc from mid to late July; a Paul Aden introduction from 1983 or earlier; similar to 'Antioch' & 'Fortunei Albomarginata'

'Snow Crust': {1985r, M. Zilis & T & Z N} listed as a 'Fortunei Gigantea' sport but actually from another green Fortunei; 23" by 50" md of white-mgd, dark green-centered lvs, 12" by 8"; pale lav fls, mid-late July; outstanding landscape plant

'Fortunei Albopicta'

key features: medium-large mound of seasonally variegated foliage; gold-centered in spring

mound size: 23" high by 49" wide

spacing: 36"

leaves: 10 1/2" long by 6 3/4" wide; chartreuse to gold-centered with a 1/4" to 3/4" wide, medium green margin in spring (early May peak in northern Illinois); changes to all-green by late May; bluish bloom covers top surface until mid-June; thin underside bloom; ovate blade shape with a rounded base; slightly wavy margin; little or no corrugation; average substance; 9-10 vein pairs

flowers: July 16 to August 10 (northern Illinois); pale lavender, darker streaking on petal midrib; 2" long by 1 1/4" wide; 24-31 per scape; scapes 20-36" high; over 30 scapes on one clump; many seed pods develop

comments: For many years, 'Fortunei Albopicta' (often as *H. fortunei viridis-marginata* or *H. fortunei aureo-maculata*) was widely grown in the nursery industry in both the U.S. and Europe. Its main attractions were a vigorous growth habit and gold-centered foliage in spring. In the last fifteen years, however, such cultivars as 'Gold Standard', 'September Sun', 'Inniswood, and 'Janet' have taken its place because, not only do they possess similar good growing habits, but their variegation intensifies as the season progresses, not disappears. Even as a green-leaved plant, however, 'Fortunei Albopicta' can be a positive addition to the landscape as a background plant or ground cover.

Unlike many other Fortuneis, it is fertile, regularly forming prolific numbers of seed pods. In Europe it was an important breeding plant for many years, resulting in a few cultivars of note.

It was registered by the nomenclature committee of the AHS in 1987 as *H. fortunei* 'Albo-picta' for leaf show purposes. Schmid (1991) changed the name to 'Fortunei Albopicta'.

seedlings, sports, and other related types:

'Bensheim': sport of 'Fortunei Albopicta' from Germany; foliage green with irregular streaks of creamy yellow and white; md 26" by 46"; lvs 8 3/4" by 6 1/8" (10 vp)

'Elizabeth Campbell': {1988r, BHHS; 'Fortunei Albopicta' sport} much wider green margins, e.g., 2" wide on a 9 1/2" by 6 7/8" leaf; noticeably different

'Chelsea Babe': {1988r, BHHS; dwarf form of 'Fortunei Albopicta'}

'Fortunei Viridis': {1987r, AHS as *H. fortunei* 'Viridis'} green-lvd sport of 'Fortunei Albopicta'; used to be fairly common, now rare

'Golden Picture': {1995r, R. & D. Benedict; selfed sdlg of 'Fortunei Albopicta'} stays gold all season; lvs 8 1/4" long by 5 1/2" wide with 11 vp

'Maya': {1996r by P. Ruh for O. Meissner & A. Summers; 'Fortunei Albopicta' sport} acts like a dwarf 'Fortunei Albopicta'; 14" by 39" md; lvs 8 1/4" by 5 1/8" (9 vp); lf cntr chartreuse, mgn dk gr; changes to all-green by June 1; found and named in the early 1960's

other similar types:

'Aoki Variegated': sport of 'Aoki' wi gold-centered lvs in spring; 23" by 55" md; lvs 9 3/4" by 6 3/8" (9-10 vp); rarely grown; same as 'Sharmon'?

'Fortunei Aurea': can be considered an all-gold 'Fortunei Albopicta' **(see page 158)**

'Gold Standard': similar except that the lf center starts out green, turns gold and has limited fertility **(see page 192)**

'Julie Morss': {1983r, J. Morss; *H. sieboldiana* 'Frances Williams' sdlg} 21" by 44" md of foliage; lvs 9" by 6" (9-10 vp), chartreuse-centered, green-mgd in spring, all-green by mid-summer; narrow funnel-shaped, pale lav fls from late July into August on 32" sc; actually a Fortunei, not a Sieboldiana

'Mary Marie Ann': gold-centered 'Aoki' sdlg **(see page 289)**

'Phyllis Campbell': {1988r, BHHS; a 'Fortunei' mutation} gold-cntrd in spring, turning green

'Revelations': {1993r, E. Moore; 'Fortunei Hyacinthina' sport; lvs light green-centered wi a med green margin}

'Sharmon': {1986r by the AHS for T. Donahue} lf center chartreuse overlaid wi a bluish bloom in spring, turning green by June 1; 23" by 46" md; lvs 8" by 6" (10 vp); lav fls, late July to mid-Aug; typical Fortunei foliage and fls; from the 1950's but now rarely grown

'Zager Green Rim': {1987r by P. Ruh for H. Zager} gold-centered, green-mgd lvs in spring; from 1943

'Fortunei Aurea'

key features: medium-large mound of foliage; gold in spring, green by early summer
mound size: 19" high by 48" wide

spacing: 36"
leaves: 10" long by 6 1/4" wide; chartreuse to bright gold in spring, depending upon location, medium green by July; thin underside bloom; ovate shape with a rounded base; no marginal waviness or corrugation; average substance; 9-10 vein pairs
flowers: mid-July into early August; pale lavender; 1 7/8" long by 1" wide; narrow funnel shape; scapes 24-30" high; fertile

comments: Like many other Fortuneis, 'Fortunei Aurea' once had much wider usage in the nursery trade than today. As a garden plant it has interest in spring when the foliage is a shade of gold, ranging from chartreuse in deep shade to bright gold under direct sunlight. By July 1 in northern Illinois, it becomes hard to distinguish from 'Fortunei Viridis' and 'Fortunei Albopicta' to which it is closely related.

Eric Smith and others in England used this plant for hybridizing, resulting in a few seedlings of note. 'Fortunei Aurea' has been sold under a variety of names including 'Twinkles', "Mackwoods No. 33", *Hosta fortunei albo-*

picta aurea, *H. fortunei aurea*, and Gold Beauty Hosta. The nomenclature committee of the AHS registered the name *Hosta fortunei* 'Aurea' in 1987 and in 1991 it became 'Fortunei Aurea' (Schmid, 1991).

seedlings, sports, and other related types:

'Gold Haze': {1988r by the BHHS for E. Smith; 'Fortunei Aurea' sdlg} gold in spring, pale green thereafter; 9 1/2" by 6 1/4" lvs (9 vp); sometimes listed as 'Golden Haze'

'Gold Leaf': {1988r, by the BHHS for E. Smith; 'Fortunei Aurea' sdlg} not grown much in the U.S.

'Golden Age': {1988r by the BHHS for E. Smith; 'Fortunei Aurea' sdlg}

'Goldsmith': {1988r by the BHHS for E. Smith; 'Fortunei Aurea' sdlg} 18" by 44" md; lvs 10" by 6"; gold early, light green by late June

'Granary Gold': {1988r by the BHHS for E. Smith; 'Fortunei Aurea' sdlg} 20" by 63" md; lvs 9 1/2" by 5 1/2" (10 vp); gold lf color slowly changes to green by August

other similar types:

'Golden Picture': {1995r, R. & D. Benedict; selfed sdlg of 'Fortunei Albopicta'} stays gold all season; lvs 8 1/4" long by 5 1/2" wide with 11 vp

'Windsor Gold': gold-lvd Fortunei from England; onc juvenile md 17" by 35" wi lvs 6" by 4 1/2" (10 vp); gold early, turning green; not common in the U.S.

'Fortunei Aureomarginata' ('Gold Crown')

key features: medium-large mound of gold-margined foliage

mound size: 23" high by 52" wide

spacing: 36"

leaves: 8 3/4" long by 6 1/2" wide; 1/8" to 1/2" wide gold margin, deep green center; slightly shiny top, thin underside bloom; ovate shape with a subcordate base; little or no marginal waviness; slight corrugation; average substance; 9-11 vein pairs

flowers: July 26 to August 14 (northern Illinois); pale lavender with whitish petal margins and throat, darker streaking in mid-petal; 2 1/4" long by 1 1/8" wide; narrow funnel shape; closely clustered near the top of 29-45", very sturdy scapes; as many as 21 scapes in a mature clump; bracts that subtend flowers remain for a few weeks following flowering; sparse seed pod formation, about 3-4 per scape

comments: Despite being one of the longest-standing hostas in cultivation, 'Fortunei Aureomarginata' remains on the "recommended" list of hostas to grow. Its yellow margins are generally consistent from leaf to leaf and the plant itself has ornamental value virtually the whole growing season. In addition to having attractive variegation from April through September, the floral bracts add an interesting dimension for a few weeks after flowering. It also has a good growth rate and better than average sun tolerance. In short it makes a great landscape plant.

It has been sold under a variety of names over the years including *H. fortunei* 'Obscura Aureomarginata', 'Gold Crown', 'Golden Crown', and *H. fortunei* 'Yellow Edge'. The AHS registered it in 1987 as *H. fortunei* 'Aureo-marginata'. Schmid (1991) changed the name to its current 'Fortunei Aureomarginata'.

seedlings, sports, and other related types:

'Academy Redundant': {1998r, S. Chamberlain; sport with

pure white margins}

'Broad Band': sport with chartreuse margins very similar to 'Fortunei Aureomarginata'; originated before 1975 by Gus Krossa; a Sieboldiana-type with gold margins also bears this name creating confusion

'Crown Royalty': {1990r, Fairway Enterprises; 'Carol' X 'Fortunei Aureomarginata'} 24" by 56" md; 10" by 7" lvs (11 vp); mgn greenish yellow, golder in bright light, dk gr cntr; pale lav fls, late July-Aug; much like 'Fortunei Aureomarginata' except for margin color

'Ellerbroek': {1996r, P. Ruh for P. Ellerbroek & N. Hylander} med-lg md of ylw-mgd foliage; a selection of 'Fortunei Aureomarginata' that is very consistent; interchangeable with 'Fortunei Aureomarginata' in landscapes

'Fortunei Obscura': same as 'Fortunei Aureomarginata' except for all-green foliage

'Holiday White': {1990r, Fairway Enterprises; sport of "Krossa L7" (='Ellerbroek')} white-centered, green-mgd foliage; difficult to grow

'Jester': Fortunei wi chartreuse margins briefly in spring, green thereafter; also called 'Joker'; an oddity

'Kiwi Treasure Trove': {1999r, H. Redgrove & B. Sligh; sport wi greenish yellow mgns (green-centered)}

'Owen Online': {1998r, R. Snyder; sport; lvs dark green-margined wi a narrow gold center}

'Patience Plus': {1999r, R. Snyder; sport of 'Owen Online'; lvs gold-centered with a narrow dark green mgn}

'Twilight' (PPAF): {1997r, G. Van Eijk-Bos, G. Van Buren, & D. Van Erven; sport} from the Netherlands; introduced by Walters Gardens, Inc. in their 1998-1999 Wholesale Perennial Price List; wider gold margins, better substance, and longer, more distinct tip than 'Fortunei Aureomarginata'

'Viette's Yellow Edge': {1986r by the AHS for A. Viette} similar to 'Fortunei Aureomarginata' except for the 1/4" margin which starts out the season greenish yellow, changing to yellow; 21" by 51" md, lvs 8 1/2" by 5 5/8" (9-10 vp)

other similar types:

'Brass Horn': {1999r, Walden West, J. Hyslop & C. Purtyman; sport of 'Fortunei Stenantha'} greenish yellow margins, med green center; appears same as 'Fortunei Stenantha Aureomarginata', 'Fool's Gold', and "Mackwoods No. 23"

'Bridgeville': {1999r, P. Ruh for J. Craig & A. Summers; unknown parentage} 23" by 46" md of 9" by 5" (11 vp) lvs that are green-centered wi a 1/2" mgn that changes

161

from chartreuse to yellow; lav fls, late July into Aug, on 31" sc; known since the 1960's as "Craig H7"; fast grower

'Heliarc': {1986r, Kuk's Forest} listed in the 2000 Kuk's Forest catalog as a sport of 'Fortunei Hyacinthina'; 23" by 72" md; lvs 10" by 8" (11 vp) wi a 1/2" greenish ylw mgn all season; an attractive mound

---

'Fortunei Gigantea'

key features: large mound of rippled, green foliage; not related to other Fortuneis
mound size: 30" high by 70" wide

spacing: 60"

leaves: 15 1/2" long by 11" wide; dark green; stays green later than most hostas, developing an attractive, golden fall color very late if not damaged by frost; thin bloom underneath; broadly oblong-ovate shape with a deeply lobed, slightly cupped base; distinctly rippled margins with 14 or so per side; slight to moderate corrugation; good substance; 15-16 vein pairs

flowers: June 23 to July 19 (northern Illinois); pale lavender color, medium lavender in bud; 2 1/2" long by 1" wide; narrow funnel shape; scapes 30-43" high; 28 scapes on one clump with 20-46 flowers per scape, 1-9 flowers open per scape per day; prolific seed pod formation

comments: Long known under the name *Hosta fortunei gigantea*, this plant is truly an imposing, yet elegant hosta. A mature specimen is always impressive for its massive mound size, huge leaves, and ornamental flowering. The marginal rippling is also quite attractive. Such traits, as well as its good fertility, made 'Fortunei Gigantea' a good breeding plant for early hybridizers such as Frances Williams,

Eunice Fisher, and others. In fact most piecrust-edged hostas have descended from 'Fortunei Gigantea'.

Though long-considered as one of the Fortuneis, it shows little relation to any other Fortunei-type. Its flowering habits, foliage characteristics (including vein pairs), and overall appearance point to it being a form of *Hosta montana*. Unfortunately, there have been a few plants that do not fit this description that have been sold as 'Fortunei Gigantea'. One of these becomes a medium-large mound of green foliage, has only 9-10 vein pairs, and produces lavender flowers on short scapes in late July. This form yielded the sports 'Snow Crust' and 'Emerald Crust' in my tissue culture lab. Additionally, there appears to be no difference between 'Fortunei Gigantea' and most plants grown under the name *Hosta elata.*

The popularity of 'Fortunei Gigantea' has declined in the last fifteen or so years, but it certainly is still worth growing.

The American Hosta Society's 1993 checklist lists 'Fortunei Gigantea' as a registered cultivar (IRA, 1993).

seedlings, sports, and other related types:

'Big Sam': {1986r by the AHS for M. Klopping} lg md of rippled, dk gr foliage; 25" by 63" md; lvs 14" by 12" (13-15 vp); very pale lav fls on 36" sc, June-July; attractive huge mound; a 'Fortunei Gigantea' sdlg introduced in 1963 but rarely grown anymore

'Challenger': {1971r, E. Fisher; 'Fortunei Gigantea' sdlg} 23" by 56" md; med gr lvs, 13" by 10" (15 vp); v pale lav fls, late June into mid-July on 30-38" sc; many seed pods; close to 'Fortunei Gigantea' in both foliage and flower

'Emerald Crust': {1988r, M. Zilis & T & Z N; as a 'Fortunei Gigantea' sport but actually is not (see previous note); 17" by 37" md; 11" by 6" (9-10 vp) lvs with a creamy white center & 1" mgn; pale lav fls in July; good grower for a white-centered plant

'Fall Emerald': {1997r by P. Ruh for A. Summers; unknown parentage} prob a sdlg of 'Fortunei Gigantea' to which it shows many similarities in foliage & flower; 23" by 60" md of broad, dark green foliage, 13" by 11" (13-15 vp); v pale lav fls, mid-June into mid-July, on 24-36" sc; many seed pods; a cultivar from the 1960's, known for staying green into late fall (as does 'Fortunei Gigantea')

'Fountain': {1983r, K. Hensen; formerly *H. sieboldiana* 'Longipes' & *H. elata* 'Fountain'} 22" by 60" md of green lvs, 12" by 8" (13 vp); near-wh fls, late June into mid-July on 30-45" sc

'Golden Anniversary': {1998r by P. Ruh for G. Holly & E. Fisher; parentage unknown} probably a sdlg of 'Fortunei Gigantea'; 23" by 54" md of shiny, deep green foliage that is chartreuse when first emerging in spring; lvs 11" by 8 1/4" (11 vp) & distinctly rippled along the margin; pale lav fls, early to late July, on 40" sc; one of the early American cultivars, developed in the 1950's & described in the first issue of *The American Hosta Society Bulletin* (Summers, 1969); the pod parent of other Eunice Fisher cvs from the 1960's including 'Carefree' (1971r), 'Crinkle Cup' (1971r), 'Pale Gold' (1997r), 'Green Platter' (1997r), & 'Satin Flare' (1971r)

'Goliath': {1986r by the AHS for J. Harrison} 31" by 61" md of med green lvs, 13" by 9" (13-15 vp), that are slightly rippled; pale lav fls, late June into mid-July on sc up to 48" high; probably a 'Fortunei Gigantea' sdlg; introduced in the early 1960's but is now rarely grown; useful hybridizing plant

'Green Ripples': {1986r by C. Williams for F. Williams; sdlg of 'Fortunei Gigantea'} lg md of heavily rippled, green foliage; lvs 11" by 8" (10 vp) wi 12 or more regular ripples per lf half

'Jolly Green Giant': {1986r by the AHS for M. Armstrong, parentage unknown} large md of huge, green lvs; 25" by 57" md; 17" by 12" lvs (14 vp); pale lav fls, late June into mid-July on 39" sc; both lvs & fls close to 'Fortunei Gigantea' of which it is probably a seedling; dates back to the early 1970's

'Snow Crust': {1985r, M. Zilis & T & Z N} listed as a 'Fortunei Gigantea' sport but actually from another green Fortunei-type; 23" by 50" md of white-mgd, dark green-centered lvs, 12" by 8"; pale lav fls, mid-late July; outstanding landscape plant

'Woodland Green': {1990r by P. Ruh for L. Simpers; 'Fountain' sdlg} lg md of green lvs with impressive, rippled margins

other similar types:
'Colossal', 'Green Acres', 'Green Piecrust', 'Her Grace', 'Rippling Waves', 'Sea Drift'

'Fortunei Hyacinthina'
key features: large mound of dark green leaves; excellent landscape plant
mound size: 23" high by 55" wide

spacing: 36"

leaves: 9 1/4" long by 7 1/4" wide; thick bloom creates bluish appearance in early spring, becoming medium to dark green by June 1; outside edge (not margin) whitish; moderate underside bloom; ovate shape with a rounded to subcordate base; slight marginal waviness; little or no corrugation; better than average substance; 9-11 vein pairs; brilliant gold fall color in mid-October

flowers: July 26 to August 18; pale lavender color; 2" long by 3/4" wide; narrow funnel shape; about 36 per scape; most in the upper 5-6" of the 25-36" scapes; 20 scapes on one mature clump; sparse seed pod formation with few viable seeds

comments: Grown for many years in the United States and Europe, 'Fortunei Hyacinthina' still has good value for landscaping. Like many other Fortuneis, it grows rapidly and has better than average sun tolerance (meaning it might take 2 hours of direct sunlight per day) and attractive flowers. The bluish color in early spring and the good gold fall color (before frost) are additional ornamental features.

'Fortunei Hyacinthina' is not especially fertile and has not been used much for hybridizing, but has been the source of a large number of sports. 'Gold Standard' is its most famous sport which has, in turn, produced a large number of sports itself including 'Moonlight', 'Richland Gold', 'Striptease', 'Brenda's Beauty', and 'Captain Kirk'.

'Fortunei Hyacinthina' has been known under a wide assortment of names including *Hosta fortunei* var. *hyacinthina, Hosta hyacinthina, Hosta fortunei glauca,*

Hosta fortunei, Hosta glauca, and *Hosta sieboldiana for-tunei.* The name finally became 'Fortunei Hyacinthina' (Schmid, 1991) and is listed as such in the American Hosta Society checklist of registered cultivars (IRA, 1993).

More than any other cultivar, 'Fortunei Hyacinthina' is considered the archetypical "Fortunei". In fact when its sports have been registered, *H. fortunei* or 'Fortunei' is often listed as the name of the source plant. It bears all of the characteristics typical of the Fortunei cultivar group for foliage, flowers, mound habits, fertility, mutability, and growing habits. It probably originated in Japan, but its exact derivation is unknown.

seedlings, sports, and other related types:

'Alaskan Halo': {1997r, P. Ruh; sport} creamy white-margined foliage; 22" by 48" md, 11 1/2" by 6 1/4" lvs wi a 1/2" mgn

'Arctic Rim': {1993r, R. Lydell; sport} 3/8" wide, creamy white mgn on a 8 1/2" by 5 5/8" lf; impressive plant

'Banana Sundae': {1980r, E. Minks; sport of a 'Fortunei' sdlg} 16" by 30" md of creamy white-centered, green-margined lvs, 9" by 5 1/2" (8 vp); pale lav fls in July; once "the rage", it has become almost extinct due to its tendency to sport green foliage & a slow growth rate; still used for breeding

'Confused': {1999r, R. Beal; sport; lf center white wi green streaks; green mgn}

'Crowned Imperial': {1988r. Walters Gardens; sport} lvs 9" by 6 1/8" wi a 1/2", white margin

'Fisher's Cream Edge': {1992r, P. Ruh for E. Fisher} a sport of 'Fortunei Hyacinthina' found in the 1960's; med-lg md of gr-cntrd lvs wi mgns that change from creamy in spring to chartreuse by mid-summer; lvs 8 1/2" by 6 1/2" (9-10 vp); formerly sold as *H. fortunei* 'Cream Edge', not to be confused with 'Krossa Cream Edge', an *H. sieboldii*-type

'Helen Field Fischer': {1970r, E. Minks; unknown origin} 16" by 39" md; 6 3/4" by 4 1/2" lvs (9 vp) bluish in spring, green thereafter; pale lav fls in mid-July; like a dwarf 'Fortunei Hyacinthina' in both foliage and flower; formerly called 'Dwarf Grey Leaf', 'Gray Leaf Dwarf and 'Small Grey Leaf'; collector's plant in the 1970's and early 1980's

'Gold Standard': {1976r by P. Banyai as a sport of 'Fortunei'} certainly from 'Fortunei Hyacinthina'; gold-centered, green-margined foliage; one of the most important hosta cultivars ever introduced; source of numerous sports **(see page 192)**

'Goosebumps': {1998r, E. Elslager; sport} heavily corrugated, green foliage

'Heliarc': {1986r, Kuk's Forest} listed in Kuk's Forest catalog as a sport of 'Fortunei Hyacinthina'; 23" by 72" md; lvs 10" by 8" (11 vp) wi a 1/2" greenish ylw mgn all season; an attractive mound

'Imperial Potentate': {1999r, R. & D. Benedict; sport of 'Crowned Imperial'} lvs center-streaked and white-margined; first saw in 1988

'Itasca': {1974r, A. Johnson; variegated cream and white-streaked foliage} first sport registered with the AHS; listed as being a sport of 'Fortunei Hyacinthina' (Fisher, 1979); no longer exists

'Julia': {1994r, P. White; sport} lg md of white-mgd, green-centered foliage

'La Vista': {1988r, Walters Gardens; sport} white-centered, green-margined foliage; weak grower

'Praying Hands': {1996r, G. Williams; parentage unknown} semi-upr md of white-mgd, green-centered foliage that is very wavy & folded upward; one of the weirdest cultivar introductions in many years; exact origin unknown, but most likely a sport of some Fortunei; grow this alongside 'Lunar Eclipse', 'Embroidery', 'Ugly Duckling', 'Tortifrons', 'Outhouse Delight', 'Gray Streaked Squiggles', 'Cynthia', 'Stetson', 'Cupid's Dart', and 'Lunatic Fringe'

'Raven': {1993r, R. Savory; 'Fortunei Hyacinthina' sdlg; dark green foliage}

'Revelations': {1993r, E. Moore; sport; lvs light green in the center, med green margin}

'Rossing's Pride': {1993r, R. Rossing; sport} impressive gold-centered foliage

'Silver Streak': {1986r by the AHS for H. Zager; unknown parentage} 8" by 19" md of heavily contorted, white-centered (green-mgd) lvs, 4 1/2" by 1 3/4" (6-7 vp); lvs heavily corrugated in margin, smooth in the narrow, white center & have a thin underside bloom; have never seen flower; acts like a sport of 'Fortunei Hyacinthina'; developed before 1963

'Thea': {1985r, N. Statham & Goldbrook Plants; sport} lvs generally streaked in center but range from all-green to creamy white-centered wi green mgns on the same clump

'Thelma M. Pierson': {1988r, R. Pierson; sport of a 'Fortunei Hyacinthina' sdlg} bright yellow foliage; similar to 'Sun Power'

'Twilight Zone': {1999r, A. Haskell & A. Malloy; sport; lvs green wi cream speckling & yellow streaking}

'Wayne': {1999r by P. Ruh for G. Krossa; sport} lvs have a

med green center & greenish ylw mgns; found in many gardens over the years, but not named until now

other similar types:

'Aoki':{1987r, AHS as *H. fortunei* 'Aoki'} use the name 'Aoki'; 21" by 52" md of med to dark green lvs that are bluish in spring, 9 1/2" by 6 3/8" (9-10 vp); pale lav fls, late July into August, on 23-33" sc; virtually indistinguishable from 'Fortunei Hyacinthina' though some claim differences

'Simper's Blue Leaf': 20" by 40" mound of medium green foliage that has a bluish cast in spring; very similar in overall appearance to 'Fortunei Hyacinthina'

'Zager Blue': {1987r by P. Ruh for H. Zager} (formerly 'Zager Blue Leaf') medium-large mound of green foliage (bluish in spring); leaves 9 3/4" by 6 3/4" (11 vein pairs)

'Fragrant Blue'
key features: medium-large mound of blue foliage; fragrant, lavender flowers in August
mound size: 20" high by 48" wide

spacing: 36"
leaves: 8" long by 6 1/2" wide; blue-green, gradually turning green; moderate underside bloom; ovate to nearly heart-shaped blade that is slightly wavy; slight corrugation; good substance; 11-12 vein pairs
flowers: early to late August; pale lavender; fragrant; scapes 30" high
comments: This Paul Aden introduction represents a breakthrough in hybridizing, being a blue-leaved hosta bearing fragrant flowers. The attractive foliage retains its blue color well into the summer and has decent slug resistance.

Paul Aden registered 'Fragrant Blue' in 1988 as a hybrid of two seedlings.

seedlings, sports, and other related types:
none listed (but I have seen an unnamed, center-variegated sport)

other similar types:
'Fried Green Tomatoes': 'Guacamole' sport forming a lg md of medium to dark green lvs; fragrant pale lav fls in August **(see next page)**

'Moonlight Sonata': 24" by 68" md of blue foliage; fragrant, very pale bluish white fls that bloom a few weeks earlier than 'Fragrant Blue'; lvs 12" by 11" (14 vp); a Greg Johnson introduction

'Sombrero': {1991r, R. Savory; 'Honeybells' sdlg with blue-green lvs} described in the 1998 Savory's Gardens catalog as being a large plant that produces very fragrant, pure white flowers in August

---

'Fragrant Bouquet'
key features: medium-large mound of creamy yellow-margined foliage; large fragrant flowers
mound size: 22" high by 48" wide (up to 28" by 52")

'Fragrant Bouquet' (center) with its sports 'Fried Green Tomatoes' (left); 'Fried Bananas' (back); 'Guacamole' (right)

spacing: 48"
leaves: 10" long by 8" wide; 1/2" to 3/4" wide margin that changes from yellow to creamy white, center pale green to chartreuse; thin underside bloom; blade ovate to broadly ovate that is moderately wavy; better than average substance; 10-12 vein pairs
flowers: mid-August into September; very pale lavender, nearly white; 3" long by 2 1/2" wide; wide open, trumpet shape; very fragrant; clustered in the top 6" of the 30-45" scapes; sparse pod formation

169

comments: 'Fragrant Bouquet' has gained great popularity recently for its combination of highly colorful foliage and large, fragrant flowers. It makes a beautiful mound that can be effectively used as a specimen plant. The vigorous growth rate also lends itself to usage as a ground cover.

Being widely propagated by tissue culture, it stands at the apex of a wonderful family of sports, starting with 'Guacamole' which sported to 'Fried Green Tomatoes' and 'Fried Bananas'. All of these grow slightly larger than 'Fragrant Bouquet'. It has been used in hybridizing work, but when seed pods form, the number of viable seeds is often limited.

Paul Aden registered 'Fragrant Bouquet' in 1982 as a hybrid of 'Fascination' X 'Fragrant Summer'.

seedlings, sports, and other related types:

'Avocado': {1998r, J. & B. Diesen; 'Guacamole' sport} very wide leaf margins (1 3/4" wide margin on a 7 3/4" by 6 1/2" leaf for 'Avocado' vs. 5/8" margins on a mature, 11" by 8 1/2" 'Guacamole' leaf); distinct

'Color Parade': green-margined, streaked-centered 'Fragrant Bouquet' sport; 2000 Q & Z N introduction

'Fragrant Candelabra': {1982r, P. Aden; 'Fragrant Bouquet' X a sdlg} have never seen

'Fried Bananas': {1994r, R. Solberg} 'Guacamole' sport; beautiful, fast-growing mound of golden foliage; color intensifies in bright light

'Fried Green Tomatoes': {1995r, R. Solberg} 'Guacamole' sport; medium to dark green leaves; most vigorous member of 'Fragrant Bouquet' family; 25" by 59" md; 11 1/2" by 7 3/4" lvs; excellent, fast-growing ground cover or background plant

'Guacamole': {1994r, R. Solberg; sport} gold-centered, green-margined foliage; 24" by 54" md; center color intensifies during the season and wi bright light; excellent grower **(see page 216)**

'Miss Saigon': {1999r, H. Hansen & Shady Oaks N; 'Fragrant Bouquet' sport; lvs green-centered, creamy white-mgd}

'Redolent Nosegay': {1999r, J. Hawes; 'Fragrant Bouquet' sport; lvs white-mgd with a dark green center streaked with yellow}

'So Sweet': {1986r, P. Aden; 'Fragrant Bouquet' X a sdlg} med-lg md of creamy white-margined foliage; fragrant, pale lav fls; widely grown; outstanding **(see page 429)**

'Stained Glass': {1999r, H. Hansen & Shady Oaks N; 'Guacamole' sport; lvs gold-centered with very wide, dk gr mgns}

'Sweetie': {1988r, P. Aden; 'Fragrant Bouquet' X 'Fragrant

Candelabra'} 20" by 50" md of pale green to gold-centered, white-margined foliage; 9 1/4" by 6" lvs; fragrant lav fls in Aug; narrower lvs, but almost identical to 'Fragrant Bouquet' in every other way; fast-growing

other similar types:
'Sugar and Cream'

'Fragrant Gold'
key features: large mound of chartreuse to gold foliage; fragrant flowers
mound size: 24" high by 53" wide

spacing: 36"

leaves: 10" long by 8" wide; chartreuse changing to medium gold; thin bloom on top surface in spring; thin underside bloom; ovate to broadly ovate blade; slightly wavy; slight corrugation at maturity; better than average substance; 12 vein pairs

flowers: late July into mid-August; pale lavender with lighter petal margins; 2" long by 1 3/4" wide; widely flared trumpet shape; narrow petals; light fragrance; scapes 34" high

comments: At best 'Fragrant Gold' offers fragrant, pale lavender flowers over a mound of chartreusey gold foliage in August. I have never been particularly impressed with its color, a "muddy" gold at best. 'Fried Bananas' makes a much brighter gold mound (with fragrant flowers, too).

Paul Aden registered 'Fragrant Gold' in 1982 as a hybrid of 'Sum and Substance' X a seedling.

seedlings, sports, and other related types:
none listed

other similar types:
'Fried Bananas': {1994r, R. Solberg} 'Guacamole' sport;

171

beautiful, fast-growing mound of golden foliage; color intensifies in bright light

---

'Francee'

key features: medium-large mound of white-margined foliage; premier landscaping hosta

mound size: 21" high by 50" wide

spacing: 40"

leaves: 8 3/4" long by 6 1/4" wide; 1/8" to 5/8" wide, creamy to pure white margin, medium to dark green center; thin underside bloom; ovate shape with a slightly lobed base; not wavy; slight corrugation with age; average substance; 10-13 vein pairs

flowers: late July into early August; medium lavender color; 2" long by 7/8" wide; narrow funnel shape; clustered near the top of the 23-33" scapes; 14 scapes on one mature clump; limited seed pod formation with few viable seeds

comments: 'Francee' has proven to be one of the best white-margined hostas for landscaping purposes. The variegation pattern is attractive from early in the growing season until fall and the growth rate is moderately fast. All in all, it is easy to understand why 'Francee' has become the accepted substitute for 'Undulata Albomarginata' for landscape usage. Perhaps the only hostas that may become more popular are 'Patriot' and 'Minuteman', sports of 'Francee'.

'Francee' was developed by Minnie Klopping of Nebraska and has been known by collectors since the early 1970's. It was registered by the American Hosta Society in 1986. 'Francee' has only limited utility in breeding work but has been the source of several sports.

seedlings, sports, and other related types:

'Academy Fire': {1997r, S. Chamberlain; sport wi light green-centered (white-margined) lvs}

172

'Counter Point': {1982r, P. Aden; sport} 25" by 60" md; lvs 10 3/4" by 6 1/4" (10 vp); 1/64" to 1/8" white margin; looks like a thin-margined 'Francee though an occasional plant will be streaked

'Jade Beauty': {1988r, M. Zilis & T & Z N} green-lvd sport of 'Francee'; 25" by 65" md, 10" by 7 3/4" lvs (10-13 vp); good in combination wi 'Francee'

'Kiwi Splash': {1999r, B. Sligh; sport; lvs streaked in center, white-mgd}

'Matrix': 'Francee' sport from Q & Z N; under evaluation since 1998, named in 1999; lvs green-mgd with a center that changes from gold to white to streaky green & white

'Minuteman': 'Francee' sport with dark green center, wide, pure white margins **(see page 296)**

'Pathfinder': {1999r, Briggs N; sport; white-centered, green-mgd lvs}

'Patriot': 'Francee' sport with medium green center, wide, creamy white margins **(see page 331)**

'Snowdrift': {1985r, M. Zilis & T & Z N; 'Francee' sport} white-centered, green-margined leaves; 13" by 26" md; lvs 6" by 2 1/4"; not vigorous; only a few collectors still have it

'Tracy's Emerald Cup': {1997r, T. Heuermann; 'Francee' sdlg} 22" by 48" md; lvs 8 1/4" by 8" (13 vp), dark green, shiny & cupped; good substance; very attractive

'Trailblazer': {1999r, M. Zilis} sport of 'Francee' developed at my nursery (Q & Z N); sharp contrast between wide, creamy white margins and dark green center; slight differences from 'Minuteman' and 'Patriot'

other similar types:

'Carol': {1986r by the AHS for F. Williams} 21" by 61" md; white-margined lvs, 8 1/2" by 6" wi a 1/16" to 1/4" white mgn (9-10 vp); typical Fortunei flowering; very close to 'Francee'; from the early 1960's

'Fisher's Cream Edge' **(see page 166)**

'Fringe Benefit': Paul Aden introduction from the late 1970's; 22" by 56" md of dark green-centered foliage with mgns that change from yellow to creamy white; lvs 9 1/2" by 7 1/2" (10-12 vp); pale lav fls, mid-July into Aug on 24-36" sc; fertile

'Green Gold': {1986r by the AHS} developed in the 1950's by Carl Mack (his "Mackwoods No. 22"), later named by Bob Savory; dense, 23" by 50" md of 8 3/4" by 5 7/8" (10 vp) lvs wi a 1/8" to 1/2" mgn that changes from creamy yellow to white by early summer; pale lav fls on 20-34" sc, July 26-Aug 18 (n IL); differs from 'Francee' in margin color; attractive & fast-growing

'Klopping Variegated': {1988r, P. Ruh} 18" by 42" md; lvs

white-mgd wi a dark green center, 9 1/2" by 5 1/2" (9-10 vp); attractive; not widely grown; developed by Minnie Klopping

'North Hills': {1986r, by AHS for A. Summers; sport} 21" by 44" md wi lvs 10" by 6 1/4" with a 1/8" to 1/4" wide creamy wh mgn; typical Fortunei fls; sets seed; developed in the early 1970's

'Patriot's Fire': {1996r, A. Summers & K. Walek; sport of 'Patriot'} white-margined lvs wi a center that changes from green to gold; an interesting, colorful mound when actively growing; closer to 'Francee' than 'Patriot'

'Sundance': {1984r, Walters Gardens; sport of 'Aoki'} white-mgd, green-centered lvs

'Zager's White Edge': {1980r, L. Simpers as a 'Fortunei' mutation} 19" by 50" md; 8 1/4" by 5 1/2" lvs (11 vp) wi a 3/8" wide, pure white mgn; one of the best white-margined Fortunei-types; sometimes listed as 'Zager White Edge'

'Frosted Jade'
key features: large mound of white-margined foliage; distinctive
mound size: 32" high by 63" wide (as much as 36" by 78")

spacing: 48"
leaves: 14" long by 10" wide; distinct, 1/4" to 5/8" wide, white margin, medium green center; irregularly rippled margin causes the blade leaf to cup slightly up or downward; some gray-green streaking to the center; thin underside bloom; oblong-ovate shape with a heart-shaped base; slight corrugation when mature; good substance; 14-15, deeply impressed vein pairs

flowers: early to late July; pale lavender with paler petal margins; 2 1/2" long by 1 1/4" wide; 26-40" scapes (32-36" typical); many seed pods develop

comments: The relatively narrow, rippled, white margins that often turn upward and its leaf shape give 'Frosted Jade' a unique and attractive look that can be mistaken for no other hosta. The unusual appearance of the margin is produced because of the difference in cellular expansion between it and the center of the leaf. The flowering habit is an ornamental plus with the scapes in balance to the foliage mound and not excessively drooping. Lillian Maroushek registered 'Frosted Jade' in 1978 as a *Hosta montana* seedling. It has become very popular and that should continue for many years to come.

What is probably most surprising about this wonderful hosta is that it is not more widely used in breeding work. Not a single registered cultivar lists 'Frosted Jade' as a parent; also surprising since it does form prolific amounts of seed.

seedlings, sports, and other related types:
none!!!

other similar types:
'Crispula', *H. montana* 'Mountain Snow'

'Galaxy'

key features: medium-large mound of highly variegated foliage; good plant for breeding
mound size: 18" high by 40" wide

spacing: 36"
leaves: 10" long by 8" wide; green margins surrounding a streaky center of creamy white, green, chartreuse, and creamy-green mottle; thin underside bloom; broadly ovate shape with a heart-shaped base; slightly wavy; slight to moderate corrugation; good substance; 13 vein pairs
flowers: late June into mid-July; medium lavender with darker striping down mid-petal; 2 5/16" by 1 5/8" wide; slightly inflated funnel shape; 19-24" scapes; fertile

comments: As a streaked and mottled specimen plant, 'Galaxy' makes a colorful addition to any shaded garden. At its best, the green-margined leaves are streaked and mottled throughout the center of the leaf, though it often sports to a variety of forms. The sport with green-margined, gold-centered leaves is called 'Galaxy Light'. Besides producing sports, it has also become a very popular breeding plant.

'Galaxy' was registered by Bill and Eleanor Lachman in 1987 as a cross of a 'Beatrice' seedling X a 'Frances Williams' seedling.

seedlings, sports, and other related types:

'Dee's Golden Jewel': {1996r, K. Walek; 'Royal Standard' X 'Galaxy'} bright gold, sun-tolerant foliage

'Galaxy Light': {1991r, W. & E. Lachman; sport} gold-centered, dark green-margined leaves

'Lollapalooza': {1998r, E. Elslager; a 'Galaxy' sdlg} lf center dk green with an occasional streak of mottled green & yellow; v wide, creamy ylw lf margin

'Mack the Knife': {1996r, J. Dishon; 'Galaxy' X 'Hadspen Heron'} attractive, yellow-margined, green-centered leaves

176

'Resurrection Galaxy': {1999r, E. Elslager; 'Galaxy' sport; lvs dk green streaked wi white & ylw}

'Rosedale Black Ice': {1999r, J. Hadrava; 'Galaxy' X 'Elegans'} 22" by 53" md of very dark green, intensely corrugated lvs, 9" by 8" (17 vp); bluish in spring & thick-substd

'Rosedale Tractor Seat': {1999r, J. Hadrava; 'Galaxy' X 'Elegans'} lg md of huge, cupped, medium to dk green lvs, 13" by 11" (21 vp); lf blade shape like the name

'Waving Winds': {1991r, W. & E. Lachman; selfed seedling of 'Galaxy'} very wavy, yellow-margined foliage; lvs 6 1/4" by 3 3/8" wi a 1/2" mgn; excellent contrast between leaf center and margin

'Wizard's Turbin': {1996r, J. Hadrava; 'Galaxy' X 'Wahoo'} creamy yellow-centered foliage, dark green margin; pale purple fls in July

other similar types:
'Christmas Tree Gala'

'Gay Blade'
key features: dense, wide-spreading mound of wavy, white-margined foliage; attractive all season
mound size: 20" high by 53" wide

spacing: 36"
leaves: 8 1/2" long by 5" wide; 1/32" to 1/16" wide, creamy white margin, medium to dark green center; slightly shiny top; thick underside bloom; elliptic blade shape; very wavy margins; smooth texture; better than average substance; 8-10 vein pairs
flowers: early to late August; medium lavender; 2 1/4" long by 1" wide; 28" high scapes covered with deep purple dots
comments: 'Gay Blade' may be thought of as "the hosta for

all seasons". I've seen 'Gay Blade' growing in a variety of gardens across the U.S., from May to October, and it always looks great. I once visited the Wade and Gatton Nurseries display in mid-October when most hostas had been beaten into the ground by frost and heavy fall rain. 'Gay Blade', though, looked every bit as good as it did in the middle of July.

The extent of its value, however, does not end with its durability. The leaves are attractively wavy, and this characteristic is greatly enhanced by the creamy white margins. The flowering habits are also an ornamental plus. 'Gay Blade' has a good growth rate, rapidly forming a dense mound of foliage that can be useful as a ground cover or a specimen plant.

'Gay Blade' is another great Bill and Eleanor Lachman introduction. It was registered in 1988 as a hybrid of a 'Resonance' seedling cross X 'Halcyon'.

seedlings, sports, and other related types:
none listed

other similar types:
'Chantilly Lace' **(see page 111)**

'Dark Star': {1999r, R. Herold; 'Swoosh' X 'Hadspen Heron'} med-sized md of blue-green-centered, creamy white-mgd foliage that is attractively wavy; good substance

'Lacy Belle': {1992r, W. & E. Lachman; 'Neat Splash' sdlg X 'Halcyon'} 16" by 37" md of wavy lvs, 7" by 4", wi a 1/4" ylw to creamy white mgn & green center

'Gay Feather'

key features: medium-sized mound of narrow, cream-centered foliage; purple flowers
mound size: 12" high by 30" wide

spacing: 24"
leaves: 7" long by 3" wide; 1/8" to 9/16" wide green margin, creamy yellow to white center; very shiny underside; blade elliptic and slightly wavy; no corrugation; thin substance; 7 vein pairs
flowers: late July into mid-August; bright purple; narrow funnel shape; scapes 23" high
comments:
'Gay Feather' makes an attractive, low mound of narrow, white-centered foliage. Herb Benedict developed this reversed sport of 'Yellow Splash' in his Michigan garden and noted to me that it had been rhizomatous in his sandy soil. Though Herb has grown it with ease, others report more difficulty in getting 'Gay Feather' to mature size. In any case it is much less vigorous than 'Yellow Splash' itself. Herb registered 'Gay Feather' in 1983.

seedlings, sports, and other related types:
none listed

other similar types:
'Celebration': {1978r, P. Aden; a hybrid of two seedlings} 17" high by 33" md; lvs 7" by 3" wi a 1/4" green mgn and creamy white center; bright purple fls on 30" sc in Aug; close to 'Gay Feather' in foliage and flower; not easy to grow; increasingly scarce

'Goody Goody': {1987r, R. Benedict; selfed 'Neat Splash' sdlg} v sm md of narrow, white-centered foliage; edger or rock garden plant; smaller than 'Gay Feather'

'Hot Lips': {1993r, H. Gowen, F. Riehl, & R. Benedict; parentage unknown} 16" by 38" md; 7 1/2" by 3 1/4" lvs wi a 3/4" wide, green mgn and wh center; purplish red petioles

'Indian Feather': {1992r, C. Owens; a selfed 'Yellow

Splash' sdlg} white-centered, dark green-margined leaves; 18" by 49" md; lvs 9 5/8" by 6 3/8" (14 vp) wi a 1-2" wide mgn; strikingly beautiful

'Noel': {1983r, R. Benedict; 'Beatrice' sport} sm md of white-centered lvs 4 1/2" by 2"; br purple fls, July-Aug

'Richland Royal Prince': 'Neat Splash' sdlg from Van Wade; dense, 13" by 29" md of green-mgd, white-centered lvs, 8" by 3 3/4" (7 vp); purple fls, mid-July into Aug; dense md habit

'Sea Thunder' (see page 383)

'Squiggles': {1978r, P. Aden; 'Yellow Splash' X 'Neat Splash'} sm md of white-centered, green-mgd, wavy foliage; center pale yellow in spring; slow-growing; rare

---

'Ginko Craig'

key features: small mound of narrow, white-margined foliage; premier edging plant
mound size: 14" high by 44" wide

spacing: 30"

leaves: 7" long by 3 1/2" wide (mature form); 6" by 2 1/4" (juvenile form); 3/8" wide, white margin that produces gray-green streaks into the dark green center; dull top surface, slightly shiny underside; narrowly elliptic blade when juvenile, elliptic at maturity; moderately wavy margins; smooth texture when young, slightly corrugated at maturity; thin substance; 8-9 vein pairs

flowers: August 16 to September 1; medium purple with darker mid-petal striping; whitish throat and petal margins; 1 3/4" long by 1 1/4" wide; open funnel shape; 16-28" scapes held well above the foliage; many seed pods develop

comments: The good growth rate, attractive white-margined leaves and low, dense mound habit have made 'Ginko

Craig' the preeminent edging plant for shady gardens. The purple flowers in August are held well above the foliage and are an ornamental plus. The shape of 'Ginko Craig' leaves changes significantly from juvenile to mature stages of growth. Young plants exhibit a fairly narrowly elliptic-shaped blade with no corrugation. This stage often persists for many years, leading to the common perception that this is what 'Ginko Craig' looks like. At some point, a well-maintained clump of 'Ginko Craig' will develop mature foliage that is larger, with wider, white margins and some puckers of corrugation.

The story of how this plant was found in Japan by Jack Craig has changed over time, but evidently he procured it in the 1960's in Japan and named it for his wife, Ginko. Some astute plant collectors change the spelling to match the "Ginkgo" tree, but that is incorrect.

In investigating the origins of *Hosta rohdeifolia* and *Hosta helonioides* 'Albo-picta' in the late 1980's, Peter Ruh and I stumbled upon the possibility that 'Ginko Craig' might actually be the latter plant. After examining several specimens of Hakama Giboshi (the Japanese name for *Hosta helonioides* 'Albo-picta') imported from Japan, we could find no difference from 'Ginko Craig'. Further observations of plants growing in Japan and the U.S. confirmed our conclusions. 'Ginko Craig' is *Hosta helonioides* 'Albopicta', or more correctly, 'Helonioides Albopicta' (Schmid, 1991). (The old plant that we used to grow as *Hosta helonioides* 'Albo-picta' is actually *Hosta rohdeifolia* **(see page 368)**. Despite this, I recommend retaining the name 'Ginko Craig' and not use 'Helonioides Albopicta'.

Additionally, there are several other cultivars that so closely resemble 'Ginko Craig' that it is difficult to tell them apart. Included in this group are 'Bunchoko', 'Elsley', 'Excalibur', 'Hime Karafuto', 'Mr. Asami Improved', and 'Swarthmore Supreme'. Examine these cultivars, keeping in mind the two distinct stages of growth, and make your own judgements.

The American Hosta Society registered 'Ginko Craig' in 1986 for Jack Craig and later gave credit to Alex Summers for a role in developing this plant (IRA, 1993).

seedlings, sports, and other related types:

'Buckwheat Honey': {1984r, R. Benedict; 'Ginko Craig' X *H. plantaginea*} 22" by 48" md; lvs 10" by 4 3/4" (9 vp); 2" long, med purple, fragr fls in mid-Aug on 32-46" sc; fls only slightly open; mound resembles 'Honeybells'

'Curly Top': {1985r, R. Benedict; 'Ginko Craig' X *H. plantaginea*} small mound (9" by 20") of thin-substanced, narrow, wavy, green lvs (5" by 1 1/8" with 4 vp); purple fls in Aug; not especially exciting

'Gosan Hildegarde': {1989r, W. Schmid; 'Golden Prayers' X 'Ginko Craig'} low md of narrow, bright gold foliage; purple fls in late July; more correctly listed as 'Little Aurora' X 'Ginko Craig'??

'Green Smash': {1988r, M. Zilis & D. Lohman; sport} 21" by 44" md; lvs 9" by 4 3/4" (8-9 vp); fast-growing mound of narrow green foliage

'Hi Ho Silver': {1997r, Walters Gardens; sport} wider white margins, even when juvenile

'Sweet Marjorie': {1983r, R. Benedict; 'Ginko Craig' X *H. plantaginea*} dense md of slightly shiny, wavy, med green foliage; 26" by 58" md; lvs 9 3/8" by 5 3/4" (9 vp); fragrant, narrow, 3" long fls in mid-Aug on 42" sc; fast-growing; similar mound habit to 'Honeybells'

'Sparkling Burgundy': 'Ginko Craig' sdlg from Bob Savory; green foliage, outstanding flower effect **(see page 432)**

other similar types:

'Bunchoko': has the appearance of a mature 'Ginko Craig'

'Elsley': 15" by 29" md of narrow, white-mgd foliage (6 1/2" by 2 7/8" wi 6 vp & a 1/4" white mgn); like a mature 'Ginko Craig'

'Excalibur': {1986r by the AHS} low, dense mound (13" by 25") of narrow, white-margined foliage; lvs 6" by 3" wi a 1/4", pure white mgn (4-5 vp); introduced by Piedmont Gardens in 1979; not much different from 'Ginko Craig'

'Hime Karafuto': Japanese plant; strong similarities to 'Ginko Craig' in mature foliage & flowering

'Jadette': {1982r, K. Anderson; unknown parentage} dense, 11" by 23" md of narrow, creamy mgd lvs, 4 5/8" by 1 1/16" (4 vp) that is also sl rippled

H. sieboldii 'Mr. Asami Improved': resembles mature 'Ginko Craig'

'Ototo San': {1990r, P. Ruh} narrow, white-mgd lvs; 12" by 26" md; br purple fls on 31" sc in Aug

'Princess of Karafuto': {1984r, M. Soules} same as 'Hime Karafuto' (name is one translation of it)

'Swarthmore Supreme': virtually indistinguishable from 'Ginko Craig'

'Tiddlywinks': {1989r, P. Banyai; unknown parentage} white-margined foliage; resembles 'Ginko Craig'

'Gloriosa'

key features: medium-sized mound of leaves with very thin, upturned, white margins
mound size: 18" high by 46" wide (up to 21" by 60")

spacing: 36"
leaves: 7 7/8" long by 4 1/2" wide; very thin, 1/32" to 1/16" wide, white margin that cups upward; center dark green; thin underside bloom; ovate to elliptic blade at maturity, narrowly elliptic when young; rounded base; noticeably upturned at tip; moderately corrugated at maturity; slight marginal waviness; better than average substance; 8-9 vein pairs

flowers: late July into early August; pale lavender; 2 1/4" long by 1" wide; bunched near the top of 20-30" scapes; many scapes per clump; typical 'Fortunei' characteristics

comments: Despite being a long-established hosta cultivar, 'Gloriosa' continues to retain its distinctive reputation. The narrowness of the upturned, white margins creates interesting cupping and corrugated effects in mature plants. It does not "drawstring" (tearing and browning of the margin) unless very heavily fertilized and watered. 'Gloriosa' has a good growth rate, rapidly becoming a dense mound of foliage that can be very effective as a ground cover or specimen plant.

I have seen some variation in 'Gloriosa' from garden to garden. Most plants have thin, white margins, but I noted one with even thinner margins, probably no wider than 1/64" on all of its leaves. There also is a form with a greenish yellow margin that gradually changes to white. At first I thought this plant was just an early season stage of 'Gloriosa' until I saw it growing alongside the typical, pure white-margined form growing in "The Hosta Glade" at the Minnesota Landscape Arboretum. These plants were labeled *Hosta rhodeifolia aureo-marginata* and *H. rhodeifolia albo-marginata*. These incorrect names were occasionally used for 'Gloriosa' before 1990, further confusing the identity of the true *Hosta rohdeifolia* **(see page 368)**.

Peter Ruh informed me that 'Gloriosa' was imported by Gus Krossa from Japan in the 1960's and later was named by Alex Summers. It was known as *H. fortunei* 'Gloriosa' for many years and registered as such by the AHS in 1986. 'Gloriosa' certainly is closely related to many Fortuneis as evidenced by both foliage and flowering characteristics.

seedlings, sports, and other related types:
'Miss Maddie': {1999r, N. Simes & R. Snyder; sport; lvs white-mgd with a dk green, yellow-streaked center}
Two other unnamed sports exist:
   (1) very thin, white margins
   (2) greenish yellow-margined (incorrectly labelled, *H. rhodeifolia aureo-marginata*)

other similar types:
H. lancifolia 'Change of Tradition'

'Goddess of Athena'
key features: medium-sized mound of foliage with distinct, creamy white margins; purple flowers; rhizomatous
mound size: 16" high by 40" wide

spacing: 36"
leaves: 7 1/2" long by 5" wide; 1/4" to 1/2" wide margin that changes from creamy yellow to white; medium to dark green center; oblong-elliptic blade that is slightly wavy with limited corrugation; top slightly shiny, underside very shiny; average substance; 7-9 vein pairs
flowers: early to late August; medium purple color; 3 1/8" long by 1" wide; bell-shaped; scapes up to 40" long; many pods develop

comments: 'Goddess of Athena' stands out because of the sharp contrast between the wide, creamy white margins and the dark green center. Bob Kuk (as Kuk's Forest) registered 'Goddess of Athena' in 1987 as a self-pollinated seedling of

184

'Decorata' for which it can be substituted in the landscape. In flower it comes very close to 'Decorata' bearing many beautiful, bell-shaped purple flowers in August.

seedlings, sports, and other related types:

'First Impressions': {1991r, R. Kuk; sport} same as 'Goddess of Athena' except for the white and mottled streaks running through the green leaf center; could be a good source of streaked seedlings

other similar types:

'Abiqua Delight', 'Bold Edger', 'Decorata'

'Gold Drop'

key features: small, dense mound of chartreuse to golden foliage

mound size: 12" high by 33" wide

spacing: 30"

leaves: 5 1/2" long by 3 7/8" wide; color changes from light green to chartreuse to medium gold, depending upon the season and light level; thin underside bloom; ovate shape with a heart-shaped base; little or no waviness; average substance; 9-10 vein pairs

flowers: June 25 to July 14 (northern Illinois); medium lavender with darker mid-petal striping; 1 5/8" long by 15/16" wide; narrow funnel shape; 15-21" scapes; 15 scapes on one clump; many seed pods develop

comments: 'Gold Drop' became very popular in the 1980's, being widely used as an edging plant, ground cover, and rock garden subject. It rapidly grows into a mature-sized clump, offers a bright show of golden foliage, and is fairly attractive in flower.

'Gold Drop' was one of the first hostas to be propagated by tissue culture in the late 1970's. Its widespread propagation led to a series of sports being named from it or its sports, creating a large, continually expanding sport family.

185

Ken Anderson registered 'Gold Drop' in 1977. It was the result of a cross of *Hosta venusta* X 'August Moon' (Solberg, 1988).

seedlings, sports, and other related types:

'Amy Elizabeth': reversed sport of 'Abby' developed at my nursery (Q & Z N); 13" by 35" md; lvs 5 1/4" by 3 3/4" (9-10 vp); 1/8" wide, medium to dark green margin; center chartreuse to gold; introduced for sale in 1999

'Abby': {1990r, P. Ruh; sport} gold-margined, green-centered leaves; 1/2" wide, gold margin on a 5 1/2" by 3 1/2" leaf; outstanding

'Crown Jewel': {1984r, Walters Gardens; sport} leaves gold-centered with very thin, white margins that can drawstring; poor grower

'Dew Drop': {1988r, Walters Garden; sport} lvs green-centered wi a pencil-thin, white margin

'Drip Drop': {1988r, Walters Garden; sport} white-mgd, chartreuse-centered lvs

'Fairway Green': {1990r, Fairway Enterprises; sport} small, dense mound of thick-substanced, very wavy, green foliage; lvs 5" by 3 3/4" (10 vp)

'Forest Shadows': {1999r, K. Engel; 'Gum Drop' sport; lvs med green wi a dark green margin}

'Gold Cadet': {1974r, P. Aden; hybrid of two seedlings} dense mound of heart-shaped, chartreuse to bright gold foliage; 13" by 29" md; lvs 6" by 4 3/8" (9-10 vp); lav fls in July; difficult to distinguish from 'Gold Drop' (and 'Gold Edger'); never widely grown and now is very rare

'Gum Drop': {1987r, L. Englerth} sport of 'Gold Drop'; med-sized, dense md of green foliage

'Honey Moon': {1982r, K. Anderson} 'Gold Drop' sibling (*H. venusta* X 'August Moon') (Solberg, 1988); 21" by 49" md; chartreuse, heart-shaped lvs, 5 1/4" by 5" (9 vp); larger than 'Gold Drop'

'Jelly Bean': {1990r, C. Harstad; sport of 'Gum Drop'} 12" by 33" md of streaked foliage with a chartreuse margin; sometimes stabilizing to other forms including chartreuse-centered, gold-mgd lvs

'Marilyn': {1990r, M. Zilis; 'Gold Drop' X 'Green Piecrust'} 17" by 43" md of slightly wavy, golden foliage; lvs 7" by 5" (11 vp), chartreuse early, medium gold by mid-summer; lav fls on 25" sc, late June into July; brighter gold, larger and more open mound habit than 'Gold Drop'

'Panache': {1999r, B. Arnold; sport; lvs gold wi a bl-green mgn}

'Peedee Absinth': {1990r, U. Syre-Herz; 'Gold Drop' X 'Subcrocea'} 12" by 33" md of chartreuse to gold lvs, 5"

by 3 1/2" (7 vp)

'Peedee Treasure': {1989r, U. Syre-Herz; 'Gold Drop' X *H. ventricosa*; br yellow-green foliage}

'Pooh Bear': {1988r, C. Falstad; sport} gold-centered, green-margined foliage

'Sun Drop': {1999r, B. Banyai; sport; lvs green-centered, pale yellow-mgd}

other similar types:

'Birchwood Parky's Gold', 'Gold Edger', 'Golden Spider'

'Gold Edger'
key features: dense mound of heart-shaped, golden foliage
mound size: 13" high by 38" wide (up to 16" by 59")

spacing: 36"

leaves: 5 1/4" long by 3 7/8" wide; color changes from light green to chartreuse or gold by mid-summer, depending upon location; yellow fall color in late October; slight bloom on the top and underside surfaces; ovate blade with a heart-shaped base; slightly wavy; slightly corrugated; average substance; 10 vein pairs

flowers: June 23 to July 12 (northern Illinois); medium lavender with a darker petal midrib; 1 9/16" by 1" wide; many 15-22" scapes with 29 buds per scape; fertile

comments: 'Gold Edger' develops into a very symmetrical, dense mound of heart-shaped, golden foliage that is very similar to 'Gold Drop'. The flowers develop in tight clusters over the foliage and are ornamentally attractive. 'Gold Edger' has been (and continues to be) propagated by both division and tissue culture, making it widely available in garden centers and through mail order catalogs.

'Gold Edger' was registered by Paul Aden, Baldwin, NY

in 1978 as a hybrid of 'Blue Cadet' X 'Gold Cadet'. It has been the source of a number of sports, building a group similar to that of 'Gold Drop'.

seedlings, sports, and other related types:

'Bilben Little Atlantis': {1998r, W. Bennett; sport wi lvs that are gold, streaked with medium green}

'Double Gold Edger': sport from Ron Simmering of Iowa with leaves that have a light gold margin and medium gold center; have only seen in the originator's garden; differs from 'Radiant Edger' in having a gold (not green) center

'Gold Edger Supreme': sport from my nursery (Q & Z N); lvs bluish to dark green-centered wi an extremely thin, white margin; a collector's curiosity but not a very good plant

'Gold Edger Surprise': sport from my nursery (Q & Z N); lvs gold-centered wi a very thin, white margin that is sometimes immeasurable; another collector's curiosity of dubious value

'Hawkeye': {1999r, L. Maroushek; sport wi green-centered, yellow-mgd lvs}

'June Bug': {1999r, R. Lydell; sport wi gold-centered, green-mgd lvs}

'Olympic Edger': {1999r, Naylor Creek N; sport; lvs greenish ylw wi a thin, creamy white mgn}

'Radiant Edger': {1990r, M. Zilis; sport} gold-margined, green-centered lvs, 4 1/2" by 4" wi a 1/2" mgn; md 14" by 39"; colors intensify during the season and in brighter light

'Timothy': {1998r, D. Ruh & P. Ruh; sport} lvs chartreuse to gold-mgd wi a dk green center; noticeably different from 'Radiant Edger'

other similar types:

'Golden Spider': {1987r, P. Ruh for G. Harshbarger; unknown parentage} low, dense md of bright gold (chartreuse early) lvs, 4 5/8" by 3 7/8" (9 vp); med lav fls, late June into mid-July, on 20-24" sc; outstanding foliage color, md habit & flower show

'Gold Regal'

key features: large, semi-upright mound of chartreuse to gold foliage

mound size: 32" high by 63" wide

spacing: 48"

leaves: 11 1/4" long by 8 1/2" wide; color changes from pale green in spring covered with a grayish bloom to chartreuse or medium gold by mid-June with increasing light levels and as the bloom wears away; yellowish gold fall color in early October; thick bloom on underside; blade ovate to oblong-ovate with a squarish base; petioles at 45 degree angle creating semi-

upright mound shape; slight marginal waviness; moderate corrugation; slight cupping, especially near the base; good substance; 14-16 vein pairs

flowers: July 4 to 29; medium lavender with lighter margins; 2 3/4" long by 1 1/2" wide; narrow funnel shape; scapes 39" high and covered with a thick bloom; many seed pods develop

comments: 'Gold Regal' makes an impressive specimen or background plant that is interesting in both foliage and flower. It has achieved "classic" status because of its great popularity over a long period of time and good durability in a wide variety of landscape situations. The intensity of the gold color is mostly dependent upon the amount of light it receives. In northern Illinois, two hours of direct sunlight will produce a beautiful mound of bright gold foliage. Plant 'Gold Regal' in very dense shade and it will remain pale green or chartreuse all season long.

It has been an excellent parent and a source of numerous mutations. Paul Aden registered 'Gold Regal' in 1974 as a hybrid of two seedlings and it ranks as one of his best introductions.

seedlings, sports, and other related types:

'Alex Summers': {1989r, V. Santa Lucia; sport} medium

189

green center; 1/4" to 1 1/2" wide, medium gold margin which is wider and brighter than that of 'Independence Day'

'Big Dipper': {1995r, R. Kuk; 'Gold Regal' sdlg} leaves chartreuse becoming gold

'Blue Betty Lou': {1987r, C. Owens; 'True Blue' X 'Gold Regal'} semi-upr md of bl foliage **(see page 85)**

'David Reath': {1998r by R. Klehm for D. Reath; sport wi dark green-centered, golden yellow-mgd lvs}

'Fort Knox': {1989r, J. & J. Wilkins; 'Gold Regal' X 'Aspen Gold'} 24" by 60" md of light gold lvs, 12" by 8" (14 vp); lav fls on 33" sc, mid-July into Aug; one of the best 'Gold Regal' seedlings

'Golden Cascade': {1984r, R. Benedict; 'Gold Regal' X a 'Gold Regal' sdlg} lvs 11 1/2" by 6 3/4" (14 vp); brighter gold and wavier margins than 'Gold Regal'

'Golden Eagle': {1998r, R. Benedict; 'Gold Regal' sdlg wi golden-yellow-mgd, bl-green-centered lvs}

'Golden Teacup': {1989r, J. & J. Wilkins; 'Aspen Gold' X 'Gold Regal'} deeply cupped, gold leaves; near-white flowers in July; beautiful plant

'Golden Torch': {1984r, R. Benedict; selfed 'Gold Regal' sdlg} vase-shaped md of chartreuse to gold foliage that is somewhat cupped and corrugated; 24" by 55" md; lvs 10" by 7 1/2" (14 vp); brighter gold and more vase-shaped habit than 'Gold Regal'

'Heartache': a Benedict hybrid of 'Gold Regal' X *H. ventricosa*; large, golden, heart-shaped leaves topped by purple flowers **(see page 223)**

'High Style': {1984r, R. Benedict, a selfed 'Gold Regal' sdlg} 23" by 44" md of bright gold leaves, 9" by 5 1/2" (14 vp); similar mound habit and leaf to 'Gold Regal' but a much brighter gold color

'Independence Day': {1998r, V. Wade; sport} gold-margined, chartreuse-centered sport; impressive, vase-shaped mound, 35" by 79"; lvs 11 1/2" by 8" (16 vp); mgn 3/8" or less; named by Van Wade on July 4, 1996 when he viewed the plant in bloom; outstanding mound habit and flower performance

'Midwest Majesty': {1983r, E. Minks; 'Gold Regal' sdlg; chartr wi green markings} have never seen

'Misty Regal': {1996r, J. & E. Stratton; sport} medium green margin, streaky chartreuse in center; lvs 13" by 7" with a 1/2" margin

'Prairie Fire': {1994r, R. Kuk; 'Gold Regal' X a golden 'Tokudama' sdlg} 12" by 25" md of corrugated, brilliant gold foliage that is somewhat wavy; lvs measure 9" by 4 3/8" (10 vp); near-wh fls on 26" sc, mid to late July

'Rascal': {1991r, R. Solberg; sport} 25" by 55" md, chartreuse margin, gold center; lvs 10" by 7" wi a 1/2" wide margin and 14 vp; lf center lightens during the season; outstanding plant

'Regal Skies': {1999r, B. Banyai; sport; blue-green foliage}

'Straka Gold': {1994r, C. Owens; 'Gold Regal' X *H. montana*; deep gold foliage}

'Ugly Duckling': {1999r, Q & Z N, M. Zilis & P. Ruh; sport} lvs gold-centered with a thin, white margin that may drawstring wi maturity; for collectors only

'Ultraviolet Light': {1989r, J. & J. Wilkins; 'Gold Regal' sdlg} semi-upr md of golden foliage topped by bright purple flowers in July; leaves smaller than 'Gold Regal' **(see page 483)**

'Unforgettable': {1999r, R. Kuk; sport of ('Gold Regal' X a gold 'Tokudama' sdlg)} 22" high, semi-upright mound of gold-mgd, green-centered foliage; lvs 9" by 7 1/2" (12 vp); lav fls from late July into mid-August on 41" sc; very impressive; sports to gold-leaved 'Skyrocket' {1999r, R. Kuk}

'Yellow Highness': {1990r, C. Owens; selfed 'Gold Regal' sdlg} strongly upright md of lvs that closely resemble 'Gold Regal' except for a much brighter gold color; 32" by 58" md; lvs 12" by 8" (16 vp); aptly named; worth growing

other similar types:

'Daybreak', 'Rising Sun'

'Gold Standard'

key features: medium-large mound of gold-centered foliage; symmetrical habit; fast grower
mound size: 22" high by 60" wide

spacing: 48"
leaves: 9" long by 6 1/4" wide; 1/4" to 1/2" wide, dark green margin; center changes from green (May 1) to medium green (May 20), chartreuse (June 10), and gold (June 25) (medium to almost white-gold with bright light); thin underside bloom; oblong-ovate blade with a rounded base and distinct tip; no marginal waviness; slight corrugation at maturity; average substance; 10-11 vein pairs
flowers: July 15 to August 6 (northern Illinois); pale lavender color with darker mid-petal striping; 1 3/4" long by 7/8" wide; narrow funnel shape; 22-36" scapes; rarely forms seed pods
comments: 'Gold Standard' will always be at the top of my list of hosta favorites. The dense mound of brightly variegated foliage makes an effective impact in any landscape and the rapid growth rate means that small plants will become full-sized clumps within a few years. I have seen 'Gold Standard' used in just about every way in the landscape: as a showy specimen, an edger, and a ground cover, even as a background plant.

Pauline Banyai found 'Gold Standard' in a batch of 'Fortunei Hyacinthina' that she received from a wholesale nursery, and in 1976 she registered it with the AHS. It created quite a sensation among members of the fledgling American Hosta Society and gave everyone a glimmer of the future of hostas. It continued to command fairly high prices into the mid-1980's and is now considered one of the staples of the perennial industry.

Like 'Fortunei Hyacinthina', its "mother plant", 'Gold

Standard' has been at the center of an incredible array of mutations, and more are being found all the time. Perhaps the most talked about sport has been 'Striptease', a narrow-centered form. Other variations on the same theme include 'Captain Kirk' and 'G String'. When 'Gold Standard' is propagated by tissue culture, sports are frequently produced. Most often is the green-leaved 'Fortunei Hyacinthina', but many unstable, white-streaked mutations also develop. Rarely seen are high quality sports on the level of 'Striptease', 'Brenda's Beauty', 'Something Different', 'Captain Kirk', or 'Moonlight'.

seedlings, sports, and other related types:

'Bob Sanders': {1998r, B. Sanders & E. Elslager; sport; lvs heavily streaked wi green, yellow & creamy white}

'Brenda's Beauty': {1992r, R. Keller; sport} lvs green-mgd with a chartreuse center early, changing to a very light yellow center by late May (n. Illinois); 18" by 46" md; 8" by 5 7/8" lvs (11 vp); one of the best 'Gold Standard' sports

'Caesar': {1999r, A. Malloy; sport wi a streaked green & white center, bl-gr mgn}

'Captain Kirk': {1999r, K. Brill; sport} impressive, narrow-centered lvs, 8" by 7" wi a 2" mgn (3" center); different from 'Striptease' and 'Gold Standard'

'Darwin's Standard': sport of 'Gold Standard' from Holland; gold-centered, green-mgd foliage

'G String': {1996r, J. Mann, Jr.; sport wi leaves that have narrow gold centers}

'Gamma Ray': {1999r, A. Malloy; 'Striptease' sport; lvs green-mgd wi a thin, white center}

'Landmark': sport of 'Gold Standard' found in 1998 at Landmark Gardens, Plattsmouth, NE; v narrow gold center & wide green mgn

'Moonlight': {1977r, P. Banyai} first 'Gold Standard' sport; go-cntrd, wh-mgd lvs **(see page 312)**

'Richland Gold': {1987r, V. Wade} all-gold sport that makes a bright, attractive mound, 18" by 45"; br gold foliage (8 1/2" by 6"); slower growing than 'Gold Standard'

'Richland Gold's Moonlight': {1999r, V. Wade; sport of 'Richland Gold'} gold-centered, white-mgd lvs

'Sam-Tina Gold': {1998r, J. Orlando; sport; light green foliage that turns white}

'Sarah Jane': {1997r, D. & J. Ward} reversed 'Gold Standard' sport; 8 1/2" by 6 1/4" (11 vp) lvs green-centered wi a 1/4" wide margin that turns gold on the same schedule as the gold center of 'Gold Standard'; 26" by 57" md; first saw in 1986; have seen this mutation develop many times

193

'Silver And Gold': {1995r, R. Lydell; sport wi gold-centered lvs bordered by a green and white margin}

'Something Different': {1990r, P. Banyai; sport} center gold (wi a green mgn) as lvs emerge in spring

'Striptease': sport with a narrow, gold center and wide, dark green margin **(see page 437)**

'Standard Deviation': {1998r, C. Helsley; sport wi streaked center & green margin}

'Zodiac': gold-centered, yellow-margined sport of 'Richland Gold'; lvs 8" by 5" (11 vp) wi a 1/8-1/4" margin; a Mark Zilis-Peter Ruh introduction; unusual color combination; named in 1999

other similar types:

'Janet': similar gold-centered, green-margined foliage, though smaller than 'Gold Standard' **(see page 244)**

'Marion Bachman': {1992r, L. Bachman; a 'Fortunei' mutation} gold-centered foliage that resembles 'Gold Standard'; one lf 7" by 4 1/2" (9 vp) wi a 1" green mgn & a lighter center

'Okay Dokey': gold-centered, green-margined sport of 'Aoki' from Herb Benedict; 22" by 58" md; lvs 9 1/2" by 6" (11 vp) wi a 1/2" dk gr mgn & br gold center; a stunning plant

'Rossing's Pride': {1993r, R. Rossing; 'Fortunei Hyacinthina' sport} impressive gold-centered foliage

---

'Golden Medallion'

key features: medium-large mound of heavily corrugated, gold foliage; slug-resistant

mound size: 16" high by 40" wide

spacing: 36"

leaves: 8" long by 7" wide; chartreuse early, turning

medium to bright gold; thick underside bloom; blade broadly ovate and slightly wavy; very heavily corrugated; thick substance; 14-16 vein pairs

flowers: late June into mid-July; near-white with a pale lavender mid-petal stripe; deeper lavender in bud; 2" long by 1 1/4" wide; in dense clusters on scapes up to 28" high; many seed pods develop

comments: 'Golden Medallion' has been around for many years under an assortment of names including *H. tokudama* 'Golden' and "Golden Tokudama". Both of those names have also been used for the very, very similar 'Golden Bullion'. The "true" 'Golden Medallion' is the all-gold sport from the tissue culture production (very rarely from the garden) of 'Tokudama Aureonebulosa' and, until 'Golden Bullion' was named, it no doubt was used for gold-leaved sports of 'Tokudama Flavocircinalis'. 'Golden Medallion' makes a nice, slug-resistant garden plant that complements other Tokudamas such as 'Buckshaw Blue', 'Bright Lights', and 'Tokudama Flavocircinalis' in the landscape. A big plus is that the foliage does not "burn" in the spring as do the golden Sieboldianas to which they are genetically related. There are many other similar golden Tokudamas that only differ by the amount of corrugation, shade of gold, cupping, leaf shape, etc. For general landscaping purposes, they can be used interchangeably. Unfortunately most in this group (including 'Golden Medallion') exhibit a fairly slow growth rate, so heavy fertilization and watering, especially in the first few years after planting, is essential to maximize growth.

The American Hosta Society registered 'Golden Medallion' in 1984.

seedlings, sports, and other related types:
none listed

other similar types:
'Aspen Gold': gold-leaved Tokudama **(see page 69)**
'Barbara White': {1990r, S. Bond; 'Tokudama' sdlg} thick-substanced gold foliage; 15" by 44" md; 12" by 9 1/2" lvs (17 vp)
'Bengee': {1999r by P. Ruh for J. Harrison, Palmer, & R. Bemis} 15" by 31" md; chartreuse, Tokudama-type lvs; probably a sdlg of 'Tokudama Aureonebulosa' (Summers, 1971b); a blue-lvd plant has erroneously been labelled this
'Bright Glow': {1986r, P. Aden} known for many years as "Golden Tardiana"; 13" by 36" md of thick-substd, br gold lvs, 7" by 6" (11-12 vp); near-wh fls, late June into mid-July on 20" sc; impressive golden Tardiana-type
'Cardwell Yellow': {1981r by P. Ruh for G. Krossa;

unknown parentage} 26" by 63" md; heavily corrugated, bright gold foliage; lvs 9 3/4" by 8 1/4" (15 vp); near-white fls, late June into July

'Estelle Aden': {1978r, P. Aden; 'Golden Waffles' X 'Gold Cup'} 16" by 42" md of heavily corrug, very bright gold lvs; thick subst; pale lav fls, late June into July; becoming rare

'Gold Cup': {1978r, P. Aden; 'Tokudama Aureonebulosa' X 'Golden Prayers'} 17" by 34" md; 9 3/8" by 8 1/2" lvs that are med to br gold; intensely corrugated, deeply cupped, & thick-substanced; differs fr 'Golden Medallion' by more deeply cupped foliage; popular breeding plant

'Golden Bullion': {1989r by P. Ruh for P. Bennerup} gold-leaved sport of 'Tokudama Flavocircinalis; virtually indistinguishable from 'Golden Medallion' though some consider it a brighter gold

'Golden Waffles' **(see page 202)**

'Goldilocks': {1970r, M. Armstrong; "Variegated Glauca" sdlg} probably from 'Tokudama Aureonebulosa'; 17" by 47" md of thick, heavily corrugated, br gold lvs, 9" by 7" (14 vp)

'Ledi Lantis': {1978r, P. Aden; 'Gold Cup' X 'Golden Waffles'} 14" by 31" md of heavily corrugated, cupped, bright gold lvs, 7" by 5 1/2" (14-16 vp); near-wh fls, late June into July; rarely grown anymore

'Peedee Dew Catcher': {1992r, U. Syre-Herz; 'City Lights' X 'Bold Ruffles'} 18" by 57" md of heavily corrugated, thick-substanced, gold lvs 11" by 8 1/2" (17 vp); changes from chartreuse to gold; has sported to 'Dippity Dew', which has green-centered, gold-mgd leaves {1999r, J. Schwarz}

'Summer Gold': {1998r, P. Ruh for S. Hamblin & F. Williams} long-standing cv that is rarely grown anymore; 14" by 38" md of thick-subst, gold foliage that becomes greener during the growing season; lvs 10" by 8" (16 vp)

'Super Bowl': medium-sized mound of deeply cupped, golden foliage; 17" by 44" md; lvs 10 1/2" by 10 1/2" (16 vp), chartreuse in spring, brighter by mid-summer; lvs also thick-substd; cupping 3" at deepest point; near-wh fls, June-July; one of the best cupped hostas; a Paul Aden introduction from the mid-1980's

'Thai Brass': {1972r, F. Woodroffe; unknown parentage} 20" by 44" md; slightly cupped, corrugated foliage; brilliant gold by mid-summer; lvs 11 1/2" by 9" (15 vp); a tremendous plant

'Treasure' **(see page 481)**

'Golden Prayers'

key features: medium-large mound of heavily corrugated golden foliage; a Tokudama-type
mound size: 21" high by 45" wide

spacing: 36"

leaves: 8 1/2" long by 8" wide; medium to bright gold color; moderate underside bloom; blade very broadly ovate, somewhat wavy, and heavily corrugated; thick substance; 14-16 vein pairs

flowers: late June into mid-July; near-white; scapes 24" or lower; some pods develop

comments: This plant has been the source of great confusion for some years. I first encountered it as a small-sized mound of bright golden foliage in various hosta collections. Later I found a plant labelled 'Golden Prayers' that fit the description of a golden Tokudama and was told that this was the true form. Much discussion at conventions centered around the presumption that the plant being widely sold as 'Golden Prayers' was the same as 'Little Aurora'. Data that I had examined in the AHS Registrar's office in 1983 was inconclusive and basically did not describe either plant! Paul Aden registered 'Golden Prayers' in 1976 as a hybrid of "Aden 381" X 'Golden Waffles'. Certainly the widely sold form of 'Golden Prayers' did not match 'Golden Waffles' but I did not know the identity of "Aden 381". Over time, though, in a wide variety of collections and nurseries, extensive data collection and observation led me to the conclusion that the commonly sold 'Golden Prayers' was indeed the same as 'Little Aurora'. Just to confirm my conclusion, I went back to Paul Aden's 1979-80 "Hosta List" to see how 'Golden Prayers' and 'Little Aurora' were depicted. Sure enough, 'Golden Prayers' is described on the third page as

197

"medium-large; unique form of upright leaves held like hands in prayer; choice gold-cupped Tokudama type". On the other hand, the description (also on the third page) for 'Little Aurora' read "small, neat clump of bright gold from Tokudama parentage; heavy substance".

What this all means is if your mature clump of 'Golden Prayers' has small foliage, roughly 5" long by 4" wide with 11-12 vein pairs forming a mound about 12" high by 22" wide, relabel it 'Little Aurora'. A mound of true 'Golden Prayers' will reach over 20" in height with leaves roughly 8" by 8" with around 16 vein pairs.

This also calls into question the origins of any sports or seedlings of 'Golden Prayers'. A few are from the true, Tokudama-type form, but most are descendants of 'Little Aurora'. I have indicated the probable origins of each in the following sections.

seedlings, sports, and other related types:
'City Lights': {1978r, P. Aden; 'White Vision' X 'Golden Prayers'} correct listing, pollen from the true 'Golden Prayers' **(see page 119)**

'Delia': {1995r, R. & M. Ford (England); as a sport of 'Golden Prayers' with a light yellow center and medium green margin; 6" high md; 3" long lvs wi 8 vp} should be listed as a sport of 'Little Aurora'

'Goldbrook Grace': {1989r, S. Bond; as a sport of 'Golden Prayers' with a pale yellow center and medium green margin forming a 6" high md and lvs that are 4" long with 8 vp} should be listed as a sport of 'Little Aurora'

'Gosan Gold Midget': {1989r, W. Schmid; *H. venusta* X 'Golden Prayers'; glossy, bright yellow-green foliage that forms a 3" high md with lvs 1 1/2" long (5 vp)} more correctly *H. venusta* X 'Little Aurora'

'Gosan Hildegarde': {1989r, W. Schmid; 'Golden Prayers' X 'Ginko Craig'} low md of narrow, bright gold foliage; purple fls in late July; more correctly listed as 'Little Aurora' X 'Ginko Craig'??

'Lakeside Leprechaun': {1991r, M. Chastain; as a sport of 'Golden Prayers'} lvs chartreuse changing to green by mid-June (Ohio); md 15" by 40"; 6" by 4 1/2" lvs; probably a sport of 'Little Aurora'

'Tucker Irish Heart': {1993r, R. Stephens; dark gr-lvd sport of 'Golden Prayers'; 8" high md wi 4" long leaves (9 vp)} another green 'Little Aurora' sport

'Zounds': {1978r, P. Aden; 'Golden Waffles' X 'Golden Prayers'} pollen from the true 'Golden Prayers' **(see page 513)**

other similar types:
'Aspen Gold', 'Estelle Aden', 'Gold Cup', 'Golden Bul-

lion', 'Golden Medallion', 'Golden Waffles', 'King Tut', 'Thai Brass', 'Treasure'

'Golden Sculpture'
key features: large, vase-shaped mound of bright gold foliage
mound size: 33" high by 72" wide

spacing: 60"

leaves: 16 1/4" long by 10 3/4" wide; chartreuse early, medium to bright gold by mid-summer; thin bloom on top and underside surfaces; blade ovate with a heart-shaped base, a long, distinct tip, and slight waviness; moderate to heavy corrugation; thick substance; 18 vein pairs

flowers: late June into early July; near-white color; 2 5/8" long by 1 1/2" wide; funnel-shaped; tall scapes

comments: 'Golden Sculpture' has long been underrated. At one time it was destined for the scrap heap of another hybridizer, but Ken Anderson realized its value and saved it. 'Golden Sculpture' has turned out to be one of the most impressive of the large, gold-leaved hostas. A mature specimen stands out in any collection with its heavily corrugated, golden leaves forming a beautiful, vase-shaped mound. The leaf blades jut out horizontally from the almost upright petioles resulting in the leaves resting no lower than 22" above soil level. In northern areas, it also has fairly good sun tolerance. Ken registered 'Golden Sculpture' in 1982.

seedlings, sports, and other related types:
none listed

other similar types:
'Fort Knox', 'Gold Regal', 'High Noon', 'Yellow Highness'

'Golden Tiara'

key features: fast-growing, medium-sized mound of gold-margined foliage
mound size: 16" high by 39" wide (up to 19" by 46")

spacing: 36"
leaves: 4 1/4" long by 3 1/2" wide; irregular, 1/8" to 3/4" wide, chartreuse to gold margin (color brighter gold in brighter light); medium green center; shiny underside; ovate blade that is slightly wavy; slight corrugation at maturity, none when young; average substance; 7-8 vein pairs
flowers: July 15 to August 2 (northern Illinois); pale purple in deep shade, medium purple with some direct sunlight; 2 1/8" long by 1 1/4" wide; funnel-shaped; 25-34" scapes; 21, 22, and 27 scapes on three mature clumps in different gardens; at the peak of flowering 2-4 flowers open per scape each day; sparse seed pod formation; sometimes reblooms in late summer if scapes removed just after flowering

comments: When introduced to collectors in the late 1970's, 'Golden Tiara' elicited great excitement by being the first hosta with gold-margined foliage in a small-sized mound. Since then it has been propagated by just about every nursery that grows hostas, but that has not diminished its value. Not only are the leaves attractive and the growth rate fast, but the flowers are an ornamental plus and it can be used in many ways in the landscape (edging, ground cover, and specimen). Needless to say, it has achieved "classic" status and will continue to be grown for a long time to come. 'Golden Tiara' is an origination of Bob Savory who registered it in 1977 as a sport of a *Hosta nakaiana* seedling.

At the 1980 AHS convention, I purchased my first 'Golden Tiara' plant at the society's auction for $40 and thought I had a bargain for this "rare" plant (since it was going for about $50 at the time). Immediately following the auction we took a tour of Savory's Greenhouse and Gardens in Edina, Minnesota where I was astounded to see a planting bed of several thousand 'Golden Tiara' divisions.

'Golden Tiara' has been extensively propagated by both division and tissue culture. One unexpected result has been the development of a huge family of related sports. Most share 'Golden Tiara's good growing and flowering habits, making excellent plants for landscaping.

seedlings, sports, and other related types:

The chronological sequence of sports related to 'Golden Tiara' is as follows:

'Golden Scepter': {1983r, R. Savory} gold-leaved 'Golden Tiara' sport; md 16" by 35"; lvs 5" by 3 3/4" (7 vp); bright gold in spring; slower growing than 'Golden Tiara'

'Diamond Tiara':{1985r, M. Zilis & T & Z N} white-margined, green-centered 'Golden Tiara' sport

'Platinum Tiara': {1987r, Walters Gardens} white-margined, gold-centered sport of 'Golden Scepter'

'Emerald Tiara': {1988r, Walters Gardens} green-margined, gold-centered sport of 'Golden Scepter'

'Jade Scepter': {1988r, M. Zilis & T & Z N} green-leaved sport of 'Golden Tiara'; good grower, serviceable ground cover but not exciting; 16" by 43" md

'Royal Tiara': {1988r, M. Zilis & T & Z N} green-margined, narrow white-centered sport of 'Golden Tiara'; odd collector's plant that grows surprisingly well; md 8" by 17" wi twisted, gnarled lvs; flower color differs from 'Golden Tiara' (lavender)

'Silver Tiara': {1988r, Walters Gardens} gold-mgd, white-centered sport of 'Golden Scepter'; very weak; no longer grown

'Emerald Scepter': t.c. sport of 'Golden Tiara' from my nursery (Q & Z N) introduced in 1991; 8" by 20" md of lvs wi a light green mgn & a gold center that can turn creamy white in bright light; originally thought to be the same as 'Emerald Tiara' but is not; less vigorous than 'Emerald Tiara' and smaller

'Grand Tiara': {1991r, A. Pollock} wide gold-margined sport of 'Golden Tiara' **(see page 206)**:

'Grand Gold': gold-leaved sport of 'Grand Tiara'; first saw in 1996

Additionally in 1998 Walters Gardens registered the following 'Grand Tiara' sports **(see page 206)**:

'Amber Tiara', 'Crystal Tiara', 'Gilded Tiara', 'Grand Prize', 'Heavenly Tiara', 'Topaz Tiara'

Seedlings related to 'Golden Tiara':

'Concordia Petite': {1996r, U. Syre-Herz; *H. venusta* X

'Golden Tiara'; small md of dk gr lvs}

'Sweet Tater Pie': {1995r, T. Avent; 'Golden Scepter' X *H. yingeri*} small md of foliage that is a shade of gold just like the name; turns green by mid-summer

'Teaspoon': {1998r, F. Nyikos; 'Birchwood Parky's Gold' X 'Golden Tiara'; margined, med gr lvs}

other similar types:

'Abby', 'Radiant Edger', 'Sultana', 'Warwick Curtsey'

'Golden Waffles'
key features: medium-large mound of intensely corrugated, bright gold foliage
mound size: 23" high by 50" wide

spacing: 36"

leaves: 11 5/8" long by 9 1/4" wide; bright gold with some direct light, chartreuse in dense shade; slight bloom on underside; broadly ovate blade with a deeply lobed and puckered base; slightly wavy; slight cupping; moderate to heavy corrugation increasing with maturity; good substance; 14-16 vein pairs

flowers: late June into mid-July; pale lavender, darker in mid-petal; 2 1/4" long by 1 3/8" wide; open funnel shape; 30" scapes; many pods develop

comments: In the areas of intense corrugation, bright gold color, and good substance, 'Golden Waffles' ranks highly. The gold color especially stands out on cloudy days or at dusk. Its growth rate is slow, so heavy watering and fertilization are necessary to achieve a mature size rapidly. Use it as a specimen plant or as a complement to gold-edged or blue Sieboldianas and Tokudamas. It also has value for hybridizers.

'Golden Waffles' was registered as a hybrid of two seedlings in 1976 by Paul Aden.

seedlings, sports, and other related types:

'Aztec Treasure': {1987r, K. Vaughn; 'Golden Waffles' X 'Rough Waters' sdlg} med-lg md of brilliant gold foliage; pale purple fls, June-July; underrated

'Gold Pan': {1978r, P. Aden; 'Golden Waffles' X 'Gold Cup'} 16" by 37" md of chartreuse to bright gold lvs, 9" by 6 3/4" (14-16 vp); lvs also heavily corrugated & somewhat cupped; near-wh fls, late June into mid-July; rarely grown

'Golden Prayers': {1976r, P. Aden; "Aden 381" X 'Golden Waffles'} the "true" form, not 'Little Aurora' **(see page 197)**

'Ledi Lantis': {1978r, P. Aden; 'Gold Cup' X 'Golden Waffles'} 14" by 31" md of heavily corrugated, cupped, bright gold lvs, 7" by 5 1/2" (14-16 vp); near-wh fls, late June into July; rarely grown anymore

'Maui Hana': {1991r, W. Vaughn; *H. sieboldiana* sdlg X 'Golden Waffles'} 23" by 57" md; medium to dark green lvs, 14" by 8 1/2" (14 vp) wi many slight, marginal ripples; long, graceful, smooth leaves; like a green 'Crispula'

'Shocking Chartreuse': {1982r, K. Vaughn; seedling X 'Golden Waffles'} luminescent gold color; moderate corrugation and cupping; rare

'Sunshine Glory': {1982r, K. Vaughn; 'William Lachman' sibling X 'Golden Waffles'} 28" by 60", semi-upr md; lvs 10" by 7" (15 vp) with a 3/8" to 1", creamy white mgn surrounding a center that changes from med gold to green during the season; worthwhile

'Tijuana Brass': {1988r, K. Vaughn; 'Golden Waffles' X 'Polly Bishop'} medium-sized md of unruly gold foliage **(see page 467)**

'Zounds': {1978r, P. Aden; 'Golden Waffles' X 'Golden Prayers'} outstanding gold-leaved Sieboldiana **(see page 513)**

other similar types:

'Centerfold': {1994r, G. Kamp; parentage unknown} 21" by 47" md of heavily corrugtd, unruly gold lvs, 10" by 7 3/4" (16 vp); striking specimen pl

'Golden Rajah': {1976r, P. Aden; 'Aspen Gold' sdlg X a 'Tokudama Aureonebulosa' sdlg} heavily corrugated, deeply cupped, bright gold foliage; 18" by 43" md; thick-substanced lvs, 9" by 9" (16 vp); excellent cultivar but not grown much anymore

'Midas Touch' **(see page 292)**

'Sea Bunny': {1986r, M. Seaver; parentage unknown} 14"

by 30" md of very heavily corrugated, 7" by 6" (13 vp) lvs; color iridescently shiny gold early, turning chartreuse by mid-summer, creating an interesting two-tone effect; near-white fls, late June into mid-July

'Sun's Glory': gold-lvd sport of 'Sunshine Glory'; semi-upright md (32" by 64") of heavily corrugated, chartreuse to bright gold foliage; lvs 12" by 8 1/4" (18 vp); pale lav fls, early to late July on scapes that just reach the top of the foliage mound; like a narrow-leaved 'Golden Waffles' in a vase-shaped md

---

Hosta gracillima (Hime Iwa Giboshi)
key features: low, very dense mound of small green foliage; purple flowers in September
mound size: 12" high by 31" wide

spacing: 18"

leaves: 4 1/4" long by 1 7/8" wide; medium green color; slightly shiny top, very shiny underside; narrowly ovate shape (elongated tear drop) with a rounded base and long, curved tip; noticeably rippled margin, 4-6 per side; reddish purple dots on much of petiole; thin substance; 4-6 vein pairs

flowers: mid-September into early October; medium purple color; a sharply contrasting band of white on the lower half of the petal margin leading into the throat creates a star-shaped center; slightly inflated funnel shape with reflexed tips; 9-15" scapes that have red-purple dots; only a few flowers per scape; fertile

comments: *Hosta gracillima* offers a combination of a very dense mound habit, small size, excellent growth rate, and late-blooming flowers. The latter characteristic should not be overlooked as there are few plants for shade gardens that bloom so late in the season. Some gardeners have used it effectively as an edger or as a specimen in the shaded rock garden.

In the wild, *Hosta gracillima* can be found in various locations around Shikoku Island. Most examples of *H. gracillima* in U.S. gardens resemble plants collected from wild populations in Japan, but a few other forms have been listed under this name.

seedlings, sports, and other related types:

Hosta gracillima "Lachman Strain": a form of the species with much narrower, wavier foliage; lvs 3 1/8" by 1" wi 4-5, distinct ripples; purple fls in Aug well above the foliage on 25" sc; resembles a form of *H. sieboldii* found wild in Japan; presumably from Bill & Eleanor Lachman

Hosta gracillima alba: white-flowered form of the species found in Japanese collections

Hosta gracillima albo-marginata: narrow, white margins; two plants may bear this name: one found in a natural population on Shikoku Island, Japan and one that has been grown in the U.S. since the early 90's; both appear to be sports of the true species

'Hydon Sunset': {1988r by the BHHS; no description supplied} identity of the true plant a thoroughly confusing situation-- listed as a hybrid of *H. gracillima* X 'Wogon Gold' that begins the season gold, turning green by Diana Grenfell (1990) who also indicated that it has been confused in the trade with 'Sunset', a much smaller gold; have seen at least 3 forms in U.S. gardens: (1) small md (8" by 22") of lvs that are gold in spring, green by mid-summer; (2) small md (10" by 27") of lvs that stay gold all season ('Sunset'?); & (3) med-lg md (21" by 42") of green lvs (8" by 6"); further complicating the issue, 'Sunset' name changed to 'Dawn' (Bond, 1994); true pl probably form #1, but most gardens have #2

'Sugar Plum Fairy': {1987r, Briggs N; as a possible hybrid of *H. gracillima* X *H. venusta*} sm md of narrow, wavy, green foliage; pale purple fls from v late Aug into mid-Sept; similar to *H. gracillima* "Lachman Strain"; probably not related to *H. venusta*

'Vera Verde': {1990r, Klehm N.} formerly *H. gracillima* 'Variegated' & *H. gracillima variegata*; dense, low md of narrow, white-margined foliage; 13" by 26" md; lvs 4 1/4" by 1 1/2" wi 4-5 vp, 1/16", white mgns, and a med gr center; blade wavy, narrowly elliptic, smooth, and thin-substd; med purple fls (1 3/4" by 1"), mid-Aug into Sept on sc up to 29" high; excellent low edger

other similar types:

'Rock Princess'

'Grand Tiara'

key features: sport of 'Golden Tiara' with wider, gold margins

mound size: 16" high by 44" wide

spacing: 36"

leaves: 5" long by 4 1/2" wide; 1" wide, gold margin, dark green center; shiny underside; broadly ovate blade with a deeply lobed base; slightly wavy; smooth texture; better than average substance; 8 vein pairs

flowers: mid-July into early August; medium purple; 30" scapes; many seed pods develop

comments: I think of 'Grand Tiara' as a "souped-up" version of 'Golden Tiara'. Not only are the margins much wider and more prominent than for 'Golden Tiara', but the substance is thicker. The speculation surrounding the origins of this plant (found by Ali Pollock, 1991 registration) range from it being a tetraploid conversion to some type of epidermal sport.

It probably came from the same type of mutation that resulted in 'Night Before Christmas' out of 'White Christmas' and 'Patriot' out of 'Francee'. Further proof of 'Grand Tiara's unusual derivation comes from the fact that 'Amber Tiara', its all-gold sport, has considerably thicker foliage than 'Golden Scepter', the all-gold sport of 'Golden Tiara'. It also has a much different overall appearance. Walters Gardens of Zeeland, Michigan registered a series of 'Grand Tiara' sports in 1998 that closely matches the range of sports found out of 'Golden Tiara'.

seedlings, sports, and other related types:

'Amber Tiara': {1998r, Walters Gardens} gold-leaved sport; introduced for sale in 1999 by W.G.

'Crystal Tiara': {1998r, Walters Gardens; sport wi lvs creamy white wi a pale ylw mgn}

'Gilded Tiara': {1998r, Walters Gardens; sport wi yellow-mgd, chartreuse-centered lvs}

'Grand Gold': gold-leaved sport; first saw in 1996

'Grand Prize': {1998r, Walters Gardens; sport; lvs med gr wi a pale ylw mgn that turns creamy white}

'Heavenly Tiara': {1998r, Walters Gardens; sport wi white-mgd, gold-cntrd lvs}

'Topaz Tiara': {1998r, Walters Gardens; sport wi yellow to greenish ylw-centered, green-mgd lvs}

other similar types:

'Golden Tiara', 'Radiant Edger', 'Sultana', 'Warwick Curtsey'

'Great Expectations'

key features: large mound of creamy yellow-centered foliage; slug-resistant

mound size: 29" high by 58" wide

spacing: 48"

leaves: 12 1/2" long by 10" wide; somewhat variable, 2 1/2" wide blue-green margin (becoming green); center yellow in May to creamy yellow or white by late June depending upon light level; margin streaks into center; moderate underside bloom; very broadly ovate blade that is slightly wavy and cupped near the deeply lobed base; heavily corrugated; thick substance; 18 vein pairs

flowers: late June into early July; near-white with a pale lavender mid-petal stripe; 2 1/4" by 1 1/8"; narrow funnel shape; creamy white scapes, 29" high; seed pods form, but seeds generally nonviable

comments: As one of the largest, center-variegated hostas ever introduced, a mature clump of 'Great Expectations' makes an impact in any garden. The beautiful creamy yellow leaf center contrasts sharply with the deep blue-green margin. Such a color combination on a large-sized leaf begs for attention from any garden visitor. The good slug resistance and attractive, typical *H. sieboldiana* flowers add to its ornamental value and the leaf center does not develop "spring burn" as many gold-centered 'Elegans' sports do.

The only negative aspect to 'Great Expectations' is its slow growth rate. On top of being a mutation of *H. sieboldiana* 'Elegans' (slow grower), it has less vigor because of the yellow leaf center. A small division of 'Great Expectations' planted in the average, shaded garden and not given special treatment most likely will not achieve its full dimensions (and may actually become smaller). New plantings must be heavily watered and fertilized all season long. An extreme, but helpful, measure is to plant 'Great Expectations' "pot and all" into the garden. This allows more moisture and fertilizer to remain near the surface of the soil around the slow-growing root system. The plant should become root-bound in about 1-2 years and the pot can be removed.

'Great Expectations' was developed by John Bond of Savill Gardens in England and introduced for sale by Klehm Nursery in 1989 (Perennial Catalog 1989, p. 31). Paul Aden registered it in 1988 as a sport of *Hosta sieboldiana* 'Elegans'.

seedlings, sports, and other related types:

'Dream Weaver': {1996r, B. Ruetenik & K. Walek; sport} much wider, blue-green margins; a 10 1/2" by 9" leaf (17 vein pairs) had a 3" to 3 1/2" margin with a 2-3" center at its widest point (versus 5" on a normal 'Great Expectations')

'Great American Expectations': {1999r, V. Wade & E. Elslager; sport of 'Great Expectations'; listed as having larger lvs, taller sc & a faster growth rate}

'Richmond Blue': blue-leaved sport of 'Great Expectations' from tissue culture propagation; named by Bill Zumbar in 1995

other similar types:

H. sieboldiana 'Borwick Beauty', *H. sieboldiana* 'Northern Lights'

'Green Acres'

key features: huge mound of green foliage
mound size: 35" high by 78" wide

spacing: 60"

leaves: 12 3/4" long by 8 1/4" wide (up to 16 3/4" by 9"); medium to dark green, thin underside bloom; elliptic-ovate blade; several large marginal waves; slightly corrugated; good substance; 15 vein pairs

flowers: early to late July; pale lavender with a whitish throat; 2 1/2" long by 1 1/4" long; open funnel shape; 36-43" scapes

comments: 'Green Acres' has gained a great deal of popularity because of its immense size. The leaf blade is distinctive in being so large but having a relatively narrow shape and distinct waviness. It can be very effective as a background plant or space-eating ground cover. How about using it as a replacement for shrubs on the north side of your home?

'Green Acres' was registered by Julia Geissler of Nebraska in 1970 with unknown parentage, but it has many characteristics in common with 'Fortunei Gigantea' in both foliage and flower.

seedlings, sports, and other related types:

'Corduroy': {1983r, S. Moldovan; 'Green Acres' sdlg; huge md of dark green foliage}

other similar types:

'Big John', 'Big Sam', 'Birchwood Elegance', *Hosta sieboldiana* 'Mira'

'Green Fountain'
key features: fountain-like, medium-large mound of
shiny green foliage; cascading scapes
mound size: 22" high by 52" wide

spacing: 48"
leaves: 11 1/8" long by 4 3/8" wide; bright, shiny green;
very shiny underside; oblong-elliptic blade with a long, narrow tip and rounded base; margin heavily rippled; no corrugation; better than average substance; petioles nearly
upright, but leaf blade droops downward at a 45 degree
angle, giving the mound a fountain-like habit; 8-9 vein pairs
flowers: mid-August into early September; pale lavender
with much white on inside; 3" long by 1 1/2" wide; most in
the top 8" of the 24-38" scapes that cascade downward,
especially in late flower; on a 21" by 50" clump in late
flower, a 31" long scape drooped downward, 22" above the
ground; intense purple-red dots on scape; much like *H.
kikutii caput-avis*
comments: A mature mound of 'Green Fountain' in full
flower impresses even the casual observer. The fountain-
like mound habit, shiny green foliage, and cascading, dense
clusters of lavender flowers give it distinction and tremendous beauty. Used along rock walls or ledges, the very
attractive flower habit can be appreciated to its fullest.

It has been used in some breeding programs with great
results. The foliage shape and mound habit are traits that its
seedlings usually bear. I have also seen a beautiful sport of
'Green Fountain' with a creamy yellow margin, unnamed as
of this writing.

Though 'Green Fountain' was registered in 1979 by Paul
Aden as a hybrid between 'Green Wedge' and *Hosta
longipes*, it more strongly resembles *Hosta kikutii caput-
avis* than *H. longipes*.

210

seedlings, sports, and other related types:
'Elvis Lives': {1995r, T. Avent; 'Peter Pan' X 'Green Fountain'} bluish foliage; mound habit strongly reminiscent of 'Green Fountain' **(see page 140)**
'Golden Fountain': {1993r, J. Dishon; 'Beatrice' X 'Green Fountain'} 23" by 45", fountain-like md of shiny, golden foliage; lvs 14 1/2" by 5 1/2" (8 vp); basically a gold-leaved 'Green Fountain'
'Spritzer': {1986r, P. Aden; "Aden 349" X 'Green Fountain'} gold-centered, green-margined version of 'Green Fountain' **(see page 434)**

other similar types:
H. kikutii caput-avis: roughly similar to 'Green Fountain' in its flowing mound of green foliage but flowers more recumbent **(see page 250)**

'Green Piecrust'
key features: large mound of heavily rippled, dark green foliage
mound size: 30" high by 57" wide

spacing: 48"
leaves: 15" long by 10 1/2" wide; dark green; thin underside bloom; blade broadly oblong-ovate, drooping downward from center to tip; deeply lobed base and long, twisted tip; as many as sixteen regular ripples along the margin of each blade half; slight corrugation; good substance; 15-16 vein pairs; an orangy gold fall color develops late, in early November (if heavy frosts haven't destroyed the foliage)
flowers: June 18 to July 15 (July 4 peak, northern Illinois); very pale lavender; 2 3/8" long by 1 3/4" wide; open funnel shape; 36-52" scapes open an average of 23 days with 2.5 flowers open per scape per day; as many as 9 flowers open

per scape near the peak of bloom; scapes eventually droop due to the weight of the numerous, developing seed pods, sometimes touching the ground by early August; 21-43 seeds per pod

comments: 'Green Piecrust' has long set the standard for piecrust-edged hostas. A "piecrust" edge is composed of many distinctive ripples that are regularly spaced along the whole length of the margin. The number of ripples per leaf blade half varies by variety, 16 in the case of 'Green Piecrust'. The large size of 'Green Piecrust' foliage further enhances the piecrust effect.

In the garden 'Green Piecrust' becomes a large, flowing mound of deep green foliage. It makes an outstanding background plant or large ground cover. I've even seen it used as an effective "centerpiece" in island beds.

With the prolific number of seed pods forming, it is not surprising that 'Green Piecrust' has been used in breeding programs. Though not all of the seedlings of 'Green Piecrust' exhibit a strong piecrust edge, many will bear this characteristic. 'Birchwood Ruffled Queen' and 'Ruffled Petticoats' are seedlings that retain the rippled edge. 'Marilyn', my cross of 'Gold Drop' X 'Green Piecrust', has only a slightly wavy margin.

The AHS nomenclature committee registered 'Green Piecrust' for the late Frances Williams in 1986. Her records at the Andersen Horticultural Library of the Minnesota Landscape Arboretum indicate that 'Green Piecrust' was an open-pollinated seedling of unknown origins that was named in 1957. Based upon both foliage and flowering characteristics, 'Fortunei Gigantea' is the likely pod parent.

seedlings, sports, and other related types:

'Birchwood Ruffled Queen': {1986r by the AHS for F. Shaw; 'Green Piecrust' sdlg} 24" by 60" mound of irregularly rippled, dark green leaves, 12 1/2" by 9"; lav fls, late June into mid-July

'Black Beauty': {1984r, K. Carpenter; 'Green Piecrust' sdlg} med-lg mound of dark green foliage; 22" by 45" md; 9 1/2" by 8" lvs (10 vp); lav fls in July; one of the best dark green hostas

'Circus Clown': {1983r, E. Minks; 'Ruffles' X 'Green Piecrust'} lg md of intensely ruffled, green foliage

'Classic Delight': {1973r, E. Fisher; 'Green Piecrust' sdlg} 30" by 72" md of neatly rippled, dark green lvs, 14" by 9" (17 vp); impressive background plant but rarely grown

'Marilyn': {1990r, M. Zilis; 'Gold Drop' X 'Green Piecrust'} 17" by 43" md of slightly wavy, golden foliage; lvs 7" by 5" (11 vp), chartreuse early, medium

212

gold by mid-summer; lav fls on 25" sc, late June into July

'Ruffled Petticoats': {1998r, J. & B. Diesen; 'Green Piecrust' sdlg} large, semi-upr md of heavily rippled, dark green foliage

'Sea Drift': {1978r, M. Seaver; 'Green Piecrust' sdlg} large mound of heavily rippled green foliage; md 24" by 48"; lvs 14" by 10 1/2" (14 vp); pale lav fls in July on 36" sc

'Trill': introduced in the 1993 Hatfield Gardens catalog as a hybrid of 'Donahue Piecrust' X 'Green Piecrust' from Kevin Vaughn; heavily rippled green lvs, 11 1/2" by 6 1/8" (12 vp); pale lav fls in July; fast growth rate

other hostas with rippled margins include:

'Big Sam': {1986r, AHS for M. Klopping} 25" by 63" md of dark green foliage wi rippled margins

'Blue Piecrust': {1986r, AHS for A. Summers} bluish, Sieboldiana-type lvs with a lightly rippled margin; 29" by 50" md; 12 3/4" by 10" lvs (19 vp)

'Chartreuse Piecrust': {1985r, C. Owens} 20" by 46" md; br gold, unruly, sl rippled lvs, 11" by 9" (19 vp)

'Choo Choo Train': {1999r, T. Sears & T. Avent} bright gold, heavily rippled lvs, 14" by 10" (17 vp); 22" by 60" md

'Crested Reef': {1975r, E. Minks} 25" by 66" md of irregularly wavy, green lvs, 10" by 8 1/2" (14 vp)

'Curls': {1990r, Fairway Enterprises} 32" by 56" md of intensely rippled, green lvs, 11" by 5" (9 vp)

'Cynthia': lg md of gold-splotched lvs wi a piecrust edge **(see page 130)**

'Donahue Piecrust': lg md of intensely rippled, green foliage **(see page 136)**

'Fortunei Gigantea': parent of 'Green Piecrust'; less pronounced rippling **(see page 162)**

'Frilly Puckers': {1986r, AHS for E. Fisher} green Sieboldiana wi sl wavy mgns; intro ~1970 or earlier

'Green Ripples': {1986r, F. Williams & C. Williams} lg md of piecrust-edged, green foliage

'Grey Piecrust': {1986r, AHS for T. Donahue} identical to 'Green Piecrust' except for a hint of blue in spring

'Holly's Velvet Piecrust': {1995r, R. & D. Benedict} 16" by 39" md; v rippled, shiny, dk green lvs, 6 3/4" by 5 3/4" (11 vp); *H. ventricosa*-type

'Komodo Dragon': Mildred Seaver introduction; 28" by 72", semi-upr md of moderately rippled, dk green lvs, 15" by 11" (14 vp); first saw in 1995

'Lakeside Ripples': {1991r, M. Chastain} lg, heavily rippled, green lvs, 13" by 9 1/2" (16 vp)

'Lime Piecrust': {1990r, W. & E. Lachman} a true "golden piecrust"; 25" by 60" md; 12" by 9" lvs

'Mesa Fringe': 27" by 72" md of elegant, ruffled, green lvs, 17" by 10"; outstanding 1991 Eldren Minks introduction

'Niagara Falls': {1991r, W. Brincka & O. Petryszyn} lg md of piecrust-edged dk green lvs **(see page 322)**

'Permanent Wave': large mound of green foliage that is nicely wavy along the margin **(see page 338)**

'Phantom': {1995r, R. Solberg & J. & J. Wilkins; 'Riptide' sdlg} med-lg md of heavily rippled, med gr lvs; pale purple fls on 36" sc in Aug

'Piecrust Power': huge green lvs with an irregular piecrust edge; md 24" by 45"; lvs 14" by 12"; lav fls in July on 36" sc; an early 1990's Paul Aden introduction

'Pioneer': {1984r, C. Tompkins} 32" by 83" md of lightly rippled, green lvs, 16" by 10" (15 vp)

'Regal Ruffles': {1990r, E. Minks} large, ruffled, blue-green foliage **(see page 364)**

'Ruffles': {1986r, AHS for D. Lehman} regularly rippled, green leaves; large mound

'Sea Frolic': 'Donahue Piecrust' sdlg from Mildred Seaver; 24" by 53" md of intensely rippled, wavy, green lvs, 13" by 9"; widely admired in the landscape & as a breeding plant

'Sum Piecrust': {1999r, E. Elslager; 'Sum and Substance' sport; lvs medium green with a rippled mgn}

'Woodland Green': {1990r by P. Ruh for L. Simpers} lg md of green lvs with impressive, rippled margins

'Ground Master'

key features: medium-sized mound of creamy-margined foliage

mound size: 16" high by 40" wide

spacing: 24"

leaves: 6" long by 2 3/4" wide; 1/2" to 3/4" wide, yellow to creamy white margin; deep green center; moderately shiny underside; blade elliptic with fairly wavy margins; slight corrugation develops with age; thin substance; 7 vein pairs

flowers: late July into mid-August; bright purple with mid petal striping; darker purple in bud; 2 1/4" long by 1 1/2" wide; thin (1/16" wide) scapes that reach 18-24" in height

comments: The low, wide-spreading mound habit of 'Ground Master' makes it ideal for ground cover or edging purposes, though it is susceptible to slug damage. Since its widespread propagation in the 1980's, it has become well-known and used in the landscaping industry. The wide, creamy white leaf margins stand out, especially under overcast conditions or at dusk.

Paul Aden registered 'Ground Master' in 1979 as a hybrid of 'Yellow Splash' X 'Neat Splash'.

seedlings, sports, and other related types:
none listed

other similar types:

'Coquette': {1987r, R. Benedict; 'Neat Splash' sdlg} med-sized md of white-mgd lvs **(see page 124)**

'Resonance': {1976r, P. Aden; hybrid of two sdlgs} small, dense mound of narrow, creamy white-margined foliage; md 9" by 24", lvs 5 3/4" by 2 7/8" wi a 1/4" to 1/2" wide margin and 5 vp; pale purple fls in August on 21" sc; important breeding plant

'Spartan Gem': {1989r, P. Banyai; parentage unknown} much like 'Ground Master' except for all-green foliage; 22" by 48" md; lvs 8" by 5" (8 vp)

'Yellow Brick Road': medium-sized mound of creamy white-margined foliage; from Chet Tompkins; very similar to 'Ground Master'

'Guacamole'
key features: large mound of chartreuse-centered foliage; large, fragrant flowers
mound size: 24" high by 54" wide (up to 31" by 64")

spacing: 48"
leaves: 11 1/4" long by 8 5/8" wide; medium to dark green margin, 5/8" wide; center chartreuse early, becoming brighter gold during the season and in brighter light; thin underside bloom; ovate to broadly ovate, moderately wavy blade; better than average substance; 12-13 vein pairs
flowers: mid-August into September; pale lavender, nearly white; 3 1/4" long by 2 3/4" wide; open, trumpet shape; very fragrant; 30-41" scapes; sparse pod formation

comments: 'Guacamole' represents one of the most exciting, new introductions of the 1990's. As a sport of 'Fragrant Bouquet', it has the same large, fragrant flowers and very fast growth rate, but the contrast between the green margin and the chartreuse to gold-centered foliage produces a striking effect. The gold center becomes brighter during the season, and even more so with 1-2 hours of morning sunlight (in northern Illinois). It can be used in a variety of ways in the landscape and also makes an excellent container plant because of its fast growth rate.

It is possible to have 'Guacamole' in bloom at almost any time of the year if grown in a greenhouse with supplemental lighting. I have seen 'Guacamole' and its sports, 'Fried Bananas' and 'Fried Green Tomatoes', flowering in the greenhouses at my nursery even during the dark months of December and January.

Bob Solberg registered 'Guacamole' in 1994.

seedlings, sports, and other related types:

'Avocado': {1998r, J. & B. Diesen; sport} very wide leaf margins (1 3/4" wide margin on a 7 3/4" by 6 1/2" leaf for 'Avocado' vs. 5/8" margins on a mature, 11" by 8 1/2" 'Guacamole' leaf); distinct

'Color Parade': green-margined, streaked-centered 'Fragrant Bouquet' sport; 2000 Q & Z N introduction

'Fried Bananas': {1994r, R. Solberg} 'Guacamole' sport; beautiful, fast-growing mound of golden foliage; color intensifies in bright light

'Fried Green Tomatoes': {1995r, R. Solberg} 'Guacamole' sport; medium to dark green leaves; most vigorous member of 'Fragrant Bouquet' family; 25" by 59" md; 11 1/2" by 7 3/4" lvs; excellent, fast-growing ground cover or background plant

'Stained Glass': {1999r, H. Hansen & Shady Oaks N; 'Guacamole' sport; lvs gold-centered with very wide, dk gr mgns}

other similar types:

'Chelsea Ore', 'Hoosier Harmony', 'Royal Accolade'

'Hadspen Blue'

key features: medium-sized mound of broad, blue foliage; slug-resistant; a Tardiana

mound size: 18" high by 48" wide

---

spacing: 36"

leaves: 7 1/4" long by 6 1/4" wide (typical) up to 8 1/4" by 6 7/8"; thick bloom creates deep blue-green color; thick underside bloom; blade broadly ovate with a cupped, cordate base; slight to moderate corrugation; thick substance; 12-13 vein pairs

flowers: late July into mid-August; very pale lavender, darker in mid-petal; 1 5/8" long by 1" wide; in tight clusters on scapes, 20-24" high; fertile

comments: 'Hadspen Blue' rates as one of the bluest cultivars ever developed. The slug-resistant foliage usually remains blue well into July, even August in some parts of the country. 'Hadspen Blue' has been widely propagated and can now be found in most nurseries and mail order catalogs. It certainly has earned the status of a hosta "classic".

Paul Aden registered 'Hadspen Blue' in 1976 for the originator, Eric Smith of England. It is a second generation Tardiana seedling that tends toward its Sieboldiana origins. It can be thought of either as a medium-sized 'Elegans' or comparable to 'Tokudama' but faster growing.

seedlings, sports, and other related types:
'Aristocrat': {1997r, Walters Gardens; sport} PPAF; blue-green-centered, white-margined foliage
'Buffy': {1986r, H. Weissenberger; 'Hadspen Blue' sdlg} blue foliage
'Edward Wargo': {1986r, H. Weissenberger; 'Hadspen Blue' sdlg} blue foliage

other similar types:
'Blue Danube', 'Blue for You', 'Blue Horizon', 'Brother Ronald', 'Camelot', 'Happiness', 'Osprey', 'Sherborne Songbird', 'Tokudama'

'Hadspen Samphire'
key features: brilliant yellow foliage in a medium-sized mound; turns green by late summer
mound size: 17" high by 40" wide

spacing: 36"
leaves: 9 1/2" long by 4" wide; shiny, luminescent gold in spring, medium green by late summer; shiny underside; narrowly ovate blade that is distinctly wavy; smooth texture; average substance; 8 vein pairs
flowers: mid to late August; pale lavender; 2 1/8" long by 1" wide; narrow funnel shape; few seed pods develop

comments: 'Hadspen Samphire' stands out like a beacon of gold light on a cloudy day. The graceful, flowing, dense mound of shiny yellow foliage is brightest in spring, slowly receding into the background as it turns an attractive green by August. It has a fast growth rate and can be effective either as a specimen or ground cover. Peter Ruh registered 'Hadspen Samphire' in 1997 for Alan Eason and Eric Smith of England who developed this plant in the early 1970's. It is a cross of *H. sieboldiana* X 'Kabitan' (Grenfell, 1990).

seedlings, sports, and other related types:

none listed

other similar types:

'Chartreuse': {1998r by P. Ruh for E. Fisher & G. Holly} dvlpd in 1955; compact md of foliage that changes from chartreuse to bright gold in early May (northern Illinois), then to med green by late May; 16" by 41" md; lvs 8" by 4 1/2" (8-10 vp); med purple fls on 21-31" sc, July 24-August 10; incredible show of brilliant gold lvs in spring; one of the first American cvs; probably an *H. rectifolia* sdlg

'Chiquita': {1979r, M. Eisel} another "spring gold" that makes a splash of color before turning green; 22" by 50" md; lvs 11" by 6" (10 vp); thin subst; med lav fls, late July on 24" scapes; emerges fairly early when crocuses and blue-flowered Puschkinia are in bloom creating a beautiful contrast; only effective for about a month, but what a month!

'Fortunei Aurea' **(see page 158)**

'Sea Fire' **(see page 381)**

'Halcyon'

key features: dense, medium-sized mound of slug-resistant blue-green foliage; a Tardiana

mound size: 18" high by 43" wide (up to 22" by 54")

spacing: 36"

leaves: 8" long by 5 1/2" wide; deep blue-green color; thick underside bloom; blade ovate to oblong-ovate with a slightly lobed base; smooth texture; slight waviness; thick substance; 12-13 vein pairs

flowers: late July into mid-August; pale bluish lavender (with whitish petal margins); 2 1/8" long by 1 1/16" wide; 18-28" scapes; many seed pods form

comments: 'Halcyon' has proven to be one of the best Tardianas. Its thick substance, dense growth habit, good blue color, and attractive show of flowers make it an excellent landscape plant. During the 1980's one European tissue culture lab propagated huge numbers of 'Halcyon'. As a result, it has become very common in the nursery trade, but that has not lessened its value in the shade garden.

Several sports have been found from 'Halcyon' including 'June', which has become a very important cultivar in its own right, and at least six green-leaved sports. 'Halcyon' has also been an important breeding plant both as a pod parent and for its pollen. Bill and Eleanor Lachman, in particular, made use of 'Halcyon' pollen in quite a number of their crosses.

'Halcyon' is a first generation Tardiana (TF 1 x 7), being originated in the early 1960's by Eric Smith. It leans more toward its 'Tardiflora' parentage in many ways except for the rich blue foliage color which hearkens back to 'Elegans'. The British Hosta and Hemerocallis Society registered 'Halcyon' in 1988 for Eric Smith.

seedlings, sports, and other related types:

'Border Bandit': {1992r, W. & E. Lachman; "81-8" X 'Halcyon'} leaves creamy yellow-margined, dark green-centered; 16" by 34" md; 7" by 5" lvs (8 vp); very attractive

'Canadian Shield': {1993r, K. Knechtel} green-leaved sport of 'Halcyon'

'Chantilly Lace': {1988r, W. & E. Lachman; 'Halcyon' pollen parent} white-margined lvs **(see page 111)**

'Crusader': {1989r, W. & E. Lachman; 'Halcyon' pollen parent} white-margined foliage **(see page 129)**

'Devon Green': dark green-leaved sport of 'Halcyon' from England

'Dress Blues': {1995r, W. Zumbar; 'Breeder's Choice' X 'Halcyon'} semi-upright, 22" by 54" md of yellow-edged, blue-green foliage

'Edge of Night': {1988r, R. Savory; 'Green Gold' X 'Halcyon'} medium to dark green foliage

'Emerald Crown': {1990r by the Lachmans; ('Resonance' X a sdlg) X 'Halcyon'} dense, 16" by 44" md of deep green foliage; sported to 'Polychrome' {1998r, A. Malloy; lvs streaked green & white}

'Indigo': {1984r, R. Savory; 'Halcyon' X a sdlg; blue-grey lvs}

'Gay Blade': {1988r, W. & E. Lachman; 'Halcyon' pollen parent} white-edged lvs **(see page 177)**

'Goldbrook Glimmer': sport of 'Halcyon' from Goldbrook Plants (Bond, 1994); one md 12" by 33" wi chartreuse-centered lvs, 6 1/2" by 4 1/2" (11 vp); 1 1/2" wide, blue-green margins

'Grunspecht': green-lvd sport of 'Halcyon' from Heinz Klose of Germany (Pollock, 1997); shiny, thick-substanced, dark green lvs that are "whitish shiny" on the underside

'June': gold-centered, green-mgd 'Halcyon' sport from NEO-plants in England **(see page 245)**

'Kryptonite': 'Halcyon' sport from Weir Meadow N (Pollock, 1997); at one time thought to be a 'Blue Wedgwood' sport; attractive, shiny, dark green foliage

'Lacy Belle': {1992r, W. & E. Lachman; 'Neat Splash' sdlg X 'Halcyon'} 16" by 37" md of wavy lvs, 7" by 4", wi a 1/4" ylw to creamy white mgn & green center

'Paradise Joyce': gold-centered, bl-green-mgd sport of 'Halcyon' from Marco Fransen of Holland; center a much lighter gold than 'June'

'Peridot': {1995r, R. Lydell} 'Halcyon' sport wi shiny dark green foliage

'Silver Creek Sunshine': {1996r, D. Savory; 'Halcyon' sdlg; lvs gold in spring, turning med green}

'Sleeping Beauty': {1997r, Walters Gardens; sport; lvs wi a creamy white mgn, bl-green center}

'Tambourine': {1987r, W. & E. Lachman; sdlg wi 'Halcyon' pollen parent} white-mgd lvs **(see page 450)**

'Torchlight': {1990r, W. & E. Lachman; "81-8" X 'Halcyon'} white-mgd lvs **(see page 479)**

'Valerie's Vanity': {1991r, R. Keller} first registered green-leaved 'Halcyon' sport; impressive, shiny, dark green foliage

other similar types:

'Blue Arrow', 'Dorset Charm'

'Heart's Content'

key features: large mound of heart-shaped, white-margined foliage

mound size: 22" high by 46" wide

spacing: 40"

leaves: 8 1/2" long by 6" wide; 1" wide margin that is yellow early changing to creamy white; center medium to dark green; thin underside bloom; blade broadly ovate with a deeply lobed, heart-shaped base; slight waviness and corrugation; better than average substance; 11-12 vein pairs

flowers: mid-July into August; pale lavender; 2 1/4" long; scapes 36" high; many seed pods develop

comments: Rarely do I get excited when viewing a cultivar for the first time. 'Heart's Content' was one of those rare times. I was struck by the way the wide, creamy margins sharply outlined the heart-shaped leaf blade. Since that time I have come to appreciate it as a mature-sized plant and am still impressed. The overall mound habit is wide-spreading and the growth rate is good both in nursery containers and in the garden.

'Heart's Content' is a Kevin Vaughn introduction first offered in the 1992 Hatfield Gardens catalog. It was listed as a hybrid of 'Breeder's Choice' X 'Polly Bishop' and sold for $150.

seedlings, sports, and other related types:
none listed
other similar types:
'Formal Attire', 'Robert Frost'

'Heartache'
key features: medium-large mound of large, heart-shaped gold foliage; purple flowers
mound size: 20" high by 42" wide

spacing: 36"

leaves: 9" long by 8" wide; medium gold; thin underside bloom; blade heart-shaped and slightly wavy; distinct tip; slight to moderate corrugation at maturity; better than average substance; 10 vein pairs

flowers: mid-July into August; bright purple; 36-40" scapes; many seed pods develop

comments: After I observed this plant in Herb and Dorothy Benedict's garden in 1985, I could not stop thinking about its combination of large, heart-shaped gold leaves and purple flowers. At the time Herb was not sure if he would keep his seedling, but my enthusiasm probably worked in its favor. It brings together the best of both parents (gold leaf color from 'Gold Regal'; heart-shaped leaf and purple flowers from *H. ventricosa*). 'Heartache' becomes a showy specimen that can brighten up any shaded area.

seedlings, sports, and other related types:
none listed

other similar types:
'Golden Friendship': {1991r, H. Gowen; unknown parentage} 22" by 44" md of thick-substanced, gold lvs, 9" by 7 3/4" (13 vp), smooth-textured when young, becoming moderately corrugated wi age; lav fls from early to late

July on 31" sc; unusual & attractive

'Holly's Gold': {1991r, R. & D. Benedict; selfed sdlg of 'Holly's Honey'} 22" by 44" md of light gold, 8" by 6" (9 vp) lvs; br purple fls on 33" sc fr early to late July; leaves gold and heart-shaped but not corrugated; close to 'Heartache' in both foliage and flower

---

'Helonioides Albopicta' (Hakama Giboshi) = 'Ginko Craig'

key features: small mound of white-margined foliage; also known as 'Ginko Craig'

mound size: 14" high by 44" wide

comments: For many years a very attractive white-margined plant that produced late season purple flowers was known as *Hosta helonioides albopicta*. I was very familiar with this plant, having a row growing in a display at my nursery. In a sequence of events described in an article that I co-authored with Peter Ruh in *The Hosta Journal* (Ruh & Zilis, 1989), I came to the conclusion that this plant was actually the true *Hosta rohdeifolia*. Schmid (1991) partially disputed this claim based upon anther color. After numerous comparisons of plants that have been growing in the United States and Japan since 1989, I stand by my original conclusion that the plant that we had been growing as *Hosta helonioides albopicta* is really the true *Hosta rohdeifolia*.

What then is the true *Hosta helonioides albo-picta*? My observations of Hakama Giboshi imported from Japan and growing in Peter Ruh's collection first made me suspect that it was the same as 'Ginko Craig'. Further study of Hakama Giboshi in collections during my two trips to Japan and a thorough re-examination of Fumio Maekawa's photos and description of *H. helonioides albo-picta* and *H. helonioides* in the 1973 issue of *The Bulletin of the American Hosta*

Society (photos on p. 37, descriptions on p. 41), confirmed my suspicions. I now have no doubt that the plant we have long-known as 'Ginko Craig' is Hakama Giboshi. This brings up the somewhat confusing issue of what to label this plant. The AHS registered it as *H. helonioides* 'Albo-picta' in 1987 and Schmid (1991) further modified it to 'Helonioides Albopicata'. Owing to the fact that the name 'Ginko Craig' has been widely used for at least 30 years, I will continue to use it instead of 'Helonioides Albopicta'.

Before I realized its relationship to *Hosta* 'Helonioides', Doug Lohman and I registered the all-green form of 'Ginko Craig' in 1988 as 'Green Smash'. This, of course, is the equivalent of 'Helonioides' (or *Hosta helonioides*).

'High Fat Cream'
key features: medium-sized mound of heavily streaked foliage; breeding plant
mound size: 13" high by 40" wide

spacing: 36"
leaves: 7" long by 5" wide; chartreuse with gold, chartreuse, and white streaking; thin underside bloom; ovate blade; average substance; slightly corrugated; 12 vein pairs
flowers: late July into August; pale lavender with thin purple stripes; 2 1/4" long by 1 3/8" wide; 23-30" scapes; fertile
comments: 'High Fat Cream' saw its popularity peak in the early 1980's when it had the reputation of being an outstanding breeding plant. It was only grown by a few collectors then, and because of its unstable nature, it has become increasingly difficult to find the true, streaked cultivar. The last good clump that I can remember seeing was back in 1984. Even in Van Wade's collection, I could only find

one-half of one leaf true-to-type on his clump of 'High Fat Cream'. On the other hand, its two, stable sports, 'American Dream' and 'Golden Guernsey', have become available from a wide variety of sources.

'High Fat Cream' was registered by Paul Aden as a hybrid of two seedlings in 1976.

seedlings, sports, and other related types:

'American Dream': {1999r, V. Wade; sport} discovered in the Wade & Gatton N. collection in 1993; wh-mgd, go-cntrd lvs, 9" by 6"; 24" by 65" md; lav fls on 30-36" sc in Aug; vigorous, attractive plant

'Amy Aden': {1980r, P. Aden; 'Fascination' X 'High Fat Cream'} low md; lvs strkd wi thin, ylw mgns; variable; lav fls in July on 17" sc

'Golden Guernsey': {1992r, P. Ruh; sport} 19" by 50" md of gold foliage; a bright splash of color

'Fascination': {1978r, P. Aden; 'Flamboyant' X 'High Fat Cream'} heavily streaked; breeding pl **(see page 147)**

'Intrigue': {1978r, P. Aden; 'Flamboyant' X 'High Fat Cream'} 20" by 40" md of highly variable foliage; some lvs green-mgd wi a creamy white center; almost as rare as 'High Fat Cream'

'Jambeliah': {1978r, P. Aden; 'Flamboyant' X 'High Fat Cream'} 16" by 48" md of heavily mottled, creamy-mgd lvs, 9" by 7" (12 vp); rarely grown

'Sunshine Kid': {1980r, P. Aden; 'Fascination' X 'High Fat Cream'} neat sm md of gold-mgd, green-centered lvs; attractive, but rarely grown

'Yellow Bird': {1991r, R. & D. Benedict; 'High Fat Cream' X 'Flamboyant'} 17" by 38" md of pale ylw lvs (10" by 6 1/2" wi 12 vp); a striking plant

other similar types:

'Hoopla', 'Flamboyant', 'Splish Splash', 'Whoopee'

'High Noon'

key features: large mound of bright golden foliage with a semi-upright habit
mound size: 26" high by 46" wide

spacing: 40"
leaves: 14" long by 9 1/2" wide; medium to bright gold, brighter with more light; thin underside bloom; blade broadly oblong-ovate with a long, distinct tip; moderately wavy; moderate to heavy corrugation; good substance; 17 vein pairs

flowers: late June into mid-July; pale lavender; scapes 32" high or more; very long seed pods

comments:
'High Noon' makes an impressive vase-shaped mound of gold foliage that can be effectively used as a focal point of an island bed or as a background plant. It normally appears bright gold but can become lighter if given a few hours of direct sunlight.

'High Noon' is a Mildred Seaver introduction and was originally called 'Sea Tall' and 'Sea High Noon'. It made such a sensation at the 1987 American Hosta Society national convention that a plant of 'High Noon' sold for a record-breaking $700 at that year's auction.

seedlings, sports, and other related types:
'Midnight Sun': {1996r, D. & J. Ward; 'High Noon' X *H. montana macrophylla*; gold foliage}
Two unnamed sports are known:
    (1) gold-centered, chartreuse-margined
    (2) green-centered, gold-margined

other similar types:
'Fort Knox', 'Golden Sculpture', 'Gold Regal', 'Rising Sun', 'Yellow Highness'

'Hime Tokudama'

key features: medium-sized, dense mound of dark green foliage

mound size: 17" high by 44" wide

spacing: 36"

leaves: 6" long by 4 1/2" wide; medium to dark green color; thin underside bloom; ovate to nearly heart-shaped blade; slightly wavy; slight corrugation with age, smooth when young; average substance; 9 vein pairs

flowers: early to late July; pale lavender; 24-30" scapes

comments: 'Hime Tokudama' grows into a wide, dense mound of green foliage that can be used as a ground cover or edging plant. The lavender flowers emerge from ball-like buds at the end of the scapes and are held well above the foliage. It was developed in Japan before 1985. From its name you'd expect a dwarf ("hime") form of 'Tokudama' but that is not the case. It is probably a *Hosta nakaiana* seedling as it shows strong similarities to it in both foliage and flowering habit. So far it has not been widely propagated by nurseries in the U.S. but several collectors have it on display.

seedlings, sports, and other related types:

'Ogon Hime Tokudama': a gold-leaved version of 'Hime Tokudama' from Japan

other similar types:

'Happy Hearts', 'Jade Scepter', 'Pearl Lake'

'Hirao Majesty'

key features: large, broad mound of shiny green foliage; dense flower clusters
mound size: 26" high by 67" wide

spacing: 60"

leaves: 17 1/2" long by 10 1/4" wide; medium green with a shiny top and very shiny underside; blade broadly oblong-ovate with a slightly lobed base and long tip; whole blade wavy and tending to droop downward from the midrib; no corrugation; smooth texture; thick substance; 13 vein pairs

flowers: July 8 to August 1 (northern Illinois); deep lavender; petal margin whitish halfway from the tip to the base; 2 7/8" long by 2" wide; open funnel shape with petals reflexed at the tips; scapes 36-48" high; 5-10 scapes per clump; clustered in the top 7" of each scape; sparse seed pod formation with few viable seeds

comments: 'Hirao Majesty' becomes an impressive mound of shiny, green foliage that commands attention. The shiny green leaves tend to be "floppy", creating a wide-spreading flowing mound effect. In July the focus shifts to the dense clusters of fairly large, deep lavender flowers. On average 60 flowers are produced in the top 7" of each scape, meaning about 9 flowers per inch. All in all 'Hirao Majesty' makes a sensational addition to any shaded garden.

The origins of this plant are somewhat obscure, but apparently Dr. Shuichi Hirao of Japan sent hosta seeds to a nursery in the U.S. labelled as "Japanese Tet". Two seedlings were selected and named "T66-01" and "T66-02" and later, "Japanese Tet. #1" and "Japanese Tet. #2". I first encountered these plants in the North Aurora, Illinois garden of Nate and Thelma Rudolph during the 1981 American Hemerocallis Society national convention. During another visit to the Rudolph garden in July 1985, both seedlings

229

were in full, gorgeous bloom. It was then that I realized the great value of these plants. Unfortunately, over the years in various gardens, #1 and #2 became mixed-up, with the result that both types were simply labelled "Japanese Tet". To avoid further confusion, in 1993 I gave #1 the name, 'Hirao Majesty' and #2, 'Hirao Supreme' and introduced them for sale. In 1997 Peter Ruh registered them with the AHS. Though both are outstanding plants, I rate 'Hirao Majesty' slightly higher because of its shinier, darker green foliage and deeper lavender flowers.

'Hirao Majesty' and 'Hirao Supreme' can be used in a breeding program, but have limited fertility. I have formed a few seed pods and have successfully used the pollen, but they are, at best, "reluctant" parents. Still, because of their unusual nature, it is worth a little frustration to use them.

seedlings, sports, and other related types:

'Brigadier': *H. sieboldiana* 'Elegans' X 'Hirao Supreme' seedling that I hybridized in 1990; 28" by 60" md of smooth, blue-green foliage; 1999 Q & Z N introduction

'Hirao Supreme': {1997r, S. Hirao, M. Zilis & P. Ruh} 25" by 69" md; lvs 15 1/4" by 9 1/2" (15 vp), slightly shiny, medium green color; same "floppy" character as 'Hirao Majesty'; med lav fls in dense clusters from mid to late July

'Miki': {1991r, P. Ruh & W. Zumbar; 'Hirao Majesty' X 'Hirao Supreme'} large, dense mound of medium gold leaves; md 22" by 60", lvs 12" by 8 1/2" (14 vp)

other similar types:

'Colossal': {1977r, R. Savory; sdlg of an unknown Japanese hybrid} 28" by 80" md of dk green lvs, 15" by 11" (13-15 vp), wi slightly rippled mgns; pale lav fls, late June into July on 30-40" sc; impressive, space-eating ground cover

'Honeybells'

key features: large, flowing mound of wavy green foliage; fragrant lavender flowers in August

mound size: 24" high by 50" wide

spacing: 48"

leaves: 10 1/4" long by 6 1/2" wide; light to medium green; slightly shiny top, very shiny underside; blade elliptic when young, broadening at maturity; 3-4 long waves cause blade to pucker downward along margins and at tip; no corrugation; average substance; 9 vein pairs

flowering: mid-August into early September; very pale lavender with 3-5 pencil-thin lines in mid-petal; 2 7/8" long by 2 1/4" wide; open funnel shape; nicely fragrant; scapes generally 39-45" (occasionally up to 52"); 15-25 scapes in a mature clump, about forty flowers per scape; at peak, 2-3 flowers open per day on each scape; opening in morning (about 10 a.m., but exact time temperature dependent); sparse pod formation with few viable seeds; pods generally misshapen

comments: When introduced for sale in the 1950's, 'Honeybells' was the most exciting hosta on the market. Its fast growth rate, fragrant flowers and large mound size fit all of the requirements of a great landscaping plant for shade. A large planting of 'Honeybells' in full bloom was not only an impressive sight but a perfumey treat as well. Its good sun tolerance and distinctive appearance only added to its appeal. All of the above is still true, except for the "exciting" part, but only because many newer cultivars have been introduced into the trade. Many nurseries continue to propagate 'Honeybells' and it is still used for general landscaping purposes.

The distinctive appearance of 'Honeybells' puts it into the class of plants that I never have a problem identifying.

231

The individual leaves pucker downward and are broadly wavy in a way that is different from most other hostas. This characteristic is accentuated by the large mature mound size. Also, the scapes are much taller than most other fragrant-flowered hostas. Of further interest is the mid-morning start time for individual flowers to open.

'Honeybells' has been utilized in a few breeding programs, but it rarely forms seed pods. During an occasional summer, however, some seed pods develop, but only a few viable seeds can be found. Unfortunately, most of the resulting seedlings do not have fragrant flowers. On the other hand, 'Honeybells' has produced some sensational mutations in tissue culture. 'Sugar and Cream' is one such sport that has become a very important cultivar in the nursery trade.

Frances Williams had a keen interest in the development of 'Honeybells'. Frances corresponded extensively with its originator, Alex Cumming of Bristol Nurseries in Connecticut. In a June 9, 1945 letter to her, he wrote that his yet unnamed seedling was a cross between *Hosta plantaginea* X *Hosta lanceolata* from before 1945. After much inquiry, Frances found out in September, 1952, from Alex's son, Rod Cumming, that it had been named 'Honeybells' and that Bristol Nurseries would offer it for sale. At the time of introduction, it was the only fragrant hosta in the nursery trade other than *Hosta plantaginea*. Although the pollen parent is assumed to be *Hosta lancifolia*, it probably was a green-leaved form of *Hosta sieboldii*. At that time the latter species was often listed as *Hosta lancifolia albomarginata*, so the confusion is understandable. The American Hosta Society registered 'Honeybells' in 1986, crediting Alex Cumming.

seedlings, sports, and other related types:

'Sombrero': {1991r, R. Savory; 'Honeybells' sdlg with blue-green lvs} described in the 1998 Savory's Gardens catalog as being a large plant that produces very fragrant, pure white flowers in August

'Sugar and Cream': sport of 'Honeybells' wi white-margined lvs **(see page 439)**

'Sweet Standard': sport of 'Honeybells' wi streaky lvs that are also white-margined **(see page 439)**

'Whipped Cream': {1988r, M. Zilis & T & Z N; sport} gr-mgd, white-cntrd lvs; very weak; very rare

other similar types:

'Bennie McRae': {1989r, N. Suggs; *H. plantaginea* sdlg; produces fragr lav fls} 24" by 60" md; light to med green lvs, 11 1/2" by 7" (11-12 vp); flowers in August; similar to 'Honeybells'

'Buckwheat Honey': {1984r, R. Benedict; 'Ginko Craig' X *H. plantaginea*} 22" by 48" md; lvs 10" by 4 3/4" (9 vp); 2" long, med purple, fragr fls on 32-46" sc in mid-Aug; fls only slightly open; mound resembles 'Honeybells'

'Royal Standard': *H. plantaginea* seedling; lg md of shiny gr lvs; fragr white fls in Aug **(see page 371)**

'Savannah Emerald': green-lvd form of 'Savannah'; 1998 Q & Z N introduction; lg md of wavy, green foliage; fast-growing; 22" by 52" md, 10 3/4" by 6 1/2" lvs; fragrant, lav fls

'Sweet Marjorie': {1983r, R. Benedict; 'Ginko Craig' X *H. plantaginea*} dense mound of slightly shiny, wavy, medium green foliage; md 26" by 58"; lvs 9 3/8" by 5 3/4" (9 vp); fragr, narrow, 3" long fls in mid-Aug on sc up to 42" high; fast-growing; similar mound habit to 'Honeybells'

'Sweet Susan': {1986r by C. Williams for F. Williams; *H. sieboldii* X *H. plantaginea*} 24" by 51" md of green lvs, 10 1/4" by 6 1/4" (8-9 vp); fragr lav fls in Aug on sc up to 40"; introduced by Fairmount Gardens in 1966 (Nesmith, 1966); similar to 'Honeybells' but differing in leaf shape, deeper flower color, slightly earlier blooming season and greater fertility

Hosta hypoleuca (Urajiro Giboshi)

key features: large, shiny green leaves, one per division; found on cliffs in Japan
mound size: 15" high by 47" wide (single leaf clumps); 23" by 60" (seedling clumps)

spacing: 36"
leaves: 15" long by 11 1/2" wide; medium to dark green; very thick underside bloom; blade broadly ovate with a deeply lobed base and a long, curled tip; 20 or so slight marginal ripples; no corrugation; good substance; sharply curved petiole covered with dark reddish purple dots, intense near the base; 11-12 vein pairs
flowers: very late July into late August; pale lavender; subtended by large, purplish white bracts; 2 3/4" long by 1 1/4" wide; scapes, 30" long, bend over with heavy weight of flowers (and later, seed pods) in the upper 3-4"; 27 flowers on a typical scape; reddish purple dots cover the scape, intense near base; fertile

comments: *Hosta hypoleuca*, the White-Backed Hosta (translation of Urajiro Giboshi), distinguishes itself through a combination of characteristics. First, each division bears only one leaf, leading to a much looser mound habit. Often in the wild, a "clump" consists of a single division with a single leaf. Secondly, the flower scapes tend to be recumbent, but only as flowering proceeds. The weight of the flowers clustered at the end of the scapes pull them downward, and when seed pods develop they often lie nearly flat. This habit may be evolutionarily related to its native habitat being the sides of hills or cliffs in a few isolated areas in Aichi Prefecture of Honshu Island in Japan. In one locale *H. hypoleuca* can be found growing out of large, vertical cracks in the sheer side of a rocky cliff. Bits of organic matter had accumulated in these cracks where *H. hypoleuca* seeds could germinate. The hanging scapes presumably would allow for better distribution of seed in such an unusual environment. The thick white bloom on the underside surface also is a distinctive feature of *Hosta hypoleuca* and the source of its common name.

As a garden plant, *Hosta hypoleuca* makes an unusual specimen plant, and is best used along a rock wall or on a shaded hillside. A "mound" slowly develops over the years, but never becomes the "typical rounded mound". Interestingly, seedlings of *H. hypoleuca* tend to be more mound-like than the species itself. In fact great diversity exists in the seedlings that arise from it. Peter Ruh grew a large patch of *H. hypoleuca* seedlings and found variations in flower color, leaf color, intensity of the underside bloom, and amount of purple dotting along the

scape and leaf petioles. Three of these seedlings were named and represent a range of foliage color possibilities: 'Azure Snow' (blue-green), 'Lemon Meringue' (gold) and 'Thor' (green).

seedlings, sports, and other related types:

'Azure Snow': blue-green *H. hypoleuca* sdlg **(see page 72)**

'Lemon Meringue': {1991r, P. Ruh; *H. hypoleuca* sdlg} 26" by 50" md of bright gold lvs, 16" by 12" (13-15 vp); sl corrug & lightly rippled; pale lav fls fr mid-July into August

'Happy Valley': {1995r, W. & E. Lachman; open-pollinated *H. hypoleuca* sdlg} leaves creamy white-margined with centers green, sometimes streaked

'Glacier Cascade': {1999r, M. Zilis & P. Cross; *H. kikutii* X *H. hypoleuca*} large, flowing md of long, wavy, green foliage; intense white lf underside; pale lav fls in August

'Maekawa': a selection of *Hosta hypoleuca* introduced by Klehm Nursery in 1989; md 17" by 50"; lvs 16" by 10" (12-13 vp), shiny, medium green wi a thick underside bloom and many marginal ripples; pale lav fls, late July into late Aug (Aug 5 peak, n Ohio); same "mound" habit as species

'Merry Sunshine': {1998r, E. Elslager; 'Fascination' X *H. hypoleuca*} green-cntrd, creamy yellow-mgd foliage; very attractive

H. hypoleuca 'Murasaki Kuki': Japanese sdlg wi purple dots covering the petiole; lav fls

H. hypoleuca 'Shirobana': Japanese sdlg wi white fls and green petioles

'Olive Oil': {1996r. J. Dishon; 'Yellow Splash' X *H. hypoleuca*} med to bright gold foliage; 13" by 40" md, 9" by 6" lvs (12 vp)

'Thor': {1994r, P. Ruh} green-leaved *H. hypoleuca* sdlg; 17" by 28" md; lvs 14" by 8" (12 vp); pale lav fls in Aug; sibling of 'Azure Snow'

other similar types:

Hosta pycnophylla: another white-backed species native to isolated areas of Japan, further south than *H. hypoleuca* with which it shares many characteristics; at one time probably part of the same species but separated geographically thousands of years ago **(see page 353)**

'Inniswood'
key features: medium-large mound of heavily corrugated, gold-centered foliage
mound size: 22" high by 48" wide

spacing: 40"
leaves: 11 1/2" long by 7 3/8" wide; dark green margin, 1/2" to 1 1/2" wide; medium to bright gold center; moderate underside bloom; ovate blade with a deeply lobed base; moderately wavy; heavily corrugated at maturity; good substance; 14-16 vein pairs
flowers: very late June into mid-July; very pale lavender; funnel-shaped; 30" scapes; many seed pods

comments: 'Inniswood' rates highly for bright foliage color and good slug resistance. It becomes a fairly large mound of gold-centered foliage that makes a great specimen plant. The growth rate is slow to moderate, definitely slower than 'Gold Standard'.

'Inniswood' sported out of 'Sun Glow' at the Inniswood Botanical Gardens in Westerville, Ohio (near Columbus). The original plant on display at the garden during the 1986 AHS national convention elicited much discussion, receiving the Savory Shield Award as the best new hosta on the convention tour that year. It did not become widely available in the commercial trade for several years, but has been extensively propagated in the last five or so years.

The Inniswood Metro Gardens registered 'Inniswood' in 1993.

seedlings, sports, and other related types:

'Handy Hatfield': {1996r, D. & J. Ward; 'Sun Glow' sport} essentially a reversed 'Inniswood'; one mound (less than mature) 17" by 40" wi 10" by 7 1/8" lvs that had a 1" to 1 1/2" wide, gold mgn & a green center

'Innisjade': green-lvd sport out of t.c.; 1997 Q & Z N intro; nice landscape contrast to 'Inniswood'

'Innisglow': gold-lvd sport out of t.c.; 1995 Q & Z N intro; close to 'Sun Glow'

'Sun Glow': {1974r, P. Aden; 'Aspen Gold' sdlg} 20" by 55" md of med to bright gold lvs, 9" by 7 3/4"; pale lav fls, late June into July on 30" sc; gold-leaved "mother plant" of 'Inniswood'

other similar types:

'Lucy Vitols', 'Paul's Glory', 'Spinning Wheel'

'Invincible'

key features: medium-large mound of shiny, dark green foliage; fragrant, pale lavender flowers
mound size: 20" high by 48" wide

spacing: 36"
leaves: 8" long by 6" wide; shiny, medium to dark green; shiny underside; blade ovate with a deeply lobed base; several slight ripples along the margin; smooth texture; average substance; 9-11 vein pairs
flowers: early to late August; pale lavender; fragrant; 2 1/4" long by 1 1/2" wide; scapes 30" high; forms seed pods
comments: 'Invincible' may not resist slugs or the sun very well but it makes an impressively shiny mound of dark green foliage that can be used in a variety of ways in the landscape. The pale lavender flowers produce a good show in August and are nicely fragrant. Like many other *H. plantaginea* seedlings, it has an excellent growth rate. Unlike many fragrant-flowered cultivars, it readily forms seed pods. Several hybridizers have utilized 'Invincible' for its shininess and dark green leaf color as well as its flower fragrance.

'Invincible' was registered in 1986 by Paul Aden as a hybrid of two seedlings.

seedlings, sports, and other related types:

'Lakeside Emerald Lights': {1993r, M. Chastain; *H. ventricosa* X 'Invincible'} small mound of shiny, dark green, slightly rippled foliage; md 11" by 30"; lvs 5 1/2" by 3 3/4" (9 vp); fls from mid-July into Aug; *H. ventricosa*-like scape bud

'Red Stepper': {1996r, G. Goodwin; 'Invincible' sdlg} dense mound of very shiny medium green lvs; petioles purple-red almost to blade; 13" by 32" md; 7 3/4" by 5" lvs (7 vp)

238

'Rippled Honey': hybrid of *H. ventricosa* X *H. plantaginea* from Herb Benedict; med-lg md of shiny, dark green foliage; fragrant, pale lav fls in Aug; closely resembles 'Invincible'

'Rosedale Barnie': {1999r, J. Hadrava; *H. ventricosa* X 'Invincible'} 13" by 40" md of dark green lvs, 6 3/4" by 5" (10 vp); med purple fls on 19" sc in dense clusters from mid to late July; impressive dark green color & purple fls

'Rosedale Dough Boy': {1999r, J. Hadrava; *H. ventricosa* X 'Invincible'} 18" by 36" md of thick, noticeably rippled, dark green lvs, 11" by 8" (14 vp); many seed pods

'Slick Willie': {1996r, J. Hadrava; *H. ventricosa* X 'Invincible'} impressive, med-sized md of shiny, very dark green foliage; one of the darkest greens ever developed

'Sweet Bo Peep': selfed 'Invincible' sdlg from Herb Benedict before 1991; 16" by 40" md of shiny, dark green lvs, 6 1/2" by 4 1/2"; fragr, pale lav fls on 34" sc in Aug; impressive, shiny, dark green leaves

other similar types:
'Iron Gate Bouquet', 'Joseph', 'Second Wind'

IRON GATE SERIES

The "Iron Gate" series of hostas was developed by Van Sellers, owner of Iron Gate Gardens in Kings Mountain, NC. In a 1987 article that appeared in *The Hosta Journal*, Van described how he crossed the pollen of 'Tokudama Aureonebulosa' onto flowers of *Hosta plantaginea*, resulting in mostly variegated, fragrant-flowered plants. Three cultivars were introduced from this cross. 'Iron Gate Supreme' was the first registered seedling (in 1980) and in 1981 Van registered a stable sport of it as 'Iron Gate Glamour'. Also registered in 1981 was another seedling from the original cross, 'Iron Gate Delight'. In 1983 'Iron Gate Bouquet' was registered along with its sport, 'Garden Bouquet'. Van was not sure of the parentage of the former (Sellers, 1987), but it no doubt is related to *H. plantaginea* owing to its fragrant flowers. The *Hosta Finder 2000* (Greene, 2000) mentions another Iron Gate introduction, 'Iron Gate Special'. The 1997 Powell's Gardens catalog describes this plant as the stable, white-margined, green-centered form of 'Iron Gate Supreme'.

'Iron Gate Glamour' has been the most stable of all the variegated "Iron Gates" with creamy white-margined, green-centered foliage. In contrast the heavily streaked foliage of 'Iron Gate Delight' and 'Iron Gate Supreme' varies considerably from plant to plant. 'Iron Gate Bouquet' is the only green-leaved selection in the series, producing fragrant, purple flowers over shiny, dark green foliage. 'Garden Bouquet' sported out of 'Iron Gate Bouquet' and has streaky foliage.

All of the "Iron Gates" are worthy plants that add a valuable splash of color to the garden. Adding to their ornamental value are the fragrant flowers which range from lavender to bright purple.

'Iron Gate Bouquet'
key features: medium-large mound of dark green foliage; purple, fragrant flowers
mound size: 19" high by 37" wide

---

spacing: 36"
leaves: 6 3/4" long by 3 1/4" wide; dark green; average substance; 7-8 vein pairs
flowers: August; purple; 2" long by 2 1/4" wide; widely flared shape; 32" scapes
comments: Though the wide-open, fragrant, purple flowers of 'Iron Gate Bouquet' have ornamental value, most of the

growing season it is just an average mound of green foliage. 'Garden Bouquet' sported from it, with streaky, variable foliage. A stable form of the latter could prove to be a more valuable garden plant.

'Iron Gate Delight'
key features: medium-sized mound of variable, streaky foliage; fragrant, pale purple flowers
mound size: 16" high by 36" wide

spacing: 30"
leaves: 7" long by 4 3/4" wide; color varies but usually green with creamy white streaking and mottling; sometimes predominantly streaked and mottled with solid creamy white areas; some also margined with creamy white; colors change from spring to summer, with the creamy whites of mid-summer being yellow in spring; slightly shiny top and underside surfaces;

margin slightly wavy; faintly corrugated; average substance; 10 vein pairs
flowers: mid to late August; very pale purple with lavender mid-petal lines; 3" long by 2 1/2" wide; open funnel shape; fragrant; scapes over 24" high
comments: Like 'Iron Gate Supreme', 'Iron Gate Delight' becomes a highly variable mound of streaky foliage. In fact that may be one of the positive aspects of this plant, i.e., you never know what to expect. The fragrant flowers are an ornamental plus.

A stable, white-margined form of this plant has been propagated but not named.

'Iron Gate Glamour'

key features: medium-large mound of creamy white-margined foliage; fragrant lavender flowers
mound size: 19" high by 40" wide

spacing: 36"
leaves: 9" long by 5 3/4" wide; 1/8" to 3/16" wide margin that changes from yellow to creamy white during the season; shiny, dark green center; occasionally streaked in center; shiny top and underside; blade ovate with a rounded base; slight corrugation at maturity; slight marginal waviness; average substance; 9 vein pairs
flowers: early to late August; pale lavender; 2 1/4" long by 2 1/4" wide; wide-open funnel shape; fragrant; scapes up to 43" high
comments: 'Iron Gate Glamour' represents the most stable of the variegated Iron Gate cultivars. It becomes a very attractive mound of white-margined foliage with the bonus of fragrant flowers.

'Iron Gate Supreme'

key features: medium-sized mound of highly variable foliage; fragrant, pale lavender flowers
mound size: 17" high by 32" wide

spacing: 30"
leaves: 7 1/4" long by 5 1/2" wide; color varies but often green with creamy yellow or white streaking and mottling; some clumps with many leaves developing solid, white centers with green margins, while others show white margins and streaked (and mottled) centers; shiny top and underside surfaces; blade ovate with a slightly lobed base and slightly wavy margin; average substance; 9 vein pairs
flowers: August; pale lavender with lighter petal margins; 2 3/4" long by 1 3/4" wide; fragrant; scapes 24" or more;

forms seed pods

comments: I once compared the leaves of seven 'Iron Gate Supreme' clumps growing in different gardens and came up with the expected result. Only two clumps had leaves that were consistently streaked. The leaves of three clumps had sported to the more stable, green-margined, white-centered form, one had white-margined, streaky-centered leaves, and one had all-green foliage

seedlings and sports of the Iron Gate Series:

'Garden Bouquet': {1983r, V. Sellers} 'Iron Gate Bouquet' sport; streaked foliage, fragrant fls

'Iron Gate Special': stabilized, white-mgd, gr-cntrd sport of 'Iron Gate Supreme'

'Peedee Laughing River': {1992r, U. Syre-Herz; 'Neat Splash' X 'Iron Gate Glamour'} green-centered, white-margined foliage topped by bright purple fls; 15" by 46" md; 10" by 4" lvs (9 vp) wi a 1/2", wavy margin; fast-growing, interesting, and a valuable addition to any garden

'Sugar Babe': {1996r, R. Solberg; 'Iron Gate Supreme' X 'Saishu Jima'} white-margined, green-centered foliage; 15" by 30" md; nice combination of attractive foliage and purple, fragrant flowers

'Sweet Jill': {1986r, R. Benedict} 'Iron Gate Supreme' sport; white-centered, green-margined foliage; fragr, pale lav fls; attractive, but not a good grower

'Valencia': {1995r, W. Zumbar; 'Beatrice' X 'Iron Gate Delight'; streaked, creamy white-mgd lvs}

'Janet'

key features: medium-large mound of gold-centered foliage; fast-growing Fortunei

mound size: 17" high by 40" wide (up to 23" by 49")

spacing: 40"

leaves: 7 3/16" long by 5" wide; thin, 1/8" wide, green margin; center chartreuse in spring turning gold by mid-summer, almost a white-gold with bright light; blade ovate with a slightly lobed base, broadening with age; thin underside bloom; little or no corrugation or waviness; average substance; 9-10 vein pairs

flowers: late July into early August; pale lavender, striped in mid-petal; 1 3/4" long by 1 1/4" wide; narrow funnel shape; scapes 30" high; typical Fortunei flower habits; not very fertile

comments: 'Janet' can be thought of as a smaller version of 'Gold Standard' with a thinner green margin. Like 'Gold Standard' it has a fast growth rate, becomes a dense mound of foliage, and changes from green in spring to gold-centered by mid-summer. It produces a bright splash of color in the garden that can be useful as a specimen plant or ground cover.

I first became aware of 'Janet' in 1981 at the AHS mini-convention in Iowa City. That year it was the "talk" of the meeting and sold for a fairly high price during the auction. Over the years it has been widely propagated and distributed but, because of its similarity to 'Gold Standard', will probably never attain a huge following.

Russ O'Harra registered 'Janet' in 1981. Its origins are obscure but it certainly is of 'Fortunei' heritage.

seedlings, sports, and other related types:

'Changing Moods': {1983r, K. Vaughn; 'Janet' X a
    'William Lachman' sibling; gold foliage that turns to

244

cream} have never seen in any garden

'Janet Day': {1996r, M. Soules; 'Janet' sport} introduced in the 1994 Soules Garden catalog which described it as "spectacular in spring with the center of the leaves ivory, bordered with a 1/4" to 3/8" satiny deep dark green" margin; have only seen this plant after the center turned light green (in late June) but was very impressed with it even at that stage; 20" by 43" md; 6 1/4" by 4 1/4" lvs (10 vp) wi a 3/8", green mgn

'Lakeside Shadows': {1990r, M. Chastain; sport} leaves have splotchily variegated gold centers

'White Lightning': {1994r, J. & B. Diesen; sport} white-margined, gold-centered foliage

other similar types:

'Fan Dance', 'Gold Standard', 'Something Different'

'June'

key features: dense, medium-sized mound of gold-centered foliage; thick substance
mound size: 16" high by 37" wide

spacing: 36"
leaves: 6" long by 4" wide; 1/8" to 3/4" wide, blue-green margin that often streaks into the center which is medium gold by mid-summer, light green earlier; thick underside bloom; blade ovate, broadening with age; slightly wavy; no corrugation; thick substance; 11-12 vein pairs
flowers: late July into mid-August; pale bluish lavender; 2" long by 1" wide; 24" scapes; many seed pods form

comments: When first introduced to the U.S. in 1993, 'June' created a lot of excitement being a gold-centered sport of the popular 'Halcyon'. Things have since calmed down, but 'June' has become a staple of the hosta industry.

There has been a bit of debate about the "true" form of

'June'. Some say it should have a light center, others say darker. The true plant undergoes significant seasonal changes. In spring the leaf center is light green (overlaid with a bluish bloom), but turns medium or light gold by early July (in northern Illinois). Under deep shade, however, the center will remain chartreuse. The two other sports of 'Halcyon' noted here differ in the ultimate intensity of the gold center.

'June' developed as a tissue culture sport from NEO Plants, Ltd. (England) who registered it in 1991.

seedlings, sports, and other related types:

'Goldbrook Glimmer': sport of 'Halcyon' from Goldbrook Plants (Bond, 1994); one md 12" by 33" wi chartreuse-centered lvs, 6 1/2" by 4 1/2" (11 vp); 1 1/2" wide, blue-green margins; center greener than 'June'

'Kiwi Gold Star' {1999r, B. Sligh; 'June' sport; all-gold foliage}

'May': {1999r, H. Hansen & Shady Oaks N; sport; greenish yellow foliage}

'Paradise Joyce': gold-centered, bl-green-mgd sport of 'Halcyon' from Marco Fransen of Holland; center a much lighter gold than 'June'

'Touch of Class': {1999r, H. Hansen & Shady Oaks N; sport; lvs gold-centered wi a wide, bl-gr mgn}

other similar types:

'Emerald Tiara', 'Green With Envy', 'Little Sunspot', 'Punky', 'Wylde Green Cream'

'Just So'

key features: small-sized mound of gold-centered foliage

mound size: 10" high by 23" wide (up to 14" by 31")

spacing: 18"

leaves: 4 1/4" long by 3 1/4" wide; medium to dark green margin, 1/16" to 1/4" wide; center chartreuse early, bright gold by mid-summer; ovate blade shape; moderate corrugation and cupping; better than average substance; 9-10 vein pairs

flowers: late June into mid-July; pale lavender; 1 3/4" long; scapes 18" high; fertile

comments: 'Just So' makes a neat, small mound of gold-centered foliage. It has a fairly good growth rate making it useful as a low edging plant, as well as a specimen for the shaded rock garden. It has been widely propagated in recent years and is becoming fairly common.

'Just So' was registered by Paul Aden in 1986 as a hybrid of a seedling X 'Little Aurora'. It shows a strong relationship to the latter plant and is very similar to green-margined versions of it.

seedlings, sports, and other related types:

'Puck': green-lvd t.c. sport; 1996 Q & Z N introduction; vigorous, low md; excellent edger; named by Bill Zumbar

'Shere Khan': {1995r, M. Zilis & W. Zumbar; sport} lvs gold-cntrd wi a thin, white mgn; dense md; collector's plant

other similar types:

'Amy Elizabeth', 'Emerald Tiara', 'Green with Envy', 'Little Sunspot', 'Wylde Green Cream'

Hosta kikutii (Hyuga Giboshi)

key features: green-leaved species native to Japan; late season flowers
mound size: 16" high by 42" wide

spacing: 36"

leaves: 11 1/2" long by 4 3/4" wide; shiny, dark green color; glabrous, whitish shiny underside; blade elliptic-ovate at maturity, elliptic when young; lightly rippled margin; no corrugation; average substance; 9-11 vein pairs

flowers: late August into mid-September (northern Illinois); very pale lavender with whitish petal margins, halfway from the tip toward the base, and a whitish throat; 2 1/2" long by 1 3/4" wide; funnel-shaped with reflexed tips; long pedicels; distinct, silvery bracts surround buds; bunched near the end of 26" scapes with as many as 80 flowers in the top 4 1/2" of the scape; can remain open for 2 days under cool temperatures; will form seed pods

comments: *Hosta kikutii* can be found in many areas of Japan including Honshu, Shikoku, and Kyushu Islands. The common name, Hyuga Giboshi, is derived from an area on Kyushu Island where it can be found growing. Horticulturally *Hosta kikutii* falls into the following four groups: (1) *Hosta kikutii* (var. *kikutii*), i.e. the plant described above; (2) *H. kikutii caput-avis*; (3) *H. kikutii leuconata*; and (4) *H. kikutii yakusimensis*. *H. kikutii polyneuron* is considered distinct by some, but any differences from *H. kikutii yakusimensis* are hard to find. I have treated the two together in this book. *H. kikutii tosana* could also be included but it has yet to become an important garden plant. Most of these have green leaves that reach 9-11" in length by 4-5" wide, no corrugation and 9-11 vein pairs. The flowering habits also tend to be similar. Most bloom late in the season (August or September) and have similar flower shapes, col-

248

ors, scape buds, and arrangement on the scapes. In general they are good garden plants and have a medium to fast growth rate making them appropriate ground covers.

H. kikutii and its various forms have been the source of numerous hybrids and sports, especially in Japan.

seedlings, sports, and other related types:

'Ahwaneeh': {1990r, U. Syre-Herz; *H. montana* X *H. kikutii*; lvs emerge green, turn pale ylw} not widely distributed

'Finlandia': {1997r, P. Ruh for A. Busse & Alex Summer; *H. kikutii* sdlg} long-standing, "historical" cv; med-sized md of dark green lvs; fls whitish, opening earlier than most *H. kikutii* types, late July into mid-Aug on 30" sc; sometimes listed as *H. kikutii* 'Finlandia'

'Glacier Cascade': {1999r, M. Zilis & P. Cross; *H. kikutii* X *H. hypoleuca*} large, flowing md of long, wavy, green foliage; intense white lf underside; pale lav fls in August

'Harvest Delight': {1997r by P. Ruh for A. Summers; *H. kikutii* sdlg} md 18" by 50"; med gr lvs 10" by 4 3/8" (10 vp); fls from mid-Sept into Oct; scapes dark reddish purple on lower half

'Harvest Desire': {1997r by P. Ruh for A. Summers; *H. longipes* X *H. kikutii*} 18" by 50" md of shiny, dk gr lvs 12" by 6 1/2"; pale lav fls open above the foliage fr early to late Sept; largest of the "Harvest" series and best for substance

H. kikutii caput-avis **(see page 250)**

H. kikutii 'Kifukurin Hyuga': yellow-margined foliage; 18" by 34" md; lvs 9" by 5 1/2" (11-12 vp) wi a 1/4" wide, yellowish green mgn; deep lav fls fr early to late Sept; becoming increasingly popular; sometimes incorrectly listed as *H. kikutii* 'Aureomarginata'; from Japan

H. kikutii leuconata: very attractive, medium-sized mound of shiny, green foliage with an intense underside bloom; 15" by 38" md; lvs 12 1/2" by 4" (10-12, deeply impressed vp); near-white fls in September; long known as *H. kikutii* 'Pruinosa', *H. kikutii* 'Urajiro', and as Urajiro Hyuga Giboshi in Japan where it is found in the wild; listed as *H. kikutii* var. *kikutii* f. *leuconata* (Schmid, 1991)

H. kikutii polyneuron **(see page 252-253)**

H. kikutii tosana: medium-sized mound of shiny, green leaves (9 1/4" by 5" wi 8-9 vp); lf blade ovate (coming to a long, thin tip), very shiny on the underside, and smooth-textured; considered to be a separate species, *Hosta tosana*, by Maekawa (1973) who listed it as being native to Shikoku Island in Japan; in U.S. collections for 20+ years but only recently propagated and sold

H. kikutii yakusimensis **(see page 252)**

'Roy's Pink': hybrid of *H. kikutii* X *H. rupifraga* from Herb Benedict; blooms earlier than either parent (in August); med-sized md of gr lvs 8 1/2" by 4 1/2" (10 vp); fls pale purple, 2 1/4" by 1"

other similar types:

'Katsuragawa': plant recently found on Shikoku Island with an intense red color from the petioles into the midrib of the blade; leaf characteristics reminiscent of *H. kikutii* to which it is closely related; grows alongside a nearly identical form that has green petioles

'Mikawa-no-Yuki': {1997r, H. Sugita & P. Ruh; *H. kikutii* "White-backed" X *H. longipes* "White-backed"} 17" by 42" md wi 12" by 4 1/8" lvs (11 vp); beautiful green foliage with a thick underside bloom; lav fls in Sept, tightly bunched near the top of the scapes; from Hajime Sugita of Okazaki, Japan; once dubbed 'Okazaki Special' by me but this is not correct; translation of name = "snow of Mikawa"; a tremendous plant

---

Hosta kikutii caput-avis (Unazuki Giboshi)

key features: dense, medium-sized mound of shiny, green foliage; late season flowers on recumbent scapes
mound size: 19" high by 40" wide (large form); 8" by 32" (dwarf form)

spacing: 36"
leaves: 13" long by 5 1/8" wide; shiny, medium green; very shiny underside; blade elliptic with a wedge-shaped base and long, narrow tip; blade arches from just above the base, creating a drooping effect; margin noticeably rippled, about ten per side; smooth texture; better than average substance; 10-11 vein pairs
flowers: mid-August into September; lavender; 2 1/8" long by 1 1/8" wide; 38" long scapes that hang downward; fertile

comments: I have seen two types of *Hosta kikutii caput-avis*, a large form (described above) and a dwarf form which bears whiter flowers (described below). This probably represents the normal range of diversity present in this unusual plant. Plant collector Yoshimichi Hirose of Iwakuni City, Japan informed me in 1995 that *H. k. caput-avis* can be found growing wild on the eastern end of Shikoku Island and just across the Kii Strait on the Kii peninsula on Honshu Island, near Wakayama. Kenji Watanabe (1985) and many others consider this plant a species separate from *Hosta kikutii*, i.e. *Hosta caput-avis*, and it is easy to see why considering its distinct features.

Watanabe (1985) described it as growing on cliffs with hanging scapes and white or purple flowers. The pendulous scapes make "Caput-avis" an ideal subject for growing out of a rock wall or on a hillside. The dwarf form can be used in the same ways and also makes a good rock garden plant.

Both forms can be utilized in breeding programs. Several sports have been selected in Japan including the following leaf types: (1) mottled; (2) streaked, mottled, and green-centered; (3) white-margined (with white flowers); and (4) yellow-margined.

seedlings, sports, and other related types:

H. kikutii caput-avis 'Kinokawa': mottled foliage; from Japan

H. kikutii caput-avis 'Unazuki Dwarf': small, white-flowering form; md 8" by 32"; lvs 7 1/2" by 2 1/4" wi 7 vp; shiny green top and underside leaf surface; whitish flowers on 17" long scapes that hang downward, sometimes creeping along the ground; sometimes sold as "Unazuki" which is not correct since this is the common name for all forms of *H. kikutii caput-avis*

'Red Neck Heaven': {1998r, T. Avent; selfed sdlg of *H. k. caput-avis*} 13" by 30" md; 7 1/2" by 2 3/8" lvs (9 vp) that are med green wi a thick underside bloom and purple red petioles

other similar types:

'Green Fountain': many similarities to the large form of *H. k. caput-avis* **(see page 210)**

Hosta kikutii yakusimensis
(Hime Hyuga Giboshi)

key features: dense, medium-sized mound of narrow, green foliage; lavender flowers in August-September
mound size: 16" high by 40" wide

spacing: 36"
leaves: 9 1/2" long by 3 1/4" wide; medium to dark green; slightly shiny top, very shiny underside; narrowly elliptic to lanceolate shape with a rounded base and long, curved tip; lightly rippled margin; no corrugation; average substance; 9-10, deeply impressed vein pairs
flowers: late August into September; pale lavender with a white throat and whitish margins halfway from the tip toward the base; 2" long by 1 1/2" wide; densely clustered near the end of 18" high scapes; forms many seed pods

comments: *H. kikutii yakusimensis* develops into a flowing, dense mound of narrow, green foliage. It can be utilized in many ways in the landscape, as a ground cover, edging plant or as a specimen to show off its late season flowers. When comparing it side-by-side with *H. kikutii*, the differences are evident. The foliage of *H. k. yakusimensis* tends to be narrower, the veins more closely set and more deeply impressed and the overall mound habit is denser. It, however, is not a dwarf plant as its common name implies (Hime = Dwarf). Mature specimens reach nearly the same dimensions as *H. kikutii*. There is also a debate as to the differences between *H. k. yakusimensis* and *H. k. polyneuron* (Sudare Giboshi). Some consider the two distinct, but garden specimens of both can be easily confused. One difference lies in their native habitats. *H. k. yakusimensis* is native to Yaku Island (off the south end of Kyushu Island, Japan). *H. k. polyneuron* can be found 250 miles away, on the western end of Shikoku Island (conversation with Yoshimichi Hirose, 7-7-95). Schmid (1991) described *H. k. polyneuron*

252

as bearing more veins (9-11) than *H. k. yakusimensis* (7-9), but my observations of the two have not found this (both about 10). It may be that at one time the two were one and the same plant but, over time, became geographically separated.

Many variegated seedlings and sports have been found from both *H. k. yakusimensis* and *H. k. polyneuron*. The most popular form of the latter in recent years has been "*H. kikutii polyneuron albomarginata*", more correctly *H. k. polyneuron* 'Shirofukurin' (Schmid, 1991). More than one white-edged sport of *H. k. polyneuron,* however, has been identified in Japan which may lead to some confusion. Sports of *H. k. yakusimensis* that I observed in Japan include (1) white-margined (3 forms); (2) creamy white-centered; and (3) streaked, 'Kabitan'-like leaves.

seedlings, sports, and other related types:

'Ogon Sudare': small, dense mound of golden foliage; red petioles; *H. k. polyneuron* sdlg fr Japan; md 9" by 31"; lvs 8" by 3" (8 vp); blade elliptic and moderately wavy

'Yoshinogawa': *H. k. polyneuron* sport found along the Yoshino River on Shikoku Island, Japan; streaked green and gold foliage

other similar types:

'Blythe Spirit': {1990r by P. Ruh for G. Schenk} very close to *H. k. yakusimensis*

'Hirao Splendor': {1997r, S. Hirao, M. Zilis & P. Ruh} formerly "Hirao 59" which I renamed in 1993; imported into the U.S. before 1970; 17" by 43" md; med green lvs 10" by 3 3/4" (10 vp, deeply impressed); lav fls in dense clusters on 36" sc in Sept; closely related to *H. kikutii yakusimensis*

'Kinbotan'

key features: small mound of yellow-margined foliage; purple flowers in July
mound size: 6" high by 20" wide

spacing: 18"
leaves: 2 1/2" long by 1 1/2" wide; narrow (1/8" wide) yellow margins that turn greenish during the season; medium green center; blade slightly wavy and ovate in shape with a rounded base; smooth texture; average substance; 3-4 vein pairs
flowers: early to mid-July; purple; 12-18" scapes; fertile
comments: 'Kinbotan' is a common plant in Japanese hosta collections and increasingly so in the U.S. It makes a neat small mound of yellow-edged foliage that can be useful in rock gardens. It is a seedling of *H. venusta* to which it shows a strong affinity in many foliage and flower traits.

I have seen a yellow-margined sport of *H. venusta* similar to 'Kinbotan' except that the margins become a brighter gold as the season progresses.
seedlings, sports, and other related types:
none listed
other similar types:
'Gaijin', 'Kifukurin Otome', *H. pulchella* 'Kifukurin' (*H. pulchella aureo-marginata*)

'King Tut'

key features: medium-large mound of heavily corrugated, bright gold foliage; slug-resistant
mound size: 19" high by 46" wide

spacing: 40"

leaves: 9 3/4" long by 8" wide; brilliant gold color by late June; thin bloom on top surface early in season; moderate bloom on underside; broadly ovate shape with a heart-shaped base; moderate corrugation; thick substance; 13-14 vein pairs

flowers: late June into mid-July; near-white with a pale lavender stripe in mid-petal; 2 1/2" long by 1 3/8" wide; narrow funnel shape; scapes up to 37" high

comments: During a July 1996 visit to the Dubuque Arboretum and Botanical Gardens, I noted that 'King Tut' was the brightest gold hosta in their large collection. 'King Tut' was registered in 1981 by Gretchen Harshbarger as a seedling of 'Tokudama Aureonebulosa' and is a sibling of 'Blondie' and 'Treasure'.

seedlings, sports, and other related types:

'Brother Stefan': {1998r, O. Petryszyn; 'King Tut' X a 'Mildred Seaver' sdlg; gold-centered, green-margined foliage}

'Mister Watson': {1999r, L. Jones; sport wi gold-centered, green-mgd lvs}

other similar types:

'Aspen Gold', 'Blondie', 'Centerfold', 'Golden Medallion', 'Golden Nugget', 'Golden Rajah', 'Golden Waffles', 'Treasure'

'Kisuji' (Kisuji Giboshi)

key features: small mound of heavily streaked, gold and green foliage; thin substance
mound size: 13" high by 29" wide

spacing: 24"
leaves: 5 3/4" long by 2 1/2" wide; green-margined with a mottled green-chartreuse-yellow center; shiny top and underside surfaces; lightly rippled margin; blade narrowly ovate; very thin substance; 6 vein pairs
flowers: early to late August; medium purple; deep purple in bud; 2 1/4" long; scapes up to 33" high
comments: 'Kisuji' forms a dense mound of brightly variegated foliage. The streaked and mottled yellow and green foliage makes it an ideal small specimen plant. It has such thin substance that it is very susceptible to slug damage, but that should not discourage anyone from growing this pretty plant. I found 'Kisuji' in just about every hosta collection in Japan where it is admired for its brightly variegated foliage. It has been known by at least two other names, 'Inaho' and *H. tardiva aureo-striata*, and can still be found in nursery lists and collections as such. Various authors have attributed 'Kisuji' to be of *H. sieboldii* origin, but I was emphatically told in Japan that this was not so.

seedlings, sports, and other related types:
none listed

other similar types:
'Fruehlingsgold': some plants sold under this name appear to be the same as 'Kisuji'

Hosta kiyosumiensis (Kiyosumi Giboshi)

key features: medium-sized mound of green foliage; native to isolated areas of Japan
mound size: 12" high by 30" wide

spacing: 24"

leaves: 6 1/2" long by 3" wide; medium green; elliptic blade shape; dull top, moderately shiny underside; smooth texture; average substance; 7 vein pairs

flowers: listed as being white on scapes about 11-14" high by Maekawa (1973)

comments: This species has made very little impact amongst hosta growers in the U.S. with the exception of a few collectors. The *Hosta Finder 2000* (Greene, 2000) lists only one U.S. retail source. *Hosta kiyosumiensis* is native to Mt. Kiyosumi (Maekawa, 1973), but it can also be found in many other areas of Japan. I have seen it growing out of rocks along a stream in Aichi Prefecture in Japan (pictured above), far from Mt. Kiyosumi and I was told of native sites from Tokyo on south into western Japan, as well as in Chiba Prefecture where Mt. Kiyosumi is located.

A much larger plant labelled *Hosta kiyosumiensis* exists in a few American collections. This plant reaches dimensions of 28" high by 56" wide with leaves 11" long by 5 1/2" wide (11-13 vein pairs). Its medium lavender flowers are produced from late July into August on scapes up to 70" long.

A number of sports can be found in Japanese collections including those with (1) yellow and green-striped leaves; (2) green and white-striped leaves; (3) mottled foliage; (4) white-centered foliage; (5) streaked and white-centered leaves; and (6) yellow-margined leaves. Most of these were collected in the wild. Several *H. kiyosumiensis* X *H. pycnophylla* hybrids were registered by Peter Ruh in 1998 and

257

H. kiyosumiensis "Busen'

1999. These include 'Amethyst Joy', 'Belle of the Ball', 'Inland Sea', 'Lavender Doll', 'Lavender Stocking', 'Quaker Lady', 'Qualifying Queen', and 'Swan Lake'. He also registered 'Toots', a hybrid of *H. pycnophylla* X *H. kiyosumiensis*.

seedlings, sports, and other related types:

'Amethyst Joy': {1999r, H. Sugita & P. Ruh; *H. kiyosumiensis* X *H. pycnophylla*} 19" by 58" md of med green lvs, 12" by 6" (11 vp); bluish cast early; one of my favorites of the Sugita-Ruh series of hybrids

H. kiyosumiensis 'Busen': gold-centered sport found in the wild by Hajime Sugita of Japan; also called *H. kiyosumiensis medio-picta*; a gold seedling from this plant also exists

'Inland Sea': {1998r, H. Sugita, M. Zilis & P. Ruh; *H. kiyosumiensis* X *H. pycnophylla*} 17" by 48" md of smooth, shiny, dark green lvs, 12 1/2" by 4 3/4" (10 vp); pale purple fls, 3" by 2", subtended by large, whitish bracts, in Aug; 26" long scapes lie on the foliage or are flat on the ground; hybridized in 1986 by Hajime Sugita of Japan; named for the sea between Honshu and Shikoku islands in Japan; tremendous plant

H. kiyosumiensis "Marginata": 27" by 63" md; lvs 11" by 5" with a 3/8" wide, greenish yellow margin; tall sc of lav fls in Aug

'Koryu' (Koryu Giboshi)

key features: small mound of twisted, irregular, narrow leaves; leaf color a combination of dark and light green areas

mound size: 7" high by 15" wide

spacing: 12"

leaves: 5 1/4" long by 1 1/4" wide; dark green along the margin and in raised areas, lighter green in the center and lower areas; top and underside surfaces shiny; narrowly elliptic blade that is twisted and wavy; uneven texture; good substance; 3-4 vein pairs that are difficult to see

flowers: early to mid-September; pale purple with lighter petal margins; 2 1/8"

long by 1" wide; narrow funnel with reflexed tips; arranged around the scapes that are 14" high

comments: 'Koryu' belongs to a select group of twisted, contorted hostas which also includes 'Fused Veins' and 'Tortifrons'. It originated in Japan where it can be commonly found in collections. Kenji Watanabe (1985) described 'Koryu' as having "swollen variegation", no doubt referring to the way some of the raised areas are darker green. The venation pattern tends to be somewhat irregular as well. The flowering characteristics of 'Koryu' strongly resemble those of 'Tardiflora', blooming at the same time, being close in color, having a similar flower shape, and being arranged on the scape in the same way.

seedlings, sports, and other related types:
none listed

other similar types:

'Emerald Necklace' **(see page 142)**

'Fused Veins': {1983r, R. Benedict} an import from Japan that appears the same as 'Hamada Contorted', a Japanese cultivar; 12" by 23" md of semi-upr, twisted, wavy lvs, 6" by 2" (4, irregularly arranged vp); leaf pale green in the center, dark green along the margin; fls from late

Aug into mid-Sept; lvs wider and larger than 'Koryu' wi
a more vigorous growth rate; a collector's plant
'Tortifrons' **(see page 480)**

'Krossa Regal'
key features: huge, vase-shaped mound of powdery
blue foliage; 5-foot scapes bearing lavender flowers in
August
mound size: 33" high by 71" wide

spacing: 72"
leaves: 11 1/4" long by 7" wide; grayish blue-green in May
and June, created by a thick bloom; dark green by early
July; very thick underside bloom; ovate shape with a
slightly lobed base and small, distinct tip; margin distinctly
wavy, 4-5 per side; no corrugation; petioles nearly vertical,
creating the vase-shaped habit; outer leaves 8-12" from the
soil surface; in some years, an orangy gold fall color develops in late October; thick substance; 12-13 vein pairs
flowers: July 26 to August 12; evenly colored, medium
lavender throughout except for a distinct, white margin
from the throat to mid-petal; 2 3/8" long by 1 1/4" wide;
funnel-shaped; very sturdy scapes covered with a thick
bloom; scape height ranges from 36" to 63"; 30-40 flowers
in the top 8-12" of each scape; as many as 25 scapes per
mature clump; does not form seed pods
comments: 'Krossa Regal' has become a hosta "classic" for
many reasons. The large-sized, vase-shaped mound of
frosty blue foliage is slug-resistant and makes the perfect
centerpiece plant for almost any garden. It also can be utilized effectively as a background plant. The vase-shaped
mound habit adds an interesting structural element and
opens the possibility for creative combination plantings.

While small to medium-sized hostas are often planted at the base of 'Krossa Regal', other perennial or annual flowers can also be quite effective.

The flowering habits of 'Krossa Regal' are notable. The scapes are borne well above the foliage, generally reaching four to six feet tall. At my first AHS convention I can recall being impressed by the sight of 'Krossa Regal' in bloom (against the background of a white house). I hadn't realized that hosta scapes could attain such magnificent heights. Since seed pods do not develop, the scapes need to be cut off immediately after flowering since they turn into "brown sticks" within 2-3 weeks.

Though 'Krossa Regal' is known for its "blue" foliage, its early season color is actually more of a "powdery gray" that differs from the blues of the Sieboldianas and Tokudamas. Comparing 'Krossa Regal' side-by-side with *H. s.* 'Elegans' in spring is a good way to understand the difference. Once the bloom has disappeared (usually by mid-summer), the subsequent dark green color is also quite attractive.

'Krossa Regal' was named for its introducer, Gus Krossa of Michigan who imported the plant from Japan. His wife, Alma, registered it for her late husband in 1980. It is a seedling of *Hosta nigrescens* which it strongly resembles in mound habit, scape height, and leaf color. The two differ, however, in foliage shape and texture. I do not know the source of 'Krossa Regal' in Japan, but while touring Japan in 1991, I was shown the cultivar 'Chodai Ginyo' in Okazaki which reminded me of 'Krossa Regal'.

Despite being pod sterile, 'Krossa Regal' pollen has been utilized by a few persistent breeders with a small amount of success. Herb Benedict once showed me a hybrid of 'Color Glory' X 'Krossa Regal' that he called 'Regal Glory'. 'Peedee Apollo' is another cultivar with 'Krossa Regal' listed as the pollen parent.

'Krossa Regal' has been the source of a few sports, the most prominent being 'Regal Splendor', a wonderful hosta in its own right. I introduced a white-centered sport, 'Porcelain Vase', many years ago that looked great in containers; however, it failed to thrive in garden situations, no doubt due to the lack of chlorophyll. Other white-centered sports, however, have proven to be much stronger growers. Most of those turn green during the season accounting for their greater vigor.

seedlings, sports, and other related types:

'Dress Whites': sport of 'Sail's Ho' (a 'Krossa Regal' mutation) from Ran Lydell; leaves green-margined with a white center that does not turn green

'Peedee Apollo': {1996r, U. Syre-Herz; 'Peedee Gold

Flash' X 'Krossa Regal'; gold lvs; purple fls on 50"
scapes in Aug}

'Porcelain Vase': {1988r, M. Zilis; sport} white-centered
foliage; beautiful in containers, not in gardens

'Regal Chameleon': sport from Walters Gardens; lvs light
gr-cntrd, dk gr-mgd

'Regal Glory': from Herb Benedict; 'Color Glory' X
'Krossa Regal'; med-lg md of heavily variegated
foliage; lav fls from mid-July into Aug much like
'Krossa Regal'

'Regal Promenade': {1994r, R. Snyder; sport; lvs emerge
bl-gr, cream streaks appear in 2-3 weeks}

'Regal Providence': {1994r, R. Snyder; sport} gold-cntrd,
bl-gr mgn; stable form of 'Regal Promenade'; very
attractive

'Regal Splendor': {1987r, Walters Gardens} creamy margined sport; a classic **(see page 365)**

'Regalia': {1992r, K. Anderson; sport} med to lt gr cntr, dk
gr, 1" margin; lvs 10" by 7 1/2" (12-13 vp); md 24" by
47" or more

'Sail's Ho': {1995r, R. Lydell; sport} lvs frosted white in
the center, dk gr-mgd; turns green

'Tom Schmid': {1995r, T. Schmid; sport wi pure white-
mgd, bl-green-centered lvs}

other similar types:

Hosta nigrescens, 'Pewter Frost', 'Tenryu'

Hosta laevigata

key features: dense mound of very wavy, bright green foliage; narrow-petalled, purple flowers in August
mound size: 12" high by 29" wide

spacing: 24"
leaves: 8" long by 2 1/2" wide; shiny, dark green; very shiny underside; blade narrowly elliptic to lanceolate; very wavy margins; smooth texture; good substance; 4-5 vein pairs
flowers: late August into September; pure purple except for two areas of white at the petal base; thin petals; very thin flower buds; scapes up to 43" high; fertile
comments: *Hosta*

laevigata makes a very attractive mound of shiny, dark green foliage that can be thought of as a narrower, wavier version of *Hosta yingeri*. The late season, spidery purple flowers open well above the mound and are an ornamental plus. It makes a positive addition to any garden and is worth using in breeding programs for its unusual foliage and flowering characteristics.

Until 1990 or so, *Hosta laevigata* was an unknown entity. Schmid (1991) reported that the original material was obtained from seed collected out of wild populations growing on islands off the coast of Korea.

seedlings, sports, and other related types:
none listed

other similar types:
'Curly Top', *H. gracillima* "Lachman Strain", *H. sieboldii angustifolia*, 'Sugar Plum Fairy', *H. yingeri*

'Lakeport Blue'

key features: large mound of heavily corrugated, blue-green foliage; slug-resistant
mound size: 27" high by 63" wide

spacing: 60"

leaves: 16 1/2" long by 12 3/4" wide; blue-green much of the growing season; thick bloom on top and underside; blade broadly ovate with a deeply lobed base; moderately wavy and heavily corrugated; blade usually puckers downward; thick substance; 17-18 vein pairs

flowers: mid-June into early July; near-white color with a pale lavender midrib; 2 1/4" long by 1" wide; scapes 26-35" high; forms seed pods

comments: 'Lakeport Blue' ranks highly for its excellent blue color which lasts into late summer. The leaves also possess the thick substance and attractive corrugation typical of *H. sieboldiana* 'Elegans' types, as are its dense clusters of near-white flowers. One factor that may distinguish it from the mass of heavily corrugated, blue-green Sieboldianas is its ability to grow well in the southern U.S. Reports from Bob Solberg of Green Hill Farm indicate that 'Lakeport Blue' does fairly well during the hot and humid summers of North Carolina.

Chet Tompkins registered 'Lakeport Blue' in 1984 as a cross of two seedlings.

seedlings, sports, and other related types:

'Blue Ox': {1999r by P. Ruh for C. Tompkins; *H. sieboldiana* hybrid} md 23" by 44" (probably larger); blue-green lvs, 9 1/2" by 9 1/2" (19 vp), heavily corrugated, thick subst, & somewhat unruly; introduced in the 1990 Fleur de Lis Gardens catalog (p. 30) as a descendant of 'Lakeport Blue'

'Rhubarb Blue': from Chet Tompkins; 'Lakeport Blue' sibling; lg md of broad, bright blue foliage; rare

'Tattletale Gray': another 'Lakeport Blue' sibling from Chet Tompkins; 26" by 48" md of heavily corrugated, blue-green lvs, 11" by 9" (14 vp); 35" sc; available from a few retail sources (Greene, 2000)

'Lakeside Accolade'

key features: large mound of shiny, dark green foliage
mound size: 28" high by 68" wide

spacing: 60"

leaves: 9" long by 8 3/8" wide; shiny, dark green; moderate underside bloom; blade very broadly ovate with a long, distinct tip; sometimes cupped; slight corrugation; average substance; 12 vein pairs

flowers: late July into mid-August; pale lavender; 2 3/4" long by 3/4" wide; scapes up to 42" high; some pods develop

comments: 'Lakeside Accolade' is notable for its shiny, dark green foliage. It is a bit surprising that it becomes so large since it is an open-pollinated seedling of 'Little Aurora' (1988 registration by Mary Chastain). It is among the first (with 'Lakeside Symphony') registrations of Mary's very large "Lakeside" series of hosta introductions.

seedlings, sports, and other related types:
none listed

other similar types:
'Black Hills', 'Joseph', 'Lakeside Black Satin', 'Lakeside Lollipop', 'Second Wind', 'Spinach Patch', *H. ventricosa*

'Lakeside Black Satin'

key features: medium-large mound of shiny, dark green foliage

mound size: 22" high by 48" wide

spacing: 40"

leaves: 10" long by 9" wide; shiny, dark green; very shiny underside; blade very broadly ovate with a deeply lobed base creating a large heart shape; long, thin tip; many slight ripples along the margin; smooth texture; better than average substance; 8-9 vein pairs

flowers: late July into mid-August; light to medium purple; 2 3/4" long by 1 1/2" wide; bell-shaped; like *H. ventricosa*

comments: 'Lakeside Black Satin' holds true to its name, bearing shiny, dark green foliage. The very small marginal ripples nicely accent the heart-shaped leaf blade. Its flowering habits are close to that of *Hosta ventricosa*, of which it is a seedling. Mary Chastain registered 'Lakeside Black Satin' in 1993. If you are attracted to dark green foliage (and purple flowers), this is worth growing.

seedlings, sports, and other related types:
none listed

other similar types:
'Holly's Honey', 'Holly's Shine', 'Lakeside Accolade', 'Lakeside Blue Cherub', 'Lakeside Lollipop', 'Lakeside Emerald Lights'

'Lakeside Neat Petite'

key features: low, dense mound of heart-shaped green foliage; bright purple flowers in July

mound size: 11" high by 24" wide

spacing: 24"

leaves: 3" long by 2" wide; medium green; dull top surface; thin underside bloom; blade ovate and slightly cupped; smooth texture; average substance; 8 vein pairs

flowers: July; bright purple; narrow funnel shape; clustered in top 2-3" of 16" high scapes; many seed pods develop

comments: Though 'Lakeside Neat Petite' makes a neat, small mound of foliage, the bright purple flowers are its most outstanding feature. They are borne in tight clusters in neat proportion to the foliage. It can be used as a low edger, rock garden plant or ground cover.

'Lakeside Neat Petite' was registered in 1991 by Mary Chastain as a hybrid of *H. venusta* X 'Blue Cadet'.

seedlings, sports, and other related types:

none listed

other similar types:

'Lakeside Little Gem'

'Peedee Elfin Bells'

'Quilting Bee': {1999r, Russ O'Harra Hosta Society for R. O'Harra; parentage unknown} dense, 13" by 30" md of corrugated, shiny, dark green lvs, 4 1/2" by 3 5/8" (8 vp); pale purple, semi-bell-shaped fls in July on 28" sc; impressive for dark green color, corrugation, & dense md habit

Hosta lancifolia (Akikaze Giboshi)
(Narrow-leaved Plantainlily)

key features: medium-sized mound of narrow green foliage; late season lavender flowers; most planted landscaping hosta ever

mound size: 19" high by 44" wide

spacing: 36"

leaves: 6 3/4" long by 2 5/8" wide; shiny, medium green; very shiny underside; blade elliptic to narrowly ovate shape with a rounded base; margin not wavy or rippled; smooth texture; distinct purple-red dots on petioles; thin substance; 6-7 vein pairs; green until late fall when they turn yellow-green or frost affects them

flowers: mid-August into early September (northern Illinois); medium lavender throughout except for a thin, white margin extending from the throat halfway to the petal tip; 1 7/8" long by 1 1/8" long; many scapes ranging from 19-30" in height; 69 scapes on one mature clump with 20-25 flowers per scape; very limited pod formation but not completely sterile

comments: Perhaps the best testament to the value of *Hosta lancifolia* is the fact that it is almost synonymous with the word "hosta" to many people in the United States. Millions of plants have been sold, grown, and divided over the course of the twentieth century, making it the premier landscaping hosta of all time. In many older cities it can be found in great numbers around homes and parks, growing in sun or shade. In the Chicago suburb of Winnetka where miles of it line city streets, it once became so common that it was known as "The Winnetka Weed". My own first recognition of a hosta was a planting of *Hosta lancifolia* in front of my grandparent's home in Chicago.

Its rapid growth rate and early introduction into the

268

United States in the 1800's certainly accounts for the large numbers that can be found. When a need for shade plants developed in the U.S. in the early twentieth century, *Hosta lancifolia* was readily available at very reasonable prices. The 1933 Wayside Gardens catalog (p. 59) listed *Funkia lancifolia* (its old name) at three for 75 cents, a dozen for $2.00, or 100 for $15.00. The rapid multiplication rate also made it an easy plant for neighbors to share divisions. At the same time, it became so common and ordinary, that it quickly lost its popularity in the 1980's when many new hybrids with thicker substance were introduced. Today it is still available to some extent at most nurseries and with the huge numbers that have been planted, *Hosta lancifolia* will continue to be a familiar sight for many years to come.

Perhaps the most understated feature of *Hosta lancifolia* is the late summer flowering. Its lavender flowers can be quite attractive, especially in mass plantings. With a mature clump producing as many as 60 scapes, several plants can produce a great multitude of flowers over its three week blooming season.

There is a bit of controversy surrounding the nomenclature of *Hosta lancifolia*. The true form is native to China, but I have never heard of anyone claiming to have seen a wild population. Schmid (1991) listed it as the cultivar 'Lancifolia' and stated that *Hosta cathayana* is often mistaken for 'Lancifolia'. Though he agreed that the two are very similar, he claimed that 'Lancifolia' is sterile and that *H. cathayana* is not and that the latter blooms later, has shorter scapes, and has smaller leaves (Schmid, 1991). He also listed 'Chinese Sunrise' (as *H. cathayana* 'Nakafu') as a form of *Hosta cathayana*. Based upon my extensive observations of *Hosta lancifolia* and 'Chinese Sunrise', the only possible conclusion that I can draw is that 'Chinese Sunrise' is derived from what we know as *Hosta lancifolia*. Further, if 'Chinese Sunrise' is actually representative of *Hosta cathayana*, *Hosta lancifolia* and *Hosta cathayana* must be one and the same plant. Some of my reasons for this conclusion are the following:

(1) Both *Hosta lancifolia* and *Hosta cathayana* bear identical flowers (medium lavender throughout except for a thin, white margin extending from the throat halfway to the petal tip);

(2) Both form similar-sized mounds (19" by 44" for *H. lancifolia*, 18" by 40" for *H. cathayana*);

(3) foliage size is identical;

(4) foliage shape is identical;

(5) leaf underside, both shiny;

(6) same number of vein pairs;

(7) purple-red dots on the petioles of both;

(8) blooming season is the same;

(9) same level of seed pod formation, i.e. limited, but not completely sterile.

From what I have observed, the form of *H. lancifolia* that we have extensively propagated in the U.S. will form only a limited number of seed pods. This, however, does not eliminate the possibility of it being a species. It could be that the selection of *H. lancifolia* that we have propagated is a clone with limited fertility. More fertile clones probably exist. A similar situation occurs in *Hosta plantaginea*, where the form that has been widely distributed in the U.S. and Europe has limited fertility (though greater than *Hosta lancifolia*). Yet, there is no denying its species designation. Interestingly, like *H. lancifolia*, *H. plantaginea* is also native to China and wild populations have not been recently identified.

The name, *Hosta lancifolia*, should be retained. I do not recommend using the names 'Lancifolia' or *Hosta cathayana*.

seedlings, sports, and other related types:

'Change of Tradition': {1988r, M. Zilis & T & Z N} t.c. sport with very thin (1/32" to 1/16"), white mgns; md 18" by 33"; lvs 5 3/4" by 2" (6 vp); interesting collector's plant

'Chinese Sunrise': {1992r by P. Ruh for R. Schaeffer & A. Summers} found as a sport of *H. lancifolia* in the garden of Robert Schaeffer in 1960, later named by Alex Summers; gold-centered foliage in spring, turning green thereafter; 18" by 40" md; 6 1/2" by 3" lvs (7 vp) that are bright gold with a thin (1/16" wide), green margin; center changes to chartreuse, then med green by July; elliptic to narrowly ovate blade that is shiny on both top and underside surfaces; thin subst; lav fls from late Aug into mid-Sept on 23" sc; a.k.a. 'Oriental Sunrise' & *H. cathayana variegata*; also listed as *H. cathayana* 'Nakafu' (Schmid, 1991)

H. lancifolia 'Aurea': a name sometimes incorrectly used for 'Wogon Gold' or 'Fortunei Aurea'

H. lancifolia 'Dwarf': invalid name used over the years for several plants including a green-leaved, *H. sieboldii* sdlg; the white-mgd cultivar, 'Louisa'; and others

H. lancifolia 'Gracilis': another invalid name for a green *H. sieboldii* seedling

H. lancifolia tardiflora: used for a form of *H. lancifolia* that is supposed to bloom later, but it does not; the same as *H. lancifolia;* name also sometimes incorrectly applied to 'Tardiflora'

270

'Irish Mist': {1994r, R. Savory; seedling of *H. lancifolia*; white-centered, green-mgd lvs}

'Little Dart': {1995r by P. Ruh & R. Lydell for E. Fisher as an *H. lancifolia* sport} called *H. lancifolia* "Dwarf" by Eunice Fisher; purple flowers in Aug; probably actually a green-lvd sdlg of *H. sieboldii*

'New Tradition': {1988r, M. Zilis & T & Z N} t.c. sport; white-cntrd, gr-margined lvs; weak grower

'Pineapple Poll': {1988r, BHHS for Eric Smith; *H. sieboldiana* X *H. lancifolia*} dense mound of narrow, wavy foliage; better substance than *H. lancifolia*, making a good replacement for it in landscapes **(see page 341)**

'Silverado': {1987r, Kuk's Forest; *H. lancifolia* sport} dense md of yellow to creamy white-margined foliage; 12" by 33" md; 6 1/2" by 2" lvs; margin 1/8" wide; pale to med purple fls, early to late Aug; listed as an *H. lancifolia* sport but it blooms earlier and flowers more purple; very attractive

'Small Talk': {1991r by P. Ruh for L. Simpers; *H. lancifolia* 'Aurea' sdlg} small mound of gold foliage that turns green

other similar types:

'Kelsey': {1996r, P. Ruh for H. Kelsey & F. Williams} a plant selected by Frances Williams; same as *H. lancifolia*

'Olga's Shiny Leaf': listed as a cultivar but is the same as *H. lancifolia*

'Pauline': {1987r by P. Ruh for D. Stone} almost identical to *H. lancifolia* in foliage and flower; sm md of elliptic, green foliage; lav fls in Aug-Sept

'Pollyanna': {1983r, P. Banyai; a probable seedling of *H. lancifolia*} sm md of elliptic, green lvs

'Sentinels': {1986r by C. Williams for F. Williams; *H. sieboldii* X *H. lancifolia*} medium-sized mound of lance-shaped, green foliage topped by a tremendous show of purple flowers in August; 17" by 44" md; lvs 6" by 2 1/4" (4-5 vp); scapes 23-30"; 62 scapes on one clump, 18-24 fls per scape; can be mistaken for *H. lancifolia* except for the purple fls and earlier blooming season; introduced by Fairmount Gardens in 1966 (Nesmith, 1966); sported to 'Silver Lance', which has white-margined foliage; from Savory's Gardens {1982r, R. Savory}

'Leather Sheen'

key features: dense, medium-sized mound of shiny, dark green foliage
mound size: 17" high by 48" wide

spacing: 36"

leaves: 7 1/2" long by 4 1/4" wide; shiny, dark green; blade ovate and moderately wavy; smooth texture when young, slightly corrugated at maturity; good substance; 8-10 vein pairs

flowers: early to mid-July; medium purple; 2 1/8" long by 1 1/4" wide; 23" scapes; does not readily form seed pods

comments: 'Leather Sheen' originated from a 1985 cross between 'Sum and Substance' and a *Hosta venusta* seedling. What has always amazed me about that cross was the great diversity of plants that resulted. Siblings to 'Leather Sheen' include 'Little Razor', 'New Wave', and 'Golden Decade'. All of these plants are fairly small-sized, a far cry from the mammoth 'Sum and Substance', and all exhibit a fairly fast growth rate. That, however, is where their similarities end. From the narrow-leaved gold 'Little Razor' to the shiny, blackish 'Leather Sheen' to gold, rounder-leaved 'Golden Decade' to olive green, wide-petioled 'New Wave', the diversity represented by these plants from the same seed pod is almost unbelievable. 'Leather Sheen' is probably the most useful landscaping plant of the bunch, making an excellent specimen, edger, or ground cover.

I registered 'Leather Sheen' in 1988 with Doug Lohman who gave it its appropriate name.

seedlings, sports, and other related types:

'Golden Decade': sibling to 'Leather Sheen'; sm md of golden foliage; rare but still offered by 4 retail sources (Greene, 2000)

'Little Razor': {1988r, M. Zilis, D. Lohman & T & Z N} 'Sum and Substance' X a *H. venusta* sdlg; low, dense md

272

of narrow, gold foliage; sibling to 'Leather Sheen', 'Golden Decade' and 'New Wave'

'New Wave': {1988r, M. Zilis & D. Lohman & T & Z N} 13" by 35" md of olive gr lvs, 6" by 5" (9 vp); wide, flat petioles; sibling to 'Leather Sheen', etc.; unusual

other similar types:

H. clausa, *H. longissima*, 'Maraschino Cherry', 'Slick Willie', *H. takahashii*, 'Tardiflora', *H. tardiva*, 'Temple Bells'

'Lemon Lime'

key features: small, dense mound of greenish gold foliage; purple flowers in July; may rebloom
mound size: 12" high by 36" wide

---

spacing: 30"
leaves: 3 5/8" long by 1 5/8" wide; pale green except in areas of bright light where it becomes chartreuse; dull top surface, whitish shiny underside; blade narrowly ovate with a rounded base; slightly wavy; smooth texture; thin substance; 3-5 vein pairs
flowers: early to late July; bright purple color with white petal margins leading into a white throat;

'Lemon Lime' bordering 'Halcyon'

1 5/8" long by 1" wide; open funnel shape with reflexed tips; 35 scapes on one mature clump ranging in height from 12-25"; scapes stand fairly erect, well above the low, dense clump of foliage; fertile
comments: 'Lemon Lime' is notable for its rapid growth rate, very dense mound habit, and attractive mass of purple flowers. It also offers the possibility of reblooming in September if the first scapes are cut to the ground right after flowering. In the landscape it is one of the top edging plants and makes a great, low ground cover.

'Lemon Lime' was registered by Bob Savory in 1977 as a seedling of *Hosta venusta*, though it certainly shows hybrid character. It can be successfully used as a breeding plant due to its good fertility and the readily available supply of flowers. Two sports of note have been named.

seedlings, sports, and other related types:

'Lemon Delight': a gold-margined, green-centered sport from England

'Shiny Penny': {1997r, R. Solberg; 'Lemon Lime' X 'Shining Tot'} sm md of bright gold foliage; pale purple fls on 13" sc in late July

'Twist of Lime': {1991r by R. Solberg for B. Banyai; sport} green-mgd, gold-centered lvs

other similar types:

'Alma', 'Chartreuse Waves', 'Feather Boa', 'Limey Lisa', 'Wogon Gold'

'Leola Fraim'

key features: medium-large mound of creamy white-margined foliage

mound size: 22" high by 51" wide

spacing: 48"

leaves: 10 1/2" long by 7 1/2" wide; 3/4" to 1 1/2" wide margin that changes from creamy yellow to creamy white during the season; dark green center; thin underside bloom; blade ovate with a slightly lobed base and distinct tip; slight cupping; three broad waves per margin; moderately corrugated; average substance; 11-13 vein pairs

flowers: early to late July; medium lavender; funnel-shaped; 2 1/4" long by 1 1/4" wide; 30-42" scapes; many seed pods

comments: With 'Swoosh' as its pod parent, something less than consistent might be expected. 'Leola Fraim', however, is the exception. It develops very attractive foliage with creamy margins that nicely contrast the dark green center. Though registered back in 1986 by Bill and Eleanor Lachman, it has been greatly underrated, being ornamentally equal to 'Patriot' and 'Minuteman' which have gained much greater popularity. It has a fast growth rate, making it useful as a ground cover and is striking enough to be used as a specimen plant.

seedlings, sports, and other related types:
none listed

other similar types:
'Heart's Content', 'Minuteman', 'Patriot', 'Scooter', 'Trailblazer'

'Little Aurora'
key features: small mound of very bright gold foliage
mound size: 14" high by 40" wide (up to 17" by 54")

spacing: 30"
leaves: 5 3/4" long by 4 1/2" wide (up to 6 3/8" by 5 3/4"); bright gold all season long; thin underside bloom; broadly ovate shape with a heart-shaped base; blade slightly wavy; moderately corrugated with age, none when young; better than average substance; 11-13 vein pairs
flowers: late June into mid-July; very pale lavender to near-white; scapes 12-22" high; fertile

comments: 'Little Aurora' becomes a dense mound of foliage that can brighten up any shaded area (even when labelled 'Golden Prayers'!). It makes a nice low accent plant and can be used effectively as an edger. It has a good growth rate and its flower performance is acceptable.

Paul Aden registered 'Little Aurora' in 1978 as a seedling of 'Tokudama Aureonebulosa' X 'Golden Waffles', though the number of vein pairs and foliage size do not match what can be expected from this parentage. It has been the source of several mutations and the number continues to grow. In addition, since most plants labelled 'Golden Prayers' are actually 'Little Aurora', many of the sports listed as being from 'Golden Prayers' can be rightfully attributed to 'Little Aurora'.

seedlings, sports, and other related types:

'Delia': {1995r, R. & M. Ford (England); as a sport of 'Golden Prayers' with a light yellow center and medium green margin; 6" high md; 3" long lvs wi 8 vp} should be listed as a sport of 'Little Aurora'

'Elfin Cup': {1988r, W. Zumbar; 'Little Aurora' sport} white-mgd, gold-cntrd lvs; saw in Bill's garden in 1986 but not since

'Enchantress': {1988r, W. Zumbar; 'Little Aurora' sport} chartreuse to gold-margined, white-centered foliage; attractive, but slow-growing; available from only one retail source (Greene, 2000)

'Goldbrook Grace': {1989r, S. Bond; as a sport of 'Golden Prayers' with a pale yellow center and medium green margin forming a 6" high md and lvs that are 4" long with 8 vp} should be listed as a sport of 'Little Aurora'

'Just So': {1986r, P. Aden; "Aden 421" X 'Little Aurora'} gold-cntrd, gr-mgd lvs; acts like a sport of 'Little Aurora' **(see page 247)**

'Lakeside Accolade': {1988r, M. Chastain; 'Little Aurora' sdlg} dark green lvs; larger than 'Little Aurora' **(see page 265)**

'Little Sunspot': {1996r, Briggs N, 'Little Aurora' sport} lvs gold-cntrd wi a dk green mgn; sensational

'Paula San Martin': {1988r, P. Balletta; sport wi white-cntrd, ylw-gr-mgd lvs} haven't seen

'Subtlety': sport of 'Little Aurora' introduced by Alan Tower of Tower Perennial Gardens in 1997; lvs chartreuse-centered, gold-mgd; appropriately named

'Sultana': {1988r, W. Zumbar; 'Little Aurora' sport} lvs gr-cntrd, gold-mgd; outstanding **(see page 441)**

'Tattoo': {1998r, T. Avent; 'Little Aurora' sport} chartreuse-margined, gold-centered lvs with a distinctive darker green "watermark" in the area between the margin and center; rapidly gaining popularity; first saw exhibited in a leaf show in 1995; PPAF

'Tucker Irish Heart': {1993r, R. Stephens; dark gr-lvd sport of 'Golden Prayers'; 8" high md wi 4" long leaves (9 vp)} another green 'Little Aurora' sport

'Vanilla Cream': {1986r, P. Aden; "Aden 456" X 'Little Aurora'} one of the best small gold hostas ever introduced **(see page 493)**

other similar types:
'Bright Glow', 'Gold Drop', 'Gold Edger', 'Golden Scepter', 'Maui Buttercups', 'Spun Sulphur'

'Little Wonder'
key features: low, dense mound of white-margined foliage; bright purple flowers in July
mound size: 9" high by 28" wide

spacing: 24"
leaves: 4 3/8" long by 2 1/4" wide; 1/8" to 1/4" wide, creamy white margins, medium green center; whitish shiny underside; blade narrowly ovate with a moderately wavy margin; smooth texture; average substance; 6 vein pairs
flowers: mid-July into early August; deep purple; funnel-shaped; 1 3/4" long by 1 1/4" wide; 24" scapes

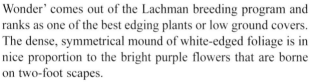

comments: 'Little Wonder' comes out of the Lachman breeding program and ranks as one of the best edging plants or low ground covers. The dense, symmetrical mound of white-edged foliage is in nice proportion to the bright purple flowers that are borne on two-foot scapes.

The Lachmans (Bill and Eleanor) registered 'Little Wonder' in 1989. It was introduced for sale in the 1990 Hatfield Gardens catalog where it was listed as a seedling of 'Neat Splash'.

seedlings, sports, and other related types:
none registered, though a streaked sport has been used for breeding

other similar types:
'Bunchoko', 'Ginko Craig', 'Ototo San', 'White Dove'

Hosta longipes (Iwa Giboshi)

key features: small to medium-sized mound of green foliage; a highly variable, common Japanese species
mound size: 10" high by 20" wide (16" by 40" for large form)

spacing: 18-36"
leaves: 8" long by 5" wide; shiny, medium to dark green; very shiny underside; slightly wavy, ovate blade with a slightly lobed base; reddish purple dots on petioles; smooth texture; thick substance; 8-9 vein pairs
flowers: late August into late September; pale purple; petal margins whitish from base to halfway to tip; 2 1/2" long by 1 1/2" wide; long pedicels; scapes 20-30" high; many pods form
comments: *Hosta longipes* ranks as one of the most commonly found species native to Japan. I have seen it growing in a variety of situations on Honshu Island ranging from wooded hillsides to rocky cliffs. Many different plants have been sold in the U.S. and Japan under the name "Iwa Giboshi" (meaning "rock hosta"). Some are true to name, but I suspect that many are hybrids or open-pollinated *H. longipes* seedlings. Based upon my observations of *H. longipes* in the wild and plants collected from the wild, Iwa Giboshi can be described as a small to medium-sized mound of thick-substanced, shiny, green foliage that produces pale purple flowers from late August well into September. Tremendous variation, however, exists in the amount of reddish purple on the petioles, amount of underside bloom, the flower color, plant size, and scape height. A large number of *H. longipes* sports have also been found in the wild. *Hosta longipes* has a medium to fast growth rate in gardens and can be used as an edger, specimen, or low ground cover. It is valuable in breeding programs for its
278

many unusual traits and is both an excellent pod and pollen parent.

The nomenclature surrounding *Hosta longipes* is almost as confusing as the number of forms. Fumio Maekawa (1972) listed *Hosta longipes* with forma *hypoglauca*, forma *viridipes* and var. *latifolia* as botanical variants. He also classified *Hosta sparsa*, *Hosta tortifrons*, and *Hosta rupifraga* as species closely related to *Hosta longipes*. Under *H. longipes*, Fujita (1978) lumped *H. longipes* var. *longipes* (typical form), *H. longipes* var. *caduca*, and *H. longipes* var. *latifolia* with *H. gracillima* and *H. aequinoctiiantha* as *H. longipes* var. *gracillima* and *H. longipes* var. *aequinoctiiantha*. Schmid (1991) listed several botanical varieties and formas of *Hosta longipes* including *H. longipes* var. *longipes* (typical form), *H. longipes* var. *caduca*, *H. longipes* f. *hypoglauca*, *H. longipes* var. *latifolia*, *H. longipes* f. *sparsa*, *H. longipes* f. *viridipes,* and *H. longipes* var. *vulgata*. Needless to say, the situation is somewhat confusing, though understandable considering the great diversity of *Hosta longipes* in the wild.

In the gardening trade, *Hosta longipes* is currently represented by a much smaller group of plants including *H. longipes* and *H. longipes hypoglauca*. *H. longipes* 'Urajiro' and *H. longipes viridipes* can be found in a number of collections and sometimes in the collector's trade, but have not been widely propagated. In Japan many beautiful *Hosta longipes* sports exist, some of which I have described. In the future, more of these will no doubt become important plants in the trade.

seedlings, sports, and other related types:

H. longipes latifolia 'Amagi Nishiki': lvs gold with green mgns in spring changing to all-green by mid-summer; found in the wild (Watanabe, 1985); leaves shiny on top and underside; very impressive

H. longipes 'Aurea': an invalid name for several golden-leaved forms of *Hosta longipes*; one form common in U.S. collections reaches 14" by 37" (md) wi lvs 7 5/8" by 3 3/4" (7 vp) & pale lav fls on 30" sc, mid-Aug into Sept

H. longipes caduca: a listed form (Schmid, 1991); rarely offered for sale

'Dim Sum': {1994r, Belle Gardens, *H. longipes latifolia* sdlg; lvs change from green to yellow gold}

'Fire Island': {1998r, W. Brincka; *H. longipes* X 'Crested Surf'; greenish yellow foliage}

H. longipes 'Golden Dwarf': small, dense mound of chartreuse foliage; narrowly elliptic lvs, 3 1/2" by 1" (4 vp); intense purple dots on petioles; not widely propagated

H. longipes 'Gotemba Nishiki': Gotemba Nursery sport; beautiful mound of creamy margined foliage

'Grand Finale': {1995r, R. Benedict & J & J Wilkins; 'Maruba Iwa' sdlg} 13" by 38" md of shiny, med green lvs, 6 7/8" by 3 7/8" (9 vp); attractive foliage but highly rated for its late season flowering {fls registered as pale purple in Sept-Oct}

'Grand Slam': {1990r, R. Benedict & H. Gowen} 16" by 43" md; shiny, rippled, dark green lvs, 7" by 4 3/4" (9-10 vp), wi a thick underside bloom and good subst; purple-red dots cover petioles; impressive mound of shiny green foliage; *H. longipes latifolia* seedling

H. longipes 'Hakuho': sport of 'Okutama Nishiski' with white-centered foliage that turns green by mid-summer; name translates to "white bird"; saw in the collection of Yoshimichi Hirose; tremendous

'Harvest Dandy': {1997r by P. Ruh for A. Summers; *H. longipes* sdlg} 16" by 50" md of sl shiny, dk gr lvs, 12" by 6" (10 vp); good subst; pale purple fls, early to late Sept

'Harvest Desire': {1997r by P. Ruh for A. Summers; *H. longipes* X *H. kikutii*} 18" by 50" md of shiny, dk gr lvs 12" by 6 1/2"; pale lav fls open above the foliage fr early to late Sept; largest of the "Harvest" series and best for substance

H. longipes hypoglauca: intense, purple-red dotting on the petioles **(see page 282)**

H. longipes 'Komyo Nishiki': pure white-centered, green-margined lvs; noticeably wavy; fr Japan

H. longipes lancea: listed as *H. longipes* f. *sparsa* (Schmid, 1991) but known in Japan under this name; have seen two forms growing along the Tenryu River in Japan amongst grasses at water's edge; very narrowly ovate to elliptic, green lvs; closely related to 'Tardiflora'

H. longipes latifolia: listed form that may be confused with *Hosta rupifraga* according to Schmid (1991)

'Maruba Iwa': 8" by 20" md of very smooth, shiny, med green lvs, 6" by 4 1/2" (9 vp); thick substance; wavy; shiny underside; fls in Sept; also listed as *H. longipes latifolia* 'Maruba' (Schmid, 1991)

'Mikawa-no-Yuki': {1997r, H. Sugita & P. Ruh; *H. kikutii* "White-backed" X *H. longipes* "White-backed"} 17" by 42" md wi 12" by 4 1/8" lvs (11 vp); beautiful green foliage with a thick underside bloom; lav fls in Sept, tightly bunched near the top of the scapes; from Hajime Sugita of Okazaki, Japan; once dubbed 'Okazaki Special' by me but this is not correct; translation of name = "snow of Mikawa"; a tremendous plant

H. longipes 'Okutama Nishiki': a Japanese sport; stunningly beautiful green-margined, creamy yellow, green and streaky-centered leaves

'Rock Happy': {1992r, P. Ruh, sdlg of *H. longipes* wi yellow-green lvs}

H. longipes 'Tama-no-Yuki': white-margined lvs; observed at Gotemba Nursery

H. longipes 'Urajiro': intensely white-backed foliage; md 15" by 32"; 11" by 7" lvs (10 vp); deep purple-red dots on petiole; excellent substance; have seen in U.S. & Japanese collections

H. longipes viridipes: form with green petioles (no purple-red dots); 19" by 55" md of slightly shiny, green lvs, 7" by 5 1/2" (10-11 vp); blade broadly ovate and very shiny on the underside; can be found in collections in the U.S. but not widely propagated

H. longipes vulgata: listed form (Schmid, 1991); some plants being grown as *Hosta longipes* or "Iwa Giboshi" could be this

H. longipes 'Tenryu Nishiki': 22" by 64" md of shiny lvs that are green-centered with a margin that changes from yellow to greenish white; lvs 10" by 6 7/8" (12 vp)

other similar types:

Hosta rupifraga: similar to *H. longipes latifolia* with which it may be mixed in the trade **(see page 374)**

Hosta longipes hypoglauca (Kofuki Iwa Giboshi)

key features: medium-sized mound of green foliage; red petioles
mound size: 12" high by 33" wide

spacing: 30"
leaves: 6" long by 4" wide; medium green; thick underside bloom; blade ovate with a rounded base and distinct tip; petioles intensely covered with purplish red dots well into the blade along the midrib; good substance; 6-7 vein pairs
flowers: September; lavender
comments: Notable for the intense coating of purple-red dots on the petiole, *H. longipes hypoglauca* has been extensively used by breeders for this characteristic. Like other Iwa Giboshi types, it makes an attractive mound of green foliage topped by late season flowers. This plant was fairly rare until recently and still commands a high retail price.

seedlings, sports, and other related types:

'Best of Twenty': *H. longipes hypoglauca* sdlg from Van Wade; green leaves with red petioles

'Brandywine': {1993r, R. Herold; (*H. montana* 'Aureomarginata' X *H. venusta*) X *H. longipes hypoglauca*} green lvs with intense purple-red dots on petioles and scapes; thick underside bloom

'Cinnamon Sticks': listed in the 1996 Hatfield Gardens catalog as a hybrid of *H. l. hypoglauca* X 'Maruba Iwa'; from Roy Herold; small, pale green foliage with many red dots on the petiole and a moderate underside bloom; also listed as producing lav fls in Sept on dark red sc (1996 Hatfield Gardens cat.)

'Fall Bouquet': {1986r, P. Aden; hybrid of two sdlgs} strongly resembles *H. longipes hypoglauca;* med-sized md of shiny dk gr lvs; petioles covered with purple-red dots into the midrib of the blade; thin underside bloom

'Grandaddy Redlegs': *H. longipes hypoglauca* sdlg from Van Wade; green lvs wi bright red petioles

'One Man's Treasure': {1999r, R. Benedict & R. Solberg; *H. longipes hypoglauca* sdlg} smooth, shiny, green lvs, 6 1/2" by 4 1/2" (10 vp); very striking red petioles and a whitish shiny underside

H. longipes 'Tagi': small mound of dark green foliage that is covered with a bluish bloom in early spring; thick underside bloom; petioles covered with reddish purple dots; smooth texture; blade narrowly ovate when young, widening with age; close to *H. longipes hypoglauca* but with narrower, bluer lvs

other similar types:
'Cinnamon Bun', 'Cinnamon and Sugar', 'Chopsticks', *H. longipes viridipes*, 'Party Time', 'Raspberry Sorbet', *H. rupifraga*

Hosta longissima (Mizu Giboshi)
key features: dense mound of narrow, dark green foliage; purple flowers in September-October
mound size: 13" high by 30" wide

---

spacing: 24"

leaves: 5 3/4" long by 1 1/2" wide; medium green; dull top surface, shiny underside; narrowly elliptic shape; not wavy; no corrugation; average substance; 3-4 vein pairs

flowers: mid-September into early October; medium purple color with white petal margins halfway from tip to base and darker mid-petal striping; 2" long by 1 3/4" wide; wide-open funnel

shape with reflexed tips; 18" scapes; seed pods often damaged by frost before seed maturation

comments: *Hosta longissima* makes an attractive, very dense mound of narrow, green foliage that has been successfully used as an edging plant and ground cover. It has a

283

fast growth rate and is easily divided. The purple flowers are valuable for a last bit of color in the shady garden before killing frosts. One year I found *Hosta longissima* flowering on November 2 in my northern Illinois garden.

For a while there has been a debate as to the origins of *Hosta longissima*. For many years it was known as *H. longissima brevifolia*, but is now simply *Hosta longissima*. It is completely different from *H. longissima longifolia* and in most ways seems closer to *Hosta sieboldii* in origin. The late blooming season, though, sets it apart from the latter species.

A number of sports exist, but none of them have yet been widely grown. A white-flowered form is known.

seedlings, sports, and other related types:

H. longissima longifolia: much smaller pl with lighter, fewer fls; very narrow, straplike lvs **(see page 285)**

'Bitsy Gold': {1985r, R. Savory; *H. longissima* X a gold sdlg} low mound of narrow, gold foliage

'Bitsy Green': {1985r, R. Savory; *H. longissima* X a green sdlg} low, dense mound of narrow, green foliage much like *H. longissima*

'Purple Lady Finger': {1982r, R. Savory} 16" by 45" md of narrowly elliptic green lvs, 7" by 1 1/2"; closed purple flowers in August-September on 24" scapes; overall appearance closely resembles *H. longissima* (In 1983 Bob told me that this was a hybrid of *H. longissima* X *H. clausa* and that the flowers reminded him of lady finger firecrackers.)

other similar types:

H. rectifolia, *H. sieboldii spathulata*

Hosta longissima longifolia
(Hosoba Mizu Giboshi)

key features: dwarf mound of straplike, green leaves; grows best in a very moist environment
mound size: 4" high by 15" wide

spacing: 12"

leaves: 6" long by 1" wide (up to 8 5/8" long); medium green; dull top, shiny underside; blade very narrowly elliptic, almost linear; not wavy; smooth texture; average substance; 2-3 vein pairs

flowers: September 10-18 (northern Illinois); pale lavender color with three, darker, mid-petal stripes; wide open funnel shape with reflexed tips; 1 3/4" long by 1 1/4" wide; scapes 14-23"; few (4 or 5) flowers per scape; pods develop

comments: One of the most unusual hostas in existence, the Hosoba Mizu Giboshi (hosoba = thin, mizu = water) can be found in a variety of habitats on Honshu Island in Japan with one thing in common: moisture. I have observed it growing amongst grasses at the edge of a rice paddy, at the bottom of a wooded hillside where moisture collected, and in a small waterfall area. I once thought that this species could serve as a replacement for *Liriope spicata*, for which it can be easily mistaken. Its requirement for moisture, however, is essential for its success in gardens, thus limiting its usage as a landscape plant. In drier situations it will survive but may go dormant early.

Another unusual aspect of *H. longissima longifolia* is the limited number of flowers per scape. About five flowers are generally produced, making for the shortest blooming season of any hosta. It is interesting, though, that it readily forms seed pods, each containing many seeds. This probably ensures its survival in the wild and makes it a useful hybridizing plant.

Several sports have been developed from this diminutive species with white-margined, yellow-margined, and yellow-centered leaves.

Yoshimichi Hirose informed me (July 1995) that while the common name is Hosoba Mizu Giboshi, some people incorrectly use the name Nana Mizu Giboshi.

seedlings, sports, and other related types:

'Asahi Comet': {1984r by W. Zumbar for K. Kato} sport of *H. longissima longifolia*; pale yellow margins that change to white during the season; observed in a Japanese collection

'Asahi Sunray': {1984r by W. Zumbar for K. Kato} sport of *H. longissima longifolia*; chartreuse margins change to yellow during the season; observed in a Japanese collection

H. longissima mediopicta: yellow-centered foliage; observed in a Japanese collection

H. longissima aureomaculata: yellow-centered, green-margined foliage; observed in an American collection; possibly the same as *H. longissima mediopicta*

other similar types:

Liriope spicata: Creeping Lilyturf; the only plant that comes close to *Hosta longissima longifolia*

'Love Pat'
key features: medium-large mound of slug-resistant, blue foliage; 'Tokudama'-type
mound size: 19" high by 40" wide (up to 24" by 50")

spacing: 36"
leaves: 9 1/4" long by 9" wide; deep blue-green into midsummer, dark green thereafter; thick bloom on top and underside; broadly ovate to rotund shape with a deeply

lobed base and distinct tip; heavily corrugated; deeply cupped at maturity, up to 3" deep; thick substance; 16-17 vein pairs

flowers: late June into early July; near-white color; 1 3/4" long by 1" wide; narrow funnel shape; 25" scapes; many seed pods develop

comments: 'Love Pat' has been one of the premier blue-foliaged, slug-resistant hostas for many years. At one time it was generally thought that 'Love Pat' would only become the size of 'Tokudama' to which it is closely related. After 5-10 years under good growing conditions, however, it can achieve much larger proportions, almost the size of *H. sieboldiana* 'Elegans'. In the landscape it can be used as a background plant, specimen, or ground cover.

'Love Pat' will form prolific amounts of seed but has not been widely used in hybridizing work.

Paul Aden registered 'Love Pat' in 1978 as a hybrid of 'Blue Velvet' X 'Blue Vision'.

seedlings, sports, and other related types:

'Blue Splendor': med-lg md of thick-substanced, cupped, blue-green foliage; 19" by 40" md; lvs 9" by 8 1/2"; near-wh fls, mid-June into July; mistakenly propagated as 'Blue Moon' during the 1980's; named by me in 1990; similar, if not the same as 'Love Pat'

'Kit Kat': {1994r, D. Smetana & A & D Nursery; sport wi lvs that are lt green-centered and streaked along the margin}

'Love Burst': {1994r, D. & D. Ballantyne; sport with gold-centered, blue-margined lvs}

'Peace': {1987r, P. Aden; "Blue Hugger" X 'Love Pat'} med-sized md of creamy yellow-mgd lvs; 13" by 29" md; 5 1/4" by 3 3/4" (9 vp) wi a 1/2" margin; thick subst; thick und bloom

other similar types:

'Blue for You', 'Blue Horizon', 'Blue Rock', 'Blue Velvet', 'Hirao Zeus', 'Fleeta's Blue', 'I'm So Blue', 'Something Blue', 'Wayside Blue'

'Lucy Vitols'
key features: medium-sized mound of gold-centered, green-margined foliage
mound size: 18" high by 40" wide

spacing: 36"

leaves: 8" long by 7" wide; green margin, medium gold center; blade broadly ovate with age and somewhat cupped; moderately corrugated; good substance; 12 vein pairs

flowers: late June into mid-July; medium lavender; 2 1/2" long by 1 3/4" wide; scapes purplish; fertile

comments: 'Lucy Vitols' matures as an attractive mound of gold-centered, green-margined foliage that is nicely cupped and corrugated. It can be effective as a specimen plant in the landscape. Mildred Seaver registered it in 1989 and introduced it for sale in the 1991 Hatfield Gardens catalog (p. 3) as a sport of 'Christmas Gold'. She remarked to me on more than one occasion that this may be her best introduction.

'Lucy Vitols' has become fairly popular in the nursery trade in recent years. The *Hosta Finder 2000* (Greene, 2000) lists 24 retail mail-order sources selling 'Lucy Vitols'.

seedlings, sports, and other related types:

'Christmas Gold': pl from which 'Lucy Vitols' sported; med-sized md of round, gold foliage; sport of 'Christmas Tree'; from Mildred Seaver

'Jason and Katie': introduced in 1997 by Hatfield Gardens as a sport of 'Christmas Gold' with reverse foliage colors of 'Lucy Vitols', i.e. green-centered, gold-margined leaves; credited to Handy Hatfield

other similar types:

'Aardvark', 'Bright Lights', 'Inniswood', 'Spinning Wheel'

'Mary Marie Ann'

key features: medium-sized mound of wavy, center-variegated foliage; seasonal color changes
mound size: 14" high by 30" wide

spacing: 24"
leaves: 6 1/4" long by 4 1/8" wide; medium to dark green, 1/2" to 3/4" wide margin; center changes from creamy yellow in early spring to a very light, whitish gold by mid-summer which holds if grown in some direct sunlight, otherwise changing to pale green by mid-August; thin underside bloom; heavily twisted, ovate blade; little or no corrugation; average substance; 9 vein pairs
flowers: late July into August; medium lavender; funnel shape; held well above foliage
comments: 'Mary Marie Ann' has intrigued collectors for many years because of its twisted, wavy foliage that seems to be changing color all the time. The twisting is due to the difference in growth rate between the green margin and lighter center which changes in color depending upon the time of the year and how much sunlight it receives. In the average shaded garden, the leaves start out with a creamy yellow center, turning lighter by mid-summer, and then to chartreuse or green by the end of summer. Give 'Mary Marie Ann' a few hours of direct sunlight and cool conditions, however, and the center continues to lighten by August, often with the veins turning green.

'Mary Marie Ann' was registered by Larry Englerth in 1982 as a seedling of 'Aoki'. It is much smaller than other center-variegated 'Fortunei'-types.
seedlings, sports, and other related types:
none listed
other similar types:
'Aoki Variegated', 'Ani Machi' ('Geisha'), 'Maya'

289

'Masquerade' (*Hosta venusta* 'Variegated')
key features: dwarf mound of white-centered foliage;
purple flowers
mound size: 6" high by 18" wide

spacing: 18"
leaves: 3 3/4" long by 1 1/2" wide; 1/8" wide, green margin; pure white center that can turn green in mid-summer;
elliptic shape; no corrugation; thin substance; 5 vein pairs
flowers: late June into mid-July; medium purple; 2 1/8"
long by 1 1/4" wide; scapes range from 6" to 22" with most
13-18" high
comments: Long known under the name *Hosta venusta*
'Variegated', 'Masquerade' makes a small mound of white-
centered foliage that is best used as a dwarf specimen in the
shaded rock garden. It grows fairly well for a white-centered plant, but its tendency to sport green leaves relegates
it to the role of a high-maintenance, collector's plant. Its
also lacks substance so slug damage can be a problem.

When *Hosta venusta* 'Variegated' was determined to be
an illegal name according to nomenclatural rules, Diana
Grenfell of England named it 'Masquerade'. The origins of
this plant have been debated since the early 1980's when it
first arrived in the U.S. from Japan. Based upon the fact that
some foliage characteristics, the blooming season, and
flowers (with a less distinct, white throat) are close to *Hosta
venusta*, it could be a hybrid of *H. sieboldii* X *H. venusta*
backcrossed to *Hosta venusta*, possibly a second or third
generation seedling. Such a system of hybridizing is followed by the noted plant collector Yoshimichi Hirose of
Iwakuni City, Japan who described his hybridizing techniques in a speech in Tokyo on June 30, 1995.

A number of sports have been identified from 'Masquerade'. Over the long haul, I suspect that some of them will
290

continue to be grown while 'Masquerade' will become a rarity.

seedlings, sports, and other related types:

'Little White Lines': {1988r, M. Zilis & T & Z N} sport of 'Masquerade'; white-margined, green-centered foliage; 11" by 32" md; lvs 4 3/8" by 2 1/4" wi a 1/16" white mgn; purple fls v late June into mid-July on 18-30" sc; many seed pods develop; attractive low edger or rock garden subject

'Munchkin': green-leaved sport of 'Masquerade' from Q & Z N; 10" high md; vigorous grower; prolific seed formation and good sun-tolerance; not exciting but a useful ground cover; introduced in 1995

'Venessa': {1999r, V. Wade; sport} low, dense md of green foliage

'Whippersnapper': {1994r, Belle Gardens; 'Masquerade' sdlg; creamy wh-mgd, green-centered lvs}

other similar types:

'Bobbin': small mound of creamy white-centered foliage that has a very narrow (1/16-1/32" wide), green margin; introduced by Russ O'Harra in the early 1980's

'Island Charm': {1997r, G. Rasmussen & A. Malloy; 'Flamboyant' sdlg} 10" by 22" md of white-centered, gr-mgd lvs, 4 1/4" by 3 1/8", wi purple red petioles; pale purple fls in July on 18" sc; a striking, v attractive, low md of center-variegated foliage; sported to 'Pink Panther' {1998r, A. Malloy; lvs white & green-streaked center wi a green margin}

'Little Willie': Bill Zumbar intro; dwarf-sized md (7" by 16") of white-centered foliage that greens up; lvs 3 7/8" by 1 1/2" (4 vp); differs from 'Masquerade' in the color of the lf center & having a more vigorous growth rate

'Pinwheel': {1983r, R. Savory; H. venusta sdlg mutation} leaves white-centered with a streaky green border; leaf center changes from very pale green to pure white during the season; dark green margin on older leaves tends to pucker and causes twisting of leaf

'Yellow Jacket': {1998r, M. Zilis & P. Ruh; H. venusta sport} small md of lvs wi creamy yellow mgns; like a yellow-margined 'Little White Lines'

'Midas Touch'

key features: medium-large mound of intensely corrugated, bright gold foliage; thick substance
mound size: 21" high by 45" wide (up to 25" by 53")

spacing: 40"
leaves: 8 1/2" long by 7" wide (up to 10 1/4" by 8 1/2"); chartreuse early, becoming bright gold; moderate underside bloom; blade broadly ovate and deeply cupped; heavily corrugated; thick substance; 15-17 vein pairs
flowers: mid-June into early July; near-white with a pale lavender mid-petal stripe; 1 7/8" long by 1 1/8" wide; scapes about 24" high

comments: 'Midas Touch' distinguishes itself by its bright gold leaf color, cupping, and intense corrugation. The latter characteristic is notable, with almost every square inch of blade surface affected. In the landscape, it can be used to brighten up deeply shaded areas as a ground cover or specimen.

'Midas Touch' was registered in 1978 as a hybrid of 'Gold Cup' X 'Golden Waffles' by Paul Aden.

seedlings, sports, and other related types:
none listed

other similar types:
'Aspen Gold', 'Golden Medallion', 'Golden Waffles', 'Sun Glow', 'White Vision', 'Zounds'

'Midwest Magic'

key features: medium-large mound of gold-centered, green-margined foliage; lavender flowers
mound size: 21" high by 47" wide

spacing: 48"

leaves: 8" long by 6" wide; 1/2" to 3/4" wide, dark green margin; center medium gold, turning chartreuse by mid-summer; thin underside bloom; blade ovate with a deeply lobed base and slight waviness; slightly corrugated; better than average substance; 12-13 vein pairs

flowers: mid to late July; pale lavender; 2 3/8" long by 1 1/4" wide; scapes 18-28" high; fertile

comments: 'Midwest Magic' was introduced with great fanfare at the 1994 MRHS meeting in Dubuque, Iowa. At one time it was thought to be a sport of 'Zounds', i.e. something akin to 'Dick Ward', but that is not the case. Instead it is a mutation of a gold-leaved seedling that may have originated in Holland (since named 'Prairie Glow'). Whatever its origin, it makes an excellent specimen in the landscape, exhibiting a nice blend of dark green margins sharply contrasting the gold to chartreuse center. If grown in fairly bright light, the center tends to stay gold later in the growing season.

I registered 'Midwest Magic' in 1999.

seedlings, sports, and other related types:

'Erie Magic': {1999r, M. Zilis} reversed sport of 'Midwest Magic'; muted green center, gold margins; introduced in the 1999 Q & Z N catalog

'Prairie Glow': gold-lvd "mother plant" of 'Midwest Magic'; med-sized md; lvs gold, turning chartreuse; 1998 introduction

'Prairie Magic': sport of 'Erie Magic' with dark green-centered, gold-margined foliage; sharp contrast between

293

margin and center; found in 1999 at Q & Z N

other similar types:
'Guacamole', 'Hoosier Harmony', 'Paradigm', 'September Sun', 'September Surprise'

'Mildred Seaver'
key features: large mound of white-margined foliage
mound size: 27" high by 62" wide

spacing: 60"
leaves: 10" long by 7 1/2" wide; 1/2" to 3/4" wide margin that changes from yellow to creamy white by mid-summer; medium to dark green center; thin underside bloom; blade broadly ovate and very slightly wavy; slight to moderate corrugation; slightly better than average substance; 10-12 vein pairs
flowers: early to late July; pale lavender color with white petal margins; 2 1/2" long by 1 3/4" wide; 24" scapes
comments: 'Mildred Seaver' has become very popular in recent years. It ranks highly among white-margined hostas for the sharp contrast between the creamy margins and green center. In the garden 'Mildred Seaver' exhibits a moderate growth rate and can be utilized as a ground cover or specimen. Kevin Vaughn bred this plant, registering it as a hybrid of "Vaughn 73-2" X *H. s.* 'Frances Williams' in 1981.

This plant honors the originator of the "Sea Series" of hostas. From her average-sized, Needham Heights, Massachusetts yard, Mildred Seaver has developed an extremely diverse and beautiful group of hybrids that rank near the top. Among her best "Sea Series" introductions are such classics as 'Sea Lotus Leaf', 'Sea Drift', 'Sea Dream', 'Sea Gold Star', 'Sea Sapphire', 'Sea Monster', 'Sea Frolic', and

'Sea Fire'. Additionally such top-selling cultivars as 'Lucy Vitols', 'Christmas Tree', 'Don Stevens', 'Spilt Milk', 'Spinning Wheel', 'High Noon', 'Komodo Dragon', and 'Richmond' resulted from her efforts. Her work has not only been superior, but has served as an inspiration to many new hybridizers.

seedlings, sports, and other related types:
none listed

other similar types:
'Crusader', 'Fringe Benefit', 'Leola Fraim', 'Minuteman', 'Patriot'

Hosta minor (Keirin Giboshi)
key features: small mound of green foliage; purple flowers in July
mound size: 8" high by 22" wide (up to 14" by 28")

spacing: 18"

leaves: 3 1/4" long by 2 3/16" wide (up to 5 1/4" by 3 7/8"); medium green; dull top surface; whitish shiny underside; ovate blade; no corrugation; little or no marginal waviness; purple-red dots on petioles; average substance; 5-6 vein pairs

flowers: early to mid-July; purple; petal margins white from the throat, halfway up to the tip; three mid-petal stripes; 2 1/4" long by 1" wide; hollow, ridged scapes up to 22" high; will form many seed pods

comments: *Hosta minor* has been a much confused plant as cultivated in the United States. Many plants being sold as *Hosta minor* are actually *Hosta sieboldii* seedlings or hybrids of *Hosta minor* itself. My data stems from plants labelled *H. minor* "Korean", indicating its native habitat. This form has distinctly ridged, hollow scapes, traits of the true plant. The petioles also exhibit some purple-red dotting. Maekawa (1973) listed native sites in both Korea and Japan, but Schmid (1991) stated that *H. minor* is native to Korea and that any Japanese wild populations are "undoubtedly escaped transplants from cultivation" (ibid, p. 74). Whatever the original source, it evidently can be found growing wild in both Korea and Japan.

In cultivation *Hosta minor* makes a low, dense mound of green foliage that can be used in the shaded rock garden or as an edger. It has a good growth rate and the flowers are an ornamental positive. It can form large numbers of seed pods, making it useful in hybridizing programs. I have not seen any *H. minor* sports.

seedlings, sports, and other related types:

H. minor 'Alba': the plant by which we knew *Hosta minor* for many years, but actually is a white-flowered version of *H. sieboldii* (*H. sieboldii* 'Alba'); evidently there is a true *H. minor alba*, a white-flowering version of the true species, which was listed by Maekawa (1973) as "Shi-robana-keirin-giboshi"

'Mrs. Minky': {1993r, P. Hall; *H. minor* X 'Piedmont Gold'; medium yellow foliage}

other similar types:

H. capitata, H. nakaiana, H. venusta

'Minuteman'

key features: medium-large mound of white-margined, dark green-centered leaves
mound size: 23" high by 50" wide

spacing: 48"
leaves: 8 1/2" long by 6" wide; 1/2" to 1" wide, white margin; dark green center; thin underside bloom; blade ovate with a deeply lobed base; sometimes cupped; slightly wavy; slightly corrugated at maturity; better than average substance; 10-13 vein pairs
flowers: late July into early August; medium lavender; 2"

long by 7/8" wide; narrow funnel shape; 23-33" scapes; limited seed pod formation with few viable seeds

comments: As a mutation of 'Francee', 'Minuteman' carries all of 'Francee's good attributes: fast growth rate, attractive foliage, and versatility in the landscape. The big difference is in the much wider, whiter margins. In comparing 'Minuteman' to 'Patriot' (the other major 'Francee' sport), the former has a darker green center and purer white margin.

John Machen of Mobjack Nurseries in Virginia selected 'Minuteman' from the same group of plants that yielded 'Patriot' and he registered it in 1994. Since that time, 'Minuteman' has quickly become one of the top-selling white-margined hostas in the nursery industry.

seedlings, sports, and other related types:
none listed

other similar types:
'Francee', 'Leola Fraim', 'Mildred Seaver', 'Patriot', 'Trailblazer'

Hosta montana (Oba Giboshi)

key features: large mound of green foliage; scape bud distinctly flower-like as it unfurls
mound size: 28" high by 78" wide (cultivated); 24" by 47" (wild)

---

spacing: 60"
leaves: 12 3/8" long by 9 1/4" wide; medium green; moderately shiny top, very shiny underside; blade ovate with a lobed, puckered base and long, distinct tip; slight to moderately wavy; slight corrugation at maturity; no purple-red dots on petioles; good substance; 14-16, deeply impressed vein pairs
flowers: early to late July; very pale lavender with a slightly

darker petal midrib; 2 3/4" long by 1 1/8" wide; open funnel shape; scapes 50" tall, occasionally 60" or more; whitish bracts of the unfurling scape buds create a distinctive, flower-like look; many seed pods form weighing down scapes

comments: *Hosta montana*, the Oba Giboshi, can be commonly found in many areas of Japan. I have seen it growing in a wide variety of sites from Tokyo on south into western Honshu. Most often it is found on wooded hillsides, but also is native to more open sites. In fact one of the greatest examples of a hosta species in the wild exists in an artillery range at the base of Mt. Fuji where plants of *Hosta montana* grow by the thousands, shaded only by the tall Maiden Grass (*Miscanthus sinensis*). In this area, at about 700 meters elevation, the Koba Giboshi (*Hosta sieboldii spathulata*), Sensitive Fern, Japanese Astilbe, *Pulsatilla*, and other plants can be found growing in between large lava floes with *Hosta montana*. The Watanabes of Gotemba Nursery in Gotemba City have made an almost lifelong crusade searching this area for sports of Oba Giboshi. I was told that in a typical eight hour day of careful "sport-hunting", one or two new sports are usually identified. Over the years, this has resulted in an incredible array of new variegated *H. montana* forms plus a few flower variations (e.g., double flowers; unusual scapes).

Over the whole range of *H. montana*, some differences in foliage traits can be identified such as shininess of the leaf surfaces and shape of the blade. Another variation is the time of emergence in spring. The "typical" *H. montana*, as represented by *H. montana* 'Aureomarginata', emerges early in the growing season, often subjecting it to late spring frosts in many U.S. gardens. The form of *H. montana* growing near Mt. Fuji, however, has evolved over many centuries to be a late emerger. Thus, the hundreds of forms collected by the Watanabes and others from this area and other high elevations potentially are the best types of *H. montana* for our gardens. Cultivars that have come from or descended from Mt. Fuji "Montanas" include *H. m.* 'Choko Nishiki', *H. m.* 'Mountain Snow', and *H. m.* 'Mountain Sunrise'. *Hosta montana* can also be a great source of seedlings as it readily forms seed pods loaded with viable seeds.

One of the main identifying features of *Hosta montana* and its various forms is the flower-like appearance of the scape bud as it unfurls and the whitish bracts separate. As the scape elongates, it loses this character, though the bracts remain. On occasion some *H. montana* plants will produce double flowers. In 1991 the Watanabes showed me pictures of a beautiful double-flowered *H. montana* that they had discovered near Mt. Fuji. For a few years in my own hosta display, the first flower of *H. montana* 'Aureomarginata' tended to be double and I have heard others describe similar occurrences.

In the garden, *Hosta montana* ranks highly as a specimen or background plant. It can also be utilized as a large ground cover on shaded hillsides (as found growing wild in Japan).

Like all of the other common species, the taxonomy of *Hosta montana* has been somewhat confused. Maekawa (1972) listed *Hosta montana* along with *H. montana* f. *aureo-marginata*, *H. montana* var. *transiens*, *H. montana* var. *liliiflora*, and *H. montana* var. *praeflorens* as variations of the species. Fujita (1978) lumped *H. montana* and *H. sieboldiana* into one species, which creates confusion and is a bit hard to justify. Schmid (1991) carefully sorted through the nomenclature and listed numerous sports and botanical varieties. One of his significant discoveries is that the plant that we have grown under the name *H. montana* 'Praeflorens' for many years is not the same as Maekawa's *H. montana* var. *praeflorens* and should now be called *H. montana* f. *macrophylla*.

From a horticultural perspective, I have broken *H. montana* into the six groups most commonly found in collections and nurseries. Each is represented by one form in this book:

> (1) *H. montana*, the "typical" green-leaved species;
> (2) *H. montana* 'Aureomarginata' (yellow-margined);
> (3) *H. montana* 'Mountain Snow' (white-margined);
> (4) *H. montana* 'Choko Nishiki' (gold-centered);
> (5) *H. montana* 'Emma Foster' (gold-leaved);
> (6) *H. montana macrophylla*.

An unbelievable array of *H. montana* seedlings and sports have been introduced as cultivars. Many of the sports are wild-collected plants from Japan, while many seedlings originated in both Japanese and American breeding programs.

seedlings, sports, and other related types:

'Big Mo': {1990r, R. Stephens; *H. montana* sdlg; dark blue-green foliage}

'Borsch 1': {1999r by P. Ruh for Borsch N; parentage unknown} large, semi-upright md of green foliage; v pale lav fls on tall sc from late June into late July, typical of *H. montana*

H. montana 'Chirifu': streaked sdlg from Mt. Tochigiken in Japan; huge md of mottled foliage; scapes up to 77" high; a favorite of a few hybridizers; in the U.S. since 1990; some 'Chirifu' pl infected wi a virus

'Dragon Wings': {1996r, W. Lefever} *H. montana* X 'Fortunei Albomarginata'; large md of green lvs

'Hatsushimo Nishiki': speckled white & green lvs; distinctive among the "Montanas"; fr Gotemba N

'Honey': {1977r, R. Savory; *H. montana* sdlg} lg md of shiny, smooth, bright green lvs, 11" by 7" (14 vp); v shiny lf underside; v pale lav fls in July

'Immense': {1991r by P. Ruh for L. Simpers; *H. montana* X 'Ibaraki-K'} lg md of br green lvs

'Mount Everest': {1996r, J. Dishon; 'Sea Prize' X *H. montana*; dk green, wh-mgd lvs}

'Mount Fuji': {1989r, J. & J. Wilkins; sdlg of *H. montana* 'Aureomarginata'} lg md of green foliage; 32" by 75" md; lvs 16" by 9" (14-15 vp); v pale lav fls on 3-4' sc in July; fertile; the archetypical green *H. montana*

'Peppermint Ice': {1994r, Belle Gardens; 'William Lachman' X *H. montana*} 16" by 38" md of creamy white-centered lvs, 8 1/2" by 6"; margins 2" wide; very attractive

'Pewter Frost': {1996r, J. Dishon, *H. pycnophylla* X *H. montana*} bl gr lvs, 11 1/4" by 7" (11 vp), smooth & slightly wavy; individual lvs roughly have the appearance of 'Krossa Regal'

'Satin Beauty': {1986r, AHS for E. Fisher; parentage unknown} 31" by 81" md of shiny, green lvs, 13" by 11" (15 vp); lf blade broadly ovate & v shiny on the underside; v pale lav fls, late June into mid-July on scapes that avg 50", but can reach as high as 70"; flower-like scape bud; closely related to *H. montana* in foliage & flower

'Sunami': {1990r, C. Soules; *H. montana* sdlg} 24" by 70" md of shiny, bright green lvs, 15" by 8 1/4" (14 vp); whitish fls open in top 12" of 48-72" sc; attractive foliage & tall scapes

'Taika': *H. montana* form listed as having thick, branched scapes (Watanabe, 1985)

'Temple Great': {1986r, B. Jernigan; *H. montana* X a sdlg; blue-green lvs}

'Tucker Blues': {1990r, R. Stephens; *H. montana* X 'Fortunei Aureomarginata'; v blue lvs}

'Tucker Friendly Folk': {1991r, R. Stephens; 'Wolcott' sdlg X *H. montana*; dark green foliage}

'Tucker Pucker': {1993r, R. Stephens; *H. montana* sdlg X 'Big Daddy'; bl-gr lvs}

'Tucker Tommy Little': {1991r, R. Stephens; 'Wolcott' sdlg X *H. montana*; leathery, dark green lvs}

'Urajiro Oba': white-backed form fr Kyushu (Watanabe, 1985)

other similar types:

Hosta fluctuans, 'Fortunei Gigantea'

Hosta montana 'Aureomarginata' (Kifukurin Oba Giboshi)

key features: large, vase-shaped mound of gold-margined foliage; emerges early
mound size: 27" high by 68" wide

spacing: 60"
leaves: 15" long by 8 1/4" wide; 1-2", variable, bright gold margin that often streaks into the shiny, medium green center; margin gradually fades to chartreuse if grown in deep shade (can bleach to white with direct sunlight); slightly shiny underside; ovate to oblong-elliptic, arching blade that has a deeply lobed, puckered base and a pointed, downwardly curved tip; slightly

wavy throughout blade; faintly corrugated at maturity; no reddish purple dots on petiole; good substance; 14-15 deeply impressed vein pairs; gold fall color
flowers: early to late July; very pale lavender, lavender in mid-petal; 2 1/4" long by 1 1/2" wide; scapes up to 47" high, tending to droop as flowering proceeds; many seed pods develop
comments: Not that long ago, *Hosta montana* 'Aureomarginata' was rarely seen in American gardens. In fact one of the charter members of the American Hosta Society, Eunice Fisher, wrote that "*H. montana aureo-marginata* is a new one for me and I just wonder if anyone else has it in the U.S. Alex has only one single plant" (Fisher, 1968). "Alex" refers to the first president of the American Hosta Society, Alex Summers, who at the time had the most complete hosta collection in the U.S. Others conjectured that it would never become popular because of its slow formation of new divisions. The situation has changed dramatically since those early days of the American Hosta Society. Every hosta collector has seen *Hosta montana* 'Aureomarginata', and most own at least one clump of it. Many nurseries and popular mail-order houses dealing in perennials offer it with a

good response from the gardening public.

H. montana 'Aureomarginata' has become readily available through mass propagation by tissue culture, but the reason for its popularity is the plant itself. From early spring on, the gracefully drooping, long-pointed foliage produces a bright splash of color. This color is created by the very wide, bright yellow leaf margins that often streak into the green center. Also adding to its "look" is the way the foliage protrudes horizontally from nearly upright petioles, creating a semi-upright mound habit. As in *H. montana*, whitish bracts produce an attractive, flower-like appearance as the scape bud unfurls. The pale lavender flowers open well above the foliage in nice proportion to the mound. The foliar substance is good, giving it some resistance to slugs and other insect pests. In short, it is an impressive and durable landscape plant. Perhaps the only negative aspect is the fact that *H. montana* 'Aureomarginata' emerges early in the spring, making it susceptible to late spring frosts in areas from Indianapolis on south. In northern Illinois it normally is not affected.

Hosta montana 'Aureomarginata' makes an excellent breeding plant, both as a pod and pollen parent. Often its seedlings carry the vase-shaped mound habit. It has also been the source of a limited number of sports, most from tissue culture.

The AHS registered the name, *H. montana* 'Aureo-marginata' in 1987. Schmid (1991) modified the name to *H. montana* 'Aureomarginata'.

seedlings, sports, and other related types:

'Ebb Tide': {1997, E. Elslager; *H. montana* 'Aureomarginata' sport} gold-margined, green-centered leaves that have a very wavy, crinkled margin; mottled streaks often present

'Emma Foster': all-gold sport; difficult to grow **(see page 305)**

'Gohon Matsu Fukurin' : a yellow-margined sport listed by Kenji Watanabe (1985)

'Mountain Haze': {1990r, M. Zilis; *H. montana* 'Aureomarginata' sport} t.c. mutation; gold-centered, green-mgd lvs; not yet widely grown; emerges early

'O Fuji Fukurin': splashed and yellow-margined sport listed by Kenji Watanabe (1985)

'Outrageous': hybrid of 'Dorothy Benedict' X *H. montana* 'Aureomarginata' from Herb Benedict; stunning, large, vase-shaped mound of heavily streaked and mottled foliage; md 20" by 50"; lvs 13" by 10"; "mother" plant of 'My Child Insook', a white-centered, green-mgd sport {1995r, R. & D. Benedict}

'Tsunotori Fukurin': yellow-mgd sport listed by Kenji Watanabe (1985)

other similar types:

'Sagae' (*H. fluctuans* 'Variegated'), 'Yellow River'

Hosta montana 'Choko Nishiki'

key features: large mound of gold-centered, green-margined foliage; late-emerging

mound size: 22" high by 48" wide

spacing: 40"

leaves: 13 1/2" long by 8 1/2" wide; 1/4" to 3/8" wide, green margin surrounds the center which is bright gold in spring; center changes to chartreuse by mid-July, green by August if grown in shade; shiny underside; blade ovate and slightly wavy; little or no corrugation; good substance; 14-15 vein pairs

flowers: early to late July; very pale lavender; 2 1/2" long by 1 3/4" wide; scapes around 40" high; forms seed pods

comments: 'Choko Nishiki' exhibits some of the brightest, most highly variegated foliage among hostas in spring. The bright gold leaf center is neatly accented by the green margins which often streak into the center. The gold color will fade to green unless some direct sunlight is provided. Under bright light the center can turn to creamy white and remain so through the growing season. I learned this one year when growing 'Choko Nishiki' in pots. Part of each plant was completely shaded, the other part exposed to a few hours of midday sun. In late June I noticed that the shaded parts were turning green, while the leaf centers of the sun-exposed portions were changing to creamy white.

I was told by the Watanabes of Gotemba Nursery that 'Choko Nishiki' was found in the wild and given to them

(April 27, 1991 conversation). They also have found a sport that is nearly identical to it.

In both the garden and nursery, it has proven to be a good grower and rates as one of the finest specimen plants for the shaded garden. One of the great advantages of 'Choko Nishiki' and any related sports is their late emergence in spring. This has a great impact for anyone growing them from about Zone 6 on south in the U.S. where spring frosts can be a problem.

seedlings, sports, and other related types:

H. montana 'Mountain Sunrise': {1999r, M. Zilis} gold-leaved t.c. sport of *H. montana* 'Choko Nishiki'; 22" by 45" md; 11" by 6" lvs that are bright gold early, turning green unless exposed to some direct sunlight; late emerger; better grower than other gold Montana sports; 1995 Q & Z N intro

other similar types:

'Kinkaku': *H. montana* sport collected in the wild in Japan; thin (1/64"), rippled, green margins, light gold center; variegated all season long; 18" by 43" md; 11 1/2" by 8" lvs (14 vp); introduced for sale in the U.S. in the late 1980's; less vigorous than 'Choko Nishiki'

'Mountain Haze': {1990r, M. Zilis; *H. montana* 'Aureo-marginata' sport} t.c. mutation; gold-centered, green-mgd lvs; not yet widely grown; emerges early

'On Stage': {1986r, P. Aden; sport of *H. montana*} lg md of gold-centered, green-margined foliage; center becomes green by mid-summer; nearly identical to 'Choko Nishiki'

'Shuho Nishiki': *H. montana*-type with gold-centered foliage; from Gotemba Nursery; pictured in *Variegated Plants in Color* (Hirose & Yokoi, 1998)

Hosta montana 'Emma Foster'

key features: medium-sized mound of gold foliage; difficult to grow

mound size: 18" high by 36" wide

spacing: 36"

leaves: 11" long by 6 1/2" wide; bright gold early, turning chartreuse; shiny underside; ovate blade; smooth texture; average substance; 13 vein pairs

flowers: early to late July; very pale lavender; 30-40" scapes

comments: 'Emma Foster' was registered in 1985 by Gene Foster as the all-gold sport out of *H. montana* 'Aureomarginata'. My experience with the plant has been mixed. As the gold-leaved sport from *H. montana* 'Aureomarginata', it has proven difficult to grow to any appreciable size. I have seen, however, an occasional, large specimen in a few collections. One measured 24" high by 45" wide with 13 1/4" by 6 1/4" leaves (15 vein pairs) in an Iowa garden.

Similar, but not the same, is 'Mountain Sunrise', a sport of 'Choko Nishiki' developed at my nursery. It has proven to be much more vigorous, presumably because of its tendency to turn green if grown in shade. It is probably close to the Japanese 'Ogon Oba' Giboshi.

All of the gold-leaved *H. montana* sports probably should only be considered collector's plants as they require extra care to reach mature size. On the other hand, gold-leaved seedlings of *Hosta montana* and related forms (e.g., 'Grand Canyon' and 'Jackpot') have much more vigor, making much better landscape plants.

seedlings, sports, and other related types:
none listed

305

other similar types:

'Ahwaneeh': {1990r, U. Syre-Herz; *H. montana* X *H. kikutii*; lvs emerge green, turn pale ylw} not widely distributed

'Mountain Pride': gold-leaved sdlg of *H. montana macrophylla* from Herb Benedict; huge mound; lvs 13" by 10" (16 vp)

H. montana 'Mountain Sunrise': {1999r, M. Zilis} gold-leaved t.c. sport of *H. montana* 'Choko Nishiki'; 22" by 45" md, 11" by 6" lvs that are bright gold early, turning green unless exposed to some direct sunlight; late emerger; better grower than other gold Montana sports; 1995 Q & Z N intro

'Ogon Oba': Japanese form of the species with golden foliage; could represent more than one plant

'Straka Gold': {1994r, C. Owens; 'Gold Regal' X *H. montana*; deep gold foliage}

'Yellow Emperor': {1987r, R. Savory; sdlg of 'Honey'} large, bright gold foliage; one lf 10 1/2" by 8" (12 vp); margin slightly wavy; thin underside bloom

---

Hosta montana macrophylla (formerly *H. montana* 'Praeflorens')

key features: huge, vase-shaped mound of green foliage; flowers open at top of mound
mound size: 35" high by 75" wide

spacing: 60"
leaves: 18" long by 12" wide; medium green; slightly shiny on top, slight bloom on underside; blade ovate to broadly elliptic with a deeply lobed base and long, skinny tip; petioles carried nearly upright with the leaf blades almost perpendicular creating a semi-upright mound habit; tips of

outer foliage about 18" above soil level; lightly rippled margins, 13 or so per side; no corrugation; good substance; 17-21, deeply impressed vein pairs

flowers: late June to mid-July; very pale lavender color; whitish petal margins; 2 5/8" long by 1 1/2" wide; scapes reach just above top of foliage, 37-40" high; as scape bud unfurls, first set of bracts distinctly starlike; forms seed pods

comments: Long-known under the name, *Hosta montana* 'Praeflorens', *H. montana macrophylla* distinguishes itself as being, perhaps, the ultimate "centerpiece" plant for the shaded garden. Strategically placed in the center of an island bed, it always draws attention for its large, semi-upright mound habit. Also distinctive are the flowers which open just above the top of the foliage mound, unlike any other *H. montana*-type. All of this, combined with the attractively rippled leaf margins and many pairs of deeply impressed veins, creates an effect that only its seedlings can imitate.

H. montana macrophylla has been utilized by a few hybridizers with outstanding results. Olga Petrysyn used it in developing 'Grand Canyon' and 'Niagara Falls', two premier cultivars. Dick and Jane Ward have recently introduced several hybrids with *H. montana macrophylla* as the pollen parent.

In the garden and as a containerized nursery plant, *H. montana macrophylla* is an average to slow grower. Extra water and fertilizer helps it reach a mature size faster.

The name was changed to *H. montana* f. *macrophylla* by Schmid (1991).

seedlings, sports, and other related types:

'Alice Gladden': {1998r, D. & J. Ward; 'White Vision' X *H. montana macrophylla*; lg, gold leaves}

'Big Boy': {1980r, L. Simpers; *H. montana* sdlg} large *H. montana macrophylla* type; md 32" high by 74" wide; green lvs, 18 3/4" by 10 1/2" (21 vp); pale lav fls on 32-41" sc, late June to mid-July; also listed as a 1986 AHS reg.

'Emerald City': {1996r, D. & J. Ward; 'Big John' X *H. montana macrophylla*} huge gr lvs, 17" by 12" (19 vp)

'Godzilla': {1996r, D. & J. Ward; 'Big John' X *H. montana macrophylla*; med green foliage}

'Grand Canyon': {1995r, O. Petryszyn & W. Brincka; 'Sum and Substance' X *H. montana macrophylla*} lg, upright md of ruffled, golden foliage

'Jackpot': {1996r, D. & J. Ward; 'White Vision' X *H. montana macrophylla*} brilliant gold foliage; one imm leaf reached 12 1/2" by 7 1/2" (16 vp)

'Midnight Sun': {1996r, D. & J. Ward; 'High Noon' X *H. montana macrophylla*; gold foliage}

'Niagara Falls': {1991r, O. Petryszyn & W. Brincka; *H. montana macrophylla* X 'Sea Drift'} lg md of dark green leaves with piecrust edges **(see page 322)**

'Stardust': {1998r, D. & J. Ward; 'White Vision' X *H. montana macrophylla*; 28" high md of large, gold lvs}

other similar types:

'Behemoth': {1988r, R. Savory; *H. montana* sdlg} med gr foliage; resembles *H. montana macrophylla*

'Bethel Big Leaf': {1979r, C. Lantis; *H. montana* sdlg} v lg md of rippled, dark green lvs, 14" by 11" (14 vp); pale lav fls in early July on 34" sc

'King James': {1992r by P. Ruh for G. Krossa & A. Summers; *H. montana* sdlg} 27" by 68" md of bluish green lvs, 17" by 12" (15-18 vp); thin, underside bloom; near-wh fls, late June into mid-July

'King Michael': {1992r by P. Ruh for G. Krossa & A. Summers; *H. montana* sdlg} 32" by 56" md; med green lvs, 15" by 11" (18, deeply impressed vp); lightly rippled mgn; near-wh fls, late June, 37" sc

'Mikado': {1982r, P. Aden; *H. montana* 'Aureomarginata' X 'Big Sam'} 37" by 76", vase-shaped md; lvs 18" by 12" (18-21, deeply impressed vp); pale lav fls just above or below the mound top on 37" sc

H. sieboldiana 'Mira': similar large mound of green foliage **(see page 393)**

Hosta montana 'Mountain Snow'

key features: large, vase-shape mound of white-margined foliage; late emerging
mound size: 27" high by 60" wide

spacing: 60"

leaves: 12" long by 8" wide; 1/16" wide, pure white margin; medium green center; many gray-green and white streaks into the center; shiny underside; ovate to oblong-ovate blade that is also slightly wavy; smooth texture; good substance; 17 vein pairs

flowers: early to late July; very pale lavender; 40" scapes; fertile

comments: 'Mountain Snow' originated as a tissue culture sport at my nursery in the mid-1980's. At that time, I expected it to be a white-margined version of *H. montana* 'Aureomarginata', i.e. with wide, white margins streaking into a green center. At maturity, however, the margins turned out to be much narrower (1/16" for 'Mountain Snow' vs. 1-2" for *H. m.* 'Aureomarginata') than I had anticipated. Still, the variegated effect is attractive, though more subtle. 'Mountain Snow' blends in well with other hostas in a mixed garden and can also be effectively used as a background plant or specimen.

I registered 'Mountain Snow' in 1988. It emerges late, being out of the Mt. Fuji strain of *Hosta montana* so it is not normally subject to late spring frosts.

seedlings, sports, and other related types:
none listed

other similar types:
'Crispula' **(see page 127)**
'Frosted Jade' **(see page 174)**
'Gay Nineties': {1994r, Belle Gardens; 'William Lachman' X *H. montana*} med-sized md of creamy white-mgd

309

(green-cntrd) lvs, 8" by 6 1/2" (13 vp); mgns 3/4" wide; pale lav fls on 25" sc, late June into July

'Lakeside Cha Cha' {1994r, M. Chastain; 'Fascination' X *H. montana*; lvs lt gr wi a creamy wh mgn}

Hosta montana albomarginata: displayed as such in some Japanese collections but probably more accurately 'Shirofukurin Oba'; probably represents more than one white-margined sport from the wild

'Mount Everest': {1996r, J. Dishon; 'Sea Prize' X *H. montana*; dk green, wh-mgd lvs}

'My Friend Nancy': {1991r, R. Benedict & N. Krul; 'Dorothy Benedict' X *H. montana* 'Chirifu'} graceful, white-margined foliage

'Rosie Posie': {1994r, Belle Gardens; 'William Lachman' X *H. montana*; creamy white-mgd lvs}

'Summer Snow': {1978r, L. Cannon; *H. sieboldiana* X 'Tokudama'} big md of wh-mgd foliage that acts like a white-edged *H. montana*

'White On': another white-margined *H. montana* sport; from Terra Nova, Portland, Oregon; very close to 'Mountain Snow'

'Moon Glow'
key features: medium-sized mound of gold-centered, white-margined foliage
mound size: 17" high by 40" wide

spacing: 36"
leaves: 8" long by 6" wide; 1/16" to 1/8" wide, creamy white margin; center changes from chartreuse to medium gold; slightly shiny underside; blade broadly ovate and moderately cupped with age; somewhat unruly; moderately corrugated; thick substance; 9-11 vein pairs
flowers: mid-July into early August; near-white color with a pale lavender mid-petal stripe; 1 7/8" long by 1 1/4" wide;

narrow funnel shape; 24" scapes

comments: Ken Anderson registered 'Moon Glow' in 1977 as a seedling of 'August Moon', almost appearing to be a white-margined version of it. Unlike 'Lunar Eclipse', which develops the drawstring effect with age, 'Moon Glow' is not usually plagued with this problem, despite also having a relatively narrow margin. An occasional clump will have a few leaves torn along the margin, but this can be avoided by not overfertilizing. In general it makes an attractive specimen plant, but I would not advocate using it as a ground cover. The growth rate is medium to slow.

There are no registered seedlings from 'Moon Glow', but a few related sports have been identified. Its gold-leaved sport, 'Harvest Glow', has been the source of sports with chartreuse margins and light yellow centers and two similar mutations with chartreuse centers and gold margins. These have not yet been named or registered.

seedlings, sports, and other related types:
'Harvest Glow': {1988r, Walters Gardens; sport} med gold lvs, 9 1/2" by 7" (11 vp); 19" by 44" md

other similar types:
'Hoosier Homecoming', 'Lunar Eclipse', 'Moonlight'

'Moon River'
key features: small mound of white-margined foliage; a Lachman introduction
mound size: 11" high by 29" wide (up to 13" by 36")

spacing: 24"
leaves: 4 1/2" long by 4" wide; 1/8" to 1/2" wide margin that changes from yellow to creamy white; blue-green center; thin underside bloom; blade broadly ovate, almost rotund; margins not wavy; smooth texture when young,

slightly corrugated at maturity; slightly better than average substance; 8-9 vein pairs

flowers: mid-July into early August; pale lavender; 2" long by 1 1/8" wide; semi-bell shape; scapes 24" high; have only seen a few pods develop

comments: 'Moon River' matures as a dense, rounded mound of white-margined foliage that can be useful as a small specimen plant, a low edger, or ground cover. It comes out of the breeding program of Bill and Eleanor Lachman who registered it in 1991 as a hybrid of 'Crepe Suzette' X 'Blue Moon'.

seedlings, sports, and other related types:
none listed

other similar types:
'Cherub', 'Heartsong', 'Tea and Crumpets', 'Thumbelina', 'Winsome'

'Moonlight'
key features: dense, medium-large mound of white-margined, gold-centered foliage
mound size: 20" high by 50" wide

spacing: 48"

leaves: 9 1/2" long by 5 1/2" wide; 1/8" wide, white margin, center chartreuse (spring) to gold (by mid-summer); thin underside bloom; ovate shape with a rounded base; slight corrugation; little or no marginal waviness; average substance; 10 vein pairs

flowers: late July into mid-August; pale lavender; 2" long by 1" wide; narrow funnel shape; 24-36" scapes; no seed pods

comments: 'Moonlight' ranks as the first sport out of 'Gold Standard', found by Pauline Banyai (1977 registration). Its bright color stands out in shaded areas, especially on over-cast days and will rapidly form a full, dense mound.

A note of caution is in order. For a few years, I have seen so-called "sports" of 'Moonlight' in a few gardens. These are characterized by raised, dark green areas on a light gold background. The number of these raised areas varies from plant to plant with a few per leaf to many that nearly cover the blade. This variation is the result of a viral infection. Do not grow or propagate these plants. Even if you are attracted to such distortion (why?!?), it is not worth any risk to the rest of your collection.

seedlings, sports, and other related types:
'Richland Gold's Moonlight': {1999r, V. Wade; sport of 'Richland Gold'} gold-centered, white-mgd lvs; slightly different appearance from 'Moonlight'

other similar types:
'Gaiety', 'Moon Glow', 'Patriot's Fire', 'Saint Elmo's Fire', 'White Lightning'

Hosta nakaiana (Kanzashi Giboshi)
key features: low, dense mound of heart-shaped, green foliage
mound size: 12" high by 32" wide

spacing: 30"
leaves: 3 3/4" long by 2 7/8" wide; medium green; dull top surface, moderately shiny underside; blade heart-shaped; margin lightly wavy; no corrugation; average substance; 6-7 vein pairs; gold fall color develops in mid-October
flowers: July 10 to 23 (northern Illinois); medium purple color with lighter throat; 1 3/4" long by 1" wide; narrow funnel shape; 15-23" scapes (most 19-20"); many scapes per clump; three mature clumps had 53, 57, and 70 scapes;

13-18 flowers clustered in the top 2 1/2" of each scape; many seed pods

comments: *Hosta nakaiana*, as found in the U. S., becomes a very dense, symmetrical mound of heart-shaped foliage. The flowers are attractive, being produced in neat proportion to the mound; however, the blooming season is fairly short in duration. In the landscape, it can be utilized as an edger, low ground cover, or rock garden plant. Probably due to the copious amounts of seed it produces, many seedlings were selected and introduced as cultivars in the 1970's. Interestingly, most of these are significantly larger than *Hosta nakaiana* itself. This points to the great amount of heterozygosity existing in the species and indicates that what we have been growing in the U.S. is a dwarf-sized *H. nakaiana* clone.

Maekawa (1973) stated that *Hosta nakaiana* could be found growing wild in both Korea and Japan. On the other hand, Schmid (1991) indicated that the plants found in Japan are probably escapees from cultivation. This is analogous to the occurrence of *Hosta minor* in Japan (Schmid, 1991).

The names 'Burke's Dwarf', "Krossa E6", 'Bell's Baby', and *H. nakaimo minor* have been used incorrectly for *H. nakaiana*. It has also been misspelled "*Hosta nakiana*". For some reason, the name "nakaimo" has frequently been attributed to this plant. The cultivar 'Nakaimo' actually grows into a much larger plant (25" by 52" mound with 10" by 6" leaves that have 10-11 vein pairs) and is not closely related to *H. nakaiana*. Additionally its Japanese name, Kanzashi Giboshi, is shared by another species, *Hosta capitata*.

seedlings, sports, and other related types:

'Apple Green': {1982r, K. Anderson; *H. nakaiana* sdlg} medium-sized, dense mound of chartreuse foliage (lighter gold with more sun); md 13" by 30"; lvs 4" by 2 3/4" (7 vp); pale purple fls, early July on 21" sc; fast-growing, very attractive edger or ground cover

'Bacchanal': {1991r by P. Ruh for L. Davidson; *H. nakaiana* sdlg} formerly "Davidson 101"; small mound of wavy, dark green foliage; purple fls on 18" sc in July

'Betty': {1983r, R. Benedict; selfed sdlg of (*H. nakaiana* X *H. ventricosa*)} dense, 13" by 36" md of heavily rippled, shiny, dark green lvs, 4 1/2" by 3 3/4" (10 vp); like a small, rippled *H. ventricosa*; attractive

'Big Hearted': {1983r, R. Benedict; *H. nakaiana* X 'Zager's Giant'} med-sized md of deep green, heart-shaped lvs, 7" by 6"

'Birchwood Gem': {1989r by P. Ruh for F. Shaw; unknown

314

parentage} sm, dense md of heart-shaped, green foliage; pale lav fls on 27" sc in July; very similar to *H. nakaiana*; developed in 1966

'Blue Boy': {1986r, AHS for D. Stone; *H. nakaiana* X *H. sieboldiana*} dense, 19" by 45" md of bl-gr lvs, 8" by 5" (10-11 vp); very popular for many years; shows traits of both parents

'Bountiful': {1971r, E. Fisher; *H. nakaiana* sdlg} 15" by 40" md; green lvs, 6 3/8" by 3 3/4" (8 vp); larger than *H. nakaiana*

'Candy Hearts': *H. nakaiana* sdlg fr Eunice Fisher; larger than *H. nakaiana*; most widely grown of its seedlings **(see page 107)**

'Dear Heart': {1975r, E. Minks; *H. nakaiana* X 'Blue Boy'} 18" by 40" md of heart-shaped, bluish green foliage; pale lav fls in July; like a large 'Blue Cadet'

'Dick's Delight': {1998r, R. Rossing; *H. nakaiana* sdlg; white-mgd, light green-centered lvs}

'Dixie Queen': {1982r, R. Savory; *H. nakaiana* X a sdlg} sm md of green lvs (4 1/2" by 3 1/2") with darker veins; a collector's curiosity

'Drummer Boy': {1983r, S. Moldovan; *H. nakaiana* X 'Ruffled Queen'} med-sized, symmetrical md of slightly cupped, heart-shaped, dark green foliage

'Duchess': {1982r, R. Savory; sport of a *H. nakaiana* sdlg} sm md of narrow, wavy lvs wi margins that change from greenish ylw in spring to pure white; fls on 20" sc in July

'Egret': {1984r, R. Savory; *H. nakaiana* X sdlg; foliage similar to *H. nakaiana* but has white fls}

'Emerald Gem': {1991r, P. Ruh for D. Stone; unknown parentage} 9" by 25" md of foliage that changes from gold to chartreuse during the season; lvs measure 4 1/8" by 2 7/8" (7 vp); purple fls on 18-24" sc, early to late July; fertile; one of the David Stone hybrids; *H. nakaiana* heritage

'Fine Points': Florence Shaw pl; probably a sdlg of *H. nakaiana*; dense md of gr lvs; rare

'Floradora': {1978r, P. Aden; *H. nakaiana* X a *H. longipes* dwarf sdlg} large numbers of lav fls in July; close to *H. nakaiana* in both foliage and flower

'Fond Hope': {1973r, E. Fisher} 25" by 63" md of bl-gr lvs, 12 1/2" by 10" (18 vp); near-wh fls, late June-July; incorrectly listed as an *H. nakaiana* sdlg; actually from *H. sieboldiana*

'Goldbrook Genie': {1989r, S. Bond; *H. nakaiana* sdlg; grey-blue foliage}

'Golden Jubilee': {1995r, R. Savory & Savory's Gardens; sdlg of a *H. nakaiana* sdlg; med gold lvs}

315

'Golden Surprise': {1991r by P. Ruh for L. Simpers} long known as *H. nakaiana* 'Aurea', a name which cannot be used; 13" by 33" md of foliage that changes from gold to chartreuse during the growing season; lvs 5 3/4" by 4 1/4" (8 vp); lav fls in dense clusters, early to late July; differs from other golden Nakaianas in being brighter early in the growing season

'Golden Tiara': {1977r, R. Savory; sport of a sdlg of *H. nakaiana*} med-sized md of gold-margined foliage; one of the all-time classics **(see page 200)**

'Happy Hearts': {1973r, E. Fisher; *H. nakaiana* sdlg} larger than *H. nakaiana* in foliage and flower; 16" by 38" md; 6 1/2" by 5 3/4" lvs

'Heartleaf': {1971r, E. Fisher; *H. nakaiana* sdlg} 19" by 48" md of green lvs, 7 3/4" by 6 3/4"; lav fls from mid to late July on 16-25" sc; much larger than *H. nakaiana*

'Kilowatt': {1970r, M. Armstrong; *H. nakaiana* sdlg} very sm md of green foliage

'Lorna': {1983r, R. Benedict; *H. nakaiana* X *H. venusta*} sm md of wavy, shiny, green foliage

'Lucky Charm': {1986r by the AHS for E. Fisher; *H. nakaiana* sdlg} dvlpd before 1976; dense, 19" by 52" md of med green lvs, 8 3/4" by 6" (10-11 vp); med lav fls in dense clusters on 30" sc; rare

'Marquis': {1982r, R. Savory; *H. nakaiana* X a sdlg} med-sized md of green foliage; br purple fls, July

'Minnie Klopping': {1975r, A. Arett} originated by Minnie Klopping around 1968; 17" by 40" md of heart-shaped lvs, 7 5/8" by 6 1/4" (10-11 vp); pale lav fls tightly bunched at the top of 23" sc, early to late July; forms a wide, flattish mound; probably a hybrid of *H. nakaiana* X *H. sieboldiana* 'Elegans'

'Oxheart': {1976, E. Minks, 'Green Platter' X *H. nakaiana*} 16" by 40" md of wide, heart-shaped, green lvs (7 1/2" by 6 1/2", 10 vp); pale lav fls, late June into mid-July on 31" sc; fertile

'Pasture's New': {1997r by P. Ruh for E. Smith & A. Summers; *H. nakaiana* sdlg} sm md of green foliage; outstanding white fls

'Pearl Lake': dense, med-sized md of heart-shaped, green foliage; *H. nakaiana* origin **(see page 334)**

'Peter Pan': {1980r, N. Minks; *H. nakaiana* X 'Helen Field Fischer'} med-sized md of heart-shaped, bluish green foliage

'Purple Bouquet': {1986r, P. Banyai; 'Nakaimo' sdlg} dense, med-sized md of heart-shaped, green foliage; spectacular show of purple flowers from mid-July into

316

August; probably a hybrid of *H. nakaiana* X *H. sieboldii*, not 'Nakaimo'

'Rim Rock': {1982r, R. Savory; *H. venusta* sdlg X *H. nakaiana* sdlg} 10" by 29" md of green foliage; purple fls in July on many, 20-29" scapes that remain erect throughout flowering

'Shells at Sea': {originally registered as 'Sea Shell' in 1980 by Anne Arett as a *H. nakaiana* sdlg} changed to 'Shells at Sea' in 1983 to preserve the "Sea" names for Mildred Seaver intro; 11" by 36" md of wrinkled, wavy, green foliage; not grown much anymore

'Soft Touch': {1977r, R. Savory; *H. nakaiana* sdlg} sm mound of heart-shaped, green foliage; bell-shaped, purple fls on 18" sc in July

'Special Gift': {1973r, E. Fisher; *H. nakaiana* sdlg} 16" by 42" md; 6 5/8" by 5 1/2" green lvs

'Valentine Lace': {1970r, M. Armstrong; *H. nakaiana* sdlg} 23" by 44" md of heart-shaped, dark green lvs, 8" by 6 1/2" (12 vp); pale lav fls, late June into July; thought to be a small plant for many years, but actually fairly large; may be an *H. nakaiana* X *H. sieboldiana* hybrid; sported to 'Ghost Spirit' with lvs that are green & white mottled in the center, bl gr-mgd {1999r, C. Isaacs}

'Warwick Curtsey': introduced for sale in the 1995 Hatfield Gardens catalog as a Gil Jones hybrid of 'Dorothy Benedict' X *H. nakaiana*; dense, 15" by 37" md of gold-mgd lvs 5" by 4 1/8" (10 vp); 1/4" to 3/4" wide, gold margin, med green center; very attractive

'Warwick Edge': {1993r, L. Jones; 'William Lachman' X *H. nakaiana*} 16" by 30" md of white-margined, green-centered foliage; outstanding grower

other similar types:

'Abiqua Ground Cover', 'Banyai's Dancing Girl', 'Blue Cadet', *H. capitata*, 'Craig's Temptation', *H. minor*, *H. venusta*

'Neat Splash'

key features: medium-sized mound of heavily streaked foliage; purple flowers in August

mound size: 16" high by 36" wide

spacing: 36"

leaves: 7 1/8" long by 2 3/4" wide; heavily streaked throughout the blade with sections of creamy white, green and a green-and-white mottle; sometimes white-margined; slightly shiny top surface, very shiny underside; blade oblong-elliptic shape with a rounded to acute base; margins slightly rippled; average substance; 6-7 vein pairs

flowers: late July into mid-August; medium purple color with whitish petal margins from tip, three-fourths of the way into the throat; petals also striped; 2 1/4" long by 1 3/8" wide; semi-bell shape with reflexed tips; scapes up to 28" high; fertile

comments: When true-to-type, 'Neat Splash' makes a striking, heavily streaked mound of foliage, but it often mutates to a wide variety of forms. In the 1985 issue of *The American Hosta Society Bulletin*, I reported on the sports that can result when 'Neat Splash' is propagated by tissue culture (Zilis, 1985). Most commonly found is 'Neat Splash Rim', the sport with white-margined, green-centered foliage. Other sports include plants with white-centered, green-margined leaves, all-green foliage or a series of mixed streaked-margined chimeras.

Paul Aden registered 'Neat Splash' in 1978 as a hybrid of 'Yellow Splash' X a 'Robusta' seedling, but its heritage is certainly *Hosta sieboldii*. It comes very close to 'Yellow Splash' in both foliage and flower and can be easily confused with it. Owing to its widespread usage in breeding to produce variegated offspring, there are many seedlings and sports which have become prominent hostas in their own

318

right. These include 'Crested Surf', 'Emily Dickinson', 'Ground Master', 'Coquette', 'Queen Josephine', 'Scooter', 'Sea Dream' and 'Sea Lightning'.

In all the fuss over the heavily variegated foliage, the value of its flowers is often overlooked. For a three week period in August, the bright purple flowers make a very nice show on scapes that stand well above the foliage.

On a commercial scale, 'Neat Splash' is becoming scarce in favor of many newer, more stable cultivars. The *Hosta Finder 2000* (Greene, 2000) lists only ten retail mail-order sources for it and even fewer (six) for the closely related 'Yellow Splash'.

seedlings, sports, and other related types:

'Artist's Palette': {1986r, Kuk's Forest; 'Neat Splash' sdlg} heavily streaked foliage; md 17" by 36", lvs 7" by 4 1/2" (9 vp); tends to sport to the gr-cntrd, creamy white-mgd form, 'Margin of Error' {1995r, R. Kuk}

'Bold Ribbons': {1976r, P. Aden; hybrid of two sdlgs} 15" by 33" md of white-margined foliage; lvs 8 7/8" by 4 5/8" (7-8 vp) wi a shiny, dark green center and 1/2" creamy white margin; bright purple fls on 29" sc, late July into Aug; very similar to 'Neat Splash Rim' and 'Yellow Splash Rim'

'Coquette': {1987r, R. Benedict; 'Neat Splash' sdlg} med-sized md of white-mgd lvs **(see page 124)**

'Cordelia': {1991r, R. Kuk; 'Neat Splash' sdlg} white-mgd lvs, deep purple fls **(see page 125)**

'Crested Surf': {1990r, R. & D. Benedict; selfed 'Neat Splash' sdlg} med-sized md of white-mgd foliage **(see page 126)**

'Eleanor Lachman': {1995r, W. & E. Lachman; ('Neat Splash' X 'Flamboyant') X 'Robert Frost'} creamy white-centered, dark green-margined foliage

'Emily Dickinson': {1987r, W. & E. Lachman; 'Neat Splash' sdlg X *H. plantaginea*} white-mgd, green-centered lvs; fragr fls **(see page 144)**

'Everlasting Love': Greg Johnson hybrid of 'Neat Splash' X 'Dorset Blue'; 14" by 38" md of white-mgd, green-centered lvs, 6" by 4 1/2" (8 vp); mgns, 1/2" to 3/4" wide, change from creamy yellow to white; lav fls in July; excellent grower

'Goody Goody': {1987r, R. Benedict; selfed 'Neat Splash' sdlg} v sm md of narrow, white-centered foliage; edger or rock garden plant

'Green Marmalade': {1987r, C. Owens; 'Neat Splash' X *H. plantaginea* (possibly)} shiny lvs streaked & margined wi creamy yellow; md 28" by 67", lvs 12" by 9" (11-13 vp); 49-62" sc bearing med lav fls, mid-July into Aug;

319

impressive foliage and tall scapes

'Ground Master': {1979r, P. Aden; 'Yellow Splash' X 'Neat Splash'} low, spreading mound of white-margined foliage **(see page 215)**

'Hertha': {1988r, R. Savory; 'Neat Splash' sdlg} low, dense md of creamy white-margined lvs; med purple fls, mid-July into Aug on 30" sc; attractive edger or ground cover; sported to 'Humility' {1997r, R. Snyder; dk green lvs}

'Josephine': {1987r, Kuk's Forest; 'Neat Splash' sdlg} "mother plant" of 'Queen Josephine' & 'Joseph'; lvs green wi an inconsistent pattern of creamy yellow streaks

'Liberty Bell': {1985r, R. Benedict, 'Yellow Splash' X 'Neat Splash'; dk purple fls in Aug} 15" by 42" md; lvs 7" by 4" (6 vp) with a 1/8" yellow mgn that turns white and occasionally produces mottled streaks into the green center

'Little Bo Peep': {1991r, R. Kuk; 'Neat Splash' sdlg} small mound of white-margined foliage

'Little Wonder': {1989r, W. & E. Lachman} 'Neat Splash' sdlg; low, dense md of white-mgd lvs **(see page 277)**

'Medusa': {1993r, R. Herold; 'Neat Splash' X *H. gracillima*} narrow, white-cntrd, green-mgd foliage; 6" by 15" md; 4 3/4" by 1 1/8" lvs

'Minnie Bell': {1985r, R. Benedict; selfed 'Neat Splash' sdlg} sm md of creamy yellow-margined lvs; like a mini-'Yellow Splash Rim'

'Neat Splash Rim': {1986r, AHS} stable, green-centered, white-margined sport found in many gardens

'Peedee Laughing River': {1992r, U. Syre-Herz; 'Neat Splash' X 'Iron Gate Glamour'} green-centered, white-margined foliage topped by bright purple fls; 15" by 46" md, 10" by 4" lvs (9 vp) wi a 1/2", wavy margin; fast-growing, interesting, and valuable addition to any garden

'Richland Royal Prince': 'Neat Splash' sdlg from Van Wade; dense, 13" by 29" md of green-mgd, white-centered lvs, 8" by 3 3/4" (7 vp); purple fls, mid-July into Aug; dense md habit

'Richland Royal Princess': {1999r, V. Wade; 'Richland Royal Prince' sport} med-sized md of white-mgd, green-centered foliage; purple fls, mid-July into August; similar to 'Neat Splash Rim'

'Richland Royal Purple': {1999r, V. Wade; 'Richland Royal Prince' sport} med-sized md of green foliage; purple fls, mid-July into August

'Sea Dream': {1984r, M. Seaver; 'Neat Splash' X sdlg} lg

md of gold-cntrd, white-mgd lvs **(see page 380)**

'Sea Lightning': {1981r, M. Seaver; 'Neat Splash' sdlg} streaked foliage; often reverts to 'Sea Thunder', white-centered, green-margined sport **(see page 383)**

'Sea Sunrise': {1982r, M. Seaver; 'Neat Splash' sdlg} sm md of brightly variegated foliage; lvs chartreuse-mgd wi a strkd center; pale lav fls in July; sports to all-gold 'Sea Yellow Sunrise' {1985r, M. Seaver}

'Squiggles': {1978r, P. Aden; 'Yellow Splash' X 'Neat Splash'} sm md of white-centered, green-mgd, wavy foliage; center pale yellow in spring; slow-growing; rare

'Swoosh': {1978r, P. Aden; 'Yellow Splash' X 'Neat Splash'} variable, heavily streaked foliage; 14" by 34" md, 7 1/2" by 3 1/2" lvs; brilliant purple fls in Aug on 24" sc; close to its parents in both foliage and flower; popular breeding plant

'Tucker Wave': {1995r, R. Stephens; 'Kabitan' X 'Neat Splash' sdlg; lvs dk green wi a lt green mgn; pale lav fls}

'Yellow Splash': {1976r, P. Aden; hybrid of two sdlgs} 18" by 43" md of heavily streaked, yellow, cream and green lvs, often wi a creamy yellow mgn; br purple fls in Aug on 30" sc; 'Neat Splash' parent; also an excellent source of variegated seedlings; frequently sports to gr-centcred, yellow-mgd form, 'Yellow Splash Rim' {1986r, AHS}

other similar types:

'Beatrice', 'Breeder's Choice', 'Don Stevens', "Robusta Variegata", 'Splish Splash', 'Starburst'

'Niagara Falls'
key features: large mound of neatly rippled, dark green foliage; semi-upright mound habit
mound size: 26" high by 52" wide

spacing: 48"
leaves: 14" long by 10 1/2" wide; dark green; shiny underside; blade broadly oblong-ovate with a deeply lobed base and a long, thin, curved tip; heavily rippled margins, 20 or more per side; smooth texture; good substance; 16, deeply impressed vein pairs **flowers:** early to late July; pale lavender, almost whitish; wide-open funnel shape; subtended by large bracts of the *H. montana*-type; 45" scapes; many seed pods develop

comments: 'Niagara Falls' was registered in 1991 as a hybrid of *H. montana praeflorens* (now *H. montana macrophylla*) X 'Sea Drift' by Bill (William) Brincka and Olga Petryszyn. It ranks near the top of hostas with piecrust margins. The dark green leaves are attractively edged with 20 or more large ripples that are noticeable even from a distance. The semi-upright mound habit further enhances the great beauty of this plant which makes a wonderful centerpiece plant in any shaded garden. It also can be utilized in a breeding program for its many good qualities and its ability to easily form seed pods. Put this plant on your "I've got to get!" list.

seedlings, sports, and other related types:
'Hoosier Dome': {1998r, O. Petryszyn; 'Niagara Falls' X ('Silver Bowl' X 'Muriel Seaver Brown') heavily rippled, domed, moderately corrugated, green leaves}

other similar types:
'Grand Canyon': {1995r, O. Petryszyn & W. Brincka; 'Sum and Substance' X *H. montana macrophylla*} lg, upright md of ruffled, golden foliage
'Manhattan': {1994r, W. Brincka & O. Petryszyn; 'Sea Frolic' sdlg} the ultimate in crinkled, rippled green

leaves; another for that "list"

'Sea Drift': {1978r, M. Seaver; 'Green Piecrust' sdlg} large mound of heavily rippled green foliage; md 24" by 48"; lvs 14" by 10 1/2" (14 vp); pale lav fls in July on 36" sc; pollen parent of 'Niagara Falls' and the closest plant to it

---

'Night Before Christmas'
key features: large mound of white-centered foliage; sport of 'White Christmas'
mound size: 25" high by 63" wide

---

spacing: 60"
leaves: 12" long by 7" wide; 2 3/4" wide, dark green margin; 1 7/8" wide, white center; thin underside bloom; blade ovate and slightly wavy; smooth texture; better than average substance; 11 vein pairs that are more closely set in white center
flowers: mid-July into early August; pale lavender; 2 1/2" long by 1" wide; narrow funnel shape; scapes up to 42" high

comments: When I heard rumors of a wider-margined version of 'White Christmas' in the early 1990's, I was a bit skeptical. I had seen other such "mutations" come and go as temporary phenomena, eventually forgotten. Well, I quickly became a believer in 'Night Before Christmas' once I had a chance to see it in a number of gardens. It is an impressive plant, perhaps one of the best white-centered hosta cultivars. It makes a much larger mound with taller scapes than 'White Christmas' and the leaves have significantly wider green margins (2 3/4" vs. about 1/2"). It can be used as a substitute for the Undulatas in the landscape, making an excellent ground cover or specimen plant. Unlike 'White Christmas', 'Night Before Christmas' is an easy plant to grow in both nursery and garden settings.

'Night Before Christmas' comes from the same nursery

(Mobjack Nurseries, Mobjack, VA) where other wide-margined sports have been found including 'Patriot', 'Minuteman', and 'Grand Tiara'. There is some debate as to how all of these plants developed their wider, thicker margins. One current theory credits tetraploid conversion for the differences seen in all of these plants. Interestingly, the green-leaved sport out of 'White Christmas' is not the same plant as the green-leaved 'Night Before Christmas', much like the difference between 'Golden Scepter' and 'Amber Tiara', gold-leaved sports of 'Golden Tiara' and 'Grand Tiara', respectively.

John Machen of Mobjack Nurseries registered 'Night Before Christmas' in 1994.

seedlings, sports, and other related types:
'Robert's Rapier': {1996r, R. Keller & White Oak N; sport of 'White Christmas'} lvs have a very narrow white center (v wide green margin); distinct from 'Night Before Christmas'

other similar types:
'Cascades', 'Middle Ridge', 'Striptease', 'Undulata Univittata', 'White Ray'

Hosta nigrescens (Kuro Giboshi)
key features: large, vase-shaped mound of cupped, blue foliage; tall scapes
mound size: 30" high by 66" wide

spacing: 60"
leaves: 12" long by 9 1/2" wide; deep blue-green early, changing to dark green by mid-summer; thick underside bloom; ovate to broadly ovate shape with a heart-shaped base and distinct tip; blade distinctly cupped upward and held perpendicular to the nearly upright petioles; moderate to heavy corrugation; no red-purple dots on petioles; thick substance; 13-14 vein pairs

flowers: late July into mid-August; pale lavender color with white petal margins and darker streaks leading into the whitish throat; 2 5/8" long by 1 3/8" wide; funnel-shaped; thick bloom on scapes that reach 54" or more; sparse seed pod formation

comments: During a visit to "The Hosta Glade" in the Minnesota Landscape Arboretum a few years back, I noted that *Hosta nigrescens* had the bluest foliage of all the hostas growing there. It has proven to be an outstanding, "impact" plant in shade gardens throughout the U.S. *H. nigrescens* makes an excellent background plant and can be a magnificent focal point of an island bed. The impressively cupped, thick-substanced foliage is carried in a semi-upright manner forming a very large mound. The flowers, though not individually striking, are impressive because they are borne on very tall, erect scapes. In one Michigan garden, I measured a scape at 86" high (see picture).

Pod formation is sparse, but several hybridizers have been able to work with it, resulting in a few significant introductions. These include 'Flower Power', 'Garnet Prince', and 'Golden Gate'. The most famous of all *H. nigrescens* seedlings, 'Krossa Regal', has achieved much greater popularity than its parent.

Hosta nigrescens is native to the northern part of Honshu island in Japan (Maekawa, 1972).

seedlings, sports, and other related types:

'Flower Power': {1987r, K. Vaughn; *H. nigrescens* X *H. plantaginea*} large, semi-upr md of shiny, br green foliage; 28" by 60" md; lvs 14" by 11" (12-13 vp) wi thick substance and a smooth texture; 3" fragr fls on 48" sc, mid-July into Aug; impressive pl wi traits of both parents

'Garnet Prince': {1991r, P. Banyai & J. Dishon; *H. nigrescens* sdlg} 22" by 40" md of shiny, dk green lvs, 7 1/2" by 5" (9 vp); better than average subst and intense, reddish purple petioles; pale purple fls on 65" sc in August; red seed pods

'Golden Gate': {1994r, W. Brincka & O. Petryszyn; *H. nigrescens* sdlg X 'Blue Whirls'} lg md of bright gold foliage that is slug-resistant; 33" by 60" md; lvs 11 1/2" by 9" (15 vp); lav fls on 42" sc from mid-July into August

'John Wargo': {1986r, H. Weissenberger; *H. nigrescens* sdlg; med green foliage} purplish red color from petioles into midrib

'Krossa Regal': *H. nigrescens* sdlg, originally fr Japan; a hosta classic; differs from *H. nigrescens* in leaf shape and cupping **(see page 260)**

'Smokerise Frosted Vase': {1994r, E. Lunsford, Jr.; 'Frances Williams' X *H. nigrescens*; grayish green-cntrd, white-mgd lvs}

'Tenryu': large, upright mound of blue-green foliage topped by tall flower scapes; avg md 28" by 60" wi lvs 10" by 6 3/4" (13 vp), but Wade & Gatton pl 44" high by 86" wide (lvs nearly identical in size, 10 1/4" by 6"); fls lavender, 2 3/4" by 1 1/2"; a Japanese pl named for the Tenryu River that is the same as or a seedling of *H. nigrescens*

'True Blue': {1978r, P. Aden; 'Chartreuse Wedge' X (*H. nigrescens* X 'Blue Vision')} 23" by 52" md of deep bl-green lvs 11 1/2" by 8 1/8" (16-18 vp); dense clusters of near-wh fls, mid-June into July; more like *H. sieboldiana* than *H. nigrescens*

Hosta nigrescens 'Elatior'
key features: huge mound of shiny green foliage; whitish flowers borne on very tall scapes
mound size: 31" high by 74" wide

spacing: 72"

leaves: 14" long by 10 1/4" wide; shiny, light green; very shiny underside; ovate to broadly elliptic with a heart-shaped base, long, distinct tip, and 3-4, broad waves; smooth texture with an occasional, faint streak of corrugation; thick substance; 14-15 vein pairs

flowers: mid-July into early August; near-white with a distinctive pattern of lavender in mid-petal; 2 3/4" long by 1 3/8" wide; funnel shape; scapes reach 71" or more; separating scape bud has a distinctive, strawflower-like appearance; forms seed pods

326

comments: As a mature specimen in flower, *Hosta nigrescens* 'Elatior' can only be viewed with awe. The massive mound of large, shiny green foliage is impressive enough, but the flower stalks that reach 6-7 feet high add a striking vertical element to the shaded landscape. It certainly needs space in the garden and can be used effectively as a background or centerpiece plant.

Though listed as a type of *Hosta nigrescens*, it likely is a hybrid. A good guess as to its parentage would be *H. nigrescens* (tall scapes, large size, upright habit) X *H. montana* (scape bud flowerlike as it unfurls, whitish flower color). *H. nigrescens* 'Elatior' readily forms seeds and has been the source of many interesting seedlings. All of these have proven to be excellent, large, landscape plants.

seedlings, sports, and other related types:

'Diva': {1999r by the Russ O'Harra Hosta Society for R. O'Harra} *H. nigrescens* 'Elatior' sdlg; lg md of bright gold foliage; 24" by 50" md, 13" by 9 1/2" lvs (15 vp); whitish fls on 3-foot scapes in July; impressive plant

'Ersatz': {1996r, P. Ruh; *H. nigrescens* 'Elatior' sdlg} lg md of green foliage; v tall scapes that tip over and spiral up and down over the top of the foliage; a collector's curiosity

'Roderick': {1999r by the Russ O'Harra Hosta Society for R. O'Harra} *H. nigrescens* 'Elatior' sdlg; huge md of green foliage topped by whitish fls on 4' sc in July; 37" by 83" md, 16 1/2" by 10 1/2" lvs (16 vp); flowers in top 8 1/2" of scape

'Russ O'Harra': {1999r, R. O'Harra, R. Olson, M. Zilis, & the Russ O'Harra Hosta Society; *H. nigrescens* 'Elatior' selection} lg md of shiny, green foliage topped by tall scapes of near-white fls in July-August

'Spotlight': {1995r, J. & J. Wilkins; 'Fort Knox' X *H. nigrescens* 'Elatior'} v lg md of br gold lvs 17" by 11"; impressive, huge bright plant

other similar types:

'Chartreuse Wedge': {1976r, P. Aden; selfed 'Green Wedge' sdlg} huge md of large, chartreuse foliage; pale lav fls from mid-July into Aug on scapes, 4' or higher

'Green Dragonet': {1999r, C. Owens; 'Butternut Hill' X 'Chartreuse Wedge'} 46" by 96" md of shiny, green lvs, 17" by 11" (16 vp); impressive, huge, semi-upright md of foliage that resembles 'Elatior'

'Green Sheen': {1978r, P. Aden; 'Green Wedge' X 'Chartreuse Wedge'} 30" by 57" md of thick, shiny green lvs, 15" by 10" (14 vp); lav fls on 40-50" sc, late July into mid-Aug; acts like a green 'Sum and Substance'

'Green Wedge': {1976r, P. Aden; *H. nigrescens* X a sdlg}

27" by 60" md of shiny, slug-resistant, light green lvs 13" by 11 1/2" (13 vp); many sc of pale lav fls, late July into Aug; scapes tend to flop over as flowering proceeds; impressively waxy, shiny appearance in a lg-sized md; resembles *H. nigrescens* 'Elatior'; popular in the 1980's

'Little Sheen': sdlg of 'Green Sheen' from Herb Benedict; dvlpd before 1991; 21" by 44" md of thick-substanced, med green (bluish early) lvs, 9 3/4" by 9 1/8" (10-12 vp); med lav fls on 24" sc, late July into Aug; essentially a small version of 'Green Sheen'

'Sum and Substance': huge mound of chartreuse to gold foliage that shows many similarities to *H. nigrescens* 'Elatior' **(see page 442)**

'Opipara' (Nishiki Giboshi) = 'Bill Brincka'
key features: large mound of yellow-margined foliage; rhizomatous; purple flowers in August
mound size: 24" high by 64" wide

spacing: 48"
leaves: 11 7/8" long by 8 1/4" wide; 3/4" to 1 3/8" wide, yellow margin that creates some gray-green streaking into the medium green center; shiny top and underside; ovate shape with a rounded to slightly angular base and wide tip; blade noticeably wavy; petiole very wide; better than average substance; 11 vein pairs
flowers: early to late August; medium purple with darker stripes in mid-petal and translucent petal margins; 2 1/4" long by 1 1/8" wide; scapes up to 46" high; many seed pods develop

comments: As a fully grown mound, 'Opipara' can only be described as spectacular. Throughout the growing season, the foliage variegation pattern is bright and colorful. Each leaf bears a wide, yellow margin that sharply contrasts the vivid green center. This effect is enhanced by the waviness of the leaf blade. 'Opipara' also has an unusual rhizomatous nature, i.e. it spreads over a wide area by underground stems. This characteristic makes it very useful as a big ground cover and could possibly be useful for hillside plantings. The August-blooming purple flowers tower above the foliage and are an ornamental plus.

There is a bad-news, good-news story surrounding this plant. The first plants of 'Opipara' grown in this country were heavily infected with a virus and, at one time, it seemed that every plant was diseased. Thanks to Bill Brincka, however, a virus-free clone was imported from Japan and has been widely propagated. Initially this clone was named 'Bill Brincka' to distinguish virus-free material from infected stock, but the name has continued to be used and was registered in 1988 (by Bill Brincka).

'Opipara' should have potential as a breeding plant, but has not been widely used.

For many years, I knew this plant as the species, *Hosta opipara*. Schmid (1991) reduced it to cultivar status due to its obviously cultivated origins.

seedlings, sports, and other related types:

'Emerald Green': {1996r, Walters Gardens & P. Ruh; sport} shiny green lvs, 9 1/2" by 5 1/2" or more; green-leaved form of 'Opipara'

H. opipara 'Kooriyama': thought to be a diminutive version of 'Opipara'; 12" by 28" md; lvs 6" by 3 3/4" (7 vp) wi a 1/4" wide yellow to creamy white margin; blade wavy and curving downward; from Japan

Hosta pachyscapa (Benkei Giboshi)

key features: medium-large mound of green foliage; native to Japan

mound size: 22" high by 48" wide

spacing: 48"

leaves: 11" long by 6" wide; slightly shiny, medium green; very shiny underside; blade narrowly oblong-ovate with a rounded base; slightly rippled margin; smooth texture; slightly above average substance; 8-9 vein pairs

flowers: early to late August; pale lavender with 3-5 darker stripes down mid-petal; 2 1/4" long by 1 1/4" wide; funnel-shaped; scapes 32" or more that tend to droop near the end of flowering; forms many long seed pods

comments: Fumio Maekawa (1973) listed *Hosta pachyscapa*, the Benkei Giboshi, as being native to Japan on Honshu Island. It has been on display in a few American collections for many years, but has never made much of an impact amongst collectors or gardeners. It readily forms seed pods, so it could be a useful hybridizing plant.

seedlings, sports, and other related types:
none listed

other similar types:

H. kiyosumiensis: closely related to *H. pachyscapa* (Schmid, 1991) **(see page 257)**

'Patriot'

key features: medium-large mound of white-margined leaves; sport of 'Francee'

mound size: 23" high by 50" wide

spacing: 48"

leaves: 8" long by 6" wide; 1/2" to 1" wide margin that changes from creamy yellow to white during the season; thin underside bloom; blade ovate; slightly wavy margins; generally smooth texture; better than average substance; 10-12 vein pairs

flowers: late July into early August; medium lavender; narrow funnel shape; 30" scapes; limited seed pod formation

comments: When first introduced, 'Patriot' made quite a sensation in the nursery trade. The significant improvement in the width of the margin over 'Francee' was very striking, and its popularity grew rapidly. 'Patriot' was found as sport of 'Francee' at Mobjack Nurseries in Virginia by John Machen who registered it in 1991. Since that time, 'Patriot' has taken over the role as the leading selling white-margined hosta. From that same group of plants came 'Minuteman', which differs by having a purer white margin and darker green center. Unfortunately the two were mixed up in the early years of 'Patriot' propagation, so some 'Patriot' plants could actually be 'Minuteman'. Most nurseries now propagating the two have correctly sorted them out and are offering true-to-type material.

seedlings, sports, and other related types:

'Fire and Ice': {1999r, H. Hansen & Shady Oaks N; sport} gr-mgd, white-centered lvs; very attractive

'Loyalist': {1998r, C. Falstad for G. Van Eijk-Bos; sport} green-margined, white-centered leaves

'Mademoiselle': {1999r, R. Klehm; sport wi white-centered, green-mgd lvs}

'Patriot's Fire': {1996r, A. Summers & K. Walek; sport of 'Patriot'} white-margined lvs wi a center that changes from green to gold; an interesting, colorful mound when actively growing; closer to 'Francee' than 'Patriot'

'Patriotic': sport of 'Patriot' with wider, white margins from Van Wade

'Paul Revere': sport of the true 'Patriot' from Q & Z N; vigorous, gr-mgd, white-centered plant

'Trailblazer': {1999r, M. Zilis} sport of 'Francee' developed at my nursery (Q & Z N); sharp contrast between wide, creamy white margins and dark green center; slight differences from 'Minuteman' and 'Patriot'

other similar types:
'Columbus Circle', 'Leola Fraim'

'Paul's Glory'
key features: large mound of gold-centered, green-margined foliage
mound size: 25" high by 55" wide

spacing: 48"
leaves: 9 1/2" long by 7" wide; 3/8" to 3/4" wide, blue-green margin becomes dark green by mid-summer; center chartreuse early changing to bright gold by mid-summer; thin underside bloom; blade ovate with a deeply lobed base and slight waviness; slight to moderate corrugation; good substance; 10-12 vein pairs
flowers: mid-July to early August; pale lavender; 2" long by 1 1/2" wide; scapes up to 40" high; many seed pods develop

comments: 'Paul's Glory' improves on such legendary gold-centered hostas as 'Gold Standard' and 'Janet' by having better substance and more intense foliage colors. In any landscape a mature specimen of 'Paul's Glory' is truly a sight to behold, but can also be effectively utilized as an eye-catching ground cover. The blue to dark green leaf margin contrasts beautifully with the gold center which begins the season chartreuse, slowly changing to medium gold.

332

I've also seen plants that received 2-3 hours of direct sunlight per day become creamy white-centered by late summer.

'Paul's Glory' has a medium to fast growth rate, forming a mature-sized clump from a single division in about three or four years. It has also been a vigorous grower in nursery containers.

Paul Hofer and Peter Ruh found 'Paul's Glory' as a sport growing in the center of a clump of 'Perry's True Blue' (an 'Elegans'-type) in 1983. This should mean that 'Paul's Glory' is a variegated Sieboldiana, but that is not the case. Both flowering and foliage habits differ significantly from the typical Sieboldiana. The flowers of 'Paul's Glory' open 3-4 weeks later than the Sieboldianas and are pale lavender versus near-white. The foliage also differs significantly from the Sieboldiana pattern in the number of vein pairs (6 fewer), substance (slightly thinner), leaf size (50% smaller), and mound size (shorter). What then is the origin of 'Paul's Glory'? Pete informed me that originally 'Perry's True Blue' was actually a mixture of blue-leaved seedlings, all thought to be 'Elegans'-types. The "mother plant" of 'Paul's Glory', however, must have been a hybrid, possibly *H. sieboldiana* X 'Fortunei'.

As it readily forms seed pods, 'Paul's Glory' can easily be incorporated into a breeding program. It has also been a source of mutations, often sporting to the blue-leaved 'Wheaton Blue' when propagated by tissue culture. Four other sports have been identified, 'American Glory Be', 'Chesterland Gold', 'Pete's Passion', and 'Peter Ruh'.

Paul Hofer and Peter Ruh registered 'Paul's Glory' in 1987.

seedlings, sports, and other related types:

'American Glory Be': {1999r, V. Wade; sport} lf center turns gold later than 'Paul's Glory'; margins a little wider

'Chesterland Gold': {1997r, P. Ruh & M. Zilis; sport} bright gold foliage; named for Peter Ruh's Ohio hometown

'Gold Glory': {1995r, R. Lydell; 'Paul's Glory' sdlg} med gold, corrug lvs, 9 1/2" by 8" (12 vp)

'Perry's True Blue': {1981r, P. & L. Hofer} mother plant of 'Paul's Glory'; large md of heavily corrugated, blue-green foliage; 30" by 68" md, lvs 15" by 11" (16-18 vp); near-wh fls, late June into July; developed in the late 1950's at Wayside Gardens when it was headquartered in Mentor, Ohio; 'Elegans'-type, though more than one blue-lvd seedling has been sold under this name

'Pete's Passion': {1997r, P. Ruh; sport} wider dark green

margins than 'Paul's Glory'; margin 1 1/4" wide vs. 1/2" for 'Paul's Glory'; side-by-side plantings show a striking difference; also more vigorous

'Peter Ruh': reversed sport of 'Paul's Glory' with green-centered, gold-margined lvs; found at Q & Z Nursery in 1999

'Wheaton Blue': {1999r, M. Zilis, sport} 26" by 50" mound of blue-green foliage; 10" by 7" lvs; named for Wheaton, IL; introduced for sale in 1995

other similar types:
'Gold Standard', 'Janet', 'Paradigm', 'September Sun'

'Pearl Lake'
key features: dense, medium-sized mound of heart-shaped, green foliage
mound size: 17" high by 48" wide (up to 22" by 56")

spacing: 40"

leaves: 6 3/8" long by 4 3/4" wide; green most of the season, thin bloom on the top surface produces a grayish green color early; moderate underside bloom; heart-shaped blade; margin slightly wavy; slight corrugation with age; average substance; 10-11 vein pairs

flowers: July 6 to July 23 (northern Illinois); pale lavender with darker mid-petal striping and a white petal margin from the whitish throat, halfway to the tip; 2" long by 1" wide; many scapes measuring 18-26" high; 30 scapes on one mature clump, about 27 flowers per scape; forms some seed pods

comments: 'Pearl Lake' grows into an attractive mound of heart-shaped, green foliage topped by a dense cluster of lavender flowers in July. It has become very popular because of its rapid growth rate and dense mound habit,

334

making an excellent edging plant. 'Pearl Lake' can be effectively used in combination with gold cultivars such as 'Gold Edger' or 'Gold Drop' or any of the variegated "Tiaras" (e.g., 'Golden Tiara' and 'Grand Tiara').

'Pearl Lake' was developed in the early 1970's and registered by Piedmont Gardens (Connecticut) in 1982 with unknown parentage. Most likely it is a seedling of *Hosta nakaiana*. It will form seed pods and has been the source of a few hybrids. Additionally a few sports have been identified, 'Veronica Lake' being the most prominent.

seedlings, sports, and other related types:

'Alston Glenn': {1998r, R. Stephens; 'Pearl Lake' X 'Tucker Pucker'; heavily rippled blue-green lvs}

'Gertie': sport of 'Pearl Lake' with chartreuse & green-streaked lvs; stabilized to 'Veronica Lake'; from Frank Riehl

'Granada': {1995r, W. Zumbar; sport} gold-margined foliage; close to 'Veronica Lake'

'Rotunda': {1988r, R. Savory; 'Pearl Lake' sdlg} 17" by 48" md of very round, cupped, medium green lvs, 9" by 8" (14 vp); sc 31" high; heavy pod formation; interesting for its rounded, cupped character

'Tucker Charm': {1993r, R. Stephens; 'Pearl Lake' X 'Herifu'; dark green foliage}

'Veronica Lake': {1993r, F. Riehl; sport} gold-margined, green-centered foliage; worth growing

other similar types:

'Blue Cadet', 'Candy Hearts', 'Jade Scepter', 'Purple Bouquet'

'Peedee Elfin Bells'
key features: medium-sized, dense mound of green foliage; purple flowers open in July
mound size: 18" high by 53" wide

spacing: 48"
leaves: 6 1/2" long by 5 1/2" wide; medium to dark green; very shiny underside; blade broadly ovate with a deeply lobed, puckered base; long, curved tip; margin lightly rippled; smooth texture; average substance; 8-9 vein pairs
flowers: July 10-31 (northern Illinois); bright purple with a distinct white petal margin from the base to the point where the petals separate; wide-open bell-shaped; 2 1/8" long by 1 3/8" wide; scapes up to 41" high; borne in the top 8-9" of the scapes; have not seen pods develop

comments: 'Peedee Elfin Bells' makes a neat, compact mound of green foliage, but the flower effect is its chief ornamental feature. Its bright purple flowers are bunched near the top of the relatively tall scapes and make quite a show in July. They resemble the flowers of its parent, *H. ventricosa*, though a bit shorter and squattier. In the landscape, it makes an excellent edging plant, low ground cover, and specimen plant.

'Peedee Elfin Bells' was registered in 1987 by Ursula Syre-Herz as a seedling of *H. ventricosa* and was among the first introductions in the "Peedee" series, named after a river in South Carolina.

seedlings, sports, and other related types:
none listed

other similar types:
'Betty', 'Bridegroom', 'Lakeside Black Satin', 'Lakeside Emerald Lights', 'Lakeside Neat Petite', 'Quilting Bee', 'Rosedale Barnie'

'Peedee Gold Flash'

key features: small, dense mound of narrow, gold-centered foliage

mound size: 12" high by 28" wide (up to 15" by 32")

spacing: 24"

leaves: 6 3/4" long by 2 3/4" wide; 1/8" to 1/4" wide green margin that sometimes streaks into the light to medium gold center; slightly shiny underside; blade narrowly elliptic-ovate and moderately wavy; smooth texture; average substance; 6-7 vein pairs

flowers: {registered as having an intense lavender color, opening from June 15 to July 15 in South Carolina} late July into August in northern areas

comments: 'Peedee Gold Flash' becomes a very attractive, fairly dense mound of gold-centered, wavy foliage. In the garden it acts like a bigger, wider-leaved version of 'Kabitan', of which it is a seedling. Its substance is average at best, but that should not discourage its usage as an edger or showy ground cover. It has become reasonably available in the last few years and is listed as being offered by 31 retail mail-order sources in the *Hosta Finder 2000* (Greene, 2000).

Ursula Syre-Herz registered 'Peedee Gold Flash' in 1987.

seedlings, sports, and other related types:

H. sieboldii 'Kabitan': parent of 'Peedee Gold Flash'; gold-centered, green-mgd lvs **(see page 420)**

'Peedee Apollo': {1996r, U. Syre-Herz; 'Peedee Gold Flash' X 'Krossa Regal'; gold lvs; purple fls on 50" scapes in Aug}

'Scarlet O'Hara': {1996r, U. Syre-Herz; 'Peedee Redlegs' X 'Peedee Gold Flash'; yellow foliage that changes to green; violet fls}

other similar types:

'Crown Prince', 'Lyme Regis'

'Permanent Wave'

key features: medium-large, flowing mound of very wavy, green foliage
mound size: 18" high by 54" wide

spacing: 48"
leaves: 12" long by 5" wide; medium green; dull top, moderately shiny underside; blade elliptic-ovate with very wavy margins, 10 or more per side; slightly corrugated; better than average substance; 7-8 vein pairs
flowers: mid-July into early August (Iowa); pale lavender with a slightly darker petal midrib; 2 1/4" long by 1 1/4" wide; funnel-shaped; scapes 33" high; many pods develop
comments: 'Permanent Wave' is, perhaps, the quintessential wavy-leaved hosta. The large waves (not small ripples as in a piecrust hosta) dominate the relatively narrow leaf and are noticeable from a good distance. The effect is further enhanced by the beautiful, flowing mound habit. 'Permanent Wave' makes an ideal specimen plant in the garden, placed in the middle or front of a shaded border where its characteristics can be fully appreciated. Though not extraordinary, the flowers are held erect, well above the foliage in good proportion to the leaf mound.

'Permanent Wave' is a Pauline Banyai origination registered in 1989 with unknown parentage. It would make an excellent component in any breeding program, especially when the goal is rippled leaf margins.
seedlings, sports, and other related types:
none listed
other similar types:
'Elvis Lives', 'Pineapple Poll'

'Piedmont Gold'

key features: large, rounded mound of bright gold, slug-resistant foliage
mound size: 25" high by 63" wide

spacing: 60"

leaves: 11" long by 9 1/4" wide; medium gold in open shade, yellowish gold in very bright light; a paler yellow fall color develops in mid to late October; thin bloom on underside; blade broadly oblong-ovate with a deeply lobed base and slight ripples along the margin; slight to moderate corrugation with maturity; good substance; 14-15 vein pairs

flowers: late June into mid-July; near-white with a pale lavender mid-petal stripe; 2 1/4" long by 1 1/2" wide; scapes just topping the foliage, up to 30-34" high; many pods develop

comments: 'Piedmont Gold' has long ranked near the top of gold-leaved *H. sieboldiana* cultivars. The foliage color tends to be consistent from early in the season to fall and appears bright under many types of lighting. As a young plant, the foliage appears smooth, but with maturity, the leaves become corrugated and the margins rippled.

'Piedmont Gold' is an origination of David Stone from the early 1970's and was registered for him by Piedmont Gardens (Waterbury, Connecticut) in 1982.

It can be utilized in hybridizing as either a pod or pollen parent. A number of sports have been found in the last dozen years with just about every variation of leaf color. Several green-centered, gold-margined sports and gold-centered, green-margined sports have been named and introduced. 'Evening Magic' and 'Lakeside Symphony' represent two that vary from the group. 'Evening Magic' has gold-centered foliage with a thin, white margin, that, unfortunately, develops the drawstring effect. 'Lakeside

339

Symphony' also has gold-centered foliage, but with a chartreuse margin. Both of these were registered in 1988 along with 'Everglades' (green-centered, gold-margined) and 'Moonshine' (gold-centered, green-margined). Unfortunately the last two were described incorrectly in the Spring '89 issue of *The Hosta Journal* (Eisel, 1989). In the last few years other 'Piedmont Gold' sports have been introduced. Many of these have leaf colors similar to 'Everglades' and 'Moonshine', but differ in the intensity or width of the margin.

seedlings, sports, and other related types:

'Cassandra': {1985r, W. Wagner; 'Petite' X 'Piedmont Gold'} low, dense mound of wavy, chartreuse to gold foliage; newer lvs gold, turning green during the summer; funnel-shaped, purple fls held well above the foliage on erect scapes, early to late July; many seed pods; attractive for its waviness and nice show of purple flowers

'David Stone': sport wi a green margin and gold center found and named by Alex Summers; center bright gold in spring; sometimes listed as 'Dave Stone'

'Evening Magic': {1988r, M. Zilis & T & Z N} t.c. sport; white-mgd, gold-centered lvs; develops the "drawstring" effect with maturity and should not be grown unless first flush of growth is removed

'Everglades': {1988r, R. Savory; sport} gold-margined, green-centered lvs, 11 1/2" by 10 1/2" wi a 1" to 1 1/4" gold mgn (14 vp); heavily corrugated; quite striking

'Hutch': {1995r, R. Stephens; "Wolcott' sdlg" X 'Piedmont Gold'; light green foliage}

'Lakeside San Kao': {1995r, M. Chastain; "Lakeside seedling" X 'Piedmont Gold'} light gold foliage

'Lakeside Symphony': {1988r, M. Chastain; sport} gold-centered, chartreuse-margined foliage; 27" by 50" md; 11" by 8" lvs (14 vp) wi a mgn up to 2 1/2" wide; lf center often turns creamy yellow by mid-summer, esp. in bright light; impressive specimen plant

'Mrs. Minky': {1993r, P. Hall; *H. minor* X 'Piedmont Gold'; medium yellow foliage}

'Moonshine': {1988r, R. Savory; sport} gold-centered, green-margined lvs

'Satisfaction': sport wi dark green center & gold margin; from Bridgewood Gardens

'Summer Serenade': {1998r, R. Klehm; sport} green-margined, gold-centered lvs; one of the best

'Tucker Tigers': {1993r, R. Stephens; 'Wolcott' sdlg X 'Piedmont Gold'; light green foliage}

'Tyler's Treasure': {1999r, C. Isaacs; 'Piedmont Gold'

sport} green-centered, gold-margined lvs, 11 1/4" by 8"
(11-12 vp); 1 1/4" gold margin; lf center very dark
green; from Moongate Farms in NC

other similar types:
'Abiqua Gold Shield', 'City Lights', 'Golden Nugget',
'Golden Waffles', 'Sea Gold Star', 'Sun Glow', 'Sunlight
Sister', 'Treasure', 'White Vision', 'Zounds'

'Pineapple Poll'
key features: medium-large, dense mound of narrow,
rippled, green foliage
mound size: 20" high by 66" wide (up to 27" by 68")

---

spacing: 60"
leaves: 10" long by
4" wide; medium to
dark green; thick
underside bloom;
blade narrowly ellip-
tic with a noticeably
rippled margin, 4-5
per side; smooth tex-
ture; good substance;
9 vein pairs
flowers: early to late
August; medium
lavender with a paler
petal margin; 2 3/8"
long by 1 5/8" wide;
scapes covered with
a thick bloom, gener-
ally 30-36" high but
as tall as 47"; 26

flowers per scape; very sparse pod formation with few
viable seeds

comments: When I first saw 'Pineapple Poll' in 1987 as the
unnamed hybrid *H. lancifolia* X *H. sieboldiana* in Peter
Ruh's collection, I was impressed with its dense mound
habit and heavily rippled leaves. While the narrow green
foliage somewhat resembles *H. lancifolia*, it gained its good
substance from *H. sieboldiana*. Where did the rippled character come from? That trait may indicate that the pod parent
may actually have been *H. sieboldii spathulata* rather than
the smooth-edged *H. lancifolia*. Regardless of parentage, it
certainly could substitute for the latter species in landscaping and provide a bit more resistance to slugs. 'Pineapple
Poll' also exhibits an excellent growth rate and is easy to
propagate by division.

It has limited breeding potential. I have attempted to set pods on it with only a minimal amount of success. Open-pollinated seed pods are very rare.

'Pineapple Poll' is an origination of Eric Smith that was registered by the British Hosta and Hemerocallis Society in 1988.

seedlings, sports, and other related types:

'Pineapple Upsidedown Cake': {1999r, M. Zilis & R. Solberg; 'Pineapple Poll' sport} developed at my nursery (Q & Z N); leaves all-green in spring changing to an attractive combination of gold centers and rippled green margins

other similar types:

H. laevigata, 'Permanent Wave', 'Sea Octopus', *H. sieboldii angustifolia*

'Pizzazz'

key features: medium-large mound of distinctive, creamy white-margined foliage

mound size: 21" high by 48" wide

spacing: 48"

leaves: 10 1/2" long by 8 1/2" wide; 3/4" to 1 1/4" wide margin that changes from yellow to creamy white and sometimes streaks into the dark green center (bluish early); thin underside bloom; blade broadly ovate with a distinct tip; blade often cupped or puckered downward and somewhat unruly; moderately corrugated; thick substance; 14-15 vein pairs

flowers: early to late July; near-white; 20-30" scapes; in dense clusters; many seed pods develop

comments: When a hosta is so distinct that it can be immediately identified in any garden, it should be appreciated. Such is the case for 'Pizzazz' which rates highly in many foliage categories including color, substance, and texture.

Its distinction is partially created by a combination of the broad blade shape that comes to an abrupt point and its tendency to be cupped. In the landscape, 'Pizzazz' can be utilized as a ground cover and makes an excellent specimen plant.

With all of its good traits and ability to form pods, 'Pizzazz' would be an excellent choice to incorporate into a breeding program.

Paul Aden registered 'Pizzazz' in 1986 as a hybrid of two seedlings.

seedlings, sports, and other related types:
none listed

other similar types:
'Carnival', 'Christmas Tree', 'Robert Frost', *H. ventricosa* 'Aureomarginata'

Hosta plantaginea
(Maruba Tama-no-Kanzashi; Fragrant Plantainlily)

key features: large mound of shiny green foliage; large, fragrant, nocturnal, white flowers in August
mound size: 25" high by 57" wide

spacing: 48"

leaves: 11" long by 7 3/8" wide; medium to light green; shiny top and underside; ovate to broadly ovate blade with a deeply lobed base and distinct tip; margin slightly wavy; smooth texture; no purple dots on petioles; average substance; 9-11 vein pairs

flowers: August 10 to September 3; pure white color; typically 4 3/4" long by 2 1/2" wide, but as much as 6 1/8" by 2 3/4"; trumpet-shaped; very fragrant; nocturnal, i.e. begins blooming at sundown, open until late afternoon of the sec-

343

ond day; scapes range from 18" to 34" high with most 25-30"; forms some seed pods, measuring 2 3/4" long by 3/8" wide, probably the largest of any hosta

comments: *Hosta plantaginea* stands out as perhaps the most horticulturally significant hosta of the last 200 years. As one of the first hostas introduced into cultivation in Europe, it also became an integral part of American gardening over 100 years ago. By the 1920's garden writers referred to this plant as long-established in American gardens. Along with *Hosta lancifolia*, *Hosta plantaginea* was commonly planted around homes in many U.S. cities in the east and midwest. *H. plantaginea* took on a unique identity because of the very large, fragrant flowers that bloomed in August. Besides the incredible number of scientific names that have been assigned to it at various times (*Funkia alba grandiflora, Funkia cordata, Funkia japonica, Funkia liliiflora, Funkia subcordata grandiflora, Hosta plantaginea cordata, Hosta plantaginea 'Grandiflora', Hosta subcordata, and Hosta subcordata grandiflora alba*), it also has been commonly known as the August Lily, Corfu Lily, Fragrant Plantainlily, Large-flowered Fragrant Plantainlily, Subcordate Plantainlily, and the White Plantainlily. In its native China, it is known as Yu-San (Maekawa, 1972). At one point someone even gave it a cultivar name, 'Fragrant Snow'. In the past, too, the name *Hosta plantaginea* 'Grandiflora' (or some form of this name) has been presumed to be a larger flowering version, but that is not the case.

The trumpet-shaped, white flowers bloom in August and are carried above the foliage in fairly dense clusters. It is the only true night blooming hosta. The flowers begin opening near sundown and are fully opened by around 8 p.m. They remain open into the next afternoon, but the exact timing is temperature dependent. If the daytime temperature remains

between 70-80°F, the flowers will stay open until about 3-4 p.m. of the next day. Subjected to 90°F or more and they begin to close by early afternoon. Many of its hybrids are "in-between", mid-morning bloomers, opening between 9 a.m. and 11 a.m. (most hosta flowers begin opening from 2-4 a.m.).

Though there seems to be some sterility in the clone of *Hosta plantaginea* that we have long grown in the U.S., this has not deterred many hybridizers from utilizing it. The list of hybrids related to it is extensive. Long-standing hybrids include 'Honeybells' and 'Royal Standard', the first significant American hosta cultivars. More recently 'Summer Fragrance', 'Invincible', 'Fragrant Bouquet', 'So Sweet', 'Emily Dickinson', and 'Fragrant Blue' have been introduced. Any hosta with fragrant flowers can be traced back to *Hosta plantaginea*, but there are also many non-fragrant *H. plantaginea* hybrids. One such plant is 'Raleigh Remembrance', a golden-leaved hybrid of 'Sum and Substance' X *H. plantaginea* that I introduced for the 1991 AHS convention. (An unnamed sibling, however, had shiny, dark green foliage with long, tubular, fragrant, white flowers.) Despite a few successes with *Hosta plantaginea* as a parent, a majority of my crosses with it have not formed pods. Interestingly open-pollinated seed pods seem to readily form, though a significant percentage of the seeds are nonviable.

After propagating *Hosta plantaginea* for several years in tissue culture, without seeing even a streak in a leaf, several sports developed in my lab. We introduced 'Ming Treasure' and 'Fragrant Flame' from this group. Walters Gardens also introduced two sports out of tissue culture, 'White Shoulders' and 'Heaven Scent'. 'Aphrodite' is a mutation of garden origin from China with beautiful double flowers.

In the landscape, *H. plantaginea* can be used in almost any way and has proven to be easy to grow. It has good sun tolerance and, at the same time, needs bright conditions for best performance. If grown in deep shade, the growth will be somewhat diminished and it may not flower. Another problem occurs in some areas of the country where late spring frosts cut back the emerging foliage. Usually the plant will recover, albeit the mound will be much reduced in size that year.

seedlings, sports, and other related types:

H. plantaginea 'Aphrodite': double-flowered form **(see page 349)**

'Austin Dickinson': {1992r, W. & E. Lachman; 'Resonance' X *H. plantaginea*} med-sized md of white-margined (creamy yellow early), green-centered foliage; fragr fls in late summer

'Bennie McRae': {1989r, N. Suggs; *H. plantaginea* sdlg; produces fragr lav fls} 24" by 60" md; light to med green lvs, 11 1/2" by 7" (11-12 vp); flowers in August; similar to 'Honeybells'

'Buckwheat Honey': {1984r, R. Benedict; 'Ginko Craig' X *H. plantaginea*} 22" by 48" md; lvs 10" by 4 3/4" (9 vp); 2" long, med purple, fragrant fls in mid-Aug on 32-46" sc; fls only slightly open

'Chelsea Ore': {1989r, J. Compton & Chelsea Physic Garden; *H. plantaginea* sdlg} green-mgd, gold-centered lvs

'Curly Top': {1985r, R. Benedict; 'Ginko Craig' X *H. plantaginea*} small mound (9" by 20") of thin-substanced, narrow, wavy, green lvs (5" by 1 1/8" with 4 vp); purple fls in Aug; not especially exciting

'Emily Dickinson': {1987r, W. & E. Lachman; 'Neat Splash' sdlg X *H. plantaginea*} white-mgd, green-centered lvs; fragr fls **(see page 144)**

'Flower Power': {1987r, K. Vaughn; *H. nigrescens* X *H. plantaginea*} large, semi-upr md of shiny, br green foliage; 28" by 60" md; lvs 14" by 11" (12-13 vp) wi thick substance and a smooth texture; 3" fragr fls on 48" sc, mid-July into Aug; impressive pl wi traits of both parents

'Forever Green': {1994r, J. Dishon; *H. rupifraga* X *H. plantaginea*; dk gr lvs; fragr lav fls}

'Fragrant Blue': {1988r, P. Aden; hybrid of two sdlgs} fragr fls, blue foliage **(see page 168)**

H. plantaginea 'Fragrant Flame': {1988r, M. Zilis & T & Z N; sport} t.c. mutation; streaked foliage; tends to produce white-centered or margined forms

'Heaven Scent': {1988r, Walters Gardens; sport} lvs center strkd, ylw-green margins; not stable

'Honeybells': {*H. plantaginea* X *H. sieboldii* hybrid} lg md of wavy green foliage; fragr lav fls in Aug **(see page 231)**

'Invincible': {1986r, P. Aden; hybrid of two sdlgs} green lvs, fragr lav fls **(see page 238)**

'Iron Gate Bouquet': {1983r, V. Sellers} *H. plantaginea* sdlg; dk green lvs; fragr purple fls **(see page 240)**

'Iron Gate Delight': {1981r, V. Sellers; *H. plantaginea* X 'Tokudama Aureonebulosa'} streaked lvs; fragr pale purple fls **(see page 241)**

'Iron Gate Supreme': {1980r, V. Sellers; *H. plantaginea* X 'Tokudama Aureonebulosa'} streaked foliage; fragr, pale lav fls **(see page 242)**

H. plantaginea var. *japonica*: differs from the species in having narrower, wavier foliage and narrower flower petals; have seen it in a few American collections

'Julia Gaede': {1994r, S. & C. Gaede; sport} lvs with thin white margins, green center

'Marbled Bouquet': {1988r, C. Falstad; sport wi streaked foliage} haven't seen in a garden

H. plantaginea 'Ming Treasure': {1999r, M. Zilis; *H. plantaginea* sport} lvs green-centered with 1/4" wide margins that change from chartreuse to gold to white, depending upon time of year and exposure to light; 1997 Q & Z N introduction

'Mistress Mabel': {1995r, W. & E. Lachman; ('Beatrice' F6 sdlg X 'Blue Moon') X *H. plantaginea*} lvs creamy white-mgd wi a shiny, dk gr cntr

'Old Faithful': {1991r, W. Brincka & O. Petryszyn; *H. plantaginea* X 'Regal Rhubarb'} large, fountain-like md of shiny, apple green foliage; red scapes and petioles; good sun tolerance

'Raleigh Remembrance': M. Zilis 1988 hybrid of 'Sum and Substance' X *H. plantaginea*; introduced at the 1991 AHS meeting in Raleigh, NC; very shiny, gold foliage; lav fls not fragrant

'Rippled Honey': hybrid of *H. ventricosa* X *H. plantaginea* from Herb Benedict; med-lg md of shiny, dark green foliage; fragrant, pale lav fls in Aug; closely resembles 'Invincible'

'Royal Standard': *H. plantaginea* seedling; lg md of shiny gr lvs; fragr white fls in Aug **(see page 371)**

'Seventh Heaven': {1994r, J. Kulpa; 'Kevin Vaughn' X *H. plantaginea*} med-lg md of streaked and mottled lvs, 8 1/2" by 6" (10 vp); fragr, white fls, late July into August; has sported to white-margined, green-centered 'Diana Remembered' {1997r, J. Kulpa}, 'Heavenly Green' {1997r, J. Kulpa; bluish green foliage}, & 'John Kulpa' {1999r, J. Kulpa; lf green-mgd, center pale ylw to creamy white}

'Spit Shine': {1986r, R. O'Harra, *H. plantaginea* sdlg; shiny, green foliage} rarely grown or seen

H. plantaginea f. *stenantha*: listed by Maekawa (1972) as having narrower flower petals; have never seen or know of anyone who has

'Summer Fragrance': {1983r, K. Vaughn; "Vaughn 73-2" X *H. plantaginea*} white-margined lvs, fragr fls; 26" by 57" md; lvs 12" by 8 3/4" wi a med green center & a 1/4" to 3/8" mgn that changes from yellow to creamy white; v pale lav fls, mid-Aug into Sept on sc 36" or higher; the first cultivar to combine white-margined foliage with fragrant flowers

'Sweet Marjorie': {1983r, R. Benedict; 'Ginko Craig' X *H. plantaginea*} dense md of slightly shiny, wavy, med green foliage; 26" by 58" md; lvs 9 3/8" by 5 3/4" (9 vp); fragrant, narrow, 3" long fls in mid-Aug on 42" sc; fast-growing

'Sweet Susan': {1986r by C. Williams for F. Williams; *H. sieboldii* X *H. plantaginea*} 24" by 51" md of green lvs, 10 1/4" by 6 1/4" (8-9 vp); fragr lav fls in Aug on sc up to 40"; introduced by Fairmount Gardens in 1966 (Nesmith, 1966)

'Warwick Essence': {1993r, L. Jones; 'Northern Halo' X *H. plantaginea*} tall, arching mound of bluish green foliage; md 31" by 51"; lvs 11 1/2" by 9" (14 vp); elegant

'White Shoulders': {1988r, Walters Gardens; *H. plantaginea* sport} white-margined foliage; created much hype when introduced because of the wide, white margins but has failed as a garden plant, i.e. the margins disappear

Other cultivars related to *Hosta plantaginea* include:
'Abba Fragrant Cloud', 'Bette Davis Eyes', 'Dee's Golden Jewel', 'Fragrant Bouquet', 'Fragrant Gold', 'Fried Bananas', 'Fried Green Tomatoes', 'Garden Bouquet', 'Guacamole', 'Hoosier Harmony', 'Iron Gate Glamour', 'Lakeside Emerald Lights', 'Peedee Laughing River', 'Red Stepper', 'Rising Sun', 'Royal Accolade', 'Savannah', 'Slick Willie', 'So Sweet', 'Sombrero', 'Sugar Babe', 'Sugar and Cream', 'Sweet Bo Peep', 'Sweet Jill', 'Sweet Standard', 'Sweet Sunshine', 'Sweetie'

other similar types:
Hosta plantaginea is so distinct that only 'Aphrodite', 'Rôyal Standard', 'Invincible', and 'Fried Green Tomatoes' would be acceptable substitutes for it in the landscape.

Hosta plantaginea 'Aphrodite' (Yae-no-Maruba Tama-no-Kanzashi)

key features: large mound of shiny green foliage; double, fragrant, white flowers in August

mound size: 24" high by 60" wide

spacing: 48"

leaves: 11" long by 7 3/8" wide; medium to light, shiny green; shiny underside; ovate to broadly ovate shape with a deeply lobed base and distinct tip; margin slightly wavy; smooth texture; no purple dots on petioles; average substance; 9-11 vein pairs

flowers: early to late August; pure white color; 5" long by 2 1/2" wide; petaloid stamens and extra petals creates double-flowered effect; very fragrant; nocturnal; 18-34" scapes; anthers, filaments, style often misshapen; have never seen a seed pod develop

comments: To most hosta collectors in the 1980's, 'Aphrodite' was nothing more than a picture and description from Maekawa's monograph in an early issue of *The American Hosta Society Bulletin* (Maekawa, 1972). Then in the late 1980's I heard reports of 'Aphrodite' being smuggled from China into Germany. Finally, a few showed up in American collections. By August 1991, I was counting petaloid stamens and extra petals on Herb Benedict's flowering clump. Since that time, 'Aphrodite' has become common among not only hosta collectors, but at just about any garden center or nursery that sells hostas. Through the efforts of several tissue culture labs and nurseries, thousands of 'Aphrodite' have been disseminated throughout the U.S. and Europe.

As a foliage plant 'Aphrodite' is no different from *H. plantaginea* and it can be utilized in the same ways in the landscape. Once in bloom, though, it takes on its distinctive character. The fully double flowers are very fragrant and very large. The only problem that I've encountered with

'Aphrodite' is that flowers on young plants sometimes do not completely open and the scapes turn brown. Usually this occurs under dry conditions. Given the proper growing environment and a few years to mature, the flowers will open fully.

So far, I haven't heard of any successful hybridizing efforts using 'Aphrodite'. I have examined numerous flowers and have not found viable pollen or a normal pistil.

Though its origins are obscure, it apparently originated as a garden sport in China. I have heard reports of old plantings in Beijing.

seedlings, sports, and other related types:

H. plantaginea 'Venus': {1993r, Walters Gardens & C. Falstad; sport of 'Aphrodite'} extra double flowers; often do not open properly due to the large numbers of petals; not yet widely grown

other similar types:

'Royal Super': double-flowered, variegated sport of 'Royal Standard'; from Clarence Falstad & Walters Gardens; lvs white-margined, sometimes heavily streaked, 7 1/2" by 4 1/4"; md 24" by 36"

'Platinum Tiara'
key features: dense, medium-sized mound of gold-centered, white-margined foliage
mound size: 11" high by 29" wide

spacing: 24"
leaves: 4 3/8" long by 3 1/8" wide; 1/8" wide, white margin that produces an occasional gray green streak into the gold center; shiny underside; ovate blade; slight corrugation; thin substance; 7 vein pairs
flowers: mid-July to early August; pale purple; 2" long by 1 1/4" wide; scapes 11-19"; sparse pod formation
comments: 'Platinum Tiara' can be used as an edging plant or low ground

cover. It is brightest in May and early June, but the gold center tends to become greener after that. The contrast between the white margin and gold center is nice but not especially striking.

Walters Gardens registered 'Platinum Tiara' as a sport of 'Golden Scepter' in 1987.

seedlings, sports, and other related types:
'Heavenly Tiara': {1998r, Walters Gardens; 'Grand Tiara' sport wi white-mgd, gold-cntrd lvs}

other similar types:
'Shere Khan'

'Popo'
key features: small mound of bluish green foliage
mound size: 8" high by 20" wide

spacing: 18"

leaves: 3 1/4" long by 2 5/8" wide; bluish green early, medium green by mid-summer; moderate underside bloom; blade ovate and slightly wavy; smooth texture; average substance; 7 vein pairs

flowers: late June into mid-July; lavender; scapes up to 17" high; forms seed pods

comments: Russ O'Harra introduced 'Popo' back in the 1980's. It created interest amongst hosta enthusiasts not only for its small-sized mound of bluish foliage, but for its unusual name. It can be utilized in a shaded rock garden or as a low edging plant. 'Popo' was registered in 1993 by Frank Riehl for Russ O'Harra with unknown parentage.

seedlings, sports, and other related types:
'Blue Monday': {1998r, R. Solberg; 'Peedee Graymulkin' X 'Popo'} heart-shaped, blue-green, thick-substanced lvs, 4 1/2" by 4" (10 vp)

351

other similar types:
'Baby Bunting', 'Gum Drop'

Hosta pulchella (Ubatake Giboshi)
key features: dwarf-sized mound of shiny, dark green foliage
mound size: 5" high by 15" wide

spacing: 12"
leaves: 3 1/2" long by 1 1/4" wide; shiny, dark green; whitish shiny underside; ovate blade; slightly wavy margins; smooth texture; better than average substance; 4-5 vein pairs
flowers: mid to late August; medium purple; 2" long by 1" wide; 6-18" scapes; fertile
comments: *Hosta pulchella* may be the smallest of all hosta species. It makes a neat, dwarf-sized mound of shiny, dark green foliage that can be effectively used in a shaded rock garden. Yoshimichi Hirose informed me that it is found growing on Mt. Ubatake at the eastern side of Kyushu Island but not many other places in Japan.

Hosta pulchella can be used in breeding programs for its dwarf size, late flowers and shiny, dark green foliage. Seedlings often exhibit excellent substance. An early blooming (June-July) form is also known in Japan.

seedlings, sports, and other related types:

'Cody': {1996r, R. Solberg; 'Shining Tot' X *H. venusta*} low md of dk green foliage; a neat small plant

'Gaijin': {1995r, M. Zilis & W. Zumbar} small (6" by 15") md of shiny foliage wi thin, yellow margins; lvs 3 3/4" by 1 1/4" (4-5 vp); fls in Aug on sc, 19" high; close to *H. pulchella* 'Kifukurin' but the fls a redder purple; a Japanese pl that I received as 'Ogon Hime' which is not correct

H. pulchella 'Kifukurin' (*H. pulchella* 'Aureomarginata'): attractive, low md of yellow-margined foliage; 12" by

'Queen Josephine'

key features: medium-sized mound of creamy yellow-margined foliage

mound size: 17" high by 42" wide

spacing: 36"

leaves: 7" long by 5 1/2" wide; 1" wide yellow to creamy yellow margin; dark green center; shiny top and underside; ovate blade with a slightly lobed base; slightly wavy margins; smooth texture; good substance; 10 vein pairs

flowers: late July into mid-August; pale purple; 2 1/2" long; scapes 33" high

comments: During a 1987 visit to Wade & Gatton Nurseries, Van showed me an interesting, thick-leaved plant called 'Josephine', a 'Neat Splash' seedling from Bob Kuk. The variegation pattern was fairly inconsistent, but its shininess and substance were notable. During a visit to Herb and Dorothy Benedict's garden in 1991, Bob surprised everyone present with a beautiful, creamy yellow-margined plant that turned out to be the stable form of 'Josephine'. Several names were tossed about with Dorothy Benedict selecting the name 'Queen Josephine' as most appropriate. Bob Kuk registered 'Queen Josephine' in 1991 and it certainly stands out as one of the best introductions from his fine breeding program.

In the garden it grows into a medium-sized mound of foliage. The leaves can be best described as having consistent, neat margins that attractively contrast the dark green center. 'Queen Josephine' exhibits a rapid growth rate both in the ground and in containers and can be used as a ground cover or specimen plant in the garden.

In a breeding program, 'Queen Josephine' can be utilized as a source of thick substance, possibly producing variegated seedlings and/or purple flowers.

357

seedlings, sports, and other related types:

'Joseph': {1990r, R. Kuk; sport of 'Josephine'} shiny, dark green foliage; slightly more vigorous than 'Queen Josephine'; mound reached 17 1/2" by 43" in one garden versus 15" by 34" for 'Queen Josephine' growing side-by-side

'Josephine': {1987r, Kuk's Forest; 'Neat Splash' sdlg} "mother plant" of 'Queen Josephine' & 'Joseph'; lvs green wi an inconsistent pattern of creamy yellow streaks

other similar types:

'Coquette', 'Ground Master', 'Neat Splash Rim', 'Scooter'

'Don Stevens': Mildred Seaver introduction from around 1991; 17" by 40" md of foliage with a yellow to creamy white margin (3/4" wide) & a dark green center; lvs 9" by 6" (9-11 vp); pale purple fls, early to late August on 31" scapes that are deep red in the upper half; sports include 'Don Juan' (green-mgd, white-centered) & 'Don Quixote' (green mgns, streaked center)

'Raspberry Sorbet'

key features: low, dense mound of shiny, wavy green foliage; purplish red scapes

mound size: 12" high by 34" wide

spacing: 24"

leaves: 7" long by 3 3/4" wide; medium to dark green; shiny top; whitish shiny underside; blade oblong-ovate with a puckered base and very wavy margins, 4-5 per side; smooth texture; petiole base bright red; average substance; 8 vein pairs

flowers: early to late August; bluish purple with white petal margins, base to tip; 2 1/8" long by 1" wide; narrow funnel shape with reflexed tips; 20" scapes purplish red, redder in the upper 7"; red pedicels

comments: While wandering through our greenhouses a few years ago, I spotted a hosta at a distance in full flower with bright red scapes. Once I calmed down and read the label, I found it to be a seedling of *H. rupifraga* X 'Shining Tot' that had been hybridized at our nursery in 1987.

Since then, I have also grown to appreciate the shiny, very wavy, dark green foliage which rapidly becomes a low dense mound that can be very useful as an edger or ground

359

cover, even as a specimen to show off the beautiful flower scapes. The upper portion of the scape is intensely red, enhancing the ornamental effect of the unusual bluish purple flowers.

'Raspberry Sorbet' was introduced for sale in 1995. It was registered in 1999 and credited to Doug Lohman and Mark Zilis.

seedlings, sports, and other related types:
none listed

other similar types:
'Brandywine', 'Chopsticks', 'Cinnamon Bun', 'Cinnamon Sticks', 'Cinnamon and Sugar'

Hosta rectifolia (Tachi Giboshi)
key features: medium-sized mound of green foliage; late season, purple flowers
mound size: 14" high by 32" wide

spacing: 30"
leaves: 6 3/4" long by 3 1/16" wide; medium green color; very shiny underside; blade narrowly ovate to elliptic shape with a moderately wavy margin; smooth texture; thin substance; 6 vein pairs
flowers: mid-August into September; medium purple with darker mid-petal striping; darker purple in bud; 2 1/4" long by 1 1/4" wide; slightly inflated funnel shape; scapes as high as 41" in a mature clump; bracts tightly wrapped around the scape; fertile

comments: *Hosta rectifolia* is notable for its late season purple flowers and makes a medium-sized mound of green foliage. Maekawa (1973) listed it as being native to northern Japan, i.e. northern Honshu and Hokkaido. Over the spectrum of varieties, cultivars and seedlings associated with *Hosta rectifolia*, it is safe to say that great diversity can be found. The upright mound habit and large size found in

'Ginbuchi Tachi', 'Kinbuchi Tachi' and 'Ogon Tachi' are not generally found in the many green forms that exist. Nevertheless, the flowering habits of all of these forms bear much in common.

The variegated types of *H. rectifolia* show great potential for a variety of purposes. Ornamentally they stand out in any collection because of their colorful foliage and strong, upright habit. The tall scapes of purple flowers in late season, too, add to their beauty. These characteristics make them ideal subjects for a breeding program. Also helpful are the large number of seed pods that generally develop. Seedlings with white flowers are possible.

seedlings, sports, and other related types:

H. rectifolia australis: 11" by 27" md of pale green lvs, 6" by 4" (9 vp); thin underside bloom; winged petioles

'Chartreuse': {1998r by P. Ruh for E. Fisher & G. Holly} dvlpd in 1955; compact md of foliage that changes from chartreuse to bright gold in early May (northern Illinois), then to med green by late May; 16" by 41" md; lvs 8" by 4 1/2" (8-10 vp); med purple fls on 21-31" sc, July 24-August 10; incredible show of brilliant gold lvs in spring; one of the first American cvs; probably an *H. rectifolia* sdlg

H. rectifolia 'Chionea': low md of white-mgd foliage; resembles 'Ginko Craig'

'Ginbuchi Tachi': white-margined form of the species from Japan; striking mound of upright leaves that have a thick, white margin; much like 'Kinbuchi Tachi Giboshi' but with a purer white margin; also called *H. rectifolia albo-marginata* but the name "Ginbuchi" is used by Watanabe (1985)

'Gosan Gold Sword': {1989r, W. Schmid; *H. alismifolia* X *H. rectifolia* 'Ogon'; lvs emerge yellow green, turning yellow}

'Hirao Grande': {1997r, S. Hirao, R. Lydell & P. Ruh; *H. rectifolia* sdlg} 18" by 46" md of med green lvs, 12 1/2" by 5 1/4"; attractive in flower; formerly "Davidson 135"

'Kinbuchi Tachi' (*H. rectifolia* 'Kinbuchi Tachi' or *H. rectifolia* 'Aureomarginata'): semi-upright mound of creamy yellow-margined foliage; very wide margins sharply contrast the shiny, dark green center; 23" by 32" md, lvs 8 1/2" by 4 1/4" (9 vp) wi a 1/2" mgn that changes from yellow to creamy white; elliptic-shaped blade; bright purple fls on 40" sc, mid-Aug into Sept; many seed pods; very striking plant that should become a "classic"; from Japan

'Montreal': {1983r, Le Jardin botanique de Montreal; possibly *H. rectifolia* X *H. ventricosa*} formerly sold as

'Japonica Blue'; 17" by 44" md of thin, green lvs, 6" by 3 1/2" (6-7 vp); large mass of purple fls, July 22- Aug 18 (n Illinois), on 20-36" sc; fast growth rate; fertile

'Mount Royal': {1983r, Le Jardin botanique de Montreal; possibly *H. rectifolia* X *H. ventricosa*} formerly sold as 'Japonica White'; 14" by 28" md of thin, narrow, green lvs, 6 3/4" by 3 3/4" (5-6 vp); white fls produced on many 36" sc from mid to late August; notable for floriferousness & fast growth rate

H. rectifolia 'Nakai': narrow foliage that has a dark green center and creamy white border; purple fls in Aug; md 12" by 26"; lvs 7 1/2" by 2 1/2" wi a thin, 1/16", white mgn; the designation of "Nakai" indicates the person who originally described the species and was mistakenly assigned to this plant

'Ogon Tachi' (*H. rectifolia* 'Ogon'): striking, semi-upright mound of golden foliage; 20" by 39" md; lvs 11" by 6" (10 vp); med to br purple fls on 40-58" sc, mid-Aug into Sept; distinctive, purple-striped bracts subtend the flowers (see the Fall '98 issue of *The Hosta Journal*, p. 20, Figures 9-10 for photos of this plant in flower); strikingly beautiful in full bloom with a good contrast betw the purple fls and golden lvs; from Japan

H. rectifolia pruinosa: 12" by 25" md of dk green lvs (bluish in spring); moderate underside bloom, lvs 6 1/2" by 3 1/4" (8 vp)

'Snowstorm': {1980r, L. Simpers; sdlg of *H. rectifolia*} low md of green lvs; white fls in Aug

'Tall Boy': {1983r, Le Jardin botanique de Montreal; *H. rectifolia* X *H. ventricosa*} lg md of green foliage; v tall scapes bearing lav fls in Aug; sibling to 'Montreal' & 'Mount Royal' **(see page 449)**

'Vilmoriniana': {1999r by P. Ruh for Vilmorin Et Andrieux; parentage unknown} long-standing cv. from the 1960's; med-sized md of green lvs, 5 3/8" by 4 3/4" (7 vp); med purple fls from dark purple buds on 30" sc, early to late Aug; mainly of historical interest, but a nice show of purple fls in Aug; shows many *H. rectifolia* traits & is similar to 'Montreal'; labelled 'Vilmoriana' for many years

H. rectifolia 'Yellow Surprise': {1983r, K. Hensen; *H. rectifolia* sdlg wi yellowish green foliage that turns green} probably the same as 'Chartreuse'

other similar types:

'Decorata Normalis', *H. sieboldii angustifolia*

'Regal Rhubarb'

key features: large, semi-upright mound of green foliage with reddish petioles
mound size: 26" high by 47" wide (up to 31" by 55")

spacing: 48"

leaves: 14" long by 9 1/4" wide; shiny, bright green; outside of petioles reddish, often into midrib of blade; thin underside bloom; blade ovate; heavily rippled margin, more than 15 per edge; moderate corrugation; good substance; 16 vein pairs

flowers: very late July into mid-August; pale purple, darker in bud; 3" long by 1 1/8" wide; scapes up to 48" high, reddish for lowest 14" or so

comments: 'Regal Rhubarb' is notable for its intense purplish red petioles, but as a landscape plant it has value for its vase-shaped mound habit, large size and tall flower scapes. The petioles are interesting but the color can only be appreciated at a close distance or in a leaf show.

'Regal Rhubarb' was registered by Van Sellers in 1983 with unknown parentage.

seedlings, sports, and other related types:
'Old Faithful': {1991r, W. Brincka & O. Petryszyn; *H. plantaginea* X 'Regal Rhubarb'} large, fountain-like md of shiny, apple green foliage; red scapes and petioles; good sun tolerance

other similar types:
'Flower Power', *H. montana*, 'Tall Boy'

'Regal Ruffles'

key features: large mound of lightly rippled, grayish green foliage

mound size: 30" high by 75" wide (up to 39 1/2" by 99")

spacing: 72"

leaves: 15 1/4" long by 12" wide; grayish green; thick underside bloom; blade broadly ovate; margin slightly rippled; moderate to heavily corrugated; good substance; 16 vein pairs

flowers: mid-June into early July (Indianapolis); near-white; 2 3/4" long by 1 1/2" wide; funnel-shaped; in dense clusters; scapes 30-40" high; fertile

comments: 'Regal Ruffles' makes a tremendous background plant in a shaded border or, even better, as the focal point of an island bed. The mature specimen of 'Regal Ruffles' in the Wade and Gatton collection is a sight to behold. At 39 1/2" high by 99" wide, it reaches incredible proportions for even a large-sized hosta. When this clump is in bloom, the flower scapes just reach the top of the foliage mound, creating an interesting effect. From the name, you'd expect incredible marginal ruffling, but that is not the case. The ripples are only slight, but that is incidental to the value of this truly magnificent plant.

'Regal Ruffles' came out of the breeding program of Eldren Minks and is a hybrid of 'Ruffles' X *H. sieboldiana* 'Elegans'. It was registered in 1980.

seedlings, sports, and other related types:

'Babbling Brook': hybrid of a sibling to 'Tutu' X 'Regal Ruffles'; semi-upr med-lg md of rippled, green leaves (bluish early); lvs 14" by 11" (16 vp); narrow funnel-shaped, pale purple fls in July on tall scapes that create a 90 degree arc as flowering proceeds; attractive foliage but the flower habit is not (cut them off); a Kevin Vaughn origination introduced for sale by Hatfield Gardens in 1992

'Crested Reef': {1975r, E. Minks; 'August Moon' X 'Ruffles'} 25" by 66" md of irregularly wavy, green foliage; lvs pucker downward and measure 10" by 8 1/2" (14 vp); lav fls, July 1-20 on 36" sc; impressive lg md of wavy foliage, but rarely seen anymore

'Ruffles': {1986r by AHS for D. Lehman; unknown parentage} 28" by 58" md of distinctly rippled, green lvs, 12" by 7" (12 vp), wi a thin underside bloom; pale lav fls on sc up to 53" high in July; outstanding for marginal ripples; parent of 'Regal Ruffles'; excellent breeding pl

other similar types:
'Blue Piecrust', 'Fortunei Gigantea', 'Green Piecrust'

'Regal Splendor'
key features: large, vase-shaped mound of creamy margined foliage; 5-foot scapes of lavender flowers; sport of 'Krossa Regal'
mound size: 30" high by 72" wide

spacing: 60"

leaves: 11" long by 7" wide; 1/4" to 3/4" wide yellow margin that turns creamy white; thick underside bloom; ovate blade shape; wavy margins; smooth texture; thick substance; 12-13 vein pairs

flowers: same as 'Krossa Regal': late July into mid-August; medium lavender; 2 1/4" long by 1 1/4" wide; funnel-shaped; scape height ranges from 36 to 60"; pod sterile

comments: 'Regal Splendor' was registered as a sport of 'Krossa Regal' by Walters Gardens in 1987. Like its mother plant, it makes a spectacular, vase-shaped mound of foliage with the added benefit of attractive variegation. The margin is often much wider near the base and toward mid-leaf, narrower near the tip and can vary in width from plant to plant.

This variability, however, should not be viewed negatively as it certainly does not affect its ornamental value. In fact 'Regal Splendor' has become a significant cultivar in the nursery trade and should continue to increase in popularity.

seedlings, sports, and other related types:

'Tom Schmid': {1995r, T. Schmid; 'Krossa Regal' sport wi pure white-mgd, bl-green-centered lvs}

'Trail of Tears': {1999r, M. Soules; sport; lvs streaked green & ylw in center, yellow-mgd}

other similar types:

'Sagae': can be mistaken for 'Regal Splendor' at a distance and when less than mature

'Snow Crust'

'Robert Frost'

key features: large mound of creamy white-margined foliage

mound size: 24" high by 50" wide

spacing: 48"

leaves: 11" long by 8 1/2" wide; 1/2" to 1" wide margin that changes from gold to creamy white; bluish green center; moderate underside bloom; broadly ovate blade with a deeply lobed base; slightly wavy and generally smooth-textured; good substance; 13 vein pairs

flowers: late June into July; whitish; very pale lavender in bud; 20-30" scapes

comments: A truly impressive plant for its large mound of foliage with very wide, creamy white borders, 'Robert Frost' is another fine Bill and Eleanor Lachman introduction. The contrast between the creamy margin and bluish center is also outstanding. In the landscape it can be utilized as a specimen or background plant. The Lachmans registered Robert Frost in 1988 as a hybrid of 'Banana Sundae' X 'Frances Williams'.

seedlings, sports, and other related types:
'Eleanor Lachman': {1995r, W. & E. Lachman; ('Neat Splash' X 'Flamboyant') X 'Robert Frost'} creamy white-centered, dark green-margined foliage

other similar types:
'Formal Attire', 'Gil Jones', 'Heart's Content', 'Showboat', *H. s.* 'Northern Exposure', *H. s.* 'Northern Halo'

'Rock Princess'
key features: small mound of green foliage; name used for two plants
mound size: 10" high by 30" wide

spacing: 18"
leaves: 4 1/4" long by 2 7/8" wide; medium green; dull top, shiny underside; blade ovate with slightly wavy margins; smooth texture; average substance; 6-7 vein pairs
flowers: late June into mid-July; pale purple; funnel-shaped; scapes 28" high
comments: I have seen two different plants labelled 'Rock Princess'. The above described plant (also pictured) is related to *Hosta nakaiana* and is more commonly found in hosta collections. It blooms in July and makes a medium-sized mound of green foliage. The other resembles *Hosta gracillima*, becoming an 8" by 20" mound of green leaves that measure 3" by 1 3/4" (3-5 vein pairs). It produces purple flowers from early to mid-September on scapes up to 15" high. Both plants make good rock garden subjects and can be effectively used as edging plants.

I suspect that part of the confusion may stem from a translation of the Japanese name for *H. gracillima*, Hime Iwa

Giboshi, being applied to an *H. gracillima* seedling at some point. "Hime" usually means dwarf when applied to plants, but can also be interpreted as "princess". "Iwa", of course, means rock. Reverse the two and you have "Rock Princess". The name probably was separately applied to a *Hosta nakaiana* seedling, hence the confusion. Needless to say, 'Rock Princess' is not a registered name with the AHS.

seedlings, sports, and other related types:
none listed
other similar types:
H. nakaiana, H. gracillima

Hosta rohdeifolia (Omoto Giboshi)
key features: medium-sized mound of narrow, white-margined foliage; late season purple flowers
mound size: 14" high by 30" wide

spacing: 30"
leaves: 6 3/4" long by 2 3/4" wide; 1/8" to 1/4" wide margin that changes from yellow to creamy white by mid-summer; medium green center color; moderately shiny underside, dull top surface; narrowly elliptic shape; smooth texture; thin substance; 5-6 vein pairs
flowers: mid to late August; light purple color with darker striping in mid-petal and a whitish margin from the throat to mid-petal; 2" long by 1 1/2" wide; semi-bell shape; emerge from a ball-like scape bud; noticeable bracts; scapes up to 43" high; fertile
comments: Plants imported from Japan as the true Omoto Giboshi make a low mound of narrow, elliptic-shaped foliage. The thin margins change from creamy yellow to white as the season progresses. I have also seen Omoto Giboshi in Japanese collections. All of them closely resemble what we had grown in our country for many years as *H. helonioides albo-picta*. The foliage and flowering characteristics of this "old" *H. helonioides albo-picta* match

Maekawa's description and photographs of *H. rhodeifolia* (Maekawa, 1973, pictures on p. 33, description on pp. 41-42). These traits include the changes in margin color, number of vein pairs, shape of the blade, foliage size, floral bracts, flower color, flower shape, flower number, flower size, and on and on. Schmid (1991) seems to dispute this conclusion on the basis of anther color (purple for the old *H. helonioides albo-picta*, yellowish white for the true Omoto Giboshi). Further comparisons should be made to confirm or deny my original claim, despite what I consider overwhelming observational evidence.

One plant that had long been grown in the U.S. under the name *Hosta rhodeifolia* has been confirmed to be 'Gloriosa'. The mistake in labelling probably occurred when the original plants from Japan were sent without a proper name. By matching the plants to information in Maekawa's monograph, it is easy to see how the confusion occurred.

The exact spelling of the specific epithet (species name) has also been in dispute for a while. George Schmid (1991) points out that the long-standing name, *Hosta rhodeifolia,* is in error. His reasoning is roughly that the Japanese name, Omoto Giboshi, indicates that this species must resemble the perennial *Rohdea*, which is called "Omoto" in Japanese. To correct the misspelling, he changed the name of the green-leaved form to *Hosta rohdeifolia f. viridis* and gave the name *Hosta rohdeifolia* 'Rohdeifolia' to the white-margined type. From a practical standpoint, these changes have led to some confusion. The name *Hosta rhodeifolia*, as representing a white-margined plant, was long-standing and any change to it was not necessary. The mistake could have been noted as an interesting historical fact and left at that. At the same time, however, I do not advocate going back to "*Hosta rhodeifolia*". For nursery and garden purposes, I suggest utilizing the name *Hosta rohdeifolia* for the white-margined plant and not bother with the overkill, *Hosta rohdeifolia* 'Rohdeifolia', as suggested by Schmid (1991). It can be used much in the same way as the name *Hosta sieboldii* represents another white-margined "species".

As for the plant itself, it can be effectively used as an edging plant and exhibits a fast growth rate, so division is fairly easy. It does form seed and has some redeeming qualities, making it useful in breeding work.

seedlings, sports, and other related types:

Hosta rohdeifolia f. viridis: listed as the green-leaved form that can be found in the wild in Japan (Schmid, 1991); rare

'Sugar Pie': {1998r, R. Snyder; sport of 'Rohdeifolia'; sm mound size; med gr-centered, white-mgd lvs}

'White Border': small mound of lance-shaped, white-margined foliage; 12" by 23" md, 5" by 1 1/2" lvs (6 vp); purple fls in Aug; imported from Japan in the 1970's; identical to *H. rohdeifolia*

other similar types:

Hosta rectifolia chionea: similar mound of white-margined foliage, but leaf blade more distinctly elliptic and margin pure white, versus creamy for *H. rohdeifolia*

'Royal Accolade'

key features: medium-large mound of gold-centered foliage; fragrant white flowers in August; sport of 'Royal Standard'

mound size: 23" high by 41" wide

spacing: 40"

leaves: 9 1/2" long by 4 1/2" wide; 3/8" to 3/4" wide, green margin; center color changes from gold in spring to greenish white by early summer, then medium green by mid-summer; shiny underside; blade ovate; margin slightly wavy; slight corrugation with maturity; average substance; 8-9 vein pairs

flowers: mid-August into early September; pure white; 3" long by 2 1/2" wide; scapes 31-42" high; limited fertility

comments: As a mutation of 'Royal Standard', 'Royal Accolade' possesses an excellent growth rate and a large number of fragrant, white flowers in August, but with attractive seasonal variegation. The gold centers are brightest in spring and usually darken to medium green by July. Occasionally a plant exposed to a few hours of direct sunlight per day will turn a lighter, greenish white for at least a few more weeks. This is similar to what happens to *H. montana* 'Choko Nishiki' when it is grown under very bright conditions.

'Royal Accolade' is similar to 'Hoosier Harmony' another gold-centered sport of 'Royal Standard'. 'Hoosier Harmony' seems to hold its variegation for a longer period of time during the growing season. Both cultivars make excellent specimen plants and can also be utilized for mass planting purposes much like 'Royal Standard'.

'Royal Accolade' was registered by Bill Zumbar in 1986.

seedlings, sports, and other related types:
'Hoosier Harmony': {1995r, Indianapolis Hosta Society} gold-centered, green-margined sport of 'Royal Standard'; introduced for sale by the Indianapolis Hosta Society in 1995; color holds well into mid-summer, especially if grown under bright conditions

other similar types:
'Chelsea Ore', 'Guacamole'

'Royal Standard'
key features: large mound of bright green foliage; many, fragrant, white flowers in August
mound size: 26" high by 63" wide

spacing: 60"
leaves: 9 3/4" long by 6" wide; medium green color; shiny top surface; very shiny underside; blade ovate with a moderately lobed base; margin slightly wavy; slight corrugation with maturity; average substance; 8-9 vein pairs
flowers: August 12 to September 5 (northern Illinois); pure white color (with a hint of lavender on some flower buds); 3" long by 2 1/2" wide; very fragrant; scapes 31-42" high, most being 35-39" high; 43 scapes on one mature clump, with 30-46 flowers per scape; very sparse seed pod formation with few viable seeds per pod

371

comments: 'Royal Standard' originated at Wayside Gardens when they were headquartered in Mentor, Ohio and was the first patented hosta cultivar. It was registered with the United States Patent Office as a hybrid of *H. plantaginea* X *H. sieboldiana* and was given Plant Patent #2467 dated Jan. 19, 1965 (originally filed on Jan. 3, 1963). Wayside had introduced it into the mail order trade in 1964 and it became an immediate hit, so much so that other nurseries propagated it and offered it under a variety of other names. Eventually it became so commonplace in the trade that apparently the patent was not enforced.

What was great about 'Royal Standard' back in the 1960's, still goes today. 'Royal Standard' makes a fast-growing landscape plant with attractive foliage and produces large numbers of fragrant, white flowers. Although the flowers are not as large as *H. plantaginea*, it produces them in much greater numbers, mainly due to the large number of scapes per plant. A mature clump of 'Royal Standard' can produce more than 1000 flowers during the 3 1/2 week flowering period. A mass planting of 'Royal Standard' can be pure olfactory pleasure on a late summer's evening.

The foliage tends to be darker green than *H. plantaginea* and the growth rate faster. An added bonus is the amount of sunlight per day that 'Royal Standard' will tolerate. In northern Ohio, a half day of direct light does not seem to negatively affect it at all. In northern Illinois, 'Royal Standard' can tolerate a daily dose of 3-4 hours of direct sunlight, especially if the site is kept adequately moist. All-day sunlight, however, scorches the foliage and dries out the margins.

'Royal Standard' has only limited fertility. In the rare instance of a pod developing, most of the seeds are not viable. One year from a large planting which produced over 100,000 flowers I was able to obtain about only 50 viable seeds. The greatest number of new plants out of 'Royal Standard' have resulted from mutations. These include the gold-centered 'Royal Accolade' and 'Hoosier Harmony', all-gold 'Prairieland Memories', and several streaked plants.

'Royal Standard' was registered by the AHS in 1986.

Despite the crush of new varieties, 'Royal Standard' still rates highly as a hosta for general landscaping purposes. The rapid growth rate, sun-tolerance, and superior flower performance continue to make it an excellent choice.

seedlings, sports, and other related types:

'Dee's Golden Jewel': {1996r, K. Walek; 'Royal Standard' X 'Galaxy'} bright gold foliage; the only registered 'Royal Standard' hybrid

372

'Hoosier Harmony': {1995r, Indianapolis Hosta Society} gold-centered, green-margined sport of 'Royal Standard'; introduced by the Indianapolis Hosta Society in 1995; color holds well into mid-summer, especially if grown under bright conditions

'Prairieland Memories': a gold-leaved 'Royal Standard' developed at my nursery (Q & Z N); basically the same as 'Hoosier Harmony' without the green margin; brightest gold in spring, slowly turning chartreuse; introduced in 1998 as the "convention plant" for the AHS meeting in Peoria, Illinois

'Royal Accolade': sport with gold-centered, green-margined foliage **(see page 370)**

'Royal Command': an alternate name for 'Royal Standard' in the 1960's; should not be used

'Royal Gold': gold-leaved 'Royal Standard' from Walters Gardens; turns green by mid-summer; rare

'Royal Standard Special': a name listed for a white-mgd 'Royal Standard' sport; rare

'Royal Splash': sport with streaked foliage; from Walters Gardens; rare

'Royal Super': double-flowered, variegated sport out of 'Royal Standard'; originally from Clarence Falstad; lvs white-margined, sometimes heavily streaked; 24" by 36" md; lvs 7 1/2" by 4 1/4"

'Sweet Winifred': {1984r, R. Benedict} same lvs and fls as 'Royal Standard'

'White Knight': another alternate name for 'Royal Standard' in Europe; should not be used

other similar types:

'Honeybells', 'Invincible', 'Sweet Bo Peep', 'Sweet Susan'

Hosta rupifraga (Hachijo Giboshi)
key features: low mound of waxy, green foliage; lavender flowers in September
mound size: 10" high by 28" wide

spacing: 24"
leaves: 8 1/4" long by 5 1/2" wide; light to medium green color; very shiny, almost waxy underside; blade ovate with a wavy margin and long, distinct tip, tending to cup downward at maturity; thick substance; 11 vein pairs
flowers: early to late September; medium lavender with whitish petal margins from tip, halfway to the throat; 2 1/4" long by 1" wide; semi-bell shape; subtended by white and purple bracts; reddish colored scapes, up to 18" high; readily forms seed pods
comments: The waxy green foliage of *Hosta rupifraga* makes it a very attractive specimen plant in the shaded garden. This characteristic, its thick foliar substance, and late season flowers contribute to its great value in breeding programs. It can also be used in the garden as an unusual edging plant.

There has been some debate as to whether plants being propagated as *H. rupifraga* are actually *H. longipes latifolia* (Schmid, 1991). This is entirely possible owing the great similarities between the two as implied in descriptions of the two plants (ibid, 1991). A major difference seems to be the presence of red-purple dots on the petioles in *H. longipes latifolia* versus the solid green petioles of true *H. rupifraga*. I suspect that the two were once part of the same population, but thousands of years of isolation on its native Hachijo Island led to *H. rupifraga* evolving slight differences.

Sports of "Hachijo Giboshi" that I observed in Japan also reflect this confusion as some conform to the true species, while others are probably mutations of *H. longipes latifolia*.

seedlings, sports, and other related types:

'Forever Green': {1994r, J. Dishon; *H. rupifraga* X *H. plantaginea*; dk gr lvs; fragr lav fls}

'Fukurin Ki Hachijo': golden foliage with a paler yellow margin; probably from the true species; in the Gotemba Nursery collection; impressive plant

'Ki Hachijo': bright golden foliage; observed at Gotemba Nursery in Japan

'Raspberry Sorbet': {1999r, D. Lohman & M. Zilis; *H. rupifraga* X 'Shining Tot'} low, dense md of shiny, green foliage; purple fls on purplish red scapes in August **(see page 359)**

'Rhapsody in Blue': {1995r, R. Benedict, J. & J. Wilkins; *H. rupifraga* sdlg} med-sized md of wide, blue-green lvs, 9 1/2" by 8 3/4" (10 vp) wi a rippled mgn; pale purple fls mid-Aug into Sept; a "blue Rupifraga"

'Roy's Pink': hybrid of *H. kikutii* X *H. rupifraga* from Herb Benedict; blooms earlier than either parent (in August); med-sized md of gr lvs, 8 1/2" by 4 1/2" (10 vp); fls pale purple, 2 1/4" by 1"

'Urajiro Hachijo' (*H. rupifraga* 'Urajiro'): 14" by 47" md of thick, green foliage that has a thick underside bloom; lvs 7 1/4" by 6" (11-12 vp); fls in September on 19" sc

other similar types:

'Grand Slam': {1990r, R. Benedict & H. Gowen} 16" by 43" md; shiny, rippled, dark green lvs, 7" by 4 3/4" (9-10 vp), wi a thick underside bloom and good subst; purple-red dots cover petioles; impressive mound of shiny, green foliage; *H. longipes latifolia* seedling

H. longipes latifolia: so close to *H. rupifraga* that they have been confused in the U.S. and Japan

'Maruba Iwa': 8" by 20" md of very smooth, shiny, med green lvs, 6" by 4 1/2" (9 vp); thick substance; wavy; shiny underside; fls in Sept; listed as *H. longipes latifolia* 'Maruba' (Schmid, 1991); almost impossible to differentiate from *Hosta rupifraga*

spacing: 72"
leaves: 13" long by 10 1/4" wide (up to 14" by 11 1/4");
1/4" to 3/4" wide margin that changes from yellow to
creamy yellow or creamy white during the growing season;
in deep shade, margins remain yellow, but are creamy white
with 2-3 hours of bright light per day; center dark green;
gray-green streaks at junction of margin and center; shiny
top surface, moderate underside bloom; blade ovate, almost
triangular, with a deeply lobed base and five or more distinct waves per margin; little or no corrugation; thick substance; 13 vein pairs
flowers: mid-July into early August; pale lavender; 2 7/8"
long by 1 5/8" wide; scapes 38-50" tall, very thick, and covered with a thick, grayish bloom; 48 flowers in the top 12"
of each scape; prolific seed pod formation
comments: Until about ten years ago, 'Sagae' (as _H. fluctu-
ans_ 'Variegated') was much admired, but not widely available. The availability has increased substantially and its
popularity continues to increase every year. It has become
one of the premier, large-sized hostas in the nursery trade.
The vase-shaped mound of yellow-margined foliage can be
utilized in many ways in the landscape, but can be most
effective as a focal point of the garden. The tall scapes bear
lavender flowers in mid-summer, but they tend to become
floppy as flowering proceeds.
  Sagae Giboshi has long been admired in Japan. In almost
every hosta collection that I visited in Japan, I found a specimen of 'Sagae'. One of the greatest surprises of my 1991
trip to Japan was finding a bonsaied 'Sagae' amongst bon-

saied pines and azaleas on display in a park in Kobe. This plant is pictured on the cover of Spring 1992 issue of *The Hosta Journal*.

The leaf margins are gold in spring, but become lighter during the growing season. How light they become depends on the siting of the plant. With a few hours of sunlight per day they turn a creamy white. In open to deep shade, the color stays a shade of yellow.

As I stated under my discussion of *Hosta fluctuans*, I believe that 'Sagae' is a sport of *Hosta fluctuans*. With this assumption the name can be correctly listed as *Hosta fluctuans* 'Sagae', though simply *Hosta* 'Sagae' is acceptable. The name *Hosta fluctuans* 'Variegated' cannot be used because 'Variegated' is not allowed as a cultivar name, even when associated with a species. The AHS registered the name *H. fluctuans* 'Variegated' in 1987, but Kenji Watanabe of Gotemba Nursery in Japan registered 'Sagae' in 1996.

Some breeders have used 'Sagae' as one of the building blocks of their programs. It has many outstanding genetic traits and is successful as a pod or pollen parent. A few sports have also been introduced. A sport with pure white margins exists in Japan.

seedlings, sports, and other related types:

'Fat Cat': {1996r, D. & J. Ward; sdlg of 'Sagae'; yellow-gold foliage and near-white fls}

'Golden Flame': {1990r, M. Zilis} gold-lvd sport of 'Sagae'; fails to grow well as the foliage turns white by mid-summer

'Great Plains': {1994r, W. Brincka & O. Petryszyn; 'Sagae' X 'Tokudama Flavocircinalis'} large, flat, powdery blue leaves, turning dark green by mid-summer; upr md, 28" by 39" (probably more); 15" by 10" lvs; slight corrug; dense clusters of near-wh fls on 31" sc in June (Ohio); outstanding large hosta

'Ivory Coast': {1999r, D. Savory; sport wi creamy white-mgd, light green-centered lvs}

'Ivory Tower': {1996r, D. & J. Ward; 'Sagae' sdlg; yellow-gold lvs, near-white fls}

'Lakeside Surf Rider': {1997r, M. Chastain; 'Lakeside Ripples' X 'Sagae'; lg md of slightly blue-green foliage and near-white fls}

'Majesty': {1999r, R. Garbe; sport; lvs med green wi pale ylw mgns}

'Midnight Express': {1996r, D. & J. Ward; 'Sagae' sdlg; blue-green lvs turning med green}

'Millennium': {1995r, J. & J. Wilkins; 'Herb Benedict' X 'Sagae'} 28" by 54", semi-upright md of thick-sub-stanced, blue-green lvs, 16" by 12" (18 vp); lvs dark green by mid-summer; pale lav fl, late June into July on 40" sc; fertile; majestic, upright mound

'Ogon Sagae': gold form of 'Sagae' from Japan; lvs change from gold to green

'Yellow Flash': {1997r, P. Ruh; 'Sagae' sport} PPAF; lvs chartreuse-centered, yellow-mgd in spring, changing to green-centered, creamy margined by early summer; outstanding

other similar types:
'Regal Splendor', 'Yellow River'

'Saishu Jima'
key features: small mound of narrow, wavy green foliage; late season purple flowers
mound size: 8" high by 20" wide

spacing: 18"

leaves: 3 3/8" long by 3/4" wide; medium to dark green; slightly shiny top, moderately shiny underside; blade narrowly elliptic, slightly rippled, and curved at tip; smooth texture; red-purple dots on petioles; thin substance; 2-3 vein pairs

flowers: late August; medium purple with darker striping in mid-petal; lighter margins on alternate petals; 1 5/8" long by 1 1/2" wide; scapes 6-12" high; few flowers per scape, 4-8 each; will form seed pods

comments: 'Saishu Jima' rapidly grows into a very dense mound of narrow, wavy foliage that makes it a suitable subject for rock gardens. I have also seen it successfully utilized as an edger in many a shaded garden. It has a very distinctive appearance, so much so that I often use it as reference point in describing other hostas ("has the 'Saishu Jima' look"). The purple flowers are ornamentally attractive up close, but from a distance do not make much of an impact.

'Saishu Jima' is Japanese in origin, literally meaning "Saishu Island". It could be related to either *H. gracillima* or *H. sieboldii angustifolia* or be a separate species. Though George Schmid (1991) states that more than one plant may be represented by this name, the plant grown as 'Saishu Jima' in the U.S. is a single, very distinct clone. The name, however, is unregistered with the AHS.

'Saishu Jima' has been incorporated into a few breeding programs, resulting in some interesting hybrids including 'Maui Rains', 'Sugar Babe', 'Lauren' and 'Saishu Jima Closed'. Herb Benedict and a few others have also found a few streaky mutants.

seedlings, sports, and other related types:

'Emerald Carpet': {1998r, P. Ruh for P. Banyai} 'Saishu Jima' sdlg that is larger in foliage and flower; dense, 12" by 26" md of narrow, green foliage; 4 3/4" by 1 1/2" lvs (4-5 vp); med purple fls on 20-27" sc in Aug; fast growth rate; excellent edger or rock garden plant; sported to gold-margined 'Magic Carpet' {1998r, R. Duback}

'Herbie': {1995r, R. & D. Benedict} sm md of white-mgd lvs; *H. venusta* X 'Saishu Jima' hybrid

'Lauren': {1991r, D. Heinz; 'Saishu Jima' sdlg} dense md (14" by 30") of long, very wavy, bright gold lvs (5 1/4" by 1 1/4"); resembles 'Chartreuse Wiggles'

'Little Jim': {1986r, R. Benedict, 'Saishu Jima' sport} 4" by 10" mound of streaky, narrow, wavy lvs, 2 5/8" by 3/4"; lav fls in August

'Maui Rains': {1991r, W. Vaughn, 'Kabitan' X 'Saishu Jima'} dense, 17" by 38" md of shiny, dk green foliage that is heavily rippled and corrugated; lvs 7" by 4"; attractive & worth growing

'Margaret': {1987r, P. Ruh for D. Stone} sm md of foliage that closely resembles 'Saishu Jima'; one of the David Stone hybrids; 5" by 13" md; 3" by 1 1/4" lvs (3 vp); 10" sc bear purple fls in late Aug

'Missy': {1992r, D. Heinz; 'Saisha Jima' sdlg} low, dense mound of rippled, bright gold foliage

'Saishu Jima Closed': seedling of 'Saishu Jima' from Herb Benedict; dense md of wavy, narrow green foliage; 16" by 34" md; 4 1/2" by 1 3/4" lvs (3-4 vp); 2" long, med to dk purple fls in Aug that incompletely open; many scapes ranging from 28" to 41"; an intriguing plant worth growing

'Sugar Babe': {1996r, R. Solberg; 'Iron Gate Supreme' X 'Saishu Jima'} white-margined, green-centered foliage; 15" by 30" md; nice combination of attractive foliage and purple, fragrant flowers

other similar types:
'Yakushima Mizu'

'Sea Dream'

key features: large, dense mound of gold-centered, white-margined foliage

mound size: 20" high by 55" wide (up to 24" high by 84" wide)

spacing: 48"

leaves: 9" long by 6" wide; 1/8" wide, creamy white margin; center pale green early, changing to bright gold by June; blade ovate with a rounded base; margins wavy, 4-5 per edge; slightly corrugated with age; slightly better than average substance; 10-11 vein pairs

flowers: mid-July into early August; medium lavender color; darker in bud; 2 1/2" long by 1 3/8" wide; funnel-shaped; held well above the foliage on scapes 38-53" high

comments: 'Sea Dream' offers a very attractive combination of gold foliage with white margins that are wavy, much in the way of 'Honeybells'. It becomes a much larger mound than I had originally expected, based on my observations of the specimen at Wade and Gatton Nurseries. The only fault may be that the flowers are held high, out of proportion to the mound of foliage. In the landscape it can be utilized as a background plant, colorful ground cover, or as the centerpiece of an island bed.

Mildred Seaver registered 'Sea Dream' in 1984 as a hybrid of 'Neat Splash' X a seedling. It has not been widely used in breeding work and has only been the source of two gold-leaved mutations.

seedlings, sports, and other related types:
'Day Dream': {1998r, G. Trucks; 'Sea Dream' sport; yellow
  gold foliage}

380

'Winfield Gold': gold-leaved sport of 'Sea Dream' developed at my nursery (Q & Z N); named for Winfield, IL; identical to 'Sea Dream' except for the white margin; introduced for sale in 1995 and listed by 8 sources in the *Hosta Finder 2000* (Greene, 2000)

other similar types:
'American Dream', 'Saint Elmo's Fire'

'Sea Fire'
key features: medium-sized; leaves bright gold in spring, green later
mound size: 18" high by 48" wide (up to 19" by 66")

spacing: 40"
leaves: 9" long by 6" wide (up to 10" by 7"); bright gold early, changing to chartreuse, then green by early summer; thin underside bloom; blade ovate; slightly wavy margins; moderately corrugated; average substance; lower portion of petioles flecked with red; 10-12 vein pairs
flowers: very late July into mid-August; pale lavender; pale purple in bud; 2" long by 1" wide; scapes 24" to 38" high; fertile
comments: 'Sea Fire' ranks as one of the brightest golds in spring (along with 'Chiquita' and 'Hadspen Samphire'). The gold leaves nicely contrast the reddish petioles, though this is only noticeable from close range. In the garden it makes a brilliant splash of springtime color and can be used to feature this characteristic. Due to its fast growth rate, it can also be an effective ground cover.

'Sea Fire' was developed in the mid-1980's and is another member of Mildred Seaver's popular "Sea Series".
seedlings, sports, and other related types:
'Dawn's Early Light': {1998r, O. Petryszyn; 'Sea Fire' sdlg;

ruffled and puckered gold lvs}

'Saint Elmo's Fire': {1995r, R. Solberg; 'Sea Fire' sport}
new lvs gold-cntrd with white mgns versus green-cntrd
and white-mgd with age creating a tricolor effect in an
active stage of growth; commonly listed as 'St. Elmo's
Fire'

'White Hot': {1998r, Walters Gardens; 'Sea Fire' sport}
white-centered, pale green-margined foliage

other similar types:

'Chartreuse', 'Chiquita', 'Hadspen Samphire'

'Sea Grotto'
key features: large mound of heavily corrugated, blue-
green foliage
mound size: 23" high by 60" wide

spacing: 60"

leaves: 11" long by 9 1/2" wide; deep blue-green; thick
underside bloom; blade broadly oblong-ovate and somewhat unruly with age; heavily corrugated; thick substance;
14-16 vein pairs

flowers: late June into mid-July; near-white; narrow funnel
shape; in dense clusters near the top of the foliage mound;
scapes 20- 30" high; many seed pods develop

comments: 'Sea Grotto' becomes a large mound of heavily
corrugated, slug-resistant foliage. It ranks highly among the
many blue hosta introductions of Mildred Seaver. Peter Ruh
registered it in 1991 for her. Though its parentage is
unknown, it falls between a Tokudama and a Sieboldiana in
mound and leaf sizes. For several years it had been known
as 'Sea Gentian', but the name was not allowed for registration.

'Sea Grotto' can be used in a breeding program for slug-resistance, good blue-green color, and attractive flower habits. In the landscape, it is effective both as a specimen and a background plant.

seedlings, sports, and other related types:
none registered

other similar types:
'Muriel Seaver Brown', 'Sea Blue', 'Sea Blue Leather', 'Sea Hero', 'Sea Lotus Leaf', 'Sea Sapphire'

'Sea Lightning' & 'Sea Thunder'

key features: medium-large mounds of center-variegated foliage

mound size: 16" high by 33" wide (up to 22" by 65")

---

spacing: 36"

leaves: 8 3/8" long by 4 3/4" wide; thick, dark green margins irregularly streak into the pale yellow to white middle, creating a very striking contrast for 'Sea Lightning'; green margins with a center that changes from gold to creamy white for 'Sea Thunder'; elliptic blade with a slightly wavy edge; moderately corrugated; average substance; 9 vein pairs

flowers: late July into mid-August; deep lavender; 2 1/2" long by 2" wide; wide-open funnel shape; scapes up to 42" high

comments: No discussion of 'Sea Lightning' would be complete without including 'Sea Thunder'. 'Sea Lightning' is the original plant that Mildred Seaver selected with heavily streaked, green, yellow and white foliage. 'Sea Thunder' is the stable, white-centered, green-margined sport of 'Sea Lightning' that often develops over time. More often than not, plants labelled 'Sea Lightning' are actually 'Sea Thunder'. A green-leaved sport (unnamed) also inevitably evolves and will take over the clump if left unchecked.

Both cultivars make nice specimens but are probably best thought of as collector's plants that need a fair amount of care to maintain. Kirk Brill of Des Moines once told me that the key to success with 'Sea Thunder' was to give it an eastern exposure. Presumably this would provide bright, morning sunlight, but avoid the intense afternoon light and heat. When 'Sea Thunder' is grown in too much light, the white center can "melt-out".

Mildred Seaver registered 'Sea Lightning' in 1981 as a seedling of 'Neat Splash'. 'Sea Thunder' had not been registered by the end of 1999.

seedlings, sports, and other related types:
none registered

other similar types:
'Don Juan', 'Don Quixote', 'Josephine', 'Neat Splash', 'Squiggles', 'Swoosh', 'Yellow Splash'

'Sea Lotus Leaf'
key features: medium-large mound of cupped, slug-resistant, blue-green foliage
mound size: 25" high by 60" wide (up to 33" by 72")

spacing: 48"
leaves: 10 1/4" long by 9" wide; blue-green early becoming dark green by late summer; thick underside bloom; blade nearly rotund shape, often heavily cupped upward, resembling a lotus leaf; moderate to heavy corrugation; thick substance; 14-15 vein pairs
flowers: late June into early July; near-white with a pale lavender mid-petal stripe; 2 1/8" long by 1 1/8" wide; in dense clusters on scapes 24-30" high; many seed pods develop
comments: The cupped foliage of 'Sea Lotus Leaf' combined with an attractive blue-green color, thick substance and dense clusters of near-white flowers make it an impres-

sive cultivar. I first saw this plant in Mildred Seaver's yard in 1983 and have been impressed with it ever since. Mildred registered 'Sea Lotus Leaf' in 1985 as a seedling of 'Wagon Wheels' and is a sibling to 'Sea Gold Star' (gold) and 'Muriel Seaver Brown' (blue).

It can be successfully incorporated into a breeding program, both as a pod or pollen parent. No sports have been identified to this point.

seedlings, sports, and other related types:

'Amethyst Blue': {1996r, C. Seaver; 'Sea Lotus Leaf' sdlg; bl-green lvs, deep purple fls}

'Muriel Seaver Brown': {1984r, M. Seaver; 'Wagon Wheels' sdlg} 25" by 60" md of thick, bl-green lvs, 14" by 11"; near-wh fls, late June into July, on 29" sc; outstanding color, corrugation & substance

'Sea Gold Star': {1984r, M. Seaver; 'Wagon Wheels' sdlg} 28" by 68" md of bright gold foliage; near-wh fls, late June into July, on 35" sc; a sport with wavier margins is called 'Sea Gulfstream' {1999r by A. Malloy for M. Zilis & M. Seaver}

'Spinnaker': {1994r, C. Seaver; 'Sea Lotus Leaf' sdlg} lg md of thick-substanced, blue-green lvs that cup upward and measure 14 1/2" by 13 1/2" (17 vp); near-white fls in June

other similar types:

'Alabama Bowl', 'Big Daddy', 'Sea Grotto', 'Sea Sapphire', 'Silver Bowl'

'Sea Monster'
key features: large mound of heavily corrugated, green foliage; slug-resistant
mound size: 26" high by 68" wide

spacing: 60"
leaves: 14" long by 12 3/4" wide; medium green; moderate underside bloom; blade rotund with a deeply cupped base; blade also generally wavy; intensely corrugated; thick substance; 15-18 vein pairs
flowers: late June into early July; near-white with a pale lavender mid-petal stripe; 2 1/4" long by 1 1/2" wide; scapes 29-36" high; fertile

comments: 'Sea Monster' owes its distinction to being a green-leaved Sieboldiana and to its intense corrugation. It becomes a very attractive, large mound of foliage that also is quite slug-resistant. Owing to its slow growth rate, it takes several years to fully develop all of its good qualities. In fact Mildred Seaver told me that it took her seven years to appreciate this 'Brookwood Blue' seedling. Although she registered it back in 1978, it continues to be fairly popular. In the garden, 'Sea Monster' can be used as a large ground cover or background plant, and can be very effective as a color contrast to blue or gold-leaved Tokudamas and Sieboldianas.

'Sea Monster' has a great deal of value in a hybridizing program if intense corrugation and slug resistance are breeding goals.

seedlings, sports, and other related types:
'Lochness': {1988r, W. & E. Lachman; 'Sea Monster' X a sdlg} lg md of blue-green foliage; leaves also heavily corrugated and unruly; near-white fls, late June into July, in dense clusters; slug-resistant
'Lochness Monster': gold-margined, green-centered sport from Kirk Brill of Iowa; very attractive

'Sea Blue Monster': a 'Sea Monster' sibling with bluish green lvs, but almost the same as 'Sea Monster' in every other way; developed by Mildred Seaver in the early 1980's

'Swamp Monster': {1991r, W. & E. Lachman; 'Sea Monster' sdlg} very heavily corrugated, shiny, dark green foliage reminiscent of alligator skin

other similar types:

'Birchwood Green', 'Nesmith's Giant', 'Puckered Giant'

'Wrinkles and Crinkles': {1985r, L. Englerth; unknown parentage} 20" by 51" md of heavily corrugated, med to dk green foliage that is also very unruly and cupped; lvs 11" by 8 1/2" (15-16 vp); near-wh fls, late June into July on 33" sc; fertile

---

'September Sun'
key features: medium-large mound of gold-centered foliage; 'August Moon' sport
mound size: 22" high by 52" wide (up to 26" by 61")

---

spacing: 48"
leaves: 9 1/2" long by 7 1/2" wide; 1/2" to 1" wide, medium green margin, medium to bright gold center; colors intensify during the season and with brighter light; thin underside bloom; broadly oblong-ovate blade that is slightly wavy and slightly corrugated; good substance; 10-12 vein pairs
flowers: mid-July to early August; pale lavender; 1 3/4" long by 1 1/2" wide; open

funnel shape; held at a right angle to the 20-27" scapes; many seed pods develop

comments: Bob Solberg found this sport of 'August Moon' in the early 1980's and registered it in 1985. It may have started a trend of sorts. Though 'Gold Standard' was prominent at that time, the craze for gold-centered hostas really began with 'September Sun'. There are other similar

'August Moon' sports including 'September Surprise', 'Lunar Orbit', and 'Lunar Magic', differing in the intensity and/or width of the green margin or the brightness of the gold center. Still, 'September Sun' ranks as the best of the bunch. Over the years, too, it has proven to be an excellent grower in both garden and nursery settings.

'September Sun' can be effectively used as a specimen plant or as a very bright ground cover. It forms many seed pods and can be used for the same breeding purposes as 'August Moon'.

seedlings, sports, and other related types:
none registered

other similar types:
'Lunar Magic', 'Lunar Orbit', 'Paradigm', 'September Surprise'

'Serendipity'
key features: medium-sized mound of heart-shaped, blue-green foliage; dense mound habit
mound size: 13" high by 36" wide (up to 18" by 48")

spacing: 36"
leaves: 5 1/2" long by 4" wide; blue-green early, changing to dark green; moderate underside bloom; blade an elongated heart shape; slightly wavy margins; smooth texture; average substance; 9-11 vein pairs
flowers: late June into mid-July; lavender; funnel shape; many scapes, 28-36" high; extensive seed pod formation
comments: The dense, rounded mound habit and bluish foliage color have contributed to the popularity of 'Serendipity'. Not to be overlooked are its attractive flowering habits. The lavender flowers are borne on many scapes held well above the foliage. 'Serendipity' can be

considered as one of the multi-purpose landscaping hostas, being useful as an edger, ground cover, or specimen.

Paul Aden registered 'Serendipity' in 1978 as a hybrid between 'Blue Cadet' X 'Tokudama'. It shares many characteristics with 'Blue Cadet' in both foliage and flower. It can be a useful breeding plant, readily forming large numbers of viable seeds.

seedlings, sports, and other related types:
'Moongate Flying Saucer': {1996r, C. Isaacs & R. Solberg; 'Serendipity' X 'Blue Blazes'} bluish green foliage early, becoming dark green; 13" by 37" md; 6 1/2" by 5" (11 vp) lvs that are slightly cupped and corrugated; avg substance; pale lav fls in mid-June in North Carolina (early July, northern Illinois), about a week later than 'Moongate Little Dipper'
'Moongate Little Dipper': {1996r, C. Isaacs & R. Solberg; 'Serendipity' X 'Blue Blazes'} shiny, dark green foliage; 13" by 36" md; 6" by 5" lvs which are cupped, moderately corrgtd, and thick-substd; pale purple fls, in whorls around 21" sc in e July; outstanding for shiny, cupped, dk gr lvs & attractive fls; underrated

other similar types:
'Blue Cadet', 'Hime Tokudama', *Hosta nakaiana*

'Shade Fanfare'
key features: medium-large mound of creamy-margined foliage
mound size: 21" high by 53" wide

spacing: 48"
leaves: 8 7/8" long by 6 3/8" wide; wide (3/4" to 1") margin that changes from yellow to creamy white, light to medium green center; thin underside bloom; blade ovate

with a slightly lobed base; whole blade curved downward toward the tip and is slightly wavy; slight corrugation; better than average substance; 10-12 vein pairs

flowers: early to late July; pale lavender; 1 7/8" long by 1 1/4" wide; narrow funnel shape; 24-36" scapes tower high over the foliage; forms many seed pods

comments: It may be hard to believe these days, but 'Shade Fanfare' was once regarded as the "poor cousin" of 'Flamboyant'. 'Shade Fanfare' originated as a stabilized sport of 'Flamboyant' that lacked the center streaking that so many collectors thought beautiful in 'Flamboyant'. Guess what? 'Shade Fanfare' has become a prominent landscaping plant, proving itself time and time again to be a good, dependable grower that also makes a colorful presence in the garden. How many collectors own 'Flamboyant' these days? How many have ever seen a true plant of it? 'Flamboyant' can be obtained from only six retail sources according to the *Hosta Finder 2000* (Greene, 2000).

'Shade Fanfare' is a Paul Aden introduction that he registered in 1986. It was found as early as 1981.

seedlings, sports, and other related types:

'Cavalcade': {1990r, W. & E. Lachman; selfed 'Flamboyant' sdlg} 10" by 7" (13 vp) lvs that are med green-centered, creamy white-mgd

'Flamboyant': {1978r, P. Aden as the result of X-ray bombardment of a gold sdlg} med-large md of heavily streaked lvs, also with creamy white margins; "mother" plant of 'Shade Fanfare'; center a combination of white, mottled chartreuse, and green streaks; unstable and difficult to maintain

'Golden Fanfare': gold-leaved sport found at my nursery (Q & Z N); md 15" by 29"; lvs 8 1/2" by 7" (11 vp); slower growing than 'Shade Fanfare' but a very nice, bright gold

'Halo': {1978r, P. Aden; 'Flamboyant' X 'Estelle Aden'} 18" by 50" md of 10 1/2" by 8 1/2" lvs (15 vp); chartreuse color changes during season to chartreuse-centered wi a 1/2" gold margin; pale lav fls in July; unusual combination of colors; sports to the all-gold 'Archangel' (Q & Z N introduction, 1997)

'Peedee Granny Smith': {1992r, U. Syre-Herz; 'Shade Fanfare' X 'Bold Ruffles'; lvs lt blue, turn green}

'Renaissance': {1983r, E. Minks; sport of 'Flamboyant'} heavily variegated foliage; rare

'Verna Jean': {1990r, W. & E. Lachman; selfed 'Flamboyant' sdlg} like a mini-'Shade Fanfare'; 12" by 36" md of chartreuse to gold-centered, creamy white-mgd lvs,

5 3/4" by 3 1/2" (8 vp); avg subst; lav fls in July on 17" sc; forms purple-red seed pods

'Vicki Aden': {1980r, P. Aden; 'Flamboyant' X a sibling} 16" by 39" md of streaked lvs, 8" by 6 3/4" (12 vp); lav fls in late July on 33" sc; highly variable pl, once popular as a breeder but now rarely grown

other similar types:

'June Moon': {1991r, E. & W. Lachman; unknown parentage} medium-sized md of chartreuse-centered, white-mgd lvs, 9" by 7 3/8" (13 vp); lvs also moderately corrugated; mgn (1/2-1" wide) changes from creamy yellow to white; v v pale lav fls in July

'Sunny Smiles': creamy-margined, light green-centered pl from Chet Tompkins that resembles 'Shade Fanfare'; md 18" by 52", lvs 9" by 7" (9-11 vp)

Hosta sieboldiana (To Giboshi)

key features: large mound of thick green foliage; near-white flowers in June-July

mound size: 24" high by 66" wide

spacing: 60"

leaves: 17 1/2" long by 10 3/4" wide; slightly blue early, medium green most of the season; thin underside bloom; blade oblong-ovate to broadly ovate with slightly rippled margins; slightly corrugated; thick substance; 16-18 vein pairs

flowers: late June into mid-July; near-white with a pale lavender mid-petal stripe; open funnel-shape; 2 1/2" by 1 1/2"; scapes 22-35" high; many long seed pods develop

comments: In American hosta collections, the plant we often think synonymous with *Hosta sieboldiana* is the cultivar, 'Elegans', developed in Germany over 90 years ago

(Fischer, 1984). Thousands of 'Elegans' seedlings have been propagated, disseminated and displayed over the intervening years, occasionally under the label "*Hosta sieboldiana*". Many of these have blue foliage, some green. In common to nearly all of them are broadly ovate, heavily corrugated leaves and near-white flowers that are produced in dense clusters from mid-June into July (northern Illinois).

In the 1980's I had a chance to study *Hosta sieboldiana* var. *sieboldiana* in Peter Ruh's collection. His plants had been obtained from Karel Hensen of the Netherlands via Eunice Fisher and should reflect "true" *H. sieboldiana*. Over the years as this clump matured, I realized that this *Hosta sieboldiana* was much different from the typical 'Elegans'. The foliage lacked corrugation. The blade was narrower and the underside bloom thin. Its overall appearance matched what Maekawa (1972) had pictured in his monograph as *Hosta sieboldiana*. During my travels in Japan, I found that the *H. sieboldiana* in collections was this same non-'Elegans' type of plant, roughly matching Hensen's *H. sieboldiana* var. *sieboldiana*. In the wild it grows in isolated areas along the north coast of Honshu, but no collector to whom I spoke had ever seen these native sites. It is much less common than *Hosta montana*, to which it is closely related. In fact all of the *Hosta sieboldiana* var. *sieboldiana* plants that I've observed have somewhat of a "Montana" look to them. The major differences from *H. montana* seem to be in flowering characteristics. *Hosta sieboldiana* var. *sieboldiana* blooms earlier, the scapes tend to be shorter, and the flowers are whiter. The mound, too, is not as vase-shaped and the individual leaves tend to be rounder and slightly more rugose (corrugated), although these characteristics are more strongly pronounced in 'Elegans'. Fujita (1978), in fact, lumped *Hosta sieboldiana* and *Hosta montana* together as *Hosta sieboldiana* (but inexplicably used "Oba Giboshi" as its Japanese common name). While I do not agree that they are the same species, *Hosta sieboldiana* var. *sieboldiana* and *Hosta montana* do share much in common.

In comparing *Hosta sieboldiana* var. *sieboldiana* to cultivated forms, it comes closest to *H. sieboldiana* 'Mira'. This has been grown in American gardens for many years and was considered a botanical variety of the species (as *H. sieboldiana* var. *mira)* by Maekawa (1972). Many characteristics of the leaves, flowers and seed pods are shared by *H. sieboldiana* var. *sieboldiana* and *H. sieboldiana* 'Mira'. 'Elegans', on the other hand, seems to represent an extreme form of *H. sieboldiana*, extreme in the sense of rounder leaves that are bluer and more heavily corrugated and producing denser clusters of flowers.

In the landscape *Hosta sieboldiana* should be used as a background plant or large ground cover. Properly placed it can become the focal point of a shaded garden bed.

With the copious amounts of seed produced, *Hosta sieboldiana* could be incorporated into a breeding program, but 'Elegans' has been more widely used. Certainly most of the seedlings and sports attributed to *H. sieboldiana* actually originated from 'Elegans'.

Various names have been assigned to *Hosta sieboldiana* including Cushion Plantainlily and the Seersucker Plantainlily as well as the scientific names, *Funkia cucullata, Funkia gigantea, Hosta robusta glauca, and Hosta glauca.*

seedlings, sports, and other related types:

H. sieboldiana 'Elegans' **(see page 400)**

H. sieboldiana var. *hypophylla*: listed by Maekawa (1972) as a botanical variety of the species that came out of cultivation; heavily corrugated, rounder foliage than the species, comes close to *H. sieboldiana* 'Elegans'; have not seen a verified specimen in the U.S. or Japan

H. sieboldiana 'Mira': 32" by 62" md of med green lvs, 17 1/2" by 13 1/2" (16-18 vp); thin underside bloom; blade oblong-ovate shape with slightly wavy margins; pale lav fls on three-foot sc; many, long seed pods develop; long known to American collectors; closest to *H. sieboldiana sieboldiana* of any hosta in cultivation

other similar types:

'Birchwood Elegance': lg md of Sieboldiana-type green foliage **(see page 79)**

'Birchwood Green': lg md of Sieboldiana-type green foliage **(see page 80)**

'Herbert': {1996r, P. Ruh for H. Zager; *H. sieboldiana* sdlg} 34" by 72" md of heavily corrugated, green (even in early spring) lvs, 13" by 9 3/4" (15 vp); formerly "Zager's Giant Sieboldiana"

'King James': {1992r by P. Ruh for G. Krossa & A. Summers; *H. montana* sdlg} 27" by 68" md of bluish green lvs, 17" by 12" (15-18 vp); thin, underside bloom; near-wh fls, late June into mid-July

'King Michael': {1992r by P. Ruh for G. Krossa & A. Summers; *H. montana* sdlg} 32" by 56" md; med green lvs, 15" by 11" (18, deeply impressed vp); lightly rippled mgn; near-wh fls, late June, 37" sc

'Lake Erie': {1998r, P. Ruh; selfed 'Perry's True Blue' sdlg} 28" by 68" md; 14 1/2" by 9 1/2", green lvs (16 vp); scapes just reach the top of the foliage

'Leviathan': {1986r by the AHS for E. Nesmith; 'Fortunei

Gigantea' X 'Blue Frost'} impressive mound of large, green foliage; md 31" by 57"; lvs 12 1/2" by 10 1/4"; near-wh fls, late June into July; not grown much anymore; first released in Elizabeth Nesmith's 1968 Fairmount Gardens catalog

H. montana macrophylla: more upright mound but foliage similar to *H. sieboldiana* **(see page 306)**

'Nesmith's Giant': {1994r, P. Ruh for E. Nesmith; *H. sieboldiana* X *H. sieboldiana* 'Elegans'} 26" by 56" md of heavily corrug, green lvs 13" by 9" (15 vp); near-wh fls on 41" sc, June-July; like a green 'Elegans' with taller scapes; long-known as *H. sieboldiana gigantea*; introduced in the 1964 Fairmount Gardens catalog

---

Hosta sieboldiana 'Borwick Beauty'
key features: large mound of gold-centered foliage; open mound habit
mound size: 24" high by 57" wide

spacing: 48"
leaves: 13 1/2" long by 9" wide; blue-green margin, 1" to 1 1/2" wide; center changes from chartreuse to gold during the season; thick underside bloom; blade broadly oblong-ovate and slightly wavy; moderate corrugation; thick substance; 16 vein pairs
flowers: mid-June into early July; near-white color with a pale lavender petal midrib; 2 1/4" long by 1 1/4" wide; narrow funnel shape; scapes up to 32" high; in dense clusters; many seed pods develop
comments: 'Borwick Beauty' stands as the first gold-centered sport of *H. sieboldiana* 'Elegans'. Like others in this category, it shares all the foliage and flowering characteristics of 'Elegans', with the exception of foliage color. The

394

large-sized leaves develop intense corrugation with age, and have heavy substance, a thick underside bloom and at least 16 vein pairs at maturity. The near-white flowers are borne in dense clusters on short scapes from mid-June into July in northern Illinois. They have a narrow funnel shape and end up forming large numbers of seed pods containing many viable seeds.

At its best, 'Borwick Beauty' makes a showy, colorful specimen. Unfortunately, 'Borwick Beauty' and most other gold-centered Sieboldianas are susceptible to the spring desiccation burn problem that plagues any gold-colored portion of the leaf. These areas tend to turn light yellow when exposed to direct sunlight, especially in the spring when the leaf is expanding. Eventually these spots turn brown or rust-colored. In contrast the green or blue-green areas never burn. In bad years, this can leave a mature clump a spotted mess. Other years the problem is minimal and only evident upon close examination. The problem also seems worse in certain parts of the country. Keeping the plant out of direct sunlight in the spring will reduce the problem significantly. At the same time, there has been a concerted effort to find "non-burning" cultivars and several show promise.

'Borwick Beauty' was registered in 1988 by the British Hosta and Hemerocallis Society. It was found by Graham and Betty McBurnie in a row of *H. sieboldiana* 'Elegans' before 1984 (1994 Homestead Division catalog).

seedlings, sports, and other related types:

none listed, though *H. sieboldiana* 'Elegans' often sports from it in tissue culture, rarely in the garden

other similar types:

'Color Glory': {1980r, P. Aden; 'Fascination' X 'Intrigue'; registration lists 26" by 36" md of heavily variegated lvs, 9" by 7", 8 vp, & lav fls, June-July} registered plant does not match the description of the gold-centered Sieboldiana sold under this name

'Dick Ward': green-mgd, gold-cntrd sport of 'Zounds'; have not seen it burn **(see page 513)**

'DuPage Delight': {1990r, M. Zilis} a reversed 'Frances Williams' from tissue culture; severe burning in bad years; named for DuPage Co., w of Chicago; md 36" by 64"

'George Smith': {1983r, G. Smith; 'Elegans' sport; lvs gold-centered, bl-green mgd} pictured on the back of *The American Hosta Society Bulletin* in 1984; much anticipated, but never distributed

'Great Expectations': {1988r, P. Aden; an 'Elegans' sport} a sport found in England by John Bond; the most spectacular plant in the whole group of center-variegated 'Elegans' types; does not burn and has become an important commercial cultivar in recent years **(see page 207)**

'Inniswood': green-margined, gold-centered sport of 'Sun Glow' **(see page 236)**

'Jim Matthews': {1998r by B. Sligh for Mrs. J. W. Matthews & Julian Matthews; selfed *H. sieboldiana* sdlg} lvs misted greenish white in the center, blue-green-margined

'Kingwood Center': {1993r, Kingwood Center, Mansfield, OH; sport of a 'Frances Williams' sdlg} gold-centered, green-margined foliage; have not seen enough to evaluate whether it burns in spring

'Mean Mama': {1995r, R. & D. Benedict; 'Dorothy Benedict' sport; gold-centered, dk gr-mgd lvs}

'Northern Sunray': {1987r, Walters Gardens; 'Elegans' sport with a white to light green center and blue-green margin} plants in gardens show only minimal variegation, pale green-cntrd at best; rarely grown anymore

'Princess Anastasia': {1998r, G. Trucks; 'Ryan's Big One' sport; lvs gold-centered wi a bl-gr mgn}

'Queen of Islip': {1990r, J. Goffery; 'Frances Williams' sport} gold-centered lvs; burns in spring

'Super Nova': {1999r, M. Zilis} reversed 'Aurora Borealis' sport; 1996 Q & Z N introduction; wider margin & does not burn as severely as others in the gold-centered, bl-green-mgd group

Hosta sieboldiana 'Dorothy Benedict'

key features: large mound of heavily streaked and mottled foliage that is slug-resistant; premier breeding plant
mound size: 26" high by 50" wide

spacing: 48"

leaves: 14" long by 11" wide; blue-green with streaks of chartreuse and green mottled areas; moderate underside bloom; blade broadly ovate, tending to cup up or downward; heavily corrugated; thick substance; 15-16 vein pairs

flowers: mid-June into July; near-white with a pale lavender petal midrib; in dense clusters; just over the top of the foliage; fertile

comments: As a selfed seedling of 'Frances Williams', Herb Benedict quickly recognized the value of a heavily streaked and mottled Sieboldiana. So much so, in fact, that he named it for his wife and hosta partner, Dorothy, and then registered it in 1983. It has become a very popular breeding plant because many of its seedlings are variegated, all with the typically good, 'Elegans' substance. Such cultivars as 'Outrageous' (and its sport, 'My Child Insook'), 'Van Wade', 'Gil Jones', 'Jim Wilkins', and 'Hideko Gowen' have resulted from hybridizing with 'Dorothy Benedict'. This is in sharp contrast to the many thin-substanced, *H. sieboldii*-type plants that have been used in the past to produce variegated seedlings (e.g., 'Beatrice', 'Neat Splash', and others).

Because of its value, 'Dorothy Benedict' has been a highly sought commodity at plant auctions where it has brought over $1000 per plant. On the retail market only one source (White Oak Nursery) lists it for sale, at $200 per plant, in the *Hosta Finder 2000* (Greene, 2000). Due to its slow growth rate and high degree of instability, it will probably continue to command such high prices for some time to come. In the garden, 'Dorothy Benedict' makes an excellent specimen plant, offering a nice contrast to 'Elegans' and its sports.

Besides 'Dorothy Benedict' and its seedlings, there are only a few other streaked 'Elegans' types. 'Doctor Reath', a seedling developed by Dr. David Reath (named by Peter Ruh) exhibits gold splotching in spring. Another is 'Homestead', a streaked and mottled sport from tissue culture that Peter Ruh grew for many years before naming and registering it. Over the years it developed very attractive, streaky foliage with similar breeding potential to 'Dorothy Benedict'.

seedlings, sports, and other related types:

'Benedict Arnold': {1996r, B. Arnold; 'Dorothy Benedict' sdlg; bl-green, greenish white-mgd lvs}

'Blast Off': {1995r, R. & D. Benedict; 'Mikado' X 'Dorothy Benedict'; green gold lvs} large-sized md

'Gil Jones': {1990r, R. & D. Benedict; selfed 'Dorothy Benedict' sdlg} lvs bl-green in the center, yellow to creamy white-margined; excellent substance

'Gold Dorothy of Richland': {1995r, S. & V. Wade, R. & D. Benedict; 'Dorothy Benedict' sdlg} lg md of very bright gold foliage

'Grandchild': {1999r, J. Schwarz; 'Dorothy Benedict' sdlg} heavily mottled foliage, often wi a bl-green mgn; near-wh fls in dense clusters in June; after several years, plants that I observed in the originator's garden still relatively small, i.e. it is a very slow grower or a small-sized Sieboldiana

'Herb Benedict': {1990r, J. Wilkins; 'Dorothy Benedict' X 'Tokudama Aureonebulosa'} foliage heavily mottled and streaked with white, cream, and green on a bl-green base; formerly "DB-86-1", winner of the 1988 AHS Savory Shield award (AHS, 1988); near-white fls, June-July

'Hideko Gowen': {1990r, R. & D. Benedict; selfed 'Dorothy Benedict' sdlg; lvs that have blue-green-margins and a center that changes from yellow-green to creamy yellow}

'Hot Flash': {1991r, R. & D. Benedict; selfed 'Dorothy Benedict' sdlg; med gr lvs, streaked wi ylw & wh}

'Huron Blue': {1990r, P. Banyai} a sibling of 'Dorothy Benedict' (selfed 'Frances Williams' sdlg); 24" by 48" md of thick, deep blue-green foliage that is somewhat cupped; lvs more than 10" by 10" (16 vp) creating a broadly ovate to rotund blade that is also heavily corrugated and fairly wavy; near-wh fls, late June into July; excellent in combination wi 'Sun Power'

'Jim Wilkins': {1990r, R. & D. Benedict; selfed 'Dorothy Benedict' sdlg} some lvs light gold-centered with a 1" bl-green mgn, others streaked and mottled throughout the leaf center; leaves also cupped, corrugtd & thick-substd; near-wh fls, late June into mid-July; gold-centered form especially striking

'Lover's Leap': {1995r, R. & D. Benedict; 'Dorothy Benedict' X 'Nooner'; lvs creamy white centered wi a dk gr mgn}

'Mean Mama': {1995r, R. & D. Benedict; 'Dorothy Benedict' sport; gold-centered, dk gr-mgd lvs}

'My Friend Nancy': {1991r, R. Benedict & N. Krul; 'Dorothy Benedict' X *H. montana* 'Chirifu'} large white-margined, blue-green-centered lvs, reminiscent of 'Sagae'; imm lf measured 12" by 8 3/4" with a 3/4" margin (13 vp); excellent substance

'My Love Dorothy': {1995r, R. & D. Benedict; selfed 'Dorothy Benedict' sdlg} lvs gold-centered in spring, white-centered in summer

'Nifty Fifty': {1986r, R. Benedict; 'Dorothy Benedict' sport} large md of creamy-margined foliage; margins yellow in spring, turning creamy white by mid-July; lvs 12 1/4" by 10 3/4" (18 vp) wi a 1/2" to 7/8" margin; very attractive; does not burn

'Outrageous': hybrid of 'Dorothy Benedict' X *H. montana* 'Aureomarginata' from Herb Benedict; stunning, large, vase-shaped mound of heavily streaked and mottled foliage; md 20" by 50"; lvs 13" by 10" (measured in 1991); "mother" plant of 'My Child Insook', a white-centered, green-mgd sport {1995r, R. & D. Benedict}

'Ruby Benedict': {1991r, R. & D. Benedict; 'Dorothy Benedict' X 'Tokudama Aureonebulosa'; lvs creamy white wi a variable bl-green margin} have seen leaves with gold centers

'Van Wade': {1990r, R. Kuk; 'Dorothy Benedict' X 'Northern Lights'} 26" by 53" md of creamy yellow-mgd, dk green-cntrd lvs, 10 1/2" by 9" (13 vp); margin 1" wide; pale lav fls on 26" sc, early July into Aug; many pods develop

other similar types:

'Doctor Reath': {1997r, D. Reath & P. Ruh} gold splotches in spring on an *H. sieboldiana* type leaf; turns green by early summer; v large mound

'Filagree': gold-splotched Sieboldiana from Dr. Reath; probably the same as 'Doctor Reath'

'Homestead': {1997r, M. Zilis & P. Ruh} t.c. sport of 'Elegans'; heavily streaked and mottled foliage; good breeding potential

Hosta sieboldiana 'Elegans'

key features: large mound of heavily corrugated, blue-green foliage; dense clusters of near-white flowers in June-July

mound size: 28" high by 61" wide (up to 33" by 75")

spacing: 60"

leaves: 15 1/2" long by 11 1/8" wide; blue-green in May and June, medium to dark green thereafter; thick bloom on top and underside surfaces; blade broadly oblong-ovate to ovate with a deeply lobed base and distinct tip; margin slightly to moderately wavy; heavily corrugated; thick substance; 16-18 vein pairs; excellent, bright gold fall color can develop from late October into early November only in years without early frosts (in northern Illinois); broad, open mound habit

flowers: June 19 to July 8 (northern Illinois); near-white with a pale lavender mid-petal stripe; 2 1/4" long by 1 1/4" wide; narrow funnel shape; scapes range from 20" to 34" high; 14 scapes on one mature clump; in tight clusters with as many as 80 flowers per scape, 50-65 typical; one to five flowers open each day per scape; many seed pods develop with the seeds maturing about four weeks after flowering

comments: Information about *Hosta sieboldiana* 'Elegans' could alone fill a book. It has become the standard to which all other large blue-green hostas are compared. The rich blue-green color, intense corrugation, and thick substance of the foliage, as well as the large plant size and dense clusters of early season near-white flowers (with a pale lavender petal midrib) are key characteristics that identify 'Elegans' and its many seedlings. Though there is some variation in the foliage among these plants, the flowers almost always have the same appearance. 'Tokudama' comes close to 'Elegans' in both flowering and foliage
400

traits, differing only by the smaller plant size. I often describe 'Tokudama' as a "down-sized" *H. sieboldiana* 'Elegans' to which it certainly has a close genetic relationship. Maekawa (1972) described *H. sieboldiana* var. *hypophylla*, which appears similar to 'Elegans'.

'Elegans' was introduced for sale in 1905 by the Arends Nursery in Germany as *Hosta fortunei* 'Robusta' (Fischer, 1984). Though Georg Arends stated that he crossed a 'Fortunei' X <u>*Hosta sieboldiana*</u> to produce "<u>Hosta fortunei</u> 'Robusta'" (ibid, p. 28), my conjecture is that he actually crossed two *Hosta sieboldiana* types. At that time, the identification and nomenclature of hostas was greatly confused. The names "Funkia fortunei" and "Hosta fortunei" were often used for what we now know as *Hosta sieboldiana*. Additionally comparing 'Elegans' to known 'Fortunei' X *H. sieboldiana* crosses reveals differences in (1) numbers of vein pairs (16-18 for 'Elegans', 13-14 for the 'Fortunei' X *H. sieboldiana* hybrids), (2) flower color (near-white with a pale lavender stripe in mid-petal for 'Elegans' versus lavender for the hybrids), (3) flowering time (mid-June into July for 'Elegans' versus mid-July into August for the hybrids), and other traits such as blade shape, underside bloom, amount of corrugation, scape height, and fertility. The Arends plant was linked to *Hosta sieboldiana* by Nils Hylander (1954) who listed it as *Hosta sieboldiana* var. *elegans* in his description of Swedish hostas. Hylander stated that it had become a fairly common plant in Sweden and that he had obtained it as *H. fortunei glauca* and *H. fortunei robusta*. He went on to say that "American nurseries have also issued different clones, originating from seed in fairly recent years" (ibid, p. 387).

Hylander really hit on the source of much confusion in the future, namely seedlings being sold as 'Elegans'. The reason for this centers around the slow growth rate of *H. sieboldiana* 'Elegans', which made propagation by division a long term process. At the same time, the copious amounts of seed that 'Elegans' produced offered a quicker source of new plants. Since most of the resulting seedlings bore the same heavily corrugated, blue-green foliage as 'Elegans', seed germination became the preferred method of increasing nursery stock until the mid-1980's. This inevitably resulted in dozens, if not hundreds, of similar-looking, slug-resistant blue-leaved plants bearing the name *Hosta sieboldiana* 'Elegans'. Though not a clone, *H. sieboldiana* 'Elegans' can be considered a cultivar in the truest sense of the word, as all of these plants share a common set of true-breeding characteristics. There, however, is some variability in the intensity of the blue-green color, mound size, amount of corrugation, leaf size, and scape height. In recent years, such slight differences have formed the basis for an absolutely staggering number of new introductions. My first encounter with an 'Elegans'-type plant was 'Helen Doriot', a David Reath cross of 'Frances Williams' X 'Elegans'. It exhibits all of the foliage and flowering traits that would be expected from 'Elegans', but matures at a slightly smaller size than typical. 'Gray Cole' and 'Ryan's Big One' probably come closest to the original 'Elegans', but they are significantly different from other 'Elegans'-types such as 'Blue Mammoth', 'Bold Ruffles', 'Big Daddy', and 'Big Mama'. Under the old system of propagation by seed, all of these plants most likely would have been given the same name, *Hosta sieboldiana* 'Elegans'.

At the same time, it is not surprising to find a dozen similar gold-margined sports or several gold-centered mutations since each could have come from a different 'Elegans' clone. That's also why cultivars such as 'Aurora Borealis' and 'Frances Williams' differ in more ways than just the size or coloring of the leaf margin. 'Aurora Borealis' has more heavily corrugated foliage, becomes a larger mound, and is a more vigorous grower than 'Frances Williams'. This does not say, however, that the same sport hasn't been given more than one name. This has occurred a few times in the case of 'Frances Williams' look-alikes.

In addition to the cultivars which are selfed 'Elegans' seedlings, many hybrids have been introduced with 'Elegans' as one of the parents. The Tardiana series, hybrids of 'Tardiflora' X *H. sieboldiana* 'Elegans' and their descendants, may be the greatest group of blue-leaved hostas ever developed. There are also hybrids with 'Tokudama', *H. nigrescens*, *H. nakaiana*, and many others. Despite the large number of hybrids related to 'Elegans', it continues to have value for hybridizing. The outstanding substance, good color, and attractive flowers are characteristics that should be part of any breeding program.

A virtual rainbow of leaf colors has sported from 'Elegans'. Most gold-margined sports were found in garden-grown plants, whereas most white-margined, white-centered and misted sports originated in tissue culture. Gold-centered sports have been found both in the ground and from tissue culture.

In 1987 *H. sieboldiana* 'Elegans' was registered by the AHS.

seedlings, sports, and other related types:

'Gray Cole': {1985r, Kuk's Forest; *H. sieboldiana* selection from Gray & Cole N} 29" by 77" md of heavily corrugated, blue-green foliage; lvs 15 1/2" by 13 1/2" (17-18

402

vp); near-wh fls on 32-40" sc, mid-June into early July; fertile; excellent example of a "typical" 'Elegans'

'Helen Doriot': {1982r, D. Reath; 'Frances Williams' X 'Elegans'} 25" by 48" md of heavily corrugated, blue-green lvs, 14" by 12" (17 vp); near-wh fls, June 21 to July 11, on 30" sc; fertile; another "typical" 'Elegans', though slightly smaller than most; some of the first t.c. experiments with hostas in the 1970's (by Dr. Martin M. Meyer at the University of Illinois) utilized this plant

'Ryan's Big One': {1982r, L. Englerth} 28" by 64" md of heavily corrugated, bl-green foliage; 15" by 13 1/4" lvs (18-20 vp); near-wh fls in dense clusters on 24-30" sc, late June into early July; gigantic, impressive md, typical of 'Elegans'

The following are just some of the registered seedlings that have either 'Elegans' or an 'Elegans' sport (e.g., 'Frances Williams', 'Northern Halo', etc.) as a parent. All of these have blue-green foliage and represent the range of 'Elegans' types that can be found. This list does not include the many members of the Tardiana Series **(see page 451)**. Green, gold, and variegated seedlings are also not listed here.

'Abiqua Drinking Gourd', 'Abiqua Pagoda', 'Abiqua Parasol', 'Alabama Bowl', 'Albert Lea', 'Birchwood Blue', 'Blue Bayou', 'Blue Frost', 'Blue Lace', 'Blue Mammoth', 'Blue Plisse', 'Blue Saucers', 'Blue Seer', 'Bold Ruffles', 'Brookwood Blue', 'Buckanon', 'Century One', 'Champion', 'Clarence', 'Cool Change', 'Crater Lake', 'Edina Heritage', 'Eleanor J. Reath', 'Ellen F. Weissenberger', 'Great Lakes', 'Jay Jay', 'Jumbo', 'June Beauty', 'Lady In Waiting', 'Lake Louise', 'Lee Armiger', 'Marge', 'Metallic Sheen', 'Nesmith's Giant', 'Polly Bishop', 'President's Choice', 'Puckered Giant', 'Quilted Hearts', 'Quilted Skies', 'Rembrandt Blue', 'Silver Award', 'Snowden', 'Sumi', 'Waterford', 'Woodland Blue'

sports:

Some of the more prominent sports from *H. sieboldiana* 'Elegans' include:

'Borwick Beauty' (gold-centered)
'Doctor Reath' (gold-spotted)
'Frances Williams' (gold-margined)
'George Smith' (gold center)
'Great Expectations' (creamy yellow center)
'Homestead' (streaked)
'Northern Halo' (white-margined)
'Northern Lights' (white-centered)
'Northern Mist' (misted center)

'Northern Star' (chartreuse-margined)
'Northern Sunray' (gold-centered)
'Northern Exposure' (white-margined)

other similar types:

'Aksarben', 'Big Daddy', 'Big Mama', 'Bigfoot', 'Blue Angel', 'Blue Max', 'Blue Ox', 'Blue Pearl', 'Blue Rock', 'Bressingham Blue', 'Buckeye Blue', 'Crinolin Petticoats', 'Evelyn McCafferty', 'Fantastic', 'Harrison', 'Hoarfrost', 'Housatonic', 'Huron Blue', 'Johanne', 'Leather Coat', 'Lochness', 'Mischief', 'Misty Waters', 'Perry's True Blue', 'Ridges', 'Rough Waters', 'Roundhouse Blues', 'Sea Lotus Leaf', 'Silver Anniversary', Stearn's Beauty', 'Trail's End', 'Versailles Blue', 'Willy Nilly', 'Zager Giant Puckered'

Hosta sieboldiana 'Frances Williams'

key features: large, open mound of heavily corrugated, gold-margined foliage; near-white flowers in June
mound size: 28" high by 63" wide

spacing: 60"
leaves: 13" long by 9 1/2" wide (up to 15 1/4" by 12"); blue-green center in spring, changing to dark green by mid-summer; 1 1/2" to 2" wide margins change from light green in early spring to chartreuse by June to medium gold by July; thick underside bloom; blade broadly oblong-ovate shape with a cordate base and slight, but distinct, tip; blade also broadly wavy and slightly cupped or puckered downward; heavily corrugated; thick substance; 15-17 vein pairs; fall color bright gold if not affected by frost

flowers: June 19 to July 10 (northern Illinois); near-white color with a pale lavender mid-petal stripe; 2 3/16" long by 1 1/8" wide; narrow funnel shape; scapes range in height from 18" to 33" with most 25-30" high; one scape had 56 flowers in a very dense cluster, 8" from the top of the scape to the bottom flower; many seed pods form

comments: 'Frances Williams' (the plant) has a long history among hosta collectors and gardeners. For many years it ranked at the top of the AHS popularity poll and became a staple of the landscaping industry. The slug-resistant, gold-margined foliage makes an imposing statement in any garden. In the last ten or so years, however, it has also become a source of controversy. Several cultivars that look very similar to 'Frances Williams' have been introduced and there is some question as to what the "true" 'Frances Williams' should be.

In researching the Frances R. Williams records at the Andersen Library of the Minnesota Landscape Arboretum, I found a great deal of information about the origins of 'Frances Williams'. The original plant was found at a nursery in Bristol, Connecticut in 1936 by Frances Williams, a garden writer, gardener, and hosta collector from Winchester, Massachusetts, who did more to promote the genus *Hosta* than anyone before the advent of The American Hosta Society. In a 1957 letter to Ellen Carder of Cheshire, CT, Frances Williams related "I got originally from Bristol Nursery the only gold edge that I know of. It was September 17, 1936 that I stopped at Bristol on my way back from Vassar...I got one of these gray leaved plants and in the bed there was a plant with a yellow edge to the leaf. I said I would take that and they stuck on the name Hosta lancifolia variegata." The bed had been labelled "Hosta caerulea". In a letter to Frances Williams dated June 2, 1962, G. W. Robinson of Oxford, England wrote that "I have taken the liberty of naming your Hosta sieboldiana 'Frances Williams' as I think it only right that your name as the finder should be properly named." It was registered with the American Hosta Society in 1986 by Frances' daughter, Connie Williams as a sport of *H. sieboldiana* 'Elegans'.

Since the advent of the American Hosta Society, several other gold-margined Sieboldianas have been named. Some such as 'Squash Edge', 'Samurai', and 'Holly's Green and Gold' appear to be the same as 'Frances Williams'. Any differences they display from 'Frances Williams' are within the realm of normal variability that can be found in this plant. In the Spring 1987 issue of *The Hosta Journal*, I reported on such variability that I had found in examining an undivided, ten-year-old clump of 'Frances Williams' (Zilis, 1987). Other cultivars, however, are distinct. 'Aurora Borealis', 'Louise Ryan', 'Olive Bailey Langdon', and 'Northern Star' differ significantly from 'Frances Williams'.

A problem noted under the discussion of 'Borwick Beauty' is the so-called "burning" of the gold leaf portions that occurs some years. The 'Frances Williams' group of cultivars is generally plagued with this problem in spring. As for 'Borwick Beauty', siting the plant properly (out of direct sunlight in spring) may be the best solution to reduce the burning. The search for non-burning forms has resulted in 'Olive Bailey Langdon' being purported to be the best. Another solution, however, may be in the development of gold-edged *Hosta sieboldiana* hybrids that do not burn. One such plant is Kevin Vaughn's 'Standing Ovation' which becomes an imposing, large mound of gold-edged foliage with a "Sieboldiana look". Perhaps the closest, non-burning, gold-margined plant to 'Frances Williams' may be 'Tokudama Flavocircinalis' which differs only in having smaller leaves and mound size. Other recommended gold-margined cultivars include 'Alvatine Taylor', 'Garden Treasure', 'Everglades', and 'Tyler's Treasure'.

'Frances Williams' has been utilized extensively in breeding work, much like 'Elegans'. When it has been used as the pod parent, most seedlings are solid-colored, blue-green or green-leaved plants, but an occasional variegated seedling will show up. Herb Benedict found the heavily mottled 'Dorothy Benedict' in a batch of selfed 'Frances Williams' seedlings. Using 'Frances Williams' as the pollen parent, Kevin Vaughn and Bill and Eleanor Lachman were able to develop such outstanding variegated cultivars as 'Bold Edger', 'Breeder's Choice', 'Cascades', 'Celebrity', 'Formal Attire', 'Mildred Seaver', 'Robert Frost', and 'William Lachman'. A few sports of 'Frances Williams' have also been identified, most notably 'Golden Sunburst', the gold-leaved form.

seedlings, sports, and other related types:

H. sieboldiana aureo-marginata: former name of various gold-margined 'Elegans' sports

'Aurora Borealis': {1986r, Wayside Gardens; 'Frances Williams' sport} formerly "Chicago Frances Williams" from Nate & Thelma Rudolph of North Aurora, IL (observed in 1983); lvs have highly variable gold margins and heavy corrugation; distinct from 'Frances Williams' with which it is thoroughly mixed in the nursery trade, i.e. many plants labelled 'Frances Williams' may actually be 'Aurora Borealis'

'Breeder's Choice' {1987r, K. Vaughn; "Vaughn 73-2" X 'Frances Williams'} 12" by 31" md of heavily streaked & mottled lvs, often wi a creamy white mgn, 6 1/8" by 4 3/4" (8-10 vp); lav fls on 22" sc, late June into July; outstanding breeding plant **(see page 101)**

'Broadway Frances': {1997r, C. Crockett; 'Frances Williams' sport; lvs bl gr-cntrd wi wide, gold mgns}

'Cascades': {1993r, W. & E. Lachman; 'Banana Sundae' X 'Frances Williams'} fountain-like md of white-cntrd lvs 11" by 4 1/2" wi a 1 1/4" mgn & 9 vp

'Celebrity': {1995r, W. & E. Lachman; hybrid of a 'Beatrice' F6 sdlg X 'Frances Williams'} impressive 26" by 56" md; lvs green-cntrd, gold-mgd, 10 1/2" by 7 1/2" (13 vp)

'Chippewa': {1986r, AHS for A. Arett; *H. sieboldiana* 'Aureo-marginata' sport} light gold margin

'Christmas Tree': {1982r, M. Seaver; 'Frances Williams' X 'Beatrice'} lg md of wh-mgd lvs **(see page 116)**

'Dorothy Benedict': selfed seedling of 'Frances Williams' from Herb Benedict; a breakthrough for breeders due to its heavily mottled Sieboldiana foliage **(see page 397)**

'DuPage Delight': {1990r, M. Zilis} a reversed t.c. sport of 'Frances Williams'; severe burning in bad years; named for DuPage Co., w of Chicago; md 36" by 64"

'Exotic Frances Williams': sport of 'Frances Williams' from the early 1980's; thin white mgns that drawstring; not recommended

'Forever Frances': {1996r, U. Syre-Herz; 'Frances Williams' sport; green-cntrd, deep gold-mgd lvs}

'Formal Attire': {1988r, K. Vaughn; 'Breeder's Choice' X 'Frances Williams'} lg md of creamy white-mgd foliage **(see page 151)**

'Golden Circles': {1998r by P. Ruh for F. Williams; sport} large mound of heavily corrugated, gold-mgd, blue-green-centered lvs; found growing under a clump of 'Frances Williams' in 1954 by Frances Williams who thought it was a seedling (Williams, 1962a); 24" by 50" md, 15" by 13" lvs wi a 2 1/2" wide margin & 15 or more vp; does not burn much

'Golden Sunburst': golden-leaved sport; tends to burn heavily **(see page 409)**

'Kiwi Blue Sunrise': {1999r, B. Sligh; *H. sieboldiana* sport; lvs have bl-green center and greenish yellow margins that change to creamy white}

'Linda Sue': {1999r, V. Wade; 'Frances Williams' sport; bl-gr center wi a 4" wide, greenish ylw mgn; listed as being a non-burning form}

'Louise Ryan': {1993r, Walters Gardens & C. Falstad; 'Ryan's Big One' sport} lvs wi bl-green in center, chartreuse margin that colors late

'Maple Leaf': {1972r, E. Minks; 'Frances Williams' sport} lg md of heavily corrugated lvs wi variable, wide gold margins; sported to all-gold, 'Golden Maple' {1980r, E. Minks}

'Northern Star': {1993r, Walters Gardens & C. Falstad; 'Elegans' sport} 12" by 7 1/2" leaves wi margins that slowly change from chartreuse to gold; lf shape tends to become distorted as the center grows faster than the margin, unusual for a gold-margined hosta; md 27" by 64"; not recommended

'Olive Bailey Langdon': {1999r by the Russ O'Harra Hosta Society for R. O'Harra; *H. sieboldiana* sport} gold-margined, bl-green-centered leaves; 31" by 58" md; 13" by 10" lvs (17 vp); has the reputation of being the best non-burning 'Frances Williams'-type; have seen limited brown spots on margins but the problem is so minor that it is almost unnoticeable

'Queen of Islip': {1990r, J. Goffery; 'Frances Williams' sport} gold-centered lvs; burns in spring

'Sara's Sensation': (1998r, P. & L. Hofer; 'Frances Williams' sport} very wide gold margins, narrow bl-green center; mgn 2 3/4" wide on an imm, 8 1/2" by 7 1/2" leaf

'William Lachman': {1981r, K. Vaughn; "Vaughn 73-2" X 'Frances Williams'} med-lg md of heavily streaked foliage; 20" by 48" md; 8 3/4" by 6 3/4" lvs (11 vp); important breeding plant

other similar types:

'Alvatine Taylor' **(see page 64)**

'Connie': {1987r, R. Benedict; 'Sunlight' sport X a 'Frances Williams' sport} lvs lt green in the center with a gold margin; md 19" by 47"; lvs 11" by 9 3/4" (17 vp); margin width about 1 1/2" but is irregular; named for Connie Williams, daughter of Frances Williams

'Gilt Edge': gold-margined 'Elegans' type from Chet Tompkins; 26" by 63" md; heavily corrugated lvs 12" by 11" (18 vp) wi 1-2" gold margins

'Holly's Green and Gold': {1997r by P. Ruh for G. Holly, F. Williams, & E. Fisher} lg md of 'Elegans'-type leaves with wide gold margins; previously 'Holly's Green Gold'

'June Dove': {1999r, M. Soules; unknown parentage} med-lg md of thick-substanced foliage that is blue-green-centered, chartreuse-mgd; lgst md I've seen = 15" by 30" wi 9" by 6" lvs (15 vp) (could get larger); near-wh fls late June into July

'Samurai': 26" by 48" md of gold-mgd lvs 14" by 11 7/8" (17 vp); introduced by Paul Aden before 1981; have not been able to distinguish from 'Frances Williams'

'Squash Edge': described in Paul Aden's 1979-80 "Hosta List" as "flatter & more compact than Frances

Williams"; plant seems to fall within normal variability of 'Frances Williams'

'Wagon Wheels': {1971r, E. Minks; 'Golden Nugget' sport} 19" by 48" md of gold-mgd, bluish green-centered lvs, 10 1/2" by 10" (17 vp); near-wh fls, late June into July on 28" sc; acts like a smaller version of 'Frances Williams'; slight to moderate burn along the margin; sports to all-gold, 'Golden Wheels' {1976r, E. Minks}

'Zager's Pride': {1987r, P. Ruh for H. Zager} formerly "Zager's Frances Williams", a name that could not be used; lg md of 'Elegans'-type foliage with wide, chartreuse margins; worth growing

---

Hosta sieboldiana 'Golden Sunburst'

key features: medium-large mound of heavily corrugated, golden foliage; tends to develop brown spots in spring

mound size: 20" high by 50" wide

---

spacing: 48"

leaves: 11 1/2" long by 9 7/8" wide; chartreuse in spring, medium gold by mid-summer; moderate underside bloom; blade broadly oblong-ovate with a deeply lobed base; blade also generally unruly at maturity; moderate corrugation; thick substance; 16 vein pairs

flowers: late June into July; near-white color with a pale lavender mid-petal stripe; 2" long by 1 1/2" wide; narrow funnel shape; in tight clusters on 29" scapes; many seed pods develop

comments: Because of the previously described "burning" problems that afflict some types of golden Sieboldiana forms, I do not recommend growing 'Golden Sunburst'. At best it becomes a medium-large mound of slug-resistant, gold foliage. Many years, however, the whole leaf can be afflicted with unsightly brown spots. If you are required by law to grow this plant, place it in a fairly protected site and avoid any exposure to direct sunlight in spring. Even if you can avoid the browning, the slow growth rate makes it a long process to maturity. There are, however, other golden 'Elegans' types that do not burn or only have minimal problems with it. Grow those plants instead!

'Golden Sunburst' originated as a sport of 'Frances Williams' in the ground many years ago. It went by the name *H. sieboldiana* 'Golden' or simply as "Golden Sieboldiana" in the few gardens that had it on display. When several tissue culture labs began producing significant numbers of it as an offtype of 'Frances Williams', the American Hosta Society registered it in 1984 with a more formal name, 'Golden Sunburst'. Two other golden Sieboldianas, 'Sunlight' and 'Midwest Gold', are almost identical.

Like 'Elegans', 'Golden Sunburst' forms large numbers of seed pods. The only reason to put any effort into growing its seedlings would be to search for non-burning, golden Sieboldiana plants.

seedlings, sports, and other related types:

'Frances Williams Baby': {1980r, E. Minks; unknown parentage} med-lg md of golden, Sieboldiana-type foliage; have seen some "spring desiccation burn"

'Golden Nugget': {1969r, V. Cooley; sdlg of *H. sieboldiana aureo-marginata*} med-sized md of cupped, bright gold foliage; near-wh fls from late June into July; slight to moderate spring desiccation burn; not grown much anymore but has been the source of numerous sports including several gold-mgd, green-centered cultivars ('Wagon Wheels', 'Cart Wheels') & green-mgd, gold-centered types ('Green Rim Nugget', 'Spinning Wheel', 'Larry Englerth')

'Midwest Gold': {1969r, V. Cooley; sdlg of *H. sieboldiana aureo-marginata*} 20" by 41" md of chartreuse to med gold lvs, 9 1/2" by 8 1/4" (16 vp); near-white fls on 24" sc, late June into July; one of the first AHS registered cultivars; slow growth rate and subject to spring desiccation burn; rarely grown; not recommended

'May T. Watts': {1985r, M. Zilis & T & Z N} white-mgd sport of 'Golden Sunburst'; margin drawstrings; combined with the burning, plant can become unsightly; named to honor a wonderful environmentalist from the Morton Arboretum in Lisle, Illinois--she deserves better!!!; luckily, not many distributed

'Sea Foam': {1978r, M. Seaver; *H. s.* 'Frances Williams' sdlg} med-sized md of gold foliage; very rare

'Sea Gold': {1985r, M. Seaver; 'Ledi Lantis' sdlg} 23" by

53" md of bright gold lvs, 11" by 8" (17 vp); 28" sc; fertile

'Sunlight': sport of *H. sieboldiana* 'Frances Williams' found by Frances Williams in 1954 (Williams, 1962b); 20" by 44" md of med gold lvs, 11" by 9" (15 vp); subject to spring burn & not recommended

'Sunlight Sister': {1986r, by the AHS for E. Nesmith} originated in the early 1960's; 23" by 60" md of med to bright gold lvs, 14 3/4" by 10 1/2" (15 vp); near-wh fls, v late June into mid-July, on 36" sc; does not develop spring desiccation burn; considered to be a sibling to 'Sunlight' but is far superior; sported to 'Neeta' {1999r, C. Owens; lvs dk green-centered, gold-mgd}

other similar types:

    'Abiqua Gold Shield'**, **'City Lights'****, 'Goldbrook Gold', 'Golden Maple', **'Golden Waffles'****, 'Golden Wheels', **'King Tut'****, **'Lime Krinkles'****, **'Piedmont Gold'****, 'Sea Gold Star', *H. sieboldiana* 'Semperaurea', 'Sun Glow', **'Treasure'****, **'White Vision'****, **'Zounds'**** **=**recommended replacements** for 'Golden Sunburst' in the landscape

---

Hosta sieboldiana 'Northern Halo'

key features: large mound of heavily corrugated, white-margined foliage

mound size: 27" high by 74" wide

spacing: 60"

leaves: 14" long by 10 1/2" wide; 3/4" wide margin creamy white in spring, sometimes turning greenish white by late summer; center blue-green early, medium green by mid-summer; moderate underside bloom; broadly oblong-ovate shape with a cordate base; margin slightly wavy; heavily corrugated; thick substance; 16-18 vein pairs

flowers: mid-June into early July; near-white with a pale lavender stripe in mid-petal; 2 1/4" long by 1 5/8" wide; narrow funnel shape; 32" scapes; many seed pods develop

comments: Walters Gardens registered 'Northern Halo' as a sport of *H. sieboldiana* 'Elegans' in 1984. Its introduction into the marketplace created quite a stir, as it was purported to essentially be a white-margined version of the very popular 'Frances Williams'. The initial enthusiasm, however, was met with disappointment in a few years when it was found that more than mutation had occurred. The result was a mixture of sports varying by width of the margin being sold as 'Northern Halo'. I can remember sorting through and identifying at least six different forms of 'Northern Halo'. Some of these had wide, white margins, while others developed pencil-thin, "drawstring" margins with age. Eventually a form with wide, white margins won out and has been sold as 'Northern Halo' for a number of years. In the mid-1990's, another form of 'Northern Halo' with the wider, whiter margins was introduced as 'Northern Exposure'.

Unlike the gold-margined 'Elegans' types, 'Northern Halo' does not develop spring "burning", for reasons that I do not understand.

For breeding purposes, 'Northern Halo' can be utilized like 'Elegans' to produce blue-leaved seedlings. The only advantages to doing this would be the availability of it in flower and the slight possibility of producing variegated seedlings.

seedlings, sports, and other related types:

'American Halo': {1999r, V. Wade; sport of 'Northern Halo'; wide, white margin}

'Northern Exposure': {1997r, Walters Gardens; 'Elegans' sport} selected form of 'Northern Halo'; very wide, white margin; 28" by 74" with lvs 15 1/4" by 10 1/2" (19 vp and a 1" to 1 1/2" wide margin)

other similar types:

'Allegan Gent': Englerth Gardens introduction; similar to 'Northern Halo' but with a mottled, greenish white margin that is 1" wide on a 10 1/2" by 8 1/2" lf (16 vp)

'Benedict Arnold': {1996r, B. Arnold; 'Dorothy Benedict' sdlg; bl-green, greenish white-mgd lvs}

'Creme de Menthe': 'Elegans' sport; thin white mgns that drawstring if overfertilized; not recommended

'Exotic Frances Williams': sport of 'Frances Williams' from the early 1980's; thin white mgns that drawstring; not recommended

'Formal Attire': {1988r, K. Vaughn; 'Breeder's Choice' X

'Frances Williams'} lg md of creamy white-mgd foliage **(see page 151)**

'Gil Jones': {1990r, R. & D. Benedict; selfed 'Dorothy Benedict' sdlg} lvs bl-green in the center, yellow to creamy white-margined; excellent substance

'Nifty Fifty': {1986r, R. Benedict; 'Dorothy Benedict' sport} large md of creamy-margined foliage; margins yellow in spring, turning creamy white by mid-July; lvs 12 1/4" by 10 3/4" (18 vp) wi a 1/2" to 7/8" margin; very attractive; does not burn

'Robert Frost': {1988r, W. & E. Lachman; 'Banana Sundae' X 'Frances Williams'} lg md of creamy white-mgd foliage **(see page 366)**

'Snow Cap': {1980r, P. Aden; 'Wide Brim' X 'Royal Rainbow'} 19" by 42" md; 7 1/2" by 6 1/4" lvs (13 vp) wi wide, white margins; near-wh fls in June-July; difficult to grow; margins often tear (not drawstring); smaller than 'Northern Halo'; not recommended

---

Hosta sieboldiana 'Northern Lights'
kcy features: medium-sized mound of white-centered foliage
mound size: 14" high by 30" wide

spacing: 30"

leaves: 10" long by 9" wide; blue-green margin, creamy white center; moderate underside bloom; broadly ovate blade with moderately wavy margins; slightly corrugated; average substance; 14-15 vein pairs

flowers: mid-June into July; near-white with a pale lavender stripe in the petal midrib; narrow funnel shape; 24-30" scapes

comments: At one time I thought 'Northern Lights' would turn out to be an important cultivar because of its splashy variegation and thick, slug-resistant leaves. It has turned out to be a collector's curiosity at best. 'Northern Lights' is not a particularly good grower, but a few gardeners have persisted and grown beautiful specimens. 'Northern Lights' is also somewhat variable with some plants having wider blue-green margins.

'Northern Lights' is a sport out of tissue culture that was registered by Walters Gardens in 1984 as a sport of *H. sieboldiana* 'Elegans'.

seedlings, sports, and other related types:
'Little Lites': {1993r, P. Banyai, J. Kulpa, & N. Krul; 'Northern Lights' sport} low md of curly, white-centered, green-mgd lvs; lf center turns pure white
'Northern Comet': variation of 'Northern Lights' with very wide, blue-green margins, narrower white center; a much better grower; rare
'Van Wade': {1990r, R. Kuk; 'Dorothy Benedict' X 'Northern Lights'} 26" by 53" md of creamy yellow-mgd, dk green-cntrd lvs, 10 1/2" by 9" (13 vp); margin 1" wide; pale lav fls on 26" sc, early July into Aug; many pods develop

other similar types:
'Great Expectations', 'Northern Mist'

Hosta sieboldiana 'Northern Mist'
key features: medium-sized mound of foliage with a mottled green and white center
mound size: 19" high by 50" wide

spacing: 36"
leaves: 12 1/2" long by 10" wide; thick, blue-green margin streaking into the green and creamy yellow mottled center; thick underside bloom; blade broadly ovate and slightly wavy; heavy corrugation; thick substance; 14-16 vein pairs
flowers: mid-June into early July; near-white with a pale lavender stripe in mid-petal; 2" long by 1 1/4" wide; narrow

funnel shape; 20-30" scapes; many seed pods develop

comments: Though closely related to 'Northern Lights', 'Northern Mist' is proving to be a much better plant for the garden. The beautifully mottled centers have just enough chlorophyll to support a decent growth rate which is a problem for 'Northern Lights'. I have seen it used effectively as a specimen plant in a number of gardens. It readily forms seed pods and could be a useful breeding plant.

'Northern Mist' was registered in 1988 by Clarence Falstad as a sport of *H. sieboldiana* 'Elegans'.

seedlings, sports, and other related types:

'American Masterpiece': {1999r, V. Wade; 'Northern Mist' sport} lvs wi wide, blue-green mgns, streaked and mottled in the center; listed in *The Wade Descriptive Hosta Catalog and Cultural Guides* for 1996-1997 as found in 1992 by Van Wade and introduced in 1996; an impressive plant

'Northern Mystery': a 'Northern Mist' sport from Clarence Falstad & Walters Gardens; lvs streaked & mottled in the center, wide bl-green mgns; md 19" by 48"; 12" by 10" lvs (17 vp) wi a 2" margin; impressive but not much different from 'Northern Mist' at maturity

'Odd Ball': {1995r, R. & D. Benedict; 'Northern Mist' sdlg; bl-green foliage}

other similar types:

'Photo Finish': {1988r, Kuk's Forest; 'Hoarfrost' sdlg} lvs misted yellow-green-white in spring with a bl-green mgn, turning medium green by mid-summer; variegation persists later in cooler climates (e.g., Pacific Northwest); md 25" by 62"; lvs 12 1/2" by 9 1/4" (16 vp), moderately corrugated, and thick-substanced; unusual collector's plant

'Spilt Milk': much like 'Northern Mist' but smaller in size
(see page 433)

Hosta sieboldii (Koba Giboshi)
key features: small, dense mound of leaves with thin, white margins; purple flowers in August
mound size: 13" high by 32" wide

spacing: 30"
leaves: 6 3/8" long by 2 3/4" wide; medium green center surrounded by a thin (1/32" to 1/8" wide), white margin; some gray-green streaking from the margin into the center; moderately shiny underside and top surfaces; blade elliptic to narrowly ovate; slightly wavy; little or no corrugation; thin substance; 4-5 vein pairs
flowers: mid to late August; medium purple with whitish petal margins and mid-petal striping; 2 1/8" long by 1 7/8" wide; open funnel shape; scapes 22-31" high, about 12 flowers per scape; develops seed pods

comments: As a garden plant *Hosta sieboldii* makes an attractive edger or ground cover. The thin, white margins add a subtle touch of color and the purple flowers produced in August make a nice show and are an ornamental plus. Its rapid growth rate and usefulness as a ground cover made it popular in the nursery industry at one time, but it has fallen out of favor with many newer, flashier varieties with better substance being introduced. Its main claim to fame may be its ability to produce variegated seedlings. Many of the popular hostas used for producing variegated seedlings have *Hosta sieboldii* in their background. Plants such as 'Beatrice', 'Neat Splash', 'Kabitan' and 'Subcrocea' are descendants of some form of *Hosta sieboldii*.

When I first started in the nursery business, I encountered this plant as *Hosta lancifolia albomarginata* and *Hosta albomarginata*, and only later as *Hosta sieboldii*. Being a variegated species makes it one of the taxonomic oddities in the genus *Hosta*. Though its origins are obscure, *Hosta sieboldii* probably originated as a single mutation from a wild population in Japan. It was collected and has been

416

maintained in cultivation for many years. Since a species must be able to sustain itself in the wild, it seems that *Hosta sieboldii* should not qualify. The reason for leaving *Hosta sieboldii* with a species designation is solely taxonomic, i.e., this plant is the "type for a large group" in the genus *Hosta* (Schmid, 1991, p. 99). Changing its name would involve a lot of taxonomic reshuffling!

The green-leaved plant commonly found in the wild was classified as *Hosta sieboldii f. spathulata* by Schmid (1991) and is also known as Koba Giboshi in Japan.

seedlings, sports, and other related types:

'Beatrice': *H. sieboldii* sdlg from Frances Williams; streaked foliage; breeding pl **(see page 74)**

'Butter Rim': {1986r by the AHS for A. Summers; *H. sieboldii* sdlg} 13" by 33" md of lance-shaped, thin, yellow-mgd, green-centered lvs, 6 3/4" by 3 1/2" (8 vp); pure white fls, July 20-Aug 7, on 35" sc; unusual combination of yellow-mgd lvs & white fls; a cultivar of long-standing; sported to 'Silver Spoon' which has white-centered, green-mgd lvs (1985r, O. Langdon)

'Carrie Ann': {1988r, P. Ruh for D. Stone; unknown parentage} 9" by 24" md of narrow, white-mgd lvs, 4" by 1 3/8" (4 vp); pure white fls on 20" sc in August; *H. sieboldii* heritage; nice combination of white-mgd lvs & white fls

'Green Beatrice': {1987r by P. Ruh for F. Williams; *H. sieboldii* sdlg} green foliage, purple flowers; sibling of 'Beatrice'

'Harvest Dawn': {1997r by P. Ruh for A. Summers; *H. sieboldii* 'Paxton's Original' sdlg} 9" by 23" md of shiny, dark green lvs, 6" by 1 3/4"; purple fls, Aug-Sept on 21" sc

'Honeybells': {*H. plantaginea* X *H. sieboldii* hybrid} lg md of wavy green foliage; fragr lav fls in Aug **(see page 231)**

'Kabitan': long-standing, gold-centered, green-mgd *H. sieboldii* form from Japan **(see page 420)**

'Krossa Cream Edge': {1997r by P. Ruh for G. Krossa} 10" by 20" md of *H. sieboldii*-type lvs, 4 3/4" by 1 7/8" (5 vp); purple fls in Aug on 24" sc, 11 per scape; long-standing garden hybrid

'Lavender Lady': {1986r by Connie Williams for her mother, Frances Williams} 13" by 27" md of med green foliage; lav fls in Aug; lvs 5 1/2" by 2 1/2"; 1948 hybrid of *H. sieboldii* X *H. plantaginea* from Frances Williams and named in 1960 (Williams, 1960b); shows no characteristics of pollen parent

'Louisa': {1986r by C. Williams for F. Williams} *H. sieboldii* sdlg; 11" by 31" md of narrow, white-mgd lvs,

5 1/2" by 2" (4-5 vp); pure white fls on 15-22" sc, Aug; few fls per scape; found by Frances Williams on Sept. 1, 1946 (Williams, 1946); introduced by Fairmount Gardens in 1959 as *H. lancifolia* hybrid (FRW #537) (Nesmith, 1959); also known as *H. lancifolia albo-marginata alba*

'Mentor Gold': {1978r, P. Ruh} dense, 12" by 38" md of white-margined lvs with centers that change from gold to green; lvs 6" by 2 1/2" (5-6 vp); med purple fls on 24" sc in Aug; *H. sieboldii*-type originated in the 1960's at the old Wayside Gardens in Mentor, Ohio

'Painted Lady': {1984r, R. Benedict; *H. sieboldii* sport} 13" by 40" md of streaked foliage; lvs sometimes white-mgd

'Purple Profusion': {1986r by C. Williams for F. Williams} *H. sieboldii* X *H. plantaginea* (sibling to 'Lavender Lady', etc.); introduced in the 1962 Fairmount Gardens catalog (Nesmith, 1962); 16" by 38" md, 6 1/2" by 3 5/8" green lvs (6 vp); beautiful purple fls, mid-Aug into Sept; worth growing

'Snow Flakes': {1986r by the AHS for F. Williams} 14" by 32" md of green lvs, 5 1/2" by 2 1/2"; nice, pure white fls in Aug; thin subst; sibling to 'Lavender Lady' (Williams, 1960b); *H. sieboldii* X *H. plantaginea*

'Slim Polly': {1986r by the AHS for F. Williams} sm md of narrow, gr lvs; med purple fls on 15" sc in August; sibling to 'Lavender Lady' (Williams, 1960b); *H. sieboldii* X *H. plantaginea*

'Subcrocea': form of *H. sieboldii* wi golden foliage; low md **(see page 426)**

'Sweet Susan': {1986r by C. Williams for F. Williams; *H. sieboldii* X *H. plantaginea*} 24" by 51" md of green lvs, 10 1/4" by 6 1/4" (8-9 vp); fragr lav fls in Aug on sc up to 40"; introduced by Fairmount Gardens in 1966 (Nesmith, 1966)

'Tinker Bell': {1986r by C. Williams for F. Williams} sm md of green foliage; listed as having white flowers; sibling to 'Lavender Lady'; *H. sieboldii* X *H. plantaginea*

other similar types:
H. lancifolia 'Change of Tradition', 'Elfin Power', 'Ginko Craig', 'Hime Karafuto', 'Little White Lines', 'Marble Rim', 'Margin of Error', 'White Dove'

Hosta sieboldii 'Alba'
(formerly *Hosta minor* 'Alba')

key features: small mound of green foliage; white flowers in August
mound size: 13" high by 30" wide

spacing: 24"

leaves: 6 1/4" long by 3" wide; medium green; slightly shiny underside; elliptic to narrowly ovate shape; slightly wavy margin; little or no corrugation; thin substance; 4-5 vein pairs

flowers: mid to late August; pure white; 2 1/4" long by 1 3/4" wide; wide open funnel shape; thin scapes up to 24" high; forms seed pods

comments: *Hosta sieboldii* 'Alba' was mistakenly sold for many years in the U.S. as *H. minor* 'Alba'. It becomes a fairly dense mound of green foliage, but is more known for its good show of white flowers in August. In the landscape it can be used effectively as a ground cover or edging plant. The true *H. minor alba* is similar but flowers earlier and is a rarely grown collector's plant. Although plants being sold as *Hosta sieboldii* 'Alba' should be fairly consistent, I suspect that over the years a number of white-flowered seedlings have been propagated as such. At the same time, several white-flowered seedlings have been introduced as separate cultivars including 'Snow Mound' and 'Snow Flakes'. Frances Williams grew many seedlings of *H. sieboldii* 'Alba' and reported that they produced either white or purple flowers (Williams, 1958).

seedlings, sports, and other related types:

'Kika': *H. sieboldii* 'Alba' sdlg wi deeply cut white fls, 3 petals per fl; in Japanese collections

'Polly Mae': {1982r, R. Savory; *H. sieboldii* 'Alba' X a sdlg; white-flowering} sm md of green lvs

419

'Snow Cream': Alex Summers introduction from the 1960's; med-sized (18" by 40") md of narrow green foliage; pure white fls on 33" sc, mid to late August; not grown much anymore

'Snow Mound': {1997r by P. Ruh for A. Summers & Sky-lands N} 11" by 33" md of narrow, green foliage; excellent show of white fls in Aug; probably a seedling of *H. sieboldii* 'Alba' or *H. sieboldii*; cultivar of long-standing

'Snow Mound Variegated': white-mgd sport of 'Snow Mound', hence white-mgd lvs plus white fls; can be found in collections and some nursery lists

other similar types:
'Mount Royal', 'Snow Drop', 'Snow Flakes', 'Snowstorm', 'Tinker Bell', 'White Mule', *H. sieboldii* 'Weihenstephen'

Hosta sieboldii 'Kabitan'
key features: low mound of narrow, gold-centered, green-margined foliage
mound size: 14" high by 32" wide

spacing: 30"
leaves: 6 1/4" long by 2" wide; 1/16" to 1/4" green margin; center gold to chartreuse, brighter with more light; slightly shiny underside; blade lanceolate to narrowly elliptic; 4-5 marginal waves; no corrugation; thin substance; 3-4 vein pairs
flowers: early to mid-August; pale purple color with darker striping in mid-petal; thin scapes, 16-24" high; few flowers per scape; will form seed pods
comments: *Hosta sieboldii* 'Kabitan' has long been a fixture in both Japanese and American hosta collections. Fumio Maekawa (1973) listed it as *Hosta lancifolia* var. *thunbergiana* f. *kabitan*, a name to scare even the most

420

ardent hosta collector! Cooler heads have prevailed and the current thinking is that 'Kabitan' is actually an *H. sieboldii* seedling and can be listed as 'Kabitan' or *H. sieboldii* 'Kabitan'. The AHS registered 'Kabitan' in 1987.

In the garden it rapidly becomes a very dense mound of variegated foliage that looks especially bright in spring. The thin, green margins sharply contrast the center which varies from pale yellow to chartreuse, depending upon the time of year and lighting. The relatively thin substance can make it a feast for slugs but it can be effective as a specimen in rock gardens or as an edger.

Despite its lack of substance, several breeders have selected and named 'Kabitan' seedlings, most of which have merit on the basis of foliage color or form. The all-green sport of 'Kabitan' was provisionally dubbed 'Green Kabitan' at my nursery, but the name has now been used in collections and gardens. 'Haku Chu Han', which should be rightly called 'Shiro Kabitan', in essence, is a white-centered version of 'Kabitan', but whether it actually sported from it is not known.

seedlings, sports, and other related types:

'Bizarre': {1986r, Kuk's Forest; 'Kabitan' sdlg} 6" by 2 1/2" gold lvs edged with a thin (1/16"), white margin; lvs also becoming corrugated with age & thin-substd; md 15" by 30"

'Blackfoot': {1994r by R. Solberg for M. Plater-Zyberk; 'Kabitan' sdlg} glowing gold lvs, 6" by 3 1/2" (6 vp); low, dense md, 12" by 36"

'Golden Spades': {1986r, Kuk's Forest; 'Kabitan' sdlg} 9" by 30" md of br gold lvs, 4" by 3" (7 vp); pale purple fls on 18" sc from mid to late July; nice, dense md of gold foliage, brightest in spring

'Golden Oriole': {1988r by the BHHS for E. Smith, 'Kabitan' X 'Hadspen Heron'} med-sized md of br gold foliage that changes to green by Aug; 16" by 40" md, 8" by 5" lvs; lav fls on 30" sc in Aug

'Green Eyes': {1990r, R. & D. Benedict; selfed 'Kabitan' sdlg} dwarf-sized md of gold-centered, green-mgd foliage; 6" by 15" md, 3" by 1" lvs

'Green Kabitan': green-lvd sport of 'Kabitan' that is much larger; 21" by 44" md, lvs 7" by 2"; 26-33" sc; vigorous md of narrow foliage; many on display at the Dubuque Arboretum and Botanical Gardens; named in 1983

'Hart's Tongue': {1987r, Kuk's Forest; 'Kabitan' sport; lvs chartreuse, turning med green} unusual plant

'Kerplunk': 'Kabitan' seedling from Herb Benedict who said that the name reflects the sound made as he discarded the original seedling into a ravine only to later recover it after having second thoughts; med-sized md of gold foliage that is much broader than 'Kabitan'; 17" by 41" md, 8" by 4 1/2" lvs (7 vp)

'Lakeside Twiddle Dee': {1996r, M. Chastain; 'Kabitan' X a sdlg; med green foliage}

'Maui Rains': {1991r, W. Vaughn, 'Kabitan' X 'Saishu Jima'} dense, 17" by 38" md of shiny, dk green foliage that is heavily rippled and corrugated; lvs 7" by 4"; attractive & worth growing

'Peedee Gold Flash': {1987r, U. Syre-Herz; 'Kabitan' sdlg} gold-centered, green-mgd foliage becoming larger than 'Kabitan' **(see page 337)**

'Sea Sprite': {1978r, M. Seaver; 'Kabitan' sdlg} gold-centered, green-mgd foliage; good contrast between margin & center; unfortunately infected with a virus and should not be grown; virus evident by large yellow spots on the foliage; some lvs may not show spots **(see page 580)**

'Shima Kabitan': green and white streaked 'Kabitan' sdlg from Gotemba Nursery in Japan

'Shiro Kabitan' ('Haku Chu Han'): white-centered sport of *H. sieboldii* or 'Kabitan' **(see page 423)**

'Tucker Wave': {1995r, R. Stephens; 'Kabitan' X 'Neat Splash' sdlg; lvs dk green wi a lt green mgn; pale lav fls}

other similar types:

'Crown Prince': {1978r, P. Ruh & H. Ross; unknown parentage} 12" by 25" md of gold-centered, pale green-mgd lvs, 5" by 3" (6-7 vp); purple fls in Aug on 21" sc; foliage greens during the season

'Lyme Regis': 12" by 24" md of gold-centered, green-margined lvs, 5 1/2" by 2 1/8" (5 vp); dk green margin, 1/4" wide; white flowers on 18" scapes in Aug; originated by Ed Skrocki; notable for its combination of gold-centered foliage and white flowers

'Moon Shadow': {1988r, R. Savory; 'Butter Rim' X a sdlg} small md of gold-centered, green-mgd lvs, 6 1/2" by 3" (6 vp); pale purple fls; have seen a few (not all) plants of this cv. infected with the 'Sea Sprite' virus

Hosta sieboldii 'Shiro Kabitan' (Shiro Kabitan Giboshi) ('Haku Chu Han')

key features: small, dense mound of white-centered foliage

mound size: 6" high by 18" wide

spacing: 18"

leaves: 4 1/2" long by 1 1/8" wide; 1/8" wide, green margins often streak into the white center; center becomes greenish by late summer; shiny underside; narrowly elliptic shape; moderately rippled margin giving the clump an overall wavy appearance; no corrugation; thin substance; 4 vein pairs

flowers: mid-August; purple with striping on petals leading into the whitish

throat; bright purple buds; 1 7/8" long by 1" wide; scapes up to 17" high; will form seed pods

comments: Sometimes one name can represent several different plants, inevitably leading to confusion. Here is a case of one plant being represented by several different names. It has been sold and known in the U.S. as 'Haku Chu Han' (or 'Haku-chu-han') for many years, but due to a translation problem, this name is apparently not correct. Kenji Watanabe (1985) stated that 'Shiro Kabitan' is actually the proper name for this plant, not 'Haku Chu Han'. Schmid (1991), on the other hand, wrote that the name "Shirokabitan" has been used taxonomically in conjunction with *H. sieboldii* 'Subcrocea', and therefore cannot be used in place of 'Haku Chu Han'. Instead he advocates the usage of a third name, 'Silver Kabitan'. What a confusing mess! (Unfortunately the AHS registered the name *Hosta sieboldii* 'Haku-chu-han' in 1986 before all the controversy about the name ensued.)

In cultivation 'Shiro Kabitan' makes a very attractive, low mound of brightly variegated foliage. The centers tend to green up by late summer, probably accounting for its good growth rate as a white-centered plant. On the negative side, it has fairly thin foliage that is susceptible to slug dam-

423

age and cannot tolerate dryness. I have seen flattened clumps of 'Shiro Kabitan' during very dry summers.

It can be utilized as a breeding plant, with the caution that it always should be hybridized with something that has better substance.

seedlings, sports, and other related types:
'Heart of Chan': {1987r, C. Owens; 'Haku Chu Han' sdlg}17" by 52" md of green lvs; many lav fls open on 30" scapes in July

other similar types:
'Celebration', 'Cupid's Arrow', 'Gay Feather', 'Island Charm', 'Masquerade', 'Royal Tiara', 'White Swan', 'Undulata'

Hosta sieboldii spathulata (Koba Giboshi)
key features: small mound of elliptic-shaped, green foliage; purple flowers in August
mound size: 14" high by 42" wide

spacing: 30"
leaves: 6" long by 2 1/8" wide; medium to dark green; shiny top surface; shiny underside; blade elliptic to lanceolate; margin slightly wavy, especially when juvenile; thin substance; 5-6 vein pairs
flowers: mid to late August; medium purple color with darker striping in mid-petal; darker purple in bud; 2 1/8" long by 1 1/2" wide; thin (1/8" wide) scapes, 22-31" high; many seed pods develop
comments: *Hosta sieboldii* f. *spathulata* is the form of *Hosta sieboldii* commonly found in the wild in Japan. Schmid (1991) classified it as such though it has been more widely known as *H. sieboldii* 'Viridis', *H. albomarginata* 'Viridis', and *H. lancifolia thunbergiana*. It shares its Japan-

424

ese common name, Koba Giboshi, with the white-margined *H. sieboldii*, but *H. sieboldii spathulata* is the plant that is more frequently associated with it. *H. sieboldii spathulata* can be found in a wide variety of habitats in Japan, but most often can be located in wooded areas. Perhaps the most interesting site I observed was the same artillery range at the base of Mt. Fuji where thousands of *Hostas montana* grew. Like the latter, *H. sieboldii spathulata* could be found between large lava floes amongst Sensitive Fern, Japanese Astilbe, and other perennials beneath the tall Maiden Grass. The two hosta species occupied isolated, distinct patches throughout the artillery range, but the *H. sieboldii spathulata* generally grew in lower, wetter areas than *H. montana*. There were also a few pockets of hybrids between the two species, usually growing near *H. sieboldii spathulata*.

Wild populations of Koba Giboshi exhibit incredible diversity. In Japanese collections of wild-collected specimens, not only did I see the typical, slightly rippled form, but also a very dwarf, round-leaved form, and one with extremely narrow, elliptic leaves that seems to come close to *H. longissima* but not *H. longissima longifolia*. There are also heavily rippled forms including one that Schmid (1991) identified as *H. sieboldii* f. *angustifolia*. This, or something similar, is probably in the background of such cultivars as 'Chartreuse Wiggles' and 'Saishu Jima'. Seedlings vary in flower color ranging from purple to pure white. Several white-flowered seedlings have been introduced as cultivars.

H. sieboldii spathulata is rarely used as a landscape plant, but would make a good edger or ground cover. The growth rate is excellent, but the foliar substance is thin.

seedlings, sports, and other related types:
none listed (most attributed to the white-margined form, *H. sieboldii*)

other similar types:
'Green Beatrice', 'Green Wiggles', 'Gypsy's Boa', 'Harvest Dawn', 'Jingle Bells', 'Lavender Lady', 'Purple Profusion', 'Royal Lady', 'Sea Octopus', 'Sentinels', *H. sieboldii* 'Alba', 'Slim Polly', 'Snow Mound', 'Temple Bells', 'The Twister'

Hosta sieboldii 'Subcrocea'
(Ki Kabitan Giboshi)

key features: low, dense mound of wavy, golden foliage
mound size: 14" high by 29" wide

spacing: 24"
leaves: 6 1/4" long by 1 3/4" wide; color varies from chartreuse (deep shade) to bright gold (open shade); slightly shiny underside; blade lanceolate to narrowly elliptic; slight to moderate marginal waviness; little or no corrugation; thin substance; 4 vein pairs
flowers: early to mid-August; pale purple with darker striping; 1 3/4" long by 1" wide; scapes up to 22" high; fertile

comments: *Hosta sieboldii* 'Subcrocea' makes a very dense mound of narrow gold foliage. The color varies according to the amount of light that it receives. I have seen it almost white-gold in sunny areas and chartreuse when grown in deep shade. The purplish flowers offer a nice contrast to the foliage. It has been a fairly popular plant for hybridizing, but nearly all of the seedlings share its one negative: poor foliar substance. Extra protection from slugs and dry conditions is an absolute necessity.

Maekawa (1973) listed this plant as *Hosta lancifolia* var. *thunbergiana* f. *subchrocea*. Over the years, the "subchrocea" was corrected to "subcrocea" and the species designation became *Hosta sieboldii*. The common name listed by Maekawa (1973), Shiro Kabitan Giboshi, was incorrect since the plant commonly known by this name in Japan has white-centered foliage. The more accurate common name, Ki Kabitan Giboshi, has been listed by Hajime Sugita (1984). Plants resembling 'Subcrocea' can be found in Japanese nurseries under a third common name, Ogon Koba Giboshi (*H. sieboldii* 'Ogon Koba').

The AHS registered 'Subcrocea' in 1987.

seedlings, sports, and other related types:

'Anne Arett': {1975r, A. Arett; 'Subcrocea' sport} 12" by 28" md of white-margined, gold-centered lvs, 5" by 1 1/4" (4 vp), thin-substd; pale purple fls from mid to late August on 20" sc

'Cheatin Heart': {1995r, W. Zumbar; 'Subcrocea' sdlg X 'Birchwood Gem'} 8" by 18" md of light gold foliage that is oval-shaped & lightly wavy; lvs measure 4" by 3 1/4" (6 vp); thin-substd; pale purple fls in mid-July on 18" sc; sported to 'Faithful Heart' {1999r, K. Brill; green-mgd, gold-centered lvs}

'Feather Boa': {1991r, R. O'Harra; 'Subcrocea' sdlg; bright yellow in spring} forms a low, neat mound of foliage that becomes chartreuse by July; 11" by 27" md, 3 3/4" by 2" lvs (5 vp); attractive purple fls in July on 16" sc; fast grower, thin substance

'Gypsy's Boa': {1999r by the Russ O'Harra Hosta Society for R. O'Harra; listed as producing purple fls in July} low md of wavy green foliage; probably sdlg of 'Subcrocea' or one of its seedlings

'Gingee': {1986r, R. O'Harra; 'Subcrocea' sdlg} sm, very dense md of narrow, heavily rippled, bright gold foliage; 10" by 26" md, 5 3/8" by 1 3/8" lvs; thin substance

'Ground Sulphur': {1986r, R. O'Harra; parentage unknown} 8" by 20", ground-hugging md of narrow, gold lvs, 4" by 1 3/4"; pale purple fls on 18" sc, mid to late July; probably a 'Subcrocea' sdlg

'Little Ann': {1998r, P. Ruh for D. Stone} 9" by 25" md of gold-centered, white mgd lvs, 4" by 1 5/8" (4-5 vp); med purple fls on 19" sc in mid-Aug; thought to be smaller than 'Anne Arett', but differences are minimal

'Rosanne': {1999r by the Russ O'Harra Hosta Society for R. O'Harra} bright gold foliage forming a 10" by 24" md; 6 1/2" by 1 3/4" lvs that are also wavy; probably a 'Subcrocea' sdlg

'Wogon Gold': {1986r, AHS} long-established name, but some feel the name should be changed to 'Wogon'; sm md of foliage that changes from br yellow in spring to chartreuse by late summer; lvs 6 1/4" by 2 1/2" (4-6 vp); purple fls on 19" sc in Aug; imported from Japan in the 1960's

'Yellow Boa': {1991r, R. O'Harra; 'Subcrocea' sdlg} 11" by 28", dense md of narrow, wavy gold lvs

'Yellow Eyes': {1999r, P. Ruh; sport of 'Green Eyes'} low, dense md of very wavy, med gold to chartreuse lvs, 3" by 1 1/4" (4 vp); md 7" by 14"; brilliant purple fls in July on 14" sc; sent to originator as 'Green Eyes'; nice combination of gold lvs & purple fls

other similar types:
'Blackfoot', 'Chartreuse Wiggles', 'Estrellita', 'Lauren', 'Orange Joy', 'Purple and Gold', 'Royalty', 'Sea Wiggles', 'Yellow Submarine', 'Yellow Waves'

'Silver Bowl'
key features: medium-large mound of deeply cupped, blue-green foliage
mound size: 23" high by 57" wide

spacing: 48"
leaves: 13" long by 11" wide (up to 15" by 12"); blue-green early, changing to a shiny, dark green; thick underside bloom; blade broadly ovate to rotund, deeply cupped (2-3") and somewhat unruly; heavily corrugated; thick substance; 17-19 vein pairs
flowers: mid-June into early July; near-white with a pale lavender stripe in mid-petal; 2 1/4" long by 1 1/2" wide; scapes 20-24" high; many seed pods develop

comments: Though 'Silver Bowl' can be considered an "older" cultivar, it still ranks highly for its deeply cupped foliage. The blue-green color, thick substance, and near-white flowers are common to many other Sieboldianas, but the cupping almost puts it into a class by itself. Even after the bluish bloom has washed away and 'Silver Bowl' has become an "emerald bowl", it remains quite attractive and distinctive.

'Silver Bowl' is a Eunice Fisher origination from the 1970's that the AHS registered in 1986. It should make an excellent parent owing to its many good qualities, but no related hosta has been registered.

seedlings, sports, and other related types:
none listed
other similar types:
'Alabama Bowl': {1986r, N. Suggs; 'Elegans' X 'Big

428

Mama'} med-lg md of deeply cupped foliage that is bl-green early turning to shiny green by July; whitish fls from mid to late July; differs from the typical Sieboldiana, especially in flower

'Julia Hardy': {1978r, P. Aden; 'Tokudama' X 'Big Mama'} 22" by 40" md of blue-green lvs, 11 3/4" by 9" (17 vp), that are also thick-substanced & deeply cupped; near-wh fls, late June into July

'Lochness Blue': {1999r, K. Brill; sport of 'Lochness'} 24" by 42" md of deeply cupped, bl-green lvs, 13" by 10" (18 vp)

'Love Pat': cupped, blue foliage **(see page 286)**

'Puckered Cup': lg md of heavily corrugated, deeply cupped, blue-green foliage; lvs 14" by 12" (18 vp); near-wh fls; outstanding blue color & deep cupping; observed in the Wade and Gatton N collection

---

'So Sweet'
key features: large mound of white-margined foliage; fragrant pale lavender flowers in August
mound size: 22" high by 50" wide (up to 26" by 60")

spacing: 48"
leaves: 7" long by 5" wide; 1/4" to 1/2" wide margin that changes from yellow in spring to creamy white by mid-summer; medium to dark green center; shiny top and underside; blade ovate with age, elliptic-ovate when younger; slightly wavy margins; smooth texture; average substance; 7-8 vein pairs
flowers: early to late August; pale lavender; 3" long by 2 1/2" wide; very fragrant; open funnel shape; scapes up to 36" high; limited pod formation

comments: The rapid growth rate, white-margined foliage and large numbers of fragrant flowers make 'So Sweet' an outstanding choice for almost any shaded landscape situation. It has been held in such high regard that the American Hosta Growers Association honored it in 1996 as its first "Hosta of the Year". It not only does well in nursery containers, but rapidly reaches maturity in the garden. The foliage does not become as large as other fragrant-flowered, white-margined cultivars such as 'Fragrant Bouquet', 'Sugar and Cream', and 'Summer Fragrance', but the flower size and fragrance rank near the top.

'So Sweet' was registered by Paul Aden in 1986 as a hybrid between 'Fragrant Bouquet' X a seedling.

seedlings, sports, and other related types:
"Green So Sweet": unnamed sport with all-green foliage; 28" by 60" md; 7 3/4" by 3 3/4" lvs (8 vp); attractive lg md of shiny, green foliage

other similar types:
'Bold Edger', 'Emily Dickinson', 'Savannah', 'Summer Fragrance', 'Sugar and Cream'

'Solar Flare'
key features: large, arching mound of bright gold foliage
mound size: 32" high by 73" wide (up to 40" by 120")

spacing: 72"
leaves: 14" long by 10 3/8" wide (up to 17" by 13"); chartreuse in spring, changing to brilliant gold by mid-summer; veins and midrib remain chartreuse; thin bloom on top in spring, washing away by early summer; moderate underside bloom; blade broadly ovate with a cordate base; many slight ripples along the margin; slight to moderate corrugation;

good substance; 17-20 vein pairs

flowers: late June into mid-July; very pale lavender with a slightly darker stripe in mid-petal; color bleaches to near-white with exposure to direct sunlight; 2 3/4" long by 1 5/8" wide; scapes 28-35" high; about 39 flowers per scape, most in the upper 6" of the scapes; many seed pods form, weighing down the scapes

comments: 'Solar Flare' becomes a bright and imposing plant in the landscape with its large, broad mound habit and brilliant gold foliage. The color intensifies during the season but the veins and midrib stay pale green and offer an interesting contrast. I have seen it effectively used as the centerpiece of an island bed and as a background plant. It has a semi-upright, arching mound habit that requires smaller plants to be grown in front of it. Pink-flowering Impatiens makes a very effective foreground plant.

The foliage color varies considerably by location and season of year. Early in the season, the color can best be described as dusky chartreuse, but it generally lightens as the season progresses. In mid-summer it will be even brighter if exposed to direct sunlight. The flower effect is not especially great once 'Solar Flare' reaches its immense proportions. At that point the scapes are mostly hidden within the foliage.

Henry Ross developed 'Solar Flare' and registered it in the name of his Gardenview Horticultural Park in Strongsville, Ohio in 1981. Though the parentage is unknown, it shows traits of both *H. sieboldiana* and *H. montana*. 'Solar Flare' has been patented (PP# 7046), so propagation is strictly licensed. This, however, should not discourage anyone from growing this magnificent plant in their garden.

seedlings, sports, and other related types:
none listed

other similar types:
'Fort Knox', 'Gold Regal', 'Golden Sculpture', 'Sunlight Sister', 'Yellow Emperor', 'Yellow Highness'

'Sparkling Burgundy'

key features: medium-sized mound of narrow, green foliage; outstanding show of purple flowers in August

mound size: 18" high by 36" wide

spacing: 36"

leaves: 7" long by 4" wide; shiny, medium green; whitish shiny underside; blade elliptic and moderately wavy; smooth texture; average substance; 8-10 vein pairs

flowers: early to late August; pale purple, darker in bud; 2 1/4" long by 1 1/8" wide; wide-open funnel shape; many 28", reddish-colored scapes; develops a few pods

comments: 'Sparkling Burgundy' has developed the reputation of being one of the best hostas for flower effect. Large numbers of pale purple flowers are produced in August on scapes which are in good proportion to the foliage mound. When used as a ground cover in a mass planting, the flower effect is further enhanced. It ranks as one of Bob Savory's most popular introductions (after 'Golden Tiara', no doubt) and was registered as a hybrid between 'Ginko Craig' X a seedling in 1982.

seedlings, sports, and other related types:

'Kiwi Parasol': {1999r, B. Sligh; sport; lvs med bl-green wi a margin}

'Obsession': {1998r, T. Avent; sport; lvs med green wi v dark gr margin}

'Party Time': {1995r, R. & D. Benedict; 'Nooner' X 'Sparkling Burgundy'} 17" by 37" md of shiny, dark green lvs, 8 5/8" by 5 3/4" (11 vp) wi irregularly rippled margins

other similar types:

'Green Smash', 'Maraschino Cherry'

'Spilt Milk'

key features: large mound of thick-substanced leaves with misted, green and white centers
mound size: 24" high by 52" wide

spacing: 48"
leaves: 10 1/2" long by 8" wide; 1-2" wide, blue-green margin changing to green by mid-summer flowing into the misted green and white center which often produces solid white streaks; moderate underside bloom; broadly ovate blade with a deeply lobed base; wavy margins; moderately corrugated; thick substance; 15 vein pairs

flowers: very late June into mid-July; near-white; 2 1/4" long by 1 1/4" wide; scapes 29" high

comments: Occasionally a hosta is so distinctive that it becomes the archetype for a specific group. Such is the case with 'Spilt Milk'. Its misted green-and-white-centered leaves, overlaid with a bluish bloom in spring, caught everyone's attention when displayed at various hosta conventions in the late 1980's. 'Spilt Milk' won recognition as the best "Unregistered Seedling" at the leaf show during the 1987 AHS convention (AHS, 1987) and then received the prestigious Nancy Minks Award during the 1989 AHS convention held in Indianapolis (AHS, 1989). It ranks as one of Mildred Seaver's finest introductions and one of the few not bearing her "Sea series" designation. In the landscape, its best usage is certainly as a specimen plant, perhaps in combination with slightly smaller blue-leaved Tokudamas.

One of my initial worries about 'Spilt Milk' was that it would continually sport to a white-centered plant as it tends to produce pure white-centered streaks in many leaves. This fear proved unfounded, however, as thousands of true-to-type 'Spilt Milk' plants have been propagated and are being offered from a wide variety of sources. The Hosta Finder 2000 (Greene, 2000) lists 30 retail mail-order sources of this plant, being sold for an average of $40.48 per plant. Though its parentage is unknown, 'Spilt Milk' no doubt has *H. sieboldiana* in its lineage, though the flowering occurs about two weeks later than *H. s.* 'Elegans'.

Mildred Seaver registered 'Spilt Milk' in 1999.

seedlings, sports, and other related types:
none listed

other similar types:
'American Masterpiece', 'Northern Mist', 'Northern Mystery', 'Sea Mist'

'Spritzer'
key features: medium-large, cascading mound of gold-centered, green-margined foliage
mound size: 22" high by 50" wide

spacing: 48"
leaves: 9 1/2" long by 5" wide; thin, green margin that often streaks into the gold center; shiny top, very shiny underside; blade narrowly ovate with a rounded base and long, curved tip; margins slightly, but noticeably rippled; smooth texture; average substance; 8 vein pairs
flowers: mid-August into early September; pale lavender; leafy scapes; fertile
comments: The flowing, dense mound habit of 'Spritzer' in combination with its bright variegation produces a spectacular sight. Paul Aden registered it in 1986 as a hybrid of a seedling X 'Green Fountain'. It definitely shows a strong relationship to its pollen parent, almost appearing to be a variegated version of it.

It can be utilized in a breeding program, passing on its flowing mound habit to its seedlings.

Unfortunately I have seen a few specimens of 'Spritzer'

infected with a virus (see the "Hosta Problem Solving Guide"). It is characterized by concentric, light yellow circles, 1-2" in diameter. Such plants should be discarded and the garden area sanitized. Unlike 'Sea Sprite', where apparently every known specimen is infected, I have only seen a few plants of 'Spritzer' infected with this virus.

seedlings, sports, and other related types:
'Katrina Jo': {1998r, F. Nyikos; seedling; light greenish yellow foliage}
'Lakeside Party Dress': {1997r, M. Chastain; a "Lakeside Seedling" X 'Spritzer'; lt green to gold-centered, creamy white-mgd lvs}

other similar types:
'Golden Fountain'

'Standing Ovation'
key features: large mound of gold-margined foliage
mound size: 28" high by 60" wide (up to 32" by 65")

spacing: 60"
leaves: 12" long by 9 1/2" wide; 1/2" wide gold margin, deep green center; thin underside bloom; blade broadly ovate with a deeply lobed base and lightly rippled margin; slightly corrugated; good substance; 13-14 vein pairs
flowers: late June into mid-July; pale purple; 1 3/4" long by 1 1/4" wide; funnel-shaped; borne well above the foliage on scapes up to 51" high; many seed pods develop
comments: 'Standing Ovation' was registered in 1987 by Kevin Vaughn as a hybrid between a variegated seedling X a green 'Goliath' seedling. It makes a tremendous mound that can be effectively utilized as either a background plant or specimen. The gold margins do not burn and should sat-

isfy the needs of those who want a non-burning Sieboldiana-type that is also a better grower. The purists may point to the differences in flower habit, i.e. they are borne on tall scapes and are purplish, but the foliage and mound habit definitely is Sieboldiana-like.

seedlings, sports, and other related types:
none listed

other similar types:
'Carnival', 'Celebrity', 'El Capitan'

'Stiletto'
key features: low, dense mound of narrow, heavily rippled, white-margined foliage
mound size: 12" high by 32" wide

spacing: 24"

leaves: 5 1/2" long by 1 1/2" wide; 1/8" wide margin that changes from yellow to creamy white; medium to dark green center; margin heavily rippled when young, less so at maturity; shiny top and underside; blade narrowly elliptic; smooth texture; thin substance; 3-4 vein pairs

flowers: early to late August; medium purple with three mid-petal stripes into a white base; 2 1/4" long by 1 1/8" wide; slightly bell-shaped; scapes up to 25" high; fertile

comments: The very dense, low mound habit and fast growth rate make 'Stiletto' one of the best hostas for edging a shaded border. The feature that gives 'Stiletto' its distinction, however, is the combination of the heavily rippled, white margin and a very narrow leaf shape. Though the rippled effect diminishes with maturity, division every three to five years helps maintain this trait. Not to be overlooked are the purple flowers which are an ornamental plus throughout the month of August.

'Stiletto' exhibits *H. sieboldii* heritage in both foliage and flower. Paul Aden registered 'Stiletto' in 1987 as a hybrid of 'Amy Aden' X *H. pulchella* variegated.

seedlings, sports, and other related types:
'Boogie Woogie': {1998r, C. Helsley; sport; lf center streaked, mgns white}

other similar types:
'Ginko Craig', 'Jadette', 'Ototo San'
'Wiggleworms': listed as a Glen Draper introduction in the *Hosta Finder 2000* (Greene, 2000); sm md of heavily rippled, narrow, yellow-mgd lvs

---

'Striptease'
key features: medium-sized mound of green-margined leaves with a narrow band of gold in the center; 'Gold Standard' sport
mound size: 20" high by 50" wide

---

spacing: 48"
leaves: 8" long by 6" wide; dark green margin; narrow gold center, 2" wide; some streaks of white at the junction of the center and margin; thin underside bloom; blade ovate and slightly wavy; smooth texture; average substance; 9-10 vein pairs
flowers: mid-July into early August; pale lavender; 1 3/4" long by 1" wide; funnel-shaped; 20-30" scapes

comments: When the late Rick Thompson first described 'Striptease' to me in the late 1980's, I thought that it could be a temporary phenomenon. After all, I had seen literally thousands of 'Gold Standard' mutations, most never amounting to much. Once I was actually able to see a leaf (in 1991) and then fully grown clumps, I became thoroughly convinced that Rick had really discovered something valuable. The wider dark green margin and narrower gold center of 'Striptease' differs so much from 'Gold Standard' that the two almost do not look related. Individual leaves give the appearance of a narrow gold leaf within a leaf. Another distinctive feature are the white lines that develop between the leaf center and margin.

'Striptease' is part of the trend toward identifying wider margined forms of many established cultivars. 'Night Before Christmas' out of 'White Christmas', 'Patriot' (and 'Minuteman') out of 'Francee', 'Dream Weaver' from 'Great Expectations', and 'Avocado' from 'Guacamole', are just a few examples of this current craze. Even 'Gold Standard' has yielded a few more such sports. Several older examples of this "fine-tuning of sports" include 'Undulata Univittata' coming out of 'Undulata' and 'White Ray' and 'Middle Ridge' from 'Undulata Univittata'.

'Striptease' multiplies fairly rapidly making division an excellent means of propagation. Tissue culturing 'Striptease' can be successful, but the results are often inconsistent.

Rick and Criss Thompson registered 'Striptease' in 1991.

seedlings, sports, and other related types:

'Captain Kirk': {1999r, K. Brill; 'Gold Standard' sport} impressive, narrow-centered lvs, 8" by 7" wi a 2" mgn (3" center); different from 'Striptease' and 'Gold Standard'

'G String': {1996r, J. Mann, Jr.; 'Gold Standard' sport wi leaves that have narrow gold centers}

'Gamma Ray': {1999r, A. Malloy; 'Striptease' sport; lvs green-mgd wi a thin, white center}

'Landmark': sport of 'Gold Standard' found in 1998 at Landmark Gardens, Plattsmouth, NE; v narrow gold center & wide green mgn

other similar types:

'Banana Boat', 'Robert's Rapier', 'Silver Streak', 'White Ray'

'Sugar and Cream'

key features: large, flowing mound of wavy, white-margined foliage; fragrant flowers in August

mound size: 28" high by 58" wide

spacing: 54"

leaves: 12 1/2" long by 5 1/2" wide; 1/4" to 1/2" wide margins that change from creamy yellow to white, medium green center; very shiny underside; elliptic-ovate, becoming broader with age; blade distinctly wavy and puckered downward; smooth texture; average substance; 9-10 vein pairs

flowers: August 12 to September 7; very pale lavender,

slightly darker in bud; 2 9/16" long by 2 1/2" wide; very fragrant; many scapes up to 43" high; sparse pod formation with few viable seeds per pod

comments: 'Sugar and Cream' has become established as one of the leading variegated, fragrant-flowered hosta cultivars. It rapidly becomes a large-sized, flowing mound of white-margined foliage that is an excellent choice for many landscaping purposes. 'Sugar and Cream' originated as a tissue culture sport of 'Honeybells' that I developed and registered in 1984. During the 1985 AHS convention it received the Savory Shield Award as the best new introduction in a tour garden.

Like 'Honeybells' it reluctantly develops pods and there are few viable seeds in the ones that do.

seedlings, sports, and other related types:

'Sweet Standard': {1984r, M. Zilis} sport of 'Honeybells'; from the same cultures as 'Sugar and Cream'; leaves creamy wh-mgd, green-and-white-streaked centers; fast-growing, splashy specimen plant in the garden, but off-color divisions need to be culled

'Whipped Cream': {1988r, M. Zilis & T & Z N; sport of 'Honeybells'} gr-mgd, white-cntrd lvs; very weak; very rare

other similar types:

H. plantaginea 'Ming Treasure': {1999r, M. Zilis; *H. plantaginea* sport} lvs green-centered with 1/4" wide margins that change from chartreuse to gold to white, depending upon time of year and exposure to light; 1997 Q & Z N introduction

'Savannah': {1999r, N. Suggs & M. Zilis} sport of a plant selected by N. Suggs; 1996 Q & Z N introduction; 25" by 60" md; lvs 11" by 7 1/2" with a 1/2" creamy white mgn; fragr, lavender fls on three-foot sc in Aug; similar to 'Summer Fragrance'

'So Sweet': {1986r, P. Aden; 'Fragrant Bouquet' X a sdlg} med-lg md of creamy white-margined foliage; fragrant, pale lav fls; widely grown; outstanding **(see page 429)**

'Summer Fragrance': {1983r, K. Vaughn; "Vaughn 73-2" X *H. plantaginea*} white-margined lvs, fragr fls; 26" by 57" md; lvs 12" by 8 3/4" wi a med green center & a 1/4" to 3/8" mgn that changes from yellow to creamy white; v pale lav fls, mid-Aug into Sept on sc 36" or higher; the first cultivar to combine white-margined foliage with fragrant flowers

'Sweet Serenity': {1990r, M. Zilis} white-margined t.c. sport of 'Sweet Susan'; fast-growing, large mound; margins change from yellow to creamy white; very rare

'Sultana'

key features: medium-sized mound of gold-margined foliage; 'Little Aurora' sport
mound size: 16" high by 30" wide

spacing: 30"

leaves: 5 1/2" long by 4 1/2" wide; 1/2" to 1" wide, medium gold margins, dark green center; thin underside bloom; blade broadly ovate and slightly wavy; slightly corrugated; good substance; 11 vein pairs

flowers: late June into mid-July; very pale lavender; scapes up to 24" high; fertile

comments: 'Sultana' was registered as a sport of 'Little Aurora' in 1988 by

Bill Zumbar and it may be his best introduction to date. It ranks highly among medium-sized gold-edged hostas, perhaps surpassing 'Golden Tiara' as the top plant in this category. The sharp contrast between the dark green center and the gold margins gives 'Sultana' a very attractive appearance. 'Sultana' has a moderate growth rate, performing well as a ground cover or edging plant and makes an attractive combination with gold-leaved 'Little Aurora' or green-leaved 'Puck'. Like 'Little Aurora' the flowering is not especially exciting, but does not detract from the foliage.

seedlings, sports, and other related types:
none listed

other similar types:

'Carousel': {1989r, W. & E. Lachman; sdlg X 'Reversed'} 16" by 30" md of gold-mgd, green-centered lvs, 6 1/2" by 5 1/4" (9 vp); lvs also heavily corrugated; striking contrast betw lf mgn & center

'Golden Tiara', 'Grand Tiara', 'Radiant Edger', 'Warwick Curtsey'

'Sum and Substance'
key features: immense mound of chartreuse to medium gold foliage; largest hosta cultivar
mound size: 31" high by 70" wide (up to 48" by 114")

spacing: 72"
leaves: 16" long by 14" wide (up to 19 3/4" by 17"); light green in early spring becoming chartreuse to medium gold depending upon light level; shiny on top, thin underside bloom; broadly oblong-ovate shape with a slightly cupped, deeply lobed base and long, skinny tip; blade also generally wavy and somewhat downwardly cupped; slight to moderate corrugation; thick substance; 14-17 vein pairs
flowers: late July into mid-August; pale lavender color with a thin white petal margin; 3" long by 1 1/2" wide; funnel shape; scapes up to 48" long, tending to droop as flowering progresses; will form seed pods
comments: 'Sum and Substance' rates as one of the most significant hosta cultivars ever developed. It combines a huge mound size, outstanding substance, and attractive foliage. In the landscape, it becomes an imposing plant with a very broad mound habit and has a relatively rapid growth rate for a large-sized hosta. Plan its placement well because it will certainly occupy a very large space within a few years. The foliage color is subject to light level, becoming brighter with more light. The substance is thick and quite slug-resistant. Perhaps its only fault is that the scapes have a tendency to droop as flowering proceeds and can look a bit messy.

Van Wade's clump of 'Sum and Substance' ranks as the largest hosta I've measured and may be a world record. Growing to proportions of 48" high by 114" wide, this mound has not only become famous for its dimensions, but for the special "fertilizer" that Van placed at the bottom of the planting hole. When you visit the magnificent Wade & Gatton Nurseries hosta collection, ask Van about his "secret to success".

'Sum and Substance' has become a top breeding plant, as well as the source of a large number of mutations. In my own hybridizing program, I have used 'Sum and Substance' with a fair amount of success. With it as the pod parent, I've introduced 'Leather Sheen', 'Little Razor', 'New Wave', 'Golden Decade', 'Metallic Sheen', and 'Raleigh Remembrance'. The number of sports out of 'Sum and Substance' keeps increasing, especially those with green-centered, gold-margined foliage. 'Beauty Substance', 'Bottom Line', 'Corona', 'David A. Haskell', 'Lady Isobel Barnett', 'Sum It Up', 'Sum of All', 'Sum Total', 'Supersonic', and 'Tiffney's Godzilla' are included in this group. Though there is some debate as to the merits of all of these, some definitely have wider, showier margins. As well, four green-leaved sports have been registered: 'Domaine De Courson', 'Green Gables', 'Irish Hills', and 'Sum Piecrust'.

Paul Aden registered 'Sum and Substance' in 1980. The parentage is unknown, but it does show traits of both *H. nigrescens* 'Elatior' and *H. hypoleuca*.

seedlings, sports, and other related types:

'Abiqua Recluse': {1989r, Walden West; 'White Vision' X 'Sum and Substance'} med-lg md of bright gold foliage **(see page 60)**

'Bottom Line': green-centered, gold-mgd sport from Pine Forest Gardens in Fayetteville, GA

'Beauty Substance': green-centered, gold-mgd 'Sum and Substance' sport from Tower Perennial Gardens

'Bubba': {1998r, T. Avent; 'Sum and Substance' sdlg} 20" by 44" md of shiny, moderately corrug, green lvs, 8 1/2" by 4 7/8" (10 vp); petioles purplish red

'Corona': {1996r, G. Braun-Nauerz & P. Warmerdam; sport; lvs green wi deep gold mgns}

'David A. Haskell' {1999r, A. Haskell & A. Malloy; sport; lvs green wi a wide yellow margin}

'Domaine De Courson': {1996r, I. Van Doorslaer & D. Grenfell; sport with med green foliage}

'Eagle's Nest': sport of 'Sum and Substance' from Ran Lydell; described in his Cooks Nursery and Eagle Bay Gardens 2000 Hosta List (p. 8) as a "most unusual sport of 'Sum and Substance'" with very wide yellow-margined, green-centered foliage that is also cupped and puckered; a much-anticipated plant

'Fragrant Gold': {1982r, P. Aden; 'Sum and Substance' X a sdlg} gold lvs; fragr fls **(see page 171)**

'Golden Decade': sibling to 'Leather Sheen', etc.; sm md of rounded gold lvs; rare

'Grand Canyon': {1995r, O. Petryszyn & W. Brincka; 'Sum and Substance' X *H. montana macrophylla*} lg, upright md of ruffled, golden foliage

'Green Gables': {1997r, Walters Gardens; green-leaved sport}

'Gunther's Prize': sport of 'Sum and Substance' wi heavily mottled foliage; 1998 Stark Gardens introduction, pictured on the cover of their 2000 catalog

'Jim Cooper': {1982r, P. Aden; 'Sum and Substance' X a sdlg} lg md of foliage wi thick subst; changes from chartreuse to med gold by mid-summer; lvs heavily corrugtd, 11" by 9" (14 vp); near-wh fls, late June into July on 35" sc; named for a former AHS president; rare

'Joyce Trott': {1988r, K. Vaughn; 'Flamboyant' X 'Sum and Substance'} creamy white-centered lvs wi wide, gr mgns, 5 1/2" long by 3 1/2" wide; md 10" high by 23" wide

'Irish Hills': {1996r, K. & L. Anderson, sport with dark green lvs}

'Kevin Kelley': {1996r, G. Goodwin; 'Sum and Substance' sdlg; light greenish yellow foliage}

'Lady Isobel Barnett': {1996r, D. Grenfell; sport} lvs gr-cntrd wi narrow gold mgns

'Leather Sheen': {1988r, M. Zilis & D. Lohman} 'Sum and Substance' X a *H. venusta* sdlg from a 1985 cross; med-sized md of shiny, dk green lvs **(see page 272)**

'Little Black Scape': {1995r, T. Avent; 'Sum and Substance' sdlg; med gold lvs; near black scapes}

'Little Razor': {1988r, M. Zilis, D. Lohman & T & Z N} 'Sum and Substance' X a *H. venusta* sdlg; low, dense md of narrow, gold foliage; sibling to 'Leather Sheen', 'Golden Decade' and 'New Wave'

'Lodestar': {1999r, S. & V. Wade; sport} lvs have very wavy, wide gold margins, green center; impressive for its waviness and wide margins

'Lovely Loretta': M. Zilis 'Sum and Substance' X 'Ginko Craig' hybrid introduced for sale by Homestead Division of Sunnybrook Farms in 1998; 14" by 36" md of wavy, bright gold lvs, 8" by 6 3/8" (10 vp); pale purple fls on sc up to 42" high, late July into mid-August; fast grower

'Metallic Sheen': {1999r, M. Zilis} 'Sum and Substance' X *H. s* .'Elegans'; hybridized in 1986; 28" by 60" md of thick-substd, gray-blue lvs 14" by 10"; 1994 Q & Z N introduction; 'Elegans'-type lvs

'Nancy Gill': from Kevin Vaughn; introduced for sale in the 1995 Hatfield Gardens catalog as a hybrid of 'Sum and Substance' X *H. pycnophylla*; very upright, bluish green (turning dk gr) lvs, 10 1/2" by 9" (20 vp), with thick underside bloom; thick-substanced; pale purple fls in early August

'New Wave': {1988r, M. Zilis & D. Lohman & T & Z N} 13" by 35" md of olive gr lvs, 6" by 5" (9 vp); wide, flat petioles; unusual; sibling to 'Leather Sheen', etc.

'Parhelion': {1997r, Walters Gardens; sport wi lt green lvs that have creamy white margins}

'Small Sum': {1996r, G. Goodwin; 'Sum and Substance' sdlg; yellow-gold lvs; near-white fls}

'Sum It Up': {1999r, M. Zilis} sport with gold-margined, green-centered foliage; margins tend to be narrow, about 1/4" wide on a 16" by 12" leaf; 1998 Q & Z N introduction

'Sum of All': sport with very wide, gold margins; introduced for sale by Q & Z N in 2000

'Sum Piecrust': {1999r, E. Elslager; sport; lvs medium green with a rippled margin}

'Sum Total': {1991r, S. Pedrick; sport wi dark green-centered, chartreuse-margined lvs}

'Supersonic': {1996r, K. & L. Anderson; sport wi dark green-centered, med gold-mgd lvs}

'Tiffney's Godzilla': {1996r, J. Dreessen; sport} gr-cntrd, gold-mgd lvs; one of the best in this category

'Titanic': {1999r, H. Hansen & Shady Oaks N; sport; lvs green-centered wi a wide (3") greenish ylw mgn}

'Tossed Salad': from Kevin Vaughn; introduced for sale in the 1995 Hatfield Gardens catalog as a hybrid of 'Sum and Substance' X *H. pycnophylla*; impressive, shiny, dk green foliage that acts like an unruly, green version of 'Sum and Substance'

'Winter Snow': sport of 'Sum and Substance' introduced in 1999 by Pine Forest Gardens; leaves gold-centered with a wide, white margin

'Zebson': {1998r, L. Jones; sport} gold-centered lvs edged with a lighter yellow margin

other similar types:

'Chartreuse Wedge', 'Green Sheen', 'Green Wedge'

'Summer Music'

key features: medium-sized mound of white-centered, green-margined foliage
mound size: 18" high by 41" wide

spacing: 36"
leaves: 7 3/4" long 1 1/2" wide, pale to medium green margin, center yellow to creamy white; shiny underside; broadly ovate blade; slightly wavy; slight corrugation at maturity; average substance; 10-11 vein pairs
flowers: early to late July; pale lavender; not fragrant; 24" scapes
comments: When Roy Klehm showed me his sport of 'Shade Master' in his collection back in 1987, I was immediately impressed with its multi-colored foliage. Each leaf offered an attractive combination of a creamy white center and a border of pale to medium green with areas of gold in between. At the time, I wondered how well it would thrive in the average shade garden, but 'Summer Music' has subsequently proven to be a good grower for a white-centered hosta. In the landscape it can be used most effectively as a specimen plant, but could also serve as a replacement for the overused 'Undulata Univittata'.

'Summer Music' is now fairly common in the nursery trade and should continue to increase in popularity. It has not been used in breeding work and only sports have been identified.

Roy Klehm registered 'Summer Music' in 1998.

seedlings, sports, and other related types:

'Last Dance': {1999r, H. Hansen & Shady Oaks N; sport of a chartreuse 'Summer Music' sport; medium green wi a 1 1/4" wide, pale yellow margin}

'Lakeside Meter Maid': {1998r, M. Chastain; 'Summer Music' sport; dk green-mgd, white-cntrd lvs}

'Nickelodeon': {1998r, T. Schmid; 'Summer Music' sport; lvs med green wi a greenish yellow mgn}

'Shade Master': {1982r, P. Aden; 'White Vision' X 'Golden Rajah'} med-sized md of bright gold lvs 10" by 7 1/2" (11 vp); pale lav fls in July; gold color stands out in any collection; "mother plant" of 'Summer Music'

'Summer Breeze': {1999r, M. Zilis & J. Diesen; sport of 'Summer Music'} lvs dark green-centered wi wide (1 1/2"), gold margins; introduced for sale in the 2000 Q & Z N catalog

other similar types:

'Reversed': {1978r, P. Aden; sport of an *H. sieboldiana* sdlg} 16" by 46" md of creamy white-centered, dark green-mgd lvs, 8" by 6" (10 vp); center color changes from gold to creamy white; lav fls on 24" sc from early to late July; slow growth has limited its use in the garden; popular breeding plant; not Sieboldiana-like

---

'Sun Power'

key features: large, dense mound of wavy, bright gold foliage

mound size: 28" high by 70" wide

spacing: 72"

leaves: 12" long by 7 1/4" wide; brilliant gold by mid-summer, especially bright with direct sunlight; thin underside bloom; blade ovate with a cupped base and a curved tip; distinctly wavy; slight corrugation; good substance; 14-16 vein pairs

flowers: early to late July; pale lavender with lighter petal margins; 2 1/4" long by 1 5/8" wide; scapes up to 43" high; reluctant pod former

comments: A mature clump of 'Sun Power' becomes the focal point of any landscape where it resides. The very bright gold color jumps out in almost any shaded garden, even from a distance. It has become a standard item in nurseries and is essential for any complete hosta collection. In the landscape it not only can be utilized as a specimen, but also as a large, background plant.

Though 'Sun Power' forms only an occasional seed pod, it is worth trying to hybridize with it owing to its many good qualities. Several sports have been named including the very popular 'Abba Dabba Do'.

Paul Aden registered 'Sun Power' in 1986 as a hybrid of two seedlings.

seedlings, sports, and other related types:

'Abba Aloft': {1990r, P. Aden; sport; med green-cntrd, chartreuse-mgd lvs} have never seen

'Abba at Large': {1990r, P. Aden; sport; dark gr-mgd, gold-centered lvs} have never seen

'Abba Dabba Do': {1998r, T. Avent; sport} green-centered, gold-margined lvs **(see page 57)**

'Abba Dew': {1999r; K. Brill; sport} lvs have a muted, light green center & gold mgns; originator's 5-year-old plant 20" by 57" wi 11" by 7" lvs; introduced for sale in 1999

'Eternal Father': {1999r, J. Willetts; sport; mottled green & yellow lvs}

'Flint Hill': {1999r, S. Matthews; sport; lvs med green wi gold mgns}

'Gold Wares': {1995r, L. Powell; 'Sun Power' X 'Gold Cover' with yellow-gold foliage}

'Paradise Power': sport with gold-centered, green-mgd lvs; from Marco Fransen of Holland

'Sun Banner': {1999r by the Russ O'Harra Hosta Society for R. O'Harra; sport} medium to dark green-centered, gold-mgd lvs

'Tiffney's Gold Digger': {1999r, J. Dreessen; sport; lvs emerge greenish ylw, turning yellow; also heavily rippled}

other similar types:

'Thelma M. Pierson'

'Tall Boy'

key features: large mound of green foliage; lavender flowers on 75" scapes
mound size: 26" high by 62" wide

spacing: 60"
leaves: 13 3/4" long by 8 1/4" wide; medium green; very shiny underside; blade elliptic when young, ovate at maturity; margins slightly wavy; little or no corrugation; better than average substance; 9 vein pairs

flowers: July 25 to August 17; medium lavender with a whitish throat and darker mid-petal streaks; 2 3/4" long by 1 1/8" wide; long,

narrow funnel shape; thick, sturdy scapes up to about 50-60" high in normal soils, as high as 75" tall in moist soil; about 1-2 seed pods form per scape with few viable seeds

comments: In flower 'Tall Boy' impresses even the casual observer with its towering scapes rising out of a large mound of smooth, green foliage. The scape height is directly related to the amount of moisture the plant receives early in the growing season. I can remember a plant in a display bed at my nursery whose scapes only reached 4-5 feet high, probably because the site was a bit dry. On the other hand, I've seen plants growing in moist conditions in Ohio that produced scapes 6-7 feet tall. I suspect that even greater heights could be achieved with constant moisture and heavy fertilization.

Besides utilizing 'Tall Boy' as a background plant, carefully placed specimens can offer some "floral drama" to the garden in August. On the average, a clump produces 22 scapes bearing about 49 flowers each. This means that over 1000 flowers open during the three week blooming period.

'Tall Boy' forms only an occasional seed pod, but if tall scapes are a breeding goal, it is probably worth working with it. No related hybrids or sports are currently registered.

Le Jardin botanique de Montreal registered 'Tall Boy' in

449

1983 as a possible hybrid between *H. rectifolia* X *H. ventricosa*, though that parentage is questionable.

seedlings, sports, and other related types:

'Montreal': {1983r, Le Jardin botanique de Montreal; possibly *H. rectifolia* X *H. ventricosa*} formerly sold as 'Japonica Blue'; 17" by 44" md of thin, green lvs, 6" by 3 1/2" (6-7 vp); large mass of purple fls, July 22- Aug 18 (n Illinois), on 20-36" sc; fast growth rate; fertile; a 'Tall Boy' sibling

'Mount Royal': {1983r, Le Jardin botanique de Montreal; possibly *H. rectifolia* X *H. ventricosa*} formerly sold as 'Japonica White'; 14" by 28" md of thin, narrow, green lvs, 6 3/4" by 3 3/4" (5-6 vp); white fls produced on many 36" sc from mid to late August; notable for floriferousness & fast growth rate; a 'Tall Boy' sibling

'Peerless': lg md of long, green foliage; very tall sc wi funnel-shaped, lav fls; from Chet Tompkins of Oregon; can see no difference from 'Tall Boy'

other similar types:

'Flower Power', 'Krossa Regal', 'Sunami'

'Tambourine'
key features: medium-large mound of white-margined foliage
mound size: 22" high by 50" wide

spacing: 48"
leaves: 8" long by 6" wide; 1/2" to 1" wide margins that change from yellow to creamy white, medium green center; thin underside bloom; blade ovate and slightly wavy; slightly corrugated; petioles covered with purple-red dots; better than average substance; 10-11 vein pairs
flowers: late July into mid-August; pale purple; funnel-shaped; 2 1/4" long by 1 1/4" wide; scapes up to 30" high
comments: 'Tambourine' is another great cultivar from Bill

450

and Eleanor Lachman who registered it in 1987 as a hybrid of ('Resonance' X a sdlg) X 'Halcyon'. It becomes a moderately dense mound at maturity and has a fairly fast growth rate. Also outstanding is the contrast between the wide, creamy margins and the green center. The pale purple flowers are borne neatly above the foliage, making an impressive show.

seedlings, sports, and other related types:
'Harmonica': {1999r, R. Snyder; sport; lvs greenish ylw wi
    a white mgn}

other similar types:
'Bold Edger', 'Crusader', 'Emily Dickinson', 'Queen Josephine'

The Tardiana Series

'Happiness' (TF 1 x 5)

The Tardianas are the result of a cross between two diverse hostas, 'Tardiflora' and *H. sieboldiana* 'Elegans'. The hybridizer was Eric Smith who worked for many years as a gardener and nurseryman in England. In creating the Tardianas, Eric gave the world a wonderful group of blue-leaved hostas for which he will forever be remembered. In *The American Hosta Society Bulletin* (March 1971, p. 57-58), Eric Smith wrote "I can quite understand that it does seem very unlikely that <u>H. tardiflora</u> could be crossed with H. <u>sieboldiana</u> <u>elegans,</u> but I can assure you that this is the cross that I made." He went on "it was pure luck that in the early autumn of one year (1961 I think) that I found a late flower on a <u>H. sieboldiana</u> <u>elegans</u> (young plant), and on the spur of the moment put some of its pollen on a fairly early flower of <u>H.</u> <u>tardiflora</u>"; and so began the Tardianas.

Out of the first generation of seedlings, four with good blue foliage were kept and used to produce a second generation from which most of the Tardianas were selected. A third generation was grown, but only one seedling was kept. At first Eric Smith used only generational numbers to identify his seedlings. For example, the four plants he saved from the first generation were listed as "TF 1 x 1", "TF 1 x 4", "TF 1 x 5", and "TF 1 x 7". The second generation, in turn, was identified as "TF 2 x 2", "TF 2 x 3", "TF 2 x 4", etc. and the one third generation seedling as "TF 3 x 1". In the early 1970's Alex Summers and Paul Aden imported the first Tardianas into the U.S. and, with Eric Smith, began naming them. Paul registered four Tardianas for Eric Smith in 1976, 'Blue Moon', 'Hadspen Blue', 'Hadspen Heron', and 'Harmony', and followed that with 'Dorset Blue' in 1977. Several other Tardianas were also named at about the same time, but they went unregistered until the late 1980's. This group included 'Halcyon', 'Blue Dimples', 'Blue Danube', and 'Blue Wedgwood'. Finally in 1988 the British Hosta and Hemerocallis Society named any remaining Tardianas still under number and published a complete list of the Tardiana names matched with their generational numbers in *The Hosta Journal* (Brickell, 1989). Two errors were made in that list, one listing 'Blue Wedgwood' as 'Wedgwood' and the other giving "TF 2 x 28" the name 'Kite' when no plant existed. The BHHS registered 25 Tardianas in 1988, while Jim Archibald (one) and Peter Ruh (two) registered the other three in 1987 and 1990, respectively. Jim Archibald had worked as Eric Smith's partner in The Plantsman, Ltd. in Dorset, England before Eric went to work as a gardener at Hadspen House in Somerset, England (Smith, 1985). Evidently, too, some of Eric Smith's original Tardiana seedlings were sent to Germany where they have been propagated and named.

In the U.S. many hybridizers have incorporated Tardianas into their hybridizing programs with outstanding results. Herb Benedict utilized 'Dorset Blue' and its offspring to produce 'Blue Chip', 'Blue Clown', 'Blue Ice', and 'Blue Jay', which are essentially 4th and 5th generation Tardianas. Herb also bred with 'Hadspen Hawk', 'Blue Moon', 'Blue Diamond' and other Tardiana seedlings. Bill and Eleanor Lachman heavily relied upon two Tardianas, 'Halcyon' and 'Blue Moon', as pollen parents for many of their fine introductions. 'Chantilly Lace', 'Crusader', 'Gay Blade', and 'Torchlight' are a few of their 'Halcyon' seedlings, while 'Moon River', 'Cherub', 'Metallica', and 'Full Moon' come out of their 'Blue Moon' line. Interestingly some Tardianas occasionally produce gold-leaved offspring. 'Bright Glow'

{1986r, P. Aden}, known for many years as "Golden Tardiana", may be the most famous of this group. Another gold-leaved Tardiana-type is 'Golden Hawk', a selfed seedling of 'Hadspen Hawk' from Herb Benedict {1984r}. He then selfed 'Golden Hawk' to produce 'Sunlight Child', another gold-leaved cultivar. There are also an ever-increasing number of sports from the Tardianas, the most prominent being 'June', a gold-centered form of 'Halcyon'. Several attractive green-leaved sports of 'Halcyon' have also been introduced.

As garden plants, the Tardianas can be generalized as medium-sized, blue-leaved plants with excellent substance and a good growth rate. Over the spectrum of all the Tardianas, characteristics that relate to both 'Tardiflora' and *H. sieboldiana* 'Elegans' can be identified, e.g., some have relatively narrow foliage, others broadly ovate leaves. The flowering occurs over a wide range of time, from late June into early September, depending upon the variety. Most produce their flowers in fairly dense clusters, but some are more spread out on the scapes. Flower colors range from near-white to purple, with many a pale bluish lavender.

In the nursery trade, only some of the Tardianas have been widely grown and propagated. Most common are 'Blue Dimples', 'Blue Moon', 'Blue Wedgwood', 'Camelot', 'Dorset Blue', 'Hadspen Blue', 'Hadspen Heron', and 'Halcyon'. Others that have been propagated to a lesser extent include 'Brother Ronald', 'Osprey', 'Blue Danube', 'Blue Diamond', 'Blue Belle', 'Blue Blush', 'Hadspen Hawk', 'Blue Skies', and 'Harmony'. Of the fifteen remaining Tardianas, only 'Eric Smith' (unfortunately, plain green foliage) and 'Hadspen Pink' (not pink-flowered and may not actually be a Tardiana) are probably not worth propagating.

When I originally encountered the Tardianas they were listed as *Hosta* x *tardiana*, and treated like a cultivated species much like the Fortuneis or Undulatas. Although most collectors knew that this was not proper taxonomy, it was a comfortable designation that showed the relationship between these plants. George Schmid (1991) categorized the Tardianas as a "Grex", a term that botanists may use, but is uncommon to horticulturists, gardeners, hosta collectors, etc. For clarity's sake, I refer to these plants instead as "The Tardiana Series" or, more simply, the Tardianas. Plants that are obviously related to them are described as being Tardiana-like.

The following is a list of Eric Smith's Tardianas by generational and seedling number. Though 34 numbers are listed, only 32 plants actually exist. "TF 2 x 25"

('Goldilocks') and "TF 2 x 28" ('Kite') are invalid cultivars.

TF 1 x 1 'Dorset Charm'
TF 1 x 4 'Dorset Flair'
TF 1 x 5 'Happiness'
TF 1 x 7 'Halcyon'
TF 2 x 2 'Blue Moon'
TF 2 x 3 'Harmony'
TF 2 x 4 'Dorset Blue'
TF 2 x 5 'Curlew'
TF 2 x 6 'Blue Skies'
TF 2 x 7 'Hadspen Blue'
TF 2 x 8 'Blue Dimples'
TF 2 x 9 'Blue Wedgwood'
TF 2 x 10 'Hadspen Heron'
TF 2 x 13 'Grey Goose'
TF 2 x 14 'Osprey'
TF 2 x 17 'Kingfisher'
TF 2 x 18 'Purbeck Ridge'
TF 2 x 19 'Sherborne Songbird'
TF 2 x 20 'Hadspen Hawk'
TF 2 x 21 'Sherborne Profusion'
TF 2 x 22 'Blue Belle'
TF 2 x 23 'Blue Diamond'
TF 2 x 24 'Blue Danube'
TF 2 x 25 (called 'Goldilocks'; another plant is registered under this name; no plant exists?)
TF 2 x 26 'Sherborne Swift'
TF 2 x 27 'Camelot'
TF 2 x 28 'Kite' (a name only; no plant exists)
TF 2 x 29 'Sherborne Swan'
TF 2 x 30 'Brother Ronald'
TF 2 x 31 'Eric Smith'
TF 2 x 32 'Hadspen Pink'
TF 2 x 34 'Sherborne Swallow'
TF 2 x 35 'Wagtail'
TF 3 x 1 'Blue Blush'

Over the years I have collected hundreds of measurements from the Tardianas in various gardens. What I have found is that most of them grow much larger than expected, especially if placed in a highly fertilized, well-watered environment. The data below reflects the largest sizes that I have seen for each cultivar. While I have observed mature specimens for most, a few probably will become larger and I have noted such possibilities. All of them show true hybrid character, combining traits of both parents. This is especially evident in the second generation (TF 2 x --). In thinking of the group as a whole, the "average" Tardiana could be described in the following way:

"medium-sized mound of deep blue-green foliage; mound size 18" by 38"; leaves 7" by 5 1/2" with 12 vein pairs, an ovate blade shape (elliptic-ovate when young), slight corrugation, slightly wavy, and thick-substanced; pale bluish lavender flowers are produced from late July into mid-August in dense clusters on scapes 22" high; many seed pods develop; dense mound habit; medium to fast growth rate".

Brief descriptions of Eric Smith's Tardianas are as follows:

'Blue Belle' (TF 2 x 22)
medium-sized mound of wavy margined, deep blue leaves; md 19" by 42"; lvs 7" by 6 1/4" (11-12 vp), blade ovate in shape and thick-substanced; purplish fls on 18-20" scapes, late July into early Aug; fertile; {1988r, BHHS}
(I used to think 'Blue Belle' would remain a small plant, but that is not the case. It makes a fairly dense mound of deep blue foliage and is certainly worth growing.)

'Blue Blush' (TF 3 x 1)
small to medium-sized mound of very deep blue-green foliage; md 13" by 37"; lvs 7" by 3 7/8" (10 vp); bluish lavender fls from mid to late Aug {1988r, BHHS}
('Blue Blush' has the reputation of being the smallest Tardiana, but with time becomes a medium-sized mound.)

'Blue Danube' (TF 2 x 24)
medium-sized mound of intense blue-green foliage; md 18" by 48"; lvs 8" by 6" (12 vp), broadly ovate, slightly wavy, slight to moderately corrugated, and thick-substanced; pale lavender fls on 20" scapes from late July into August {1988r, BHHS}
(Even as a young plant, the foliage of 'Blue Danube' is one of the bluest. It shows many Sieboldiana traits, except for the limited corrugation. This may be one of the most under-rated of the Tardianas.) **(also see page 89)**

'Blue Diamond' (TF 2 x 23)
medium-large mound of bright blue foliage; md 22" by 49"; lvs 7 1/2" by 4 1/2" (12-13 vp), ovate, slight marginal waves, slightly corrugated, thick-substanced; pale lavender fls from mid-July into August on 30" scapes {1988r, BHHS}
('Blue Diamond' becomes a fairly large mound and has excellent, blue-green foliage.)

455

'Blue Dimples' (TF 2 x 8)
medium-sized mound of deep blue foliage; dense mound habit; md 18" by 45"; lvs 8 3/4" by 5 1/2" (11-12 vp), oblong-ovate shape, slightly wavy, thick substance; very pale lavender fls from mid-July into mid-August on scapes up to 24" high; fertile {1988r, BHHS}
(One of the most widely grown of the Tardianas, 'Blue Dimples' has also been the source of controversy. Years ago a few collectors decided that plants of 'Blue Dimples' were actually 'Blue Wedgwood' and vice-versa. Labels were switched and both were widely propagated under their new designations. 'Blue Dimples' tends to have slightly longer foliage than the more "wedge-shaped" 'Blue Wedgwood'.) **(also see page 90)**

'Blue Moon' (TF 2 x 2)
small mound of deeply cupped, intensely blue foliage; md 10" by 23"; lvs 5" by 4 1/4" (10-11 vp), very broadly ovate, heavily corrugated; whitish fls from late July into early August on short scapes {1976r, P. Aden for E. Smith}
('Blue Moon' may actually be the smallest Tardiana and is also at the center of its own controversy. Some confusion occurred when a much larger plant was widely propagated in the late 1980's as 'Blue Moon'. That plant is now labelled 'Blue Splendor'. The true 'Blue Moon' rates highly for its deep blue color, deep cupping, small size, and good substance.) **(also see page 93)**

'Blue Skies' (TF 2 x 6)
medium-sized mound of bluish green foliage; md 14" by 42"; lvs 5 1/2" by 4 1/2" (10-11 vp), broadly ovate shape that is slightly cupped; also faintly corrugated and thick-substanced; pale lavender fls from mid-August into early September on 16" scapes {1988r, BHHS}
('Blue Skies' was one of the first of the Tardianas to be widely propagated, but has fallen out of favor in deference to bluer-leaved types. It does produce a nice show of late season flowers. It was the source of the first Tardiana sport, 'Emerald Skies', which is now sold as a green-leaved plant, but originally had leaves with green centers and very thin, white margins.)

'Blue Wedgwood' (TF 2 x 9)
medium-sized mound of deep blue foliage; md 19" by 44"; lvs 7 1/2" by 5 1/2" (11-13 vp), ovate blade with a slightly cupped, flattish base, slightly wavy, thick-substanced, and slightly corrugated; very pale bluish lavender fls from late

July into late August on 20-27" high scapes; fertile {1988r, BHHS}

('Blue Wedgwood' ranks as one of "the best of the best". Its blue color is quite intense and can make quite a show in any garden. It has been widely propagated.) **(also see page 96)**

'Brother Ronald' (TF 2 x 30)
medium-sized mound of frosty blue foliage; md 16" by 35"; lvs 7" by 5" (12 vp), ovate blade that is slightly cupped, moderately corrugated, and thick-substanced; white fls from mid-July into early August (July 27 peak) in dense clusters on scapes 18-20" high; some pods develop {1988r, BHHS}

('Brother Ronald' offers a very attractive combination of blue foliage and dense clusters of white flowers. It may become larger than the listed measurements.) **(also see page 104)**

'Camelot' (TF 2 x 27)
medium-sized mound of bright blue foliage; md 17" by 42"; lvs 7 3/4" by 6 1/4" (12-13 vp), broadly ovate with a deeply lobed base; slightly corrugated, slightly cupped, and thick-substanced; very pale lavender fls from late July into mid-August on scapes up to 22" high {1988r, BHHS}

('Camelot' has become very popular and is known for its brilliant blue foliage.) **(also see page 106)**

'Curlew' (TF 2 x 5)
medium-large mound of blue-green foliage; md 20" by 42" (up to 23" by 51"); lvs 7" by 6" (12 vp), broadly ovate in shape, slightly wavy and thick-substanced; pale bluish lavender fls from mid-August into early September in dense clusters on scapes up to 26" high; many seed pods {1988r, BHHS}

(Though 'Curlew' is considered one of the "lesser" Tardianas, it still rates highly for blue color and substance.)

'Dorset Blue' (TF 2 x 4)
small, dense mound of intensely blue foliage; md 10" by 24"; lvs 5 1/4" by 4" (11-12 vp), blade broadly ovate, moderately cupped, moderately corrugated, and thick-substanced; very pale lavender fls from mid to late August in dense clusters on 16" scapes; fertile {1977r, P. Aden for E. Smith}

("Small and very blue" best describes 'Dorset Blue'. It also is a fairly slow grower. 'Dorset Blue' seedlings also tend to be "small and very blue" (and slow-growing).) **(also see page 137)**

457

'Dorset Charm' (TF 1 x 1)

medium-large mound of deep blue-green foliage; md 18" by 46" (up to 23" by 60"); lvs 7 3/4" by 4 1/2" (up to 8" by 5") (11-12 vp); blade oblong-ovate shape, slightly wavy, slightly corrugated, and thick-substanced; pale lavender fls produced from early to mid-August on scapes 19" or so; fertile {1990r, Peter Ruh for E. Smith}

(Despite being one of the "original" Tardianas, 'Dorset Charm' is almost unknown to gardeners.)

'Dorset Flair' (TF 1 x 4)

medium-sized mound of rich blue foliage; md 16" by 34" (up to 21" by 54"); lvs 7 1/2" by 4 1/2" (up to 8" by 5 1/8") (11-12 vp), ovate shape with slight corrugation and waviness and good substance; near-white to pale bluish lavender fls from mid-Aug into Sept on 18" scapes {1990r, Peter Ruh for E. Smith}

('Dorset Flair' is another first generation Tardiana seedling that rates highly for blueness and substance. It has not been widely grown.)

'Eric Smith' (TF 2 x 31)

medium-sized mound of green foliage (slightly blue in spring); md 16" by 41"; lvs 5 1/4" by 4 1/2" (10-11 vp) with an ovate blade shape, moderate corrugation and average substance; lavender purple fls from early to late July on scapes up to 31" high; fertile {1987r, J. Archibald}

('Eric Smith' stands as the greenest of the Tardianas, possibly selected for flower performance.)

'Goldilocks' (TF 2 x 25)

a gold-leaved 'Tokudama Aureonebulosa' seedling from Maxine Armstrong bears this name and cannot be used for a Tardiana; there may be no plant grown as TF 2 x 25

'Grey Goose' (TF 2 x 13)

medium-sized mound of bluish green foliage; md 12" by 30" (probably larger); lvs 6 1/4" by 5 3/4" (11-13 vp), ovate shape with a heart-shaped base and long, distinct tip; leaves also slightly corrugated and wavy, above average substance; pale lavender fls, early to late July, on scapes 16" or more {1988r, BHHS}

('Grey Goose' will probably achieve greater dimensions. It is not one of the bluest but is worth growing.)

'Hadspen Blue' (TF 2 x 7)

medium-large mound of broad, blue-green foliage; md 18" by 48"; lvs 7 1/4" by 6 1/4" (up to 8 1/4" by 6 7/8") (12-13

vp), broadly ovate with a deeply cupped base, slightly corrugated and thick-substanced; very pale lavender fls from
late July into mid-August in tight clusters on scapes 20-24"
high; fertile {1976r, P. Aden for E. Smith}
(I often think of 'Hadspen Blue' as coming close to 'Tokudama' in many ways, particularly mound and foliage sizes.
It has become one of the most popular in the Tardiana
Series.) **(also see page 217)**

'Hadspen Hawk' (TF 2 x 20)
medium-sized mound of blue-green foliage; md 18" by 43";
lvs 7 1/2" by 4" (10-11 vp), blade elliptic-ovate in shape,
widening with age; slightly wavy, smooth texture, and thick
substance; pale lavender fls in tight clusters from late
August into early September {1988r, BHHS}
('Hadspen Hawk' shows many 'Tardiflora' traits in its
foliage and blooming season, but its dense flower clusters
hearken back to 'Elegans'. The blue color and substance are
excellent.)

'Hadspen Heron' (TF 2 x 10)
small to medium-sized mound of deep blue foliage; md 14"
by 32"; lvs 5" by 2 1/2" (9 vp); leaves narrowly elliptic when
young, widening with age; moderately wavy, thick-substanced, and smooth-textured; pale lavender fls open from
late July into mid-August {1976r, P. Aden for E. Smith}
('Hadspen Heron' has fooled many a collector. As a young
plant the leaf blade has a narrowly elliptic shape, but widens
considerably with age.)

'Hadspen Pink' (TF 2 x 32)
medium-sized mound of bluish green foliage; md 15" by
38"; lvs 6" by 3 1/4"; pale purple fls from late July into mid-
August {1988r, BHHS}
('Hadspen Pink' may have been selected for pink flowers,
but they are not and the foliage is average at best. There
really is nothing to warrant growing this plant other than to
collect the complete Tardiana series.)

'Halcyon' (TF 1 x 7)
medium-sized mound of blue-green foliage; md 18" by 43";
lvs 8" by 5 1/2" (12-13 vp), blade ovate to oblong-ovate,
slightly wavy, smooth-textured, and thick-substanced; pale
bluish lavender fls from late July into mid-August on 18-
28" scapes; many seed pods develop {1988r, BHHS}
(As the top-selling Tardiana, 'Halcyon' has been widely
propagated in Europe and the U.S. It is also the "mother
plant" of 'June', a gold-centered sport.) **(also see page 245)**

'Happiness' (TF 1 x 5)
medium-large mound of deep blue foliage; md 18" by 46"; lvs 8 1/2" by 6 1/4" (11-12 vp), ovate shape, slightly corrugated, and thick-substanced; pale bluish lavender fls from late July into mid-August on 30" scapes; many seed pods develop {1988r, BHHS}
('Happiness' is quite underrated as a landscape and breeding plant. It tends more toward 'Elegans' than 'Tardiflora'.)

'Harmony' (TF 2 x 3)
medium-sized mound of bluish green foliage; md 15" by 33"; lvs 5" by 3 3/4" (10 vp), blade ovate at maturity (elliptic when young) and thick-substanced; bluish purple flowers from late Aug into Sept on 18" scapes {1976r, P. Aden for E. Smith}
('Harmony' is notable for its late season purplish flowers. Its leaves are small relative to its mound size.)

'Kingfisher' (TF 2 x 17)
medium-sized mound of very dark green foliage that is bluish in spring; md 13" by 30"; lvs 7" by 3 1/2" (10 vp), ovate, slightly wavy, smooth texture, and thick-substanced; pale lavender flowers from mid-August to early September {1988r, BHHS}
('Kingfisher' becomes an attractive, medium to small-sized mound of dark green foliage.)

'Kite' (TF 2 x 28)
(No plant exists under this name, though it was registered in 1988 by the BHHS.)

'Osprey' (TF 2 x 14)
medium-sized mound of blue-green foliage; md 17" by 39"; lvs 7 1/2" by 6" (12 vp), broadly ovate blade, slight cupping, moderate corrugation, and good substance; white fls from very late June into late July on 26" scapes {1988r, BHHS}
('Osprey' has always been one of my favorites because of its combination of blue foliage and early season white flowers.)

'Purbeck Ridge' (TF 2 x 18)
medium-sized mound of bluish green foliage early, turns dark green; md 16" by 33"; lvs 8 3/8" by 4" (9-11 vp), oblong-ovate shape tapering to a long point, wavy and thick-substanced; pale lavender fls from late July into early August {1988r, BHHS}
(Another of the "lesser" Tardianas and not one of the bluest, 'Purbeck Ridge' offers foliage that tends more to its 'Tardiflora' ancestry.)

460

'Sherborne Profusion' (TF 2 x 21)
medium-sized mound of blue-green foliage; md 13" by 30"; lvs 6" by 3 3/4" (10 vp) with an ovate shape, slight corrugation and good substance; medium lavender fls from late June into mid-July on 18" scapes; fertile {1988r, BHHS}
(Plants that I have seen of 'Sherborne Profusion' have been smaller than most Tardianas and are quite floriferous.)

'Sherborne Songbird' (TF 2 x 19)
medium-large mound of deep blue-green foliage; md 20" by 38" (up to 26" by 50"); lvs 8 1/4" by 6 1/4" (12-13 vp) with a broadly ovate blade, moderate corrugation and good substance; pale bluish lavender fls from late July into mid-August in very tight clusters near the top of 22" scapes {1988r, BHHS}
(My biggest Tardiana mound measurement came from 'Sherborne Songbird' growing in the Wade & Gatton collection. Its blue color rates highly but is a shade less intense than 'Camelot'. It also produces dense clusters of flowers that are very attractive.)

'Sherborne Swallow' (TF 2 x 34)
{1988r, BHHS}
(This is the only Tardiana that I have not been able to fully evaluate. I have only seen a very small specimen of this plant.)

'Sherborne Swan' (TF 2 x 29)
medium-large mound of deep blue foliage; md 19" by 42"; lvs 9" by 6" (10-11 vp); blade ovate and widest near the base, arching downward to the long, slender tip; also slightly corrugated and wavy, and thick-substanced; very pale lavender fls from mid-July into early August on 20" scapes {1988r, BHHS}
(The foliage of 'Sherborne Swan' has an excellent bright blue color and a very graceful appearance.)

'Sherborne Swift' (TF 2 x 26)
medium-sized mound of thick-substanced, blue-green foliage; md 14" by 31" (up to 19" by 33"); lvs 5 1/2" by 2 1/2" (10 vp) {1988r, BHHS}
('Sherborne Swift' rates highly for substance and blue-green color, but has not been widely grown.)

'Wagtail' (TF 2 x 35)
medium-sized mound of bluish green foliage; md 16" by 39"; lvs 5" by 4" (9 vp); pale lavender fls from late June into

mid-July on 24" scapes; unusual internal markings on flowers; fertile {1988r, BHHS}

('Wagtail' makes an attractive mound of foliage but is not one of the bluest. It does produce a nice show of flowers.)

There are also several cultivars that exhibit many Tardiana traits, but they are not a part of Eric Smith's original group. I often describe such plants as "Tardiana-like", a category unto itself. Some of these include the following: 'Birds of Happiness', 'Blaufink', 'Blauemeise', 'Blue Arrow', 'Blue Beard', 'Blue Border', 'Blue Cherub', 'Blue Chip', 'Blue Clown', 'Blue Dwarf', 'Blue Heaven', 'Blue Ice', 'Blue Jay', 'Blue June', 'Blue Melody', 'Blue Urchin', 'Blue Whirls', 'Bright Glow', 'Buffy', 'Canadian Shield', 'Deep Blue Sea', 'Devon Blue', 'Devon Green', 'Devon Tor', 'Edward Wargo', 'Full Moon', 'Glockenspiel', 'Golden Hawk', 'Irische See', 'June', 'Kayak', 'Microtardiana', 'Nordatlantik' ('North Atlantic'), 'Peridot', 'Reginald Kaye', 'Rhein', 'September White', 'Silvery Slugproof', 'Sunlight Child', 'Valerie's Vanity', 'Winfield Blue', 'Winsome Blue'

'Tardiflora' (Aki Giboshi)

key features: small mound of thick, dark green foliage; lavender flowers in September-October
mound size: 12" high by 26" wide

spacing: 24"
leaves: 6 7/8" long by 3" wide; shiny, dark green; very shiny underside; narrowly elliptic to elliptic blade; margin slightly wavy; smooth texture; thick substance; many reddish purple dots on the petioles; 7-8 vein pairs

flowers: late September into October; medium lavender; wide, whitish petal margins into throat; 2" long by 1 1/4" wide; narrow funnel

shape with reflexed petal tips; radiating around scapes that are 20" or so; forms many seed pods

comments: 'Tardiflora' continues to be highly respected for many reasons. The thick, slug-resistant foliage has an attractive, shiny, dark green color and forms a dense mound. The late-season flowers appear when few other plants are blooming in the garden. It can be effectively used as an edger or low ground cover in the landscape.

'Tardiflora' has been used extensively in breeding work, most notably for the Tardianas. Because of its late blooming habits, the maturing seed pods are often damaged by frost in northern areas before the seeds mature. If bringing the whole plant indoors is not an option, some hybridizers have cut off scapes with nearly mature seed pods, placed them in water, and finished seed ripening inside.

The origins of 'Tardiflora' are unclear. It was known for many years as the species, *Hosta tardiflora*. Schmid (1991) relegated it to cultivar status owing to the fact that no wild populations have been identified. Its closest relative is *H. longipes lancea*, which some claim is the same as 'Tardiflora'. Schmid (1991) listed *H. longipes lancea* as *H. longipes* f. *sparsa* and stated that this name represents the fact that it bears few flowers. He points out that 'Tardiflora', on the other hand, bears many more flowers per scape and has yellow anthers (versus purple for *H. l. sparsa*). I have seen *H. longipes lancea* (the accepted name in Japan, not *H. longipes sparsa*) growing along the Tenryu River in Japan and have viewed wild, collected plants in Japanese gardens. There is a strong resemblance between 'Tardiflora' and *H. l. lancea*, but I think it is likely that 'Tardiflora' is a seedling selection of *H. longipes lancea*.

seedlings, sports, and other related types:

'Gala': {1978r, P. Aden; selfed sdlg of 'Tardiflora'} 15" by 35" md of thick, variegated lvs, 8 1/4" by 3 7/8" (8-9 vp); lf color variable wi some completely streaked, others green-centered wi a streaky mgn; pale purplish lav fls on 18-24" sc from mid-Aug into Sept; unusual, highly variable foliage & attractive fls

H. lancifolia tardiflora: a name used for plants of *H. lancifolia* thought to bloom later than normal but such plants are just *H. lancifolia*

The Tardiana Series: hybrids of 'Tardiflora' X *H. sieboldiana* 'Elegans' developed by Eric Smith in the 1960's; included in the first generation are 'Dorset Charm', 'Dorset Flair', 'Happiness', and 'Halcyon' with the latter being the closest to 'Tardiflora' **(see pages 451-462)**

'Tardiflora Hybrida': (1992r, P. Ruh for G. Arends; 'Tardiflora' X *H. ventricosa*} developed by George Arends of Germany from around 1911; 15" by 34" md of shiny, medium green lvs, 6 1/2" by 3" (6 vp); blade smooth, shiny on the underside and thin-substanced; purple fls from early to late Aug on 21" sc; lvs & fls not at all like 'Tardiflora'; notable for its early date of development and is of interest mainly to collectors

H. tardiflora minor: a name of no-standing for a plant thought to be a dwarf 'Tardiflora' but is not

'Tortifrons': formerly listed as the species, *Hosta tortifrons*, but actually a sport of 'Tardiflora'; twisted, curled foliage; difficult to propagate; great collector's plant **(see page 480)**

'Venetian Blue': M. Zilis hybrid of ('Marilyn' X 'Tardiflora') X 'Tardiflora'; dense, 14" by 36" md of sl rippled, blue foliage; 6" by 3" lvs become med green by mid-summer; lav fls in July; fast grower; introduced for sale by Q & Z N in 2000

other similar types:

'Fused Veins': sm md of twisted, chartreuse-centered lvs related to 'Tardiflora' **(see page 259)**

'Koryu': sm md of twisted, chartreuse-centered lvs; could be a 'Tardiflora' mutation **(see page 259)**

464

Hosta tardiva
(Nankai Giboshi; Late Plantainlily)

key features: medium-sized mound of shiny, green foliage; purple flowers in September

mound size: 16" high by 32" wide

spacing: 30"

leaves: 6 5/8" long by 3" wide; shiny, dark green; very shiny underside; blade narrowly ovate to ovate with a rounded base; slightly wavy margins; smooth texture; average substance; 7 vein pairs

flowers: September; medium purple with distinct, white petal margins from the throat halfway to the tip; 2 1/4" long by 1 1/4" wide; semi-bell-shaped; 24" scapes

comments: *Hosta tardiva* was once a species that almost every hosta collector thought he or she knew. In 1990 imports of *Hosta tardiva* from its native Japan revealed that the true species was much different from what we had grown in our gardens. The foliage was a shinier, darker green and the mound habit fairly dense. Also, it bloomed later (September) on shorter scapes. The incorrect, older plant has now been named 'Southern Comfort'. Also, the plant labelled *H. tardiva aureo-striata* in some gardens is not closely related to *H. tardiva* and is actually the cultivar 'Kisuji' (Kisuji Giboshi in Japan).

One negative is the thin foliar substance, making it somewhat susceptible to slug damage. Though a few nurseries offer this plant for sale (Greene, 2000), it has not made much of an impact in the nursery trade.

seedlings, sports, and other related types:

H. tardiva "Margined" ('Kifukurin Nankai'??): sport with a neat, yellow margin that I observed in one Japanese collection

other similar types:

'Southern Comfort': {1992r, P. Ruh; unknown parentage}

465

15" by 36" (up to 21" by 48") md of green lvs, 8 1/4" by 3 1/2", 7 vp; light purple fls hang on one side of 52" scapes; many seed pods develop; avg subst; collector's plant; thought to be *H. tardiva* for many years

---

Hosta tibae (Nagasaki Giboshi)
(formerly *Hosta chibai*)

key features: dense, medium-sized mound of green foliage; purple flowers on branched scapes in September
mound size: 16" high by 44" wide

spacing: 36"
leaves: 8 3/8" long by 5" wide; medium green; slightly shiny top, very shiny underside; blade ovate with a long, curved tip and slightly puckered base; slight marginal rippling; faintly corrugated; purple-red dots near the base of the petiole; average substance; 7-8 vein pairs
flowers: mid to late September; purple with unusual white stripes in both bud and opened flower; 2 3/8" long by 1 7/8" wide; 19-23" scapes that are branched; forms seed pods
comments: *Hosta tibae* is notable for its branched flower scapes and makes a fairly dense mound of slightly rippled, green foliage. It can be found wild in Japan around Nagasaki on Kyushu Island (Fujita, 1978, p. 39), hence the common name of Nagasaki Giboshi. Its scientific name has been altered a few times over the years. It was known as *Hosta chibai* in gardens for many years, then briefly *Hosta tibai*. Finally the name became *Hosta tibae* (Schmid, 1991).

A few hybridizers are attempting to incorporate the branched scape characteristic of *Hosta tibae* into their breeding programs. What they are ultimately seeking is a hosta version of the sturdy, branched scapes of daylilies. The branching in *H. tibae* is fairly wispy in comparison to

466

that of a daylily, but certainly is a good starting point. I once carefully examined a 21 3/4" high *H. tibae* scape and found branches at 5 1/2", 10", and 12 3/4" high. The main scape produced 28 flowers while each of the branches had 6-7 flowers.

In Japan I was shown a wild-collected sport with beautiful creamy yellow margins. Also, its petioles had an attractive red color.

seedlings, sports, and other related types:
'Gold Piece': {1983r, K. Vaughn; complex hybrid involving *H. ventricosa*, *H. tibae*, *H. plantaginea*, and *H. nigrescens*} introduced many years ago, but have only seen a few times, never in bloom; foliage thick-substanced and gold; combines the best-flowering species in one plant

other similar types:
Hosta capitata

'Tijuana Brass'
key features: medium-sized mound of very unruly, gold foliage; slug-resistant
mound size: 16" high by 40" wide

spacing: 36"
leaves: 10" long by 8 1/2" wide; chartreuse, becoming a shiny, medium gold; thin underside bloom; blade broadly ovate and extremely twisted, unruly, and heavily corrugated; thick substance; 13 vein pairs
flowers: early to late July; pale lavender; 2" long by 7/8" wide; held well above the foliage on scapes up to 32" high; many seed pods develop
comments: 'Tijuana Brass' has an intriguing quality that few other hostas possess. The foliage is so unruly and twisted that sometimes the exposed parts of the leaf become gold while the more shaded, sunken areas remain chartreuse to pale green. The

slug resistance is also outstanding. It can be used as a specimen plant or in small groups. How about growing 'Tijuana Brass' with 'Fantastic', 'Bold Ruffles', 'Spinach Patch' and 'Twist and Shout' (plus 'Tortifrons'?) for a comparison of hostas with "disturbed" foliage.

Kevin Vaughn crossed 'Golden Waffles' with 'Polly Bishop' to produce this fine plant which was registered in 1988. Consider using 'Tijuana Brass' in your breeding program.

seedlings, sports, and other related types:
none listed

other similar types:
'Spinach Patch': Kevin Vaughn hybrid introduced by Hatfield Gardens in 1993; heavily corrugated, unruly, twisted, dark green foliage; 22" by 50" md, lvs 11 1/2" by 9" (13 vp); tremendous!

'Twist and Shout': {1988r, K. Vaughn; 'Gold Piece' X a sibling of 'Aztec Treasure'} 28" by 50", semi-upright md of heavily corrugated, cupped, and unruly, shiny green foliage; leaves 11" by 9" (14" vein pairs); 36" scapes of pale purple flowers from late June into mid-July; greener and larger than 'Tijuana Brass' but with a similar unsettled appearance

'Twisted Sister': Kevin Vaughn introduction; deeply cupped and corrugated, dark green foliage

---

'Tiny Tears'
key features: small mound of teardrop-shaped, green foliage
mound size: 6" high by 21" wide

spacing: 18"
leaves: 3 1/2" long by 2 1/2" wide; medium green; moder-

ately shiny underside; blade ovate; not wavy or corrugated; average substance; 6 vein pairs

flowers: late June into mid-July; medium purple; 1 1/2" long by 1" wide; scapes 13" to 21" high; 21 scapes on one clump; fertile

comments: 'Tiny Tears' rapidly grows into a dense mound of teardrop-shaped foliage that is very similar to *Hosta venusta*. Its ultimate size is subject to soil fertility. In poor soil 'Tiny Tears' remains very small, but with greater fertility the mound can reach the listed dimensions of 6" by 21". It makes an excellent rock garden plant or edger for special situations. At maturity it is very difficult to distinguish 'Tiny Tears' from *H. venusta* and others such as 'Abiqua Miniature', 'Suzuki Thumbnail', 'Thumb Nail', and 'Tot Tot'.

'Tiny Tears' was registered in 1977 by Bob Savory as a seedling of *Hosta venusta*.

seedlings, sports, and other related types:
none listed

other similar types:
'Abiqua Miniature', 'Alpine Dream', 'Cody', 'Popo', 'Suzuki Thumbnail', 'Thumb Nail', 'Tot Tot', *H. venusta*

'Tokudama'
key features: medium-sized mound of heavily corrugated, slug-resistant blue foliage
mound size: 18" high by 44" wide

spacing: 36"
leaves: 9 1/4" long by 7 1/2" wide; deep blue-green until late June, dark green thereafter; blade broadly ovate to oblong-ovate and slightly cupped; heavily corrugated; no purple-red dots on petioles; thick substance; 15-17 vein pairs; good orangy gold fall color in late October

flowers: late June into early July; near-white with a pale lavender mid-petal stripe; 2 1/4" long by 1" wide; narrow funnel shape; scapes up to 24" high; many seed pods develop; distinctive pod shape

comments: In the garden, 'Tokudama' can be thought of as a smaller version of *H. sieboldiana* 'Elegans'. The heavily corrugated, blue-green mound of foliage makes a striking specimen plant in the landscape and its thick substance gives 'Tokudama' excellent slug resistance. Its only negative trait is a slow growth rate, but that should not stop anyone from growing it.

For many years, 'Tokudama' was considered a species, i.e. *Hosta tokudama*. Maekawa (1972) listed it as such, though he stated that "It is often cultivated in Japan. The plant seems to be spontaneous in Inaba province". The term "spontaneous" indicates that some plants had escaped from cultivation and were "naturalized" in the wild. Plant collector Hajime Sugita (1984) listed 'Tokudama' as being a cultivar and not found in the wild. During my first trip to Japan in 1991, I did not see any wild specimens of 'Tokudama' and, in fact, very few cultivated ones either. Due to its presumed cultivated origins, this plant and its sports have been relegated to cultivar status (Schmid, 1991). Recently I have spoken to a few sources in Japan who claim that they know of wild locations of 'Tokudama', but these could just be naturalized specimens.

Nomenclature aside, 'Tokudama' can be a wonderful addition to any shaded garden. It has been extensively used in breeding work, and there are a large number of related cultivars. Many of its seedlings grow larger than 'Tokudama' itself, but smaller than *H. sieboldiana* 'Elegans'. Variegated versions of 'Tokudama' include 'Tokudama Aureonebulosa' and 'Tokudama Flavocircinalis'. They originated in Japan and are presumed to be sports of 'Tokudama'.

seedlings, sports, and other related types:

'Abiqua Drinking Gourd': {1989r, Walden West; 'Tokudama' X *H. sieboldiana*} lg md of cupped blue-green foliage **(see page 58)**

'Barbara White': {1990r, S. Bond; 'Tokudama' sdlg} thick-substanced gold foliage; 15" by 44" md; 12" by 9 1/2" lvs (17 vp)

'Betcher's Blue': {1986r, AHS} long-standing cultivar from Carl Betcher; 'Tokudama' sdlg; 16" by 40" md; 9 7/8" by 7 1/2" lvs that are deep bl-green (dk gr later); blade sharply turned upward along margin; near-wh fls in June-July; limited seed pod formation; notable for its interesting cupping habit

'Blue Cadet': {1974r, P. Aden; 'Tokudama' sdlg} dense

470

med-sized md of bluish green foliage; acts like a seedling of *H. nakaiana* **(see page 87)**

'Blue Dome': {1980r, E. Minks; self of 'Tokudama' tet.} med-lg md of heavily corrugated, bl-green foliage; larger than 'Tokudama', as much as 32" by 67" with 12 1/2" by 10" lvs (16 vp)

'Blue Fan Dancer': {1976r, P. Aden; self of a 'Tokudama' sdlg} 21" by 38" md of heavily corrugtd, bl-gr lvs, 8" by 7"; thick-subst; near-wh fls, June-July on 24" sc; highly thought of, rarely grown

'Blue Horizon': {1985r, L. Englerth; 'Tokudama' sdlg} 17" by 32" md of v heavily corrugated, deep bl-green lvs, 8" by 7" (16 vp); outstanding color, corrugation and substance

'Blue Lagoon': {1972r, F. Woodroffe; 'Tokudama' sdlg} 15" by 36" md of unruly, blue-green lvs, 8" by 8"; notable for unruliness

'Blue Tiers': {1976r, P. Aden; 'Tokudama' sdlg} rare

'Blue Umbrellas': {1978r, P. Aden; 'Tokudama' X 'Elegans'} lg md of bluish green lvs **(see page 94)**

'Blue Velvet': {1976r, P. Aden; 'Tokudama' X a 'Tokudama' sdlg} med-sized md of heavily corrugated, bl-green foliage

'Bon Voyage': {1980r, E. Minks; 'Tokudama' X 'Dearheart'} rare

'Carder Blue': {1986r by the AHS} long-standing 'Tokudama' form from Ellen Carder; 18" by 38" md of heavily corrugtd, thick, bl-green lvs, 8 1/2" by 7 1/2"; long known as *H. tokudama* 'Carder Blue'

'Fleeta's Blue': {1999r by P. Ruh for F. Woodroffe & R. O'Harra} 'Tokudama' sdlg wi thick, blue-green foliage; v close to 'Tokudama'

'Fleeta Brownell Woodroffe': {1986r, R. O'Harra; 'Tokudama' sdlg} gold-margined, bl-green-centered foliage; v close to 'Tokudama Flavocircinalis'

'Hime Tokudama': Japanese hybrid actually related to *H. nakaiana*, not 'Tokudama' **(see page 228)**

'Hirao Zeus': {1997r, S. Hirao & P. Ruh} long known as "Tokudama Tet." indicating that it could be a tetraploid form of 'Tokudama'; lg md of heavily corrugtd, bl-green foliage (deep green by late summer); md 24" by 58"; lvs 14" by 10 1/2" (16-18 vp) that are also heavily corrugated and v thick-substanced; near-wh fls, late June into July on 34" sc; fertile; outstanding

'Kiwi Forest': {1999r, B. Sligh; 'Tokudama' sport wi mottled foliage that turns green}

'Lady In Waiting': {1980r by A. Arett; hybrid of 'Tokudama' X 'Elegans'} 24" by 52" md; bl-gr lvs (14" by 11"

wi 17-18 vp); near-wh fls, June-July, on sc up to 42";
"mother plant" of 'Alvatine Taylor'

'Lake Louise': {1975r, E. Minks; 'Tokudama' X *H.
sieboldiana*} 22" by 44" md of heavily corrugated, bl-
green lvs 11" by 9" (18-19 vp); thick subst; near-wh fls
in June-July; rarely grown

'Lime Krinkles': {1988r, M. Soules; 'Tokudama' sdlg} 17"
by 36" md of heavily corrugated, unruly foliage that is
med to br gold; near-wh fls in June-July

'Moscow Blue': {1986r by the AHS for A. Arett; unknown
parentage} 21" by 48" md of heavily corrugated, thick,
deep bl-green lvs, 10" by 8" (16-17 vp); near-wh fls, late
June into July on 26" sc; one of the best blue Tokudamas

'Pelham Blue Tump': {1986r, R. Kitchingman; 'Tokudama'
sdlg} low, dense md of green foliage; similar to 'Blue
Cadet'

'Quilted Cup': {1980r, E. Minks; 'Tokudama' X 'Crinkle
Cup'} 18" by 37" md of heavily corrugated, bl-green
lvs, 9 1/2" by 8 1/8" (15 vp); lvs also thick-substanced,
unruly and deeply cupped

'Rabinau': a 'Tokudama' selection found in the early
1960's; no differences from 'Tokudama'

'Rough Waters': {1969r, M. Armstrong; 'Tokudama' sdlg}
lg md of intensely corrugated, bluish green foliage; md
29" by 56", lvs 11" by 8" (16 vp); near-wh fls in June-
July; one of the first hostas registered with the AHS;
popular breeding plant for many years

'Silver Rim': {1980r, E. Minks; selfed 'Tokudama' sdlg}
17" by 36" md; 8 1/2" by 5 3/4" blue-green lvs (15 vp)

'Smokey Tokey': {1998r, E. Elslager, 'Tokudama' sport}
17" by 38" md of rich blue-green lvs, 10 1/2" by 8" (18
vp); heavily corrugated

'Tokudama Aureonebulosa': long-standing gold-centered
form of 'Tokudama' from Japan; most likely a sport **(see
page 473)**

'Tokudama Flavocircinalis': long-standing gold-margined
form of 'Tokudama' from Japan; most likely a sport **(see
page 477)**

'Warwick Cup': {1993r, L. Jones; 'Tokudama' sdlg} 21" by
48" md of bl-green lvs, 10" by 9" (18 vp); heavily corrugated and cupped; fertile

'Wayside Blue': {1989r, P. Ruh; 'Tokudama' sdlg} found in
a field formerly used by Wayside Gardens in Perry, OH;
was sold as *H. tokudama* 'Wayside'; med-sized md of
blue-green lvs; near-wh fls, June-July; slight differences
from 'Tokudama'

other similar types:
'Birchwood Parky's Blue', 'Black Limerick', 'Blue for You', 'I'm So Blue', 'Julia Hardy', 'Krinkled Joy', 'Love Pat', 'Mood Indigo', 'Peek-A-Boo', 'Samual Blue', 'Seersucker', 'Skookumchuck'

'Tokudama Aureonebulosa'
key features: medium-sized mound of gold-centered, blue-margined foliage; slug-resistant
mound size: 18" high by 42" wide

spacing: 30"
leaves: 7 3/8" long by 6" wide (up to 8 1/2" by 7 1/4"); center changes from chartreuse early to medium gold by midsummer with many pale green and blue-green streaks from the 1" to 1 1/2" wide blue-green margins; colors not as distinct and margin thinner when young; orangy gold color may develop in late fall; thick underside bloom; blade rotund to broadly oblong-ovate, cupped and somewhat wavy; heavy corrugation; thick substance; 16-18 vein pairs
flowers: late June into early July; near-white with a pale lavender mid-petal stripe; 1 3/4" long by 1" wide; narrow funnel shape; densely clustered on scapes that are as high as 24"; many seed pods develop
comments: 'Tokudama Aureonebulosa' originated in Japan, most likely as a mutation of 'Tokudama'. Despite its relatively slow growth rate, it is one of the most highly respected hostas among gardeners, collectors and nurserymen. The appeal of 'Tokudama Aureonebulosa' stems from its colorful, slug-resistant foliage. The intensity of coloration varies with light level, being brighter gold with more direct light. The intense corrugation, unruliness, and cupping also add to its ornamental value. Although the

473

flowers seem incidental, they are produced in attractive, dense clusters and are an ornamental plus.

This plant was known for many years as *H. tokudama aureo-nebulosa* when 'Tokudama' was considered a species. The AHS registered it as *H. tokudama* 'Aureo-nebulosa' in 1987. Schmid (1991) reduced it to cultivar status, hence the name, 'Tokudama Aureonebulosa'. A closely related form, *Hosta tokudama* f. *flavo-planata*, was described as "very yellow, on the margin very narrowly green" by Maekawa (1972, p. 58). Over the years I have seen a few specimens labelled as such and have even propagated them, but they appear no different from 'Tokudama Aureonebulosa'. In fact the juvenile form of the latter can easily be described as yellow in the center with a narrow, green margin, so I do not believe that the name 'Tokudama Flavoplanta' (or *H. tokudama flavo-planta)* can be correctly ascribed to any plant.

'Tokudama Aureonebulosa' has been a popular hybridizing plant for many years. A number of variegated, gold, and blue cultivars have been the result including 'Iron Gate Supreme' (streaked), 'Iron Gate Delight' (streaked), 'Eventide' (white-margined), 'King Tut' (gold), 'Peek-A-Boo' (blue), 'Sweet Sunshine' (gold), and 'Treasure' (gold) among others. A few sports have also been identified including 'Golden Medallion' (gold) and 'Blue Shadows' (chartreuse-centered, rather than gold).

seedlings, sports, and other related types:
'Bengee': {1999r by P. Ruh for J. Harrison, Palmer, & R. Bemis} 15" by 31" md; chartreuse, Tokudama-type lvs; a blue-lvd plant has erroneously been labelled this; probably a sdlg of 'Tokudama Aureonebulosa' (Summers, 1971b)

'Bingo': {1993r, Belle Gardens; 'Tokudama Aureonebulosa' sdlg} 16" by 38" md of bluish green-centered, gold-margined lvs

'Blondie': {1982r, G. Harshbarger; 'Tokudama Aureonebulosa' sdlg} sibling to 'Treasure' and 'King Tut'; med-lg md; lvs chartreuse early, changing to bright gold, 10" by 9" (16 vp); heavily corrugated; near-wh fls, late June into early July; fertile; an attractive bright mound

'Blue for You': {1991r, R. & D. Benedict; selfed 'Tokudama Aureonebulosa' sdlg} med-lg md of blue-green lvs, 8" by 7" (14-16 vp), md 16" by 40" (up to 24" by 55"), heavily corrugated, cupped & unruly

'Blue Shadows': {1980r, K. Anderson; 'Tokudama Aureonebulosa' sport} differs from 'Tokudama Aureonebulosa' in its chartreuse to pale green leaf center rather than gold; very attractive variation

'Boots and Saddles': {1983r, E. Minks; a 'Tokudama Aureonebulosa' sport with more gold splashing} similar to
'Tokudama Aureonebulosa'

'Brenner Pass': {1972r, F. Woodroffe; as a "variegated form
of *H. glauca*"} med-sized md of gold-centered, blue-
mgd foliage; very close to, if not the same as, 'Tokudama Aureonebulosa'

'Eventide': {1992r, W. & E. Lachman; sdlg X 'Tokudama
Aureonebulosa'} green-centered, white-mgd lvs, 13" by
8" wi a 3/8" wide, white margin

'Fleeta's Fantasy': {1999r by P. Ruh for F. Woodroffe & R.
O'Harra} gold-centered, bl-green-mgd lvs; almost identical to 'Tokudama Aureonebulosa' and 'Brenner Pass'

'Gold Cup': {1978r, P. Aden; 'Tokudama Aureonebulosa' X
'Golden Prayers'} 17" by 34" md; 9 3/8" by 8 1/2" lvs
that are med to br gold; intensely corrugated, deeply
cupped, & thick-substanced; differs fr 'Golden Medallion' by more deeply cupped foliage; popular breeding
plant

'Golden Medallion': gold-leaved sport of 'Tokudama Aureonebulosa' **(see page 194)**

'Golden Rajah': {1976r, P. Aden; 'Aspen Gold' sdlg X a
'Tokudama Aureonebulosa' sdlg} heavily corrugated,
deeply cupped, bright gold foliage; 18" by 43" md;
thick-substanced lvs, 9" by 9" (16 vp); excellent cultivar
but not grown much anymore

'Goldilocks': {1970r, M. Armstrong; "Variegated Glauca"
sdlg} probably from 'Tokudama Aureonebulosa'; 17" by
47" md of thick, heavily corrugated, br gold lvs, 9" by 7"
(14 vp)

'Herb Benedict': {1990r, J. Wilkins; 'Dorothy Benedict' X
'Tokudama Aureonebulosa'} foliage heavily mottled
and streaked with white, cream, and green on a bl-green
base; formerly "DB-86-1", winner of the 1988 AHS
Savory Shield award (AHS, 1988); near-white fls, June-
July

'Iron Gate Delight': {1981r, V. Sellers; *H. plantaginea* X
'Tokudama Aureonebulosa'} streaked lvs; fragr pale
purple fls **(see page 241)**

'Iron Gate Supreme': {1980r, V. Sellers; *H. plantaginea* X
'Tokudama Aureonebulosa'} streaked foliage; fragr,
pale lav fls **(see page 242)**

'King Tut': {1981r, G. Harshbarger; 'Tokudama Aureonebulosa' sdlg} sibling to 'Blondie' and 'Treasure'; med-lg
md of heavily corrugated, bright gold foliage **(see page
255)**

'Little Aurora': {1978r, P. Aden; sdlg of 'Tokudama Aureonebulosa' X 'Golden Waffles'} sm md of br gold

foliage; number of vp and lf size do not match parentage **(see page 275)**

'Newberry Gold': {1996r, Carter, Holmes & N. Plemmons; 'Tokudama Aureonebulosa' sdlg} broadly ovate gold foliage

'Peek-A-Boo': {1976r, P. Aden; 'Tokudama Aureonebulosa' X "Aden 355"} 19" by 51" md, 11 1/2" by 9 1/2" lvs (15 vp) that are a deep bl-green, heavily corrugated, and slug-resistant; sc 30" high

'Princess Diana': {1997r, G. Trucks; 'Tokudama Flavoplanata' sport; lvs wi a bl-green-mgn that streaks into the gold center}

'Ruby Benedict': {1991r, R. & D. Benedict; 'Dorothy Benedict' X 'Tokudama Aureonebulosa'; lvs creamy white wi a variable bl-green margin} have seen leaves with gold centers & bl-green mgns

'Serene': {1983r, E. Minks, 'Tokudama Aureonebulosa' sport} gold-cntrd, bl-gr-mgd foliage; md 15" by 40", lvs 10" by 7 3/4" (18 vp) wi 1 1/2" mgns; center lighter gold than 'Tokudama Aureonebulosa'

'Sweet Sunshine': {1997r, R. Solberg; 'Sweet Susan' X 'Tokudama Aureonebulosa'}gold lvs rounded, cupped and heavily corrugated; fragr white fls; very attractive

'Treasure': {1981r, G. Harshbarger; 'Tokudama Aureonebulosa' sdlg} sibling to 'Blondie' and 'King Tut'; med-lg md of bright gold foliage **(see page 481)**

'Wahoo': {1976r, P. Aden; 'Tokudama Aureonebulosa' X 'Tokudama Flavocircinalis'} med-sized md of heavily variegated foliage; md 17" by 38", lvs 7 1/2" by 5 1/2" (10 vp); foliage colors variable, ranging from heavily streaked to yellow-mgd or all-green; pale lav fls in July on 22" sc; popular breeding pl; foliage, flower color, and blooming season not 'Tokudama'-like

'Winning Edge': {1988r, M. Zilis & T & Z N; as a selfed 'Tokudama Aureonebulosa'} bl-gr lvs wi mgns that change from creamy yellow to white; can drawstring; cut off first flush of foliage; no longer widely grown

other similar types:

'Aardvark': {1991r, D. Savory; 'Aspen Gold' sdlg} med-sized md of chartreuse to gold-centered, green-margined foliage that is also thick-substanced & heavily corrugated; dense clusters of near-white fls from about early to late July (Ohio); resembles 'Tokudama Aureonebulosa' in foliage & flower

'Abiqua Hallucination': {1999r, Walden West, J. Hyslop & C. Purtyman; 'Tokudama Flavocircinalis' sport} heavily corrugated, gold-centered, bl-green-mgd lvs; very similar to Tokudama Aureonebulosa'

476

'Bright Lights': 19" by 52" md of gold-centered, bl-green-mgd lvs, 9" by 7" (15 vp); mgns 3/4" to 1 1/2" wide; lvs also thick-substd wi a thin underside bloom; blade not as round as 'Tokudama Aureonebulosa'; near-wh fls, June-July; very popular in the last ten years; a Paul Aden introduction

'Inniswood' **(see page 236)**

'Larry Englerth': {1986r, H. Benedict} gold-centered, bl-green-mgd lvs; close to 'Spinning Wheel'

'Lucy Vitols' **(see page 288)**

'Spinning Wheel': sport of 'Golden Nugget' from Mildred Seaver; introduced for sale in 1988 by Hatfield Gardens; 20" by 50" md of gold-cntrd, bl-green-mgd lvs, 11 1/2" by 10 1/2" (18 vp); near-wh fls, late June into July on 25" sc; similar to 'Green Rim Nugget' and 'Larry Englerth'

'Tokudama Flavocircinalis'

key features: medium-large mound of gold-margined foliage; slug-resistant

mound size: 17" high by 48" wide (up to 23" by 70")

spacing: 48"

leaves: 9" long by 6 7/8" wide; 1" to 1 3/4" wide, chartreuse to medium gold margin; center blue-green becoming dark green by mid-summer; moderate underside bloom; blade broadly ovate; blade also generally wavy, heavily corrugated and slightly cupped; thick substance; 16 vein pairs

flowers: late June into early July; near-white with a pale lavender mid-petal stripe; lavender overtones in bud; 2" long by 1 1/4" wide; in dense clusters on 25" scapes; will form seed pods

comments: 'Tokudama Flavocircinalis' becomes an impressive, broad mound of thick-substanced, heavily corrugated foliage with wide, gold margins. It can be thought of as a medium-sized version of 'Frances Williams' with the added benefit of not "burning" along the margin. Like the other Tokudamas, it was once considered a form of the species, i.e. *H. tokudama flavo-circinalis*, but is now listed as a cultivar (Schmid, 1991). The AHS registered it as *H. tokudama* 'Flavo-circinalis' in 1987. It can be utilized as a ground cover or specimen plant.

'Tokudama Flavocircinalis' readily forms seed and can be successfully incorporated into a breeding program. Three sports have been identified.

seedlings, sports, and other related types:

'Abiqua Hallucination': {1999r, Walden West, J. Hyslop & C. Purtyman; 'Tokudama Flavocircinalis' sport} heavily corrugated, gold-centered, bl-green-mgd lvs; very similar to 'Tokudama Aureonebulosa'

'Cat's Meow': {1998r, C. Falstad; 'Tokudama Flavocircinalis' sport; lvs wi a light green center, gold margins}

'Fleeta Brownell Woodroffe': {1986r, R. O'Harra; 'Tokudama' sdlg} gold-margined, bl-green-centered foliage; v close to 'Tokudama Flavocircinalis'

'Golden Bullion': {1989r by P. Ruh for P. Bennerup} gold-leaved sport of 'Tokudama Flavocircinalis; virtually indistinguishable from 'Golden Medallion' though some consider it a brighter gold

'Great Plains': {1994r, W. Brincka & O. Petryszyn; 'Sagae' X 'Tokudama Flavocircinalis'} large, flat, powdery blue leaves, turning dark green by mid-summer; upr md, 28" by 39" (probably more); 15" by 10" lvs; slight corrug; dense clusters of near-wh fls on 31" sc in June (Ohio); outstanding large hosta

'Jack of Diamonds': {1985r, R. Savory; as a hybrid of *H. sieboldiana* X a seedling mutation} appears very similar to 'Tokudama Flavocircinalis' in both foliage and flowering

'Mood Indigo': {1996r, D. & J. Ward; 'Tokudama Flavocircinalis' sdlg} med-lg md of heavily corrugated, deep blue lvs; wh fls in June-July (Ohio); impressive combination of blue lvs & white fls

'Wahoo': {1976r, P. Aden; 'Tokudama Aureonebulosa' X 'Tokudama Flavocircinalis'} med-sized md of heavily variegated foliage; not 'Tokudama'-like **(see page 476)**

other similar types:

'Abiqua Moonbeam', 'Alvatine Taylor', 'Bingo', 'Cart Wheels', 'Celebrity', 'Dippity Dew', 'June Dove', 'Mayan Moon', 'Sunnybrook', 'Tranquility', 'Wagon Wheels'

'Torchlight'

key features: semi-upright, medium-large mound of white-margined foliage; reddish petioles

mound size: 22" high by 45" wide

spacing: 40"

leaves: 6" long by 4 1/2" wide; 1/2" wide, white margin; dark green center; purple-red dots on petioles that are especially dense on lower petiole; shiny top and very shiny underside; blade ovate, more elliptic when young; slightly wavy margins; smooth texture; average substance; 8-9 vein pairs

flowers: mid-July into early August; lavender; 2 1/2" long by 1" wide; narrow funnel shape; scapes up to 35" high

comments: 'Torchlight' is another fine plant from the Bill and Eleanor Lachman hybridizing program. They registered it with the AHS in 1990 as a hybrid of seedling #81-8 X 'Halcyon'. It is known for its vase-shaped mound habit, attractive, white-margined foliage and red petioles, but there are more positives to 'Torchlight' than that. It exhibits a fairly fast growth rate, making it a great nursery plant, but, more importantly, a good garden plant that can be utilized as a showy specimen. The flowers are an ornamental plus, being a rich lavender and are borne on scapes well above the foliage.

A factor often overlooked in hostas is the durability of the foliage over the course of the season. 'Torchlight' begins and ends the season looking great. In fact one of my greatest impressions of 'Torchlight' is seeing a beautiful specimen in Van Wade's collection---in mid-October---a time when 90% of the hostas had been affected by frost or were going dormant.

It should be noted that while the red petioles can be attractive, they certainly are not the dominant feature of 'Torchlight'. The vase-shaped mound habit allows them to be seen close-up, but from a distance they cannot be easily viewed.

seedlings, sports, and other related types:

'Border Bandit': {1992r, W. & E. Lachman; "81-8" X 'Halcyon'} leaves creamy yellow-margined, dark green-centered; 16" by 34" md; 7" by 5" lvs (8 vp); very attractive; out of the same cross as 'Torchlight'

'Shady Choice': {1998r, J. & B. Diesen; sport} 23" by 42" md; 7 3/4" by 5 1/2", green lvs (9 vp)

other similar types:

'Chantilly Lace', 'Crusader', 'Gay Blade', 'Tambourine'

'Tortifrons'
(Kogarashi Giboshi; Arechi Giboshi)

key features: small mound of twisted, contorted, green foliage

mound size: 8" high by 17" wide

spacing: 18"

leaves: 5" long by 1" wide; dark green; very shiny underside; blade very narrowly elliptic with a very long, tapered tip; heavily twisted and contorted; not corrugated but very irregular texture; good substance; 4 vein pairs that arc hard to see

flowers: mid to late September; pale bluish lavender; funnel-shaped with slightly reflexed tips; 2 1/4" long by 1 1/2" wide; scapes 15" or so

comments: 'Tortifrons' has intrigued hosta collectors for many years. The heavily twisted, dark green foliage always makes it an interesting conversation piece in the garden. It is best utilized in a special spot in the garden where its strange foliar habits can be observed closely. For even better viewing, it should be grown in containers.

Its desirability is partly related to its scarcity. Attempts to successfully propagate 'Tortifrons' by tissue culture have generally met with failure. The plants that result turn out to be 'Tardiflora'. This, of course, means that 'Tortifrons' is a sport of 'Tardiflora'. Evidently, the leaf distortion seen in 'Tortifrons' is caused by the same type of epidermal chimera that prevents 'Embroidery' and a few others from being accurately propagated by tissue culture.

Maekawa (1973) considered 'Tortifrons' a species (*Hosta tortifrons*). This is a bit hard to understand since he was aware of its close relationship to 'Tardiflora' and only cited cultivated specimens. Schmid (1991) reduced it to cultivar level, hence its current nomenclature.

seedlings, sports, and other related types:
'Tornado': seedling of 'Tortifrons' from Japan that is twisted and white-backed

other similar types:
'Emerald Necklace', 'Fused Veins', 'Koryu'

'Treasure'
key features: medium-large mound of bright gold foliage; slug-resistant
mound size: 22" high by 55" wide

---

spacing: 48"
leaves: 10 3/4" long by 9 1/2" wide; medium to bright gold, intensity depending upon site and season; moderate underside bloom; blade cupped and broadly ovate with a deeply lobed base; very heavily corrugated; thick substance; 14-16 vein pairs

flowers: late June into July; very pale lavender with a slightly darker stripe

in mid-petal; 2 1/4" long by 1" wide; scapes 26-35" high with 30" typical; many seed pods develop

comments: 'Treasure' ranks highly among gold cultivars for its brilliant color and intense corrugation. Though registered in 1981 by Gretchen Harshbarger (as a seedling of 'Tokudama Aureonebulosa'), its popularity has steadily increased as hosta enthusiasts realize the value of this plant. 'King Tut' and 'Blondie' are similar, gold-leaved siblings of 'Treasure'.

seedlings, sports, and other related types:
'Garden Treasure': {1997r, J. Schwarz; sport} gold-mgd, green-centered (bluish early) lvs; attractive

other similar types:
'Aspen Gold', 'Newberry Gold'

Hosta tsushimensis (Tsushima Giboshi)
key features: medium-sized mound of green foliage
mound size: 12" high by 31" wide

spacing: 24"
leaves: 7 3/4" long by 3 3/4" wide; medium green; narrowly ovate blade; moderately wavy margin; no corrugation; intense purple-red dots on petioles; thin substance; 5-6 vein pairs
flowers: mid-August; medium purple, striped and a whitish margin from the throat halfway to the petal tip; 2" long by 1 5/8" wide; open funnel shape with heavily reflexed tips and a thin corolla tube; scapes 24-30" high; readily forms seed pods that have a distinct spike at the tip
comments: Tsushima Island lies in the Korean Strait, northwest of Kyushu Island and southeast of the Korean peninsula. Fujita (1978, p. 39) stated that *Hosta tsushimensis* could be "found all over Tsushima". It becomes a fairly dense mound of wavy green leaves and makes an attractive addition to any hosta collection. There are a number of flower color variants as well as a gold-leaved version. While red-flowered and tri-colored flower forms are purported to exist, the ones I've seen in bloom are just shades of purple.

seedlings, sports, and other related types:
H. tsushimensis albiflora: have seen at the peak of bloom in

mid-Sept producing pure white fls measuring 2" by 1";
probably the same as *H. tsushimensis* 'Shirobana'
(Schmid, 1991), which could be listed as listed as the
cultivar 'Shirobana Tsushima'

'Ogon Tsushima': gold-leaved form from Japan; dense
mound of foliage, 10" by 26"; 6" by 3" lvs (6 vp); med
purple fls in August

H. tsushimensis 'Sanshoku': reported to have tricolor flowers including shades of purple, red, and white; have only
seen it produce bright purple flowers with thick white
petal margins

other similar types:

Hosta jonesii: low md of green lvs 6" by 2 7/8" (7 vp); dull
top, whitish shiny underside; blade elliptic-ovate;
described by Schmid (1991) as a species native to several Korean islands and closely related to *H. tsushimensis*; at this point, a "collector's plant"

'Ultraviolet Light'
key features: dense, medium-sized mound of bright
gold foliage; purple flowers; distinctive
mound size: 19" high by 41" wide

spacing: 36"
leaves: 8" long by 5"
wide; bright gold
into mid-summer;
thin underside
bloom; ovate blade
that is slightly wavy;
smooth texture; bet-
ter than average sub-
stance; 10-11 vein
pairs
flowers: early to late
July; bright purple;
2" long; 36" scapes;
many seed pods
develop
comments: Though
'Ultraviolet Light' is
a 'Gold Regal'
seedling (registered in 1989 by Jill and Jim Wilkins), it differs significantly in its smaller overall mound size and
brighter gold foliage. Another difference is the bright purple
flowers which are centered neatly above the mound of
foliage. Its combination of characteristics creates a distinct

appearance that makes 'Ultraviolet Light' a top-class plant.

seedlings, sports, and other related types:
none listed

other similar types:
'Fort Knox': {1989r, J. & J. Wilkins; 'Gold Regal' X 'Aspen Gold'} 24" by 60" md of light gold lvs, 12" by 8" (14 vp); lav fls on 33" sc, mid-July into Aug; some similarities to 'Ultraviolet Light' but the two will not be confused

---

'Undulata' (Suji Giboshi)
key features: small mound of very wavy, white-centered foliage
mound size: 12" high by 32" wide

spacing: 30"
leaves: 6" long by 2 5/8" wide; 1/8" to 1/2" wide green margin plus some pale green areas at the junction between the center and the margin; center color white, 1 3/4" wide, becoming mottled green or green after flowering; shiny underside; narrowly elliptic shape with a rounded base and twisted tip; two to three broad, prominent waves in the blade, causing twisting throughout, especially near the tip; thin substance; 6-8 vein pairs
flowers: early to late July; pale lavender with whitish petal margins; 2 1/2" long by 1 3/4" wide; narrow funnel shape; scapes up to 40" high; sterile
comments: 'Undulata' has been used in landscapes throughout the United States for many years, but is much less common than 'Undulata Univittata'. The difference between the two lies in the percentage of white in the leaf. In 'Undulata' the white center accounts for two-thirds of the leaf versus only one-third for 'Undulata Univittata'. 'Undu-

lata' is also much smaller and less vigorous.

As a landscape plant, it reaches its peak early in the season. The white-centered foliage produces a refreshing splash of variegation in May and June that is hard to equal, even by dozens of newer cultivars. Many a hybridizer has sought to reproduce the springtime 'Undulata' look in their seedlings. On the other hand, the 'Undulata' flower effect can best be described as "gangly". The lavender flowers are widely spaced on scapes that are very tall in proportion to the mound size. Near the end of July, the scapes begin to turn brown and, if not removed, become an unattractive mess of tall, brown sticks. After flowering the foliage goes through a color metamorphosis of sorts. What were interesting white-centered leaves quickly begin turning green or mottled green. The uninitiated think they are witnessing the formation of a sport. At the same time, any damage caused by slugs throughout the summer becomes noticeable. Small and large holes may riddle the foliage. This unsightliness is enhanced by dry conditions or exposure to direct sunlight which leads to browning in the slug holes and along the leaf margins. By September 'Undulata' is often so poor-looking that it needs to be cut down to the ground.

Like 'Crispula' and 'Decorata', Maekawa (1973) listed 'Undulata' as a species (*Hosta undulata*) despite being a variegated plant not found in the wild. Most hosta collectors had long suspected the cultivated origins of 'Undulata' because of its variegated nature and the fact that it cannot reproduce itself by seed. Even Maekawa (1973, p. 56) described its habitat as "cultivated in gardens of Japan". George Schmid (1991) finally put into print the obvious, that *Hosta undulata* should be considered a cultivar, i.e. 'Undulata'. Thankfully he converted the specific epithet into the cultivar name, thus avoiding the inevitable confusion. The only other acceptable name would have been 'Suji' from the Japanese common name.

As a breeding plant, 'Undulata' is difficult to work with, though an occasional seed pod will develop with one or two viable seeds. Tony Avent has had the greatest breeding success with 'Undulata', introducing two seedlings related to it. Three other cultivars were once considered to be varieties of the species *Hosta undulata* including 'Undulata Albomarginata' (white-margined), 'Undulata Erromena' (green), and 'Undulata Univittata' (wider green margins, smaller white center). Whether all of these are sports of 'Undulata' or seedlings of it is unclear. 'Undulata Univittata' acts like a sport of 'Undulata' and 'Undulata Albomarginata' seems to be a sport of 'Undulata Erromena' but there are slight differences between the two groups. Unbelievable as it may seem, I worked with 'Undulata' in tissue culture for a few years. It often produced a sport with foliage that emerged all-white in spring and gradually turned green, first along the veins and then the whole leaf, i.e., something akin to Tony Avent's 'Outhouse Delight'.

seedlings, sports, and other related types:

'Kiwi Spearmint': {1999r, B. Sligh; 'Undulata' sport; lvs pure white wi a green mgn}

'Outhouse Delight': {1998r, T. Avent; sdlg of 'Undulata'} new lvs emerge white, turning green during the season; unusual & strange collector's plant

'Paintbrush': {1976r, E. Minks; 'Undulata' X *H. ventricosa* 'Aureomaculata'} med-sized md of heart-shaped lvs that are chartreuse in the center & green-mgd; turns green by early summer

'Shichu-no-Tama': a seedling of 'Undulata' from Gotemba N in Japan; lvs emerge pure white early in the spring, turns green, starting along the veins; observed in 1991; similar to 'Outhouse Delight'

'Snow White': {1983r, A. Arett; *H. undulata* 'Undulata' sport; more white in the foliage and more vigor} lvs 6" by 3 1/2" (9 vp)

'Unducosa': {1986r, AHS} hybrid of 'Undulata' X *H. ventricosa* developed by Alex Summers and described in *The American Hosta Society Bulletin* in 1971 (Summers, 1971a); med-sized md of shiny, wavy-margined, green lvs 8 3/8" by 6 1/4" (8 vp); intermediate between its parents; collector's plant

'White Wall Tire': {1995r, T. Avent; 'Outhouse Delight' sdlg} lvs white early, changing to white with greenish veins, and finally to green by early summer; lvs also wavy , measuring 8" by 3 3/4" (8-9 vp); unusual collector's plant; md 12" by 30"

other similar types:

'Gay Feather' **(see page 176)**

'Gray Streaked Squiggles': {1978r, H. Ross & P. Ruh; unknown parentage} sm md of narrow, wavy foliage; elliptic-shaped lvs green, overlaid with fine, white dotting; rarely ever fls (pale lav in July); truly one of the oddities of the hosta world that should be grown side-by-side with 'Outhouse Delight' and 'White Wall Tire'

Hosta koreana 'Variegated': plants sold under this name the same as 'Undulata'

'White Christmas' **(see page 504)**

'Undulata Albomarginata'
(Fukurin Ohatsuki Giboshi)

key features: medium-sized mound of white-margined foliage; most commonly planted white-margined hosta in the last 100 years

mound size: 18" high by 44" wide (up to 23" by 51")

spacing: 36"

leaves: 8 1/4" long by 4 1/2" wide; 1/4" to 1/2" wide, creamy white margin with gray-green gradations at the junction of the margin and center which is a medium green; very shiny underside; blade elliptic with a rounded to acute base and slightly curved tip; slightly wavy margin, 3-5 per side; slight corrugation at maturity, none when younger; thin substance; 7-10 vein pairs

flowers: July 12 to August 2 (northern Illinois); pale lavender with a midpetal stripe and whitish petal margin; 2 1/4" by 1 1/2" wide; scapes 31-45" high; 25 scapes on one mature clump; sterile

comments: 'Undulata Albomarginata' has been the most widely used white-margined hosta in American landscapes in the twentieth century. It has a fairly vigorous growth rate and looks great during April, May, and June. Like 'Undulata', it typically starts to deteriorate in July when the scapes turn into tall, brown sticks after flowering. The thin foliage also is extremely susceptible to slug damage. I have seen plants of 'Undulata Albomarginata' where the foliage has become skeleton-like by August. As well, it tends to brown along the margins and in slug holes when subjected to dryness or direct sunlight.

Some of the damage can be attributed to the fact that it is such an ordinary part of the landscape that no special care is given. The same plants look bad, year after year. Adding to the problem, 'Undulata Albomarginata' is often grown in unsuitable areas, i.e. in full sun or hard-packed clayey soil. The mature size of such plants is much reduced and the ornamental value is significantly reduced. When 'Undulata Albomarginata' is given the proper care, it can be attractive for much of the growing season. Slug-bait, fertilizer, and water make a great deal of difference.

Before being relegated to cultivar status (Schmid, 1991), it was considered a botanical variety of *Hosta undulata*, under the name *Hosta undulata albo-marginata*. I am sure that many garden labels will continue to bear this name for a long time to come. It is called the Fukurin Ohatsuki Giboshi in Japan, where it originated many years ago and is still commonly found in gardens. Also, the AHS registered it as *H. undulata* 'Albo-marginata' in 1987. Apparently in England, 'Undulata Albomarginata' has been known as 'Thomas Hogg', a name formerly used for 'Decorata' in the U.S. Other names have also been used including 'Frank Sedgewick', "Mackwoods No. 5", and *Hosta japonica undulata aureo-marginata*.

Like 'Undulata' its breeding potential is very limited, but I have a seen a few pods develop. It does not readily sport, though one has been registered. I have never seen it mutate to the all-green form, 'Undulata Erromena', in the garden.

seedlings, sports, and other related types:
'Spartan Flash': {1998r, E. Elslager; sport; streaked, green, yellow and white foliage}

other similar types:
'Hauser Silver Edge': same as 'Undulata Albomarginata'
'Rocknoll Snow Edge': same as 'Undulata Albomarginata'
'See Saw': white-mgd sport of 'Undulata Erromena'; differs from 'Undulata Albomarginata' in having narrower, more cupped leaves but is fairly similar in other ways **(see page 490)**

'Undulata Erromena' (Ohatsuki Giboshi)

key features: medium-large mound of wavy, green foliage

mound size: 21" high by 47" wide (up to 25" by 65")

spacing: 48"

leaves: 8 1/4" long by 4 1/2" wide; medium green; slightly shiny top, very shiny underside; elliptic to broadly elliptic shape with a rounded base and distinct tip; light marginal ripples, 5-7 per side; smooth texture; no purple-red dots on petioles; average substance; 8-10 vein pairs

flowers: July 6 to 29; pale lavender color with whitish petal margins and throat; 2 3/4" long by 1 1/2" wide; funnel-shaped; scapes typically up to 45" high, but can reach 58" high under good conditions; many scapes per clump; very rarely forms seed pods with even fewer viable seeds

comments: 'Undulata Erromena' may be the most durable of the Undulatas. It forms a relatively large mound of foliage that is not as susceptible to slug or sun damage as the other types. As well, while the flower scapes are tall, they are in better proportion to the mound. Though grown for many years in American landscapes, it is not as common as its variegated counterparts. There has been some question about how 'Undulata Erromena' relates to the other Undulatas. It shows many similarities to 'Undulata Albomarginata', but its relationship to 'Undulata' and 'Undulata Univittata' is less clear. Its long-standing name, *Hosta undulata erromena*, was changed to 'Undulata Erromena' by Schmid (1991). The AHS had registered it as *H. undulata* 'Erromena' in 1987.

Its breeding potential is limited though an occasional seed pod will develop. 'See Saw' is an Alex Summers 'Undulata Erromena' sport from the early 1970's.

'Undulata Erromena' can be found growing in Japanese landscapes, used much in the same way as in the U.S. In fact it is one of the few hostas that I saw being used for general landscaping purposes in Japan.

seedlings, sports, and other related types:

'Kathy-O': {1994, D. O'Donnell; sport; lvs streaked creamy white & green}

'Mary Scholl': {1999r, R. Lamlein; sport; lvs greenish ylw wi a green mgn}

'See Saw': {1986r by the AHS for A. Summers} sport of 'Undulata Erromena' from the early 1970's; pictured in *The American Hosta Society Bulletin* (Summers, 1974); 18" by 40" md of white-margined lvs, 6 1/4" by 2 3/4", with a 1/8" to 1/4" wide, white margin; slightly more cupped & narrower lvs than 'Undulata Albomarginata'

other similar types:

'Nakaimo': {1986r, AHS} 25" by 52" md of med green lvs, 10" by 6" (10-11 vp), slightly rippled and v shiny on the underside; med lav fls, early to late July on 30-40" sc; sterile; 60+-year-old cultivar thought to have Japanese origins; similar to 'Undulata Erromena'

'Unducosa' **(see page 497)**

'Undulata Univittata'
key features: medium-sized mound of wavy, white-centered foliage; very common
mound size: 18" high by 45" wide (up to 20" by 49")

spacing: 40"
leaves: 7" long by 4 1/4" wide; deep green margin, 1 1/2" wide; creamy white to white center; some pale green streaks between margin and center; shiny underside; blade broadly elliptic with a rounded base and curved tip; generally wavy, especially near tip; smooth texture; average to thin substance; 7-8 vein pairs

490

flowers: July 10 to August 5; pale lavender with darker mid-petal stripes; 2 3/8" long by 1 1/4" wide; funnel shape; scapes typically 32-45" high; 33 scapes on one clump with about 30 flowers per scape; sterile

comments: 'Undulata Univittata' has been the most commonly planted white-centered hosta in the U.S., much more so than 'Undulata'. It differs from 'Undulata' by having a much wider green margin that covers 2/3 of the leaf, versus 1/3 for 'Undulata'. 'Undulata Univittata' is also more vigorous and certainly has made a greater impact in American landscaping. In the garden it tends to emerge fairly early, often a week ahead of most hostas. Like the other Undulatas it makes a fairly good show of variegated foliage in April-May-June, but begins to deteriorate in July. It is plagued with the same problems that necessitate special care (slug-bait, water, fertilizer, and shade) for it to look its best.

Also like the other Undulatas, 'Undulata Univittata' went through a series of name changes. It was not described by Fumio Maekawa in his monograph, but Hylander (1954) listed it as *Hosta undulata* var. *univittata*, a name which continued to be used into the late 1980's. The AHS registered it in 1987 as *H. undulata* 'Univittata', and finally Schmid (1991) designated it as 'Undulata Univittata'.

Though it has been historically popular in the U.S., I do not recall seeing it in any Japanese garden or collection.

Its breeding potential is limited, though an occasional pod will develop. Several sports, mostly based upon the width of the margin, have been identified and named.

seedlings, sports, and other related types:

'Middle Ridge': {1979r, P. Ruh, R. Boonstra, & C. Lewis; sport} named for a road in northern Ohio near where it was found; differs from 'Undulata Univittata' in having the margin cover about 75% of the leaf blade, versus 67% for 'Undulata Univittata' and 33% for 'Undulata'; interchangeable with 'Undulata Univittata' in the landscape; formerly called 'Ella Sedgewick'

'Unitalis': named by Herbert A. Zager of Des Moines, Iowa before 1959; forms a med-sized md of lvs with a narrow, white stripe down the center; lacks the pale green sections usually found between the margin and center of 'Undulata Univittata' to which it is very close; haven't seen in many years

'White Ray': {1974r, E. Minks; sport of 'Undulata Univittata'} 19" by 38" md of foliage with a very narrow white center; on a 6 1/2" by 3 5/8" wide leaf, center only 1/2" wide (versus 1 1/2" for 'Undulata Univittata'); sometimes sports all-green foliage

other similar types:
'Color Riot', 'Indian Feather', 'Night Before Christmas', 'Sea Thunder', 'Silver Streak'

'Uzu-no-Mai'
key features: tiny rosettes of green foliage; best as a container-grown plant
mound size: 2 1/2" high by 5" wide

spacing: 6"
leaves: 2 1/2" long by 1 1/2" wide; medium to dark green; shiny top, whitish shiny underside; blade ovate and wavy, often curling at tip; smooth texture; average substance; 3-4 vein pairs
flowers: purple-striped; in a dense cluster on short scapes just above the foliage
comments: 'Uzu-no-Mai' deserves mention because it has the reputation of being the smallest hosta. The measurements listed above may not reflect what it actually can become (I suspect larger), but that is what I have seen in a few gardens. My experiences with it, however, have been less than encouraging. I have seen it die in both gardens and containers. I once gave a talk in Illinois to about 150 people and asked how many had grown 'Uzu-no-Mai'. A large number of hands went up. When I asked how many had plants that survived for more than one year, only two hands went up. Both were residents of the state of Washington, where the climate closely matches that of Japan where it originated. In Japan I did see a number of beautiful 'Uzu-no-Mai' specimens in containers, probably the best growing environment for this odd, little plant.

For a short time, 'Uzu-no-Mai' was being sold as 'Dancing Eddy'.
seedlings, sports, and other related types:
none listed

492

The only plant that comes close is a dwarf form *Hosta sieboldii* that I observed in one Japanese collection.

'Vanilla Cream'
key features: small mound of bright gold foliage
mound size: 11" high by 26" wide

spacing: 24"
leaves: 5 1/2" long by 4 1/2" wide; bright gold; thin underside bloom; blade a broad heart shape and puckered downward, adding to the rounded mound appearance; moderate corrugation; average substance, 10-11 vein pairs
flowers: late July; lavender; 2 1/8" long by 1 1/4" wide; 16" scapes
comments: 'Vanilla Cream' becomes a dense, rounded mound of very bright gold foliage. It has a fast growth rate and can be utilized as a bright specimen, ground cover or edger. At dusk or on cloudy days, the foliage will stand out in any collection.

It has not been incorporated into many breeding programs, but has been the source of a few significant mutations, most notably 'Wylde Green Cream'.

Paul Aden registered 'Vanilla Cream' in 1986 as a hybrid of a seedling X 'Little Aurora'.

seedlings, sports, and other related types:
'Ice Cream': {1998r, R. Rossing; sport; dark green lvs with a light green margin}
'Peppermint Cream': sport found at Hatfield Gardens in 1988; lvs gold with a subtle, pale green margin; variegation noticeable only upon close examination
'Pistachio Cream': green-leaved sport of 'Vanilla Cream' developed at my nursery (Q & Z N) and named by Elizabeth Stratton; dense, medium-sized mound of dark green foliage

'Shell Bell': {1999r, L. Jones; sport; lvs greenish ylw early, developing a yellow mgn later}

'Wylde Green Cream': {1996r, J. & E. Stratton; sport} gold-centered, dark green-margined foliage; margins about 1/4" wide; v striking contrast between leaf center and margin

other similar types:

'Bright Glow', 'Little Aurora', 'Maui Buttercups'

'Spun Sulphur': {1986r, R. O'Harra; unknown parentage} 10" by 24" md of v bright gold lvs, 5 7/8" by 4 3/8" (9 vp); fertile; dense md habit; effective specimen plant

---

Hosta ventricosa (Ovate-leaved Plantainlily; Murasaki Giboshi)

key features: medium-large mound of shiny, dark green foliage; bell-shaped purple flowers in July

mound size: 22" high by 50" wide (up to 26" by 60")

spacing: 48"

leaves: 9 1/2" long by 7 3/4" wide; shiny, dark green; very shiny underside; blade broadly ovate with a heart-shaped base and long, thin, twisted tip; many tiny ripples along the margin, especially noticeable early in the season; smooth texture; average substance; 8-9 vein pairs

flowers: July 12 to 30 (northern Illinois); medium purple with distinctive striping and whitish petal margins and throat; 2 3/8" long by 1" wide; distinctive bell shape; widely spaced on the scapes that typically measure 40", but can be as high as 53"; 22 scapes on one mature clump; 18 to 25 flowers per scape; numerous, very thick seed pods form with many viable seeds per pod

comments: As one of the three hosta species known to be native to China (*H. plantaginea* and *H. lancifolia* being the others), *Hosta ventricosa* has a long history in gardening. It was one of the first hostas exported to the West and has long

494

been a fixture in American shade gardens as a ground cover. The value of the tall scapes bearing bell-shaped purple flowers should not be overlooked. They make quite a show in July and are particularly striking in mass plantings.

One unusual characteristic of *H. ventricosa* is the formation of asexual (apomictic) seedlings. The flowers need to be fertilized for seed formation to occur, but instead of just developing a single, sexually produced embryo like all other hostas, multiple embryos, asexual in nature, develop out of endosperm tissue in the seed. I have examined *H. ventricosa* seeds under a dissecting microscope and have found as many as ten embryos of various sizes growing in a single seed. In a test tube, nearly all of the embryos become seedlings, whereas in a greenhouse or garden bed, only 3 or 4 generally survive. The asexual seedlings are genetically identical to the mother plant, meaning that *H. ventricosa* can be clonally propagated by seed with the caveat that an occasional seedling (from the sexually produced embryo) will be different. Some of these slightly different seedlings have been selected and introduced by a few persistent hybridizers. These include 'Holly's Honey', 'Little Blue', 'Lakeside Black Satin', 'Slick Willie', and 'Waving Wuffles'.

Two sports of *H. ventricosa* have been significant. *H. ventricosa* 'Aureomarginata', a sport with white-margined foliage, has become one of our most beloved variegated hostas. The other, *H. ventricosa* 'Aureomaculata', has been grown in nurseries for many years, though it has never achieved the popularity it deserves.

seedlings, sports, and other related types:

H. ventricosa 'Aureomaculata': sport with gold-centered, green-margined foliage in spring, changing to all-green by early summer; beautiful in spring; a good breeding plant; registered by the AHS as *H. ventricosa* 'Aureo-maculata' in 1987

H. ventricosa 'Aureomarginata': sport found in Europe; white-margined foliage that varies considerably from leaf to leaf, plant to plant; margins yellow early in the season, hence the origin of "aureo" **(see page 498)**

'Betty': {1983r, R. Benedict; selfed sdlg of (*H. nakaiana* X *H. ventricosa*)} dense, 13" by 36" md of heavily rippled, shiny, dark green lvs, 4 1/2" by 3 3/4" (10 vp); like a small, rippled *H. ventricosa*; attractive

'Bridegroom': {1990r, R. & D. Benedict & Hideko Gowen; 'Holly's Honey' sdlg} 16" by 34" md of rippled, shiny, dark green lvs, 6" by 4" (9 vp); purple fls in July; very unusual mound appearance created by upturned leaf tips; similar to 'Stirfry'

'Crystal Fountain': {1999r, B. Banyai; *H. ventricosa* sport wi gold lvs}

'Fury of Flame': {1985r, M. Zilis & T & Z N} *H. ventricosa* 'Aureomaculata' sdlg; lvs emerge yellow, changing to cream and green mottled by June and finally all-green; an odd, unusual collector's plant

'Gold Flush': {1984r, A. Bloom; sport of *H. ventricosa*} nearly identical to *H. ventricosa* 'Aureomarginata' except for a few gold streaks and mottled sections projecting into the leaf center

'Heartache': a Benedict hybrid of 'Gold Regal' X *H. ventricosa*; large, golden, heart-shaped leaves topped by purple flowers **(see page 223)**

'Holly's Honey': {1986r, AHS for G. Holly} a 1963 sdlg of *H. ventricosa*; 23" by 40" md of shiny, rippled, dk green lvs, 9 1/2" by 9"; bell-shaped purple fls in July on 33" sc; shinier and more heavily rippled than *H. ventricosa*; used by Herb Benedict to produce such shiny, dark green-leaved seedlings as 'Holly's Dazzler' {1987r}, 'Holly's Shine' {1987r}, 'Holly's Velvet Piecrust' {1995r}, 'Bridegroom' {1990r}, 'Stirfry' {1990r}, and 'Rippled Honey' plus the gold-leaved 'Holly's Gold' {1991r}

'Kiwi Black Magic' {1999r, B. Sligh; *H. sieboldiana* X *H. ventricosa*} very dark green foliage

'Lakeside Black Satin': *H. ventricosa* sdlg; med-lg md of shiny, dark green foliage **(see page 266)**

'Lakeside Emerald Lights': {1993r, M. Chastain; *H. ventricosa* X 'Invincible'} small mound of shiny, dark green, slightly rippled foliage; md 11" by 30"; lvs 5 1/2" by 3 3/4" (9 vp); fls mid-July into Aug; *H. ventricosa*-like scape bud

'Little Blue': {1976r, L. Englerth} no doubt a seedling of *H. ventricosa*; 16" by 42" md of shiny, dark green lvs, 9" by 5"; lvs narrower than *H. ventricosa;* bell-shaped, bright purple fls in July; sterile

'Minnesota Nice': {1997r, R. Snyder; sport of *H. ventricosa* 'Aureomaculata' with 3 seasonal flushes of variegated foliage}

'Paintbrush': {1976r, E. Minks; 'Undulata' X *H. ventricosa* 'Aureomaculata'} med-sized md of heart-shaped, center-variegated foliage; center color chartreuse surrounded by a thick green margin

'Peedee Elfin Bells': {1987r, U. Syre-Herz; *H. ventricosa* sdlg} med-sized md of dark green foliage **(see page 336)**

'Peedee Picotee': {1992, U. Syre-Herz; *H. ventricosa* sdlg; lvs begin yellow green, turn yellow}

'Peedee Treasure': {1989r, U. Syre-Herz; 'Gold Drop' X *H.*

ventricosa; br yellow-green foliage}

'Purple Flame Forever': {1988r, M. Zilis & T & Z N} gold-lvd sdlg of *H. ventricosa* 'Aureomaculata'; weak grower; 'Holly's Gold' a much better golden *H. ventricosa* form

'Rosedale Barnie': {1999r, J. Hadrava; *H. ventricosa* X 'Invincible'} 13" by 40" md of dark green lvs, 6 3/4" by 5" (10 vp); med purple fls on 19" sc in dense clusters from mid to late July; impressive dark green color & purple fls

'Rosedale Dough Boy': {1999r, J. Hadrava; *H. ventricosa* X 'Invincible'} 18" by 36" md of thick, noticeably rippled, dark green lvs, 11" by 8" (14 vp); many seed pods

'Slick Willie': {1996r, J. Hadrava; *H. ventricosa* X 'Invincible'} impressive, med-sized md of shiny, very dark green foliage; one of the darkest greens ever developed

'Stirfry': {1990r, R. & D. Benedict; 'Holly's Honey' selfed} 18" by 36" (up to 26" by 72") md of green lvs, 7" by 4 1/4" (7 vp); purple fls, mid-July into Aug on sc up to 48" high; lvs also heavily rippled along the margins & upturned at the tips like 'Bridegroom'

'Tall Boy': {1983r, Le Jardin botanique de Montreal; *H. rectifolia* X *H. ventricosa*} lg md of green foliage; v tall scapes bearing lav fls in Aug; parentage in question **(see page 449)**

'Tardiflora Hybrida': (1992r, P. Ruh for G. Arends; 'Tardiflora' X *H. ventricosa*} developed by George Arends of Germany from around 1911; 15" by 34" md of shiny, medium green lvs, 6 1/2" by 3" (6 vp); blade smooth, shiny on the underside and thin-substanced; purple fls from early to late Aug on 21" sc; lvs & fls not at all like 'Tardiflora'; notable for its early date of development and of interest mainly to collectors

'Tucker Valentine': {1991r, R. Stephens; 'Herifu' X *H. ventricosa*; glossy green lvs & white fls}

'Unducosa': {1986r, AHS} hybrid of 'Undulata' X *H. ventricosa* developed by Alex Summers and described in *The American Hosta Society Bulletin* in 1971 (Summers, 1971a); med-sized md of shiny, wavy-margined, green lvs 8 3/8" by 6 1/4" (8 vp); intermediate between its parents; collector's plant

'Venucosa': {1986r, AHS} *H. venusta* X *H. ventricosa* hybrid found by Alex Summers in the late 1960's; 20" by 55" md of heart-shaped, green lvs 6 5/8" by 5" (8 vp); bell-shaped purple fls, July 14-31; sparse pod formation; intermediate characteristics between the two parents; collector's plant

'Waving Wuffles': {1995r, T. Avent; *H. ventricosa* sdlg}
   25" by 47" md of rippled, green lvs, 8" by 5" (7-8 vp)
   with 13 or so marginal ripples
other similar types:
'Second Wind', 'Taffeta'

Hosta ventricosa 'Aureomarginata'
key features: medium-large mound of variable, white-margined foliage; purple flowers
mound size: 22" high by 47" wide

spacing: 48"
leaves: 8 1/2" long by 7" wide; 1" to 1 1/2" margin that changes from yellow early to creamy white by mid-June; center medium to dark green; shiny top and underside; broadly ovate shape with a heart-shaped base and long, twisted tip; smooth texture; average substance; 8-10 vein pairs
flowers: mid to late July; bright purple, striped; 2 3/8" long by 1 1/2" wide; bell-shaped; scapes up to 39" high; many seed pods form

comments: *Hosta ventricosa* 'Aureomarginata' has reached the level of a hosta "classic". It is highly respected for not only its strikingly variegated foliage, but by doing well under a wide variety of conditions. No hosta collection can be complete without *H. ventricosa* 'Aureomarginata'. Although the name "Aureomarginata" translates to "yellow-margined", it is so for only a few weeks in spring, turning to white by early summer. The margins are very irregular and nicely contrast the dark green center, standing out even from a long distance. Adding to its ornamental value are the bell-shaped purple flowers which contrast nicely with the variegated foliage.

   The origins of *Hosta ventricosa* 'Aureomarginata' are not entirely clear. When the AHS registered the name *H. ventricosa* 'Aureo-marginata' in 1986, it listed Alan Bloom of

Bressingham Gardens in England as the originator. Later, in "The Genus Hosta List of Registered Cultivars" (1993, p.85), the AHS gave credit for this plant to Karel Hensen of the Netherlands. Over the years it has been known under a variety of names including *H. ventricosa aureo-variegata*, *H. ventricosa variegata*, and *H. ventricosa* 'Variegated'.

seedlings, sports, and other related types:

'Flame Stitch': {1991r, C. Falstad; *H. ventricosa* 'Aureo-marginata' sport} reversed sport, i.e. dk green mgns that streak into the creamy white center; needs more garden evaluation

'Gold Flush': {1984r, A. Bloom; sport of *H. ventricosa*} nearly identical to *H. ventricosa* 'Aureomarginata' except for a few gold streaks and mottled sections projecting into the leaf center

'Taffeta': {1991r, R. O'Harra; selfed sdlg of *H. ventricosa* 'Aureomarginata'} shiny, dark green foliage; resembles *H. ventricosa*

'Yellow Flame': {1999r, J. Hawes; sport; lvs gold-centered wi a wide, green margin}

other similar types:

'Pizzazz', 'Robert Frost'

Hosta venusta (Otome Giboshi)
key features: small, dense mound of teardrop-shaped green leaves; purple flowers in July
mound size: 7" high by 30" wide

spacing: 24"
leaves: 2 1/2" long by 1 3/4" wide; medium green; dull top surface, moderately shiny underside; blade ovate with a rounded base; slightly wavy; smooth texture; average substance; 3-5 vein pairs

flowers: June 25 to July 10 (northern Illinois); bright purple with a whitish throat; 1 3/4" long by 1" wide; funnel-shaped; many 14-22" scapes with prominent ridges; 8-14 flowers per scape; forms seed pods

comments: *Hosta venusta* has been a popular plant in hosta collections and rock gardens because of its small size and very dense, rounded mound habit. A mature clump in flower can be quite attractive owing to the large number of scapes that develop. One 20-year-old clump that I observed (measuring 7 1/2" by 36") produced 41 scapes. With 10 flowers per scape, more than 400 flowers opened over its blooming season. *Hosta venusta* can also be used very effectively as an edger and low ground cover in the landscape.

Maekawa (1973) listed *H. venusta* as being native to Quelpaert Island, off the coast of Korea, sometimes escaping into the wild in Japan. It is well-known to Japanese collectors who have utilized it extensively in hybridizing work. Several variegated *H. venusta* seedlings have been bred in Japan including 'Nishikigawa' and 'Kinbotan'. 'Suzuki Thumbnail' and 'Masquerade' are among a number of *H. venusta* hybrids of Japanese origin given English names. *H. venusta* hybrids from the U.S. include 'Alpine Dream', 'Cody', 'Gosan Gold Midget', 'Tiny Tears', and 'Tot Tot'. Many of the green-leaved seedlings closely resemble *H. venusta* and, with maturity, become almost impossible to distinguish from it. Several beautiful sports of *H. venusta* have been developed in Japan including types with gold-margined leaves and two gold-centered plants (one of these becomes golder in the center (lutescent) while the other greens up in the middle (viridescent).

seedlings, sports, and other related types:

'Abiqua Miniature': {1988r, Walden West} sm md of green, *H. venusta*-type foliage; lvs dull on top, whitish shiny on the underside; purple fls in early July; fertile

'Alpine Dream': {1982r, R. Savory; *H. venusta* X an *H. venusta* sdlg} compact md of green foliage; bright purple fls in mid-July

'Amanuma': Fumio Maekawa hybrid of *H. venusta* X *H. capitata* named for his address (Watanabe, 1985); 10" by 28" md of green lvs, 3 1/2" by 2" (7 vp); many purple fls in early to mid-July on 22-30" scapes; dense mound habit & very floriferous

'Ballerina': {1982r, R. Savory; *H. venusta* X sdlg} small md of narrow, green lvs, 4" by 2", with a slightly wavy margin; white fls in July

'Blue Eyes': {1996r, R. Herman; *H. venusta* sdlg with blue-green foliage} a name also used for a Herb Benedict hybrid with bright blue foliage

500

'Cody': {1996r, R. Solberg; 'Shining Tot' X *H. venusta*} low md of dk green foliage; a neat small plant

'Concordia Petite': {1996r, U. Syre-Herz; *H. venusta* X 'Golden Tiara'; small md of dk gr lvs}

'Craig's Temptation': 11" by 32" md of oval-shaped, green lvs, 4 3/8 by 2 7/8" (6-7 vp); large numbers of med purple fls in July on 19" sc; probable hybrid of *H. venusta* X *H. nakaiana*; found growing on a tree in a temple garden in Kyoto, Japan in 1968 by George Schenk & Jack Craig

'Gosan Gold Midget': {1989r, W. Schmid; *H. venusta* X 'Golden Prayers'; glossy, bright yellow-green foliage that forms a 3" high md with lvs 1 1/2" long (5 vp)}

'Herbie': {1995r, R. & D. Benedict} sm md of white-mgd lvs; *H. venusta* X 'Saishu Jima' hybrid

'Honey Moon': {1982r, K. Anderson} 'Gold Drop' sibling (*H. venusta* X 'August Moon') (Solberg, 1988); 21" by 49" md; chartreuse, heart-shaped lvs, 5 1/4" by 5" (9 vp)

'Kinbotan': *H. venusta* seedling; sm md of greenish yellow-mgd lvs **(see page 254)**

'Lakeside Neat Petite': {1991r, M. Chastain; *H. venusta* X 'Blue Cadet'} sm, dense md of gr foliage **(see page 267)**

'Little Fellow': {1990r, C. Owens; selfed sdlg of *H. venusta*} tiny md of green foliage

'Lorna': {1983r, R. Benedict; *H. nakaiana* X *H. venusta*} sm md of wavy, shiny, green foliage

'Masquerade': formerly *H. venusta* 'Variegated', probably *H. sieboldii* X *H. venusta*; 'Little White Lines' (white-margined) and 'Munchkin' (green) sported from this cultivar **(see page 290)**

'Minuta': small md of teardrop-shaped, green foliage; purple fls on 14" sc in July; no doubt a sdlg of *H. venusta*; have seen in collections for many years; also known as 'Minata' & 'Minutissima'

'Misty Morning': {1986r, Kuk's Forest; *H. venusta* sdlg} 16" by 57" md of heart-shaped, chartreuse to med gold lvs, 6 1/2" by 5 1/2" (10 vp); lav fls in July on 26" scapes

'Nishikigawa': hybrid of ('Swoosh' X *H. venusta*) X *H. venusta* from Yoshimichi Hirose of Iwakuni City, Japan; white-margined, green-centered foliage in the shape of *H. venusta*

'Rock Master': {1982r, P. Aden; *H. venusta* X a sdlg} v sm md of lance-shaped, shiny green leaves

'Shining Tot': {1982r, P. Aden; *H. venusta* X 'Rock Master'} 5 1/2" by 16" md of shiny, dark green lvs, 3 1/4" by 2 1/4" (5-6 vp); pale purple fls in Aug; much like *H. pulchella* in both foliage and flower, not *H. venusta*; a good hybridizing plant

'Suzuki Thumbnail': {1987r, P. Ruh for K. Suzuki} *H. venusta* sdlg from Kichigoro Suzuki of Japan; small md of green foliage that closely resembles *H. venusta* & 'Thumb Nail'

'Surprised By Joy': {1998r, A. Malloy; 'Flamboyant' X *H. venusta*; wh-cntrd, gr-mgd lvs}

'Thumb Nail': {1982r, P. Aden; *H. venusta* X a sdlg} 7" by 21" md of green lvs 3" by 2 1/2" (3-4 vp); dull top, moderately shiny underside; blade a teardrop shape and smooth-textured; pale violet fls from late June into mid-July, differing from *H. venusta* only by the shade of purple in the throat

'Tiny Tears': {1977r, R. Savory; *H. venusta* sdlg} low md of green lvs; varies slightly from its parent **(see page 468)**

'Tot Tot': {1978r, P. Aden; 'Blue Cadet' X *H. venusta*} sm mound (7" by 21") of green lvs, 2 1/2" by 2", with 6 vp and a thin underside bloom; pale purple fls with whitish petal margins, early to mid-July on 13-19" sc; useful rock garden pl; effective in flower, one clump having 45 scapes

'Venucosa': {1986r, AHS} *H. venusta* X *H. ventricosa* hybrid found by Alex Summers in the late 1960's; 20" by 55" md of heart-shaped, green lvs 6 5/8" by 5" (8 vp); bell-shaped purple fls, July 14-31; sparse pod formation; intermediate characteristics between the two parents; collector's plant

other similar types:

'Abiqua Jim Dandy', 'Awesome', *H. minor*, *H. nakaiana*, 'Rim Rock'

'Whirlwind'
key features: medium-large mound of greenish white-centered foliage
mound size: 19" high by 40" wide (up to 23" by 45")

spacing: 36"

leaves: 8" long by 6 1/2" wide (up to 10" by 8"); dark green margin, 2 1/8" wide; center whitish with green veins, turning to light green by mid-summer, dark green by August; thin underside bloom; blade broadly ovate and noticeably curved and wavy; long, distinct tip; slightly corrugated; good substance; 11 vein pairs

flowers: late July into August; lavender; 3" long; 30" scapes; some pod formation

comments: 'Whirlwind' is a standout in any hosta collection for its variegation and wavy, unruly mound habit. The leaf center undergoes continual color changes, being white with greenish tints early in the season, slowly becoming pale green, then darker green. The shiny, dark green margin offers a nice contrast to the center even when it is pale green. 'Whirlwind' has a fairly fast growth rate and makes a very nice specimen plant, but could also be an effective ground cover. All in all, 'Whirlwind' rates as one of the most distinctive and attractive hosta introductions of the last twenty years.

John Kulpa registered 'Whirlwind' in 1989 as a possible sport of 'Fortunei Hyacinthina'. Though it may have some 'Fortunei'-like characteristics, it does not act like 'Fortunei Hyacinthina' at all.

seedlings, sports, and other related types:

'Dust Devil': {1999r, M. Zilis; sport of 'Whirlwind'} lvs dk green-centered with a mgn that changes from greenish yellow to creamy white during the season; "reverse sport" of 'Whirlwind'; med-lg md

'Eternal Flame': {1999r, H. Hansen & Shady Oaks N; sport; lvs dk green-mgd wi a creamy white center that stays white}

'Second Wind': {1991r, J. Kulpa; 'Whirlwind' sport} shiny, dk green lvs, 9 1/2" by 7 1/2" (12 vp); md 23" by 48"; dense md habit and one of the best dk green hostas; greatly underrated

'Trade Wind': {1994r, J. Kulpa; 'Second Wind' sport; dk green lvs streaked with white}

'Whirlwind Tour': sport of 'Whirlwind' named in England; lf center starts green, turns creamy white by mid-summer

other similar types:
'Whirligig'

'White Christmas'
key features: medium-sized mound of white-centered foliage
mound size: 15" high by 35" wide

spacing: 36"

leaves: 8" long by 4 1/4" wide; narrow, green margin, 1/4" to 1" wide; center creamy white, becoming green during the season in juvenile plants; thin underside bloom; blade narrowly ovate with a rounded base; slightly wavy margins; smooth texture; thin substance; 8-9 vein pairs

flowers: mid-July into early August; pale lavender; narrow funnel shape; scapes 22-30" high; have never seen a seed pod develop

comments: Probably due to the seemingly insatiable demand for white-centered hostas, 'White Christmas' has continued to be very popular despite being introduced in the early 1970's. I have seen many fine specimens in display gardens, but some gardeners have had trouble growing it. Like many other white-centered hostas, it needs some direct sunlight each day. As a juvenile plant the foliage will turn almost completely green by the end of summer and this may account for its ability to eventually grow into a decent-sized mound.

'White Christmas' is often thought of as a substitute for 'Undulata' cultivars in the landscape, though they are not closely related. 'White Christmas' is the stable form of a plant known for many years as *Hosta fortunei* 'Krossa Variegated', a cultivar with unstable, streaky foliage. 'White Christmas' was registered in 1999 by Peter Ruh for Gus Krossa (and "Palmer"). Information that I gathered from the AHS registrar's office in 1983 indicated that it was introduced in 1971 by Gus Krossa and, at one time, was known as 'Krossa White'.

I have never seen any seed pods develop from 'White Christmas', but it has yielded the very famous sport, 'Night Before Christmas'.

seedlings, sports, and other related types:
'Calypso': {1987r, W. & E. Lachman; sdlg X 'White Christmas'} 10" by 23" md (often smaller) of creamy white-centered, green margined lvs, 6" by 2 3/8" (6-7 vp); 1 1/2" long, purple fls on 17" sc, late July into Aug; striking pl, but difficult to grow; center tends to "melt-out" by late summer; useful breeding plant
'Robert's Rapier': {1996r, R. Keller & White Oak N; sport of 'White Christmas'} lvs have a very narrow white center (v wide green margin); center 1/4" wide on a 7" by 3 3/4" lf
'Night Before Christmas': sport with wider green margins; much more vigorous and makes a much larger mound than 'White Christmas' **(see page 323)**

other similar types:
'Ani Machi', 'Banana Sundae', 'Celebration', 'Emerald Crust', 'Gay Feather', 'Silver Streak', 'Undulata'

'White Vision'
key features: medium-large mound of heavily corrugated, gold foliage
mound size: 20" high by 42" wide and probably larger

spacing: 36"
leaves: 9 1/2" long by 7" wide; medium gold, becoming a light gold by midsummer; thick bloom on top and underside; blade broadly ovate with a heart-shaped base and generally wavy; moderate to heavy corrugation; thick substance; 16 vein pairs
flowers: late June into mid-July; very pale lavender with a slightly darker mid-petal stripe; 2 1/4" long by 1 1/2" wide; open-funnel shape; scapes up to 37" high; forms many seed pods

comments: 'White Vision' makes an attractive mound of brilliant gold foliage. A side-by-side comparison I once made between 'White Vision' and 'City Lights', however, resulted in the latter being a more impressive plant. In the early 1980's 'White Vision' was fairly popular but is no longer widely grown. It has been useful in breeding programs. It not only readily forms seed pods, but offers excellent slug resistance, an attractive gold color, and good corrugation. 'White Vision' was registered by Paul Aden in 1978 as a hybrid of 'Sun Glow' X 'Gold Cup'.

seedlings, sports, and other related types:

'Abiqua Gold Shield': {1987r, Walden West; 'White Vision' sdlg} bright gold foliage that is heavily corrugated, slightly cupped, unruly, and slug resistant; md 29" by 66" with lvs 14" by 10 1/2" (14-15 vp); near-wh fls in dense clusters on 31" sc, late June into July; many seed pods; worth growing

'Abiqua Recluse': {1989r, Walden West; 'White Vision' X 'Sum and Substance'} med-lg md of bright gold foliage **(see page 60)**

506

'Alice Gladden': {1998r, D. & J. Ward; 'White Vision' X *H. montana macrophylla*; lg, gold leaves}

'City Lights': {1978r, P. Aden; 'White Vision' X 'Golden Prayers'} bright gold foliage that is even brighter than its mother **(see page 119)**

'Jackpot': {1996r, D. & J. Ward; 'White Vision' X *H. montana macrophylla*} brilliant gold foliage; one imm leaf reached 12 1/2" by 7 1/2" (16 vp)

'Shade Master': {1982r, P. Aden; 'White Vision' X 'Golden Rajah'} med-sized md of bright gold lvs 10" by 7 1/2" (11 vp); pale lav fls in July; gold color stands out in any collection; "mother plant" of 'Summer Music'

'Stardust': {1998r, D. & J. Ward; 'White Vision' X *H. montana macrophylla*; 28" high md of large, gold lvs}

other similar types:

'Golden Prayers' (true form)

'Wide Brim'
key features: medium-large mound of creamy yellow-margined foliage
mound size: 18" high by 45" wide

spacing: 40"

leaves: 8 1/2" long by 6" wide; 1" to 2" wide margin that changes from yellow to creamy white, somewhat dependent upon light level; margin streaks into the medium to dark green center; thin underside bloom; blade broadly ovate and slightly wavy; moderately corrugated; above average substance; 10-12 vein pairs

flowers: late July into August; pale lavender with darker mid-petal striping; 2 1/8" long by 1 5/8" wide; scapes 24" high

comments: Its striking foliage colors and fast growth rate make 'Wide Brim' one of the best hostas for landscaping purposes. It can be utilized in almost any way, but is most effective as a ground cover or specimen. The vivid contrast between the green center and wide, irregular, creamy yellow margin is quite striking. Paul Aden registered 'Wide Brim' back in 1979 as a hybrid of 'Bold One' X 'Bold Ribbons'.

seedlings, sports, and other related types:

'Brim Cup': {1986r, P. Aden; "Aden 392" X 'Wide Brim'} med-sized md of cupped, white-mgd, green-centered foliage; often tears along the margin **(see page 103)**

'Honeysong': found by Alex Summers in the mid-1990's; same foliage and flowers as 'Wide Brim'

'Kissing Cousin': {1998r, E. Elslager; 'Wide Brim' sport} creamy white-margined lvs; distinctly different from 'Wide Brim'

'Pegasus': sport found in 1998 at Homestead Division of Sunnybrook Farms; white-centered, green-margined leaves

'Pretty Kitty': {1999r, E. Elslager; sport} dk green-centered lvs with a creamy white mgn, i.e. whiter than 'Wide Brim'

'Snow Cap': {1980r, P. Aden; 'Wide Brim' X 'Royal Rainbow'} 19" by 42" md; 7 1/2" by 6 1/4" lvs (13 vp) wi wide, white margins; near-wh fls in June-July; difficult to grow; margins often tear (not drawstring); not recommended

'Stetson': {1997r, Walters Gardens; 'Wide Brim' sport} differs in having very wavy, "folded" lvs

other similar types:

'Carnival'

'Yakushima Mizu'

key features: small mound of narrow, wavy foliage
mound size: 6" high by 14" wide

spacing: 12"
leaves: 3" long by 1" wide; medium to dark green; shiny top and underside surfaces; blade narrowly elliptic and rippled along the margin; smooth texture; thin substance; 3 vein pairs

flowers: late August; lavender; 9 1/2" scapes; few flowers (about 6) per scape

comments: As a truly dwarf hosta, 'Yakushima Mizu' can be useful as a rock garden plant or low edger. It blooms for a very short period of time, much like *H. longissima longifolia* to which it is not closely related. The origins of 'Yakushima Mizu' are somewhat obscure, though it certainly came from Japan. A translation of the name implies that it comes from Yakushima, an island south of Kyushu Island, and can be found around water (mizu). Kenji Watanabe (1985) listed this as being from the "albo-marginata" (*H. sieboldii*) group of hostas as did Hajime Sugita (1984); however, it is not closely related to *H. kikutii yakusimensis*.

seedlings, sports, and other related types:
none listed

other similar types:
H. gracillima, 'Saishu Jima'

'Yellow River'
key features: large mound of yellow-margined foliage
mound size: 30" high by 66" wide (up to 38" by 80")

spacing: 60"

leaves: 12" long by 8" wide (up to 16" by 9 1/2"); 3/8" to 1 3/8" wide yellow margin, medium to dark green center; thin underside bloom; broadly oblong-ovate blade that is also slightly wavy along the margin; not corrugated; better than average substance; 12-15 vein pairs that are deeply impressed; mound habit semi-upright

flowers: early to late July; near-white; 2 1/4" long by 1 1/8" wide; scapes just above the top of the foliage, up to 39" high; many seed pods develop

comments: Though developed many years ago in England by Eric Smith, 'Yellow River' was relatively unknown until about a dozen years ago. I first viewed this magnificent, yellow-margined cultivar in Herb Benedict's garden in 1985 and wondered why it had not become more popular. The sharp contrast between the dark green center and consistent yellow edge immediately impressed me. Van Wade and others began growing it and displaying leaves at AHS conventions. Soon the word was out and it began to be intensively propagated, so much so that it has become commonly found at nurseries and in just about every hosta collection of significance.

The ultimate size of 'Yellow River' surprised me. The first few plants that I viewed in the Benedict garden were medium-sized (9" by 4 1/2" leaves) and gave no indication of the immense proportions as seen in the Wade and Gatton Nurseries hosta display (where I measured the 38" high plant). With its great size, it makes an excellent background plant or large ground cover and also can be an effective
510

specimen plant.

It has not been used much in hybridizing, despite its many good characteristics and excellent pod set. The only known sport is 'Green River', the green-leaved form.

Peter Ruh registered 'Yellow River' for Eric Smith and Paul Aden in 1993.

seedlings, sports, and other related types:
'Green River': {1999r, V. Wade; sport} all-green foliage; md 34" by 69"; a great background plant

other similar types:
'Abba Dabba Do', 'Sun Banner'

Hosta yingeri
key features: small to medium-sized mound of shiny, smooth foliage; narrow-petalled, purple flowers in September
mound size: ranges from 9" high by 30" wide to 19" by 38"

spacing: 24"

leaves: ranges from 5 7/8" long by 4" wide (7 vein pairs) to 10 3/4" long by 5 1/2" wide (8-9 vein pairs); shiny, dark green, lighter green along the veins; whitish shiny underside; narrowly elliptic-ovate blade that is also moderately wavy; generally smooth but sometimes slightly corrugated; good substance

flowers: late August to mid-September; medium purple; narrow petals; 15-18" scapes for smaller form, 27-31" for larger types; many seed pods develop

comments: *Hosta yingeri* becomes a fairly dense mound of shiny, smooth, dark green foliage. The late season flowers are an attractive shade of purple and have fairly narrow petals. Being a species, the range of sizes and forms that exist is not surprising. The most common types could be classified as "medium-sized" plants, but I have seen smaller ones as well. It can be used as a ground cover or specimen plant in the landscape.

When introduced to hosta collectors in the late 1980's, *Hosta yingeri* created quite a stir. It represented the first hosta species discovered in many years and was strikingly different from anything else available. Hybridizers looked upon it as a source of new genetic material for their breeding programs and wisely began using it. The results have been outstanding.

H. yingeri is native to islands off the coast of Korea and was named for horticulturist Barry Yinger (Schmid, 1991). It appears to be very closely related to *H. laevigata* **(see page 263)**.

seedlings, sports, and other related types:

'City Slicker': {1996r, J. Dishon; 'Yellow Splash' X *H. yingeri*; dk green lvs wi gold mgns that turn creamy}

'Korean Snow': {1999r, Niche Gardens & R. Solberg; *H. yingeri* sdlg} flecked green and white foliage; purple, *H. yingeri*-like flowers

'Lakeside Looking Glass': {1997r, M. Chastain; *H. yingeri* sdlg} v attractive, shiny, dk green foliage

'Potomac Pride': {1995r, T. Avent; *H. yingeri* X 'Blue Umbrellas'} 24" by 50" md of shiny, dark green lvs 12" by 8 1/2", good substance; bluish purple fls on 36" sc in July; 1995 AHS "convention" plant; fast growth rate

'Sweet Tater Pie': {1995r, T. Avent; 'Golden Scepter' X *H. yingeri*} small md of foliage that is a shade of gold just like the name; turns green by mid-summer

H. yingeri 'Treasure Island': {1998r, T. Avent as a selection of *H. yingeri*} dk green lvs 7 1/2" by 5" wi 10 vp, shiny on top, whitish shiny underneath; purple fls from late August into September

other similar types:

Hosta laevigata: similar medium-sized mound of shiny, dark green foliage; similar in flower; major difference from *H. yingeri* is its narrower, wavier leaf blade

Zilis, Mark R. 1987. "Classifying the Variability in *Hosta sieboldiana* 'Frances Williams'." *The Hosta Journal* 18 (1): 39-41.

The Frances R. Williams Hosta Records

The records of Frances R. Williams are archived at the Andersen Horticultural Library of the Minnesota Landscape Arboretum, Chanhassen, MN. The following letters have been cited in *The Hosta Handbook*.

Cumming, Alex. 1945. Letter to Frances Williams. June 9, 1945.

Cumming, Rod. 1952. Letter to Frances Williams. September 16, 1952.

Nesmith, Elizabeth. 1959. Letter to Frances Williams. Feb. 16, 1959.

Nesmith, Elizabeth. 1962. Letter to Frances Williams. Feb. 5, 1962.

Nesmith, Elizabeth. 1966. Letter to Frances Williams. Aug. 20, 1966.

Williams, Frances R. 1946. Letter to Alex Cumming. Sept. 2, 1946.

Williams, Frances R. 1958. Letter to Ellen Carder. May 7, 1958.

Williams, Frances R. 1959a. Letter to Carl Mack. Oct. 31, 1959.

Williams, Frances R. 1959b. Letter to Elizabeth Nesmith. Dec. 18, 1959.

Williams, Frances R. 1960a. Letter to Elizabeth Nesmith. July 6, 1960.

Williams, Frances R. 1960b. Letter to Elizabeth Nesmith. Aug. 8, 1960.

Williams, Frances R. 1961. Letter to Elizabeth Nesmith. June 6, 1961.

Williams, Frances R. 1962a. Letter to George W. Robinson. Sept. 10, 1962.

Williams, Frances R. 1962b. Letter to Elizabeth Nesmith. Sept. 25, 1962.

Williams, Frances R. 1966. Letter to Elizabeth Nesmith. April 1, 1966.

Catalog Listings

Aden, Paul. 1979-1980. Hosta List. Baldwin, NY.

Adrian's Flowers of Fashion Nursery. 1995. Price List. Alliance, OH.

American Hostas, Daylilies, and Other Perennials (Wade & Gatton Nurseries). 1996-1997. Catalog. Bellville, OH.

Banyai Hostas. 1993, 1995. Mail Order Catalogs. Hockessin, DE

Caprice Farm Nursery. Spring 1990. Catalog. Sherwood, OR.

Cooks Nursery and Eagle Bay Gardens. 2000 Hosta List. Dunkirk, NY.

Fairway Gardens. 1980-82; 1983-85. Price Lists. Albert Lea, MN.

Fisher, Eunice. 1977-1978. Price list. Oshkosh, WI.

Fleur de Lis Gardens. 1990. Catalog. Canby, OR.

Freeman Tree Farm. 1998 Hosta & Perennials. Price list. Davenport, IA.

Goldbrook Plants. 1998. Catalog. Suffolk, England.

The Green Hill Gossip. Green Hill Farm. 1998. Catalog. Chapel Hill, NC.

Hatfield Gardens. 1989-1993, 1995-1997. Catalogs. Circleville, OH.

Homestead Division of Sunnybrook Farms. 1994-2000. Catalogs. Chesterland, OH.

The Hosta Patch. 1998. Price list. Barrington, IL.

Jim's Hostas. 2000. Price List. Dubuque, IA.

Klehm Nursery Perennials. 1989-1994. Perennial Catalogs. South Barrrington, IL.

Kuk's Forest Nursery. 2000. Catalog. Brecksville, OH.

Mackwoods Gardens. 1960. Hosta Listing. Spring Grove, IL.

Naylor Creek Nursery. *Plant List 2000*. Chimacum, WA.

Pine Forest Gardens. 1999. Price list. Fayetteville, GA.

Plant Delights Nursery, Inc. 2000 Catalog. Raleigh, NC.

Powell's Gardens. 1989-1998. Catalogs. Princeton, NC.

Q & Z Nursery, Inc. 1996-2000. Wholesale Catalogs. Rochelle, IL.

Reath Gardens. 1993. Price List. Vulcan, MI.

Robyn's Nest Nursery. 2000. Catalog. Vancouver, WA.

Savory's Gardens, Inc. 1994-1998. Catalogs. Edina, MN.

Schmid Nursery & Gardens. 1999. Catalog. Jackson, MI.

Sea Made. 1996. Hosta Catalog. Wilmington, DE.

Shady Oaks Nursery, Inc. 2000 Catalog. Waseca, MN.

Soules Garden. 1994-1995. Catalogs. Indianapolis, IN.

Stark Gardens. 2000. Hosta & Daylily Catalog. Norwalk, IA.

Tower Perennial Gardens. *New Introductions 1997*. Price List. Spokane, WA.

Walden West Hosta. 1996 Hosta Listing. Scotts Mills, OR.

Walters Gardens. 1998-1999, 1999-2000. Wholesale Perennial Price List. Zeeland, MI.

Wayside Gardens. 1933. Catalog. Mentor, OH.

Wild Garden Catalog. 1976-1977. Bethell, WA.

GENERAL INDEX

A & D Nursery 287

Aden, Paul 29, 57, 68, 77, 83, 87, 88, 92, 93, 95, 96, 103,
112, 115, 118, 119, 132, 137, 141, 142, 147, 148, 149,
155, 168, 169, 170, 171, 173, 179, 180, 186, 187, 189,
195, 196, 197, 198, 203, 208, 210, 211, 214, 215, 218,
226, 237, 238, 247, 275, 276, 282, 287, 292, 304, 308,
315, 318, 319, 320, 321, 326, 327, 343, 346, 353, 354,
389, 390, 391, 395, 408, 413, 429, 430, 434, 437, 440,
443, 444, 447, 448, 452, 453, 456, 457, 459, 460, 464,
470, 471, 475, 476, 477, 478, 493, 501, 502, 506, 507,
508, 511, 513, 517

American Hosta Society (AHS), history 18, 28-30

Anderson, Ken 29, 71, 84, 182, 186, 199, 262, 311, 314,
444, 445, 474, 501, 516

Anderson, L. 445

apomixis 42

Archibald, Jim 452, 458

Arends, George 401, 464, 497, 515

Arends Nursery 401

Arett, Anne 64, 99, 146, 316, 317, 407, 427, 471, 472, 486

Armstrong, Maxine 164, 196, 316, 317, 458, 472, 475

Arnold, Beth 186, 398, 412

Avent, Tony 57, 71, 95, 134, 140, 202, 211, 213, 251, 276,
432, 443, 444, 448, 485, 486, 498, 512

Bachman, Lloyd 194

Bailey, Liberty Hyde 19

Ballantyne, Diana 287

Ballantyne, Don 287

Balletta, P. 276

Banyai, Bruce 187, 191, 274, 496

Banyai, Pauline 19, 70, 76, 88, 108, 128, 166, 182, 192,
193, 194, 215, 271, 312, 316, 325, 338, 379, 398, 414

Beal, R. 166

Belle Gardens 99, 126, 279, 291, 300, 309, 310, 474

Bemis, Royal 195, 474

Benedict, Dorothy 14, 29, 54, 76, 124, 126, 138, 157, 159,
167, 213, 223, 224, 226, 302, 319, 357, 379, 396, 398,
399, 413, 415, 421, 432, 474, 476, 495, 497, 501

Benedict, Ralph (Herb) 14, 29, 54, 74, 76, 91, 93, 104,
113, 114, 121, 124, 126, 137, 138, 145, 157, 159, 167,
179, 180, 181, 182, 190, 194, 213, 215, 223, 224, 226,
233, 239, 243, 250, 259, 261, 262, 280, 283, 302, 306,
310, 314, 316, 319, 320, 328, 346, 347, 357, 373, 375,
379, 396, 397, 398, 399, 406, 407, 408, 413, 415, 418,
421, 432, 452, 453, 474, 476, 477, 495, 496, 497, 500,
501, 510

520

Hosta Name Index

Main listings are in boldface type. Boldface numbers indicate descriptions. Names in parentheses can represent simply an identification of a common name, e.g., Aki Giboshi (*H.* 'Tardiflora'); an alternate name (both names are acceptable), e.g., *H.* 'Frances Williams' (or *H. sieboldiana* 'Frances Williams'); or an updated, correct name that should be used, e.g., *H.* 'Burke's Dwarf' (= *H. nakaiana*).

533

548

HOSTA NAME INDEX *(Continued)*

HOSTA NAME INDEX *(Continued)*

HOSTA NAME INDEX *(Continued)*

HOSTA NAME INDEX *(Continued)*

580

HOSTA PROBLEM SOLVING GUIDE

Problem: SLUGS

Characteristics: night-feeding; prosper with high humidity

Symptoms: small holes in leaves, generally between the veins; in extreme cases, leaf totally eaten except for midrib & veins

Prevention: remove mulches around older plantings; grow thick-substanced, slug-resistant varieties

Control: apply granular bait early in the growing season to limit slug population; stale beer popular non-chemical control (one can in a 3-4" deep container; replenish in 3 days or after it rains)

Problem: FOLIAR NEMATODES

Characteristics: microscopic worms that feed on leaf tissue; spread by splashing water during the growing season; eggs overwinter in crowns or dried-up foliage

Symptoms: interveinal areas begin yellowing in mid-summer, turn dark brown by late summer

Prevention: isolate plants for one growing season from suspect sources; limit overhead watering

Control: destroy infected plants unless extremely valuable; soak divisions of infected valuable plants in a 120°F hot water bath for 15-20 min., plant in a container and isolate for six months before replanting; some sprays and granular pesticides have proven effective but must be applied by a licensed applicator

Problem: BLACK VINE WEEVILS

Characteristics: night-feeding; hard-shelled insects

Symptoms: edges of leaves notched out

Prevention: do not plant hostas near Yews (*Taxus*) and other trees and shrubs which may harbor weevil populations

Control: chemical sprays; catch weevils and crush with pliers

Problem: CUTWORMS (VARIEGATED)

Characteristics: night-feeding; 1 1/2" long, brown insects; can attack virtually all types of hostas

Symptoms: large sections of leaf tissue suddenly gone

Control: granular insecticides; place white cloth under plant, shine flashlight on cutworms as they feed at night, & squash worms after they fall to the ground

Problem: 'SEA SPRITE' VIRUS

Characteristics: all 'Sea Sprite' plants infected; a few
    other *H. sieboldii* types susceptible

Symptoms: circular, yellow dots sprinkled on foliage;
    some leaves non-symptomatic but still infected

Prevention: avoid susceptible cultivars; clean pruning
    shears or knives used in dividing or maintaining hostas
    in a 50% bleach solution

Control: none; destroy infected plants and remove sur-
    rounding soil

Problem: 'SPRITZER' VIRUS

Characteristics: 'Spritzer' & 'Green Fountain' most susceptible but can affect other cvs.

Symptoms: 1/4" to 1/2", concentric, yellow circles in small numbers on leaves; some leaves non-symptomatic

Prevention: carefully examine any plant of 'Spritzer' for symptoms before planting; clean pruning shears or knives used in dividing or maintaining hostas in a 50% bleach solution

Control: none; destroy infected plants and remove surrounding soil

Problem: 'OPIPARA' VIRUS

Characteristics: all 'Opipara' plants in U.S. before 1987 were infected; can spread to other cultivars through mechanical means

Symptoms: grainy, brown flecking gradually overtakes foliage

Prevention: only grow 'Bill Brincka' clone of 'Opipara'; clean pruning shears or knives used in dividing or maintaining hostas in a 50% bleach solution

Control: none; destroy infected plants and remove surrounding soil

Problem: SOUTHERN BLIGHT

Characteristics: leaves pull away easily when tugged; worse with high humidity, high temperatures and poor air circulation

Symptoms: pale areas develop on foliage; crown of plant a mass of fibrous, white threads; untreated crowns will rot

Prevention: provide good aeration between plants in areas of the country where this is a problem; in nursery settings spray or drench with fungicides during susceptible times; do not use high nitrogen fertilizers

Control: dig infected plants out of the garden, remove any leaf tissue, and soak clump in a 10-20% bleach solution for 1-2 hours; dry plant for 1-2 days, repot and isolate for 3 months; remove any soil that would have been in contact with the infected plant; in nursery settings spray or drench with fungicides once symptoms appear

Problem: HEAVY FROST DAMAGE

Characteristics: *H. montana* 'Aureomarginata', *H. lancifolia*, & *H. plantaginea* often affected; temperatures below 28°F

Symptoms: foliage of newly emerging plants wilts and turns watery the morning after a heavy frost

Prevention: choose later emerging cultivars if possible; keep a continuous water spray on plants overnight during nights of heavy frost or protect plants with heavy cloth or a frost blanket

Control: cut back foliage of frost-damaged plants

Problem: LIGHT FROST DAMAGE

Characteristics: in late spring when nighttime
   temperatures reach 28-32°F; any hosta susceptible
Symptoms: light yellow dotting in interveinal areas,
   sometimes followed by browning later
Prevention: same as for "Heavy Frost Damage"
Control: cut back foliage if it becomes unsightly

Problem: FAIRY RING (CENTER CLUMP DIEBACK)

Characteristics: old, established clumps can be affected; have seen in Fortuneis the most

Symptoms: a perimeter ring of buds emerge first in spring; center buds dead, rotted, or very slow to grow

Prevention: divide fast-growing hostas every 5-6 years

Control: dig up clump and replant healthy portions in fresh soil once a fairy ring develops; if no rot, amend soil in area of old clump with peat moss and fertilizer; if rot present, remove soil and do not replant hostas in same hole

Problem: SPRING DESICCATION BURN ("SPRING BURN")

Characteristics: primarily on Sieboldianas with gold color in the foliage; does not affect non-gold areas

Symptoms: small to large brown areas develop on gold sections of leaf in spring

Prevention: plant "non-burning" cultivars

Control: grow susceptible cultivars in protected sites, out of exposure to direct sunlight to limit damage

Problem: DRAWSTRING EFFECT

Characteristics: fast-growing leaf center outgrows the narrow, white margin; becomes evident with maturity; only affects a few cultivars

Symptoms: leaves develop cupping and distortion early in season, followed by ripping & tearing of margin

Prevention: do not grow known "drawstring" plants; do not overfertilize hostas which can cause the drawstring effect in other white-margined hostas

Control: cut back the first flush of foliage of "drawstring" plants, usually 4-6 weeks after leaves emerge in spring

Problem: CHEMICAL DAMAGE

Characteristics: occurs as hostas are in a rapid stage of growth, often in spring

Symptoms: leaves curled, distorted, and thickened; scapes flattened, producing unusual flower effects

Prevention: do not spray herbicides on windy days in spring; avoid using wood preservatives in areas where they might leach into garden soil

Control: if possible remove affected plant and replant in a new site; provide adequate moisture and fertilizer if symptoms develop; foliage removal not necessary

Problem: MELTOUT

Characteristics: affects some white-centered cultivars after receiving direct sunlight for several weeks

Symptoms: center of leaf lightens, dries, turns brown, and falls out by mid to late summer

Prevention: grow susceptible cultivars in protected, shaded sites

Control: cut back affected foliage and move to a shadier site

About the Author

Mark Zilis is the owner of Q & Z Nursery, Inc., Rochelle, IL, a leading supplier of hostas to the wholesale nursery market. Mark received a B.S. in ornamental horticulture in 1976 and an M.S. in horticulture in 1979 from the University of Illinois. He has been an active member of the American Hosta Society since 1980, serving on its Board of Directors, judging leaf shows, and as an auctioneer at its national conventions. Mark has studied hostas in gardens throughout the U.S. and during two trips to Japan. He has also been a leader in the development of plant tissue culture techniques and is a frequent speaker on the subject as well as a number of topics related to hostas, herbaceous perennials and wildflowers. Over the last 15 years, Mark has introduced over fifty varieties of hostas including 'Sugar and Cream', *H. montana* 'Mountain Snow', 'Pineapple Upside-down Cake', 'Dust Devil', 'Leather Sheen', and 'Summer Breeze'.

Mark resides in Rochelle with his wife, Katie, and their four children, Andy, Amy, Anthony, and Becky.

The author studying hostas in a native setting in Japan.

NOTES

NOTES